T0305945

Resourcing the Start-up Business

Drawing on the most up-to-date and relevant research, this concise text-book is an accessible guide to harnessing the appropriate resources when launching a new start-up business. The focus is on the wide range of tangible and intangible resources available to entrepreneurs in the early stages of a new venture. This second edition brings in material on crowdfunding, digitalization and Covid-19, and dedicates new chapters to:

- lean start-ups and business models
- idea generation and opportunity development and
- business incubators and accelerators.

The book supports students with learning objectives, a summary, discussion questions and a practical call to action in each chapter. A teaching guide and slides are also available for instructors. *Resourcing the Start-up Business* will be a valuable textbook for students of entrepreneurship and new venture creation globally.

Oswald Jones is Emeritus Professor of Entrepreneurship at the University of Liverpool Management School.

Allan Macpherson is Senior Lecturer in Entrepreneurial and Organizational Learning at the University of Liverpool Management School.

Dilani Jayawarna is Professor of Entrepreneurship at the University of Liverpool Management School.

Routledge Masters in Entrepreneurship
Edited by Janine Swail and Robert Wapshott

The *Routledge Masters in Entrepreneurship* series offers postgraduate students specialist but accessible textbooks on a range of entrepreneurship topics. Collectively, these texts form a significant resource base for those studying entrepreneurship, whether as part of an entrepreneurship-related programme of study, or as a new, non-cognate area for students in disciplines such as science and engineering, helping them to gain an in-depth understanding of contemporary entrepreneurial concepts.

The volumes in this series are authored by leading specialists in their field, and although they are discrete texts in their treatment of individual topics, all are united by a common structure and pedagogical approach. Key features of each volume include:

- a critical approach to combining theory with practice, which educates its reader rather than solely teaching a set of skills
- clear learning objectives for each chapter
- the use of figures, tables and boxes to highlight key ideas, concepts and skills
- an annotated bibliography, guiding students in their further reading, and
- discussion questions for each chapter to aid learning and put key concepts into practice.

Managing Human Resources in Small and Medium-Sized Enterprises
Entrepreneurship and the Employment Relationship
Robert Wapshott and Oliver Mallett

Building an Entrepreneurial Organisation
Simon Mosey, Hannah Noke and Paul Kirkham

Family Business
Carole Howorth and Nick Robinson

Women's Entrepreneurship
Maura McAdam

Resourcing the Start-up Business
Creating Dynamic Entrepreneurial Learning Capabilities
Oswald Jones, Allan Macpherson and Dilani Jayawarna

For more information about this series, please visit: www.routledge.com/ Routledge-Masters-in-Entrepreneurship/book-series/ME

Resourcing the Start-up Business

Creating Dynamic Entrepreneurial Learning Capabilities

Second Edition

Oswald Jones, Allan Macpherson and Dilani Jayawarna

Routledge
Taylor & Francis Group

LONDON AND NEW YORK

Cover image: © Getty Images

Second edition published 2023
by Routledge
4 Park Square, Milton Park, Abingdon, Oxon, OX14 4RN

and by Routledge
605 Third Avenue, New York, New York 10158

Routledge is an imprint of the Taylor & Francis Group, an informa business

© 2023 Oswald Jones, Allan Macpherson, and Dilani Jayawarna

First edition published by Routledge 2013

British Library Cataloguing-in-Publication Data
A catalogue record for this book is available from the British Library

Library of Congress Cataloging-in-Publication Data
Names: Jones, Oswald, author. | Mcpherson, Allan, author. | Jayawarna, Dilani, author.
Title: Resourcing the start-up business: creating dynamic entrepreneurial learning capabilities / Oswald Jones, Allan Mcpherson, and Dilani Jayawarna.
Description: Second Edition. | New York, NY : Routledge, 2023. |
Series: Routledge masters in entrepreneurship |
Revised edition of the authors' Resourcing the start-up business, 2014. |
Includes bibliographical references and index. |
Identifiers: LCCN 2022021103 (print) | LCCN 2022021104 (ebook) |
ISBN 9781032321196 (hardback) | ISBN 9781032320038 (paperback) |
ISBN 9781003312918 (ebook)
Subjects: LCSH: New business enterprises–Management. |
Small business–Management. | Business planning. | Entrepreneurship.
Classification: LCC HD62.5 .J6585 2023 (print) |
LCC HD62.5 (ebook) | DDC 658.1/1–dc23/eng/20220725
LC record available at https://lccn.loc.gov/2022021103
LC ebook record available at https://lccn.loc.gov/2022021104

ISBN: 978-1-032-32119-6 (hbk)
ISBN: 978-1-032-32003-8 (pbk)
ISBN: 978-1-003-31291-8 (ebk)

DOI: 10.4324/9781003312918

Typeset in Optima
by Newgen Publishing UK

Access the Support Material: www.routledge.com/9781032321196

Contents

Introduction to the Case Studies

The authors have worked together on the study of entrepreneurship and the management of small businesses for more than 20 years. During that time, we have published articles on a wide-range of topics related to the problems associated with starting and managing smaller firms. Throughout this book we use a number of core case studies to illustrate key points related to dynamic entrepreneurial learning. All ten cases provide important insights into how entrepreneurs overcome the practical problems of establishing new businesses and dealing with decisions about the growth of those businesses.

Active Profile

Anna Heyes graduated from the University of Liverpool and established Active Profile in 2004 and has since won many awards including young entrepreneur of the Year, Northwest Women in Business 2008 and 2010. Active Profile is based on Liverpool Science Park and offers a wide range of services in the area of public relations and marketing. The company grew steadily in the first eight years, employed eight staff and had a turnover more than £500,000 in 2012. Active Profile has developed an extensive client base and now delivers communication strategies for brands by focusing on each client's business goals ensuring they meet their strategic object-ives. Under Anna Heyes's leadership, the company has continued as a fast-growing agency and now has offices in Manchester and London as well as Liverpool (www.activeprofile.co.uk/company/).

DOI: 10.4324/9781003312918-1

Fit Co

Fit Co was first established by a personal trainer who wanted to use his expertise in fitness to start a gym. However, while he was well known and respected in the industry, he lacked business experience. His real passion was in delivery fitness, not running the business. He encouraged an old school friend to join him. Together they were able to take responsibility for different parts of the business and acquire a new gym to expand the opportunities to deliver classes and attract membership of the gym.

Fume Co.

Fume Co. was a small fume cabinet company manufacturer in the Northwest of England. The owner struggled for many years achieve any growth, and his products were not known for quality or on-time delivery. He hired a new manager with experience in both manufacturing and sales to help address the problems. Bringing in this expertise helped to turn around this small, struggling firm and develop into an established manufacturing company with a reputation for on-time delivery of quality products. New systems and experience helped to grow turnover from £800,000 to £4.5 million over five years.

Innospace (Manchester Metropolitan University Business School)

Innospace was established in 2007 by staff from the Centre for Enterprise at Manchester Metropolitan University Business School to provide incubation space for graduates from all faculties of the University. The quotations from graduate entrepreneurs in Innospace were collected by PingPing Meckel during her doctoral research. The first objective in establishing Innospace was to provide graduates with support for the creation of knowledge-based businesses. The second objective was to encourage a 'community of practice' among those based in the incubator. Nascent entrepreneurs were provided with 12 months accommodation and access to knowledge, expertise and support available from MMUBS as well as other organizations within Manchester City-region. Within six months of launch Innospace had attracted 74 graduated entrepreneurs. Innospace was originally hosted within a self-contained floor of a Grade II listed building less than two minutes' walk from Manchester city centre. Currently, Innospace is located in Turing House, close to the city centre and continues to promote entre-preneurship within Manchester and details can be found on the following website: www.innospace.co.uk/

Jazooli

While still at school Sam Wilson began to buy and sell mobile phones on eBay to supplement his pocket-money. Sam's brother Ben formerly established Jazooli in 2008 while taking a year out before going to uni-versity and the business was run from Ben's bedroom in the family home for the first nine months. Ben began to source accessories for electronic goods directly from China and because higher volumes demanded more space their parents agreed to convert the family's garage into a storage unit. By October 2009 the business was doing so well that it was decided that Martin, their father, should join Jazooli on a full-time basis. On completing sixth form in 2010 Ben also joined the company on a full-time basis and they moved to a large warehouse with better transport links for deliveries and mail collections. The business continued to grow and four full-time staff had joined the company by May 2012 as well as three part-timers. In the first year of operation (2008) business turnover was £70,000 and this had increased to more than £3 million by 2015 with 12 employees. Business activities extended from mobile phones and accessories for tablet computers to include a wide range of consumer goods and electronic cigarettes.

Machine Co.

The owner of this company started with a small machine shop. The industry was changing with the introduction of CNC machines and so were customer expectations. They were a supplier to the aerospace industry, which was under financial pressure. They were in danger of losing the small amount of business they had. However, their customer helped set up a supplier development project, which they joined, and the owner embedded new continuous improvement systems he learned on the programme into the business. Academics from a nearby university as well as consultants provided other expertise such as quality management and tooling procedures. He was also able to show the system to prospective customers as evidence of the legitimate manufacturing practices in the business and he won new clients that reduced his reliance on one main customer and thus spread the risk. He managed to grow the business from £500,000 to £1.8 million, by leveraging weak ties and embedding new systems.

Packaging Co.

Packaging Co was the second new firm for the owner who had previously owned a small contract business selling pre-packaged 'kits' including bicycle repair gear. The owner-director's strategy was to develop business opportunities by first proving his firm's capability through successful 'small jobs' with a view to obtaining larger contracts. Through this strategy, the firm grew slowly over eight years from three to 12 employees, and from £200,000 to £650,000 in turnover. A local competitor came up for sale and he managed to purchase the business expanding through acquisition and moved his packaging company to the new premises. He did not, however, hire any new management and he struggled to cope with both the merger and the development of more complex manufacturing scheduling. The owner was constantly trying new methods and eventually introduced a new management information system and changed the management structure. He also attempted a range of options to improve internal efficiencies, enhance staff involvement and further develop the business. He learned about these ideas from his business contacts, but he always tried to achieve them on his own. Despite a number of initiatives, the firm struggled to reach its potential. It eventually failed.

PPE Ltd.

This small firm was established by a husband-and-wife team. The husband had worked in BNFL (British Nuclear Fuels Ltd.) and used his experience and relationships to establish a small manufacturing facility for personal protective equipment (PPE), including protective non-slip boots, protective tenting and a more versatile protective suit. For a number of years this was a very small operation, but over time, the husband (technical director) leveraged his relationships and addressed some of the problems he had experienced while working in protective equipment at BNFL. He embedded these solutions into product lines. Over 5 years he grew the firm to a turn-over of £800,000. His relationships and growing reputation as a solution provider, allowed him to win a contract as a PPE supplier to BNFL. As part of the contract, PPE were required to value-engineer existing supplies, which required rationalization and improvement of PPE products. Part of this process involved taking on manufacturing assembly work of products they co-innovated with supply network partners, and it also required that they encourage suppliers to innovate products to meet the demanding standards required in the nuclear industry. Over 18 months turnover grew from around £800,000 to approximately £3.5 millions and number of staff increased from eight to 32 personnel. Despite its rural location with poor transport connections, which limits access to technical networks and edu-cational institutions, PPE established relationships in their business network to facilitate development of the firm into a successful, innovative and prof-itable small business.

Spark Revolutions Ltd.

Phil and Adam established Spark Revolutions to offer website design and consultancy. Spark Revolutions was based on Liverpool Science Park and comprised five individuals who covered a broad area of expertise. Both developers have deep knowledge sets and achieved 1st class degrees in their respective disciplines. This allows Spark Revolutions to be driven by innovation not be constrained by a narrow knowledge base. Spark Revolutions have worked for Apple in their headquarters in California and are SAP qualified ERP consultants. Spark Revolutions create robust systems while also implementing stunning visuals by leveraging the latest technolo-gies. Spark Revolutions works closely and efficiently with all their clients and customers. The company combines with Ashgrove Marketing to offer a broad range of scaleable solutions comparable to those provided by larger organizations while maintaining the innovativeness and flexibility of a small business.

Wigan Recycling

While working at a community partnership project, Paul developed an interest in the topic of recycling. Seeing the potential for establishing a social enterprise Paul contacted local hospitals, schools and universities about the collection of redundant computers. Paul then found a derelict supermarket that he was able to use free of charge to set-up his computer recycling business in 2009. Despite all his cost-saving measures he still managed to build up debts of £20,000 on his credit cards, which he eventually settled with the help of a grant from Liverpool City Council. Later, he entered into an agreement with another recycling company to share staff on a part-time basis. Along with free support from family and friends, Paul was able to extend his operations outside of the Liverpool area. Wigan Recycling provides an excellent example of bootstrapping the business – see Chapter 9.

Developing Your Entrepreneurial Learning Capabilities

1.1 Introduction

As the topic has grown in importance over the last 20 years there has been a steady increase in the number of textbooks dealing with entrepreneurship, business start-up and the management of small firms (Baron & Hmieleski, 2018; Blundel, Lockett, Wang & Mawson, 2021; Burns, 2018; Morris & Kuratko, 2020; Zacharakis, Corbett & Bygrave, 2020). In this book, we adopt a different approach from those already available to students. Our focus is considerably narrower than most textbooks, which generally cover the whole business life cycle from opportunity identification to maturity. Here we concentrate on what we regard as the most important period associated with student ventures: the decision to start a business and the first 12 months of operation. All chapters in this book are focused on how nascent entrepreneurs obtain, mobilize and apply their resources in this crucial period. Although Chapters 10 and 11 do examine business growth, we are primarily concerned with encouraging new entrepreneurs to establish a sound basis for businesses that are viable in the longer-term. Few new entrepreneurs will be concerned with employees in the early stages and, therefore, we do not spend time discussing issues related to small-firm management. Most new entrepreneurs should concentrate on managing themselves and mobilizing their resources rather than trying to deal with the complexity of employment-related issues. At the same time, the principle of this book is that the 'blue-print' or template established in the immediate pre- and post-start-up phase will have significant implications for the future of the business (Baron, Hannan & Burton, 1999). Hence, we stress the importance of 'dynamic entrepreneurial learning' and the need to create new businesses based on the principles of dynamic

DOI: 10.4324/9781003312918-2

capabilities. There has been much intellectual effort expended on defining the term entrepreneur (Shane, 2012). We adopt a very general definition in which an entrepreneur is someone attempting to start their own business or those currently managing their own businesses (Aldrich & Yang, 2012).

While there are critics who find little evidence of 'entrepreneurial learning' (Storey, 1994, 2011) our approach is based on the principle that learning is central to long-term success of start-up businesses (Haneberg & Aaboen, 2021; Jones, Meckel & Taylor, 2021b). There is certainly evidence which supports the view that there is a positive relationship between higher levels of human capital and entrepreneurial success (Davidsson & Honig, 2003; Kim, Aldrich & Keister, 2006; Kurczewska & Mackiewicz, 2020; Unger, Rauch, Frese & Rosenbusch, 2011). For example, the concept of 'absorptive capacity' is based on the principle that possession of knowledge makes it easier to recognize the value of new information and apply to commercial ends (de Jong & Freel, 2010; Witt, 2004). While Cohen and Levinthal (1990, p. 129) were referring to learning in R&D-based organizations the concept of absorptive capacity was established according to the principles of cognitive learning: 'accumulated prior knowledge increases both the ability to put new knowledge into memory, what we would call the acquisition of knowledge, and the ability to recall and use it'. Building resilience (Chadwick & Raver, 2020) into start-up businesses means that young and inexperienced entrepreneurs must develop the ability to make the best of their own skills and knowledge. However, they must also have the social skills to mobilize the resources of those 'close ties' belonging to their immediate networks of family and friends. Based on an extensive review of the absorptive capacity literature, Flechas Chaparro, Kozesinski and Camargo Júnior (2021) distinguish between internal and external approaches to the acquisition of knowledge for new businesses. The authors identify four internal strategies: experiential learning (learning from experience), vicarious learning (learning from others), searching (learning by searching for specific information) and congenital learning (drawing on intrinsic knowledge gained from personal experiences). External strategies include grafting (learning by incorporating people that possess knowledge), human mobility (knowledge transfer from the exchange of experiences), partnerships with universities and social networks (Flechas Chaparro et al., 2021, p. 75). Establishing partnerships with other nascent entrepreneurs also offers an extremely effective way of enhancing the absorptive capacity of start-up businesses (Jones, Meckel & Taylor, 2021a).

The authors have been teaching and researching entrepreneurship for a considerable amount of time. At the same time, our thinking about entrepreneurial learning has been influenced by the work of Allan Gibb and Jason Cope (Cope, 2005; Cope & Watts, 2000; Gibb, 2011; Gibb & Ritchie, 1982). Learning from critical incidents (crises) or even from failure is a crucial element of Jason's contribution to our understanding of the way in which entrepreneurs learn in practice (Cope, 2003, 2011; Pittaway & Thorpe, 2012). We believe that such principles can be applied in the classroom by encouraging students to engage in a process of active learning (Lourenco & Jones, 2006). We acknowledge that conventional lectures still have a place in terms of transmitting ideas, facts and theories about entrepreneurship. Real learning will, however, only take place if students engage in activities which give them some experience of undertaking tasks associated with entrepreneurship. Such experience can take a variety of forms including vicarious learning from experienced entrepreneurs, engaging with computer simulation games or experiencing real business start-up, ideally guided by experienced 'mentors' (see Chapter 5).

1.2 Learning Objectives

- To appreciate the growing importance of entrepreneurship especially for younger people.
- To be able to articulate the nature of the learning approach advocated in this book.
- To understand the significance of developing an entrepreneurial mindset.
- To consider the opportunities and threats associated with the Covid-19 pandemic.
- To recognize that the knowledge associated with entrepreneurship is dynamic and rapidly changing.

1.3 Growing Importance of Entrepreneurship

Entrepreneurship has become a topic of major importance to politicians and to those involved with higher education. The advent of a new political agenda became apparent with the first Thatcher government of 1979 which began to promote the idea of an enterprise culture within the UK (Anderson,

Drakopoulou-Dodd & Scott, 2000; Anderson, Jack & Drakopoulou-Dodd, 2010). Similar changes were also occurring within other developed counties as the 'post-war' consensus between politicians of the left and right about the role of the State and commitment to public spending based on Keynesian economic theory began to disintegrate. A political realignment with the emergence of New Labour under the leadership of Tony Blair meant the politicians of the left were as enthusiastic about entrepreneurship as previous Conservative governments (Hesmondhalgh, Oakley, Lee & Nisbett, 2015). Both Blair and his successor as prime-minister, Gordon Brown, were keen to ensure that the UK was 'the best place in the world to start a business'. This phrase was regularly used by David Cameron's Conservative government (2010–2016). Growing interest in entrepreneurship as an alternative to paid employment is not simply associated with developed countries such as the UK (see Chapter 13). According to the GEM studies, 'factor-driven econ-omies' (the least developed) such as Egypt and Indonesia have high levels of entrepreneurial activity. Efficiency-driven economies including Brazil, China and Russia also have levels of entrepreneurial activity which exceeds levels in most innovation-driven economies including France, Germany, Italy, Japan and Spain. As discussed in Chapter 13, it is important to consider the distinction between opportunity-based entrepreneurship and necessity-based entrepreneurship. Necessity-based entrepreneurship, which is usu-ally very low value, accounts for a greater proportion of entrepreneurial activity in less developed economies. Therefore, it is not simply the level of entrepreneurship which is important but also the extent to which such activity contributes to National economic and social well-being.

Despite growing interest in entrepreneurship, the failure rates of new businesses remain high although it is difficult to obtain definitive figures. Some suggest that 90% of new businesses fail in the first year. However, recent UK figures provide a more optimistic picture for survival rates.[1] There are approximately 650,000 start-ups every year in the UK and 89% survive the first year while 42.4% survive for five years. Baron et al. (1999) proposed that all entrepreneurs begin with a blueprint which informs their approach to the process of building a business. Drawing on a survey of 76 technology-based companies in Silicon Valley the authors identified five basic employ-ment models (engineering, star, commitment, bureaucracy and autocracy) based on three dimensions: attachment, selection and coordination/con-trol (Baron et al., 1999). Such blueprints are associated with a number of factors including the entrepreneur's business strategy and the influence of key resource providers (Baron et al., 1999). Aldrich and Yang (2012, p. 1) extend these ideas by suggesting that a key reason for failure is that most young people attempting to start their own businesses have not acquired 'the blueprints and associated tools they need to build organizations'.

The first and most important of those tools is knowledge: what entrepreneurs need to know and how they apply that knowing. Aldrich and Yang (2012) suggest that there are three interrelated personal 'dispositions' associated with entrepreneurial actions which they describe as routines, habits and heuristics (Box 1.1). The term routine was developed by Nelson and Winter (1982, p. 197) and it refers to 'regular and predictable patterns of behavior'. Latour (1986) differentiates between ostensive routines (abstract patterns) and performative routines (specific actions). From the perspective of a nascent entrepreneur, ostensive routines encompass such activities as the need to produce a well-researched business plan as a means of engaging with resource providers. Performative routines concern those actions entrepreneurs undertake to obtain and analyse the data necessary to convince potential funders that their business idea is worthwhile.

Habitual behaviour is an essential element of human activity as well as the underpinning of future 'organizational routines' (Hodgson, 2009). Individual habits are the basis on which nascent entrepreneurs enact emerging routines in their new businesses (Aldrich & Yang, 2012; Jones & Li, 2017). As pointed out by Baron (2008) emotions and feelings are central to the habitual responses made by entrepreneurs to key decisions during business start-up. Therefore, in considering the ways in which students make the transition to entrepreneurship it is important to encourage reflection on the efficacy of those habitual behaviours which influence development of their 'business models' (Jones & Giordano, 2021).

Box 1.1

I guess the hard work was always in me and just took a while to come out. From about 11 or 12 when my mum started doing her MA, she worked 16 hours a day non-stop and still does. I am like that; people email me at 10pm and they have a response within 5 minutes, and I think if you own your own business you should expect to be on call 24 hours a day. If you don't deal with problems, there and then you don't care enough about what you do. [Ben Wilson, Jazooli]

The third element identified by Aldrich and Yang (2012) are heuristics which are distinctive from habits. With regards to nascent entrepreneurs, it is suggested that they must make the best use of information which is appropriate to their own individual situations. Hence, simple 'rules-of-thumb' inform decisions when individuals are short of both time and resources. This suggests that effective nascent entrepreneurs do not waste time and effort trying to achieve optimal solutions. Rather, they accept that they will have to compromise and make the best of the resources they have available (Anjum, Farrukh, Heidler & Díaz Tautiva, 2021; Jones & Li, 2017). As we discuss in later chapters, this approach fits very well with what we describe as entrepreneurship based on bootstrapping and bricolage.

It is widely accepted that routines are essential to the effective operation of established organizations (Cohen & Bacdayan, 1994; March & Simon, 1958; Nelson & Winter, 1982; Pentland & Feldman, 2005). According to Pentland, Feldman, Becker & Liu (2012), repetitive patterns of action form the basis of all routines (Aldrich & Yang, 2014; Macpherson, Herbane & Jones, 2015). In the context of a new business venture, the entrepreneur's habitual behaviours and heuristics (rules of thumb for problem-solving) will combine to establish some rudimentary routines concerned with activities such as the pricing of their products or services (see Box 1.2):

Box 1.2

When you start off you have no idea how to price things and it's impossible to find out about market averages. You haven't got a clue how long it's going to take to develop a product; you go off best-guesses and sometimes they are just wrong. There've been a few times when we've priced ourselves out of the market, even undercharged, been way off the mark, got caught in the enthusiasm trap and it's not the best thing we could have done [*Spark Revolutions Ltd.*].

Entrepreneurs who understand the need overcome *ad hoc* approaches to pricing and costing, as well as other business activities, are more likely to be successful in the longer term (Jones & Giordano, 2021). Routines are based on a 'substrate of individual habits' acquired as a result of influences from family, education and early work experiences (Aldrich & Yang, 2012, p. 13).

Subsequently, entrepreneurial choices about the nature of their 'business platform' will form the basis of organizational routines as the firm becomes more established (Davidsson & Klofsten, 2003). Routines will be refined *via* a process of variation and selection as entrepreneurs identify approaches which work best for their businesses. As we discuss in Chapter 2, a range of knowledges, skills and capabilities are associated with the early stages of starting a business and form the basis on which new entrepreneurs embed the appropriate routines into their commercial activities.

While we acknowledge that functional and technical skills are important in most start-up businesses it is also essential that nascent entrepreneurs develop their social competences (Holt & Macpherson, 2010; Tocher, Oswald, Shook & Adams, 2012). Entrepreneurs must create routines based on activities associated with bootstrapping and bricolage which are central to the acquisition, reconfiguration, integration and exploitation of the resources required to establish their businesses. As the business grows, bootstrapping and bricolage should become embedded routines in the fabric of the firm to ensure that it remains responsive and agile by maintaining a lean approach in its operating strategy (Timmons, 1999). For example, RSL, a small, entre-preneurial manufacturing firm, adopted a number of relatively straightfor-ward routines which helped to improve the overall business performance, and these are summarized in Table 1.1 (Jones & Craven, 2001b). As these basic routines became established in the firm it was possible to introduce more sophisticated routines associated with a new product development

Table 1.1 Developing New Routines

	ACTIONS TAKEN IN RSL
Scan trade journals	Carefully examine trade journals and supplier catalogues for new product ideas
Develop customer contacts	Build strong relationships with customers to identify their existing and future needs
Attend trade shows	Initiate informal discussions with staff from competitors to stimulate new product ideas
Competitor price check	Examine competitor prices as a basis for estimating their cost-base
Encourage supplier input	Involve suppliers in early stages of new product development – helping to reduce costs

committee and the 'reverse engineering' of competitor products (Jones & Craven, 2001a).

As we discuss in the next section, linking entrepreneurial actions to those routines which form the basis of successful business platform fits with contemporary perspectives on entrepreneurship which are known as the practice-based approach (De Clercq & Voronov, 2009; Teague, Tunstall, Champenois & Gartner, 2021). The practice-based view of entrepreneurship rejects the idea that some individuals have intrinsic attributes (such as tolerance of ambiguity, risk-taking and the need for achievement) which mean they will be more likely to become entrepreneurs (McClelland, 1962). The alternative view is that entrepreneurship is a set of social practices which are influenced by broader structures, institutions and societal norms (Elfring, Klyver & van Burg, 2021; Lounsbury, Cornelissen, Granqvist & Grodal, 2019; Lounsbury & Glynn, 2001).

1.4 A Practice-based Approach to Entrepreneurial Learning

As we discuss in Chapter 5, early approaches to entrepreneurial learning were based primarily on cognitivism (Kohler, 1925; Piaget, 1926) and behaviourism (Pavlov, 1927; Skinner, 1938; Thorndike, 1913). Gradually there have been moves to adopt approaches which incorporate experiential and social learning. Our understanding of entrepreneurial learning has certainly been influenced by David Kolb's experiential learning theory. As Kolb (1984) acknowledges his own ideas owe a strong intellectual debt to Jean Piaget's contribution to the understanding of cognitive development. The work of social psychologist Kurt Lewin on group dynamics also influenced the development of ELT. In particular, Lewin's (1951) action-research approach to planned change ranging from small groups to complex organizations had 'the most far-reaching practical significant' (Kolb, 1984, p. 8). Kolb also acknowledges his intellectual debt to the work of American philosopher John Dewey. Recent interest in the 'practice turn' has revitalized interest in Dewey's contribution to the fields of philosophy and education (Raelin, 2007). Kolb (1984) argues that Dewey's commitment to experiential learning meant that he was most influential educational theorist of the twentieth century. Dewey, along with Charles Sanders Pierce and William James was one of three scholars associated with founding the pragmatism school of philosophy. Pragmatism is based on the idea that theory and practice are linked in a process of mutual reinforcement. Practice informs theory, enhanced theory improves practice, the adoption of new practices further aids theory development. The important issue as far as we are concerned is that it is essential to identify the social practices which underpin the actions of nascent entrepreneurs as they attempt to establish new business ventures (Anderson, Drakopoulou-Dodd & Jack, 2010).

Emergence of the practice perspective was based on attempts to resolve tensions between contrasting explanations of social phenomena based on either agency (individual action) or structures such as class, family and education (Bourdieu, 1977; Giddens, 1987). Gradually the practice perspective has been adopted in the study of strategy (Whittington, 1996) management (Samra-Fredericks, 2003), organizational learning (Lave & Wenger, 1991), small firms (Stringfellow & Shaw, 2009) and entrepreneurship (De Clercq & Honig, 2011; Karatas-Ozkan, 2011; Steyaert & Katz, 2004). De Clercq and Voronov (2009) set out an explanation of entrepreneurship from a practice perspective based on Bourdieu's (2002) concept of habitus (Box 1.3). As discussed in Chapter 5, individual dispositions at the micro-level are linked to the macro-level ('the field') by habitus at the meso-level. Perhaps the most useful applications of Bourdieu's ideas concern the four types of capital which individual entrepreneurs draw on to pursue their objectives in setting up a business (Karatas-Ozkan, 2011).

- **Economic capital** refers to the financial resources to which a nascent entrepreneur has access – can include debt and equity funding;
- **Cultural capital** concerns the socialization processes associated with education and training as well as other forms of work-related experiences;
- **Social capital** refers to the resources (physical and emotional) which can be acquired via the nascent entrepreneur's various network ties (strong and weak); and
- **Symbolic capital** is the sum of the other three forms of capital as it is central to the entrepreneur's ability to legitimize themselves and their business in the eyes of potential stakeholders.

Box 1.3

Habitus focuses attention on the values, dispositions and expectations of social groups which are acquired through the activities and experience of everyday life. Habitus refers to the elements of culture that can be identified in the day-to-day practices of individuals, groups, societies and nations. It includes the habits, skills, styles and tastes which form the basis of the non-discursive knowledge on which the taken-for-granted assumptions of various social groups are founded.

The various forms of capital are used by individuals to legitimize their identity as entrepreneurs and provide credibility for the various social practices associated with acquiring the resources to start a new business (De Clercq & Voronov, 2009; Teague et al., 2021). Karatas-Ozkan (2011) uses this framework in a detailed case study of a new business venture established by five nascent entrepreneurs. She concludes that learning experiences associated with the various forms of capital are mobilized by a range of entrepreneurial practices related to starting a new business (Table 1.2).

According to Raelin (2007) higher education is dominated by pedagogical approaches which adhere to the Cartesian principle which separates theory and practice. Objectified knowledge is based on *facts* which are established through the collection of *positive* empirical data. Consequently,

Table 1.2 Routines and Entrepreneurial Practices

ROUTINES	ENTREPRENEURIAL PRACTICES
Identify business opportunities	Develop a 'feel' for the market and existing competitors
Acquiring resources	Use social networks as a basis for identifying and acquiring relevant resources
Managing oneself	Develop practical rules of thumb to make best use of own resources (time)
Managing business functions	Learn to balance various activities associated with a new business: operations, finance, customers, suppliers etc.

learning in higher education relies on the transfer of objectified knowledge from lecturer to students via theories and frameworks. In entrepreneurship education objectified facts include the psychological attributes associated with entrepreneurs such as risk-taking, tolerance of ambiguity and the need for achievement. Those whose approach is informed by a social constructionist (Berger & Luckmann, 1966) epistemology reject the idea that social phenomena can be defined by objective facts. Rather, social constructs such as 'entrepreneurship' differ according to their location in time and space in relationship to a particular culture. To give an extreme example, the way in which entrepreneurship is understood by a young male entrepreneur based in Silicon Valley will be very different from the understanding of a middle-aged African woman engaged in subsistence agriculture to feed her family. Raelin (2007) argues that an 'epistemology of practice' has major implications for the integration of classroom-based learning and work-based learning. Individuals should be encouraged to construct knowledge in conjunction with their lecturers and other students (Rawes & Renwick, 2020). Rather than being provided with objectified knowledge about the problems associated with starting a business students should be given opportunities to gain first-hand experience of such problems. They should also be encouraged to learn by reflecting on their experiences at the individual and group levels. Hence, student learning from others in a social environment is mediated through both theories which are presented in the classroom and through the norms associated with knowledge-sharing within groups (Vygotsky, 1978).

Activity theory (Engeström, 2001) has been widely adopted to develop a better understanding of organizational learning. Jones and Holt (2008) use activity theory to examine the ways in which entrepreneurial ventures change during their early years of operation. Three case studies are used to illustrate the inherent messiness associated with the transition from conception of business ideas to their actual gestation. In particular, the study indicates a range of factors such as pro-activity, risk-taking, heightened self-confidence, vision, the use of heuristics and rules of thumb which are used by entrepreneurs to identify and exploit new opportunities. During business start-up, entrepreneurial identities are formed within social and cultural environments that include family, professional and policy communities. Entrepreneurs must organize their knowledge and actions within existing structures such as business planning, marketing, limited liability and intellectual property rights (Jones & Holt, 2008).

17

Adopting a practice-based view of learning has substantial implications for those engaged in entrepreneurial education. Instead of concentrating on individual traits and cognitions there is more focus on socially embedded experiences and relations. As Higgins and Elliott (2011, p. 353) point out, 'practice as a pedagogical approach to entrepreneurial education' means that 'individual learners are encouraged to understand a situation by connecting knowing and doing'. This also means that students must be encouraged to adopt an active, rather than a passive, approach to learning by engaging in the knowledge creation process. A further advantage is that the interaction of experience and practice helps students develop the appropriate critical thinking and communication skills which are a prerequisite for entrepreneurial success (Galloway, Higgins, McGowan, Preedy & Jones, 2017; Higgins & Elliott, 2011). The ability to remember 'facts' and to describe appropriate theories such as Corbett's (2005) conceptualization of how experiential learning informs opportunity recognition and exploitation are important elements of any course/module offered in higher education. As well at the objective/explicit knowledge associated with known facts and theories about entrepreneurship, students should be encouraged to develop their tacit knowledge associated with the development of sense-making abilities related to the 'reading' of social situations and adopt the appropriate (formal or informal) language (Cornelissen, Clarke & Cienki, 2012).

1.5 Developing an Entrepreneurial Mindset

One of the key issues in entrepreneurship research focuses on those individuals who are better at identifying new business opportunities than other people. Such individuals may also be better at mobilizing the resources necessary to exploit those opportunities. It is generally accepted that an *entrepreneurial mindset* helps explain why some individuals are better able to develop new ideas, solve difficult problems, exercise higher levels of creativity as well as identifying new opportunities (Kuratko, Fisher & Audretsch, 2020). Possessing (or developing) an entrepreneurial mindset enables some individuals to make sense of a complex and rapidly changing environment. From our perspective in writing this book, we are committed to the importance of helping students develop an entrepreneurial mindset. We believe that thinking like an entrepreneur will be important to you in your future career whether or not you decide to start your own business (see Chapter 3).

Based on a review of the literature, Naumann (2017) lists several descriptions of an entrepreneurial mindset. The following definition by Haynie, Shepherd, Mosakowski and Earley (2010, p. 62) fits best with our approach in this book: 'the ability and willingness of individuals to rapidly sense, act and mobilize in response to a judgemental decision under uncertainty about possible opportunities for gain'. Hopefully, you can see that this definition covers a wide range of activities in various organizational contexts that go beyond entrepreneurs identifying new business opportunities. This fits with individuals who could be described as 'self-starters'; those who are highly motivated and willing to take the initiative without constant supervision. It would be very difficult to pursue an entrepreneurial career without being a self-starter! Naumann (2017, p. 161) then goes on to summarize the seven attributes most strongly associated with an entrepreneurial mindset in the literature.

1. **Cognitive tuning and goal orientation** – 'tuning' means that an individual's cognition should be focused on the current task that is most important to their overall goal (ie, starting a business). This is based on the recognition that cognition is dynamic, and the emphasis will change depending on those activities being undertaken by the would-be entrepreneur. Goal orientation simply means that you should have a clear objective in mind when you are undertaking various tasks. For example, you might consider whether writing a conventional *business plan* will help you start your own new business (this is discussed in Section 4.4, Lean Start-up).

2. **Heuristic-based decision logic** – heuristics are also known as 'rules of thumb', which means that individuals use their previous experiences when making decisions under conditions of uncertainty (ie, you do not possess all the relevant 'facts'). Using heuristics may be particularly difficult for students who have little previous work experience. However, vicarious knowledge (using the experience of other entrepreneurs who may be family members) can certainly provide guidance in making decisions under time pressure faced with highly dynamic situations.

3. **Alertness** – originated with Kirzner (1973) who stressed the importance of entrepreneurs possessing the alertness to spot new business opportunities. Baron (2006) suggests that alertness is partly a cognitive attribute and is also influenced by intelligence and high levels of

creativity. Alertness is discussed in Section 3.3, Entrepreneurial cognition and creative thinking.

4. **Prior knowledge** – (also discussed in Chapter 3) usually referred to as a combination of education and previous work experience. Most undergraduate and postgraduate students are unlikely to have acquired a great deal of work experience. As we discuss in Chapter 7 (human capital) there is a strong link between gaining some work experience and the chance of establishing a successful start-up business. That work experience can be relatively mundane such as undertaking a paper round or working in a fast-food restaurant. It appears to be the early establishment of good work-related routines and the opportunity to engage with customers and experienced business people that is important.

5. **Social interaction/capital** – the importance of social capital to entrepreneurs has been increasingly recognized as the role of social networks have become apparent. Social capital refers to the benefits you gain from your close family and friends (strong ties) and 'friends of friends' (weak ties). It is generally acknowledged that people with more extensive and diverse social network are able to access a wide range of tangible (finance) and intangible resources (emotional support).

6. **Metacognition** – can be defined as 'thinking about thinking' or perhaps more accurately, learning to learn. As we discuss in Sections 4.3 (Business Models) and 4.4 (Lean Start-up), the ability to learn as you move from the identification of an opportunity to the creation of a new business will influence whether you succeed or fail (see Figure 4.3).

7. **Cognitive adaptability** – any entrepreneurial business is likely to be faced with a complex and highly dynamic environment, which makes forecasting extremely difficult. Therefore, the ability to make sense of that complexity will be based on your 'cognitive resources' including understanding of other people and their motives as well as your cognitive resources built-up during previous experiences, memories and routines. As we have previously stressed, some of those cognitive resources may have been acquired vicariously via the experiences of other people.

Attributes 1 to 5 are described as the core of an entrepreneurial mindset and they 'translate into recognisable and observable behaviour' (Naumann, 2017, p. 163). In other words, there are clear linkages between each of

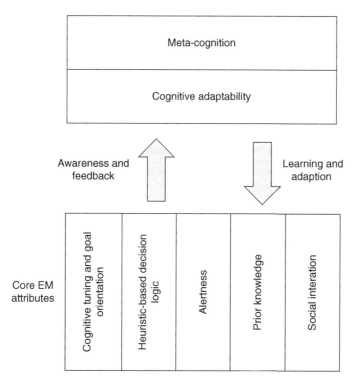

Figure 1.1 Influences on the Entrepreneurial Mindset

the five attributes and the activities undertaken by nascent entrepreneurs. While attributes 6 and 7 are described as meta-cognitive attributes and they are less easy to associate with specific entrepreneurial behaviours (Figure 1.1). Essentially, meta-cognitive attributes are associated with the individual's ability to reflect on their thinking processes and make adaptions to their cognition and, ultimately, the way in which they operate (Naumann, 2017).

Kuratko et al. (2020) also draw on the existing literature to develop a model of the EM, which has three distinct factors: cognition, emotions and behaviours. As we have discussed above, cognition describes the mental functions associated with understanding, storing, remembering, problem-solving and decision-making. Entrepreneurial cognition is concerned with the way in which entrepreneurs think when they are identifying opportunities or making decisions about whether they should grow their business (Kuratko et al., 2020). To sum up, it is generally accepted that entrepreneurs think in ways that are different from those of other people.

The second factor proposed by Kuratko et al. (2020) is the entrepreneurial behaviour associated with engaging in activities designed to identify an opportunity and, ultimately, start a new business. Simply thinking about opportunities without action will not lead to the creation of new products, services, or businesses. Particularly for young, inexperienced would-be entrepreneurs, the processes associated with identifying an opportunity, obtaining the necessary resources and starting a business (the entrepreneurial process) happen concurrently with the development of their own entrepreneurial identities. The experiential learning cycle (see Chapter 5) because of thinking and planning (cognition) and then taking action means that you will learn about yourself as well as the prospects for your business idea. You should learn whether you have the intrinsic motivation and self-efficacy to make the move into entrepreneurship. If you believe that you do have the appropriate skills (self-efficacy) then you are more likely to be motivated by a career as an entrepreneur.

The third factor identified by Kuratko et al. (2020) is described as the emotional aspect of becoming an entrepreneur. For most entrepreneurs, their activities will be framed by high levels of risk and uncertainty, which for most people means they are exposed to stressful emotions. A willingness to accept that your day-to-day lives will be typified by stressful situations is an important element in becoming an entrepreneur. This stress is not only associated with the risks of failure, but it is also a result of you, the entrepreneur, having to take on a range of different roles. As we discuss in Section 2.3, there are a number of basic skills you must obtain in in the early stages of business start-up: opportunity identification/development, sales, marketing, finance, time management, resilience and so on. As the business begins to function, then it is necessary to acquire higher-level skills such as strategic decision-making, negotiation, financial planning (see Chapters 2 and 12). While there is no doubt that you will experience plenty of emotional 'highs' associated with the successful launch of your new business there will also be plenty of 'lows' as you worry about the likelihood of the business succeeding. This points to two other key entrepreneurial attributes: resourcefulness and resilience. Resourcefulness refers to your cognitive adaptability as you draw on you prior knowledge to overcome seemingly insoluble problems. Fisher, Neubert & Burnell (2021) argue that creating a resourcefulness narrative is important for stimulating a positive response from external resource providers. In other words, if you are seen as a resourceful individual then you are more likely to convince other

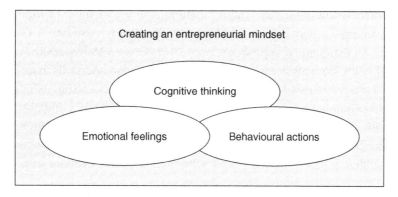

Figure 1.2 The Entrepreneurial Mindset Triad

people to support your venture. Resilience refers to your 'mental toughness' as you will be required to face numerous set-backs in your attempts to make the transition from student to entrepreneur (Chadwick & Raver, 2020). Resilience is also referred to as 'grit' in some studies of entrepreneurship success (Mooradian, Matzler, Uzelac & Bauer, 2016).

In summary, Kuratko et al. (2020) stress the importance of recognizing that the three factors illustrated in Figure 1.2 are not independent. In fact, your cognition, emotions and behaviours interact to reinforce each of the other factors. According to the authors (Kuratko et al., 2020, p. 7):

> If individuals embrace this mindset and realize that the interactive nature of the three aspects then they will likely become even more entrepreneurial over time; whereas individuals that fail to utilise the interactive aspect of their entrepreneurial mindset will find it difficult to tap into their entrepreneurial mindset as time progresses.

We also suggest that it is important you see these three factors as mutually reinforcing because that will help build resourcefulness and resilience into your daily activities as an entrepreneur.

1.5.1 Entrepreneurship Education and the Entrepreneurial Mindset

We are committed to the idea that entrepreneurship education must go beyond conventional pedagogical approaches associated with business and management programmes. It is widely accepted that effective entrepreneurship education should include a strong element of experiential learning (Lourenco & Jones, 2006; Manolis, Burns, Assudani & Chinta, 2012). An experiential approach (Cope, 2011; Cope & Watts, 2000; Politis, 2005) helps students acquire the relevant knowledge and skills associated with entrepreneurship. In the early stages, entrepreneurship education should certainly be focused on developing the right attitudes and mindsets for students to take the step into becoming entrepreneurs. The QAA[2] [Quality Assurance Association for Higher Education] (2018) distinguishes among three different modes of delivery for entrepreneurship education:

- Learning about (entrepreneurship) refers to a traditional pedagogy based on knowledge acquisition through the study of the topic based on lectures and text-books;
- Learning for (entrepreneurship) has a more practical goal and the focus in on learning how to be more entrepreneurial through experiential learning; and
- Learning 'through' the practical application of entrepreneurial activity requires the development of enhanced reflection skills and relates to practical activities including start-ups, venture creation programmes and incubators or accelerators.

We anticipate students using our book will be undertaking courses/ programmes in which the focus is on experiential learning (see Chapter 5) to help develop entrepreneurial capabilities and mindsets. A central feature of 'learning to learn' is that the various activities you undertake as part of your course should be followed by a period of critical reflection. This means that you should have a clear understanding of what you 'know' about entrepreneurship as well as your knowledge gaps. Figure 1.3 (QAA, 2018) illustrates the learning journey for entrepreneurial students and here we focus on the importance of the entrepreneurial mindset. The model suggests that learning via the curricula should be supplemented by extracurricular learning. Most universities have enterprise clubs (Pittaway et al., 2015) that provide additional opportunities to engage in entrepreneurial activities. Developing an entrepreneurial mindset means becoming more aware of your own enterprise and entrepreneurial capabilities. The QAA[3] (2018) provides a list of factors associated with an entrepreneurial mindset:

- Self-aware of personality and social identity
- Motivated to achieve personal ambitions and goals

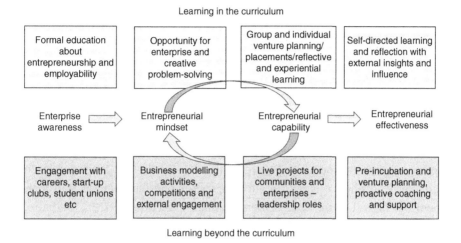

Figure 1.3 Student Learning Pipeline and the Entrepreneurial Mindset

- Self-organized, flexible and resilient
- Curious towards new possibilities for creating value
- Responsive to problems and opportunities by making new connections
- Able to go beyond perceived limitations and achieve results
- Tolerant of uncertainty, ambiguity, risk and failure
- Sensitive to personal values such as ethical, social, diversity and environmental awareness.

There are a number of recent studies from a range of different countries that investigate the importance of entrepreneurship education in developing an entrepreneurial mindset among the student population (Cui, Sun & Bell, 2021; Inada, 2020; Kwapisz, Schell, Aytes & Bryant, 2021; Lindberg, Bohman, Hulten & 2017). The results indicate that courses which are based on an experiential learning approach combined with opportunities for extra-curricular activities designed to encourage enterprising behaviours do have a positive influence on the entrepreneurial mindset. In Chapter 3, we focus on the core capability of identifying entrepreneurial opportunities and the various exercises will provide the opportunity to develop an entrepreneurial mindset.

You should now undertake the Entrepreneurial Mindset exercises at the end of this chapter.

1.6 Covid-19 and the New Economic Environment

The emergence of Covid-19 at the end of 2019 had a massive impact on global economic activity (Kuckertz et al., 2020). Most developed countries instigated 'lockdowns', which curtailed many business activities except for healthcare, food, transport, communications and emergency services. In such circumstances, starting a new business became increasingly difficult for young and inexperienced entrepreneurs. Nevertheless, as discussed in Chapter 2, resilience is a core attribute for anyone intending to start their own business (Doern, 2017; Doern, Williams & Vorley, 2019). Therefore, thinking about ways in which you can respond to the crisis by making the best use of your own resources, engaging in creative problem-solving and making effective use of your network resources can help in overcoming the crisis (Kuckertz et al., 2020). As we discuss in Chapter 9, these responses can be classified as 'bootstrapping' behaviours, which are central to the approach advocated in this book (Jayawarna, Jones & Macpherson, 2020; Jones & Jayawarna, 2010).

Kuckertz et al. (2020) also suggest that focusing on opportunities associated with the crisis can help overcome the problems facing new entrepreneurs (for example, the rise in demand for home deliveries). In their response to Covid-19, Alvarez and Barney (2020) draw on the concept of 'uncertainty' associated with the work of Frank Knight. They suggest that during periods of business, economic, medical and political stability, then the tools consistent with discovery theory (Shane, 2000), scientific methods, rationality and boundedly rational analysis are appropriate in guiding start-up businesses. In response to the higher levels of uncertainty associated with Covid-19, they argue that 'creation theory' provides a better tool for dealing with the current challenges (see Section 12.6.5). What this means in practice is entrepreneurs should 'go back to the beginning, when the virus first jumped from animals to humans and understand the human actions that started the uncertainty that disrupted the world' (Alvarez & Barney, 2020, p. 553). Developing a better understanding of the actions that set-off the uncertainty means that entrepreneurs will have a better chance of *creating opportunities* that can help humankind.

According to GEM 2020, the Covid-19 outbreak was declared a global health emergency on 30 January 2020 and a global pandemic on 11 March

2020. The report goes on to suggest the response will need businesses to become more adaptable, flexible, resilient and responsive. This means that entrepreneurs and the owners of small businesses should have significant advantages over large business which lack the ability to adapt to new circumstances. The GEM Report has the following advice for policymakers:

- **Clear and concise communication** of policies is a must, if a maximum number of entrepreneurs are to benefit from policies favourable to entrepreneurship.
- **Collaboration** and **cooperation** with entrepreneurs, academics, hubs and other enabling organizations will be essential as all stakeholders seek value-adding partnerships and synergies to exchange knowledge and know-how.
- **Responsibility** and **resilience** will be assets to all organizations; the COVID-19 pandemic showed us just how important it is to work together for the common good.
- **Innovating** and celebrating **innovation** is the name of the game moving forward as entrepreneurs grasp opportunities.
- **Simplifying** policies is also important so that new entrants from the informal sector in particular will be able to navigate the new, formal business context that they have entered.
- **Preparation**, since policymakers would do well to spend time **preparing** for a potential, many say even likely, new wave of the pandemic.

According to the most recent GEM Report (2020/21) at least 50% of total early stage entrepreneurs (TEAs) in both developed and developing countries stated that starting a business was more difficult than a year ago. In addition, there was widespread agreement that the pandemic had delayed their plans for getting new businesses operational. A more positive development suggested that in nine of the 43 countries surveyed by GEM, more than half of those starting or running a new business agreed that the pandemic had led to new business opportunities (Alvarez & Barney, 2020; Kuckertz et al., 2020). The GEM Report (2020/21) also indicates that overall rates of early-stage entrepreneurial activity did not appear to have changed significantly compared to 2019. This is certainly very surprising given the severity of ongoing Covid-19 crisis. It is suggested in the Report that the failure to identify a decline in TEA may be a result of GEM's data collection ending in August 2020. Given that we had been suffering from the impact of Covid-19 for almost 18 months (at that time), then the timing of the research is unlikely to be the primary reason for a continued commitment to business start-up. It may be that there has been a shift to 'necessity' entrepreneurship (Dencker, Bacq, Gruber & Haas, 2021) as those who have lost their jobs move into *enforced* self-employment.

In summary, there is no doubt that the Covid-19 pandemic has made life considerably more difficult for those either running their own businesses or those thinking about starting new businesses. Results from the most recent GEM reports provide some reasons for optimism as it appears that entrepreneurs and owner-managers have displayed considerable amounts of resilience in response to the crisis. At the same time, we suggest that the core principles of this book; entrepreneurial learning, bootstrapping and building extensive & diverse social networks will help all young entrepreneurs in their desire to start new businesses.

1.7 Summary and Key Learning Points

In Chapter 12 we discuss the evolution of theories related to entrepreneurship. In its early stages the field was dominated by individualist approaches associated with psychology (McClelland, 1962) and macro-level approaches associated with economics (Kirzner, 1973). Gradually, a range of theorists introduced approaches which were based on a more social understanding of entrepreneurship. Many writers have incorporated ideas associated with social network theory and social capital theory to challenge ideas associated with the entrepreneur as heroic individual (Conway & Jones, 2012). For example, based on the process perspective, Steyaert's (2007) concept of 'entrepreneuring' has begun to have an impact on our understanding of entrepreneurship. Of course, the entrepreneurial learning perspective also draws heavily on the importance of the entrepreneurs' engagement with other social actors (Cope, 2005; Jones & Li, 2017; Jones, Macpherson & Thorpe, 2010; Macpherson & Jones, 2008; Rae, 2005). Although Sarasvathy's effectuation theory has its roots in Simon's (1959) ideas about information processing her work also incorporates a strong social element via the entrepreneur's social networks (who I know).

We acknowledge that traditional views of entrepreneurship (McClelland, 1962) cannot be entirely discounted because there is no doubt that some individuals, such as Sam and Ben Wilson,[4] are *natural* entrepreneurs in the same way that other young people have an affinity for music, sport or science. We also acknowledge the importance of an internal locus of control to successful entrepreneurship (Mueller & Thomas, 2001; Ndofirepi, 2020; Rotter, 1966). Locus of control refers to the extent to which individuals believe that they are in control of events in their own lives rather than being subject to external forces (see Box 1.4).

Box 1.4

Before this I was a completely different person, most people would say that I was lazy, didn't try hard at school. I could have done much better, but I took school as a stepping stone. GCSEs, they were stepping stones, and A Levels. I always got what I needed and was offered a place at university. I declined for a year and set this up. As soon as I set this up, I watched TV programmes like Dragon's Den, I would read articles and things and I just took from that all I needed was hard work, determination and common sense. [Ben Wilson, *Jazooli*]

At the same time, we are firmly committed to the idea that entrepreneurship can be learned and that individuals can even be encouraged to develop the motivation to start their own businesses. In part, this can be explained by ideas related to self-efficacy – those who believe they have mastered the appropriate skills are more likely to undertake a particular task (Bandura, 1997; Pollack, Carr, Michaelis & Marshall, 2019; Smith & Woodworth, 2012). We also believe that the kind of 'ordinary' business established by the vast majority of new entrepreneurs are more important than the small number of so-called 'gazelles' and 'unicorns', which are the focus of much academic attention (Aldrich & Ruef, 2018).

Although our approach is very different from that of most textbooks because of our focus on the early stages of entrepreneurship there is one way in which the book is conventional. We have tried to plan the book so that the reader's understanding of entrepreneurship is cumulative building from the basics of acquiring the early resources required for start-up to issues associated with early-stage business growth in Chapters 10 and 11. While we are committed to the ideas associated with 'learning-by-doing', the book is driven by a research-based approach as we incorporate contemporary ideas and knowledge into the book. In addition, Chapter 12 provides a detailed account of contemporary entrepreneurship theories. Chapter 13 deals with policy issues associated with entrepreneurship, focusing on the key themes associated with supporting new businesses. Therefore, we suggest that most value will be obtained from this book by approaching the text in a relatively linear fashion. For the most part, we have adopted a writing style that addresses you, the student, directly to make our message more readily understood. While we remain convinced that entrepreneurship is an appropriate topic for study in Higher Education, we are also committed to the idea that the conventional lecture/tutorial format is not particularly effective in entrepreneurial education (Galloway et al., 2017; Hägg & Kurczewska, 2021). As we have briefly outlined above, a strong practice element is an essential criterion for encouraging students to develop their understanding of whether they have the skills, competences, commitment and resourcefulness to become 'real' entrepreneurs (Jones et al., 2021b).

1.8 Discussion Questions and Call to Action

- Why is this book different from most other textbooks dealing with entrepreneurship and new businesses?
- Can you explain why interest in entrepreneurship has increased over the last 20 years?
- What are the four forms of 'capital' identified by Bourdieu and why are they important to would-be entrepreneurs?
- What are the links between habits, routines and heuristics in the context of entrepreneurship?
- Do you think that enterprise education can help develop an 'entrepreneurial mindset?
- What impact has the Covid-19 pandemic had on young people wanting to start their own businesses?

The principle which underpins this book is that entrepreneurship is based on skills and competences that can be acquired by all students attending colleges and universities. Although we acknowledge that only a minority of students will go on to start their own businesses. Nevertheless, the skills and competences associated with developing an entrepreneurial mindset will benefit all students, whatever careers they pursue in the future.

Therefore, we reiterate the importance of active learning rather than passively 'absorbing' knowledge during lectures and seminars (Kwapisz et al., 2021). As discussed in Chapter 5, we stress the importance of experiential learning as the key to effective learning *for* entrepreneurship (learning how to be more entrepreneurial). As we have outlined above (and discuss in Chapter 5) active learning has several elements, which will assist you in developing an entrepreneurial mindset.

1. Active participation in lectures and classroom exercises is a fundamental starting point for entrepreneurial learning

2. Engaging in conversations with your classmates, lecturers, family members, friends about their business activities and ideas.

3. Talking to other people about potential business ideas – this is part of your 'sensemaking' process [How do I know what I think until I hear what I say' (Weick, 1995, p. 25)].

4. Observing and analysing the world around you – trying to identify potential business ideas.

5. Critically evaluating existing businesses (your college/university) – what things do they do well and what do they do badly (potential business opportunities)?

6. Learning from the experience of other entrepreneurs and business owners (vicarious learning).

7. As we discuss in Chapter 5, it is important that as well as participating in active learning you also engage in extracurricular activities associated with enterprise clubs and societies.

Exercise 1: Evaluate Your Entrepreneurial Mindset – Individual and Group Exercise

Individual Activity: work through each section evaluating your strengths and weaknesses

1. **Cognitive tuning and goal orientation**
   Consider how good you are at focusing on the task at hand – particularly when you have a clear goal to achieve (an essay deadline for

example). Do you find yourself easily distracted or likely to engage in 'displacement' activities to avoid focusing on what needs to be done?

2. **Heuristic-based decision logic**

   Think about how you make decisions when you are confronted with new or difficult problems and limited time to obtain information. Do you draw on your previous experiences or do you think about what influential people would do – your parents or older sibling for example?

3. **Alertness**

   List ten potential business opportunities based on your day-to-day experiences. Think about services that you would like to purchase but are not currently available or your experience of poor service, which could provide a new business opportunity.

4. **Prior knowledge**

   Think about your education, your travels (in your home country and abroad) and your work experience (if you have any) and consider what are the most useful factors in helping you begin an entrepreneurial career.

5. **Social interaction**

   List ten people who you know well and identify what resources they could potentially provide if you started your own business. The resources could be tangible such as finance or use of their premises for your new venture. Alternatively, the resources could be intangible such as experience of managing their own business or a willingness to provide emotional support.

6. **Cognitive adaptability**

   To what extent do you tolerate complexity and uncertainty or do you prefer to deal with situations that are straight-forward and easily resolvable?

7. **Meta-cognition**

   How effective are you at understanding what you know about a particular topic or subject? When you have been presented with a new idea/concept/theory – do you spend time reflecting on how well you understand the new information?

Group Activity

When you have completed your individual assignment, you should then join with two or three other members of your group and compare results for each of the seven factors outlined about.

There are no right/wrong answers to any of the questions – the idea of the exercise is to encourage you to think about the extent to which you have an entrepreneurial mindset.

Notes

1 www.microbizmag.co.uk/startup-statistics/
2 www.qaa.ac.uk/quality-code/enterprise-and-entrepreneurship-education
3 www.qaa.ac.uk/quality-code/enterprise-and-entrepreneurship-education
4 Our case study of Sam and Ben's start-up company, Jazooli, is discussed in Chapter 12.

References

Aldrich, H. E. & Ruef, M. (2018). Unicorns, Gazelles, and Other Distractions on the Way to Understanding Real Entrepreneurship in the United States. *Academy of Management Perspectives*, 32(4), 458–472.

Aldrich, H. E. & Yang, T. (2012). Lost in translation: Cultural codes are not blueprints. *Strategic Entrepreneurship Journal*, 6(1), 1–17.

Aldrich, H. E. & Yang, T. (2014). How do entrepreneurs know what to do? learning and organizing in new ventures. *Journal of Evolutionary Economics*, 24(1), 59–82.

Alvarez, S. A. & Barney, J. B. (2020). Insights from creation theory: The uncertain context rendered by the COVID-19 pandemic. *Strategic Entrepreneurship Journal*, 14(4), 552–555.

Anderson, A. R., Drakopoulou-Dodd, S. & Jack, S. L. (2010). Network practices and entrepreneurial growth. *Scandinavian Journal of Management*, 26, 121–133.

Anderson, A. R., Drakopoulou-Dodd, S. & Scott, M. G. (2000). Religion as an environmental influence on enterprise culture – The case of Britain in the 1980s. *International Journal of Entrepreneurial Behavior & Research*, 6(1), 5–21.

Anderson, A. R., Jack, S. L. & Drakopoulou-Dodd, S. (2009). Social capital in the capitalisation of new ventures: accessing, lubricating and fitting. In: *Handbook of Business and Finance*. M. Bergmann and T. Faust (Eds.), pp. 293–300. Nova Science Publishers Inc.

Anjum, T., Farrukh, M., Heidler, P. & Díaz Tautiva, J. A. (2021). Entrepreneurial Intention: Creativity, Entrepreneurship, and University Support. *Journal of Open Innovation, 7*(1), 1–13. doi:10.3390/joitmc7010011

Bandura, A. (1997). *Self-efficacy: the exercise of control / Albert Bandura*: New York: W.H. Freeman, 1997.

Baron, J. N., Hannan, M. T. & Burton, M. D. (1999). Building the Iron Cage: Determinants of Managerial Intensity in the Early Years of Organizations. *American Sociological Review, 64*(4), 527–547.

Baron, R. A. (2006). Opportunity Recognition as Pattern Recognition: How Entrepreneurs 'Connect the Dots' to Identify New Business Opportunities. *Academy of Management Perspectives, 20*(1), 104–119.

Baron, R. A. (2008). The Role of Effect in the Entrepreneurial Process. *Academy of Management Review, 33*(2), 328–340.

Baron, R. A. & Hmieleski, K. M. (2018). *Essentials of entrepreneurship: changing the world, one idea at a time*. Cheltenham, UK: Edward Elgar.

Berger, P. L. & Luckmann, T. (1966). *The Social Construction of Reality: A Treatise in the Sociology of Knowledge*. New York: Doubleday.

Blundel, R., Lockett, N., Wang, C. L. & Mawson, S. (2021). *Exploring entrepreneurship*. Los Angeles: Sage.

Bourdieu, P. (1977). *Outline of a theory of practice [by] Pierre Bourdieu; translated by Richard Nice* : Cambridge: Cambridge University Press.

Bourdieu, P. (2002). Habitus. In J. Hillier & E. Rooksby (Eds.), *Habitus: A Sense of Place*. Aldershot: Ashgate.

Burns, P. (2018). *New venture creation: a framework for entrepreneurial start-ups* (Second edition ed.). London: Palgrave.

Chadwick, I. C. & Raver, J. L. (2020). Psychological Resilience and Its Downstream Effects for Business Survival in Nascent Entrepreneurship. *Entrepreneurship: Theory & Practice, 44*(2), 233–255.

Cohen, M. D. & Bacdayan, P. (1994). Organizational Routines Are Stored As Procedural Memory: Evidence from a Laboratory Study. *Organization Science 4*, 554–568.

Cohen, W. & Levinthal, D. (1990). Absorptive Capacity: a new perspective on learning and innovation. *Administrative Science Quarterly, 35*(1), 128–152.

Conway, S. & Jones, O. (2012). Networks and the Small Business. In S. Carter & D. Jones-Evans (Eds.), *Enterprise and Small Business: Principles, Practice and Policy* (3rd edn. pp. 338–361). Harlow: Pearson.

Cope, J. (2003). Entrepreneurial Learning and Critical Reflection: Discontinuous Events as Triggers for 'Higher-level' Learning. *Management Learning, 34*(4), 429–450.

Cope, J. (2005). Toward a Dynamic Learning Perspective of Entrepreneurship. *Entrepreneurship: Theory & Practice*, *29*(4), 373–397.

Cope, J. (2011). Entrepreneurial learning from failure: An interpretative phenomenological analysis. *Journal of Business Venturing*, *26*(6), 604–623.

Cope, J. & Watts, G. (2000). Learning by doing – An exploration of experience, critical incidents and reflection in entrepreneurial learning. *International Journal of Entrepreneurial Behavior & Research*, *6*(3), 104–124.

Corbett, A. C. (2005). Experiential Learning Within the Process of Opportunity Identification and Exploitation. *Entrepreneurship: Theory & Practice*, *29*(4), 473–491.

Cornelissen, J. P., Clarke, J. S. & Cienki, A. (2012). Sensegiving in entrepreneurial contexts: The use of metaphors in speech and gesture to gain and sustain support for novel business ventures. *International Small Business Journal*, *30*(4), 213–241.

Cui, J., Sun, J. & Bell, R. (2021). The impact of entrepreneurship education on the entrepreneurial mindset of college students in China: The mediating role of inspiration and the role of educational attributes. *The International Journal of Management Education*, *19*(1). doi:10.1016/j.ijme.2019.04.001

Davidsson, P. & Honig, B. (2003). The role of social and human capital among nascent entrepreneurs. *Journal of Business Venturing*, *18*(3), 301–331.

Davidsson, P. & Klofsten, M. (2003). The Business Platform: Developing an Instrument to Gauge and to Assist the Development of Young Firms. *Journal of Small Business Management*, *41*(1), 1–27.

De Clercq, D. & Honig, B. (2011). Entrepreneurship as an integrating mechanism for disadvantaged persons. *Entrepreneurship & Regional Development*, *23*(5/6), 353–372.

De Clercq, D. & Voronov, M. (2009). Toward a Practice Perspective of Entrepreneurship: Entrepreneurial Legitimacy as Habitus. *International Small Business Journal*, *27*(4), 395–419.

de Jong, J. P. J. & Freel, M. (2010). Absorptive Capacity and the Reach of Collaboration in High Technology Small Firms. *Research Policy*, *39*(1), 47–54.

Dencker, J. C., Bacq, S., Gruber, M. & Haas, M. (2021). Reconceptualizing Necessity Entrepreneurship: A Contextualized Framework of Entrepreneurial Processes Under the Condition of Basic Needs. *Academy of Management Review*, *46*(1), 60–79.

Doern, R. (2017). *Strategies for Resilience in Entrepreneurship: Building Resources for Small Business Survival After a Crisis*. In N. Williams & T. Vorley (Eds.), *Creating Resilient Economies* (pp. 11–27). Cheltenham: Edward Elgar.

Doern, R., Williams, N. & Vorley, T. (2019). Special Issue on Entrepreneurship and Crises: Business as Usual? An Introduction and Review of the Literature. *Entrepreneurship and Regional Development*, *31*(5–6), 400–412.

Elfring, T., Klyver, K. & van Burg, E. (2021). *Entrepreneurship as Networking: Mechanisms, Dynamics, Practices, and Strategies*. New York: Oxford University Press.

Engeström, Y. (2001). Expansive Learning at Work: toward an activity theoretical reconceptualization. *Journal of Education & Work, 14*(1), 133–156.

Fisher, G., Neubert, E. & Burnell, D. (2021). Resourcefulness narratives: Transforming actions into stories to mobilize support. *Journal of Business Venturing, 36*(4), 106122.

Flechas Chaparro, X. A., Kozesinski, R. & Camargo Júnior, A. S. (2021). Absorptive capacity in startups: A systematic literature review. *Journal of Entrepreneurship, Management & Innovation, 17*(1), 57–95.

Galloway, L., Higgins, D., McGowan, P., Preedy, S. & Jones, P. (2017). Student-led enterprise groups and entrepreneurial learning: A UK perspective. *Industry and Higher Education, 31*(2), 101–112.

Gibb, A. (2011). Concepts into practice: meeting the challenge of development of entrepreneurship educators around an innovative paradigm: The case of the International Entrepreneurship Educators' Programme (IEEP). *International Journal of Entrepreneurial Behavior & Research, 17*(2), 146–165.

Gibb, A. & Ritchie, J. (1982). Understanding the Process of Starting Small Businesses. *International Small Business Journal, 1*(1), 26–45.

Giddens, A. (1987). *Social theory and modern sociology (by) Anthony Giddens*: Cambridge: Polity Press.

Hägg, G. & Kurczewska, A. (2021). *Entrepreneurship Education – Scholarly Progress and Future Challenges*. New York: Routledge. Retrieved from https://liverpool.idm. oclc.org/login?url=https://search.ebscohost.com/login.aspx?direct=true&db= edsswe&AN=edsswe.oai.lup.lub.lu.se.cdc6c749.76c9.4245.9d2b.7072f4e21 375&site=eds-live&scope=site

Haneberg, D. H. & Aaboen, L. (2021). Entrepreneurial learning behaviour of community insiders. International Journal of Entrepreneurial Behavior & Research, ahead-of-print. doi:10.1108/IJEBR-04-2020-0255

Haynie, J. M., Shepherd, D., Mosakowski, E. & Earley, P. C. (2010). A situated meta-cognitive model of the entrepreneurial mindset. *Journal of Business Venturing, 25*(2), 217–229.

Hesmondhalgh, D., Oakley, K., Lee, D. & Nisbett, M. (2015). *Culture, Economy and Politics. The Case of New Labour*. Basingstoke: Palgrave McMillan.

Higgins, D. & Elliott, C. (2011). Learning to Make Sense: What Works in Entrepreneurial Education? *Journal of European Industrial Training, 35*(4), 345–367.

Hodgson, G. M. (2009). The Nature and Replication of Routines. In M. C. Becker & N. Lazaric (Eds.), *Organizational Routines: Advancing Empirical Research* (pp. 26–44): Cheltenham. and Northampton, MA.: Edward Elgar.

Holt, R. & Macpherson, A. (2010). Sensemaking, Rhetoric and the Socially Competent Entrepreneur. *International Small Business Journal*, *28*(1), 20–42.

Inada, Y. (2020). The Impact of Higher Education Entrepreneurship Practical Courses: Developing an Entrepreneurial Mindset. *Journal of Applied Business & Economics*, *22*(8), 161–176.

Jayawarna, D., Jones, O. & Macpherson, A. (2020). Resourcing Social Enterprises: The Role of Socially Oriented Bootstrapping. *British Journal of Management*, *31*(1), 56–79.

Jones, O. & Craven, M. (2001a). Beyond the routine: innovation management and the Teaching Company Scheme. *Technovation*, *21*(5), 267–280.

Jones, O. & Craven, M. (2001b). Expanding Capabilities in a Mature Manufacturing Firm: Absorptive Capacity and the TCS. *International Small Business Journal*, *19*(3), 39–56.

Jones, O. & Giordano, B. (2021). Family entrepreneurial teams: The role of learning in business model evolution. *Management Learning*, *52*(3), 267–293.

Jones, O. & Holt, R. (2008). The creation and evolution of new business ventures: an activity theory perspective. *Journal of Small Business & Enterprise Development*, *15*(1), 51–73.

Jones, O. & Jayawarna, D. (2010). Resourcing new businesses: social networks, bootstrapping and firm performance. *Venture Capital*, *12*(2), 127–152.

Jones, O. & Li, H. (2017). Effectual Entrepreneuring: Sensemaking in a Family-Based Start-Up. *Entrepreneurship and Regional Development*, *29*(5–6), 467–499.

Jones, O., Macpherson, A. & Thorpe, R. (2010). Learning in owner-managed small firms: Mediating artefacts and strategic space. *Entrepreneurship and Regional Development*, *22*(7/8), 649–673.

Jones, O., Meckel, P. & Taylor, D. (2021a). *Creating Communities of Practice: Entrepreneurial Learning in a University-Based Incubator*. Cham (Switzerland): Springer.

Jones O, Meckel P, Taylor D. (2021b). Situated learning in a business incubator: Encouraging students to become real entrepreneurs. *Industry and Higher Education*, *35*(4), 367–383.

Karatas-Ozkan, M. (2011). Understanding Relational Qualities of Entrepreneurial Learning: Towards a Multi-layered Approach. *Entrepreneurship and Regional Development*, *23*(9–10), 877–906.

Kim, P. H., Aldrich, H. E. & Keister, L. A. (2006). Access (Not) Denied: The Impact of Financial, Human, and Cultural Capital on Entrepreneurial Entry in the United States. *Small Business Economics*, *27*(1), 5–22.

Kirzner, I. M. (1973). *Competition and Entrepreneurship*. Chicago: University of Chicago.

Kohler, W. (1925). *The Mentality of Apes*. Norwood, NJ: Ablex

Kolb, D. A. (1984). Experiential learning: experience as the source of learning and development / David A. Kolb. In: Englewood Cliffs, N.J.: Prentice-Hall.

Kuckertz, A., Brändle, L., Gaudig, A., Hinderer, S., Morales Reyes, C. A., Prochotta, A., and Berger, E. S. C. (2020). Startups in times of crisis – A rapid response to the COVID-19 pandemic. *Journal of Business Venturing Insights, 13*. doi:10.1016/j.jbvi.2020.e00169

Kuratko, D. F., Fisher, G. & Audretsch, D. B. (2020). Unraveling the entrepreneurial mindset. *Small Business Economics: An Entrepreneurship Journal*, 1. doi:10.1007/s11187-020-00372-6

Kurczewska, A. & Mackiewicz, M. (2020). Are jacks-of-all-trades successful entrepreneurs? Revisiting Lazear's theory of entrepreneurship. *Baltic Journal of Management, 15*(3), 411–430.

Kwapisz, A., Schell, W. J., Aytes, K. & Bryant, S. (2021). Entrepreneurial Action and Intention: The Role of Entrepreneurial Mindset, Emotional Intelligence, and Grit. *Entrepreneurship Education and Pedagogy*. doi:10.1177/2515127421992521.

Latour, B. (1986). The powers of association. In J. Law (Ed.), *Power, Action and Belief* (pp. 264–280). London: Routledge and Kegan Paul.

Lave, J. & Wenger, E. (1991). *Situated learning: Legitimate peripheral participation*. New York: Cambridge University Press.

Lewin, K. (1951). *Field Theory in Social Science*. Harper Row, London.

Lindberg, E., Bohman, H., Hulten, P., &, W., Timothy. (2017). Enhancing students' entrepreneurial mindset: a Swedish experience. *Education + Training, 59*(7/8), 768–779.

Lounsbury, M., Cornelissen, J., Granqvist, N. & Grodal, S. (2019). Culture, innovation and entrepreneurship. *Innovation: Organization & Management, 21*(1), 1–12.

Lounsbury, M. & Glynn, M. A. (2001). Cultural Entrepreneurship: Stories, Legitimacy and the Acquisition of Resources. *Strategic Management Journal, 22*, 545–564.

Lourenco, F. & Jones, O. (2006). *Learning Paradigms in Entrepreneurship Education: Comparing the Traditional and Enterprise Modes*. Retrieved from London: National Council for Graduate Entrepreneurship.

Macpherson, A., Herbane, B. & Jones, O. (2015). Developing Dynamic Capabilities through Resource Accretion: Expanding the Entrepreneurial Solution Space. *Entrepreneurship and Regional Development, 27*(5–6), 259–291.

Macpherson, A. & Jones, O. (2008). Object-mediated Learning and Strategic Renewal in a Mature Organization. *Management Learning, 39*(2), 177–201.

Manolis, C., Burns, D. J., Assudani, R. & Chinta, R. (2012). Assessing experiential learning styles: A methodological reconstruction and validation of the Kolb Learning Style Inventory. *Learning and Individual Differences*, 23, 44–52.

March, J. G. & Simon, H. A. (1958). *Organizations*. Oxford: Wiley.

McClelland, D. C. (1962). Business Drive and National Achievement. *Harvard Business Review, 40*(4), 99–113.

Mooradian, T., Matzler, K., Uzelac, B. & Bauer, F. (2016). Perspiration and inspiration: Grit and innovativeness as antecedents of entrepreneurial success. *Journal of Economic Psychology*, *56*, 232–243.

Morris, M. H. & Kuratko, D. F. (2020). *What Do Entrepreneurs Create? Understanding Four Types of Venture*. Cheltenham: Elgar.

Mueller, S. L. & Thomas, A. S. (2001). Culture and entrepreneurial potential: A nine country study of locus of control and innovativeness. *Journal of Business Venturing*, *16*(1), 51–75.

Naumann, C. (2017). Entrepreneurial Mindset: A Synthetic Literature Review. *Entrepreneurial Business and Economics Review*, *5*(3), 149–172.

Ndofirepi, T. M. (2020). Relationship between entrepreneurship education and entrepreneurial goal intentions: psychological traits as mediators. *Journal of Innovation & Entrepreneurship*, *9*(1), 1–20.

Nelson, R. R. & Winter, S. G. (1982). *An evolutionary theory of economic change*. Cambridge, MA: Belknap Press of Harvard University Press.

Pavlov, I. P. (1927). *Conditioned Reflexes: An Investigation of the Physiological Activity of the Cerebral Cortex*. Translated and Edited by G. V. Anrep. London: Oxford University Press.

Pentland, B. T. & Feldman, M. S. (2005). Organizational routines as a unit of analysis. *Industrial & Corporate Change*, *14*(5), 793–815.

Pentland, B. T., Feldman, M. S., Becker, M. C. & Liu, P. (2012). Dynamics of Organizational Routines: A Generative Model. *Journal of Management Studies*, *49*(8), 1484–1508.

Piaget, J. (1926). *The language and thought of the child*. Oxford: Harcourt, Brace.

Pittaway, L., Gazzard, J., Shore, A. & Williamson, T. (2015). Student clubs: experiences in entrepreneurial learning. *Entrepreneurship & Regional Development*, *27*(3/4), 127–153.

Pittaway, L. & Thorpe, R. (2012). A framework for entrepreneurial learning: A tribute to Jason Cope. *Entrepreneurship & Regional Development*, *24*(9/10), 837–859.

Politis, D. (2005). The Process of Entrepreneurial Learning: A Conceptual Framework. *Entrepreneurship: Theory & Practice*, *29*(4), 399–424.

Pollack, J. M., Carr, J. C., Michaelis, T. L. & Marshall, D. R. (2019). Hybrid entrepreneurs' self-efficacy and persistence change: A longitudinal exploration. *Journal of Business Venturing Insights*, *12*. doi:10.1016/j.jbvi.2019.e00143

Rae, D. (2005). Entrepreneurial learning: a narrative-based conceptual model. *Journal of Small Business and Enterprise Development*, *12*(3), 323–335.

Raelin, J. A. (2007). Toward an Epistemology of Practice. *Academy of Management Learning & Education*, *6*(4), 495–519.

Rawes, K. & Renwick, K. (2020). Transformative learning for university level students and advisors: a self study. *Professional development in education*. doi:10.1080/19415257.2020.1853591

Rotter, J. (1966). Generalized expectancies for internal versus external control of reinforcements. *Psychological Monographs*, 80(1), 1–28.

Samra-Fredericks, D. (2003). A proposal for developing a critical pedagogy in management from researching organizational members' everyday practice. *Management Learning*, 34(3), 291–312.

Shane, S. (2000). Prior Knowledge and the Discovery of Entrepreneurial Opportunities. *Organization Science*, 11(4), 448–469.

Shane, S. (2012). Reflections On The 2010 AMR Decade Award: Delivering on the Promise of Entrepreneurship as Field of Research. *Academy of Management Review*, 37(1), 10–20.

Simon, H. A. (1959). Theories of Decision Making in Economics and Behavioral Science. *American Economic Review*, 49, 253–283.

Skinner, B. F. (1938). *The Behavior of Organisms*. New York: Crofts-Crofts.

Smith, I. H. & Woodworth, W. P. (2012). Developing Social Entrepreneurs and Social Innovators: A Social Identity and Self-Efficacy Approach. *Academy of Management Learning & Education*, 11(3), 390–407.

Steyaert, C. (2007). 'Entrepreneuring' as a conceptual attractor? A review of process theories in 20 years of entrepreneurship studies. *Entrepreneurship & Regional Development*, 19(6), 453–477.

Steyaert, C. & Katz, J. A. (2004). Reclaiming the space of entrepreneurship in society: geographical, discursive and social dimensions. *Entrepreneurship & Regional Development*, 16(3), 179–196.

Storey, D. J. (1994). *Understanding the small business sector*. London: International Thompson Business Press.

Storey, D. J. (2011). Optimism and chance: The elephants in the entrepreneurship room. *International Small Business Journal*, 29(4), 303–321.

Stringfellow, L. & Shaw, E. (2009). Conceptualising entrepreneurial capital for a study of performance in small professional service firms. *International Journal of Entrepreneurial Behavior & Research*, 15(2), 137–161.

Teague, B., Tunstall, R., Champenois, C., & Gartner, W. B. (2021). Editorial: An introduction to entrepreneurship as practice (EAP). *International Journal of Entrepreneurial Behavior & Research*, 27(3), 569–578.

Thorndike, E. L. (1913). *Educational Psychology*. New York: Teachers College.

Timmons, J. A. (1999). *New Venture Creation: Entrepreneurship for the 21st Century* (Fifth ed.). New York: McGraw Hill.

Tocher, N., Oswald, S. L., Shook, C. L. & Adams, G. (2012). Entrepreneur Political Skill and New Venture Performance: Extending the Social Competence Perspective. *Entrepreneurship and Regional Development*, 24(5–6), 283–305.

Unger, J. M., Rauch, A., Frese, M. & Rosenbusch, N. (2011). Human capital and entrepreneurial success: A meta-analytical review. *Journal of Business Venturing*, 26, 341–358.

Vygotsky, L. S. (1978). *Mind in Society: The Development of Higher Psychological Processes*. Cambridge: Cambridge University Press.

Weick, K. (1995). *Sensemaking in Organizations*. Thousand Oaks, CA: Sage.

Whittington, R. (1996). Strategy as Practice. *Long Range Planning, 29*(5), 731–735.

Witt, P. (2004). Entrepreneurs' networks and the success of start-ups. *Entrepreneurship & Regional Development, 16*(5), 391–412.

Zacharakis, A. & Corbett, A. C. & Bygrave, W. D. (2020). Entrepreneurship (5th edition). Hoboken, New Jersey: Wiley.

2 Business Start-up Skills and Competences

2.1 Introduction

Being successful in occupations requires certain knowledge, skills and capabilities, some of which we acquire as we engage in work. Graduates who join larger companies will often start as 'trainees' as they are given time to acquire the skills necessary to become productive members of the organization. The reality for those of you thinking about starting your own business is that the experience will be very different. You may have had exposure to some of the important issues likely to confront new entrepreneurs as you take your first tentative steps into starting and running your own business. As mentioned in Chapter 1 and discussed in greater detail in Chapter 5, we are committed to the value of experiential learning and engagement in extracurricular activities. It is also important to develop your social networks as a means of obtaining advice and information from those more experienced in the world of business. In Chapter 5 (Section 5.6), we suggest that university-based incubators (Jones, Meckel & Taylor, 2021a, 2021b) can provide a sheltered environment in which to develop your entrepreneurial skills. It is certainly worth investigating whether there is an incubator which caters for new businesses on, or close to, your university. There are many advantages to starting your entrepreneurial career in a business incubator and these are discussed in Chapter 5. However, to begin the chapter, we set out what we regard as the basic business skills needed if you are considering working for yourself or starting your own business. This is then followed by a brief explanation of the nature of entrepreneurial skills when adopting an effectual approach to business start-up (Section 2.4).

DOI: 10.4324/9781003312918-3

In Section 2.5, we consider the knowledge, skills, knowledge and capabilities that you should develop as you are establishing the business. Some scholars suggest that there are key functional and analytical skills all entrepreneurs should have at the outset, such as those necessary to balance a budget, read a balance sheet and cope with legal requirements. There may also be key technical knowledge and the skills necessary to deliver the product and/or service produced by your firm. Clearly if you are starting a technology, or science-based business, you are more likely to succeed if you have the appropriate technical skills. In addition, the skills necessary to start and grow a business are not necessarily the same, since managing as a sole trader is very different from managing staff and developing new markets. In this regard, entrepreneurs often overlook the softer social skills necessary to engage with employees, customers, potential investors and suppliers. Such skills promote creativity in developing and generating business ideas but also help reach wider networks where resources necessary to development of the venture reside. It may also be necessary to set up production facilities, or customer service protocols, manage quality and delegate work. However, engaging with staff and others outside of the business requires 'impression management' and communication skills that are necessary to broker relationships with resource providers as well as customers, suppliers and investors.

This chapter proceeds by considering the basic business skills you will need at the start-up stage. Attention then turns to the types of knowledge, skills and capabilities identified by research necessary to develop and resource the business as it grows, and how an entrepreneur might acquire them. Finally, we consider the role of cultural entrepreneurship and the skills necessary to engage others in the development of the venture.

2.2 Learning Objectives

- To understand the importance of developing the appropriate behavioural skills required for business start-up.
- To appreciate the role of knowledge, skills and capabilities as essential resources applied to the creation of new ventures.
- To be able to distinguish between the 'casual' and 'effectual' approaches to business start-up.
- To recognize the importance of 'generic competences' as you gain experience in your entrepreneurial career.

- To understand the contribution of both formal and informal learning as the business grows in complexity.
- To understand how and why 'cultural entrepreneurship' and the concept of 'resourcefulness narratives' are key elements in your entrepreneurial attributes.
- To understand the limitations of your existing skills including your resourcefulness and resilience.

2.3 Basic Business Start-up Skills

As discussed in Chapter 7, even young entrepreneurs bring with them skills gained over their life-course through education, work experience, or even some involvement in entrepreneurship [see Box 5.1] (Hickie, 2011; Jayawarna, Jones & Macpherson, 2014). Lone entrepreneurs have a limited set of skills, while entrepreneurial teams bring a wider variety of capabilities, knowledge and experience (Patzelt, Preller & Breugst, 2021). Depending on the sector, ambition of the entrepreneur and the scope of the firm, potentially at least, the appropriate skills will vary. It is important to consider, therefore, what skills are available at the outset and what the nascent entrepreneur might need now, and in the future, and why certain skills are important. There has been some research to identify exactly what skill sets provide the best opportunities to create a successful firm. The resource-based view of the firm (Arend & Lévesque, 2010; Barney, 1991) attempts to explain how the entrepreneur's capabilities and human capital have a fundamental influence on the performance of the firm (Chapters 7 and 10). However, the results are inconclusive and, therefore, it is advisable to approach this subject with caution. The issues are complex and there is certainly not one list of skills that will fit every situation. Studies that have been conducted range across a broad assortment of contexts in terms of sector, geography, economic climate, institutional regulation, national culture, age and gender (Meoli, Fini, Sobrero & Wiklund, 2020). Studies also use a variety of measures of success – for example, profit, turnover, or number of employees – and are not necessarily comparable (Wach, Stephan, Gorgievski & Wegge, 2020).

Chang and Rieple (2018) studied the way in which students' entrepreneurial skills developed during an elective module designed for undergraduates from a range of backgrounds. All those registered for the elective had completed the 'core' business and management modules including marketing, accounting and economics. The objective was to evaluate how undergraduate students adopt 'opportunity management' (OM) behaviours identified as causation, effectuation and bricolage. OM refers to the whole process from opportunity identification to the development of the potential opportunity into a product or service that can be offered to the market. Entrepreneurs adopting a causal approach to business start-up set their goals based on a detailed analysis of the market and competitors. This information is then formalized in a business plan, which is generally used to obtain the resources necessary to start the business (Shane, 2000). An effectual approach (see Section 2.4) to business start-up begins with the means that the entrepreneur has at their disposal (skills, knowledge, finance), which is then applied to a suitable business opportunity (Sarasvathy, 2001). Bricolage (Lévi-Strauss, 1967) has some similarities with effectuation (and bootstrapping as discussed in Chapter 9) and involves a process of 'making do' with whatever resources the entrepreneur has to hand (Baker & Nelson, 2005; Fisher, 2012; Fisher, Neubert & Burnell, 2021). According to the authors, these are 'the behavioural skills that students leaving higher education should have learnt' (Chang & Rieple, 2018, p. 472).

In their study, Chang and Rieple (2018) assessed the adoption of OM behaviours by observing groups of 25 undergraduate teams (five members) who had to raise funds for six social enterprises over a period of ten weeks. Each team had to complete a weekly reflective log which was then analysed by the authors and activities categorized as causation, effectuation or bricolage. Half of the behaviours were identified as 'causation' and 25% for each of effectuation and bricolage. However, although the causal approach was dominant in the early stages of the project, reaching a peak at week 4, thereafter it declined rapidly. In contrast, effectuation and bricolage increased in importance as the project progressed and peaked at week 7. Interestingly, those teams with more experienced members were able to combine the three behavioural skills more effectively than the inexperienced groups. The authors conclude that the causal approach dominates most business school teaching and that students should be introduced to the principles of effectuation and bricolage to broaden their opportunity management behaviours and entrepreneurship skills (Chang & Rieple, 2018, p. 491).

According to Hahn, Minola, Bosio and Cassia (2020) studies designed to evaluate the impact on entrepreneurship education (EE) on entrepreneurial outcomes have produced mixed results (Chang & Rieple, 2013). The authors suggest this is because it is necessary to assess the influence of various external factors on the relationship between enterprise education and the acquisition of the appropriate entrepreneurial skills. Of particular importance is whether the course is an elective or a compulsory element of the students' degrees. Students who decide to take an entrepreneurship elective module are likely to be more highly motivated than those taking compulsory modules. Secondly, students who belong to an 'enterprising family' (Jones & Giordano, 2021) are more likely to be interested in the topic of entrepreneurship. Based on a sample of 427 students from eight European countries, Hahn et al. (2020) assess the impact of enterprise education on their entrepreneurial skills taking into account the influence of two 'boundary conditions', type of course and students' embeddedness in an enterprising family. Seven skills were measured during the study: identifying a business opportunity, creating new products or services, managing innovation, being a leader and communicator, building professional networks, commercializing new ideas and managing a business (Hahn et al., 2020). The results of the study revealed that elective modules were beneficial in enhancing students' entrepreneurial skills. Compulsory modules were only effective in enhancing the entrepreneurial skills of those students with a positive experience of family business. Students exposed to low-performing family businesses or businesses that created tensions among family members did not benefit from enterprise education.

Rayna and Striukova (2021) discuss the emergence of *fab labs* and *makerspaces*, which provide access to digital manufacturing technologies such as 3D printers, laser cutters and computer numerical controlled [CNC] machines as well as traditional woodworking and metalworking craft-based tools. One of the basic principles of *fab labs* and *makerspaces* is that they bring students studying STEM (science, technology, engineering and mathematics) subjects together with business/management students. STEM students are encouraged to share their technical knowledge with business students and business students are urged to share their knowledge of business and entrepreneurship. The advent of *fab labs* and *makerspaces* coincided with a focus on 'twenty-first century skills' including creativity, collaboration and communication as well as more the technical, digital skills (Rayna & Striukova, 2021). The authors draw on two frameworks developed by the European Union (EU) to encourage greater emphasis on entrepreneurship in member states. The digital framework (DigComp) is illustrated in Table 2.1 and while we acknowledge these skills are important for all young entrepreneurs, we do not focus on them here (Ferrari, 2013).

Table 2.1 Digital Skills (DigComp)

Information and data literacy
Browsing, searching and filtering data, information and digital content
Evaluating data, information and digital content
Managing data, information and digital content
Communication and collaboration
Interacting through digital technologies
Sharing through digital technologies
Engaging in citizenship through digital technologies
Collaborating through digital technologies
Netiquette
Managing digital identity
Digital content creation
Developing digital content
Integrating and re-elaborating digital content
Copyright and licences
Programming
Safety
Protecting devices
Protecting personal data and privacy
Protecting health and well-being
Protecting the environment
Problem solving
Solving technical problems
Identifying needs and technological responses
Creatively using digital technologies
Identifying digital competence gaps

Table 2.2 Entrepreneurship Skills (EntreComp)

Ideas and opportunities
Spotting opportunities
Creativity
Vision
Valuing ideas
Ethical and Sustainable Thinking
Resources
Self-awareness and self-efficacy
Motivation and perseverance
Mobilizing resources
Financial and economic literacy
Mobilizing others
Into Action
Taking the initiative
Planning and management
Coping with uncertainty, ambiguity and risk
Working with others
Learning through experience

The entrepreneurial framework, known as *EntreComp* (McCallum, Weicht, McMullan & Price, 2018) is illustrated in Table 2.2. As stated in the report 'EntreComp creates a shared understanding of the knowledge, skills and attitudes that make up what it means to be entrepreneurial – discovering and acting upon opportunities and ideas, and transforming them into social, cultural, or financial value for others' (McCallum et al., 2018, p. 15). The framework has three distinct sets of skills: ideas and opportunities; resources; and into action. All three of these areas are covered extensively in the following chapters: ideas and opportunities (Chapters 3 and 4), resources (Chapters 6, 7, 8 and 9), into action (Chapters 3, 4 and 5).

Many authors argue that undergraduate students need to develop 'entrepreneurial thinking skills' so that they can manage uncertainty whatever careers they pursue (Peschl, Deng & Larson, 2021). In recognition of this need, entrepreneurship education has shifted from traditional lectures to more experiential and hands-on approaches to problem-solving (Lourenco & Jones, 2006; Nabi, Linan, Fayolle, Krueger & Walmsley, 2017; Neck & Corbett, 2018). Drawing on comprehensive reviews of literature dealing with entrepreneurial skills (Bacigalupo, Kampylis, Punie & Van Den Brande, 2016; Davis, Hall & Mayer, 2016; Kier & McMullen, 2018; McCallum et al., 2018), Peschl et al. (2021, pp. 4–5) provide a list of seven major themes:

1. **Problem-solving** – is closely related to opportunity identification as it is based on the cognitive capacity to create novel business ideas (see Table 2.2, Ideas and Opportunities). Essentially, problem-solving is focused on the ability to develop innovative solutions and execute a plan to resolve the problem (creating a product or service).

2. **Tolerance for ambiguity** – this refers to the ability to be able to deal with high levels of uncertainty and risk. This is a skill which entrepreneurs need to accept the difficulty of predicting the outcome of events (starting a business) and retaining an optimistic outlook.

3. **Failing forward** – all entrepreneurs will have negative experiences during business start-up and responding positively to various setbacks requires and ability to learn from those experiences. Developing self-confidence (self-efficacy), resilience and persistence helps individual 'bounce back' from their disappointments.

4. **Empathy** – the ability to read the emotions of other people (customers, suppliers, resource providers) is a crucial skill for any would-be entrepreneur. This is related to your own self-awareness and an understanding of how your actions impact on other people. Emotional intelligence and social imaginativeness also refer to the ability to take someone else's perspective.

5. **Creativity with limited resources** – most young people trying to start their own business will have limited resources and probably the burden of financial debts. The ability to make the best of the resources in your possession is fundamental to the ideas expressed in effectuation theory, bricolage and bootstrapping.

6. **Responding to feedback** – talking to other people about your ideas is central to the sensemaking process. At the same time, you must be

willing to listen to what other people have to say and make judgements about the extent to which their views are relevant to you and your business. It is very likely that some feedback will be negative, and it is particularly important that you are open to the value of that feedback (rather than adopting a defensive posture).

7. **Teamworking** – one of the major myths is that entrepreneurship is an individual pursuit. Most new entrepreneurs must rely on their networks of strong and weak ties (Chapter 6) to provide advice, information and knowledge about the problems associated with starting new businesses. The ability to work as a team-member is also highly relevant if you decide to start your business in an incubator (see Section 5.5).

Peschl et al. (2021) acknowledge that their list does not include the more technical skills associated with starting a new business such as writing a business plan or raising finance. As the authors go on to state: 'The ET-7 were selected after an extensive review of the literature, and they capture the ability to solve complex problems, deal with uncertainty, learn from failures, see things from the perspective of another, think creatively, respond to feedback and work effectively in a team' (Peschl et al., 2021, p. 11). In other words, the above list, as well as *EntreComp*, is focused on helping students develop an entrepreneurial mindset (Section 1.5).

Although it involved a relatively small number of students, a study by Chang and Rieple (2013) reveals some important insights about the power of live projects. The objective was to examine the impact of engaging with real-life entrepreneurs on students' perception of their skills. Students from a range of different disciplines participated in an eight-week elective module, 'developing a small business'. The 27 students worked in groups to carry out a detailed business analysis based on visits to the company premises, interviews with key members of staff and customers. Each group of students then presented a business development plan to one of four companies participating in the exercise. Using an instrument with 17 categories of entrepreneurial skills, the students were required to self-rate their skills at the start, middle and end of the exercise (see Table 2.3). The authors acknowledge that because of the small sample, it was not possible to claim the results were statistically significant. Nevertheless, it is *significant* that students' perception of specific skills declined consistently from periods 1 to 2 and 2 to 3. It is clear from the study that students who were confident about their skills at the start of the project were much less self-assured following exposure

Table 2.3 Entrepreneurial Skills Development

Technical Skills	
Managing operations	Stable
Managing supplies and supply chains	Stable
Office/production space skills	Increased
Managing plant and equipment	Stable
Management Skills	
Planning, organizing and supervising	Stable
Marketing skills	Stable
Financial management	Decreased
Legal skills	Decreased
Administrative skills	Stable
Higher-order skills related to learning and problem-solving	Decreased
Entrepreneurial Skills	
Develop a concept and a business plan	Decreased
Environmental scanning	Decreased
Opportunity recognition	Decreased
Networking	Decreased
Personal Maturity Skills	
Self-awareness	Decreased
Accountability	Decreased
Emotional coping	Stable
Creativity	Decreased

to a live programme involving real-life entrepreneurs. The authors suggest that student skills did not actually decline over the period of the project. 'Our preferred explanation is that the students' contacts with real managers, companies and problems made them increasingly aware over time how inadequate their skills were' (Chang & Rieple, 2013, p. 230). What is most notable is that all the entrepreneurial and individual maturity skills, with the exception of 'emotional coping' actually declined (Table 2.3). In contrast, the technical and management skills were largely stable with the exceptions of financial and legal skills as well as higher level learning. We believe these results raise some very important issues about student perception of their skills that are certainly worth discussing in the classroom.

To summarize, we acknowledge the need for students studying entrepreneurship developing the appropriate skills as quickly as possible. There are a range of technical skills including basic financial management, preparing business plans and carrying out competitor analyses as well as various digital skills (Table 2.1) that are important for any would-be entrepreneur (Peschl et al., 2021; Rayna & Striukova, 2021). However, in this section we concentrate on what might be termed the 'softer' entrepreneurial skills as identified in *EntreComp* (McCallum et al., 2018). In our view, developing an entrepreneurial mindset (Section 1.5) improving your thinking skills (Peschl et al., 2021) as well as the ability to identify and develop new business opportunities are fundamental to becoming a successful entrepreneur (Chapter 3).

2.4 An Effectual Approach to Skill Development

Schumpeter (1934, p. 81) suggested that entrepreneurship is rare and argued that 'the carrying out of new combinations is a special function, and the privilege of a type of people who are less numerous than all those who have the "objective" possibility of doing it'. This means that entrepreneurial skills were perceived to be a unique set of capabilities that allows only some individuals to perceive and develop new opportunities (Penrose, 1959). Authors argue that opportunity recognition and exploitation is the defining skill necessary to become an entrepreneur (Shane, 2000; Venkataraman, 2004). By this, they mean the ability to leverage existing knowledge and experience in new settings to identify gaps in the market. This means that setting up a new venture requires market knowledge and experience, a willingness to use that knowledge/experience to identify new opportunities (Figure 2.1). Opportunity recognition and setting up a new venture require imagination, creative and innovative skills at the outset (see Chapter 3).

Certainly, if an entrepreneur is intending to redefine a market or create a completely new product, then high levels of innovation and creative skills are important. It is hard to imagine how successful ventures that are used

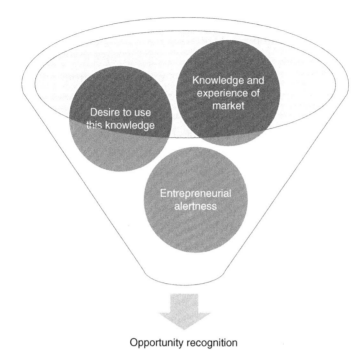

Opportunity recognition

Figure 2.1 Opportunity Recognition

as case studies, taught on entrepreneurship schools, and are identified in the business press, such as Google, Apple, Microsoft, Facebook, Twitter and so on could have been successful without the self-belief and creativity to deliver innovation. That said, many new ventures are set up, not with the intention of reinventing the marketplace, but with the purpose of leveraging a market niche and creating enough returns to meet the entrepreneur's needs and aspirations. Indeed, many new ventures are not necessarily innovative as they may take an existing idea and refine it and/or deliver a better customer experience. It is difficult to see what is truly innovative about any of Richard Branson's Virgin Group businesses that he has developed over the years including the music industry, soft drinks, finance and travel, yet many consider him as a role model of the successful entrepreneur. John Schnatter, who owns *Papa John's Pizza* with around 3,000 stores worldwide, has made a very successful business without reinventing the basic business model. *Jazooli*, the company setup by two young brothers began selling cheap mobile phone accessories online but within four years they were turning over more than £1 million (see Box 3.1). The approach adopted by the brothers to setting up and developing their company followed the principles of effectuation theory (Jones & Li, 2017).

Saras Sarasvathy developed the concept of effectuation as an alternative way of considering how new ventures emerge from contingencies and available resources (Sarasvathy, 2001, 2012; Sarasvathy & Ramesh, 2019). In this regard, she uses the concept of effectuation to suggest that new entrepreneurs can deploy the means at his or her disposal – available resources, the entrepreneur's personal characteristics, abilities and skills to exploit contingencies and shape outcomes. Conventional opportunity recognition is about identifying a current gap in the market and creating a new product to fill that gap. In contrast, an effectual approach means that ventures emerge when potential entrepreneurs develop solutions to existing problems that gradually create new opportunities to develop over time. Sarasvathy (2008) thus provides insight into the emergent nature of new ventures by showing how an individual entrepreneur, or team, can take what they know and resources they have available to solve a problem. As they do this, if they limit their exposure to risk, leverage the contingencies available in the environment and through their networks (perhaps also an unexpected event or good fortune), they eventually form a venture (Figure 2.2). The difference between the approaches is that an effectual entrepreneur seeks to take their opportunity as an uncertain future unfolds, whereas opportunity recognition approach suggests entrepreneurs predict what the future will be.

This suggests that rather than innate skills and abilities held only by a few (as proposed by Schumpeter), the principles of effectuation can be acquired and applied by anyone who is motivated to start a business. Entrepreneurial expertise is not a set of traits, characteristics or success factors, but a way of problem solving that can be learned (Sarasvathy, 2008). An entrepreneur uses the human capital available to them (resilience, prior experience and education) to make sense of problems and contingencies. As discussed in more detail later (Chapter 12), there are five distinct factors underpinning effectuation theory (Sarasvathy, 2012):

- **The bird-in-the-hand principle** - instead of starting with a formal business plan, effectual entrepreneurs begin with their own 'means' – who they are (interests and motivations), what they know (skills) and who they know (social networks). This principle simply means starting a business

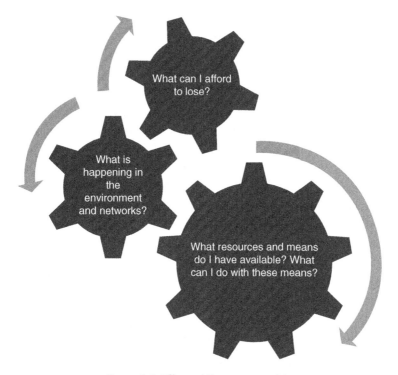

Figure 2.2 Effectual Entrepreneurship

in an area that you know by doing something that you know about. The bird-in-the-hand principle is similar to the philosophies underpinning bootstrapping and bricolage.

- **The affordable loss principle** – we have all taught entrepreneurship courses where students spend a great deal of time projecting annual sales based on the number of products or services sold in the marketplace. In most cases such projections are entirely unrealistic based as they are on optimistic assumptions related to both supply and demand. Affordable loss concerns the entrepreneur making decisions about the amount of time, effort, skills and money they are willing to invest in the venture. The focus is not on the resources (money) you need to start a new business. Rather, you should ask yourself how much can I afford to lose and how much am I willing to lose?
- **The crazy quilt principle** – as mentioned above, causal approaches to business start-up are usually based on unrealistic evaluations of 'the

market' (number of customers, response of competitors and so on). Effectual entrepreneurs do not restrict themselves to a predetermined view of the market opportunity. They begin with their means (see bird-in-the-hand principle) and then attempt to 'create' a market for their products/services. Consequently, effectual entrepreneurs can exploit opportunities as they arise instead of having a fixed vision of how they operate in the marketplace. The crazy quilt principle also encourages effectual entrepreneurs to work with other stakeholders so they can co-create new opportunities.

- **The lemonade principle** – 'when life gives you lemons make lemonade' is a well-known American saying. Starting with flexible goals, rather than fixed target, means that you can exploit unexpected events rather than being hampered by those events. Remaining open to new eventualities means you can be positive about new possibilities rather than adopting a defensive position. For example, think about those companies that responded positively to the Covid-19 crisis and were able take advantage of new opportunities presented by 'lockdown'.
- **The pilot in the plane principle** – effectual entrepreneurs are not simply at the mercy of the wider marketplace but are able to consciously create their own futures. Sarasvathy (2012, p. 143) give the example of an effectual response to climate change. Instead of relying on individual genius to invent a new energy source, an effectual approach would involve bringing together a range of stakeholders including inventors, regulators and event social movements such as *Extinction Rebellion*. Such collaboration could help stimulate the creation of new ventures to commercialize products and services based on renewal energy.

In Box 2.1 we illustrate how effectual entrepreneurship works in practice by illustrating the setting up of Manchester Metropolitan University's *Centre for Enterprise* (Jones, Macpherson & Woollard, 2008). To summarize, effectual entrepreneurs demonstrate their 'knowledge-in-practice' (Orlikowski, 2002) as they solve problems and create new business. In other words, whether one takes a view that entrepreneurs find or create opportunities, having a thorough understanding of their available human capital (skills and knowledge) is an essential consideration when deciding what type of firm to create, or what type of market to enter.

Box 2.1

Early in 2000, Manchester Metropolitan University Business School was involved in a UK government initiative to help people from disadvantaged backgrounds start their own businesses. As a result of this initiative, the *Centre for Enterprise* (CfE) was launched to deliver a training programme for 'new' entrepreneurs in Greater Manchester. Creation of the CfE was not part of any University strategic plan but simply a response to an unexpected opportunity. In the next ten years, the CfE grew from two part-time employees to 21 full-time staff who were involved with a wide range of different projects. Initially, the CfE relied on the skills and knowledge of the two founders (**bird-in-the-hand**) to initiate the programme. As the workload increased, a number of PhD students were recruited to work on a part-time basis to minimize financial risk to the University (**affordable loss**). As the CfE became established, staff responded flexibly to a range of new opportunities (**crazy quilt**), which included conventional research funding from the Economic and Social Research Council, consultancy projects for various organizations including Manchester City Council and training for owner-managers of small firms. The CfE relied on various stakeholders (PhD students and MMU staff) identifying new eventualities (**lemonade principle**) that offered the chance to take on more projects and turn part-time jobs into full-time positions. Remaining flexible to the emergence of new opportunities by utilizing various resources (**pilot-in-the-plane**) within the Business School and MMU itself, helped the CfE become established as a key actor in the Greater Manchester ecosystem with the creation of Innospace, the University's business incubator.

2.5 Early-Stage Growth: Developing Your Knowledge, Skills and Capabilities

As new ventures begin to grow, the skills and knowledge necessary to manage the various activities will change and entrepreneurs must learn to apply new skills. If this growth is slow, then the entrepreneur's development process may not be crucial; however, faster growth is more challenging because it will difficult to keep pace with the additional competences necessary to manage a growing firm (Aldrich & Ruef, 2018; Jones, Macpherson & Thorpe, 2010; Macpherson, 2005). In Chapter 11 we examine and critique a range of approaches to understanding growth in new ventures, and we also discuss entrepreneurial learning in Chapter 5. In this chapter, however, we will focus specifically on research that examines the knowledge and skills that may be necessary to develop the firm.

2.5.1 Generic Skills and Competences

Early learning research focused on the person (entrepreneur) and the development of their managerial knowledge (know-how) (Curran, 1986; Stanworth & Curran, 1991). At this time, research focused on the key entrepreneurial attributes and traits and the managerial skills appropriate for running a successful business. Entrepreneurial capabilities may be rare and inimitable, but research suggests that entrepreneurs cannot accrue profit unless managerial human capital is available to provide specialist functions and processes designed to make the most of opportunities available. Indeed, Penrose (1959) was clear in her analysis of growing firms that this required both the ability to spot opportunities, but also be able to make appropriate use of available resources to exploit such opportunities. Smith and Miner (1983), for example, suggest that managing a growing business is subtly different and they note important differences between 'entrepreneurial' and 'management' motivation. They define managerial activity as according with the desire or willingness to implement systems of bureaucracy. Based on a comparative sample of 38 entrepreneurs and 294 managers at a variety of levels in corporate organizations, they suggest that the motivation to 'manage' was lower in entrepreneurs. This, they argue, is an advantage when spotting and acting on opportunities, but may become a distinct disadvantage if they do not have the ability to put in place the structures essential to manage a growing business.

Studies have suggested a range of skills are needed by new entrepreneurs to set-up and run their businesses. It seems that these lists, implicitly at least, are influenced by the idea of a 'recipe' for the management of entrepreneurial firms. The term recipe is most widely known through the work of Spender (1989) who suggested that there are particular 'guides to action' associated with specific industries or sectors. Hence, when considering the development and skills needed by entrepreneurs there is a concern with identifying and applying 'generic' recipes for firms (Sharifi & Zhang, 2009). Man et al. (2002), for example, identify six competency areas necessary for managing a growing business. The concept of 'entrepreneurial competences' was also used widely by UK Government Agencies and business support organizations to justify particular programmes for the economic development of smaller firms (Mitchelmore & Rowley, 2010). Synthesizing the results from a wide range of earlier studies (Brinckmann, Salomo & Gemuenden, 2011; Man et al., 2002; Mangham, 1985; Martin & Staines, 1994; Matlay & Hyland, 1997; Mitchelmore & Rowley, 2010; Sadler-Smith, Hampson, Chaston & Badger, 2003) it was possible to list the most widely recognized generic 'entrepreneurial competences' (Table 2.4). We suggest that this list provides a useful summary of the areas would-be entrepreneurs need to consider as they start to develop their businesses. As we have already discussed, a 'core' entrepreneurial competence is the ability to identify and exploit market opportunities. Resourcefulness is an undervalued competence for entrepreneurs who will be confronted by many setbacks while in the process of establishing and developing their business (Chadwick & Raver, 2020; Fisher et al., 2021; Kor, Mahoney & Michael, 2007).

Some influential observers have consistently argued that the link between entrepreneurial learning and firm performance is tenuous and that policy support for such activity is inappropriate (Coad & Storey, 2021; Greene, Mole & Storey, 2015; Storey, 2004). Based on an extensive review of the literature, Soto-Simeone, Siren and Antretter (2020) are far more positive about the role of individual knowledge, skills and experience in terms of their contribution to new venture survival (Soto-Simeone, Sirén & Antretter, 2021). From the entrepreneur's perspective, while they recognize that business and management skills are important for success, they also perceive their own skills as adequate (Tagg, Mason & Carter, 2004), and often complain that the support systems provided are inappropriate for their needs (Beresford & Saunders, 2005).

Our view is that enhancing your entrepreneurial skills will certainly improve the chances of your new business surviving the crucial early stages

Table 2.4 Generic Competences

Competency	Behavioural Expectation
Entrepreneurial	The ability to keep abreast of potential changes in the market in order to recognize and exploit market opportunities.
Relational	The ability to motivate others, to engage with them to build trust, establish networks and to persuade others to join in the venture. Effective communication, symbolic management and rhetorical abilities.
Conceptual	The ability to absorb and make sense of complex information and to interpret its meaning, or be innovative in reformulating ideas based on such information.
Functional	The ability to develop and operate management systems necessary to run the business. This involves controlling and allocating all its resources, human, technological and financial.
Technical	These are specific key competences that depend on technical product or service knowledge in order to deliver the primary revenue stream for the business.
Resourcefulness	The motivation, commitment and resilience to problem solve and to apply creative solutions given limited resources and capacity.

Source: This list is developed from a number of papers and studies described above

following start-up. As the business begins to grow, then functional skills and competences, such as marketing, financial control, sales, strategic planning, customer relationship management and human resource management will become more important in developing a growing business. Specific technical knowledge of the product or service are also relevant in understanding the firm's potential in the marketplace. It is certainly appropriate to assume that once a firm is established entrepreneurs will need to continue the process of competence development. This will be required in both functional and technical skills (either through experience or education) to manage the firm's growth (see Box 2.2).

Box 2.2

The Managing Director of Machine Co, a machining company, had had an Aerospace manufacturer as its main customer for a number of years. However, the MD detected a shift in that relationship as a result of economic pressures in the industry. Although the MD of Machine Co felt he was making savings and improving product quality to meet his customer's requirements, he could not provide evidence to his customer.

> They were looking for a good business strategy you know. What are you doing to cut cost? How much scrap do you produce? I knew in my mind that we'd made cost savings but I couldn't produce evidence… My knowledge of what was going on in the company was all word of mouth you know. I knew we had scrapped a job yesterday but by tomorrow that was all forgotten…. I knew I wasn't performing well in these audits.

He relied on the informal systems that had been in use since he started the firm. It was clear to the MD that, if he was going to maintain his major customer in the long-term, he would need to provide competitive year-on-year improvements and he would need to develop systems to show what he had achieved. He was fortunate that his customer, concerned by the number of failed supply audits, set up a supplier development programme. This initiative delivered by a Further Education College in collaboration with the customer. He started to use his training at the College to consider how he might improve his business and he implemented formal continuous improvement systems and quality audits. These new skills and competences allowed him to retain the customer. He was also able to show potential new customers his professional approach to quality and cost efficiency, which allowed him to increase his customer base and to grow the business.

It is well established that there is a strong and consistent relationship between entrepreneurial competences and business success (Mitchelmore & Rowley, 2010). A recent publication suggested that an increased focus on digital technologies and innovation meant that there is a need to re-examine the nature of entrepreneurial competences (Reis, Fleury & Carvalho, 2021). For example, some authors propose that entrepreneurial competences can be categorized as personal attributes, abilities and skills, knowledge and experience (Rezaei-Zadeh, Hogan, O'Reilly, Cunningham & Murphy, 2017). Entrepreneurial competences are the various skills required for individuals or teams to transform ideas into functioning businesses (Mitchelmore & Rowley, 2010). According Rezaei-Zadeh et al. (2017, p. 183) meta-competences 'are higher-order abilities, to do with being able to learn, adapt, anticipate and create'. Based on an extensive literature review, the authors identified four distinct groups of entrepreneurial meta-competences.

1. Personal and behavioral meta-competence (PBMC) the ability to adopt appropriate behaviors during the creation of the new venture, including self-confidence, control of emotions, listening, objectivity, sensitivity to peers, conformity to professional norms

2. Functional meta-competence (FMC): the ability to perform different business-related tasks to effectively produce context-related outcomes in order to be successful in the creation and deployment of the new venture

3. Knowledge and cognitive meta-competence (KCMC): mastering appropriate business-related knowledge and the ability to apply this knowledge in practice, including theoretical and technical knowledge of the business field, tacit knowledge about the new venture, procedural knowledge of finance, project management and contextual knowledge about the environment in which the new venture will be created

4. Values and ethical meta-competence (VEMC): the possession of appropriate professional values and the ability to make sound judgements, for example, the adherence to laws, social/moral sensitivity and confidentiality.

As a result of their detailed analysis of the competences literature, Rezaei-Zadeh et al. (2017) link a range of lower-level competences to the four meta-competences and the most important are listed in Table 2.5. The greatest number of competences (43%) were associated with personal and behavioural meta-competences and had a strong focus on learning, emotional

Table 2.5 Entrepreneurial Meta-Competences

Personal and Behavioural Meta-competence (PBMC)	
Learning to learn	learning from failure & feedback, information seeking, resource allocation
Emotional stability	open to new experiences, resistant to stress, internal locus of control, self-knowledge, need for achievement
Business passion	total commitment, internal drive, direct job involvement, proactive, risk-taking
Leadership/ communication	motivate other people, networking/team-building, collaboration, delegation, complementary competences
Functional meta-competence (FMC)	
Innovation	accept new challenges, creativity, non-traditional perspective, idea generation, originality
Strategic foresight	opportunity identification, seeing big picture, responsive to customers, value-added
Knowledge and cognitive meta-competence (KCMC)	
Market analysis	commercial and sales skills, negotiation, goal-orientation, analytical ability, stakeholders
Values and ethical meta-competence (VEMC)	
Self-confidence & optimism	optimism, persistence, determination, goal-driven, link between effort and outcomes

stability and business passion. Functional meta-competences accounted for 26% of lower-level competences and were grouped under innovation (creativity, idea generation and originality) and strategic foresight (opportunity identification, responsive to customers and adding value to produces/services). The knowledge and cognitive meta-competences (KCMC) also accounted for approximately 26% of the lower-level competences and focused on the skills associated with an ability to analyse the market (analytical ability, commercial and sales skills). Based on four detailed case studies Phua and Jones (2010) demonstrated that while new entrepreneurs did not produce detailed marketing plans they did have a sophisticated cognitive approach to collecting, processing and applying marketing data.

The prevalence of 'softer' marketing skills as opposed to 'harder' analytical approaches to marketing was also confirmed by Jayawarna, Jones, Lam and Phua (2014). Values and ethical meta-competences (5%) contained items concerned with optimism, persistence and goal-driven behaviours. In summary, there is some focus on the importance of conventional analytical competences particularly associated with the market. However, similar to EntreComp (McCallum et al., 2018), discussed above, there is much greater emphasis on developing the would-be entrepreneur's softer, interpersonal skills and competences.

Based on US data, Bauman and Lucy (2021) discuss a number of trends which should be considered by those involved with enterprise education. They claim that the so-called 'millennials' expect to have a more equitable work-life balance and are resistant to the idea of working for large corporations. Also, in most developed countries the service sector is far more important than traditional manufacturing industries and this is reflected in the types of start-up businesses. In addition, the rise in importance of the Internet and associated technologies (social media) has certainly made it considerably easier to establish service-based start-up businesses (Bauman & Lucy, 2021). The implications for helping students acquire the appropriate competences to ensure that they can create successful businesses are similar to the personal and behavioural meta-competences outlined above. Blass (2018) suggested the following factors: understanding who you are and your goals, tolerance for risk, emotional intelligence, survival and developing resilience (Doern, 2017; Doern, Williams & Vorley, 2019). Encouraging students to learn about themselves and their potential to become successful entrepreneurs is central to effective entrepreneurship education (Cope, 2003). Starting a new business means that would-be entrepreneurs must be prepared to face uncertainties and overcome new challenges (Arikan, Arikan & Koparan, 2020). Emotional intelligence, the ability to manage your own feeling and empathize with other stakeholders increases the likelihood of success in your entrepreneurial endeavors (Kwapisz, Schell, Aytes & Bryant, 2021). Given the challenges of risk and uncertainty, it is also very important that young entrepreneurs build-up their psychological resilience so that they can deal positively with the inevitable setbacks they will face (Blass, 2018; Chadwick & Raver, 2020). Resilience is closely linked to resourcefulness (Fisher et al., 2021), the ability to apply creative solutions to difficult problems, outlined in Tables 2.3 and 2.4.

2.5.2 *Exploiting Innovation and Creativity*

There is potentially a tension between the need to develop skills and cap-abilities that focus on managing the firm – such as quality control, financial management and human resource management – and to develop those that support product development, innovation and creativity. The latter is neces-sary if an entrepreneur is to continue to enhance their product portfolio and to respond to market changes.

This tension between exploiting existing knowledge and exploration of new opportunities was first defined by March (1991). Technical knowledge may be required to identify a gap in the market, or to innovate and design specific products, but this advantage would be quickly lost if entrepreneurs cannot provide sufficient capability to lead production and change (Kakati, 2003). This means that the development of new processes or products can only create long-term profits if systems and capabilities are shared throughout the organization and institutionalized into new systems and routines (Crossan, Lane & White, 1999; Ghezzi, 2019; Jones & Macpherson, 2006). For example, Baker and Nelson (2005) note the difference between parallel and selective bricolage (the practice of making do with resources discarded or unused by others) among entrepreneurial firms. In their study, they argue that parallel bricolage is a habituated process of making do and a *modus operandi* for some entrepreneurs. However, selective bricolage means pursuing specific problems, or opportunities and ensuring they gen-erate long-run rents by embedding the outcomes in new processes and routines. Jones and Macpherson (2006) argue similarly in their empirical study of three mature firms undergoing periods of renewal. In these firms, they noted that new systems and processes allowed the sharing of know-ledge and the delegation of responsibility to enable entrepreneurs to insti-tutionalize innovation. Put simply, while innovative and creative skills are necessary to be able to take advantage of opportunities, functional, lead-ership and management capabilities are necessary to be able exploit those opportunities. This exemplifies arguments provided by Penrose (1959) that particular entrepreneurial and management capabilities are required in order to both understand *and* capitalize on potential opportunities within the marketplace.

The ability to balance entrepreneurial and managerial skills has been conceptualized as ambidexterity (Birkinshaw, Probst & Tushman, 2009; Wenke, Zapkau & Schwens, 2021), and describes the pursuit of two

Table 2.6 Innovation and Entrepreneurship: Potential Tensions

EXPLOITATION FOCUS	EXPLORATION FOCUS
Selection	Risk Taking
Implementation	Innovation
Refinement	Creativity
Efficiency	Experimenting
Control	Flexibility
Standardization	Variation
Proficiency	Play
Productivity	Search

simultaneous paths (see table 2.6). What is a challenging repertoire for large firms is even more difficult for a single individual (or small team); it is clear, that the deployment of innovation requires others in the firm to develop the appropriate skills and competences to be able to deliver efficient and effective processes. A study by Freel (2005) identified that the most innovative firms in his study of 1,345 SMEs invested more in developing the skills and capabilities of their staff. In other words, lists of competences tend to focus on the entrepreneur's abilities, but making the most of innovation and creativity requires attention and development of knowledge, skills and capabilities available across the venture (Evers & Andersson, 2021; Wenke et al., 2021). We discuss further the *dynamic capabilities* to be able to develop and renew the operational capacity of the venture in Chapter 10. However, below we also discuss the role of experience, education and training.

2.5.3 The Role of Experience and Informal Training

Attention has turned from trying to establish causality between education and performance and has begun to focus more on how entrepreneurs navigate the vicissitudes of starting and running a business. In terms of how entrepreneurial skills might develop, Rae and Carswell (2001) use the life stories of entrepreneurs gathered through in-depth interviews to suggest that, while entrepreneurial activity may be dependent on specific capabilities developed during earlier careers (based on technical knowledge and functional training), it is also developed through successful and failed activities and through interaction with others. These experiences are combined and organized to construct personal theories, or an 'entrepreneurial discourse', which, with self-confidence and belief, may result in business or personal success. These findings echo those of Cope & Down (2010) and Rae (2004) who both confirm in their studies that experience and entrepreneurial capability co-evolve.

Rae (2004) suggests that, entrepreneurs develop a theory of action as they are exposed to 'learning episodes' or experiences over time. Each new experience and interaction potentially develop their theory of action, but such experiences are specific to both the entrepreneur and the context. This means that any understanding of an entrepreneur's success at managing a growing business through recognizing and develop opportunities must be cognizant of the situated and contextual nature of their participation and experience. Wood, Bakker and Fisher (2021) argue that the entrepreneur's theory of action relies on what they describe as 'time-calibrated internal narratives'. Because all entrepreneurs must deal with risk and uncertainty, they create narratives of action to guide them through the start-up process. Such narratives are based on three dimensions of time:

- **Initialization** – refers to the specific time when an individual decides that they are going to start their entrepreneurial venture. So, for those studying entrepreneurship in college or university, it might be 'when I graduate'. Alternatively, it could be 'when I have acquired some experience/resources'.
- **Pace** – refers to the time between initial start-up and some other decisive action. For example, time to first sale, breakeven, profitability, first employee and so on. On the other hand, it is well established that entrepreneurs are often unrealistically optimistic about the timing of critical actions.
- **Chronology** – refers to the sequencing of entrepreneurial actions during the start-up process. The way in which entrepreneurs approach the creation of a new venture will clearly have a strong influence on the sequencing of activities. Adopting a 'causal' approach will generally entail detailed research, followed by the creation of a business plan, which aids the search for resources. Whereas an 'effectual entrepreneur' will begin their business with the resources at hand (bird-in-the-hand).

Importantly, the authors stress that these 'time-calibrated narratives' are generally cognitive constructions that occur before the narrative is shared with other stakeholders (family and friends, for example). The important point is that the construction and use of internal narratives is a principal mechanism by which entrepreneurs time calibrate future entrepreneurial action (Wood et al., 2021, p. 154).

Jason Cope has been particularly influential in arguing that venture trajectories are strongly influenced by the context within which individuals manage their enterprise (Cope, 2003, 2005). In essence, using case studies in six firms, he demonstrates how situated and context-dependent experiences can create profound changes in the way entrepreneurs negotiate the development path of the firm (Cope, 2005). He argues that we need a more nuanced appreciation that fundamental change develops from intense and discontinuous experiences that entrepreneurs have in the day-to-day management of their business. This means that entrepreneurial resources are not necessarily transferable, or replicable, but are embodied in the entrepreneur and embedded in the context of the enterprise. Whether we take the view that the attitude and perception necessary to develop and exploit opportunities can be taught, or only develop through situated experiences, this dimension of human capital is identified by Kakati (2003) as 'entrepreneurial quality'. This is defined as the broad range of capabilities necessary to be able to translate resources into rents, by adopting *appropriate strategies* to exploit opportunities. What is suggested here is that what is appropriate, or might work, depends to a significant amount on context, or even what Storey (2011) argues is blind luck. This resonates strongly with the concept of effectuation, as proposed by Sarasvathy (2001, 2008), where entrepreneurs are able deploy available resources to exploit specific contingencies and that this is how the venture emerges.

Here it is important to consider the role of sensemaking (Weick, 1995) in defining the responses by entrepreneurs to the challenges they face, and how their repertoire of available actions is continually being developed. Weick argues that sensemaking is a skill of negotiating the meaning of everyday practical experiences by comparing the available cues against the available cognitive resources, developed from prior experiences and education, to make sense of and enact, a response (Jones & Li, 2017). When faced with situations, where prior experience fails to provide solutions, entrepreneurs must create new outcomes using their sensemaking skills. In doing so, they create new traces (evident in new systems, material objects and so on) and entrepreneurs are thus deeply embedded in the environments in which they practice their craft: 'They act, and in doing so create the materials that become the constraints and opportunities they face' (Weick, 1995, p. 31). This means that experience creates their 'entrepreneurial discourse', 'repertoire' or 'industry recipe', which they then employ when managing responses to the events they face when managing the firm (Rae & Carswell, 2001; Sharifi & Zhang, 2009; Spender, 1989). Experience is a key ingredient of future action and thus highlights how a previous business failure might potentially be a useful antecedent for a future venture (Cope, 2011).

Experience is a fundamental resource influencing the development trajectory of the firm and is itself developed over time while gaining managerial experience. This has led some to argue that prior business experience, and even failure, provides new venture owners with more likelihood of success (Cope, 2011). Furthermore, research implies that knowledge resource requirements and configurations will change over time and, therefore, that a generic competence approach, while still important, does not address the specific challenges faced by an entrepreneur as they struggle to make sense of their own situation and enact their response. This suggests that policy makers may need to target their agenda at the specific challenges faced by entrepreneurs rather than delivering generic skills and competence solutions, although these generic approaches are not without merit, as we will see below (Box 2.3).

Box 2.3

A Box Manufacturer, *Packaging Co.*, attributed his management style and processes to previous experience he had gained both in industry and in other businesses he had managed. Before he decided to start his own business, the owner-director had been a senior sales and marketing position for a large packaging process and design company. In this job, he observed how his chairman retained tight fiscal control. These were principles that he applied to his own business and they were reinforced through experience as he operated within very tight profit margins. Thus, the owner-director spent a significant amount of his time on financial management to ensure that efficiencies were taken where possible.

When I used to work for (the large packaging company), which was a fifteen/twenty million pound business, it was done exactly the same way. The Chairman signed all cheques and he was the one that analysed all the margins and if it was out he'd ask the questions. He'd make sure it was never out and that's exactly the same principles that I apply. All my jobs are costed. There's no way in the world that we would ever do anything knowingly that makes a loss. I would rather not to take on the order.

2.5.4 Entrepreneurial Education and Formal Training

It is argued that a lack of relevant knowledge and skills at start-up, and in the early stages of development, is a significant reason for the high failure rate in new ventures (for example, Beresford & Saunders, 2005). They go on to suggest that policymakers can address this weakness by providing educational support in the first three years of start-up. The development of generic competence maps, such as National Vocational Qualifications and skills reports, such as Bolton (1971), influenced the content of entrepreneurship education in the UK. In the US, the Small Business Administration provides advice for new venture owners that covers key functional areas such as preparing a business plan, finance, marketing, legal requirements and internationalization. The list is similar from the Australian Government Small Business Enterprise Centres. In all these approaches, competences and/or defining key functional disciplines have significantly influenced the content of training and education programmes provided through government services, independent providers and higher education institutions. This has allowed the development of advice on how to prepare a business plan, review business strategy and specialist financial information. In all these countries, business start-up kits are available online from government sponsored or approved agencies.

However, there has also been a relatively recent change in policy that accords with the growing body of research, discussed above, that advocates a more nuanced approach to entrepreneurship education. In the UK, an initiative known as LEAD (leadership, enterprise and development) originally developed by academics at Lancaster University has been extremely successful in improving the performance of smaller firms (Gordon, Hamilton & Jack, 2012; Kempster, Smith & Barnes, 2018; Smith, Kempster & Wenger-Trayner, 2019). The main benefits are higher levels survival and growth as well as substantial improvements in financial performance (Jones, 2022). The programme is designed to create close relationships between participants to increase trust and develop social capital, which promotes knowledge sharing between members of the cohort (Jones & Macpherson, 2014). University staff and business experts deliver the content as well as individual coaching sessions and masterclasses to address specific needs. In the US, the SBA has adopted the mentoring role and recent UK Government policy provided a brokering service to experts through business advisers for entrepreneurs, which had mixed success (Mole & Keogh, 2009). In keeping with this individual and context sensitive education, Gibb (2009) advocates action learning, an approach which requires entrepreneurs to address real problems they face with the support of an action learning set (a group of peers) and a set facilitator. However, he also recognizes that the institutional norms of education providers and policy support make it difficult to achieve in practice.

Research that supports the role of education and training in developing successful businesses is ambiguous. However, much of this research focused on the relationship to firm performance and ignored the wider context including other contingent factors that might influence the relationship (Bryan, 2006; Coad & Storey, 2021; Soto-Simeone et al., 2021). Past education and experience create intellectual capital and it is this resource that entrepreneurs use in order to make sense of ambiguity; increased cognitive capacity and ability will have implications for behaviour and actions (Wiklund & Shepherd, 2003) and a broader range of education and experience is likely to allow a wider range of possible responses (Bood, 1998; Soto-Simeone et al., 2020). Since education and training, all things being equal, improve available human capital, this is likely to provide a wider repertoire of possible responses when faced with challenges by all staff within the firm. Whether such formally developed skills and capabilities result in better performance will depend on contingencies and context. Also, this implies that while many entrepreneurs may prefer informal learning, this does mean there is not a significant role for formal education in increasing the intellectual capacity of the entrepreneurs and their staff (Kempster et al., 2018). We discuss the theme further in Chapter 5, with regards to entrepreneurial education (Box 2.4).

Box 2.4

At Machine Co, as noted above in Box 2.2, the development of continuous improvement capabilities was the key factor in winning work from their customer and in expanding the customer base. While the MD was able to not only demonstrate what he had been doing informally, his college course allowed him to develop new ideas and to improve the quality of his employees' skills.

> Well, there's this college and they're telling me that all big companies use these tools and techniques and I thought, they can't all be wrong, you know. It was a realization that these must work for them to be so popular and I started to cherry pick and listen to what could work in Machine Co… I started to experiment, measuring things and trying new techniques and to encourage my staff to record and measure what they were doing. I also got in a 'set up reduction' consultant to train the staff. That helped and then they were coming to me with ideas.

This formal training allowed the MD and his staff to gain experience in quality and continuous improvement techniques used in large firms. They improved the machining systems and reduced set up times. The supplier development programme allowed the MD to learn new management skills.

2.6 Cultural Entrepreneurship

Given the range of knowledge skills and capabilities necessary to create a successful new business it is unlikely they will all be embodied in one individual. New entrepreneurs need knowledge, resources and capabilities from others inside and outside the firm's boundaries, which they must borrow, appropriate and integrate into the venture (Jayawarna, Jones & Macpherson, 2020). Even sole traders need to engage with customers, suppliers and other organizations if they are to be successful. We discuss the role of networks and social capital in Chapter 6, and there are also relevant discussions in Chapter 5 about social learning. Both chapters highlight that many resources exist outside of the firm and that appropriate knowledge, skills and capabilities are held by others within the firm. As such, relationship management is a key aspect of managing a venture. Entrepreneurs must enlist the support of others to join their firm, to buy their products/services and help them operationalize their ideas (Anderson, 2005).

This has led to an interest in what Lounsbury and Glynn (2001) define as 'cultural entrepreneurship'. They go on to argue that this is a process to help create and transmit an identity that others might see as legitimate to benefit from and engage with institutional capital and other resource (Lounsbury, Gehman & Glynn, 2019; Lounsbury & Glynn, 2019). Spender (2005) suggests that the immaterial and symbolic elements of firms carry meaning. Sensemaking is a skill of negotiating the meaning of everyday practical experience with others (Weick, 1995) and through the skilled presentation of symbolic and immaterial entities entrepreneurs can participate purposively with others to make collaborative engagement possible (Clarke, 2011; Holt & Macpherson, 2010; Jones & Li, 2017). A similar competence is labelled as 'narrative sensemaking' (O'Connor, 2002), by which she means that an entrepreneur is able to represent the firm in a coherent narrative through interconnected plot lines that make sense, and are connected, to others and other organizations. Understanding new venture creation as a performance, or narrative, shows how entrepreneurs must convince others that their ideas and proposals have merit, and provide credibility such that others will be willing to invest time, money and effort into the venture (Anderson, 2005; O'Connor, 2002).

For example, in a study of three entrepreneurs, using ethnography techniques, Clarke (2011) found that they used visual symbols: to present an appropriate scene to stakeholders; to create a professional identity and emphasize control; and to regulate emotions. These visual symbols included props, settings, dress and expressiveness and entrepreneurs 'actively seek to make sure that stakeholders experience positive emotions by carefully managing their surrounding visual environment' (Clarke, 2011, p. 1384). She argues that the more experienced entrepreneurs were more adept at this, and that such skills of symbolic management were important for securing appropriate support for their ventures. Other studies examine micro-level interactions and highlight the use of both speech and gestures by entrepreneurs to convince others of the viability and legitimacy of their business (Clarke, Cornelissen & Healey, 2019; Cornelissen, Clarke & Cienki, 2012). These authors note that entrepreneurs use metaphors in both communication modes in the early stages of the commercialization of a venture. By doing so entrepreneurs attempt to emphasize their own agency and control, but also the predictability and taken for granted nature of what is a novel venture (Clarke et al., 2019; Lounsbury et al., 2019).

Baron and Tang (2009) argue that skills associated with social perception, expressiveness and self-promotion influence new venture performance, although this is mediated by the success in obtaining information and available resources. These social skills are micro-level factors that eventually have a macro-level effect on business performance. Their findings 'point to a process in which entrepreneurs' social skills influence their effectiveness in obtaining crucial resources, and these resources, in turn, influence new venture performance' (Baron & Tang, 2009, p. 300). Micro-level-skills are important, not just for entrepreneurs, but for all actors within the business that engage with various stakeholders, since these 'boundary spanning' roles are important in facilitating access to external resources including knowledge (Jones, 2006). In short, specific social skills, such as political skills, emotional sensitivity, impression management, social adaptability and persuasiveness can influence the quality of interactions which in turn influence the ability of entrepreneurs to engage successfully with others when establishing and managing a new venture (Baron & Markman, 2000; Fearon, Furlotti, van Vuuren & McLaughlin, 2021; Lounsbury & Glynn, 2019; Tocher, Oswald & Hall, 2015; Tocher, Oswald, Shook & Adams, 2012). This understanding of 'cultural entrepreneurship' is conceptualized in Figure 2.3.

Fisher et al. (2021) link cultural entrepreneurship and the concept of entrepreneurial resourcefulness to explain how new business overcome resource constraints. There are strong similarities to both bricolage (Bernardi & Pedrini, 2020) and bootstrapping (Jayawarna et al., 2020) as resourcefulness refers to the entrepreneur's ability to make the best possible use of their existing resources (Baker & Nelson, 2005). Accessing external support is vital to the success of any entrepreneurial venture and it is essential to obtain resources from a range of stakeholders including family, friends, suppliers, partners, business networks, professional advisors as well as investors. Inevitably, there is limited information related to the viability of new businesses and entrepreneurs must use stories and narratives to mobilize the emotions and cognitions of potential resource providers

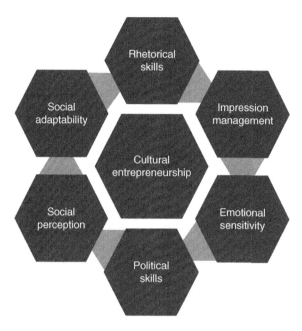

Figure 2.3 Cultural Entrepreneurship

(Lounsbury & Glynn, 2001, 2019). There are a number of entrepreneurial narratives associated with various activities within new businesses (Fisher et al., 2021):

- **Identity narratives** – focus on the entrepreneur's skills, motivations and experience in relationship to starting and managing the new venture. Such narratives should enable the entrepreneur to explain 'who I am', 'what I am doing' and 'what I hope to achieve'. An identity narrative helps resource providers understand the risks and rewards associated with offering support to the business.
- **Opportunity narratives** – are related to the nature of the potential business opportunity and the likelihood of the entrepreneur being able to successfully exploit that opportunity. This narrative will be influenced by whether the entrepreneur is adopting a causal or an effectual approach to business start-up.
- **Failure narratives** – many new businesses fail, and it is a key element of the learning process that entrepreneurs should be able to construct narratives to explain that failure. Clearly, such a narrative is central to explanations about why any new business will also not fail.

- **Projective narratives** – focus on the imagined future state of the business in terms of growth trajectories potential new market, recruitment of new staff, acquisition of new technologies etc. In other words, this is the direction I want to take the business in the future.
- **Pivot narratives** – it is widely acknowledged that many entrepreneurial businesses take a very different direction than was originally intended. For example, the adoption of a new business model (see Chapter 4) would require the entrepreneur to develop a narrative to reassure stakeholders that this change had being carefully evaluated and implemented.

Fisher et al. (2021) go on to explain that resourcefulness narratives contain two crucial elements: creativity and overcoming impediments. First, entrepreneurs must be able to demonstrate that they are making use of their existing resources in imaginative and creative ways (Baker & Nelson, 2005). Secondly, entrepreneurs should be able to explain how they overcame obstacles or impediments on their journey to starting a business: 'I was able to launch my business despite having a large amount of student debt'. As illustrated in Figure 2.4, potential resource providers will judge the level of creativity and the significance of the impediments based on the entrepreneur's narrative. Consequently, their perceptions of the entrepreneur's **resourcefulness** will strongly influence decisions about offering support to the venture. You can observe this process in action on TV programmes such as *Dragon's Den* and the U.S. version known as *Shark Tank*. Clearly, any narrative must be preceded by the entrepreneur taking some meaning **actions** (Figure 2.4).

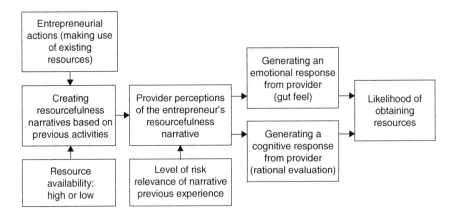

Figure 2.4 Resourcefulness Narratives and Support Provision

Simply saying 'this is what I intend to do, and this is how I will overcome any obstacles I confront' will not represent a convincing narrative.

It is then suggested by Fisher et al. (2021) that emotions and cognition influence the resource providers' decisions about whether they should offer support to the venture. The authors claim that an emotional response is based on three factors: surprise, interest and admiration (think about how you respond to a lecturer or to one of your friends telling you a 'story'). Surprise refers to the extent to which the narrative has some unexpected elements that hold the audience's attention. You need to be able to surprise the listener with explanations of your creativity and impediments. Secondly, interest is a positive emotion towards the speaker and motivates the listener to pay attention (again, think about listening to a lecturer). Interest is also stimulated by relevance of the narrative in relationship to the entrepreneur's creativity and ability to overcome impediments. Thirdly, admiration refers to the extent to which the narrative generates positive attention towards the entrepreneur. Clearly, engendering a sense of admiration among your audience will depend on your ability to 'read' what they are expecting from you. Stimulating admiration from an audience comprising family and friends is likely to be very different from pitching to a group of venture capitalists (who will probably have very different values and objectives).

Whereas an emotional response can be summarized in the colloquial term 'gut feel', the cognitive pathway is based on a more rational response to the limited amount of information that is available about the venture. Again Fisher et al. (2021) suggest that there are three factors influencing cognition: competence, commitment and credibility. The ability to demonstrate your competence as an entrepreneur is fundamental to the attraction of additional resources. Who would support a venture in which they perceived the entrepreneur to be incompetent? The ability to signal resourcefulness in your previous actions will help create confidence in resource providers' perception of your ability to succeed in the future. Beginning a career as an entrepreneur will inevitably mean you will have to overcome many obstacles and setbacks. Individuals who lack commitment are likely to become disillusioned and demotivated very quickly. The ability to demonstrate creativity in overcoming various difficulties will help demonstrate your commitment to resource providers. Thirdly, it is important that you can convince others of your credibility as an entrepreneur. Combining views of your competence and commitment will strongly influence perceptions of the extent to which you are credible to resource providers.

It is important to stress at this stage that almost anyone is a potential resource provider to your nascent business. You may be thinking that this material about resourcefulness narratives is only related to your engagement with funders such as bankers, business angels or venture capitalists. As we discuss in Chapters 8 and 9, very few new businesses can attract external funding particularly in the early stages. Also, the resources that are important to a new business include emotional support, advice, knowledge, information and network contacts. As demonstrated in the story of Innospace, working in a business incubator means that you can obtain support from a number of sources including your fellow incubates (Jones et al., 2021a). Hence, your resourcefulness narratives are important whoever you engage with in your entrepreneurial journey. It is impossible to know in advance who may be able to provide you with useful knowledge and information.

Finally, Fisher et al. (2021) identify a number of contingencies that influence the efficacy of resource narratives (Figure 2.4). The first contingency concerns the resource environment itself and the extent to which resources are readily available. In areas where resources are scarce, individuals are more likely to be forced into 'necessity' entrepreneur (becoming entrepreneurs because there are no other employment opportunities) and they must act resourcefully to survive. In such circumstances, resourcefulness becomes 'normalized' and narratives will have less impact on emotions or cognition (Fisher et al., 2021). Conversely, in areas where resources are readily available to most entrepreneurs then resourcefulness narratives have more power to persuade because they are rarer. The second factor is the level of uncertainty associated with a venture. Uncertainty is related to several factors such as: the business is at an early stage, the entrepreneur lacks experience, utilizing new technologies, creating new markets or adopting a new business model. Any one of these issues will make it difficult for resource providers to evaluate the longer-term potential of a business. Thirdly, if the entrepreneur has a track record of achievement in starting new businesses this it is likely to reassure resource providers even if other risk-factors (new technology/markets) are a feature of the new business. Clearly, most young people studying entrepreneurship in college or university are very unlikely to have gained previous experience as an entrepreneur. In Chapter 7, we discuss the importance of would-be entrepreneurs gaining some work experience during their education. Such experience is important in helping those lacking entrepreneurial experience generate resourcefulness narratives. Lastly, what Fisher et al. (2021) refer to as the 'recency of action' describes when the events described in the resourcefulness narrative took place. If your creativity in overcoming impediments happened recently then they will have more impact than if they happened in the past. So, a story about how you sold pens and pencils to fellow pupils in junior school will have little impact when you are trying start a business on completion of your university degree.

You may well become a successful entrepreneur without feeling the need to create a resourcefulness narrative. However, we suggest that the ability to draw on a range of cultural tools including language, visual artifacts, gestures and rhetoric can help inexperienced entrepreneurs create resourcefulness narratives that are meaningful for a range of different resource providers.

In this section, we have highlighted the importance of softer skills and competences in gaining access to additional resources and can also help communications with internal stakeholders. In essence, research into symbolic management, cultural entrepreneurship, rhetorical skills and resourcefulness narratives suggest new venture creation is as much about 'impression management' (Harris, Kacmar, Zivnuska & Shaw, 2007; Korzynski, Haenlein & Rautiainen, 2021) as it is about specific functional and technical knowledge.

2.7 Summary and Key Learning Points

The subject of knowledge, skills and capabilities required to create and run a new venture is complicated. However, as stated at the outset of this chapter, we are committed to the view that improving your knowledge, skills and competences will certainly enhance your chances of creating a successful business. As we discuss in greater detail in Chapter 5, the most appropriate way to develop your entrepreneurial skills is via an approach known as experiential learning. This is particularly important in terms of developing the behavioural skills that are the focus of this chapter. Table 2.2 provides a useful summary of the EntreComp skills that are discussed in Section 2.3. These skills are grouped under three headings: ideas/opportunities, resources and entrepreneurial actions. We suggest that paying attention to these skills will also reinforce the importance of developing an *entrepreneurial mindset* as discussed in section 1.5. Section 2.4 is focused on the links between the developing your entrepreneurial skills and an effectuation approach to business start-up. Effectuation theory is based on using the resources (skills) in your possession and then creating an opportunity and developing your skills as you solve the day-to-day problems of creating and growing a new business.

Although not everyone accepts the concept of 'entrepreneurial learning', we see the kind of competences discussed in Section 2.5 as the basis of successful entrepreneurial careers. The six distinct competences outlined in Table 2.1 are core to our message in this chapter. For example, developing your resourcefulness, the ability to apply creative solutions to the kind of difficult problems you will face in starting a business, will help you decide whether you are committed to a career as an entrepreneur. There is plenty of evidence to confirm that obtaining some work experience, however mundane, is important for any would-be entrepreneur. We also discuss the importance of informal learning (learning-by-doing) as well as the more formal training that helps enhance appropriate managerial skills as the business moves into a more mature phase. Finally, we discussed the concept of 'cultural entrepreneurship', which refers to the ability to use language, artifacts, gestures and rhetoric to influence others. This approach can be summarized by the term 'resourcefulness narratives' that are an essential element of accessing a wide range of resources from various stakeholders associated with your business. Drawing on the above discussion, these are the main learning points:

- Enhancing your basic business skills is an important first step in equipping yourself with the competences required to start a new business.
- Effectuation theory provides an alternative approach to starting a business that could be more appropriate for young would-be entrepreneurs with limited access to resources.
- Education and prior experiences are key factors in providing the human capital necessary to navigate the early days of venture creation.
- The broader and more varied your skills, knowledge and competences, the more likely they are to provide a wider repertoire to cope with the challenging problems faced by all new entrepreneurs.
- As the venture grows, knowledge, skills and capabilities will continue to develop through day-to-day problem solving, but they must keep pace with changing contexts.

- While informal experiences are important, formal education and training can also improve the knowledge, skills and capabilities of *all* staff and provide valuable resources for the sustainability of the firm
- Soft skills and relationship management (cultural entrepreneurship) are a crucial part of managing all stakeholders and in navigating boundaries to allow access to other resources essential for firm survival and growth.

2.8 Discussion Questions and Call to Action

1. What are the most important 'basic business skills for those intending to work for themselves or start new businesses?

2. What are the range of factors that influence the skills and knowledge necessary to set-up and run a new venture?

3. What are the implications of different theories for defining necessary skill sets within a firm: for example, the 'traditional causal approach' and effectuation theory?

4. What are the links between the entrepreneur's stocks of human capital and the success of a new venture?

5. What might be the potential sources of skills and knowledge that a nascent entrepreneur can bring to their business? How might they supplement these skills and address any deficiencies that they iden-tify? Why is experience so important in making the most of existing knowledge?

6. Why is it challenging to define a generic set of skills that a new venture owner might need to start a new business?

7. What is meant by the term 'cultural entrepreneurship' and why is it important to all would-be entrepreneurs?

If you are studying entrepreneurship as a modular element of a more general business/management degree, then there will be far lower levels of commitment to pursuing an entrepreneurial career than among students choosing entrepreneurship as an elective. Nevertheless, we believe that even if you have no intention of becoming an entrepreneur (at the present time), then the kind of skills outlined in this chapter will still be of use to you in your future career. Developing an entrepreneurial mindset, becoming a 'self-starter' and enhancing your ability to identify new business opportunities will all be valued by many future employers. Alternatively, if you are committed to starting your own business then improving your ability to communicate with other people could make the difference between a successful or an unsuccessful career as an entrepreneur. Part of the value in studying an entrepreneurial module is that it gives you the opportunity to learn about yourself as well as about entrepreneurship. Setting up a new business, or even working for yourself, is very different from being an employee of an established organization. You will face various setbacks that will test your resilience and resourcefulness and if you do not feel that you have the capacity to respond to these kinds of difficulties then you should consider alternative careers. One positive way to find out more about the demands of entrepreneurship is to work for a small business where you can gain a wide range of experiences as well as observing the challenges facing entrepreneurs without bearing all the risks of starting your own business.

References

Aldrich, H. E. & Ruef, M. (2018). Unicorns, Gazelles, and Other Distractions on the Way to Understanding Real Entrepreneurship in the United States. *Academy of Management Perspectives, 32*(4), 458–472.

Anderson, A. R. (2005). Enacted Metaphor: The Theatricality of the Entrepreneurial Process. *International Small Business Journal, 23*(6), 587–603.

Arend, R. J. & Lévesque, M. (2010). Is the Resource-Based View a Practical Organizational Theory? *Organization Science* (4), 913–930.

Arikan, A. M., Arikan, I. & Koparan, I. (2020). Creation Opportunities: Entrepreneurial Curiosity, Generative Cognition, and Knightian Uncertainty. *Academy of Management Review, 45*(4), 808–824.

Bacigalupo, M., Kampylis, P., Punie, Y. & Van Den Brande, L. (2016). EntreComp: The Entrepreneurship Competence Framework. Luxembourg: Publications Office of the European Union.

Baker, T. & Nelson, R. E. (2005). Creating Something from Nothing: Resource Construction through Entrepreneurial Bricolage. *Administrative Science Quarterly, 50*, 329–366.

Barney, J. (1991). Firm Resources and Sustained Competitive Advantage. *Journal of Management, 17*(1), 99–121.

Baron, R. A. & Markman, G. D. (2000). Beyond social capital: How social skills can enhance entrepreneurs' success. *Academy of Management Executive, 14*(1), 106–116.

Baron, R. A. & Tang, J. (2009). Entrepreneurs' social skills and new venture performance: mediating mechanisms and cultural generality. *Journal of Management, 35*(2), 282–306.

Bauman, A. & Lucy, C. (2021). Enhancing entrepreneurial education: Developing competencies for success. *The International Journal of Management Education, 19*(1). doi:10.1016/j.ijme.2019.03.005

Beresford, R. & Saunders, M. N. K. (2005). Professionalization of the business start-up process. *Strategic Change, 14*(6), 337–347.

Bernardi, C. D. & Pedrini, M. (2020). Transforming water into wine: Environmental bricolage for entrepreneurs. *Journal of Cleaner Production, 266*. doi:10.1016/j.jclepro.2020.121815

Birkinshaw, J., Probst, G. & Tushman, M. (2009). Organizational ambidexterity: balancing exploration and exploitation for sustained corporate performance. *Organization Science, 20*(4), 685–695.

Blass, E. (2018). Developing a curriculum for aspiring entrepreneurs: What do they really need to learn? *Journal of Entrepreneurship Education, 21*(4), 1–14.

Bolton, J. E. (1971). *Report of the Committee of Enquiry on small firms*. Retrieved from London: HMSO.

Bood, R. (1998). Charting Organizational Learning: A Comparison of Multiple Mapping Techniques. In C. Eden & J. C. Spender (Eds.), *Managerial and Organizational Cognition: Theory, Methods and Research* (pp. 210–230). London: Sage.

Brinckmann, J., Salomo, S. & Gemuenden, H. G. (2011). Financial Management Competence of Founding Teams and Growth of New Technology-Based Firms. *Entrepreneurship: Theory & Practice, 35*(2), 217–243.

Bryan, J. (2006). Training and Performance in Small Firms. *International Small Business Journal, 24*(6), 635–660.

Chadwick, I. C. & Raver, J. L. (2020). Psychological Resilience and Its Downstream Effects for Business Survival in Nascent Entrepreneurship. *Entrepreneurship: Theory & Practice, 44*(2), 233–255.

Chang, J. & Rieple, A. (2013). Assessing students' entrepreneurial skills development in live projects. *Journal of Small Business & Enterprise Development, 20*(1), 225–241.

Chang, J. & Rieple, A. (2018). Entrepreneurial decision-making in a microcosm. *Management Learning, 49*(4), 471–497.

Clarke, J. S. (2011). Revitalizing Entrepreneurship: How Visual Symbols are Used in Entrepreneurial Performances. *Journal of Management Studies, 48*(6), 1365–1391.

Clarke, J. S., Cornelissen, J. P. & Healey, M. P. (2019). Actions Speak Lounder than Words: How Figurative Language and Gesturing in Entrepreneurial Pitches Influences Investment Judgements *Academy of Management Journal, 62*(2), 335–360.

Coad, A. & Storey, D. J. (2021). Taking the entrepreneur out of entrepreneurship. *International Journal of Management Reviews*, 1. doi:10.1111/ijmr.12249

Cope, J. (2003). Entrepreneurial Learning and Critical Reflection: Discontinuous Events as Triggers for 'Higher-level' Learning. *Management Learning, 34*(4), 429–450.

Cope, J. (2005). Towards a Dynamic Learning Perspective of Entrepreneurship. *Entrepreneurship Theory and Practice, 29*(4), 373–397.

Cope, J. (2011). Entrepreneurial learning from failure: An interpretative phenomeno-logical analysis. *Journal of Business Venturing, 26*(6), 604–623.

Cope, J. & Down, S. (2010). *I think therefore I learn? Entrepreneurial Cognition, Learning and Knowledge and Knowing in Practice.* Paper presented at the Babson College Entrepreneurship Research Conference, Lausanne, Switzerland.

Cornelissen, J. P., Clarke, J. S. & Cienki, A. (2012). Sensegiving in entrepreneurial contexts: The use of metaphors in speech and gesture to gain and sustain support for novel business ventures. *International Small Business Journal, 30*(4), 213–241.

Crossan, M. M., Lane, H. W. & White, R. E. (1999). An Organizational Learning Framework: From Intuition to Institution. *Academy of Management Review, 24*(3), 522–537.

Curran, J. (1986). *Bolton 15 Years on: A Review and Analysis of Small Business Research in Britain 1971–1986.* London: Small Business Research Trust.

Davis, M. H., Hall, J. A. & Mayer, P. S. (2016). Developing a new measure of entrepreneurial mindset: reliability, validity, and implications for practitioners. *Consulting Psychology Journal: Practice & Research, 68*(1), 21–48.

Doern, R. (2017). *Strategies for Resilience in Entrepreneurship: Building Resources for Small Business Survival After a Crisis.* Cheltenham: Edward Elgar.

Doern, R., Williams, N. & Vorley, T. (2019). Special Issue on Entrepreneurship and Crises: Business as Usual? An Introduction and Review of the Literature. *Entrepreneurship and Regional Development, 31*(5–6), 400–412.

Evers, N. & Andersson, S. (2021). Predictive and effectual decision-making in high-tech international new ventures – A matter of sequential ambidexterity. *International Business Review, 30*(1). doi:10.1016/j.ibusrev.2019.101655

Fearon, C., Furlotti, M., van Vuuren, W. & McLaughlin, H. (2021). Developing new opportunities, entrepreneurial skills and product/service creativity: a 'Young Enterprise' (YE) perspective. *Studies in Higher Education, 46*(6), 1081–1098.

Ferrari, A. (2013). *DIGCOMP: A Framework for Developing and Understanding Digital Competence in Europe.* Luxembourg: Publications Office of the European Union.

Fisher, G. (2012). Effectuation, Causation, and Bricolage: A Behavioral Comparison of Emerging Theories in Entrepreneurship Research. *Entrepreneurship: Theory & Practice, 36*(5), 1019–1051.

Fisher, G., Neubert, E. & Burnell, D. (2021). Resourcefulness narratives: Transforming actions into stories to mobilize support. *Journal of Business Venturing, 36*(4). doi:10.1016/j.jbusvent.2021.106122

Freel, M. S. (2005). Patterns of innovation and skills in small firms. *Technovation, 25*(2), 123–134.

Ghezzi, A. (2019). Digital startups and the adoption and implementation of Lean Startup Approaches: Effectuation, Bricolage and Opportunity Creation in practice. *Technological Forecasting & Social Change, 146*, 945–960. doi:10.1016/j.techfore.2018.09.017

Gibb, A. (2009). Meeting the Development Needs of Owner Managed Small Enterprise: A Discussion on the Centrality of Action Learning. *Action Learning: Research and Practice, 6*(3), 209–227.

Gordon, I., Hamilton, E. & Jack, S. (2012). A study of a university-led entrepreneurship education programme for small business owner/managers. *Entrepreneurship & Regional Development, 24*(9–10), 767–805.

Greene, F. J., Mole, K. F. & Storey, D. J. (2015). Business Advice and the New Business. London: Palgrave Macmillan UK.

Hahn, D., Minola, T., Bosio, G. & Cassia, L. (2020). The Impact of Entrepreneurship Education on University Students' Entrepreneurial Skills: A Family Embeddedness Perspective. *Small Business Economics, 55*(1), 257–282.

Harris, K. J., Kacmar, K. M., Zivnuska, S. & Shaw, J. D. (2007). The impact of political skill on impression management effectiveness. *Journal of Applied Psychology, 92*(1), 278–285.

Hickie, J. (2011). The Development of Human Capital in Young Entrepreneurs. *Industry and Higher Education, 25*(6), 469–481.

Holt, R. & Macpherson, A. (2010). Sensemaking, rhetoric and the socially competent entrepreneur. *International Small Business Journal, 28*(1), 20–42.

Jayawarna, D., Jones, O., Lam, W. & Phua, S. (2014). The performance of entrepreneurial ventures: examing the role of marketing practices. *Journal of Small Business and Enterprise Development, 21*(4), 565–587.

Jayawarna, D., Jones, O. & Macpherson, A. (2014). Entrepreneurial potential: The role of human and cultural capitals. *International Small Business Journal, 32*(8), 918–943.

Jayawarna, D., Jones, O. & Macpherson, A. (2020). Resourcing Social Enterprises: The Role of Socially Oriented Bootstrapping. *British Journal of Management, 31*(1), 56–79.

Jones, O. (2006). Developing Absorptive Capacity in Mature Organizations: The Change Agent's Role. *Management Learning, 37*(3), 355–376.

Jones, O. (2022). Academic engagement with small business and entrepreneurship: Towards a landscape of practice. *Industry and Higher Education, 36*(3), 279–293.

Jones, O. & Giordano, B. (2021). Family entrepreneurial teams: The role of learning in business model evolution. *Management Learning, 52*(3), 267–293.

Jones, O. & Li, H. (2017). Effectual Entrepreneuring: Sensemaking in a Family-Based Start-Up. *Entrepreneurship and Regional Development, 29*(5–6), 467–499.

Jones, O. & Macpherson, A. (2006). Inter-organizational Learning and Strategic Renewal in SMEs: Extending the 4I Network. *Long Range Planning, 39*(2), 155–175.

Jones, O. & Macpherson, A. (2014). Research perspectives on learning in small firms. In D. Rae & C. L. Wang (Eds.), *Entrepreneurial Learning: New Perspectives in Research, Education and Practice* (pp. 289–312). London: Edward Elgar Publishing.

Jones, O., Macpherson, A. & Thorpe, R. (2010). Learning in owner-managed small firms: Mediating artefacts and strategic space. *Entrepreneurship & Regional Development, 22*(7/8), 649–673.

Jones, O., Macpherson, A. & Woollard, D. (2008). Entrepreneurial Ventures in Higher Education: Analysing Organizational Growth. *International Small Business Journal: Researching Entrepreneurship, 26*(6), 683–708.

Jones, O., Meckel, P. & Taylor, D. (2021a). *Creating Communities of Practice: Entrepreneurial Learning in a University-Based Incubator*. Cham (Switzerland): Springer.

Jones, O., Meckel, P. & Taylor, D. (2021b). Situated learning in a business incubator: Encouraging students to become real entrepreneurs. 35(4), 367–383.

Kakati, M. (2003). Success criteria in high-tech new ventures. *Technovation, 23*(5), 447–457.

Kempster, S., Smith, S. & Barnes, S. (2018). *Chapter 14: A review of entrepreneurial leadership learning: an exploration that draws on human, social and institutional capitals*. Cheltenham: Edward Elgar Publishing.

Kier, A. S. & McMullen, J. S. (2018). Entrepreneurial Imaginativeness in New Venture Ideation. *Academy of Management Journal, 61*(6), 2265–2295.

Kor, Y. Y., Mahoney, J. T. & Michael, S. C. (2007). Resources, Capabilities and Entrepreneurial Perceptions. *Journal of Management Studies (Wiley-Blackwell), 44*(7), 1187–1212.

Korzynski, P., Haenlein, M. & Rautiainen, M. (2021). Impression management techniques in crowdfunding: An analysis of Kickstarter videos using artificial intelligence. *European Management Journal.* doi:10.1016/j.emj.2021.01.001

Kwapisz, A., Schell, W. J., Aytes, K. & Bryant, S. (2021). Entrepreneurial Action and Intention: The Role of Entrepreneurial Mindset, Emotional Intelligence, and Grit. *Entrepreneurship Education and Pedagogy.* doi:10.1177/2515127421992521

Lévi-Strauss, C. (1967). *The Savage Mind*. Chicago: University of Chicago Press.

Lounsbury, M., Gehman, J. & Glynn, M. A. (2019). Beyond Homo Entrepreneurus: Judgement and the Theory of Cultural Entrepreneurship. *Journal of Management Studies*, *56*(6), 1214–1236.

Lounsbury, M. & Glynn, M. A. (2001). Cultural Entrepreneurship: Stories, Legitimacy and the Acquisition of Resources. *Strategic Management Journal*, *22*, 545–564.

Lounsbury, M. & Glynn, M. A. (2019). *Cultural entrepreneurship: a new agenda for the study of entrepreneurial processes and possibilities*. Cambridge: Cambridge University Press.

Lourenco, F. & Jones, O. (2006). *Learning Paradigms in Entrepreneurship Education: Comparing the Traditional and Enterprise Modes*. Retrieved from London: National Council for Graduate Entrepreneurship.

Macpherson, A. (2005). Learning to Grow: Resolving the Crisis of Knowing. *Technovation*, *25*(10), 1129–1140.

Man, T. W. Y., Lau, T. & Chan, K. F. (2002). The competitiveness of small and medium enterprises A conceptualization with focus on entrepreneurial competencies. *Journal of Business Venturing*, *17*(2), 123–142.

Mangham, I. (1985). In Search of Competence. *Journal of General Management*, *12*(2), 5–12.

March, J. G. (1991). Exploration and Exploitation in Organizational Learning. *Organization Science*, *2*(1), 71–87.

Martin, G. & Staines, H. (1994). Managerial Competences in Small Firms. *Journal of Management Development*, *13*(7), 23–34.

Matlay, H. & Hyland, T. (1997). NVQs in the small business sector: a critical overview. *Education + Training*, *39*(9), 325–332.

McCallum, E., Weicht, R., McMullan, L. & Price, A. (2018). *EntreComp into Action - Get inspired, make it happen: A user guide to the European Entrepreneurship Competence Framework*. Luxembourg: Publications Office of the European Union.

Meoli, A., Fini, R., Sobrero, M. & Wiklund, J. (2020). How entrepreneurial intentions influence entrepreneurial career choices: The moderating influence of social context. *Journal of Business Venturing*, *35*(3). doi:10.1016/j.jbusvent.2019.105982

Mitchelmore, S. & Rowley, J. (2010). Entrepreneurial competencies: a literature review and development agenda. *International Journal of Entrepreneurial Behavior & Research*, *16*(2), 92–111.

Mole, K. F. & Keogh, W. (2009). The implications of public sector small business advisers becoming strategic sounding boards: England and Scotland compared. *Entrepreneurship & Regional Development*, *21*(1), 77–97.

Nabi, G., Linan, F., Fayolle, A., Krueger, N. & Walmsley, A. (2017). The Impact of Entrepreneurship Education in Higher Education: A Systematic Review and Research Agenda. *Academy of Management Learning & Education*, *16*(2), 277–299.

Neck, H. M. & Corbett, A. C. (2018). The scholarship of teaching and learning entrepreneurship. *Entrepreneurship Education and Pedagogy, 1*(1), 8–41.

O'Connor, E. (2002). Storied Business: Typology, Intertextuality, and Traffic in Entrepreneurial Narrative. *Journal of Business Communication, 39*(1), 36–54.

Orlikowski, W. (2002). Knowing in Practice: Enacting a Collective Capability in Distributed Organizing. *Organization Science, 13*(3), 249–273.

Patzelt, H., Preller, R. & Breugst, N. (2021). Understanding the Life Cycles of Entrepreneurial Teams and Their Ventures: An Agenda for Future Research. *Entrepreneurship: Theory & Practice, 45*(5), 1119–1153.

Penrose, E. T. (1959). *The Theory of the Growth of the Firm*. Oxford: Basil Blackwell.

Peschl, H., Deng, C. & Larson, N. (2021). Entrepreneurial thinking: A signature pedagogy for an uncertain 21st century. *The International Journal of Management Education, 19*(1). doi:10.1016/j.ijme.2020.100427

Phua, S. & Jones, O. (2010). Marketing in new business ventures: examining the myth of informality. *International journal of entrepreneurship and innovation management, 11*(1), 35–55.

Rae, D. (2004). Practical theories from entrepreneurs stories: discursive approaches to entrepreneurial learning. *Journal of Small Business and Enterprise Development, 11*(2), 195–202.

Rae, D. & Carswell, M. (2001). Towards a conceptual understanding of entrepreneurial learning. *Journal of Small Business and Enterprise Development, 8*(2), 150–158.

Rayna, T. & Striukova, L. (2021). Fostering skills for the 21st century: The role of Fab labs and makerspaces. *Technological Forecasting & Social Change, 164*. doi:10.1016/j.techfore.2020.120391

Reis, D. A., Fleury, A. L. & Carvalho, M. M. (2021). Consolidating core entrepreneurial competences: toward a meta-competence framework. *International Journal of Entrepreneurial Behavior & Research, 27*(1), 179–204.

Rezaei-Zadeh, M., Hogan, M., O'Reilly, J., Cunningham, J. & Murphy, E. (2017). Core Entrepreneurial Competencies and Their Interdependencies: Insights from a Study of Irish and Iranian Entrepreneurs, University Students and Academics. *International Entrepreneurship and Management Journal, 13*(1), 35–73.

Sadler-Smith, E., Hampson, Y., Chaston, I. & Badger, B. (2003). Managerial Behaviour, Entrepreneurial Style and Small Firm Performance. *Journal of Small Business Management, 41*(1), 47–67.

Sarasvathy, S. D. (2001). Causation and Effectuation: Toward a Theoretical Shift from Economic Inevitability to Entrepreneurial Contingency. *The Academy of Management Review, 2*, 243–263.

Sarasvathy, S. D. (2008). *Effectuation: elements of entrepreneurial expertise*. Cheltenham: Edward Elgar.

Sarasvathy, S. D. (2012). Effectuation and Entrepreneurship. In S. Carter & D. Jones-Evans (Eds.), *Enterprise and Small Business: Principles, Practice and Policy* (3rd ed., pp. 135–151). Harlow: Pearson.

Sarasvathy, S. D. & Ramesh, A. (2019). An Effectual Model of Collective Action for Addressing Sustainability Challenges. *Academy of Management Perspectives, 33*(4), 405–424.

Schumpeter, J. (1934). *The Theory of Economic Development*. Cambridge, Mass: Harvard University Press.

Shane, S. (2000). Prior knowledge and the discovery of entrepreneurial opportunities. *Organization Science, 11*(4), 448–469.

Sharifi, S. & Zhang, M. (2009). Sense-making and Recipes: Examples from Selected Small Firms. *International Journal of Entrepreneurial Behavior and Research, 15*(6), 555–571.

Smith, N. R. & Miner, J. B. (1983). Type of Entrepreneur, Type of Firm, and Managerial Motivation: Implications for Organizational Life Cycle Theory. *Strategic Management Journal, 4*(4), 325–340.

Smith, S., Kempster, S. & Wenger-Trayner, E. (2019). Developing a Program Community of Practice for Leadership Development. *Journal of Management Education, 43*(1), 62–88.

Soto-Simeone, A., Siren, C. & Antretter, T. (2020). New Venture Survival: A Review and Extension. *International Journal of Management Reviews, 22*(4), 378–407.

Soto-Simeone, A., Sirén, C. & Antretter, T. (2021). The role of skill versus luck in new venture survival. *International Journal of Management Reviews, 23*(4), 549–556.

Spender, J. C. (1989). *Industry Recipes: The Nature and Source of Management Judgement*. Oxford: Basil Blackwell.

Spender, J. C. (2005). An essay on the state of knowledge management. *Prometheus, 23*(1), 101–116.

Stanworth, J. & Curran, G. (1991). *Bolton 20 Years on: The Small Firm in the 1990s*. London: Paul Chapman.

Storey, D. J. (2004). Exploring the Link, among Small Firms, between Management Training and Firm Performance: A Comparison between the UK and other OECD Countries. *International Journal of Human Resource Management, 15*(1), 112–130.

Storey, D. J. (2011). Optimism and chance: The elephants in the entrepreneurship room. *International Small Business Journal, 29*(4), 303–321.

Tagg, S., Mason, C. & Carter, S. (2004). *Lifting the barriers to growth in UK small businesses*: 2004 biennial survey of FSB membership.

Tocher, N., Oswald, S. L. & Hall, D. J. (2015). Proposing Social Resources as the Fundamental Catalyst Toward Opportunity Creation. *Strategic Entrepreneurship Journal, 9*(2), 119–135.

Tocher, N., Oswald, S. L., Shook, C. L. & Adams, G. (2012). Entrepreneur political skill and new venture performance: Extending the social competence perspective. In *Entrepreneurship & Regional Development*, *14*(5–6), 283–305.

Venkataraman, S. (2004) Entrepreneurial opportunity. In M. Hitt & D. Ireland (Eds.), *Encyclopedic Dictionary of Entrepreneurship* (100–103). Malden, MA: Blackwell.

Wach, D., Stephan, U., Gorgievski, M. J. & Wegge, J. (2020). Entrepreneurs' Achieved Success: Developing a Multi-faceted Measure. *International Entrepreneurship and Management Journal*, *16*(3), 1123–1151.

Weick, K. (1995). *Sensemaking in Organizations*. Thousand Oaks, CA: Sage.

Wenke, K., Zapkau, F. B. & Schwens, C. (2021). Too small to do it all? A meta-analysis on the relative relationships of exploration, exploitation, and ambidexterity with SME performance. *Journal of Business Research*, *132*, 653–665.

Wiklund, J. & Shepherd, D. (2003). Aspiring for, and Achieving Growth: The Moderating Role of Resources and Opportunities. *Journal of Management Studies*, *40*(8), 1919–1941.

Wood, M. S., Bakker, R. M. & Fisher, G. (2021). Back to the Future: A Time-Calibrated Theory of Entrepreneurial Action. *Academy of Management Review*, *46*(1), 147–171.

3 | The Nature of Entrepreneurial Opportunities

3.1 Introduction

The work of Shane/Venkataraman has been crucial in confirming the centrality of opportunity identification to a better understanding of entrepreneurship (Shane, 2000, 2012; Shane & Venkataraman, 2000; Venkataraman, Sarasvathy, Dew & Forster, 2012). Their work is based on the so-called 'Austrian' view that markets are in a constant state of disequilibrium underpinned by dynamic competition (Chiles, Vulture, Gupta, Greening & Tuggle, 2010; Elias, Chiles & Qian, 2020). The emergence of new business opportunities is an outcome of these constant market disturbances. Furthermore, such opportunities have an objective reality, which is distinct from the entrepreneur themselves. This suggests that 'opportunities' are out there waiting to be discovered by *alert* entrepreneurs. The alternative view is that opportunities are created through the efforts of entrepreneurs as they attempt to establish new businesses (Edelman & Yli-Renko, 2010). In this perspective, would-be entrepreneurs use their knowledge and whatever experience they possess to *create* opportunities (Gartner, Bird & Starr, 1992; Macpherson & Holt, 2007; Smith, Moghaddam & Lanivich, 2019). While this might appear to be a typical 'academic' debate, it does have implications for the way in which you approach your own entrepreneurial career. Our view is that while it is possible for you to identify a potential opportunity, it then requires the exercise of your creative skills to turn the idea into a functioning business.

It has been suggested that there are six main factors associated with opportunity identification (George, Vinit, Lahti & Wincent, 2016): prior knowledge, social capital, cognition/personality traits, environmental conditions, alertness and systematic search (see IDEATE model below). There are

DOI: 10.4324/9781003312918-4

91

several different forms of prior knowledge: understanding markets, ways to serve those markets, customer problems (Ardichvili, Cardozo & Ray, 2003; Dabrowski, 2019; Sanz-Velasco, 2006; Shane & Venkataraman, 2000). While some students may have a rudimentary understanding of the way in which markets operate it is unlikely that this knowledge will have been obtained from real-world experience. Similarly, you may well have experienced poor service from various organizations with which you have dealings (including your university!). However, it is doubtful that these experiences have been translated into potential business opportunities. There is an associated concept that is likely to be relevant in your attempt to start a new business. Personal interests influence an entrepreneur's understanding of opportunities and are related to the knowledge and understanding acquired through education, work experience, social relationships and daily life (Venkataraman, 2004, 1997b). Your own personal interests will include hobbies, participation in various sports and the arts (cinema, music, etc.), learning new skills such as a language as well as various social activities (attending concerts, exhibitions etc). Personal interests refer to any of the things that you are enthusiastic about and, therefore, likely to provide high levels of motivation in starting your own business. Your personal interests are certainly a useful starting point for trying to identify business opportunities.

Many influential scholars regard the ability to identify new business opportunities as the defining feature of entrepreneurship. At the same time, there are many myths associated with the creativity that is the basis of idea generation. The view we advocate in this book is that everyone can become more creative assuming they have the *intrinsic motivation* to learn and practice new skills. Therefore, in this chapter we concentrate on demonstrating how you can improve your thinking skills (cognition) as a basis for identifying and evaluating business opportunities.

3.2 Learning Objectives

- To understand the links between entrepreneurial cognition and creative thinking and consider why they are important to opportunity identification.
- To understand the different processes associated with divergent and convergent thinking in the context of opportunity identification.
- To understand how engaging in classroom exercises based on the IDEATE model can enhance your thinking skills.

- To recognize the differences between opportunity identification and opportunity evaluation.
- To appreciate the role of sustainable entrepreneurship in dealing with threats posed by environmental change.
- To understand the opportunities associated with green entrepreneurship.

3.3 Entrepreneurial Cognition and Creative Thinking

Much early interest in entrepreneurship focused on identifying the unique psychological attributes that entrepreneurs were believed to possess. The work of McClelland (1962) was particularly influential with traits such as tolerance of ambiguity, the need for achievement and risk-taking supposedly associated with entrepreneurship. Ultimately, the findings derived from trait-based research were inconclusive and there was a gradual shift to entrepreneurial cognition (Delmar and Witte, 2012). Entrepreneurial cognition refers to an individual's knowledge structures and the way in which they are able to make assessments, judgements and decisions related to opportunity identification (Dimov, 2011, 2020). Entrepreneurs are believed to use 'mental maps' to help them piece together unconnected pieces of information to identify new business opportunities. Gregoire, Cornelissen, Dimov and Burg (2015, p. 128) summarize what is known about entrepreneurial cognition: there is support for the theory of planned behaviour (Ajzen, 1991) as an explanation for entrepreneurial intentions; entrepreneurs prefer informal sources of information; 'entrepreneurial cognition' is a distinctive set of thought processes; finally, 'mental models' are critical for entrepreneurial decision-making (Forbes, 1999). Delmar and Witte (2012) suggest that it is particularly important to consider two cognitive models that impact on entrepreneurial behaviour: self-efficacy and intrinsic motivation.

> **Self-efficacy** focuses on your perceived capabilities related to the performance of entrepreneur-related tasks. Put simply, perceived high levels of self-efficacy mean you will be confident that you have the appropriate skills to become an entrepreneur. Therefore, you will be more likely to start your own business than someone with lower levels of self-efficacy. Acquiring the basic business skills, outlined in Section 2.3 will be a starting point for establishing higher levels

of self-efficacy (Bandura, 1997). Obtaining experience in exercising those skills is also an essential prerequisite for developing confidence in your ability to perform the tasks associated with becoming an entrepreneur. Hence, we believe that any programme designed to encourage students to start their own businesses should have a strong experiential element (see Chapter 5). Here we are focusing on opportunity identification, which is a skill regarded as central to entrepreneurship. Consequently, improving your thinking skills (cognition) is an important step in developing the self-efficacy associated with successful entrepreneurship.

Intrinsic motivation means that individuals are motivated by the task itself rather than expecting some additional reward. Consider why you are studying this particular module: is it because it will contribute to your degree? Alternatively, are you motivated by the intrinsic need to learn more about becoming an entrepreneur? Intrinsic motivation is closely associated with high levels of creativity (DeTienne & Chandler, 2004). You are unlikely to be able to identify creative new business opportunities unless you are strongly committed to the task. The level of interest you have in a task is also related to those activities that are difficult and challenging. To sum up, if you have a strong commitment to improving your skills through engagement in experiential learning you are more likely to make the transition from student to entrepreneur. If, however, you are learning about entrepreneurship because your main aim is to obtain good marks in your coursework and exams then you probably do not have the required levels of intrinsic motivation for self-employment.

The concept of creativity, similar to entrepreneurship, is widely misunderstood to be associated with a small number of highly creative individuals (or highly entrepreneurial individuals). Our view is that creativity is a skill that can be developed by engaging in experiential learning. As pointed out by Ritter and Mostert (2017, p. 244):

Creative thinking skills are thus inherent to normative cognitive functioning rather than an innate talent available to only a few genius minds. Importantly, research supports the idea that creative thinking can be trained.

94

Some suggest that the term entrepreneurial is used to describe those individuals who appear to be creative and innovative because of their ability to identify new business opportunities. As we discussed above, the ability to improve your levels of creativity will depend on your intrinsic motivation. Do you want to be a more creative thinker? If so, then there are several exercises that will help enhance your levels of creativity. Creativity training is an effective way of stimulating new and feasible business ideas (Warnick, Kier, LaFrance & Cuttler, 2021). McMullen and Kier (2017) suggest that there are three distinct dimensions to creativity: creative imagination, social imagination and practical imagination.

Creative imagination is what is generally associated with creative individuals. Conventional education does not encourage or promote creativity as there is usually more focus on learning and repeating various 'facts'. De Bono (2015) is one of the key scholars of creativity and he developed the concept of 'lateral thinking' (De Bono, 1995). This means searching for non-obvious solutions to problems by adopting different mindsets. There are several tools associated with lateral thinking such as brainstorming, which encourages individuals to generate as many ideas as possible without thinking about whether or not those ideas are 'practical'. This is also known as divergent thinking where the focus is on novelty rather than identifying conventional solutions to the immediate problem.

Social imagination refers to the ability to be able to take a different perspective than your own. This is particularly important for entrepreneur as they need to consider what their customers are thinking as well as other stakeholders and potential competitors. Rather than engaging with customer this involves 'mental simulation' (see Section 4.5) whereby you think about the problem/solution from the perspective of someone else. A starting point might be to consider how your close friends or family would react to your intention to become an entrepreneur rather than following a more traditional career path. Thinking about problems from the perspective of other people can be a trigger to creative solutions by helping you adopt a different mental frame. Clearly, social imagination has some similarities to lateral thinking as you should try to consider the same issue/problem from a range of different perspectives.

Practical imagination focuses on the implementation of new ideas by attempting to imagine potential barriers and obstacles. Practical imagination can also be described as 'convergent thinking' as you try to refine your ideas by identifying the best possible solution. Here you must engage in activities such as planning, forecasting and budgeting as you use your judgement to think things through in a critical and rigorous manner. If you have gained some previous experience (see Section 1.5, Developing an entrepreneurial mindset) then this should inform your practical imagination. At the same time, ***vicarious learning*** from the experiences of other would-be entrepreneurs can also inform your decision-making at this stage. TV programmes such as *The Apprentice*, *Dragon's Den* or the *Shark Tank* can certainly broaden your understanding of the business landscape.

McMullen and Kier (2017) go on to say that 'imaginativeness' is a skill that is based on the tacit knowledge you have gained from (vicarious) experiences and your latent imagination. The authors then suggest that use of their Imaginativeness Scale can help individuals obtain a 'baseline' for the three elements of their imagination (Kier & McMullen, 2018, 2020). Therefore, we suggest that you now complete the Imaginativeness Scale as a means of identifying your strengths and weaknesses.

Exercise 1: The Imaginativeness Scale

Creative Imaginativeness		
1	I consider myself to be inventive	1 2 3 4 5
2	I consider myself to be innovative	1 2 3 4 5
3	I demonstrate originality in my work	1 2 3 4 5
4	I like to do original work	1 2 3 4 5
5	People think I am artistic	1 2 3 4 5
6	Being creative is part of my identity	1 2 3 4 5
	Total	
Social Imaginativeness		
1	I can see things from other people's perspective	1 2 3 4 5
2	I try to see the world through other people's eyes	1 2 3 4 5
3	I find it easy to understand other people's feeling	1 2 3 4 5

4	I have a good sense of what others are feeling	1	2	3	4	5
5	I can read emotions from facial expressions	1	2	3	4	5
6	I am good at reading other people	1	2	3	4	5
	Total					
Practical Imaginativeness						
1	I am good at project management	1	2	3	4	5
2	I can anticipate bottlenecks in a project	1	2	3	4	5
3	I try to plan ahead for new situations	1	2	3	4	5
4	I can make connections between discrete pieces of information	1	2	3	4	5
5	Forming mental images helps me solve problems	1	2	3	4	5
6	I can adapt existing methods to solve new problems	1	2	3	4	5
	Total					

Creativity can be understood as a balance between ideas that are original and at the same time useful. The concept of alertness is central to the understanding of cognition and opportunity identification (Kirzner, 1973, 2009). Cognitive psychology defines alertness as 'achieving and maintaining a state of high sensitivity to incoming stimuli and indicates that alertness influences the speed of attention' (Arikan, Arikan & Koparan, 2020, p. 432). *Alertness* is usually regarded as the key factor enabling entrepreneurs to identify new opportunities (Posner, 2008; Shane, 2000). The literature on entrepreneurial cognition focuses on the question of how entrepreneurs think (Chavoushi et al., 2021). Alertness is a cognitive capability possessed by entrepreneurs to help them notice entrepreneurial opportunities (Gaglio & Katz, 2001). Based on their literature review, Chavoushi et al. (2021) differentiate between alertness to the identification of new opportunities and the creation of opportunities. Opportunity spotting in discovery mode requires entrepreneurs to be primed for objective cues from the environment. The alternative way of thinking suggests that opportunities are endogenously created by entrepreneurs themselves (Alvarez & Barney, 2007; Sarasvathy, 2012). Opportunity creation relies on the entrepreneurs' *intrinsic alertness* as they are not responding to external cues from the environment (Chavoushi et al., 2021). According to Sanz-Velasco (2006) even in the case of high-technology ventures, opportunity creation appears to be more appropriate than the identification of objective business opportunities. Based on a random sample of 114 nascent entrepreneurs, Edelman and Yli-Renko

(2010) also found that most opportunities are based on the entrepreneurs' subjective interpretation (see Section 12.6 for a more extensive discussion on the differences between opportunity identification and opportunity creation). Opportunity identification is primarily associated with the so-called *causal school* (Shane, 2003, 2012; Shane & Venkataraman, 2000). Others have suggested that the discovery approach does not capture the messiness associated with the reality of trying to create new business opportunities (Moroz & Hindle, 2012). Box 3.1 provides an illustration of opportunity creation in action as a young entrepreneur starts a new business (see also, Box 3.2).

Box 3.1 Opportunity Creation: The case of *Jazooli*

Sam Wilson began buying and selling mobile phones while still at school and at that stage had no intention of setting up a business. Gradually, Sam began to increase the amount of money that was generated by his online trading and in 2008 *Jazooli* was established as a company by Sam's bother Ben who took a year out before going to university. For the first nine months of operation Ben ran the business from his bedroom in the family home. After completing sixth form in 2010 Sam joined *Jazooli* on a full-time basis. The business continued to expand and *Jazooli* moved to a large warehouse and by 2015 employed ten full-time staff and four part-timers with a turnover of £4.5 million. Business activities had extended from mobile phones and accessories for tablet computers to a wide range of consumer goods and electronic cigarettes.

The *Jazooli* story is a great example of opportunity creation. Rather than starting out with a clearly articulated business idea, Sam began by trading mobile phones to supplement his pocket money. When Ben started to work in the business he realized that they could increase their margins by sourcing goods directly from China – instead of buying and selling on *eBay*. Gradually, as business activity increased, Ben, Sam and their father Martin began to adopt a more strategic approach to managing the business (see Jones and Li, 2017).

Regardless of whether you engage in opportunity identification or opportunity creation, creativity is crucial to ensuring you are able to establish a business that has the potential to generate real value in the longer-term. A key element in the promotion of creativity in the concept of *divergent thinking* (Acar & Runco, 2019). Divergent thinking means developing the ability to generate a large number of ideas from a single starting point. The associated concept of 'brainstorming' is a widely used technique to aid creativity through divergent thinking (Coskun, 2005). Mumford, Mobley, Reiter-Palmon, Uhlman and Doares (1991) suggest that the creative process has eight stages: problem definition, information search, information organization, concept combination (divergent thinking), evaluation, implementation, planning, monitoring (convergent thinking). There are variations in the number of suggested stages but, in general, most models share at least three processes; problem identification, idea generation and idea evaluation (Medeiros, Steele, Watts and Mumford, 2018).

Divergent thinking begins with the definition of a problem such as how do deal with the number of discarded plastic bottles. Idea generation relies on participants engaging in the reorganization of their knowledge structures; a process known as *conceptual combination* (Mobley, Doares & Mumford, 1992; Mumford et al., 1991). *Conceptual combination* refers to the synthesis of your existing knowledge structures. For example, you might consider how to motivate people to dispose of their plastic bottles in a more responsible manner + potential uses for those plastic bottles. *Generation* refers to the emergence of new concepts as a result of the combination process such as questioning why drinks companies do not use a more environmentally friendly material. Medeiros et al. (2018: 473) suggest that students' initial responses to divergent thinking tasks are typically the least original and most familiar relative to later responses. The authors go on to argue that imposing constraints can help 'jumpstart' this process by reducing time spent on less original ideas and encouraging students to consider more innovative solutions more quickly. Introducing constraints when dealing with ill-defined problems, central to creativity, decreases a reliance on easy solutions and encouraged students to search for novel and surprising solutions (Stokes & Wilson, 2010).

Idea evaluation is discussed in more detail below when the IDEATE model is introduced (Section 3.4). Here it is important to mention that there is a shift in focus from divergent thinking to convergent thinking. Convergent thinking simply means that you attempt to focus on the idea or ideas that have the most potential as practical solutions to existing problems. The key issue at this stage is to introduce you to the concepts of brainstorming and the processes associated with divergent thinking. Therefore, in the exercise that follows this section you will be encouraged to improve your creativity through divergent thinking – without being concerned about the practicality of your ideas. To summarize, our objective in introducing the idea of entrepreneurial cognition is to encourage you to develop your thinking skills; 'thinking outside the box' to use the well-known cliché! For this to be successful, you will need to be 'intrinsically motivated' in performing the various exercises that fundamental to this chapter. If you do so, then we suggest that you will be on your way to mastering a key entrepreneurial skill and enhancing your levels of self-efficacy.

Exercise 2: In Groups – Take Brainstorming Exercise (on Website)

3.4 Entrepreneurial Cognition and Opportunity Identification

Opportunity is a core concept in any attempt to understand the nature of entrepreneurship (Shane & Venkataraman, 2000; Warnick et al., 2021). 'Opportunities are central to the creation of new ventures and the social and economic benefits that flow from entrepreneurial activities, whether those are the incremental actions of Kirzner's equilibrium-seeking entrepreneur or the acts of creative destruction of Schumpeter's equilibrium-destroying entrepreneur' (Valliere, 2013, p. 432). Put more simply, an incremental action may involve offering a slightly different service from that provided by existing businesses: for example, providing live music in your café or bar. On the other hand, examples of *Schumpetarian* change would be the emergence of the original Internet-based businesses such as Facebook, Twitter and Amazon.

Academic research on entrepreneurial cognition is mainly concerned with understanding how individuals identify and then exploit new opportunities. Dew, Grichnik, Mayer-Haug, Read and Brinckmann (2015, p. 148) use the concept of situated cognition, which is based on the principle that cognitive activity 'inherently involves perception and action in the context of the human body situated in a real-world environment'. Those committed to the idea of situated cognition reject the more traditional view that cognition is primarily focused on the purely a mental activity associated with information processing. In contrast, situated cognition means that it is important to consider the 'body', the external world and other social actors. For example, Jones and Giordano (2021) identify the importance of team-based cognition among a family of four involved in the creation of a new online business. By sharing their 'mental maps' about the future directions of the company they were able to develop a coherent view of how to move from 'bedroom start-up' to a fast-growing company successfully competing against much larger rivals. This is described as 'distributed cognition' because it draws attention to the social elements of cognition (Dew et al., 2015). Distributed cognition is central to ideas associated with 'communities of practice' that are created in start-up incubators and accelerators (Jones, Meckel & Taylor, 2021a). Sharing knowledge and experiences is a crucial benefit of working with other nascent entrepreneurs who are also engaged in the identification and exploitation of new opportunities. Participating in classroom exercises are designed to help you and your fellow students share knowledge and improve the learning experience for all group members.

Entrepreneurship education should be focused on creating students who have a good chance of establishing successful entrepreneurial careers. Most students have significant disadvantages when thinking of starting their own businesses. They lack domain expertise and industry experience as well as having limited personal networks compared to experienced entrepreneurs (Hägg & Kurczewska, 2019). Consequently, the opportunities identified by students tend to be narrow and predictable. Certainly, in our experience of teaching entrepreneurship most student business ideas do not extend beyond bars, cafes and second-hand bookstores. Cohen, Hsu and Shinnar (2021) develop a teaching approach, which they describe as IDEATE, which encourages students to engage in a systematic search for new and meaningful opportunities. The IDEATE tool is also designed to help students develop new expertise and capabilities. Cognitive flexibility is central to your opportunity identification abilities in a rapidly changing business environment (Ritter & Mostert, 2017). To be successful, there needs to be a fit between the opportunity and the personal needs and aspirations of those trying to become entrepreneurs (Hsu, Shinnar, Powell & Coffey, 2017).

McMullen and Shepherd (2006) developed a conceptual model with two distinct components: attention and evaluation. This framework forms the basis of the IDEATE model. It also draws heavily on the concept of experiential learning, which enhances students' cognitive structures and ways of thinking (see Chapter 5). As you will have seen, this chapter promotes the importance of students creating innovative business ideas and that is central to our focus on entrepreneurial cognition. At the same time, as discussed in Section 3.5, we are committed to the importance of an action orientation in the exploration of business opportunities. Hence, testing out your abilities as an entrepreneur by gaining some first-hand experience is a crucial step in the learning process. Therefore, trying out a simple business idea[1] such as trading on *eBay* will help you decide whether entrepreneurship is an option for you.

Some scholars distinguish between passive and active searches for new opportunities (Cohen et al., 2021). Passive search refers to opportunities that are identified as a result of an individual's existing knowledge and capabilities as they operate within their immediate environment. That is, the kind of opportunities that you could identify as a result of experiences during your day-to-day activities. In their early paper, DeTienne and Chandler (2004) develop an approach designed to improve the opportunity identification skills among novice entrepreneurs. This is described as the 'Securing, Expanding, Exposing and Challenging' (SEEC) approach to opportunity identification. Adopting SEEC in the classroom encourages would-be entrepreneurs to identify opportunities when they encounter problems in their everyday lives (DeTienne & Chandler, 2004). *Securing* simply means that you should keep a record of any new ideas that occur to you during your daily activities. Rather than recording in a 'journal' (DeTienne & Chandler, 2004) it is now more convenient for you to keep a digital record in your mobile phone. *Expanding* means evaluating your ideas by thinking of potential solutions (ie, identify business opportunities). Select the idea with most potential and make a one-minute pitch to classmates. In the *Exposing* phase students should form groups of 3 or 4 to 'brainstorm' a range of possible solutions to the various problems identified by each of the group members. The idea here is to promote some 'creative chaos' whereby students should not feel constrained by offering practical solutions. Finally, *Challenging* involves a competitive element as students present their business ideas to classmates who are encouraged to identify potential weaknesses. This scenario creates the situation for 'low-cost' failure as students are encouraged to see the problems associated with taking their ideas to the marketplace. Passive searches are also closely associated with effectual approaches to starting a business (Sarasvathy, 2001). In contrast, IDEATE is based on the idea that active searches for new opportunities is a skill that can be acquired experientially. It is pointed out by Cohen et al. (2021) that experienced entrepreneurs generate more ideas than students because they possess greater levels of 'prior knowledge'.

Exercise 3: The SEEC Exercise:

Securing - Keep a record of all the new ideas that occur to you during your daily activities and record on your mobile phone.

Expanding - Evaluating your ideas by thinking of potential solutions (ie, identify potential business opportunities). Select the idea with most potential and make a one-minute pitch to classmates.

Exposing - Students should form groups of three or four to 'brainstorm' a range of possible solutions to the various problems identified by each group member. The idea here is to promote some 'creative chaos' and students should not feel constrained by offering practical solutions.

Challenging - A competitive element to end the exercise as students present their business ideas to classmates who are encouraged to identify potential weaknesses (again, should stick to the principles of an 'elevator pitch' – so presentation should be no more than two minutes).

The IDEATE model has six steps and they are briefly described below (see Figure 3.1). You should, however, engage in a classroom exercise to explore the application of IDEATE and its potential for improving your cognitive processes.

- **Identify** – the idea of this stage in the exercise is to encourage you to concentrate on problems that are worth solving – the 'migraine headache problem'. Rather than things that are a minor inconvenience for you (having to queue for lunch). Hence, you should try to focus on the identification of opportunities that could provide the basis of a real start-up business with prospects for growth

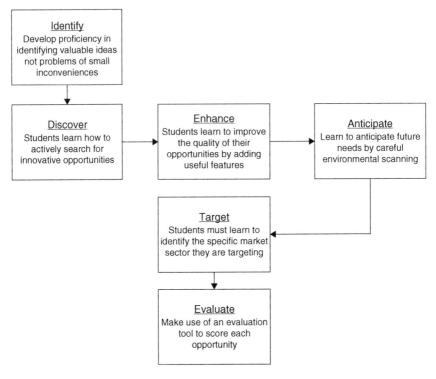

Figure 3.1 The IDEATE Model

- **Discover** – here you are encouraged to think about 'problem-rich' areas when you are searching for opportunities. The starting point could be issues that you are passionate about such as global warming or the amount of plastic waste littering our streets.
- **Enhance** – you should focus on improving the quality of the opportunity to make it more attractive and more profitable. In the Jazooli case, the boys enhanced their online offering by incorporating software that encouraged customers to leave positive comments on their website by offering a substantial reduction on their next purchase. This helped increase the number of new customers as well as more repeat sales to existing customers.
- **Anticipate** – it is important for you to consider various factors which are likely to lead to new opportunities in the future. This can be summarized in the following PESTEL model: Political, Economic, Social (including demographics), Technological, Environmental and Legal (regulations).

You should map out the changes in each category and consider the potential business opportunities.

- **Target** – exploring the customer segment that you intend to target so that you obtain a clear idea of whether your offering will be attractive to those customers. Once again, our experience is that this is an area which most students tend to take for granted. Thinking that once you have generated a business idea then that will somehow find a market.
- **Evaluate** – this is a two-stage process which begins in the classroom as your fellow students are encouraged to provide comprehensive feedback on the real value of your ideas. Once you have discarded the ideas that seem the weakest then you should engage with potential customers to obtain feedback from potential purchasers of your offering.

IDEATE is based on the principle that it is important to move beyond a passive search when attempting to identify new business opportunities. We acknowledge that there are circumstances where a passive search can lead to new opportunities and it is certainly worth practicing this skill in your everyday activities. Undertaking a more structured and active approach to the search for new opportunities should enhance your cognitive processes and develop your thinking skills. We are committed to the idea that learning is fundamental to developing the next generation of entrepreneurs who have the capabilities to build successful businesses. Participating in experiential classroom learning will help you develop the appropriate skills required to identify meaningful new business opportunities. To that end, you will be encouraged to identify many opportunities during the IDEATE exercises and, at first, this may appear overwhelming. We do, however, concur with Cohen et al. (2021, p. 1944) who confirm the value of IDEATE in the classroom:

> Our results show a significant correlation between the IDEATE teaching method and the innovativeness of the opportunities participants identified. We were also able to show that the individuals taught using the IDEATE approach identified opportunities that were more innovative than the opportunities identified by those using the passive search approach.

In an earlier study, Munoz, Mosey and Binks (2011) examined the development of what they describe as opportunity identification capabilities

(OIC). As a result of students' exposure to an entrepreneurship module, the authors confirmed that students became significantly better at making new connections when responding to external stimuli. In addition, most improved their OIC as a result of completing the module which was designed to enhance opportunity identification and develop different mental frames. In terms of adopting new ways of thinking, Munoz et al. (2011) use the analogy of learning a different language; learning a few words in a new language only requires a good memory. However, because every language has different rules in terms of grammar and meaning, it is necessary 'to communicate in a completely different way'. Therefore, developing your ability to communicate in a different language requires you to adopt different mental frames (Munoz et al., 2011, p. 292).

In Chapter 4 we introduce several concepts that are related to the topic of opportunity development (OD): business models, lean start-up and design thinking. Opportunity development is also strongly related to entrepreneurial learning as these two factors are closely interrelated for inexperienced would-be entrepreneurs. As we will explain in Chapter 5, entrepreneurial learning and opportunity development are essentially linked together as you (the entrepreneur) gain insight about yourself and the opportunity you have identified. In most cases, OD will be an iterative process rather than a linear progression from idea to a fully functioning business. In this section we expand on the earlier stages of OD as you refine ideas that you identified in the exercises discussed above.

Exercise 4: The Ideate Framework (Cohen et al., 2021)

	ACTIVITY
STEP 1	
IDENTIFY	Focus on worthwhile problems such as recycling plastic waste or Covid-19
	Try to identify 5 opportunities
STEP 2	
DISCOVERY	Actively search for opportunities in problem-rich areas you are passionate about
	Think about your main passions as well as interesting places you have visited – try to identify opportunities

	ACTIVITY
	Identify 5 opportunities related to your own interests and experiences
STEP 3	
ENHANCE	Enhance existing businesses by adding an innovative element OR by developing a new business model
	Generate 5 opportunities which add value to existing products or services
STEP 4	
ANTICIPATE	Think about the PESTLE sources of change: political, economic, social, technological, legal and environmental
	Identify 5 new opportunities related to the six areas of change
STEP 5	
TARGET	Think about your target customer and what benefits they will get from your product/services
	What customers will you target? Generate 5 opportunities
STEP 6	
EVALUATE	You now have a list of 25 opportunities – select the **five** which you think have the most potential. You should formally evaluate those five opportunities in exercise 5

3.5 Opportunity Evaluation

In the previous section we have discussed the importance of generating a range of business ideas. Our teaching experience suggests that most students do not give that stage enough attention and are happy to accept the first business idea that comes to mind. We believe that it is crucial to consider a range of business opportunities at the early stages of your entrepreneurial career. This provides you with a more realistic basis on which to consider your future as an entrepreneur. In this section, we examine how you can make decisions about which particular opportunity is the best fit with your own entrepreneurial orientation. The creativity literature discusses the differences between 'divergent' and 'convergent' thinking. Divergent thinking refers to the necessity of opening up to new ideas so that you are not constrained by your previous experiences when considering the possibilities for a new business idea. Convergent thinking refers to the need to identify the ideas that are most likely to succeed in the marketplace. The idea of opportunity evaluation means that you should try to ensure that you

Figure 3.2 Opportunity Development

will be able to establish a venture to exploit an opportunity. Based on an extensive review of the literature, Wood and McKelvie (2015) suggest that opportunity evaluation is based on four key themes (Figure 3.2).

1. **Mental models** – these are cognitive representations of the competitive environment based on your own beliefs and judgements. Factors influencing your cognitive images of the opportunity will include the likely returns, the associated risks and your personal objectives (Ardichvili et al., 2003). If your objectives are to create a very fast-growing business and make a sale as quickly as possible then your judgements about the balance of risks and rewards will be very different from your wanting to create a small sustainable business. Inevitably, cognitive images will differ between individuals, which helps explain why not all new opportunities will appeal to all entrepreneurs. Opportunity evaluation is a process by which the would-be entrepreneur uses their experience and information to develop a mental image of the opportunity's attractiveness.

2. **Integration** – focuses on how individuals integrate their idiosyncratic dispositions, knowledge and goals into representations of new opportunities. Your own aspirational levels will be a crucial influence on whether or not you decide to pursue a particular business opportunity (Lee & Venkataraman, 2006). High levels of 'positive dispositions' tend to have a negative influence of opportunity evaluation (Baron, Hmieleski & Henry, 2012). In other words, some entrepreneurs are too optimistic about the chances of their business succeeding. You need to be realistic about your own abilities and the likelihood of your business idea being successful. While Kor, Mahoney and Michael

(2007) suggest that industry-related experience provides entrepreneurs with a sound basis on which to evaluation the likelihood of the opportunity proving to be successful. As we discuss in Chapter 7, gaining any experience in the 'real world' is likely to be beneficial to your career as an entrepreneur.

3. **Congruence** – generally there will be other stakeholders involved with any start-up venture. According to Wood and McKelvie (2015) the most salient are those with a financial stake in the business (or a potential financial interest) such as venture capitalists or business angels. The evaluation of new opportunities by these stakeholders will often be based on a business plan or funding pitches made by the nascent entrepreneur. Some suggest that entrepreneur and venture capitalists use different criteria to evaluate an opportunity. Entrepreneurs concentrate on the potential for market growth and returns on their assets while VCs focus on the entrepreneurs themselves – particularly their perceived knowledge, skills and abilities (Bammens & Collewaert, 2014). Most student start-ups will not attract financial stakeholders but other people will have an interest in the business opportunity. Talking to close friends and family is a useful way of getting a wider perspective on the potential of your new business opportunity.

4. **Action Orientation** – relates to the efforts made by the nascent entrepreneur to pursue the introduction of a new product or service. Once again, this involves interpretation of the environment as the entrepreneur considers what resources (knowledge, skills, time, equipment, finance) must be mobilized to exploit the opportunity and the likely benefits. This means 'envisioning' a future pathway for your business based on your personal judgement about the desirability, feasibility and associated risks related to the opportunity. In simple terms, this means that you need to consider the exact nature of the actions you must undertake to move from the identification of an opportunity to a functioning business. As we discuss in Chapter 4, this focus on action orientation fits very well with the lean start-up methodology.

To summarize, following on from Section 3.3, having identified an 'opportunity situation' (Shane & Venkataraman, 2000) you should then begin to seriously consider whether the opportunity is for you. The starting point is the construction of a mental image of how you could exploit the opportunity based on the resources (dispositions, knowledge, skills equipment, finance and goals) in your possession as well as those you may be able to 'bootstrap' from other people or organizations (see Chapter 9). Your individual cognitive activities (mental models and integration) are also likely to be shaped by social cognitions based on interactions with various stakeholders including investors (perhaps), customers, family and close friends (Wood & McKelvie, 2015). Remember, at this stage you are evaluating a range of opportunities to identify one that has real potential for success and fits with your personal dispositions and motivations.

Others suggest that the attractiveness of an opportunity is influenced by the nature of the environment particularly the availability of resources and the potential for economic growth (Kushev, Ahuja & Carter, 2019). If the environment in which you are starting your business is thriving there will be more prospects for growth and better access to resources than is likely in times of economic uncertainty (during a pandemic for example). It should be noted that the pandemic did create business opportunities for personal protective equipment (face masks) as well as anti-Covid vaccines (see Section 1.6). Individuals do not exist in isolation from other actors and interaction with the environment (customers, competitors, resource providers) will all influence the entrepreneur's actions. In addition to an individual's knowledge, experience and skills, the nature of their social capital is important for gaining access to external resources. For example, greater diversity in your social network is the basis for higher levels of social capital and, therefore, access to a wider range of resources including information and knowledge (see Chapter 6). Following your use of the IDEATE model in the previous section, you should have several potential business ideas. We suggest you use the RAMP (returns, advantage, market and potential) model below to formally evaluate those ideas.

We now turn our attention to the links between entrepreneurial cognition and opportunity identification in the context of various environmental challenges. Given the imminent disasters associated with global warming and degradation of the natural world, it should not be too difficult to convince young people that this issue can no longer be ignored.

Exercise 5: Opportunity Evaluation

Business Opportunity

	Returns	No			Yes	
1.	Will the idea generate more money than you spend?	1	2	3	4	5
2.	Can you launch the business without external investment?	1	2	3	4	5
3.	Will the idea generate good returns?	1	2	3	4	5
	Advantages					
4.	Is your business idea better than existing competitors?	1	2	3	4	5
5.	Is your idea unique and does it have limited competition?	1	2	3	4	5
6.	Does the idea have a patent that gives an advantage?	1	2	3	4	5
7.	Does the idea have some other advantage (personal service)?	1	2	3	4	5
	Market					
8.	Do you have a clear idea of the target consumer?	1	2	3	4	5
9.	Is there a clear market for the business idea?	1	2	3	4	5
10.	Does the idea fill a market need?	1	2	3	4	5
	Potential					
11.	Will the idea provide a good financial reward?	1	2	3	4	5
12.	Does the idea have real potential for market growth?	1	2	3	4	5
13.	Are there others who believe in the business ideas?	1	2	3	4	5
14.	Are there other businesses that are similar (validation that this opportunity is worth pursuing)?	1	2	3	4	5
	Total					

Source: www.morebusiness.com/evaluating-business-opportunities/

Note: This framework is intended to help you evaluate and compare the potential of a number of business ideas generated by means of the IDEATE model

3.6 Sustainable Development: Identifying Green Opportunities

As pointed out above, there are a range of *problem-rich* areas associated with the environment, which could be a source of new opportunities. The

idea of green entrepreneurship (or ecopreneurship) has increased in importance in recent years. One well-known example in the UK is *ecotricity*,[2] a
company founded by committed environmentalist Dale Vince (Box 3.2).
Shepherd and Patzelt (2011) combine an earlier definition of entrepreneurship (Venkataraman, 1997a) with the concept of sustainable development:
'sustainable entrepreneurship is focused on the preservation of nature, life
support and community in the pursuit of perceived opportunities to bring
into existence future products, processes and services for gain, where gain is
broadly construed to include economic and non-economic gains to individuals, the economy and society'. The core of sustainable development is based
on the idea that all natural systems have limits and, to sustain the wellbeing
of future generations, it is necessary to live within those limits (Hall, Daneke
& Lenox, 2010). There are a range of sustainability-related entrepreneurship
concepts in the literature: ecopreneurship, environmental entrepreneurship,
environpreneurship, green entrepreneurship, social entrepreneurship, social
enterprise and sustainable entrepreneurship (Gast, Gundolf & Cesinger, 2017).

Box 3.2 Creating Green Opportunities: The case of *Ecotricity*

Dale Vince was born in 1961 and his father owned a garage where
he gained some mechanical experience. He left school at 15 to join a
hippy commune and eventually acquired an old fire engine in which
he lived while touring the UK and Europe. Eventually, using his mechanical knowledge he rigged up a windmill to provide electrical power
for his mobile home. He attended many festivals and his practical
skills were useful for setting up on-site power generators. At the 1994
Glastonbury festival he also set up a windmill to charge mobile phone
batteries. Then in 1995 he founded *Ecotricity* and launched his first
wind turbine to supply green energy. At that time the 'green energy
market' did not exist in the UK – so Dale Vince *created* the opportunity for a green energy supplier. *Ecotricity* now has a number of
wind farms and solar parks supplying both domestic and business
customers. Dale Vince is also well known in the UK for his ownership of *Forest Green Rovers*, which is the world's only vegan football
club and also was recognized by the United Nations and FIFA as the
world's first carbon-neutral football club.

Masciarelli and Leonelli (2020) point out several environmental threats including surface water degradation, toxic waste in groundwater, air pollution, ozone depletion, climate change and destruction of ocean fisheries worldwide. The authors go on to suggest that entrepreneurship has a key role to play in helping to solve these problems by introducing products and services that are competitive but, more importantly, do not damage the environment (Dean & McMullen, 2007). We suggest that a student's commitment to sustainable entrepreneurship will depend on two concepts introduced in Section 3.3: intrinsic motivation and self-efficacy. Starting a sustainable business will certainly be challenging and if you are not strongly committed to protecting the environment you are unlikely to be successful. Self-efficacy means being confident that you have the appropriate skills to tackle environmental problems by starting a sustainable entrepreneurial venture. This will also, we suggest, depend on your levels of *prior knowledge* about the various threats to the environment. As discussed in Section 3.1, there are various forms of prior knowledge: understanding markets, ways to serve those markets, customer problems (Ardichvili et al., 2003; Dabrowski, 2019; Sanz-Velasco, 2006; Shane, 2000). Clearly, all these forms of prior knowledge can be linked to the various environmental problems mentioned above. Young people have the most to lose from these problems and, therefore, we anticipate that most students will have some awareness of the various environmental threats. A more challenging question is: do you have the motivation and skills to do something about these challenges?

According to data from the Global Entrepreneurship Monitor (GEM) young adults in the 18 to 34 age group are most likely to engage in sustainable entrepreneurship. There is also a positive association between education levels and interest in starting a green business (Bosma et al., 2016). Those with higher level qualifications are more likely to be concerned with environmental issues. Whereas traditional entrepreneurship is primarily concerned with economic development (Kirzner, 1973), sustainable entrepreneurship attempts to balance the so-called 'triple-bottom' line: economic, social and ecological goals (Cohen, Smith & Mitchell, 2008; Munoz & Cohen, 2018). Based on a review of the literature dealing with the sustainable entrepreneurship process (SEP) and four in-depth case studies, Belz and Binder (2017) develop their own stage model of the entrepreneurial process.

Stage 1 Recognizing an ecological problem: as we discussed above, there is certainly no shortage of ecological (environmental) problems which everyone encounters in their daily lives. Plastic waste, traffic pollution, global warming, warming and rising levels of the oceans, climate change etc.

Stage 2 Recognizing an ecological opportunity: at this stage you should consider how an ecological problem can lead to an ecological business opportunity. The various problems associated with burning fossil fuels to produce electricity led Dale Vince to identify the opportunity of offering green electricity to the marketplace (see Box 3.2). Cohen and Winn (2007) suggest that various 'market imperfections' (externalities, flawed pricing, information asymmetries) provide entrepreneurial opportunities. Damaging emissions (externalities) from coal-fired power-stations mean that there are opportunities for green energy solutions. The cost of air travel does not reflect the ecological damage caused by aircraft (flawed pricing) and this provides opportunities associated with 'carbon offsetting' (tree planting). Most people may be unaware that much fashionable clothing is produced in unsafe working conditions (information asymmetries) and that provides opportunities for clothing that is ethically produced. As we have discussed above, either the SEEC or the IDEATE models can be used to help identify ecological opportunities.

Stage 3 Developing a double-bottom line solution (ecological and economic): at this stage, you must consider how an ecological problem provides a business opportunity that aligns with your own values and those of potential customers. Belz and Binder (2017) argue that ecological attributes should be aligned with core criteria such as functionality, performance, design, durability and safe disposal of products and services. Belz and Binder (2017) also include a stage for the triple bottom line (social as well as ecological and economic). While we acknowledge that many ecological solutions will also have social benefits (the creation of new jobs associated with renewal energy) that is not our focus here.

Stage 4 Forming and funding a sustainable enterprise: a core theme of this book is that it will be very difficult for students and recent graduates to obtain external funding for their new businesses. The exception may be that if you have some unique knowledge that can be legally protected (intellectual property rights) then you may be able to attract investors such as business angels or venture capitalist (see Chapter 8). Most start-ups will rely on family or friends for financial support in the early stages. Hence, we stress the value of adopting an effectual approach to starting your own business by additional 'bootstrapping' resources (see Chapter 9). 'Crowdfunding' is another potential route to external finance and this can be either formal or informal finance (see Chapters 8 and 9).

Stage 5 Creating or entering a sustainable market: assuming the characteristics of your product or service are appropriate to your target market then you must pay careful attention to the pricing of your offerings. This issue is discussed in more detail in Sections 4.3 (Business Modelling) and 4.4 (Lean Start-up). However, we believe that it is essential that you spend time talking to potential customers as early as possible in the process so that you obtain a clear understanding of their demands. It may well be that offering niche ecological products or services means that you can charge premium prices. At the same time, it may be that because your fixed costs are lower that your competitors, you can price well below current market offerings (see Box 3.1).

Eller et al. (2020) combine the sustainable entrepreneurship process model (Belz & Binder, 2017) with the model of sustainable opportunity recognition (Shepherd & Patzelt, 2011). The latter suggests that sustainable opportunity identification is a process consisting of a transition from problem to solution and sustainable opportunity identification (Figure 3.3). Furthermore, students should be inspired to recognise the importance of identifying sustainable business opportunities. As indicated above, there are no shortage of ecological problems to use as a starting point – but using the IDEATE model could aid the search for additional problems. It is essential that students become aware of the adverse consequences associated with

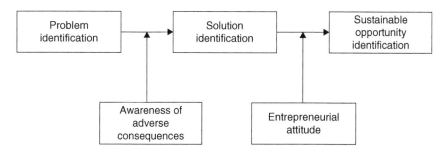

Figure 3.3 Sustainable Opportunity Identification

various environmental problems. Increasing student awareness should also improve the intrinsic motivation to seek solutions that reduce our impact on the environment. Students attitude to both entrepreneurship and the environmental will influence their willingness to seek sustainable business solutions that could form the basis of a start-up company. The more problems that are identified at the start of the process the more the likelihood of identifying potential solutions to some of those problems (Eller et al., 2020). In their study, Eller et al. (2020) confirmed that student awareness of the adverse impact of adverse consequences increased the motivation to seek sustainable solutions. Furthermore, those students with an entrepreneurial attitude were more likely to move from solution to sustainable opportunity identification.

Ideas associated with individual creativity and green entrepreneurial intentions are brought together by (Jiang, Wang, Wang & Li, 2020). They suggest that those possessing cognitive flexibility, a willingness to engage in divergent thinking and high-levels of creativity are more likely to recognise the importance of green business solutions. Green recognition focuses attention on an individual's ability to identify and act on the potential benefits of engaging in green entrepreneurship. Jiang et al. (2020) contrast 'green recognition' with what they describe a 'green disengagement'. The moderating factor which influences creative entrepreneurs to decide between green recognition and green disengagement is *green self-identity*. Those students whose commitment to sustainability is central to their self-identity will be far more likely to have green entrepreneurial intentions (Figure 3.4). Those students with low levels of green self-identity will focus their creativity on explaining why they opt for green disengagement.

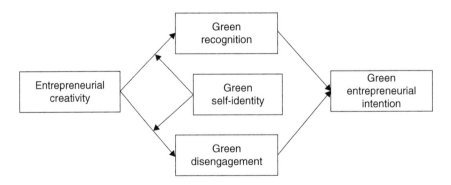

Figure 3.4 The Dual Pathway of Green Entrepreneurial Intentions

There are various forms of disengagement; moral (Detert, Klebe Trevino & Sweitzer, 2008), cultural (Gayo, 2017) and civic (Cheng & Liu, 2018). Green disengagement is defined as 'a process of specific recognition by which individuals disconnect from environmental awareness and responsibility' (Jiang et al., 2020, p. 5). Assuming the objective is to start more sustainable businesses, the practical implications of this study confirm the importance of identifying those students with a strong orientation to a green self-identity.

3.7 Summary and Key Learning Points

Chapter 3 focuses on what many scholars regard as the key skill that distinguishes entrepreneurs from non-entrepreneurs: the ability to identify new business opportunities. At the outset, it is important to recognize the distinction between opportunity identification and opportunity creation. Opportunity identification represents the traditional perspective that opportunities are 'out there' waiting to be discovered by alert entrepreneurs. In contrast, opportunity creation means that entrepreneurs create opportunities through their own efforts without responding to 'signals' from the market. Opportunity creation is generally associated with effectuation theory (Sarasvathy, 2001; Sarasvathy, 2008; Sarasvathy & Ramesh, 2019), which suggests that entrepreneurs rely on their own resources to create new business opportunities. For example, in the Jazooli case (Box 3.1), Sam started trading mobile phones on eBay and gradually began to sell various mobile phone accessories. As the volume of business increased, Sam and his brother Ben were able to establish a growing, profitable business. They certainly did not formally identify an opportunity but created and grew their business through the practical activity of trading various accessories.

Whether an opportunity is identified or created depends very much on entrepreneurial cognition. The concept of cognition focuses attention on how individuals use their mental facilities to make decisions. Hence, cognition refers to ways in which we obtain, process, store, understand and use knowledge. In terms of entrepreneurship, cognition has a direct influence on both your self-efficacy and intrinsic motivation. Cognition also influences your creative thinking skills and is important in terms of identifying new opportunities. We suggest that creativity is a skill which can be acquired experientially and the chapter contains a number of exercises that you should complete. As explained in Section 3.3, there is now acceptance that cognition is influenced by the 'situation' as well as by an individual's mental activity. We believe 'situated cognition' is particularly relevant to students engaging in entrepreneurial learning. Such learning is a social activity as well as a mental activity(Jones, Meckel & Taylor, 2021b).

Practising your thinking skills is central to improving the ability to identify new business opportunities. To obtain the most benefit from this material it is essential that you engage with the Brainstorming exercise as well as using both the SEEC and IDEATE models to identify opportunities with the potential for generating meaningful business ideas. Both SEEC and IDEATE are based on the principle that it is important to engage in an active, rather than a passive, search for new opportunities. Given the significance of threats to the environment, we also focused on the need to consider identifying opportunities that could form the basis of an ecologically sustainable business. A number of scholars see entrepreneurship as a key mechanism for shifting economic activity towards a more environmentally sustainable model. The key learning points from Chapter 3 are as follows:

- The starting point for this chapter is that you should have a clear understanding of the importance of entrepreneurial cognition. Cognition is a crucial component in the entrepreneurial ability to identify and exploit new opportunities. It is also the basis of self-efficacy (are you confident you have the appropriate skills to become an entrepreneur?) and intrinsic motivation (are you motivated by the desire to become an entrepreneur?).
- There are strong links between cognition and the ability to think creatively. Enhancing your 'imaginativeness' will help in your future career whether or not you start your own business. Divergent thinking is a crucial dimension of creativity and this is certainly a skill that can be developed through practice.
- Opportunity identification is the starting point for any new entrepreneurial business. This applies whether the opportunity is created in an incremental way or identified as a result of a systematic search. If you cannot identify an opportunity then you are very unlikely to start your own business. Practice with the SEEC and IDEATE models is central to improving your cognitive process related to opportunity identification.
- Degradation of the environment is a topic that is of increasing importance to the lives of everyone on the planet. Furthermore, threats to the environment provide a *problem-rich* source of ecological business

opportunities. You should have a clear understanding of how sustainable entrepreneurship can make a positive contribution to the environment.

- We believe that it is possible to motivate students to take seriously the issue of sustainable entrepreneurship. Adopting an instrumental (rather than an idealistic) approach means that it is possible to make money while doing good things for the environment.

- Opportunity identification is the first stage in the process and this should be followed by opportunity evaluation. This, we suggest, is similar to the distinction between divergent thinking (opening up) and convergent thinking (closing down). The process of evaluation should also involve consideration of your own skills, abilities and motivation. You may have identified a valuable opportunity but is it the right one for you?

3.8 Discussion Questions and Call to Action

1. What do you understand by the term entrepreneurial cognition and why is it important to opportunity identification?

2. Do you think creativity is an innate characteristic or skill that can be developed in the classroom?

3. What are the key differences between opportunity identification and opportunity creation?

4. What are the main barriers to students or recent graduates setting up their own businesses?

5. What are the differences between divergent thinking and convergent thinking in terms of opportunity identification?

6. Can you explain the difference between identifying opportunities by passive and active searches?

7. What are the four stages in opportunity evaluation?

8. Can you explain what you understand by the term 'sustainable development'?

9. Why do you think that younger people are more likely to engage in sustainable entrepreneurship than older, more experience people?

10. To what extent does the identification of sustainable opportunities differ from the identification of conventional business opportunities?

It is often assumed that creative people are in some way different from the rest of the population because they are believed to possess unique abilities. Similar to Ritter and Mostert (2017), our view is that creativity is a skill that can be developed and we suggest a number of exercises in this chapter. Enhancing your cognitive abilities (thinking skills) will be important in the future whether or not you decide to pursue an entrepreneurial career. The ability to approach problems in creative ways is important in any career or any organizational context. Therefore, developing the ability to engage in what De Bono (2015) calls 'lateral thinking' (or 'thinking outside the box' to use a colloquial term) will be of value to you in the future. Our experience of teaching entrepreneurship is that students are not particularly adept at identifying interesting and challenging business opportunities. We therefore encourage you to make a concerted effort to identify new business opportunities that can then be discussed with your classmates. You should experiment in using both passive searches (based on your day-to-day experiences) and a more active (systematic and structured) approach based on the IDEATE model.

Notes

1 We are grateful to our erstwhile colleague David Taylor for pointing out the importance of students gaining first-hand entrepreneurial experience.
2 www.ecotricity.co.uk

References

Acar, S. & Runco, M. A. (2019). Divergent thinking: New methods, recent research, and extended theory. *Psychology of Aesthetics, Creativity, and the Arts, 13*(2), 153–158.

Ajzen, I. (1991). The Theory of Planned Behavior. *Organizational Behavior & Human Decision Processes, 50*(2), 179–211.

Alvarez, S. A. & Barney, J. B. (2007). Discovery and creation: alternative theories of entrepreneurial action. *Strategic Entrepreneurship Journal, 1*(2), 11–26.

Ardichvili, A., Cardozo, R. & Ray, S. (2003). A theory of entrepreneurial opportunity identification and development. *Journal of Business Venturing, 18*(1), 105–123

Arikan, A. M., Arikan, I. & Koparan, I. (2020). Creation Opportunities: Entrepreneurial Curiosity, Generative Cognition, and Knightian Uncertainty. *Academy of Management Review, 45*(4), 808–824.

Bammens, Y. & Collewaert, V. (2014). Trust Between Entrepreneurs and Angel Investors: Exploring Positive and Negative Implications for Venture Performance Assessments. *Journal of Management, 40*(7), 1980–2008.

Bandura, A. (1997). *Self-efficacy: the exercise of control.* New York: W.H. Freeman.

Baron, R. A., Hmieleski, K. M. & Henry, R. A. (2012). Entrepreneurs' dispositional positive affect: The potential benefits – and potential costs – of being 'up'. *Journal of Business Venturing, 27*(3), 310–324.

Belz, F. M. & Binder, J. K. (2017). Sustainable Entrepreneurship: A Convergent Process Model. *Business Strategy and The Environment, 26*(1), 1–17.

Bosma, N.S., Schøtt, T., Terjesen, S.J. & Kew, P. (2016) *Global Entrepreneurship Monitor 2015 to 2016: Special Topic Report on Social Entrepreneurship.* Global Entrepreneurship Research Association, www.gemconsortium.org

Chavoushi, Z. H., Zali, M. R., Valliere, D., Faghih, N., Hejazi, R. & Dehkordi, A. M. (2021). Entrepreneurial Alertness: A Systematic Literature Review. *Journal of Small Business and Entrepreneurship, 33*(2), 123–152.

Cheng, T. & Liu, S. (2018). Service Cynicism: How Civic Disengagement Develops. *Politics & Society, 46*(1), 101–129.

Chiles, T. H., Vulture, D. M., Gupta, V. K., Greening, D. W. & Tuggle, C. S. (2010). The Philosophical Foundations of a Radical Austrian Approach to Entrepreneurship. *Journal of Management Inquiry, 19*(2), 138–164.

Cohen, B., Smith, B. & Mitchell, R. (2008). Toward a sustainable conceptualization of dependent variables in entrepreneurship research. *Business Strategy & the Environment, 17*(2), 107–119.

Cohen, B. & Winn, M. I. (2007). Market imperfections, opportunity and sustainable entrepreneurship. *Journal of Business Venturing, 22*(1), 29–49.

Cohen, D., Hsu, D. K. & Shinnar, R. S. (2021). Identifying innovative opportunities in the entrepreneurship classroom: a new approach and empirical test. *Small Business Economics: An Entrepreneurship Journal, 57*(4) 1931–1955.

Coskun, H. (2005). Cognitive stimulation with convergent and divergent thinking exercises in brainwriting: Incubation, sequence priming, and group context. *Small group research, 36*(4), 466–498.

Dabrowski, D. (2019). Market knowledge and new product performance: the mediating effects of new product creativity. *Journal of Business Economics & Management, 20*(6), 1168–1188.

De Bono, E. (1995). Serious creativity. *Journal for Quality and Participation, 18*(5), 12–18.

De Bono, E. (2015). *Serious creativity: using the power of lateral thinking to create new ideas.* London: Vermilion.

Dean, T. J. & McMullen, J. S. (2007). Toward a theory of sustainable entrepreneurship: Reducing environmental degradation through entrepreneurial action. *Journal of Business Venturing, 22*(1), 50–76.

Delmar, F., and Witte F.C. (2012). The psychology of the entrepreneur. In S. Carter and D. Jones-Evans, *Enterprise and small business: principles, practices and policy* (3rd edition. pp152–179). Harlow: Pearson.

Detert, J. R., Klebe Trevino, L. & Sweitzer, V. L. (2008). Moral Disengagement in Ethical Decision Making: A Study of Antecedents and Outcomes. *Journal of applied psychology*, *93*(2), 374–391.

DeTienne, D. R. & Chandler, G. N. (2004). Opportunity Identification and Its Role in the Entrepreneurial Classroom: A Pedagogical Approach and Empirical Test. *Academy of Management Learning & Education*, *3*(3), 242–257.

Dew, N., Grichnik, D., Mayer-Haug, K., Read, S. & Brinckmann, J. (2015). Situated Entrepreneurial Cognition. *International Journal of Management Reviews*, *17*(2), 143–164.

Dimov, D. (2011). Grappling with the unbearable elusiveness of entrepreneurial opportunities. *Entrepreneurship: Theory and Practice*, *35*(1), 57–81.

Dimov, D. (2020). Opportunities, Language, and Time. *Academy of Management Perspectives*, *34*(3), 333–351.

Edelman, L. F. & Yli-Renko, H. (2010). The impact of environment and entrepreneurial perceptions on venture-creation efforts: Bridging the discovery and creation views of entrepreneurship. *Entrepreneurship: Theory and Practice*, *34*(5), 833–856.

Elias, S. R. S. T. A., Chiles, T. H. & Qian, L. I. (2020). Austrian economics and organizational entrepreneurship: a typology. *Quarterly Journal of Austrian Economics*, *23*(3/4), 313–354.

Eller, F. J., Gielnik, M. M., Wimmer, H., Thölke, C., Holzapfel, S., Tegtmeier, S. & Halberstadt, J. (2020). Identifying business opportunities for sustainable development: Longitudinal and experimental evidence contributing to the field of sustainable entrepreneurship. *Business Strategy & the Environment*, *29*(3), 1387–1403.

Forbes, D. P. (1999). Cognitive approaches to new venture creation. *International Journal of Management Reviews*, *1*(4), 415.

Gaglio, C. M. & Katz, J. A. (2001). The Psychological Basis of Opportunity Identification: Entrepreneurial Alertness. *Small Business Economics*, *16*(2), 95–111.

Gartner, W. B., Bird, B. J. & Starr, J. A. (1992). Acting As If: Differentiating Entrepreneurial From Organizational Behavior. *Entrepreneurship: Theory & Practice*, *16*(3), 13–31.

Gast, J., Gundolf, K. & Cesinger, B. (2017). Doing business in a green way: A systematic review of the ecological sustainability entrepreneurship literature and future research directions. *Journal of Cleaner Production*, *147*(March), 44–56.

Gayo, M. (2017). Exploring Cultural Disengagement: The Example of Chile. *Cultural Sociology*, *11*(4), 468–488.

George, N. M., Vinit, P., Lahti, T. & Wincent, J. (2016). A Systematic Literature Review of Entrepreneurial Opportunity Recognition: Insights on Influencing Factors. *International Entrepreneurship and Management Journal*, *12*(2), 309–350.

Gregoire, D. A., Cornelissen, J., Dimov, D. & Burg, E. (2015). The Mind in the Middle: Taking Stock of Affect and Cognition Research in Entrepreneurship. *International Journal of Management Reviews, 17*(2), 125–142

Hägg, G. & Kurczewska, A. (2019). Who Is the Student Entrepreneur? Understanding the Emergent Adult through the Pedagogy and Andragogy Interplay. *Journal of Small Business Management, 57*, 130–147.

Hall, J. K., Daneke, G. A. & Lenox, M. J. (2010). Sustainable development and entrepreneurship: Past contributions and future direction. *Journal of Business Venturing, 25*(5), 439–448.

Hsu, D. K., Shinnar, R. S., Powell, B. C. & Coffey, B. S. (2017). Intentions to reenter venture creation: The effect of entrepreneurial experience and organizational climate. *International Small Business Journal: Researching Entrepreneurship, 35*(8), 928–948.

Jiang, H., Wang, S., Wang, L. & Li, G. (2020). Golden Apples or Green Apples? The Effect of Entrepreneurial Creativity on Green Entrepreneurship: A Dual Pathway Model. *Sustainability, 12*(15). doi:10.3390/su12156285

Jones, O. & Giordano, B. (2021). Family entrepreneurial teams: The role of learning in business model evolution. *Management Learning, 52*(3), 267–293.

Jones, O. & Li, H. (2017). Effectual Entrepreneuring: Sensemaking in a Family-Based Start-Up. *Entrepreneurship and Regional Development, 29*(5–6), 467–499.

Jones, O., Meckel, P. & Taylor, D. (2021a). *Creating Communities of Practice: Entrepreneurial Learning in a University-Based Incubator*. Cham: Springer.

Jones, O., Meckel, P. & Taylor, D. (2021b). Situated learning in a business incubator: Encouraging students to become real entrepreneurs. *Industry & Higher Education, 35*(4), 367–383.

Kier, A. S. & McMullen, J. S. (2018). Entrepreneurial Imaginativeness in New Venture Ideation. *Academy of Management Journal, 61*(6), 2265–2295.

Kier, A. S. & McMullen, J. S. (2020). Entrepreneurial imaginativeness and new venture ideation in newly forming teams. *Journal of Business Venturing, 35*(6), 106048.

Kirzner, I. M. (1973). *Competition and Entrepreneurship*. Chicago: University of Chicago.

Kirzner, I. M. (2009). The Alert and Creative Entrepreneur: A Clarification. *Small Business Economics* (2), 145–152.

Kor, Y. Y., Mahoney, J. T. & Michael, S. C. (2007). Resources, Capabilities and Entrepreneurial Perceptions. *Journal of Management Studies (Wiley-Blackwell), 44*(7), 1187–1212.

Kushev, T., Ahuja, M. K. & Carter, R. E. (2019). A Social Cognitive Perspective on Opportunity Evaluation. *Journal of Entrepreneurship, 28*(1), 35–67.

Lee, J.-H. & Venkataraman, S. (2006). Aspirations, market offerings, and the pursuit of entrepreneurial opportunities. *Journal of Business Venturing, 21*(1), 107–123.

Macpherson, A. & Holt, R. (2007). Knowledge, learning and small firm growth: A systematic review of the evidence. *Research Policy*, *36*, 172–192.

Masciarelli, F. & Leonelli, S. (2020). *Sustainable entrepreneurship: How entrepreneurs create value from sustainable opportunities*. Entrepreneruship Behaviour Series. Bingley (UK): Emerald Publishing Ltd.

McClelland, D. C. (1962). Business Drive and National Achievement. *Harvard Business Review*, *40*(4), 99–113.

McMullen, J. S. & Kier, A. S. (2017). You don't have to be an entrepreneur to be entrepreneurial: The unique role of imaginativeness in new venture ideation. *Business Horizons*, *60*(4), 455–462.

McMullen, J. S. & Shepherd, D. A. (2006). Entrepreneurial action and the role of uncertainty in the theory of the entrepreneur. *Academy of Management Review*, *31*(1), 132–152.

Medeiros, K.E ., Steele, L.M. , Watts, L.L. & Mumord, M.D. (2018). Timing is everything: Examining the role of constraints throughout the creative process. *Psychology of Aesthetics, Creativity, and the Arts*, *12*(4), 471-488.

Mobley, M., Doares, L. & Mumford, M. (1992). Process analytic models of creative capacities: Evidence for the combination and reorganization process. *Creativity Research Journal*, *5*(2), 125–155.

Moroz, P. W. & Hindle, K. (2012). Entrepreneurship as a Process: Toward Harmonizing Multiple Perspectives. *Entrepreneurship: Theory and Practice*, *36*(4), 781–818.

Mumford, M. D., Mobley, M. I., Reiter-Palmon, R., Uhlman, C. E. & Doares, L. M. (1991). Process analytic models of creative capacities. *Creativity Research Journal*, *4*(2), 91–122.

Munoz, C., Mosey, S. & Binks, M. (2011). Developing Opportunity-Identification Capabilities in the Classroom: Visual Evidence for Changing Mental Frames. *Academy of Management Learning & Education*, *10*(2), 277–295.

Munoz, P. & Cohen, B. (2018). Sustainable Entrepreneurship Research: Taking Stock and looking ahead. *Business Strategy and The Environment*, *27*(3), 300–322.

Posner, M. I. (2008). Measuring Alertness. *Annals of the New York Academy of Sciences*, *1129*, 193–199.

Ritter, S. M. & Mostert, N. (2017). Enhancement of creative thinking skills using a cognitive-based creativity training. *Journal of Cognitive Enhancement*, *1*(3), 243–253.

Sanz-Velasco, S. (2006). Opportunity development as a learning process for entrepreneurs. *International Journal of Entrepreneurial Behavior & Research*, *12*(5), 251–271.

Sarasvathy, S. D. (2001). Causation and effectuation: towards a theoretical shift from economic inevitability to entrepreneurial contingency. *Academy of Management Review*, *26*(2), 243–263.

Sarasvathy, S. D. (2001). Causation and Effectuation: Toward a Theoretical Shift from Economic Inevitability to Entrepreneurial Contingency. *The Academy of Management Review* (2), 243–263.

Sarasvathy, S. D. (2008). *Effectuation: elements of entrepreneurial expertise*. Cheltenham: Edward Elgar.

Sarasvathy, S. D. (2012). Effectuation and Entrepreneurship. In S. Carter & D. Jones-Evans (Eds.), *Enterprise and Small Business: Principles, Practice and Policy* (3rd ed., pp. 135–151). Harlow: Pearson.

Sarasvathy, S. D. & Ramesh, A. (2019). An Effectual Model of Collective Action for Addressing Sustainability Challenges. *Academy of Management Perspectives*, *33*(4), 405–424.

Scott, G., Leritz, L. E. & Mumford, M. D. (2004). The Effectiveness of Creativity Training: A Quantitative Review. *Creativity Research Journal*, *16*(4), 361–388.

Shane, S. (2000). Prior Knowledge and the Discovery of Entrepreneurial Opportunities. *Organization Science*, *11*(4), 448–469.

Shane, S. (2003). *A General Theory of Entrepreneurship: The Individual-Opportunity Nexus*. Cheltenham: Edward Elgar.

Shane, S. (2012). Reflections On The 2010 AMR Decade Award: Delivering on the Promise of Entrepreneurship as Field of Research. *Academy of Management Review*, *37*(1), 10–20.

Shane, S. & Venkataraman, S. (2000). The Promise of Entrepreneurship as a Field of Research. *Academy of Management Review*, *25*(1), 217–226.

Shepherd, D. A. & Patzelt, H. (2011). The new field of sustainable entrepreneurship: Studying entrepreneurial action linking 'what is to be sustained' with 'what is to be developed'. *Entrepreneurship Theory and Practice*, *35*(1), 137–163.

Smith, A. W., Moghaddam, K. & Lanivich, S. E. (2019). A set-theoretic investigation into the origins of creation and discovery opportunities. *Strategic Entrepreneurship Journal*, *13*(1), 75–92.

Stokes, D. & Wilson, N. (2010). *Small Business Management and Entrepreneurship*. Andover: Cengage.

Valliere, D. (2013). Towards a schematic theory of entrepreneurial alertness. *Journal of Business Venturing*, *28*(3), 430–442.

Venkataraman, S., Sarasvathy, S. D., Dew, N. & Forster, W. R. (2012). Reflections on the 2010 AMR decade award: Whither the promise? Moving forward with entrepreneurship as a science of the artificial. *Academy of Management Review*, *37*(1), 21–33.

Venkataraman, S. (2004) Entrepreneurial opportunity. In M. Hitt & D. Ireland (Eds.), Encyclopedic Dictionary of Entrepreneurship (pp. 100–103). Malden, MA: Blackwell.

Venkataraman, S. (1997a). The distinctive domain of entrepreneurship research: an editor's perspective. In J. Katz & J. Brockhaus (Eds.), *Advances in Entrepreneurship, Firm Emergence, and Growth* (pp. 119–138). Greenwich, CT: JAI Press.

Venkataraman, S. (Ed.) (1997b). *The Distinctive Domain of Entrepreneurship Research: An Editor's Perspective* (Vol. 3). Greenwich, CT: JAI Press.

Warnick, B. J., Kier, A. S., LaFrance, E. M. & Cuttler, C. (2021). Head in the clouds? Cannabis users' creativity in new venture ideation depends on their entrepreneurial passion and experience. *Journal of Business Venturing, 36*(2). doi:10.1016/j.jbusvent.2020.106088

Wood, M. S. & McKelvie, A. (2015). Opportunity Evaluation as Future Focused Cognition: Identifying Conceptual Themes and Empirical Trends. *International Journal of Management Reviews, 17*(2), 256–277.

Business Models and the Lean Start-up Approach

4.1 Introduction

In this chapter we introduce four concepts that have become increasingly important to all those considering starting their own businesses: business models, lean start-up methodology, design thinking and digitalization. While the ideas underpinning these four concepts are extremely diverse, we believe that they combine to provide a more effective and less risky approach to business start-up.

DaSilva and Trkman (2014) argue that the term 'business model' originates from a combination of the resource-based view (RBV) and transaction cost economics (TCE). Business models are useful for identifying the value creation potential of entrepreneurial firms (Chesbrough, 2010; Chesbrough & Rosenbloom, 2002; George & Bock, 2011; Zott & Amit, 2010). It is crucial for new firms to have flexible business models that help entrepreneurs to respond to environmental change (Baden-Fuller & Morgan, 2010; Brettel, Strese & Flatten, 2012; Demil & Lecocq, 2010). Others argue that entrepreneurs should modify their business models to suit the firm's life cycle (Andries & Debackere, 2007; Fiet & Patel, 2008). Adopting an appropriate business model is essential if entrepreneurs are to create customer value that leads to a source of revenue capable of supporting survival and growth (Afuah, 2019; Chandler, Broberg & Allison, 2014; Doganova & Eyquem-Renault, 2009).

In Chapter 9 we introduce the role of 'informal finance' during business start-up. Another term for informal finance is 'bootstrapping', which refers to the ways in which nascent entrepreneurs obtain additional resources that are either free or well below market price (Jayawarna, Jones & Macpherson,

DOI: 10.4324/9781003312918-5

2020; Jones & Jayawarna, 2010). Bootstrapping is also a way of thinking, and it means making the most effective use of your resources whatever stage of the business. For example, Harrison, Mason and Girling (2004, p. 308) provide the following definition: 'Bootstrapping involves imaginative and parsimonious strategies for marshalling and gaining control of resources'. Therefore, we suggest that the concept of bootstrapping has many parallels with the principles underpinning the 'lean start-up' approach (Ries, 2011). In fact, Ries[1] acknowledges the similarities but claims his 'approach to launching companies goes beyond bootstrapping' (Ghezzi, 2019).

Adopting a lean approach to business start-up also means having a clear vision of your business model. Business models have been linked to entrepreneurial firms since the advent of the 'dot.com boom' at the beginning of the twenty-first century (Cellan-Jones, 2001; Hedman & Kalling, 2003; Massa, Tucci & Afuah, 2017; Osterwalder & Pigneur, 2005). In their literature review, Amit and Zott (2001) suggested that business models are important because they enable entrepreneurs to test the market by examining the nature of opportunities. Business models are also useful for analysing the value-creation potential of new businesses and their longer-term sustainability (Chesbrough, 2010; Chesbrough & Rosenbloom, 2002). More recent literature has examined the role of business models in the commercialization processes of small high-technology firms (Pellikka and Malinen, 2015). Therefore, when you have identified a business opportunity, the next stage is to map out the key features on a business model canvass.

4.2 Learning Objectives

- To understand the importance of a business model as the basis for testing your ideas for starting a successful new business.
- To understand the principles of the lean start-up approach as a way of avoiding the risks associated with the traditional 'business plan' approach to starting a business.
- To understand how the concept of design thinking complements both business models and lean start-up
- To understand the importance of digitalization in terms of the creation of products and services as well as a start-up firm's interaction with suppliers, customers and other stakeholders

4.3 Business Models Supporting Start-up

Most entrepreneurs have implicit business models in mind when they are in the process of starting a new business. Our objective in this section of the book is to encourage you to think about making your ideas explicit by identifying the various components associated with a basic business model.

Having a clear business model is essential if new firms are to realize the economic value of technology-based products or services (Pellikka & Malinen, 2015). Several authors point out that new entrepreneurs have limited financial, technological, human resources and managerial resources as well as lacking the power to influence more established organizations (Ambos & Birkinshaw, 2010; Burton & Beckman, 2007; Santos & Eisenhardt, 2009). According to Andries, Debackere and Van Looy (2013) most entrepreneurs make incremental changes to their business models based on trial-and-error learning. Hence, entrepreneurs should make incremental, stepwise changes as they experiment with closely related business models. This is likely to be more effective than adopting radically new business models. The learning curve effect as entrepreneurs gain experience describes the process by which individuals improve their efficiency by regularly repeating a range of tasks and activities (Andries & Debackere, 2013; Andries, Debackere & Van Looy, 2020). As start-ups begin to deliver products or services then the business model becomes embedded in the firm's basic organizational routines (Cavalcante, Kesting & Ulhøi, 2011). Greater experience leads to higher levels of productivity as well as more effective decision-making related to reducing internal costs, pricing and marketing (Shepherd, Douglas & Shanley, 2000).

Amit and Zott (2015) claim that there are four antecedents of business model design in new firms: goals, templates, stakeholders and environmental constraints. As pointed out by Chesbrough (2010) rapid changes in information and communication technologies (ICT) has enabled entrepreneurs to fundamentally change the way in which they engage with customers and suppliers. Business models are based on a system of interdependent activities associated with a firm and its various partner organizations. While business model design is described (Amit and Zott, 2015, p. 332):

> the conceptualization of boundary-spanning activity that includes the mechanisms that connect these interdependent activities and the

identification of the party that carries out each of the activities within the system.

Early-stage business models are based on 'entrepreneurial' choices about organizational activities including procurement practices, location and assets (Amit & Zott, 2021; Casadesus-Masanell & Ricart, 2010). Drawing on the design literature (Boland & Collopy, 2004; Romme, 2003), Amit and Zott (2015, p. 334) identify four business model antecedents: goals to create and capture value; templates of incumbents; stakeholders' activities; and environmental constraints. These four factors are underpinned by four design themes: lock-in; efficiency; novelty; and complementarities. The conceptual model developed by Amit and Zott (2015, p. 346), supported by 'illustrative evidence from nine new ventures', lays the foundations 'for future research on business models'.

The main elements of a typical business model have been described by several authors (Amit & Zott, 2015; Landoni et al., 2020; Morris, Schindehutte & Allen, 2005; Osterwalder & Pigneur, 2005). Morris et al. (2005) identify six components which underpin a rudimentary business model: value creation (the offering); customers (the market); internal capabilities; competitive strategy; economic factors (how to make money); and personal factors such as motivation and ambition for growth (Andries et al., 2013). Afuah (2019) contends that business models provide a framework for creating and capturing value and have five main elements, which evolve and develop as firms grow. The first element is the *customer value proposition* (CVP); this refers to a firm's offering in terms of the products or services provided to solve customer problems and/or satisfy their needs (Afuah, 2019). A key point is that customers do not always know, in advance, what product or service they need, which is described as 'inchoate demand' (Geroski, 2003). Thus, according to Afuah (2019) an element of a firm's value proposition is to educate, inform and help customers discover their latent needs for new products or services. Afuah (2019) defines the second element of the business model as the *market segment* which is crucial because entrepreneurs need to know who will pay for their products or services. Market segment includes size of the potential market; the ability of customers to pay; customer demographics and levels of competition. Thirdly, the *revenue model* concerns those customers willing to pay a specific amount for a particular product or service. The aim is to maximize the number of customers paying for a firm's unique value proposition. Fourthly, the *growth model* focuses on questions of how firms can grow profitably. Growth concerns what must be done to increase the number of customers paying for a firm's products/services. Costs should be minimized which involves negotiating with suppliers and other stakeholders.

The fifth element, defined as the firm's *capabilities* is the fulcrum upon which the other four components hinge. Entrepreneurs create firms from an initial idea and attract financial support in order to develop their value proposition (Selden & Fletcher, 2015). Moreover, Afuah (2019) argues there are two elements to the *capabilities* component, namely 'resources' and 'activities'. Resources are what a firm owns or has access to while activities are necessary to transform resources into value capture (Mueller, Volery & von Siemens, 2012). A firm's resources include finance, equipment, products, knowledge and IPR as well as intangible assets such as social capital (Afuah, 2019).

A review of the business model literature identified three distinct groups of business model components (Wirtz, Pistoia, Ullrich & Göttel, 2016): *strategy*; *customer & market* (customer model, market offer model, revenue model); and *value creation* (service model, procurement model, financial model). The three 'customer and market' components overlap with three components identified by Afuah (2019): customer value proposition (CVP); market segment; and revenue model. The 'value creation' components are not covered by Afuah (2019) but are present in the work of other business model scholars (Hedman & Kalling, 2003; Johnson, Christensen & Kagermann, 2008; Osterwalder & Pigneur, 2005; Zott & Amit, 2017). Therefore, drawing on the 'integrated business model' developed by Wirtz et al. (2016) our proposed business model framework has two distinct blocks: 'customer and market' components and 'value creation' components. We further suggest that, unlike Afuah (2019), business growth will be an outcome of the other elements (customer and market + value creation) of the business model (see Figure 4.1). A longitudinal study of a start-up business is used to develop an evolutionary perspective on business model change based on the two distinct groupings: customer & market and value creation (Jones & Giordano, 2021).

Customer and Market Components

Customer Value Proposition – products/services that the entrepreneur supplies to his/her customers to solve their problems and/or satisfy their needs better than existing competitors;

Market Segment - the groups of customers to whom a value proposition is, or should be, offered (how many, ability to pay, attractiveness of each segment etc);

Revenue Model – calculation regarding how many customers pay how much for what product or service, when and how.

Value Creation Components

Service delivery model – the nature of relationship with customers (transactional or relational);

Procurement model – the nature of the entrepreneur's relationship with suppliers (transactional or relational);

Finance model – financial control/planning and longer-term financial structure of the business.

In the early stages of creating a business it is essential that inexperienced entrepreneurs concentrate on the three customer and market components of their business model. Hence, you should ask yourself the following questions:

1. What is the distinctive nature of my product/service and how will I out-compete existing businesses (CVP)?
2. Who exactly is my product/service aimed at and how will I attract sufficient customers willing to pay the asking price (market segment)?
3. What returns can I expect to achieve when I begin to trade (revenue model)?

Focusing on these core components should help you decide whether you have a viable business model. Our experience of student business plans suggests that usually there is a very limited understanding of the nature of their market segment. Therefore, it is crucial to the success of your business that you have a clear idea of those who will buy your offering in the early stages. We are not suggesting that service delivery and procurement are unimportant in the early stages of a new business. Clearly you will have to engage with suppliers and customers from the early stages of starting your business. Our basic proposition is that these components, together with the finance model, will become more important as the business begins to trade at higher volumes.

This evolutionary process is illustrated by means of Jazooli, a start-up company established by two young brothers while still at school (Jones and Giordano, 2021).[2] Jazooli was founded to sell cheap mobile phone accessories to young people of a similar age to themselves. Initially, the basic business model was to buy and sell as cheaply as possible making a small turnover on each item. When they began the business, it was basically a schoolboy hobby and revenue was a supplement to their pocket-money. In other words, Simon and Bill were not under any financial pressures in the very early stages of starting Jazooli. Gradually, turnover increased after the business was formally established in 2008 and within one-year they had to move activities from the family home to larger, rented premises. Gradually, as the business increased in size and the boys became more professional in managing Jazooli, then they paid more attention to the value-creating components of their business model.

1. **Procurement model** – in the early stage of the business, the boys simply obtained the cheapest products from suppliers in China. As they gained experience, they began to establish longer-term working relationships with the more reliable Chinese suppliers. Also, streamlined their activities by using the Amazon hub in Germany to deliver products directly to customers as well as introducing CRM software (see below).

2. **Service delivery model** – the introduction of sophisticated software systems including customer relationship management (CRM) enabled the boys to refine the relationships with both customers and suppliers (see above). CRM helped automate responses to customers to enhance their service by encouraging repeat purchases and responding quickly to customer complaints.

3. **Finance model** – while their business model was essentially focused on maintaining a low-cost base, they began to recognize the need to develop a more strategic approach to the financial aspects of the business. They employed a professional accountant who encouraged them to reinvest their profits in business development (building a stronger brand identity). They also began to manage financial risks associated with currency fluctuations by making hedge-payments to their Chinese suppliers in US dollars.

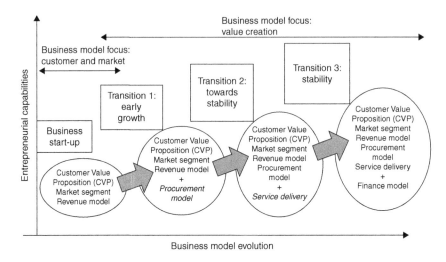

Figure 4.1 Business Model Evolution

Figure 4.1 illustrates this evolutionary process, which involves a wider range of entrepreneurial capabilities or competences as the business model becomes more sophisticated. To summarize, in the early stages of start-up, you should concentrate on the three customer & market components of your business model. Gradually, as the number of customers and sales increase then the value creation components should be given more attention. Professionalizing your links to both customers (service delivery) and suppliers (procurement) should help you reduce your operating costs while providing a better service. As transactions begin to stabilize, then you can adopt a more strategic view of managing the financial aspects of the business. The *Jazooli* case illustrates the importance of investing in the appropriate business software to professional relationships with suppliers and customers (Jones and Giordano, 2021). What we are suggesting here is that as you (the entrepreneur) enhance your capabilities and gain more experience of managing the business, you should be able to improve the way in which your organization operates.

4.4 The Lean Start-up Approach (LSA)

In their widely influential book, Womack, Jones and Roos (1990) introduced the topic of 'lean manufacturing practices' to a wider audience of academics and managers. This work focused on a Japanese management philosophy committed to reducing waste and constant incremental improvement (Deming, 1982; McMillan, 1992). There are clear links between the lean start-up approach and established management theories including the lean philosophy (Womack et al., 1990), organizational learning (Easterby-Smith, Araujo & Burgoyne, 1999) as well as key entrepreneurial theories such as effectuation (Sarasvathy, 2012) and bricolage (Baker & Nelson, 2005). In this section, we concentrate on the practical lessons associated with the lean start-up approach to those of you seriously considering setting up a new business.

The lean start-up approach was initiated by Eric Ries who authored a book about his practical experiences as a young entrepreneur. *The Lean Start-up* (Ries, 2011) was responsible for changing the approach to starting a business: 'hundreds of thousands of copies were sold in short time, and his theories became known and used worldwide, becoming a reference among entrepreneurs' (Bortolini, Danilevicz & Ghezzi, 2018, p. 1766). Lean start-up also incorporates ideas developed by Steve Blank, about the importance of regular engagement with customers (Blank, 2013; Blank & Dorf, 2020). Traditionally, teaching entrepreneurship and business start-up concentrated on the preparation of detailed business plans. Ries (2011) rejects this static approach in favour of what he described as 'business model validation' (BMV) based on incremental improvements to your basic business model. The original vision and associated business idea are usually developed prior to engaging in the lean start-up methodology. Hence, why we discuss the approaches to idea generation in Chapter 3.

Lean start-up begins with entrepreneurs transforming their business ideas into a basic business model (focusing on CVP, market segment and revenue as discussed in Section 4.2). The lean approach is intended to reduce the time and resources invested by the prospective entrepreneur (i.e., you!) in a non-viable business idea. The lean approach to start-up means minimizing time spent on product development and in favour of obtaining early customer feedback (Ries, 2011). Having established a basic business model, you should then generate hypotheses that can be tested by obtaining feedback from potential customers. This approach to business start-up can be summarized in what Ries (2011) describes as 'build-measure-learn'. In the case of a service, rather than a tangible product, build may refer to specifying the nature of the offering. For example, in the case of Jazooli, the younger brother began the business buying and selling mobile phones and accessories on eBay. While these 'hypotheses' were not explicitly stated, the underpinned Sam's approach once he realized that he could make money from his eBay activities (see Box 3.1, Chapter 3, Section 3.3).

CVP

I believe that young people (aged between 15 and 21) will buy mobile phone accessories (cases) online if they are cheaper than they can buy in high street stores.

I believe that customers are more likely to make a repeat purchase if their orders are delivered promptly

I believe incentivizing customers by offering a 10% reduction on their next purchase means they will provide positive feedback on our website

Market Segment

I believe that our offering will be most attractive to IT literate young people (15 to 21) who are in school or further/higher education.

I believe that keeping prices below our direct competitors will be the most important factor in attracting and retaining customers in our chosen segment

Revenue model

I believe that in the first month of trading we will attract a total of 200 customers making and average purchase of £10 equating to an income of £2000.

I believe that by the sixth month of trading we will attract 1000 customers per week spending an average of £10 equating to a weekly income of £10,000.

Your hypotheses should then be tested by talking to potential customers about the product/service and obtaining useful feedback. Ries (2011) refers to this stage as 'build' as he is focused on technological products. In terms of services, 'build' refers to the way in which you test your hypotheses by talking to customers. This might appear relatively straight-forward but if you are to obtain reliable results about how to proceed then you must adopt a rigorous approach. Therefore, you should consider how you will identify your sample, how many potential customers you will engage and how you will decide whether to accept or reject your hypotheses (i.e., the level of support – 70%, 80%, 90%, 95%). The latter issue falls into the category of 'measuring' your results and Ries (2011) suggests the use of statistical tools to assist analysis of the data. We believe that this is unlikely to be necessary unless you are anticipating large numbers of responses. This could, of course, be possible if you use social media (survey monkey) to elicit responses. Clearly the disadvantage of using social media is that you will have to reveal your business ideas to a very large audience. Given that you are unlikely to be able to protect your intellectual property as you could with a tangible product this is probably an unnecessary risk.

The final stage, 'learning', is when you consider whether, based on the data collected in stage two, you should accept or reject your hypotheses (Berends, van Burg & Garud, 2021). According to Ries (2011), there are three decisions you can make [persevere, perish or pivot]: a) accept the hypotheses and proceed with your existing business idea; b) reject the hypotheses and abandon the business idea; c) partially accept the hypotheses and modify your original business idea/model. For the majority, it is likely that option c) will apply and that the next stage means that you must identify the weaknesses in your idea and consider how they can be eliminated. The cycle should then be repeated until you are satisfied that your data indicate that you should proceed with your business idea (Figure 4.2). As illustrated in Figure 4.2, there are two distinct learning processes associated with the lean start-up model. Feedforward learning is based on the entrepreneur's cognition as the hypotheses associated with their business model are tested by engagement with customers. According to Berends, Smits, Reymen and

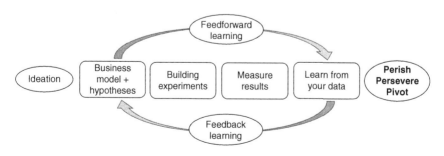

Figure 4.2 Business Model Development

Podoynitsyna (2016), this form of learning is based on 'forward-looking processes' in which entrepreneurs pursue actions based on cognitive representations (Mackay & Burt, 2015). Secondly, experiential learning is 'backward-looking' as feedback from customers is used to make decisions about the validity of the original business model (Berends et al., 2016; Jones and Giordano, 2021).

In line with lean start-up, the main point of the process illustrated in Figure 4.2 is that you learn quickly without investing a substantial amount of resource (time and finance) until you have obtained positive customer feedback (minimum viable product). This direct engagement with customers enables you to make incremental improvements to your business model enhancing the likelihood of a successful launch. As we will discuss later, this approach to business start-up has strong similarities to effectuation theory and bootstrapping. Mansoori (2017, p. 818) describes the business model development process as 'validated learning through purposeful experimentation'. The importance of the model is that it describes a 'cyclical process' as the business model is refined through regular engagement with customers. It is, of course, possible that the original business model is welcomed by customers and no modifications are required. However, in our experience this is an unusual occurrence. In summary, the outcome of the process is that you (the entrepreneur) must decide whether to **persevere** (continue with your existing business model), **pivot** (adjust your business model considering learning from customers), **perish** (decide your business model is not viable and abandon the start-up) (Berends et al., 2021).

Even if you decide that you are not going to pursue your original idea, we believe that the learning process will be valuable and should provide useful insight into your own abilities as an entrepreneur as well as the potential of your business idea (Andries et al., 2020).

4.5 Role of Design Thinking in Start-up

It is claimed by Garbuio, Dong, Lin, Tschang and Lovallo (2018, p. 45) that 'the practice of entrepreneurship education, the lean start-up approach and the business model canvas practice both build on the management discourse of design thinking' (Blank, 2013; Blank & Dorf, 2020; Ries, 2011). As we discuss above, the lean start-up approach is based on ideas associated with lean manufacturing: enhanced quality through incremental improvement and regular customer feedback. The concept of a 'minimal viable product' means that entrepreneurs can discuss their ideas with customers and 'pivot' the business model based on responses obtained from the marketplace. Similarly, the business model canvas approach shares several characteristics with design thinking: a focus on identifying users' needs, a cross discip-linary view of the business model and its customer value proposition (design of the product or service).

According to Tim Brown a leading proponent of design thinking in business, innovation (in this case, new business ideas) 'is powered by a thorough understanding, through direct observation, of what people want and need in their lives' (Brown, 2008, p. 85). Note, the direct link with the lean start-up methodology discussed above (via early contact with customers). Traditionally, design thinking has been associated with tan-gible consumer durables such as cars, television sets, hi-fi equipment and sporting goods (training shoes, tennis racquets, golf clubs etc). In recent years Apple[3] products have been successful largely because of the pleasing design of their personal computers, tablets, mobile phones and portable music devices (ipod). Design thinking influences not only the look of Apple's products but also their 'usability' in term of the interface between device and user. In fact, most electronic manufacturers follow the Apple template for the look, feel and operation of their smartphones. Swedish furniture company Ikea are also well known for the distinctiveness of their designs. Ikea adopts an approach it describes as 'democratic design,[4] which is based on five principles: form, function, quality, sustainability and low price. Increasingly, design thinking has been applied to a wide range of services as well as products. You could, for example, think about websites you regularly use and consider the ones that are well-designed and those that fail the good design test. Brown (2008, p. 87) goes on to outline the profile of a design thinker:

- **Empathy** – the ability to see the world from multiple perspectives including friends, colleagues, end users and customers. Taking a 'people first' helps design thinkers to imagine solutions that are desirable and meet customer needs. Design thinkers are good observers and they notice things that others do not see.
- **Integrative thinking** – using analytical processes is important in design but it is also essential to try and see the 'bigger picture'. In other words, try to develop the ability to see how your potential product or services

fits with other elements of the lives of your target customers. Are there complementary products and services for example?

- **Optimism** – design thinking, similar to starting a new business, is a challenge and you should be prepared to consider a wide-range of alternatives rather than settling for the first solution that comes to mind. Remaining optimistic means that you always believe that you can find a better solution to a problem.
- **Experimentalism** – design thinkers should be prepared to pose questions and explore various constraints in creative ways that could proceed in entirely new directions.
- **Collaboration** – the increasing complexity of products, services and experiences has replaced the myth of the lone creative genius with the reality of the enthusiastic interdisciplinary collaborator. Therefore, it is important to share your ideas with other people so that you can obtain useful feedback.

Garbuio et al. (2018) explicitly link design thinking to entrepreneurship education by suggesting that both disciplines encourage students to look at the world in new ways. They begin by suggesting that several recent developments support the need to adopt design thinking in entrepreneurship education. First, the wider recognition that opportunities are created rather than discovered as suggested by earlier entrepreneurship theorists (Shane etc). Secondly, opportunity creation is essentially a cognitive skill, which can be learnt and practised in the classroom. Thirdly, as we discuss in Section 4.3, there is an increasing awareness of the lean start-up approach with its focus on the generation of hypotheses. Fourthly, design is recognized as a cognitive construct rather than a process-based construct. What this means in terms of entrepreneurial education is that students should be encouraged to develop their cognitive skills (different ways of thinking) rather than instructed about design processes and tools (Garbuio et al., 2018, p. 43). The authors go on to propose that there are four cognitive foundations to design thinking related to entrepreneurship and opportunity creation.

1. **Framing** – is the foundation of creative thinking, which is associated with the need to resolve 'problematic situations' such as developing a new business idea. Framing means that you need to think more broadly about a problem related to opportunity identification and creation.

In practice, you should consider opportunity creation from extreme or opposite positions. A common business idea suggested by students is a second-hand book shop on campus, which might involve talking to potential customers who would primarily be other students. Taking an extreme position might suggest that most students no longer buy books (second-hand or otherwise). Alternatively, you might hypothesize that buying books becoming more popular among some young people. The recent revitalization of the market for vinyl records and cassette tapes is an example of the re-emergence of so-called obsolete technologies. What are the implications of these competing 'hypotheses' for the idea of a second-hand bookstore?

2. **Analogical Reasoning** – focuses on the importance of using analogies to help identify new opportunities. You might recall some appropriate knowledge from previous experiences (as a student or customer) and apply it to a new situation or problem. For example, the low-cost airlines such as EasyJet took the basic principles of fast-food delivery (McDonaldization) and applied those principle to air travel (no frills service and payment for extras such as seat reservations). Garbuio et al. (2018) give the example of Apple's iPod, which was based on the analogy of 'music on the move' as provided by the Sony Walkman (personal cassette tape player). However, Apple replaced the limited cassette tape with the flexibility of digital music storage.

3. **Abductive Reasoning** – adopting a logical approach to explain some unexpected data or phenomena; the differences between what people say they do and what they do in practice. Individuals may say that they care about the environment and worry about global warming – but at the same time – take long-haul flights to distant holiday destinations. You could hypothesize that individuals feel that aircraft would continue to fly long-haul routes even if they chose not to travel. Hence, their decision would have no impact on lessening the environmental damage. Clearly such tensions can provide entrepreneurs with opportunity creation in terms of holidays in 'green' resorts that care for the environment and establish real jobs for local people.

4. **Mental Simulation** – this refers to the testing out of ideas related to the operation of a new business opportunity based on an untried business model. As we discussed in Section 4.3, mapping the essential elements of your business idea onto the business model canvas helps test out its

potential. In other words, having identified a potential business opportunity you should 'mentally simulate' the idea by asking the following questions:

- How will your idea work in the marketplace?
- How will you scale the business?
- How will competitors react when you start your business?

In responding to a) you should concentrate on the core elements of the business model: customer value proposition, market segment and your revenue model (how are you going to make money?). You should then consider how you will scale the business by selling more to existing customers or acquiring more customers (different market segment or expanding geographically). Point c) refers to an issue which is rarely addressed by most inexperienced entrepreneurs. It is unlikely that any competitor will welcome new entrants into the marketplace and existing organizations will generally have more resources to deter start-up businesses. For example, the owner of a small, local grocery store in Newcastle (UK) decided to use the name Singhbury's for his business and was issued with a legal challenge by Sainsbury's. Not able to afford the fees to take on the supermarket he changed the name to Morrisingh's (which was not challenged by the owners of Morrison's supermarkets). McDonald's have regularly taken legal action against small businesses using Mc in their trading names. For example, McCurry, a small Malaysian restaurant, did eventually win the right to continue using the name after a legal battle that lasted more than six years.

Dziadkiewicz (2017) draws on the work of Blank (2013) to stress the importance of customer development based on the design thinking approach. As outlined above, following the 'ideation' stage, entrepreneurs use the business model framework to map-out the essential elements of the business idea. Paying particular attention to the customer value proposition (CVP) so that you can articulate the features that differentiate your product or service from existing competitors [see point a) above]. The ability to 'empathize' with customers gives greater insight into their needs and helps entrepreneurs design products/services that are attractive to those consumers. The approach we are describing here differs from the conventional 'business plan' approach because of the focus on early interaction with customers. Consequently, entrepreneurs can make adjustment (pivot) to their product/service before they have invested too much in terms of

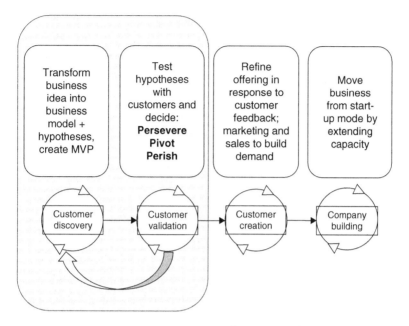

Figure 4.3 Customer Development Model

their resources (time and finance). These early activities are summarized in Figure 4.3 (customer development and customer validation), as the entrepreneur engaging the customer in a learning experience, which informs their decisions about the next stage (pivot, persevere or perish). In other words, should you proceed with the original idea (persevere), redesign your product/service (pivot) or decide to abandon your existing idea (perish). Once the idea has been validated by customers, then the final refinements are made to the offering and the entrepreneur then focuses on sales and marketing to build future demand [point c) above]. You should then be in a position to move from start-up mode into a fully operational business delivering products or services to the marketplace (customer creation and company building).

In summary, Garbuio et al. (2018, p. 55) suggest that there are several benefits to 'would-be' entrepreneurs of adopting a design thinking approach during the early stages of business start-up. First, experience in using the foundational tools (framing, analogy, abduction and simulation) helps individuals develop their cognitive abilities. Secondly, the interaction of framing and observing demonstrates the dynamics of consumer choices. In other words, it is important for students to recognize the constantly evolving nature of the marketplace as new products and services are constantly introduced. Thirdly, practice using cognitive tools helps 'demystify' the designer as 'creative genius' or the entrepreneur as having unique abilities to identify new business opportunities. Finally, early exposure to the importance of cognition in entrepreneurship helps build students' self-confidence and develops higher levels of resilience through the process of learning from experience. In other words, creativity is a skill that can be acquired with regular practice in the classroom and in your daily lives (thinking about how you could *design* a better service in your favourite café, bar, restaurant or even in the university library!).

4.6 The Role of Digitalization

In this section we discuss the relevance of digitalization to those of you who are seriously considering starting your own businesses. The emergence of digital technologies in the last 25 years has opened-up a wide-range of entrepreneurial opportunities as well as making starting a business quite straight-forward for anyone with a mobile phone or a computer. Elsewhere (Section 4.4) we discuss a company started by an 11-year-old schoolboy who began trading mobile phones on eBay and gradually built-up a substantial Internet-based business with his brother. Therefore, setting up a digital business is an effective way in which you can incorporate the ideas discussed earlier in the chapter: business models, lean start-up and design thinking.

The links between digitalization and entrepreneurship came to public attention at the end of the C20th with the emergence of the so-called dot. com boom (Cellan-Jones, 2001). Entrepreneurs making use of e-commerce to establish new firms also led to the emergence of academic interest in the concept of business models (Baden-Fuller & Morgan, 2010; Hedman & Kalling, 2003; Morris et al., 2005; Osterwalder & Pigneur, 2005; Zott & Amit, 2017). It was quickly recognized that digital businesses (clicks) had very different business models than traditional organizations (bricks). Taking retail as example, the emerging new businesses no longer had to invest in expensive stores to sell their goods. This trend has been accentuated during the recent Covid-19 pandemic when high-street retailers have lost-out to their online rivals (Kuckertz et al., 2020). Most existing retail business have responded to threat of e-commerce by investing in digital offering – the so-called 'bricks and clicks'. Certainly prior to the pandemic, some companies such as John Lewis in the UK had been reasonably successful in combing their traditional stores with goods sold online.

Digital entrepreneurship refers to businesses in which some or all the activity takes place online: the creation and/or distribution of products/services or in some cases the workplace itself (Fossen & Sorgner, 2021). Digital entrepreneurship fits neatly with the earlier themes of lean start-up and design thinking because of the focus on dynamic customer needs (Hull, Hung, Hair, Perotti & De Martino, 2007). Initially, the key enabler of electronic commerce was the Internet itself, hence the dot.com boom of the late 1990s. Subsequently, a wide range of digital technologies (mobile computing, cloud computing, social media, 3D printing, data analytics/artificial intelligence (AI) and gaming) provide numerous entrepreneurial opportunities (Landoni et al., 2020; Xu & Koivumäki, 2019). Nambisan (2017) suggest that there are three distinct categories of digital technologies that are important to entrepreneurs. First, *digital artifacts*, which are components, applications or media content that form part of a product/service and offer value to end-users. Because knowledge is stored digitally, it can be incorporated into a range of devices including PCs, tablets, mobile phones, smart watches as well as home appliances such as refrigerators, cookers, washing machines, toasters and even toothbrushes. Secondly, the term *digital platform* refers to a shared set of services with a common architecture that host a range of complementary offerings. The most widely used platforms are Apple's iOS, Google's Android and Microsoft Windows. These digital platforms provide entrepreneurs with opportunities to create specialist apps that are then widely available to consumers. Thirdly, the *digital infrastructure* including the Internet, broadband networks, mobile telecommunications, cloud computing, data analytics, online communities, social media and 3D printing, all provide complementary capabilities for entrepreneurs. For example, the emergence of crowdfunding and crowdsourcing would not have been possible without creation of the digital infrastructure (Boudreau, Jeppesen, Reichstein & Rullani, 2021; Landström, Parhankangas & Mason, 2019). Equally, digital makerspace and data analytics enable entrepreneurs to get rapid feedback on their product/services (Nambisan, 2017).

An important aspect of digitalization is that it can substantially reduce the time it takes to enact the entrepreneurial process. Ideas can be fleshed-out onto the business model canvass and hypotheses tested, modified and reintroduced (as per the lean start-up model). Digitalization also offers opportunities for entrepreneurs to rapidly scale-up in size once their business model has been validated. Another important aspect of digitalization is that it places more focus on opportunity creation rather than opportunity identification. The latter is associated with the traditional approach to starting a business based on the creation of a detailed business plan (Shane, 2003). Consequently, we suggest that digital businesses fit closely with the key themes on which this book is based: bootstrapping, effectuation and learning. We discuss these links in more detail in Chapters 5 and 9.

Digitalization has reduced the barriers to entry for those considering starting a business. The revolution in ICT (Information and Communication and Technologies) means that communicating with suppliers and customers is no longer constrained by geographical boundaries (Xu & Koivumäki, 2019; Zhao, Barratt-Pugh, Standen, Redmond & Suseno, 2021). Consequently, your business could be 'global' from the moment you begin to trade. Even in the quite recent past, most start-up businesses would have been focused on their local market and, if successful, would gradually have expanded their activities to offer products/services nationally, internationally and globally (Ben Youssef, Boubaker, Dedaj & Carabregu-Vokshi, 2021). In terms of the start-up business, digitalization is associated with several activities (Hair, Wetsch, Hull, Perotti & Hung, 2012; Hull et al., 2007). Any entrepreneur establishing a new company will almost certainly have a website as a basis for the company's *digital marketing*. Engaging in digital marketing is likely to be more effective and substantially cheaper than using traditional marketing media. In addition, social media has become increasingly widely used as a marketing channel for new businesses. Secondly, *digital sales* refer to the ability of customers to buy a company's products/services directly via their PC, tablet or mobile phone. For example, during the pandemic lockdown when conventional restaurants began to offer 'click and collect' services (or home delivery by *Deliveroo/Justeat* etc.), customers paid electronically for their food at the time of ordering.

Thirdly, *digital distribution* describes the delivery of products/services electronically rather than in traditional ways. Most software packages (such as computer operating systems, computer games etc.) are now paid for and downloaded directly from the web. Whereas, ten years ago, the majority of software products were delivered by means of a physical artifact (CD-Rom), which customers would download to their PC or laptop. Also, the emergence of services such as Amazon Marketplace allow small business to sell and distribute their products and services using the power of the Amazon brand name. Fourthly, and closely related to digital distribution, *digital operations* describe the 'modes of interaction' within the business itself. Increasingly, digitalization means that many new businesses can operate based on what might be described as a network model. What this means in practice is the entrepreneur may be able to establish their business without the need for a conventional office or storage facilities. Clearly if your business is based on a complex physical product (personal computer) or requires sophisticated processes (chemicals) you will certainly need a building with all the associated services. However, the majority of student start-ups (unless you are an engineer or a scientist) are unlikely to require anything more than a computer and a mobile phone to get the business started. This has numerous advantages because it minimizes many of the traditional risks associated with starting a new business. Digitalization lowers the financial investment required to start a business, reduces the transaction costs associated with developing both marketing and distribution channels. Digitalization also minimizes transport obstacles and eliminates the physical limitations of time and space, which helps new entrepreneurs to enlarge their customer base (Saridakis, Lai, Mohammed & Hansen, 2018).

Digital start-ups are important because they have their potential to create value and wealth to consumers (Ratzinger, Amess, Greenman & Mosey, 2018). Knowledge creation is the basis of the growth in digital start-ups and that focuses attention of university departments such as computer science and business schools (Kollmann, 2006). Ratzinger et al. (2018) attempted to examine the links between human capital (university education) and the creation of digital start-ups. Using a crowdsourced database known as *Crunchbase*, the authors obtained a sample of almost 5000 digital start-ups. They were able to confirm that human capital, measured by university education, was statistically significant in terms of reaching the 'investment milestones' measured on the following scale: self-sustaining, external funding and exit the business (Ratzinger et al., 2018, p. 767). Unsurprisingly, those with a technical education were the most successful in reaching their investment milestones. Less obviously, students with degrees from the humanities/social science were more successful than those with a business education. The level of higher education (BA/BSc, MSc and PhD) was also positively associated with entrepreneurial success, although the impact was fairly marginal (between 2% and 4%). Ratzinger et al. (2018, p. 774) summarize by say that that 'increased formal business and technical education within founding teams increases the probability of reaching investment milestones for digital 'start-ups'. The links between human capital and entrepreneurship are considered in more detail in Chapter 7.

4.7 Summary and Key Learning Points

In this chapter we have introduced four related concepts: business models, lean start-up, design thinking and digitalization. The majority of recent graduates who are thinking of starting a new business are likely to have very limited resources – particularly finance. Therefore, any initiative that helps minimize the risks associated with the failure of start-ups is worth considering. All new entrepreneurs considering starting a business should reflect on the role of digitalization. As discussed in Section 4.6, digitalization has made it much more straight-forward to set-up a new business particularly in terms of relationships with customers and suppliers. Most digital businesses will not need to invest in costly physical infrastructure such as a building or specialized equipment. This minimizes risks during the early stages of operation and also makes it easier to scale-up business activity. We suggest that digitalization fits neatly with the underlying principles of the lean start-up methodology. Similarly, lean start-up is based on the business model canvass in which the basic business idea is mapped out. We suggest that, initially, the focus should be on developing a clear understanding of the customer value proposition (CVP), market segment and the revenue model. Establishing how your offering will add value to existing products/ services in the marketplace is an essential first step. This should be followed by identification of the customers you will target and calculation of how you will make a profit. In the lean start-up approach, the next stage is to engage potential customers to obtain feedback on their response to your offering. Consequently, you must then decide on your next step: perish (give-up on the idea), persevere (continue with your original idea) or pivot (make modifications to your original idea). The latter case is the most likely outcome and this early engagement with customers means that you can modify your ideas without having made a major financial investment. The concept of design thinking ties the other three topics (business models, lean start-up and digitalization) because a well-designed product or service with features that are attractive to consumers will have more chance of succeeding in the marketplace. Good design skills are central to the pivot outcome as illustrated in Figure 4.3, because you will be required to modify your offering in response to feedback from potential customers. Therefore, the key learning points from this chapter are as follows:

- You should have a clear understanding of the key elements of a basic business model and be able to distinguish between the three **customer and market components** and the three **value creation components**. You should also be clear about why it is important to focus on the customer and market components at the early stages of start-up.
- We believe that understanding the lean start-up approach to business creation is key to minimizing your investment and the associated risks for new entrepreneurs. The principle underpinning the LSM is that you should learn from early engagement with customers as you attempt to validate your business model.
- There are two complementary learning processes associated with the lean start-up approach (Figure 4.2), feedforward learning as you test your ideas with customers and feedback learning as you reflect on what you have heard from those customers.
- Design thinking is a useful business skill that can be developed with practice rather than an attribute only associated with gifted individuals. You can improve your design thinking by exercises in the classroom but also by considering the strengths and weaknesses of existing products/ services (websites for example).
- It is almost impossible to think about the creation of new business ventures without considering the impact of digitalization. Even craft-based businesses will attract more customers if they have a *well-designed* website. But in developing your business model it is essential to think about how you can make use of the digital infrastructure to minimize costs as well as enhancing the links to customers, suppliers and other stakeholders.
- Finally, you need to take a 'holistic' view of the four concepts introduced in this chapter and think seriously about how they fit together in the development and operationalization of your business idea.

4.8 Discussion Questions and Call to Action

1. Why is it important to distinguish between the three customer & market components and the value-added components of your business model?

2. How would you describe the core features of the lean start-up model and how does it differ from conventional approaches to starting a new business?

3. What are the activities that link lean start-up to your business model?

4. What are the three possible outcomes associated with business model developing and the testing of your hypotheses?

5. Why is early engagement with customers central to both the lean start-up methodology and design thinking?

6. What are the differences between analogical reasoning and abductive reasoning and how these two concepts are linking in design thinking?

7. What are the most significant ways in which digitalization will impact on your business model?

8. What are the advantages and disadvantages associated with the use of crowdfunding?

The belief that entrepreneurs are born is one of the most persistent myths associated with business and management. We acknowledge that some individuals may have a predisposition to certain careers. Some may be very good at sport, others attracted by the arts or the sciences. Equally, there may be some people who appear to be 'natural' entrepreneurs such as Sam Wilson (Box 3.1, Chapter 3), who began his entrepreneurial careers in primary school. Clearly you do not need a BSc, MSc or PhD in business and management to become an entrepreneur. However, as we discuss in Chapter 7, there are strong links between higher levels of human capital and the success of start-up businesses.

In this chapter, we have introduced four apparently disparate concepts and it is our belief that they are strongly linked together. Therefore, developing a business model using the principles of the lean start-up approach, design thinking and digitalization is certainly something that you can practice. For example, in Section 4.2 we discuss the role of 'mental simulation' in testing-out your business ideas. Answering these three questions is a worthwhile exercise, which will benefit from discussion with your classmates and your teacher:

*   How will your idea work in the marketplace?
*   How will you scale the business?
*   How will competitors react when you start your business?

Notes

1 www.inc.com/live
2 At the time of this study, Jazooli was described as ECessori for reasons of commercial confidentiality as the company was undergoing a trade sale.
3 www.cleverism.com/why-apple-design-successful/
4 https://about.ikea.com/en/life-at-home/how-we-work/democratic-design

References

Afuah, A. (2019). *Business model innovation: concepts, analysis, and cases* (2nd ed. ed.). New York: Routledge.

Ambos, T. C. & Birkinshaw, J. (2010). How Do New Ventures Evolve? An Inductive Study of Archetype Changes in Science-Based Ventures. *Organization Science, 21*(6), 1125–1140.

Amit, R. & Zott, C. (2001). Value Creation in E-Business. *Strategic Management Journal, 22*(6/7), 493–520.

Amit, R. & Zott, C. (2015). Crafting Business Architecture: the Antecedents of Business Model Design. *Strategic Entrepreneurship Journal, 9*(4), 331–351.

Amit, R,. & Zott, C. (2021). *Business Model Innovation Strategy*. New York: Oxford University Press.

Andries, P. & Debackere, K. (2007). Adaptation and Performance in New Businesses: Understanding the Moderating Effects of Independence and Industry. *Small Business Economics, 29*(1/2), 81–99.

Andries, P. & Debackere, K. (2013). Business Model Innovation: Propositions on the Appropriateness of Different Learning Approaches. *Creativity and Innovation Management, 22*(4), 337–358.

Andries, P., Debackere, K. & Van Looy, B. (2013). Simultaneus Experiementation as a Learning Strategy: Business Model Development Under Uncertainty. *Strategic Entere[preneurship Journal, 7*(4), 288–310.

Andries, P., Debackere, K. & Van Looy, B. (2020). Simultaneous experimentation as a learning strategy: Business model development under uncertainty – Relevance in times of COVID-19 and beyond. *Strategic Entrepreneurship Journal, 14*(4), 556–559.

Baden-Fuller, C. & Morgan, M. S. (2010). Business Models as Models. *Long Range Planning, 43*(2), 156–171.

Baker, T. & Nelson, R. E. (2005). Creating Something from Nothing: Resource Construction through Entrepreneurial Bricolage. *Administrative Science Quarterly, 50*, 329–366.

Ben Youssef, A., Boubaker, S., Dedaj, B. & Carabregu-Vokshi, M. (2021). Digitalization of the economy and entrepreneurship intention. *Technological Forecasting & Social Change, 164*. doi:10.1016/j.techfore.2020.120043

Berends, H., Smits, A., Reymen, I. M. M. J. & Podoynitsyna, K. (2016). Learning while (re)configuring: Business model innovation processes in established firms. *Strategic Organization, 14*(3), 181–219.

Berends, H., van Burg, E. & Garud, R. (2021). Pivoting or persevering with venture ideas: Recalibrating temporal commitments. *Journal of Business Venturing, 36*(4). doi:10.1016/j.jbusvent.2021.106126

Blank, S. (2013). Why the Lean Start-Up Changes Everything. *Harvard Business Review, 91*(5), 63–72.

Blank, S. & Dorf, B. (2020). *The startup owner's manual: the step-by-step guide for building a great company*. Hoboken, NJ: Wiley.

Boland, R. J. & Collopy, F. (2004). Toward a Design Vocabulary for Management. In R. J. Boland, Jr. & F. Collopy (Eds.), *Managing as designing* (pp. 265–276). Stanford: Stanford University Press, Stanford Business Books.

Bortolini, R. F., M., N. C., Danilevicz, A. M. F. & Ghezzi, A. (2018). Lean Startup: a comprehensive historical review. *Management Decision, 59*(8), 1765–1783.

Boudreau, K. J., Jeppesen, L. B., Reichstein, T. & Rullani, F. (2021). Crowdfunding as Donations to Entrepreneurial Firms. *Research Policy, 50*(7). doi:10.1016/j.respol.2021.104264.

Brettel, M., Strese, S. & Flatten, T. C. (2012). Improving the performance of business models with relationship marketing efforts – An entrepreneurial perspective. *European Management Journal, 30*(2), 85–98.

Brown, T. (2008). Design Thinking. *Harvard Business Review, 86*(6), 84–92.

Burton, M. D. & Beckman, C. M. (2007). Leaving a legacy: Position imprints and successor turnover in young firms / Laisser un héritage: empreinte de la situation et le renouvellement du personnel dans les jeunes entreprises. *American Sociological Review, 72*(2), 239–266.

Casadesus-Masanell, R. & Ricart, J. E. (2010). From Strategy to Business Models and onto Tactics. *Long Range Planning, 43*(2), 195–215.

Cavalcante, S., Kesting, P. & Ulhøi, J. (2011). Business model dynamics and innovation: (re)establishing the missing linkages. *Management Decision, 49*(8), 1327–1342.

Cellan-Jones, R. (2001). *Dot.bomb: the rise & fall of dot.com Britain*. London: Aurum.

Chandler, G. N., Broberg, J. C. & Allison, T. H. (2014). Customer Value Propositions in Declining Industries: Differences between Industry Representative and High-Growth Firms. *Strategic Entrepreneurship Journal, 8*(3), 234–253.

Chesbrough, H. (2010). Business Model Innovation: Opportunities and Barriers. *Long Range Planning, 43*(2), 354–363.

Chesbrough, H. & Rosenbloom, R. S. (2002). The role of the business model in capturing value from innovation: evidence from Xerox Corporation's technology spin-off companies. *Industrial & Corporate Change, 11*(3), 529–555.

DaSilva, C. M. & Trkman, P. (2014). Business Model: What It Is and What It Is Not. *Long Range Planning, 47*(6), 379–389.

Demil, B. & Lecocq, X. (2010). Business model evolution: in search of dynamic consistency. *Long Range Planning, 43*(2/3), 227–246.

Deming, W. E. (1982). *Out of the crisis: quality, productivity and competitive position*. Cambridge: Cambridge University Press.

Doganova, L. & Eyquem-Renault, M. (2009). What do business models do?: Innovation devices in technology entrepreneurship. *Research Policy, 38*(10), 1559–1570.

Dziadkiewicz, A. (2017). Customer Value Development in the Light of Design Thinking Approach *Journal of Positive Management, 8*(3), 58–68.

Easterby-Smith, M., Araujo, L. & Burgoyne, J. (1999). *Organizational Learning and the Learning Organization: Developments in Theory and Practice*. London: Sage Publications Ltd.

Fiet, J. O. & Patel, P. C. (2008). Forgiving Business Models for New Ventures. *Entrepreneurship: Theory & Practice, 32*(4), 749–761.

Fossen, F. M. & Sorgner, A. (2021). Digitalization of work and entry into entrepreneurship. *Journal of Business Research, 125*, 548–563.

Garbuio, M., Dong, A., Lin, N., Tschang, T. & Lovallo, D. (2018). Demystifying the Genius of Entrepreneurship: How Design Cognition Can Help Create the Next Generation of Entrepreneurs. *Academy of Management Learning & Education, 17*(1), 41–61.

George, G. & Bock, A. J. (2011). The Business Model in Practice and its Implications for Entrepreneurship Research. *Entrepreneurship Theory and Practice, 35*(1), 83–111.

Geroski, P. A. (2003). *Where Do New Technologies Come From?* Oxford: Oxford University Press.

Ghezzi, A. (2019). Digital startups and the adoption and implementation of Lean Startup Approaches: Effectuation, Bricolage and Opportunity Creation in practice. *Technological Forecasting & Social Change, 146*, 945–960.

Hair, N., Wetsch, L. R., Hull, C. E., Perotti, V. & Hung, Y.-T. (2012). Market Advantage in Digital Entrepreneurship: Advantages and Challenges in a Web 2.0 Networked World. *International Journal of Innovation and Technology Management, 9*(06). doi:10.1142/S0219877012500459

Harrison, R. T., Mason, C. M. & Girling, P. (2004). Financial bootstrapping and venture development in the software industry. *Entrepreneurship & Regional Development, 16*(4), 307–333.

Hedman, J. & Kalling, T. (2003). The business model concept: theoretical underpinnings and empirical illustrations. *European Journal of Information Systems, 12*(1), 49–59.

Hull, C. E., Hung, Y.-T., Hair, N., Perotti, V. & De Martino, R. (2007). Taking advantage of digital opportunities: a typology of digital enterpreneurship. *International Journal of Networking & Virtual Organisations, 4*(3), 290–303.

Jayawarna, D., Jones, O. & Macpherson, A. (2020). Resourcing Social Enterprises: The Role of Socially Oriented Bootstrapping. *British Journal of Management, 31*(1), 56–79.

Johnson, M. W., Christensen, C. M. & Kagermann, H. (2008). Reinventing Your Business Model. (cover story). *Harvard Business Review, 86*(12), 50–59.

Jones, O. & Giordano, B. (2021). Family entrepreneurial teams: The role of learning in business model evolution. *Management Learning, 52*(3), 267–293.

Jones, O. & Jayawarna, D. (2010). Resourcing new businesses: social networks, bootstrapping and firm performance. *Venture Capital, 12*(2), 127–152.

Kollmann, T. (2006). What is e-entrepreneurship? – fundamentals of company founding in the net economy. *International Journal of Technology Management, 33*(4), 322–340.

Kuckertz, A., Brändle, L., Gaudig, A., Hinderer, S., Morales Reyes, C. A., Prochotta, A. & Berger, E. S. C. (2020). Startups in times of crisis – A rapid response to the COVID-19 pandemic. *Journal of Business Venturing Insights, 13.* doi:10.1016/j.jbvi.2020.e00169

Landoni, P., Dell'era, C., Frattini, F., Messeni, P. A., Verganti, R. & Manelli, L. (2020). Business model innovation in cultural and creative industries: Insights from three leading mobile gaming firms. *Technovation, 92–93.*

Landström, H., Parhankangas, A. & Mason, C. M. (2019). *Handbook of research on crowdfunding.* Cheltenham: Edward Elgar.

Mackay, D. & Burt, G. (2015). Strategic learning, foresight and hyperopia. *Management Learning, 46*(5), 546–564.

Mansoori, Y. (2017). Enacting the lean startup methodology: The role of vicarious and experiential learning processes. *International Journal of Entrepreneurial Behavior & Research, 23*(5), 812–838.

Massa, L., Tucci, C. L. & Afuah, A. (2017). A critical assessment of business model research. *The Academy of Management Annals, 11*(1), 73–104.

McMillan, C. J. (1992). Quality management: Lessons from Japan. *Business Quarterly, 57*(1), 111–115.

Morris, M. H., Schindehutte, M. & Allen, J. (2005). The entrepreneur's business model: toward a unified perspective. *Journal of Business Research, 58*(6), 726–735.

Mueller, S., Volery, T. & von Siemens, B. (2012). What do entrepreneurs actually do? An observational study of entrepreneurs' everyday behavior in the start-up and growth stages. *Entrepreneurship: Theory and Practice*, *36*(5), 995–1017.

Nambisan, S. (2017). Digital Entrepreneurship: Toward a Digital Technology Perspective of Entrepreneurship. *Entrepreneurship: Theory & Practice*, *41*(6), 1029–1055.

Osterwalder, A. & Pigneur, Y. (2005). Clarifying Business Models: Origins, Present, and Future of the Concept *Communications of the Association for Information Systems*, *16*, 1–25.

Pellikka, J. & Malinen, P. (2015). Fostering business growth and commercialisation processes in small high technology firms. International Journal of Business Environment, *7*(1), 98–118.

Ratzinger, D., Amess, K., Greenman, A. & Mosey, S. (2018). The Impact of Digital Start-Up Founders' Higher Education on Reaching Equity Investment Milestones. *Journal of Technology Transfer*, *43*(3), 760–778.

Ries, E. (2011). *The lean startup: how today's entrepreneurs use continuous innovation to create radically successful businesses*. New York: Crown Business.

Romme, G. L. (2003). Making a Difference: Organization as Design. *Organization Science*, *14*(5), 558–573.

Santos, F. M. & Eisenhardt, K. M. (2009). Constructing Markets and Shaping Boundaries: Entrepreneurial Power in Nascent Fields. *Academy of Management Journal*, *52*(4), 643–671.

Sarasvathy, S. D. (2012). Effectuation and Entrepreneurship. In S. Carter & D. Jones-Evans (Eds.), *Enterprise and Small Business: Principles, Practice and Policy* (3rd ed., pp. 135–151). Harlow: Pearson.

Saridakis, G., Lai, Y., Mohammed, A.-M. & Hansen, J. M. (2018). Industry characteristics, stages of E-commerce communications, and entrepreneurs and SMEs revenue growth. *Technological Forecasting & Social Change*, *128*, 56–66.

Selden, P. D. & Fletcher, D. E. (2015). The entrepreneurial journey as an emergent hierarchical system of artifact-creating processes. *Journal of Business Venturing*, *30*(4), 603–615.

Shane, S. (2003). *A General Theory of Entrepreneurship: The Individual-Opportunity Nexus*. Cheltenham: Edward Elgar.

Shepherd, D. A., Douglas, E. J. & Shanley, M. (2000). New venture survival: Ignorance, external shocks, and risk reduction strategies. *Journal of Business Venturing*, *15*(5), 393–410.

Wirtz, B. W., Pistoia, A., Ullrich, S. & Göttel, V. (2016). Business Models: Origin, Development and Future Research Perspectives. *Long Range Planning*, *49*(1), 36–54.

Womack, J. P., Jones, D. T. & Roos, D. (1990). *The machine that changed the world: the story of lean production*: New York: Rawson Associates.

Xu, Y. & Koivumäki, T. (2019). Digital business model effectuation: An agile approach. *Computers in Human Behavior, 95*, 307–314.

Zhao, F., Barratt-Pugh, L., Standen, P., Redmond, J. & Suseno, Y. (2021). An exploratory study of entrepreneurial social networks in the digital age. *Journal of Small Business and Enterprise Development, ahead-of-print* (ahead-of-print).

Zott, C. & Amit, R. (2010). Business Model Design: An Activity System Perspective. *Long Range Planning, 43*(2), 216–226.

Zott, C. & Amit, R. (2017). Business Model Innovation: How to Create Value in a Digital World. *Marketing Intelligence Review, 9*(1), 18–23.

5 | Entrepreneurial Learning and Business Start-up

5.1 Introduction

Whether entrepreneurs are 'born or made' and the extent to which entrepreneurship can be taught are two of the most persistence questions posed to those engaged in teaching enterprise-related subjects. While we acknowledge that some individuals are entrepreneurial from a very young age, our view is that entrepreneurship comprises a set of skills that can be acquired by any reasonably motivated student. A number of authors have tried to establish that there is a genetic component to entrepreneurship (Nicolaou, Shane, Cherkas, Hunkin & Spector, 2008). Shane, Nicolaou, Cherkas, and Spector (2010) examine links between genetics, the big five[1] and the likelihood of becoming self-employed by comparing a large sample of twins (monozygotic and dizygotic). The authors do concede that they were only able to identify a 'modest association' between two of the big five personality characteristics (extraversion and openness to experience) and the propensity to become an entrepreneur. In their recent paper, Ramoglou, Gartner and Tsang (2020, p. 4) dismiss the idea that there is something that can be described as an entrepreneurial gene:

> There are no 'hidden' entrepreneurial genes or necessary psychological traits. Entrepreneurs exercise a widely held agentic potential simply because they happen to believe that they can succeed entrepreneurially. And their belief is due to the way that they view the world – and worldviews are not rooted in genes, or traits, but in grammars.

DOI: 10.4324/9781003312918-6

Rather than relying on an entrepreneurial gene, an alternative explanation is that some families endow their children with attributes such as self-discipline, conscientiousness as well as good habits, including critical self-reflection and awareness of cognitive shortcuts (Aldrich & Yang, 2012). The authors go on to say that such social learning provides continuity in entrepreneurship across generations and is more important than specific entrepreneurial knowledge. We believe that the context and the influence of key individuals including parents are likely to be more important than any genetic predisposition towards entrepreneurship (Box 5.1).

Box 5.1 Parental Influence

Sam has probably told you it started off as a bit of hobby - but then it became evident, very early on, that it was something more than a hobby. I think he was about 13 when we discovered what he was up to - it started with second-hand mobile phones which he knew he could buy and sell. It became evident the amount of money he was making was becoming quite significant and I said to him, I think you should make this into a proper business. I like to think I have a bit of an entrepreneurial spirit myself because I have been self-employed for 20 years. So, whenever I have seen anything in the boys I have always tried to encourage it and that happened with Sam. Even when he was at primary school he got into a bit of trouble for selling pens [Martin Wilson, Jazooli].

Simply explaining key theoretical concepts such as opportunity identification or resource acquisition by means of conventional lectures is not an appropriate way to learn about entrepreneurship (Pfeifer & Borozan, 2011; Pocek, Politis & Gabrielsson, 2021). Effective entrepreneurship education must include a practical element in which students are able to apply ideas to which they have been introduced via lectures, tutorials or independent study. There are a number of ways in which this can be done which vary from computer simulations such as SimVenture, to starting a real business in programmes run by your university (Box 5.2), as well as extra-curriculum activities including organizations such Enactus and student societies such as the Liverpool Entrepreneurs Network Society[2] (LENS). In this chapter, we intend to demonstrate what is known about enterprise education and entrepreneurial learning (Byrne, Fayolle & Toutain, 2013; Fayolle, Kariv & Matlay, 2019). We then examine the implications for students of entrepreneurship in terms of the knowledge you need to acquire as well as your expectations about how such knowledge is acquired. The starting point is based on the view that there are a number of skills or competences associated with effective entrepreneurship. However, the ability to list or recite a set of competences, no matter how sophisticated, will not in itself turn undergraduate or postgraduate students into successful entrepreneurs. Learning has a strong social element and engaging in activities designed to encourage the sharing of knowledge and understanding is an essential element of the approach advocated in this book.

We begin by outlining the core elements of experiential learning, which has become central to our understanding of the ways in which new entrepreneurs acquire the appropriate knowledge, skills and competences.

Box 5.2 Introducing SimVenture

In SimVenture (www.simventure.co.uk/) players take on the role of entrepreneur in managing time and money to develop the business and resolve the issues that arise over the course of a game. The player makes decisions and receives feedback in monthly cycles. Any number of decisions can be made each month in four key business areas: organization; sales & marketing; finance; and operations. Based on these decisions the simulation responds each month and shows the number of enquiries, orders and sales generated - which determines the flow of money into the business.

SimVenture is designed to respond to best practice principles. Players who research markets, competitors and customers carefully and then analyse the data and take appropriate actions will always do better than those who use guesswork to drive decisions. The virtual company is managed on a month-by-month basis allowing learners to develop their business from start-up for a maximum of 36 months.

5.2 Learning Objectives

- To understand the significance of experiential learning as a basis for students making the transition to an entrepreneur career.
- To explain how social learning and cognitive learning contribute to a better the understanding of entrepreneurship.
- To identify the benefits of active learning and simulation in terms of enhancing entrepreneurial learning.
- Explain the role of extracurricular activities associated with enterprise clubs, societies and alumni associations in promoting entrepreneurial learning.
- Understand the importance of business incubators in encouraging business start-up and the role played by communities of practice.

5.3 Experiential Learning for Entrepreneurs

Until the beginning of the twenty-first century, courses offered by universities that dealt with entrepreneurship or the management of smaller firms were rare in the UK. In the US, the teaching of entrepreneurship has a much longer tradition and the first course was established in 1947 (Katz, 2003). In terms of the number of institutions offering courses in entrepreneurship, the field had reached maturity by the beginning of the C21st. This is further demonstrated by convergence in the topics of US text-books dealing with entrepreneurship and small business management (Katz, 2008). US enterprise education has also been strongly promoted by leading institutions such as the Kauffman Foundation (www.kauffman.org/) and Babson College (www.babson.edu). Kauffman has an extensive research programme designed to provide an in-depth understanding of what drives innovation and economic growth in entrepreneurship. Babson College[3] and the London Business School initiated the Global Entrepreneurship Monitor (GEM) in 1999. GEM, now a global consortium of over 500 researchers is the largest and most developed research programme on entrepreneurship in the world obtaining data from more than 120 countries. GEM is unique because it tracks rates of entrepreneurship across multiple business phases and assesses the characteristics, motivations and ambitions of entrepreneurs, as well as societal attitudes.

From around 2000, interest in entrepreneurship has grown rapidly and most UK institutions now offer courses on business start-up (Jones, 2022). Growth in teaching of entrepreneurship can be explained by increasing legitimization of the topic as an area of academic study. Allan Gibb's pioneering work focused on understanding the process of starting a new business (Gibb, 1987; Gibb & Ritchie, 1982). The authors begin by rejecting conventional 'trait' theory and, instead, argue that entrepreneurship is a social process that involves a series of transactions as individuals gain experience. Interestingly, the importance of family, friends and career development as well as primary, secondary and further education are noted as being influential (Gibb, 2002). This view fits closely with the importance of the entrepreneurial 'life-course', which is discussed in Chapter 7. In providing education for entrepreneurs and owners of small businesses, Gibb stressed the importance of entrepreneurship for creating new jobs and enhancing economic growth. In terms of entrepreneurial learning, Gibb focuses on the importance of an action learning approach which actively engages students. An extensive review of the literature considers UK and European responses to the challenge of enterprise education (Gibb, 2002). Gibb (2011) examines a programme designed to develop the skills of enterprise educators via the International Entrepreneurship Educators Programme (IEEP). A persistent theme in the literature is the central importance of entrepreneurs acquiring and developing the skills, heuristics and frameworks necessary to meet the changing demands of a growing business (Breslin & Jones, 2012) [also see Chapters 2, 10 and 11].

The importance of understanding the context in which entrepreneurial learning takes place has also been stressed by other key authors (Cope, 2005; Cope & Watts, 2000; Rae & Carswell, 2001). As indicated in Chapter 1, the concept of experiential learning (Kolb, 1984) has been widely influential in the field of entrepreneurship (Figure 5.1). In developing the learning cycle, Kolb drew extensively on a range of earlier authors (Dewey, 1938; Lewin, 1951; Piaget, 1926). The experiential learning cycle is based on the principle that knowledge is created by a combination of two dialectical processes: making sense of experience (prehension) and applying that experience (transformation). The prehension dimension varies from abstract conceptualization (comprehension) to concrete experience (apprehension). The transformative dimension varies from active experimentation (extension) to reflective observation (intention). These four basic learning modes can be summarized as follows:

Abstract Conceptualization: focuses on the 'scientific' ability to use logic, ideas and concepts as a way of understanding particular physical or social phenomena.

Concrete Experience: emphasises an artistic and intuitive approach (rather than a science-based approach) based on dealing with real situations in an intuitive manner.

Active Experimentation: focuses on directly influencing other people as a way of changing particular situations through a process of doing rather than observing.

Reflective Observation: understanding ideas and situations through a process of careful observation (rather than a focus on taking action).

Combining the two dimensions (Figure 5.1) illustrates four distinct and elementary forms of knowledge (Kolb, 1984). The essential idea underpinning the learning cycle is that knowledge creation and knowing requires the transformation of experience and the ability to be able to make sense of experience (prehension):

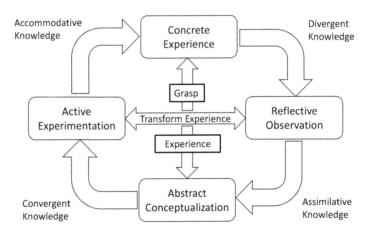

Figure 5.1 Kolb's Experiential Learning Cycle

Convergent knowledge is created by the combination of comprehension (abstract conceptualization) and transformation through extension (active experimentation).

Accommodative knowledge is created by the combination of apprehension (concrete experience) and transformed by extension (active experimentation).

Divergent knowledge is created through apprehension (concrete experience) and transformed by intention (reflective observation).

Assimilative knowledge is created through comprehension (abstract conceptualization) and transformed by intention (reflective observation).

Kolb's model has been used as the basis of a 'learning style inventory' (Honey & Mumford, 2001), which classifies learners into four types: activist, theorist, pragmatist and reflector. This is certainly a useful device for encouraging students to think about the way in which they learn. For example, 'theorists' learn best from the presentation of abstract ideas about entrepreneurship such as differences between opportunity identification and opportunity creation (Shane & Venkataraman, 2000). Alternatively, 'activists' learn best by actually trying out new things rather than listening to lectures dealing with various aspects of 'entrepreneurial theory'. Pragmatists are more concerned with trying things that actually work while reflectors learn best from observation.

The various learning style inventories based on Kolb's cycle have been criticized by a wide range of writers (Manolis, Burns, Assudani & Chinta, 2012). For example, test-retest experiments indicate that the scales do not reliably measure learning styles. Manolis et al. (2012) develop what they describe as a reduced learning style inventory (RLSI), which they suggest is superior to earlier measurement instruments. The authors argue that their instrument provides a more holistic measure of student learning styles. We suggest, however, that the benefit of such learning style inventories is not based on the extent to which they objectively measure an individual's particular approach to learning. Rather, learning style inventories can be used to encourage students to *reflect* on their responses to the various forms of pedagogy used in the teaching of entrepreneurship. Hence, rather than being a fixed psychological attribute 'learning style' is something to which students can adjust according to the context and the topic they are studying.

As we discuss in the following section, effective entrepreneurial learning has both cognitive and social elements (Cope & Down, 2010).

Some argue that Kolb's experiential learning theory (KELT) is based on the principles of cognitivism in which thinking is separated from experience and action. As Holman, Pavlica and Thorpe (1997, p. 139) argue in this model the learner is seen as an 'intellectual Robinson Crusoe'. Drawing on activity theory (Bakhtin, 1981; Vygotsky, 1978) the authors suggest that learning should be understood in the context of the learner's social relations (see Chapter 1). Learning is a process of 'argumentation' in which activities associated with thinking, reflecting, experiencing and taking action are mediated by the social, cultural and historical context in which the learner is situated (Holman et al., 1997). Kayes (2002), in particular, suggests that critics of KELT have not paid enough attention to the influence of Vygotsky's social constructivist learning theory. Eventually, Kolb and his colleagues explicitly extend KELT to account for the social processes associated with learning as well as cognitive processes (Baker, Jensen & Kolb, 2005). The authors propose that conversational learning helps learners construct new meaning and transform their collective experiences into knowledge and knowing (Baker et al., 2005, p. 412). While there are five dialectics associated with conversational learning theory, we concentrate on the two dimensions which are the basis of KELT: apprehension-comprehension and reflection-action.

Apprehension and Comprehension (Concrete Experience and Abstract Conceptualization)

The core dialectic of apprehension and comprehension means that knowledge is based on concrete knowing and abstract knowing (Kolb, 1984). There is constant tension between subjective, intuitive and emotional understanding and objective, abstract and rational understanding (this can be summarized as right brain – left brain thinking). In terms of entrepreneurial learning, this dialectic can be represented by, on the one hand, encouraging students to explore their previous experiences of entrepreneurship (perhaps through TV programmes such as *Dragon's Den*) and consider how that experience has influenced their perceptions of what it is to be an 'entrepreneur'. On the other hand, students can be presented with data related to numbers of start-ups per year, the proportion that obtain external finance as well as conceptual ideas such as resource-dependency theory or resource-deficiency theory. Promoting class conversations based on resolving the tension between students' feelings about entrepreneurship and more abstract theories/data related to entrepreneurial activity promotes deeper learning.

Extension and Intention (Reflective Observation and Active Experimentation)

The second dialectic of extension and intention means that there is a tension between the application of new knowledge (action) and a sense-making or mean-making process (reflection). Experiential learning approaches must create conversational space to help learners resolve the tension between action and reflection. In terms of entrepreneurial learning resolving this dialectic means students must engage in active experimentation by, for example, generating ideas for a potential new business. This should be combined with group (not individual) reflections on their experiences related to idea generation and encouraged to engage in conversations about the implications for their own understanding of what it means to be a nascent entrepreneur engaged in creating a new business.

This broader understanding of the experiential learning cycle is described as follows by Taylor and Pandza (2003). The four elements of the model (theorizing, action, experience and reflection) all take place within a social context. Therefore, it is essential that entrepreneurship courses provide plenty of opportunities for students to share their knowledge and understanding. Conventional activities such as preparing a business plan or participating in a simulation game (such as SimVenture) can easily be organized to accommodate social learning activities. Consequently, as we illustrate in Figure 5.2, the focus shifts from a concentration on cognitive learning (as described in the traditional Kolb cycle) to social learning as group activities encourage discussion and reflection as students move through the four stages of the model.

Cope's influential work draws heavily on KELT to stress the importance of basing entrepreneurial learning on an action-oriented process of co-participation (Cope, 2003, 2005; Pittaway & Cope, 2007; Pittaway & Thorpe, 2012; Politis, 2005). According to Cope (2005) there are five key areas which should be of concern in terms of entrepreneurial learning (Table 5.1). We have structured these five factors in a hierarchy because any

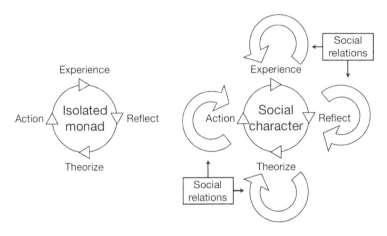

Figure 5.2 Extending Kolb' Experiential Learning Cycle

Table 5.1 Entrepreneurial Learning Tasks

LEARNING TASKS	ASSOCIATED ACTIVITIES
Learning about oneself	Evaluating strengths and weaknesses in terms of aptitude for entrepreneurship
Learning to manage relationships	Developing appropriate social skills to build relationships with resource providers
Learning about the business	Improving understanding of how the business works – making a profit
Learning about the environment and networks	Building relationships with stakeholders, customers, suppliers and competitors
Learning about business management	Acquiring the skills and knowledge necessary to grow the business

well- planned course should provide students with the opportunity to learn about themselves and the extent to which they have the attributes (persistence and resilience) to become entrepreneurs. Secondly, we see the acquisition of appropriate social skills as crucial to effective entrepreneurship (see Chapter 2). Therefore, the opportunity to learn about the nature and management of relationships is central to establishing businesses with real potential for growth. Learning about (the) business and learning about the environment and entrepreneurial networks are equally important to students of entrepreneurship. Finally, learning about small business is less important during the nascent entrepreneurship stage. Clearly, as the business becomes established, acquiring broader managerial skills such as human resource management or leadership will contribute to the longer-term success of the firm (Chapters 2 and 10).

In terms of 'learning in practice', it may be possible to accommodate the cognitive and social learning approaches to entrepreneurship education (Cope & Down, 2010). This idea builds on the work of Marshall (2008, p. 419) who suggests that the cognitive and practice perspectives are complementary because they provide a deeper understanding 'how unfolding social realities are constituted and enacted'. The earlier work of Burgoyne (1995) is also important in reconciling the cognitive and social perspectives on learning (Figure 5.3). Nascent entrepreneurs do not make decisions or undertake tasks related to starting their businesses in isolation from other social actors (Fearon, Furlotti, van Vuuren & McLaughlin, 2021). Participation refers to active encounters that are the basis of effective entrepreneurial learning. Such encounters can be formal elements of a module in which students are expected to engage in group-work: for example, brainstorming business ideas or preparing a business plan (see Chapter 3). Encounters can also be informal based on students' conversations outside the classroom (perhaps using social media) or your engagement with entrepreneurs,

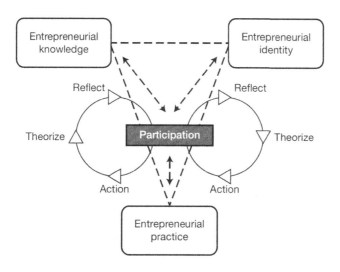

Figure 5.3 Combining Entrepreneurial Cognition and Practice

owner-managers or employees of smaller firms (this could occur as you engage in part-time work in a bar or restaurant). This idea of 'conversations' informing various activities associated with the learning cycle fits with the approach proposed by Baker et al. (2005).

Entrepreneurial knowledge is obviously a key issue for most undergraduates and postgraduates who are unlikely to have had direct exposure to the issues associated with small businesses. For such students, their understanding of entrepreneurship will be informed by the media via programmes such as *Dragon's Den* or through new-style entrepreneurs such as hip hop star Jay-Z who made the transition from drug dealer to high-profile businessman (Greenburg, 2011). Alternatively, it is well established that those who come from entrepreneurial families will generally have been exposed to the day-to-day problems of managing a small business (Zellweger, Nason & Nordqvist, 2012). Consequently, this group may have a much clearer understanding of what it takes to become an entrepreneur. As we indicated above, encouraging conversations among students about their different understanding of what it means to be an entrepreneur can be an enriching experience.

Identity refers to the extent to which the 'self' is recognized in the entrepreneurial process (Burke, 2006; Kasperova, Kitching & Blackburn, 2018). As pointed out by Down and Warren (2008) entrepreneurial identity is shaped by interactions between the individual, the venture and broader cultural influences. From a pedagogical perspective, entrepreneurial identity focuses attention on the way in which belonging to a community of practice provides opportunities for students to learn how to be an entrepreneur. For many, this will be a discomforting experience in which they must make the switch from the 'passivity' of being a student to the action associated with being an entrepreneur.

Entrepreneurial practice is not simply about doing things (capabilities); it also concerns learning the appropriate social skills such as negotiation with suppliers, customers, funders and other stakeholders. Rae (2004) suggests that immersion in practice enables entrepreneurs to develop a theory of what works which can be described as know-how, know-what and know-who (Dohse & Walter, 2012). In a study of fast-growing business set-up by young entrepreneurs, Hickie (2011) notes that 11 of the 15 participants in his study had developed informal ventures while still at school. This might be something that is difficult to replicate in the classroom with students who have had little practical exposure to entrepreneurship. However, some practices can be replicated by encouraging students to engage in meaningful tasks such as writing and presenting a business plan or setting up a business. What is crucial about such activities is that the participants must be encouraged to reflect on the whole experience to help them link practice, learning and identity through participation in a community of practice.

The work of French social theorist Bourdieu (1977) is the basis of an important attempt to locate entrepreneurial learning within the context of a multi-layered relational and contextual framework. Karatas-Ozkan and Chell (2010) distinguish between the micro, the meso levels and the macro levels based on a detailed, longitudinal study of two start-up businesses. The value of this approach is that the orientations and dispositions of individuals (micro) are located within the context of their relationships and social networks (meso) and the broader institutional context, which includes regulatory factors as well as market and sectoral influences. For example, although recent graduates in the UK, France, China and India which face similar difficulties in starting new businesses (lack of resources/experience) they will also be faced with societies in which the support and approval for entrepreneurial activity will be very different. In Chapter 13, we discuss the GEM (Global Entrepreneurship Monitor) studies which distinguish between three stages of economic development (factor-driven, efficiency-driven and innovation-driven). Similarly, those starting businesses that require limited amounts of experience or specialized knowledge face very different problems to those of a young scientist or engineer attempting to establish a technology-based business. These ideas are summarized in Figure 5.4 in which the three levels of entrepreneurial learning are identified. Cognitive learning is a central element of business education whether at the undergraduate or postgraduate levels. An individual's 'absorptive capacity' will influence their ability to learn and apply new ideas and new ways of thinking. At the same time, it is central to the perspective adopted in this book that learning has a strong social element. In the classroom, this means that group exercises such analysing case studies or undertaking business planning exercises are an extremely powerful form of learning. Outside the classroom, this means learning from our experiences as consumers (spotting potential gaps in the marketplace) as well as learning vicariously from more experienced entrepreneurs. Equally, the influence of the context in which individuals are considering starting their business will have consequences for the success or failure of those businesses. For example, there are likely to be far more business opportunities in rapidly growing economies, such as China, Brazil or India, than there

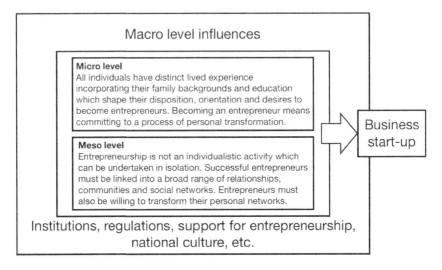

Figure 5.4 Influences on Entrepreneurial Learning

are in developed economies, such as France or the UK, which are experiencing very low levels of growth (see Chapter 13).

5.4 Active Learning and Simulation

As indicated above, there has been a shift away from simple models of the individualistic entrepreneur who is blessed with specific traits (risk-taking, internal locus of control, need for autonomy) that differentiate them from other members of the population. A broader understanding of entrepreneurship has prompted more sophisticated approaches to teaching and learning. The socially-situated view of learning increasingly influences the way in which teaching is actually delivered in the classroom. Entrepreneurship education was originally based on the transfer of knowledge and information, which followed the 'traditional' university pedagogy (Harris, Forbes & Fletcher, 2000). In this approach, students were perceived to be passive receivers of wisdom from their lecturers and professors. Allan Gibb advocated a 'mixed' approach to learning which focused on developing enterprising behaviours, skills and attributes [creativity, self-confidence, motivation] (Gibb, 1987). Such an approach to entrepreneurship education adopts a 'transformative methodology', which means that learners are engaged in constructing and owning their own learning (Pocek et al., 2021).

In contrast to lecture-based courses in which knowledge was passed to passive learners, enterprising approaches emphasize the use of experiential and action learning through which knowledge is constructed by learners in the process of 'doing' (Chang & Rieple, 2018; Lourenco & Jones, 2006; Lourenço, Jones & Jayawarna, 2013). Action learning combines periods of real-world experience with problem-based reflections on the behaviours and assumptions which limit individual or organizational performance (Chang & Rieple, 2018; Rae, 2012; Raelin, 2007; Revans, 1978).

There are a number of ways in which more enterprising approaches can encourage active learning among students. Probably the most widely used approach is to invite experienced entrepreneurs as guest speakers to inspire students to start their own businesses. Preparation of business plans (either individually or in groups) is also widely used to promote more active learning as students are required to obtain and analyse information related to the market, consumers and competitors. Business simulation games have been adopted as 'tasters' for potential students or to embed elements of a particular module/course. SimVenture is an increasingly sophisticated game that enables students to obtain a better understanding of the complexity associated with starting and running a business. The objective of SimVenture is to provide students with insight into the complexity of decision-making during the start-up process. Evidence from the literature confirms the effect-iveness of business games simulation and indicates that students gain real benefits in many aspects of entrepreneurial decision-making including finance and business planning (Gabrielsson, Tell & Politis, 2010; Gamlath, 2009; Huebscher & Lendner, 2010; Kriz & Auchter, 2016). Giving students opportunities to engage in entrepreneurial activities via business simulation fits with a 'constructivist' approach to learning. That is, you are encouraged to create your own understanding of specific situations as a result of com-bining your previous business knowledge with experience gained by engaging with the simulation (Box 5.3).

Box 5.3 Learning from SimVenture

The most positive thing I gained from SimVenture is that is gives you a 360 degree view of the business. There are practical things in business which you don't read in theory – for instance - data problems, getting payments from customers and getting a reminder letter about a legal case. Things like getting a different supplier and how to deal with problems as they happen. These are very practical things which you are not taught about in class. It is a 360 degree process looking at recruitment, what gaps you have in your business – what skills you are looking for. These were the most positive experiences of SimVenture. [Anurag, Liverpool entrepreneurship student]

During the simulation itself, lecturers/instructors should act as facilitators of students' 'learning-by-doing'. In addition, students should be encouraged to undergo 'double-loop' learning as they acquire new knowledge and understanding as well as new skills, such as decision-making. Based on a sample of more than 2000 students, Huebscher and Lendner (2010), conclude that business simulation promotes real learning and complex entrepreneurial thinking. Students in the sample indicated that they obtained real benefits in terms of developing a better understanding of entrepreneurial thinking/action, strategy, marketing, problem-solving and team-working. The authors also indicate that simulation games are useful for sensitizing non-business students to the nature of entrepreneurial action. Our own experience of using SimVenture is that simulation games are best used as part of a blended learning programme, which certainly should include some time in which students are encouraged to reflect on what they have learnt from the simulation. The importance of combining experiential learning and reflection is confirmed by Ahn (2008) who conducted a study based on three groups of students who played the game individually:

1. RO – reflective observation group (after playing the game students were asked to reflect on their decision-making)
2. RO+AC – reflective observation and abstract conceptualization (these students were asked to list the concepts/theories which related to their decision-making before they reflected on their decision-making)
3. CG – control group (were asked to evaluate performance of the company – without reflection)

The RO+AC group rated the 'educational efficacy' much higher than the RO group and the CG group scored lower than either of the other two groups. The RO+AC group also had higher levels of 'fun and excitement' while playing the game and found it technically much easier than the other two groups. The study confirms the value of actively engaging students in Kolb's experiential learning cycle (Ahn, 2008). Our own experiences confirm the value of combining *SimVenture* with conventional lectures for introducing appropriate concepts and theories as well as periods of guided reflection in which students are actively encouraged to link theory and practice. In addition, learning is enhanced when the simulation game is played by small groups (3 or 4) of students rather than individually (Ahn, 2008). They should then be encouraged to discuss and reflect on their decisions as the game progresses.

5.5 The Role of Enterprise Clubs and Societies

In addition to courses related to entrepreneurship and the management of small firms, many universities encourage students to join enterprise societies and participate in initiatives such as Enactus (Box 5.4), Junior Enterprise Europe (JEE), Collegiate Entrepreneurs Organization (CEO) and the National Association of College and University Entrepreneurs (NACUE). These bodies are generally described as 'student-led enterprise organizations' (SLEO) and are seen are crucial in shaping the intentions of their members (Sansone, Ughetto & Landoni, 2021). According to Pittaway, Rodriguez-Falcon, Aiyegbayo and King (2011), the number of active entrepreneurship clubs and societies indicates the quality of educational programmes in US universities. Enterprise educators also see clubs and societies as a way of encouraging informal learning that adds value to conventional classroom pedagogy. In the UK, clubs and societies are generally managed by students themselves and are usually affiliated to Student Unions. Clubs are important for introducing students to the idea of entrepreneurship via activities such as: meeting successful entrepreneurs; networking events to engage with the local business community; participation in seminars and competitions. Some institutions offer students opportunities to participate in investment funds or investment clubs, which involve the buying of stocks and shares or the chance to invest in start-up companies (Pittaway et al., 2011, p. 40).

Box 5.4 The Role of Enactus

Enactus at the University of Liverpool engages in a number of activities which help students develop their entrepreneurial and organizational skills and knowledge. Enactus is a student led social enterprise running social projects in and around Liverpool. Students who are involved with Enactus will Improve their leadership skills by running real-life projects in the community as well as working with corporate sponsors including Unilever, Santander, Enterprise Rent a Car and Everton Football Club. Engaging with Enactus enhances skills for internships and placement applications as well as developing students' enterprise and entrepreneurial skills.

A study to evaluate the effectiveness of clubs and societies in enhancing entrepreneurial learning concluded they are an important component in encouraging students to engage with entrepreneurial learning (Pittaway, Gazzard, Shore & Williamson, 2015). Such learning tends to be experiential and social as students engage with practical activities and share their understanding with more experienced entrepreneurs. Participants in the study had a range of motivations for engaging in clubs and societies and these included: help start their own business, develop transferrable skills, gain practical experience and, more surprisingly, enhance their curriculum vitae to improve employment prospects (Pittaway et al., 2011, p. 52). This may be because many students see entrepreneurship as something to consider in the future when they have gained real-life business experience. Students did identify real benefits from engaging in clubs and societies: gaining experience and learning-by-doing were regarded as more useful than classroom-based teaching (Box 5.5). Second, the opportunity to engage informally with other students and practitioners can create a genuine 'community of practice' in which knowledge and understanding are enhanced for all participants (Haneberg & Aaboen, 2021).

Box 5.5 Engaging in Experiential Learning

At the University of Liverpool Management School, 250 students participating in a second-year entrepreneurship module engage in a business start-up exercise as well as conventional lectures. Students work in groups of 5 or 6 and begin by identifying a business opportunity, which must be approved by the lecturer (to avoid students engaging in projects that are illegal or unethical). They then set-up a company and run it for ten weeks culminating in an 'enterprise fair' in the Students' Union. Alumni from the University of Liverpool Management Schools' Growth Catalyst programme act as mentors for each group of students.

The Growth Catalyst programme is for entrepreneurs in Greater Merseyside wanting to grow their businesses. Growth Catalyst is an eight-month part-time leadership course that has operated since 2010. In that time, 278 (11 cohorts of approximately 25) entrepreneurs have graduated from the programme. The programme's success can be measured by an average increase in turnover of 49% (average turnover was £1.05 million on entering the programme), a 38% increase in investment and more than 500 new jobs created in the region. Equally important, was the strong evidence of increased networking and peer-to-peer learning both intra- and inter-cohort. The Growth Catalyst alumni have a strong attachment to the University of Liverpool and hence their willingness to mentor students studying entrepreneurship modules.

Student clubs are 'an autonomous group of students who meet regularly with the express aim to enhance their personal learning around a given topic or theme' (Pittaway et al., 2015, p. 127). In the UK, Pittaway et al. (2015) distinguish between the support offered by Enactus and entrepreneurial clubs. Enactus is a global organization operating in 36 countries with more than 72,000 members annually. The website[4] defines their activities as follows:

Enactus UK supports students & young people across the country to engage in social action and social enterprise. Our mission in the UK is to be recognised as a leader in developing a national network of socially minded young leaders of the future, who transform communities and society through real life social action and environmentally responsible enterprise. We are dedicated to creating a better world while developing the next generation of entrepreneurial leaders and social innovators. The Enactus network of global business, academic and student leaders are unified by our vision - to create a better, more sustainable world.

A survey report that links to entrepreneurial learning include enhanced interpersonal skills, development of managerial and enterprise skills as well as increasing motivation and self-confidence (Pittaway et al., 2015). The authors go on to point out that learning activities in student clubs do not necessarily involve the four stages of the Kolb cycle (see Section 5.3). For example, listening to a talk by an experienced entrepreneur will promote 'assimilative learning' (combining reflective observation and abstract conceptualization); involvement in student-led projects may lead to 'accommodative learning' (combining active experimentation and concrete experience). Within Enactus, there appears to be a greater emphasis on active experimentation and concrete experience via engagement in community service projects and social business start-ups (Pittaway et al., 2015, p. 15). To ensure that real cognitive change takes place (development of an entrepreneurial mindset), experiential learning activities should include opportunities for individuals to reflect on their experiences (Burgoyne, 1995). Action and experience without reflective observation is unlikely to lead to changes in future behaviours among participants (Chang & Rieple, 2018; Cope, 2003; Taylor & Thorpe, 2004). Pittaway et al. (2015) summarizes their findings by suggesting that Enactus places more emphasis on learning-by-doing whereas enterprise clubs focus on social learning designed to create an interest in entrepreneurship and business start-up.

A recent survey of students from a number of European countries examined the impact of belonging to Junior Enterprise Europe (JEE) on their entrepreneurial intentions (Sansone et al., 2021). Most students were studying science/technology (47%) or business (42%) and almost 50% had some work experience. The result of the survey revealed that the more time spent in JEE and the higher the number of events students attended were positively associated with their entrepreneurial intentions. In addition, belonging to JEE enabled students to enhance both their social capital and their human capital; particularly teamworking, communication skills and self-confidence. Sansone et al. (2021, p. 23) summarize their findings:

> Our results indicate that JEE plays an important role in driving students' entrepreneurial intention and in fostering the entrepreneurial culture and ecosystem inside a university. In fact, SLEOs are fostering students' entrepreneurial spirit and competences by proactively engaging their members in decision-making, encouraging them to start their own projects and actively look for new opportunities.

Alumni Associations help ex-students in their careers by providing access to networks, skill development programmes and enhanced job opportunities. Some suggest that alumni associations have a key role in promoting student experiential learning via their engagement with alumni entrepreneurs (Pittaway et al., 2011). Alumni networks also provide access to additional resources for those students/graduates engaged in starting new businesses. It is widely acknowledged that those individuals with more extensive and diverse networks are more likely to be successful in their entrepreneurial endeavours (Davidsson & Honig, 2003; Preedy & Jones, 2017). Network ties are increasingly recognized as a key resource for nascent entrepreneurs in the form of bridging and bonding social capital (see Chapter 6). Landoni, Bolzani and Baroncelli (2021) suggest that Alumni Associations and clubs support self-employment as an alternative career path by helping develop an 'entrepreneurial mindset' among members. The authors examined the activities of 55 Italian universities with Alumni Associations in developing both members (ex-students) and existing students. Services offered for Alumni in support of entrepreneurship appear to be limited with only on-campus working space clearly related to business start-up. Although access to libraries and online facilities may be useful to some members wanting access specialized business databases. Table 5.2 lists the eight services provided by Alumni organizations in Italian universities for members and students. In total 36 Alumni organizations (65%) provided explicit entrepreneurial support in the form of incubation facilities.

In the UK, Baroncelli, Bolzani and Landoni (2019) identified alumni associations in 161 HEIs and their main services were the provision of opportunities for networking via online platforms and social media. Only 30 (17%) of Alumni Associations offered specific support for students wanting to pursue careers in entrepreneurship (see Boxes 5.6 and 5.7). The most

Table 5.2 Alumni Services for Students and Universities

Ambassador	Representing the University to potential students
Conferences	Providing on-campus conferences and speeches
Mentoring	Offering mentoring services to students
Job Offers	Job offers to existing students
Internships	Internships for existing students
Grants	Providing grants and loan to existing students
Donations	Donations to the University or University programmes
Entrepreneurship	Support and incubation for student start-ups

common forms of support included: prizes for alumni entrepreneurs, a visible community highlighting alumni profiles and biographies to serve as role models, establishment of entrepreneurship-related interest groups, associations, funding and crowdfunding initiatives sponsored by alumni, support for the HEI's initiatives to foster entrepreneurship, events, seminars, lectures and dissemination of training materials (Baroncelli et al., 2019, p. 12).

Box 5.6 University of Liverpool Alumni Association

The University of Liverpool has a large Alumni Association with more than 240000 graduates located all over the world. Graduates are encouraged to join one of the 35 academic groups associated with various departments. For example, the University of Liverpool Management School (ULMS) has 25000 graduates belonging to a world-wide network. A topical, recent addition is the Liverpool Infection and Global Health (IGH) Alumni Association, which was launched in 2012. There are also many international alumni networks based in Africa, Australia, China, Europe, India, North America and South-East Asia. These networks are run by local alumni ambassadors and volunteers. In addition, Liverpool Connect is a platform that allows past and present students to benefit from links to the alumni community by networking and sharing professional experience.

Within ULMS, there are several initiatives linking members of the alumni association with current students. For example, a popular online Masterclass series includes guidance from experienced entrepreneurs on how to start a business. ULMS Extra is a virtual insight panel that enables students to get state-of-the-art information from alumni about working a range of different sectors. ULMS encourages students to participate in Global Entrepreneurship Week, which is held annually in Liverpool to promote the benefits of entrepreneurship. ULMS has also had a partnership with Santander to provide an enterprise fund, which offers grants of up to £1000 to help students develop their business ideas. The benefits of self-employment are explained to MBA students via a careers catalyst initiative known a 'Starting a Freelance Business. A new service offered as a partnership between the University of Liverpool and Liverpool John Moore's University is an innovation coach who will encourage UG and PG students to consider co-founding their businesses. Experienced alumni from both universities will assist by acting as guest speakers and offering informal mentoring.

Box 5.7 Brett Centre for Entrepreneurship (University of Liverpool Management School)

The most obvious example of alumni support for enterprise within the University of Liverpool is the launch of the Brett Centre for Entrepreneurship (previously known as the Centre for Enterprise & Entrepreneurial Leadership). The Brett Centre is funded by a £1.25 million donation by Paul Brett as well as additional support from the University. According to the Director, Professor Robert Blackburn the Brett Centre will have three main pillars – research, enterprise education and engagement/impact. The Centre will recruit entrepreneurs in residence and a centre administrator, to support its work in education and engagement, and a number of additional PhD students. Paul Brett, University of Liverpool alumnus (BA Hons Geography 1965, Hon LLD 2017), is a long-time supporter of the University of Liverpool having previously made generous donations to the Yoko Ono Lennon Centre and The Brett Building, a dedicated MBA suite.

Whether related to clubs or Alumni associations, there has certainly been an increase in extracurricular activities in UK universities. The benefits for students are building greater self-confidence, extending social ties and enhancing interpersonal skills. With specific focus on enterprise-related extracurricular activities the most common events are business competitions, networking opportunities and business incubation as well as raising awareness of entrepreneurship and self-employment as career options (Preedy, Jones, Maas & Duckett, 2020). In addition to experiential learning, extracurricular activities can also promote self-directed learning and social learning. As Preedy et al. (2020) point out, active self-directed learning is closely associated with experiential learning where the focus is on action and reflection (Neck & Corbett, 2018). Involvement in extracurricular activities should provide opportunities to experiment as well as gaining a better understanding of the difficulties associated with entrepreneurship and the threat of business failure (Figure 5.5). As discussed in Section 5.3 (Table 5.1), self-directed learning provides you with the opportunity to learn more about yourself and your commitment to an entrepreneurial career. Social learning is also an important aspect of your involvement in extracurricular events as they provide opportunities to learn from your peers as well as more experienced entrepreneurs, managers and academics. Engaging in extra-curricular events while attending university will help you build an extensive social network and create the social capital necessary for your future career (Pocek et al., 2021).

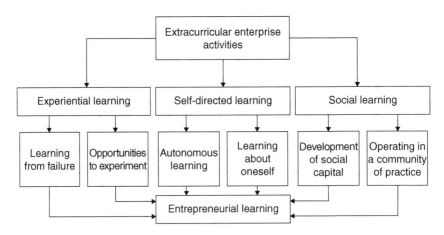

Figure 5.5 Extracurricular Activities and Entrepreneurial Learning
Source: Preedy et al., 2020

Based on their study of 24 different types of UK universities, Preedy et al. (2020) state that the main types of extracurricular enterprise activities are: networking events, socializing, guest speakers, mentoring sessions, business competitions and trading practice. The most valued outcomes for students were skills development, knowledge acquisition, personal growth, social capital development and enhanced employability (Preedy et al., 2020, p. 1093). Participants agreed that they benefitted from the three forms of learning identified in Figure 5.5. Extracurricular events such as business competitions helped develop technical skills particularly in relationship to networking and the sale of goods or services. Extracurricular activities also provided the motivation for students to become self-directed learners through the use of social media and other online sources. As a consequence, students felt that they were able to get a better sense of what it is like to be a real entrepreneur by engaging with those they could relate to in terms of their business careers. Social learning was promoted as a result of involvement with a group of students who were all motivated to learn about entrepreneurship. This sense of 'community' encourages the sharing of experience and knowledge in a way that strengthens ties between those engaged in extracurricular activities (Preedy et al., 2020).

Clubs and societies are an important element of your overall experience of studying entrepreneurship as part of a formal university course. In particular, such activities provide opportunities to engage in concrete experience and active experimentation that not only enhances learning through abstract conceptualization (classroom-based learning), but also encourages much deeper reflective learning. Hence, extracurricular activities should provide opportunities to combine Kolb's two dialectical processes: making sense of experience (prehension) and applying that experience (transformation) [see Section 5.3] (Kolb, 1984). To summarize, we believe that there are substantial benefits to be gained from your engagement in extracurricular activities including enterprise clubs, societies such as *Enactus* as well as alumni associations (Preedy & Jones, 2015, 2017). First, you will have the opportunity to meet and engage with other students who are committed to the idea of entrepreneurship as a career option. You should also have opportunities to engage with experienced entrepreneurs and business owners who can provide first-hand accounts of the highs and lows of starting and managing a new business. Secondly, you will have the chance to find out more about yourself and your motivation to become self-employed or an entrepreneur. Starting a new business is very unlikely to provide a smooth road to 'overnight' business success. Resourcefulness and resilience are essential attributes for anyone aspiring to a career as an entrepreneur. Engaging in extracurricular activities gives you the chance to find out for yourself whether you have these attributes. Thirdly, involvement with extracurricular activities is a good way to add real value to your curriculum vitae (CV). You may decide to gain some business experience before engaging in entrepreneurship and demonstrating your commitment and motivation to potential employers will certainly be helpful.

5.6 Situated Learning in a University-based Incubator

As indicated above, learning beyond the curricula involves a wide range of different activities (Figure 5.5). Therefore, we suggest that you should take the opportunity to engage with staff and incubatees based in your university's incubator. Alternatively, most large towns and cities will have business incubators which may offer opportunities to investigate their facilities. While some students do start new businesses while in the process of completing their studies the majority will begin their entrepreneurial careers after graduation. Students entering a university-based incubator (UBI) will generally have a range of different educational backgrounds. Some will have taken degrees or modules related to entrepreneurship and business start-up. Others may have been prompted to engage in an entrepreneurial career as a result of a family background in business or self-employment (Jones & Giordano, 2021). Some UBIs may also encourage entrepreneurs not associated with the university to join the incubator. This has the benefit of providing a more diverse group of people engaged in the start-up process (Jones, Meckel & Taylor, 2021b). University-based incubators (UBIs) provide opportunities for learning-by-doing as well as social learning through engagement with others involved in the start-up process (Taylor & Thorpe, 2004). Belonging to a 'community of practice' (Lave & Wenger, 1991) can help inexperienced would-be entrepreneurs acquire knowledge as a result of their participation in experiential and social learning. In addition, UBI incubation managers should act as knowledge brokers by engaging with key actors in the regional ecosystem such as resource providers in the form of larger companies, business angels and venture capitalists (McAdam, Miller & McAdam, 2016; van Weele, Steinz & van Rijnsoever, 2018; van

Weele, van Rijnsoever, et al., 2018) as well as linking to more experienced entrepreneurs and owner-managers.

Situated learning theory is based on the idea that learning takes place in communities of practice among groups of people engaged in common enterprises (Theodorakopoulos, Kakabadse & McGowan, 2014). The core of situated learning theory is what Lave and Wenger (1991) describe as legitimate peripheral participation. Legitimate peripheral participation has strong similarities to the traditional form of an 'apprenticeship' in which a craftsperson passes on their tacit knowledge to an inexperienced learner (Handley, Clark, Fincham & Sturdy, 2007). Such 'situated learning' bridges understanding based individual cognition and knowledge acquired from the social processes associated with the 'lived-in world' (Lave & Wenger, 1991). Legitimate peripheral participation is not based on a conventional pedagogy where some form of instruction takes place; instead, learning takes place as a result of the situated practices associated with a community of practice, in this case a UBI. According to Lave and Wenger (1991) individuals develop their identities and practices through participation in situated learning activities (Handley, Sturdy, Fincham & Clark, 2006; McDonald & Cater-Steel, 2017; Mercieca, 2016). The importance of situated learning for young entrepreneurs is confirmed by Haneberg and Aadland (2020, p. 135); 'the findings of this study imply that entrepreneurship education programmes in which students learn through venture creation should be organised in a way that makes students establish relationships and interact with each other on a regular basis'.

Theodorakopoulos et al. (2014, p. 611) argue that creating a community of growth-oriented businesses within an incubator requires three conditions: i) community strength, ii) boundary permeability, iii) community identity based on learning. Social interaction is important because tacit knowledge can only be acquired through direct social interaction (Nonaka & Takeuchi, 1995). What this means in practice is that there must be high levels of trust between community members so that there is a willingness to share problems, knowledge, information and practices (Brown & Duguid, 1991). At the same time, community members must engage with key actors in the ecosystem to access external knowledge, experience and resources (Nicholls-Nixon & Valliere, 2020; Nicholls-Nixon, Valliere, Gedeon & Wise, 2021; van Weele, Steinz, et al., 2018; van Weele, van Rijnsoever, et al., 2018). (Jones, Meckel & Taylor, 2021a) provide a detailed account of a UBI known as Innospace based at Manchester Metropolitan University (see Box 5.8).

Box 5.8 Entrepreneurial Learning in a UBI: the Innospace story

A University-based Incubator (UBI) established at Manchester Metropolitan University is the subject of a recent book. Innospace was launched in September 2007 to help MMU students make the transition into entrepreneurship. Take-up of the facility was excellent and by the end of year there were 75 registered users representing 56 businesses. Innospace continues to support young entrepreneurs and has been responsible for the creation of many new businesses and new jobs. From the outset, the informal design of Innospace was intended to develop a learning ethos among incubatees by encouraging the sharing of knowledge, experiences and problems. The learning community also included other groups such as MMU students, policy-makers, individuals and groups from various business communities (business angels and venture capitalists) who regularly engage with incubatees both formally and informally. The success of Innospace provides a template for other universities to establish incubation facilities in support of student entrepreneurship.

A number of studies confirm the central role of the incubator manager (or management team) in creating a learning CoP (Politis, Gabrielsson, Galan & Abebe, 2019). Previous business experience helps incubator managers adopt a 'brokerage' role linking incubatees to external business networks (Breznitz & Zhang, 2020; Redondo & Camarero, 2019). Experienced managers can also provide access to potential customers, funders, experienced entrepreneurs and owner-managers (Ahmad & Ingle, 2011; Ahmad & Thornberry, 2018). Consequently, the incubator manager/management team have a key role in helping incubatees develop their bridging and bonding social capital (Lee & Jones, 2008; Redondo & Camarero, 2019). Other actors are also important in providing inexperienced entrepreneurs with appropriate knowledge and information. Members of the CoP *peer group* are central to collaborative learning; *mentors* and *coaches* provide valuable learning based on their own 'real-world' experiences; *specialists or experts* in law, marketing, production and search engine optimization are also useful (Levesque, Minniti & Shepherd, 2009; Seet, Jones, Oppelaar & Corral de Zubielqui, 2018). Also, as discussed in Section 4.4 (lean start-up), early engagement with potential customers is essential for those entrepreneurs wanting to enhance their chances of launching successful new ventures (Blank, 2013; Blank & Dorf, 2020).

Factors associated with developing entrepreneurial learning, opportunity identification and development in a UBI are illustrated in Figure 5.7 (see Section 5.7). This process is shaped by a complex interaction of knowledge, information, skills and learning that begins before you as a potential entrepreneur enter a UBI and continues throughout the incubation process. The centre of the model focuses on the learning processes which help incubatees identify and develop ideas into feasible business propositions (see Chapter 3). At the same time, belonging to a community of practice will help develop a new identity as you make the transition from student to entrepreneur. While you are identifying and developing a business idea (Ardichvili, Cardozo & Ray, 2003) you will also be creating an entrepreneurial identity (Kasperova et al., 2018). The idea of establishing an entrepreneurial identity is commensurate with what is termed 'learning as becoming' (Farnsworth, Kleanthous & Wenger-Trayner, 2016; Wenger & Snyder, 2000). In practice this means that as you gain experience within the UBI, you will gradually begin to see yourself as a **real** entrepreneur and this is an important step in your development as you interact with potential customers, resource providers as well as members of your peer group. Inevitably, there will be dropouts during the incubation process as some incubatees decide that entrepreneurship is not for them. Being part of a UBI community of practice does, however, demand an 'entrepreneurial mindset' and we suggest that belonging to an incubator can help all recent graduates become more enterprising.

The benefits of belonging to a 'mixed' incubator such as Innospace is that the community of entrepreneurs will have different types of knowledge, experience, skills and access to resources (tangible and intangible). Hence, a community of practice is shaped by the human capital acquired by incubatees during their time spent in education (Handley et al., 2007; Handley et al., 2006; Jones et al., 2021a). We suggest that your bank of human capital includes not only the time spent in higher education but also the learning that took place during your primary and secondary schooling (Jayawarna, Jones & Macpherson, 2014). In addition, those who have gained some work experience while in school, college or university will be able to make good use of the opportunities offered by being based in an incubator

(Hickie, 2011). In Section 2.3 we discussed a range of basic business skills that you need to begin an entrepreneurial career. In addition, social skills are certainly important aspect for any young person intending to pursue a career in entrepreneurship (Tocher, Oswald & Hall, 2015). It is generally acknowledged that your family and close friends are the likeliest resource-providers during the start-up stage (Battisti & McAdam, 2012). In the longer term, it is essential that you develop your social network to ensure that you have access to a wider range of resources including knowledge, information and finance (Bøllingtoft & Ulhøi, 2005; McAdam & McAdam, 2006). A study of a Swedish venture creation programme (VCP) confirmed the significance of informal networks to the success of student start-ups (Haneberg & Aaboen, 2020). In summary, your social skills are important for creating both bridging (internal) and bonding (external) social capital while you are based in a UBI (Lee & Jones, 2008; Redondo & Camarero, 2019).

Resources possessed by those entering a UBI are more likely to be intangible rather than tangible. Most students will have incurred substantial debts during their studies and, therefore, will lack access to financial capital. For example, students graduating from English universities in 2020 had average debts of over £40,000 (Jones et al., 2021b). Adopting an effectual approach to start-up by bootstrapping additional resources will help young entrepreneurs start their businesses without incurring additional financial burdens (Jayawarna, Jones & Macpherson, 2020; Jones & Jayawarna, 2010). In fact, Haneberg (2019) suggests that entrepreneurial learning is an effectual process based on three dimensions: activity, multiple actors and context dependence. Therefore, entrepreneurial learning is action-oriented as it is based on experiential and experimental learning, which can be expressed as learning-by-doing. One of the most significant changes in understanding is recognition that entrepreneurship involves extensive social interactions rather than purely individualistic endeavours. Entrepreneurs rarely work in isolation and their activities are based on collaboration with other people (Gibb, 1997; Jack, Drakopoulou-Dodd & Anderson, 2008; Pittaway et al., 2015). This particularly apparent in the context of a UBI where inexperienced entrepreneurs can provide mutual support as well as accessing knowledge and experience from mentors, coaches and experienced entrepreneurs. According to Haneberg (2019), the 'surroundings' in which entrepreneurial activities take place also strongly influence the start-up process. Understanding entrepreneurial learning as an effectual process helps provide a better understanding of entrepreneurship as a dynamic and adaptive activity influenced and shaped by social networks and the context in which that learning occurs (Nicholls-Nixon & Valliere, 2021).

During your time in university, you may have belonged to an entrepreneurial club or society, which promoted the importance of entrepreneurship to students. Clubs and societies play a key role in enhancing the skills and knowledge of students intending to pursue an entrepreneurial career (Pittaway et al., 2015; Pittaway et al., 2011). As the authors go on to point out, club membership is an important factor in developing the social skills necessary for students to become successful entrepreneurs. Therefore, we suggest that it is essential that campus-based clubs and societies associated with entrepreneurship are encouraged to have a role in university-based incubators. The role of clubs and societies is discussed in more detail in Section 5.4).

5.7 Enterprise Education and Entrepreneurial Learning

Over the last 20 years researchers have gained a much better understanding of the links between enterprise education and entrepreneurial learning. As we emphasize throughout this book, there is now much greater focus on experiential learning rather than simply learning various theories of entrepreneurship. What this means for you as a student is that your course should be 'for' enterprise and entrepreneurship rather than 'about' the more formal elements (theories) of entrepreneurship. However, UK university researchers are also required to demonstrate the extent to which their research *impacts* on practitioners and policymakers. Based on case studies submitted to the government's Research Excellence Framework (REF), institutions are ranked according to the value of their economic and social impact. Researchers in the areas of entrepreneurship and small business management are responsible for many of the cases submitted to the REF exercise (Jones, 2022). In addition, the UK Government has also introduced the Teaching Excellent Framework (TEF),[5] which places increasing emphasis on the 'quality' of teaching by university staff members.

Consequently, the majority of those responsible for entrepreneurship programme and modules will be researchers as well as teachers (Jones, 2022). Your lecturers should be part of a 'virtuous learning circle' which brings together teaching, research and practical engagement with

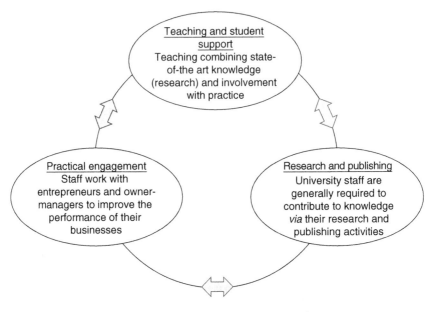

Figure 5.6 The Virtuous Learning Circle

entrepreneurs and owner-managers (Figure 5.6). In our experience, teaching does not simply involve the passing on of knowledge to students. Rather, teaching incorporates a two-way flow of knowledge as student questions in class, their responses in written coursework and examinations can provide new insights, which add to the stock of knowledge. Therefore, as Figure 5.6 illustrates, you as a student will play an active role in the generation of new knowledge which should inform both theory and practice. At the same time, you and your fellow students should benefit from programmes that are 'state-of-the-art' in terms of both theory and practice. The QAA[6] (2018) document on enterprise education distinguishes between the different ways of delivering enterprise education as follows:

> 'About' courses are intended to help students assimilate and reflect upon existing theories, knowledge and resources that enhance their understanding of a topic or theme, for example, venture creation and business growth strategies. They tend to draw upon a more traditional pedagogy involving lectures and set texts to explore the theoretical underpinnings of Enterprise and Entrepreneurship. Case studies will investigate past events and decision-making that could

inform 'for' approaches. Students may also learn how Enterprise and Entrepreneurship has evolved as a discipline and will be able to critically evaluate the relevant literature.

'For' courses focus on creating an enterprising approach, aiming to help students discover what it is to be enterprising, as well as offering insight into being an entrepreneur; it is a preparatory method. These courses are normally delivered via experiential learning opportunities that engage and enhance the student's capabilities within a meaningful and relevant context. They challenge the student to think about the future and visualise opportunities. Students will typically be engaged in scenarios that challenge their thinking and make explicit the need for creativity and innovation.

In Chapter 12 we discuss the way in which entrepreneurial theory has evolved in recent years and we believe that understanding some of the key theoretical ideas will enrich your own learning. Nevertheless, if you are serious about a future career in self-employment or in setting up your own business then your educational experience should be driven by the latter approach (the 'for' agenda). Scandinavian universities are at the forefront of using venture creation programmes (VCPs) as an integral element of the curricula. Students are required to start new ventures which facilitates entrepreneurial learning and enhances university support for entrepreneurship. VCPs are typified by five factors: experiential learning, interdisciplinarity, process-based curricula, access to external networks and contributions to the regional ecosystem (Sørheim, Aadland & Haneberg, 2021). Importantly, the authors stress that VCPs are not a 'quick-fix' and it takes time for businesses established by students and graduates to create significant 'value-added'. Consequently, it is important that university managers and policymakers are realistic in their evaluation of VCPs and UBIs.

The nature of the university in which you are studying will have a strong influence in shaping the provision of business incubation facilities. For example, a simple dichotomy is that some institutions focus on research while others give more attention to teaching and practical engagement. This can be summarized in the extent to which an institution fulfils the requirement for being an 'entrepreneurial university' (Etzkowitz, Webster, Gebhardt & Terra, 2000). The *Times Higher Education* (THE) has an annual award for the 'outstanding entrepreneurial university' (sponsored by the NCEE[7]

[National Centre for Entrepreneurship in Education]) based on the extent to which entrepreneurship and innovation are encouraged among the student population. An initiative by the Chartered Association of Business Schools, known as the 'Small Business Charter', is awarded to Business Schools that promote entrepreneurship to their students as well as offering support to the small business community. Entrepreneurial universities will demonstrate their commitment to student entrepreneurship by providing business incubation facilities as well as establishing links to the regional ecosystem (Jones et al., 2021a).

Experiential learning theory [ELT] (Kolb, 1984) has been incorporated in the curricular of many enterprise programmes. Some authors suggest that because of the importance placed on learners reflecting on their previous experiences, ELT is 'backward looking' (Berends, Smits, Reymen & Podoynitsyna, 2016). There is a limited focus on would-be entrepreneurs adopting a sensemaking approach to the future needs of their businesses (Jones & Li, 2017). As discussed extensively in Chapter 3, cognitive learning is concerned with planning for the future rather than basing actions on past experiences. Therefore, cognitive learning, in contrast to experiential learning, is described as 'forward looking' by Berends et al. (2016). Rather than being independent, we suggest that in practice, the two forms of learning are complementary and create a virtuous learning environment (Figure 5.7). In practice, experiential learning 'feeds-forward' into cognitive learning and the latter 'feeds-backward' into experiential learning (Jones &

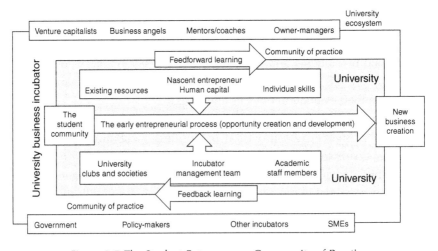

Figure 5.7 The Student Entrepreneur Community of Practice

Giordano, 2021). Figure 5.7 indicates that the two processes are part of a continual learning cycle where previous experiences and understanding are the basis for the next stages in the entrepreneurial learning process. Knowledge and skills are transformed into potential new business opportunities and participant begin to mature into their entrepreneurial identities. This is core of the community of practice where individual and group learning takes place via interactions between members of the incubator community. These interactions are based on their different types of prior knowledge as well as new information, skills, experiences and resources acquired while in the incubator. Also, individual incubatees, as well as the group, become more familiar with the issues associated with entrepreneurship (learning as becoming) then their identities as 'real' entrepreneurs are increasingly legitimized (Kasperova et al., 2018).

The outer ellipse of the model represents the incubator community of practice where incubatees' human capital (resources, skills, knowledge & experience) combine with inputs from the incubation manager to develop their business ideas and create new entrepreneurial identities. In addition, incubatees will acquire new knowledge and skills as a result of interacting with their peer group, the management team and those operating in the eco-system including business mentors/advisors, experienced entrepreneurs, business owners, potential funders (business angels & venture capitalists) and local policymakers. The transformation of existing knowledge and skills into new opportunities and the creation of new entrepreneurial identities are embedded within the inner boundary (shaded area). Feedforward and feedback learning occurs at an individual level because of interactions between members of the incubator community. These interactions are based on their different types of prior knowledge as new information, skills, experiences and resources acquired while in the incubator (Jones et al., 2021b).

The overall benefit of spending time in business incubator is that it provides a 'safe harbour' while you develop a feasible business idea and a new identity as an entrepreneur. Ultimately, students should graduate from the incubator with the knowledge and experience to create a functioning new business. However, those that decide entrepreneurship is not for them should still benefit from the skills and experience gained while in the incubator. This is confirmed by a study of 70 students engaged in a Scandinavian new venture programme: 'the results support the idea that outcomes from entrepreneurship are broader than merely producing new ventures and also entail personal development' (Haneberg & Aadland, 2020, p. 133). This is important because, as the authors point out, many of those engaged in entrepreneurship education programmes pursue conventional career paths. Creation of a successful UBI community of practice will have several advantages for the region and the University. New businesses should feed-in to the regional ecosystem building higher levels of economic activity and creating new job opportunities. For the University, a successful incubator will demonstrate the institution's support for the regional economy and help attract enterprising students to a range of different programmes.

In their conclusions, Jones et al. (2021a) suggest a number of issues that you should consider when thinking of joining an incubator. First, as discussed in Section 1.3, evaluating your stock of prior knowledge and experience is important for identifying existing strengths and weaknesses. Secondly, succeeding as a new entrepreneur is unlikely to happen without high levels of intrinsic motivation and it certainly helps if you pursue business opportunities that fit with your personal interests. The commitment many individuals have to their hobbies can play an important role in the creation of new business opportunities. Thirdly, you should also be prepared to broaden your knowledge by networking with fellow incubatees who will have different sets of knowledge, experience, skills and social contacts. Fourthly, the study of Innospace revealed that the social spaces and a supportive community learning environment are as important as the access to office facilities associated with a UBI in helping inexperienced entrepreneurs start new businesses. Therefore, when choosing a business incubator, you should try to establish whether the incubator has a cooperative learning environment. To a great extent, this depends on the skills of the management team to create the conditions for a supportive community of practice within the UBI. Therefore, we recommend speaking to the manager and, if possible, to some existing incubatees to evaluate the benefits of being based in the incubator before deciding to go ahead. At the same time, you need to be willing to become an active member of the incubator learning community, which involves sharing knowledge and information with your peers (Jones et al., 2021a). Without such engagement, even an incubator with the most sophisticated facilities would not be the basis for creating an effective learning community. Hence, you should be committed to using your social skills to extend your social networks inside the UBI as well as engaging with key actors in the ecosystem.

5.8 Summary and Key Learning Points

Entrepreneurial learning is a process rather than a classroom activity in which you absorb a few key concepts and regurgitate those ideas in an essay or an examination. Furthermore, entrepreneurial learning brings together knowledge acquired as part of your college or university education and extracurricular activities involving membership of clubs and societies. This means that learning in the classroom should be combined with learning from experience for those who want to make a success of their entrepreneurial careers. We have demonstrated how research based on experiential learning has shaped a deeper understanding of the way in which new entrepreneurs acquire appropriate skills and knowledge. Consequently, there is considerable focus on the central importance of experiential learning as a means of enhancing the skills you need to become a successful entrepreneur. As we have discussed in this chapter, there are a number of ways in which the experience of being an entrepreneur can be partially replicated in the classroom: inspirational talks by successful entrepreneurs, business start-up activities incorporated into courses/modules (see Young Enterprise example), using simulation games such as SimVenture, as well as actively engaging in clubs and societies such as Enactus or Junior Enterprise Europe. However, we believe that there is no substitute for engaging in real-life entrepreneurial activity as described in Box 5.9.

Box 5.9 Learning by Doing

It all began when I was about 13 years old and I started selling mobile phones on eBay for about £10. That's where it began because you can see the money you are making and you think, I can do this it's easy. So, I started buying and selling grander things, anything I knew I could sell on eBay and it just started from that really. It developed further when I started looking on eBay for good deals and eventually you start thinking, there has to be suppliers somewhere and that is how it led on really – just doing a little bit and then taking a big step in buying. [Sam Wilson, *Jazooli*]

There are certainly many benefits from participating in a range of extra-curricular activities including the opportunity to meet experienced entrepreneurs and owner-managers. We suggest that extracurricular activities are important in developing an 'entrepreneurial mindset' as discussed in Chapter 1 (Figure 1.3). You will also benefit from the opportunity to 'learn about yourself' with a particular focus on your resilience in the face of the kind of difficulties you will certainly face in trying to start your own business. It is important that you actively search for opportunities to get involved in extracurricular activities rather than waiting for staff members or other students to make the arrangements. For example, involvement in business competitions, community enterprise and taking a leadership role in a society or club are all important in broadening your knowledge and experience. In addition, your university will have an alumni association and many of the members will be experienced in business and entrepreneurship. It is certainly worthwhile investigating the potential of engaging with your university's alumni, who are often keen to pass on their knowledge to current students. Finally, we discussed the links between entrepreneurial learning and university-based incubators (UBI). Incubators are a key mechanism for helping you make the transition from student to entrepreneur as they provide a 'safe harbour' in which to develop your business ideas. Once again, you should use your initiative to investigate the opportunities offered by business incubators while in the process of completing your studies. The key learning points from Chapter 5 are as follows:

- Kolb's experiential learning cycle is core to understanding the principles of entrepreneurial learning. You should pay particular attention to ensuring that you understand the four types of learning based on assimilative knowledge, convergent knowledge, accommodative knowledge and divergent knowledge.
- Conventional understanding of learning focused on cognition (the way in which your mind absorbs, processes and applies knowledge). We acknowledge the importance of cognitive learning but stress the significance of social learning to entrepreneurship. Explaining your thoughts to other people is central to the sensemaking process as you evaluate your business ideas.
- It may be difficult to gain real-world experience of entrepreneurship while you are studying at university. Therefore, we believe simulation

tools such as SimVenture provide exposure to some of the key problems associated with entrepreneurship in a low-risk environment. However, our central argument in this book is that effective enterprise education has to have a strong practical bias and, hence, the focus on experiential learning.

- The course or courses you are studying in college/university will be primarily focused on learning *about* entrepreneurship. Most lecturers will introduce you to some of the key thinkers, such as Schumpeter and his concept of 'creative destruction', which is central to entrepreneurial theory (see Chapter 13). At the same, as stressed in Section 5.5, extracurricular activities are extremely important for acquiring knowledge that will be useful for your entrepreneurial career. Extracurricular include joining enterprise clubs and societies, engaging with your alumni association and undertaking projects with local businesses or social enterprises.

- Another important extracurricular activity is to seek out your local business incubator (whether managed by your university or an external body). We believe that business incubators provide a useful bridge between studying entrepreneurship and running your own business. Talking to the management team and existing incubatees is a useful way of finding the potential benefits before you graduate.

5.9 Discussion Questions and Call to Action

1. How does experiential learning fit with the distinction between learning **about** entrepreneurship and learning **for** entrepreneurship?

2. Explain how social learning complements cognitive learning in enterprise education.

3. What are the core ideas associated with Kolb's learning cycle?

4. How does your own experience of learning fit with the ideas expressed in Kolb's learning cycle?

5. What contextual factors have the most influence on students' ability to start their own businesses?

6. What do you think is the most effective way of simulating the process of starting a business?

7. Describe some of the extracurricular activities you have engaged in since joining university and explain how those activities will help your career in entrepreneurship.

8. To what extent have you considered joining a business incubator as the next step in your entrepreneurial career?

This chapter contains the central message to students who are serious about becoming entrepreneurs. As indicated in the introduction, we acknowledge that some individuals appear to be 'natural' entrepreneurs (see Box 5.1) and are able to spot opportunities for making money from an early age. Nevertheless, we are committed to the idea that the knowledge associated with entrepreneurship can be obtained via appropriately designed college and university courses. You would not expect to undergo an operation by a 'surgeon' who had not taken their medical examinations nor fly in a plane by someone claiming to be a 'natural', rather than a qualified, pilot. We are not suggesting that all entrepreneurs should be professionally qualified, but we certainly believe that there is a body of knowledge that can improve your chances of longer-term success. Ideally, your course should provide you with opportunities to obtain some direct experience by engaging with more experienced entrepreneurs and owner-managers. We recognize that this may be difficult in institutions with large classes and, therefore, some form of simulation exercises can provide useful experience of the problems associated with starting and running your own business. Developing a business model (Chapter 4) and writing a realistic business plan as part of a group exercise can certainly be a valuable learning experience. Such exercises can also develop your *entrepreneurial mindset*, which can help you identify potential business opportunities. The important 'call to action' associated with this chapter is that if you want to become an entrepreneur then you must be committed to active, rather than passive, learning. There are many ways in which you can acquire entrepreneurial knowledge:

a. TV programmes such as *Dragon's Den* can help you think through some of the issues associated with 'selling' your business ideas to other people

b. Try to identify new business opportunities in your day-to-day activities (see Chapter 3)

c. Ask family and friends who are running or working in small businesses about their positive and negative experiences

d. When engaging with a small business (bar, café restaurant etc.) try to evaluate how effective they are in offering their services [what do they do well and what do they do badly?]

e. Talk to someone who has had experience of being based in a business incubator

f. As we discuss in Chapter 7, getting any real-world business experience is invaluable in becoming an entrepreneur (even delivering papers or working in a fast-food restaurant)

Notes

1   The big five personality attributes are described as: extraversion, openness to experience, agreeableness, conscientiousness and emotional stability (see Zhao, H. and Seibert, S. E. (2006) 'The Big Five Personality Dimensions and Entrepreneurial Status: A Meta-Analytical Review', *Journal of Applied Psychology*, 91(2), 259–271.

2   www.liverpoolguild.org/groups/liverpool-entrepreneurs-network-society-lens

3   www.babson.edu/academics/centers-and-institutes/the-arthur-m-blank-center-for-entrepreneurship/thought-leadership/global-entrepreneurship-monitor/#

4   http://enactusuk.org/what-is-enact

5   www.gov.uk/government/collections/teaching-excellence-framework   (accessed 6 January 2021)

6   www.qaa.ac.uk/scotland/development-projects/enterprise-and-entrepreneurship

7   https://ncee.org.uk/about-us/ (accessed 24 September 2020)

References

Ahmad, A. J. & Ingle, S. (2011). Relationships matter: case study of a university campus incubator. *International Journal of Entrepreneurial Behavior & Research*, *17*(6), 626–644.

Ahmad, A. J. & Thornberry, C. (2018). On the structure of business incubators: de-coupling issues and the mis-alignment of managerial incentives. *The Journal of Technology Transfer*, *43*(5), 1190–1212.

Ahn, J.-H. (2008). Application of the Experiential Learning Cycle in Learning from a Business Simulation Game. *E-Learning*, *5*(2), 146–156.

Aldrich, H. E. & Yang, T. (2012). Lost in translation: Cultural codes are not blueprints. *Strategic Entrepreneurship Journal*, *6*(1), 1–17.

Ardichvili, A., Cardozo, R. & Ray, S. (2003). A theory of entrepreneurial opportunity identification and development. *Journal of Business Venturing*, *18*(1), 105–123.

Baker, A. C., Jensen, P. J. & Kolb, D. A. (2005). Conversation as Experiential Learning. *Management Learning*, *36*(4), 411–427.

Bakhtin, M. M. (1981). *The Dialogical Imagination*. Austin: University of Texas Press.

Baroncelli, A., Bolzani, D. & Landoni, M. (2019, July). Alumni Organizations in the Entrepreneurial Universities. In Academy of Management Proceedings (Vol. 2019, No. 1, p. 12736). Briarcliff Manor, New York 10510: Academy of Management.

Battisti, M. & McAdam, M. (2012). The Challenges of Social Capital Development within the University Science Incubator: the Case of the Graduate Entrepreneur. *International Journal of Entrepreneurship and Innovation*, *13*(4), 261–276.

Berends, H., Smits, A., Reymen, I. M. M. J. & Podoynitsyna, K. (2016). Learning while (re)configuring: Business model innovation processes in established firms. *Strategic Organization*, *14*(3), 181–219.

Blank, S. (2013). Why the Lean Start-Up Changes Everything. *Harvard Business Review*, *91*(5), 63–72.

Blank, S. & Dorf, B. (2020). *The startup owner's manual: the step-by-step guide for building a great company*. New Jersey: Wiley.

Bøllingtoft, A. & Ulhøi, J. P. (2005). The networked business incubator – leveraging entrepreneurial agency? *Journal of Business Venturing*, *20*(2), 265–290.

Bourdieu, P. (1977). *Outline of a theory of practice [by] Pierre Bourdieu; translated by Richard Nice*: Cambridge: Cambridge University Press.

Breslin, D. & Jones, C. (2012). The Evolution of Entrepreneurial Learning. *International Journal of Organizational Analysis*, *20*(3), 294–308.

Breznitz, S. M. & Zhang, Q. (2020). Determinants of graduates' entrepreneurial activity. *Small Business Economics: An Entrepreneurship Journal*, *55*(4), 1039–1056.

Brown, J. S. & Duguid, P. (1991). Organizational Learning and Communities-of-Practice: Toward a Unified View of Working, Learning, and Innovation. *Organization Science*, *2*(1), 40–57.

Burgoyne, J. G. (1995). Learning from experience: From individual discovery to meta-dialogue via the evolution of transitional myths. *Personnel Review*, *24*(6), 61–72.

Burke, P. J. (2006). Identity Change. *Social Psychology Quarterly* (1), 81–96.

Byrne, J., Fayolle, A. & Toutain, O. (2013). Entrepreneurship Education: What we Know and What we Need to Know. In E. Chell and M. Karataş-Özkan (Eds.), *Handbook of Research in Entrepreneurship and Small Business*. (pp. 261–288). Cheltenham UK: Edward Elgar Publishing.

Chang, J. & Rieple, A. (2018). Entrepreneurial decision-making in a microcosm. *Management Learning*, *49*(4), 471–497.

Cope, J. (2003). Entrepreneurial Learning and Critical Reflection: Discontinuous Events as Triggers for 'Higher-level' Learning. *Management Learning, 34*(4), 429–450.

Cope, J. (2005). Towards a Dynamic Learning Perspective of Entrepreneurship. *Entrepreneurship Theory and Practice, 29*(4), 373–397.

Cope, J. & Down, S. (2010). *I think therefore I learn? Entrepreneurial Cognition, Learning and Knowledge and Knowing in Practice.* Paper presented at the Babson College Entrepreneurship Research Conference, Lausanne, Switzerland.

Cope, J. & Watts, G. (2000). Learning by doing – An exploration of experience, critical incidents and reflection in entrepreneurial learning. *International Journal of Entrepreneurial Behavior & Research, 6*(3), 104–124.

Davidsson, P. & Honig, B. (2003). The role of social and human capital among nascent entrepreneurs. *Journal of Business Venturing, 18*(3), 301–331.

Dewey, H. E. (1938). Teaching Social Problems without Textbooks. *Education Digest, 3*(7), 56–57.

Dohse, D. & Walter, S. (2012). Knowledge context and entrepreneurial intentions among students. *Small Business Economics, 39*(4), 877–895.

Down, S. & Warren, L. (2008). Constructing narratives of enterprise: cliches and entrepreneurial self-identity. *International Journal of Entrepreneurial Behavior and Research, 14*(1), 4–23.

Etzkowitz, H., Webster, A., Gebhardt, C. & Terra, B. R. C. (2000). The future of the university and the university of the future: evolution of ivory tower to entrepreneurial paradigm. *Research Policy, 29,* 313–330.

Farnsworth, V., Kleanthous, I. & Wenger-Trayner, E. (2016). Communities of Practice as a Social Theory of Learning: A Conversation with Etienne Wenger. *British Journal of Educational Studies, 64*(2), 139–160.

Fayolle, A., Kariv, D. & Matlay, H. (2019). *The role and impact of entrepreneurship education: methods, teachers and innovative programmes.* Cheltenham: Edward Elgar.

Fearon, C., Furlotti, M., van Vuuren, W. & McLaughlin, H. (2021). Developing new opportunities, entrepreneurial skills and product/service creativity: a 'Young Enterprise' (YE) perspective. *Studies in Higher Education, 46*(6), 1081–1098.

Gabrielsson, J., Tell, J. & Politis, D. (2010). Business Simulation Exercises in Small Business Management Education: Using Principles and Ideas from Action Learning. *Action Learning: Research and Practice, 7*(1), 3–16.

Gamlath, S. (2009). Field testing two simulation games: do winners win consistently? *On the Horizon, 17*(4), 388–396.

Gibb, A. (1987). Education for Enterprise: Training for Small Business Initiation - Some Contrasts. *Journal of Small Business and Entrepreneurship, 4*(3), 42–47.

Gibb, A. (1997). Small Firms' Training and Competitiveness: Building upon the Small Firm as a Learning Organization. *International Small Business Journal, 15*(3), 13–29.

Gibb, A. (2002). In pursuit of a new 'enterprise' and 'entrepreneurship' paradigm for learning: creative destruction, new values, new ways of doing things and new combinations of knowledge. *International Journal of Management Reviews, 4*(3), 213–232.

Gibb, A. (2011). Concepts into practice: meeting the challenge of development of entrepreneurship educators around an innovative paradigm: The case of the International Entrepreneurship Educators' Programme (IEEP). *International Journal of Entrepreneurial Behavior & Research, 17*(2), 146–165.

Gibb, A. & Ritchie, J. (1982). Understanding the Process of Starting Small Businesses. *International Small Business Journal, 1*(1), 26–45.

Greenburg, Z. O. (2011). *Empire State of Mind: J-Zay's Journey from Street Corner to Corner Office.* New York: Penguin.

Handley, K., Clark, T., Fincham, R. & Sturdy, A. (2007). Researching situated learning - Participation, identity and practices in client-consultant relationships. *Management Learning, 38*(2), 173–191.

Handley, K., Sturdy, A., Fincham, R. & Clark, T. (2006). Within and Beyond Communities of Practice: Making Sense of Learning Through Participation, Identity and Practice. *Journal of Management Studies, 43*(3), 641–653.

Haneberg, D. H. (2019). Entrepreneurial learning as an effectual process. *The Learning Organization, 26*(6), 631–647.

Haneberg, D. H. & Aaboen, L. (2020). Incubation of technology-based student ventures: The importance of networking and team recruitment. *Technology in Society, 63.* doi:10.1016/j.techsoc.2020.101402

Haneberg, D. H. & Aaboen, L. (2021). Entrepreneurial learning behaviour of community insiders. *International Journal of Entrepreneurial Behavior & Research.* (ahead of print) doi:10.1108/IJEBR-04-2020-0255

Haneberg, D. H. & Aadland, T. (2020). Learning from Venture Creation in Higher Education. *Industry and Higher Education, 34*(3), 121–137.

Harris, S., Forbes, T. & Fletcher, M. (2000). Taught and enacted strategic approaches in young enterprises. *International Journal of Entrepreneurial Behavior & Research, 6*(3), 125–146.

Hickie, J. (2011). The Development of Human Capital in Young Entrepreneurs. *Industry and Higher Education, 25*(6), 469–481.

Holman, D., Pavlica, K. & Thorpe, R. (1997). Rethinking Kolb's theory of experiential learning in management education - The contribution of social constructionism and activity theory. *Management Learning, 28*(2), 135–148.

Honey, P. & Mumford, A. (2001). *The learning styles questionnaire.* London: Peter Honey Publications.

Huebscher, J. & Lendner, C. (2010). Effects of Entrepreneurship Simulation Game Seminars on Entrepreneurs' and Students' Learning. *Journal of Small Business and Entrepreneurship, 23*(4), 543–554.

Jack, S. L., Drakopoulou-Dodd, S. & Anderson, A. R. (2008). Change and the development of entrepreneurial networks over time: a processual perspective. *Entrepreneurship & Regional Development*, *20*(2), 125–159. doi:10.1080/08985620701645027

Jayawarna, D., Jones, O. & Macpherson, A. (2014). Entrepreneurial potential: The role of human and cultural capitals. *International Small Business Journal*, *32*(8), 918–943.

Jayawarna, D., Jones, O. & Macpherson, A. (2020). Resourcing Social Enterprises: The Role of Socially Oriented Bootstrapping. *British Journal of Management*, *31*(1), 56–79.

Jones, O. (2022). Academic engagement with small business and entrepreneurship: Towards a landscape of practice. *Industry and Higher Education*, *36*(3), 279-293.

Jones, O. & Giordano, B. (2021). Family entrepreneurial teams: The role of learning in business model evolution. *Management Learning*, *52*(3), 267–293.

Jones, O. & Jayawarna, D. (2010). Resourcing new businesses: social networks, bootstrapping and firm performance. *Venture Capital*, *12*(2), 127–152.

Jones, O. & Li, H. (2017). Effectual Entrepreneuring: Sensemaking in a Family-Based Start-Up. *Entrepreneurship and Regional Development*, *29*(5–6), 467–499.

Jones, O., Meckel, P. & Taylor, D. W. (2021a). *Creating Communities of Practice: Entrepreneurial Learning in a University-Based Incubator*. Cham (Switzerland): Springer.

Jones, O., Meckel, P. & Taylor, D. W. (2021b). Situated learning in a business incubator: Encouraging students to become real entrepreneurs. *Industry & Higher Education*, *35*(4), 367–383.

Karatas-Ozkan, M. & Chell, E. (2010). *Nascent Entrepreneurship and Learning*: Cheltenham, U.K. and Northampton, MA:Elgar.

Kašperová E, Kitching J, Blackburn R. Identity as a causal power: Contextualizing entrepreneurs' concerns. *The International Journal of Entrepreneurship and Innovation*, *19*(4), 237–249.

Katz, J. A. (2003). The chronology and intellectual trajectory of American entrepreneurship education. 1876–1999. *Journal of Business Venturing*, *18*, 283–300.

Katz, J. A. (2008). Fully Mature but Not Fully Legitimate: A Different Perspective on the State of Entrepreneurship Education. *Journal of Small Business Management*, *46*(4), 550–566.

Kayes, D. C. (2002). Experiential Learning and Its Critics: Preserving the Role of Experience in Management Learning and Education. *Academy of Management Learning & Education*, *1*(2), 137–149.

Kolb, D. A. (1984). Experiential learning: experience as the source of learning and development / David A. Kolb. In: Englewood Cliffs, N.J.: Prentice-Hall.

Kriz, W. C. & Auchter, E. (2016). 10 Years of Evaluation Research Into Gaming Simulation for German Entrepreneurship and a New Study on Its Long-Term Effects. *Simulation & Gaming, 47*(2), 179–205.

Landoni, M., Bolzani, D. & Baroncelli, A. (2021). The Role of Alumni Clubs in the Universities' Entrepreneurial Networks: An Inquiry in Italian Universities. In P. Jones, N. Apostolopoulos, A. Kakouris, C. Moon, V. Ratten & A. Walmsley (Eds.), *Universities and Entrepreneurship: Meeting the Educational and Social Challenges* (Vol. 11, pp. 49–63). Bingley: Emerald Publishing Limited.

Lave, J. & Wenger, E. (1991). *Situated learning: Legitimate peripheral participation.* New York: Cambridge University Press.

Lee, R. & Jones, O. (2008). Networks, Communication and Learning during Business Start-up. *International Small Business Journal, 26*(5), 559–594.

Levesque, M., Minniti, M. & Shepherd, D. A. (2009). Entrepreneurs' Decisions on Timing of Entry: Learning From Participation and From the Experiences of Others. *Entrepreneurship Theory and Practice, 3*(2), 547–570.

Lewin, K. (1951). *Field Theory in Social Science.* London: Harper Row.

Lourenço, F. & Jones, O. (2006). Learning paradigms in entrepreneurship education: comparing the traditional and enterprise modes. National Council for Graduate Entrepreneurship Working Paper, 27.

Lourenço, F., Jones, O. & Jayawarna, D. (2013). Promoting sustainable development: The role of entrepreneurship education. *International Small Business Journal, 31*(8), 841–865.

Manolis, C., Burns, D. J., Assudani, R. & Chinta, R. (2012). Assessing experiential learning styles: A methodological reconstruction and validation of the Kolb Learning Style Inventory. *Learning and Individual Differences, 23*, 44–52.

Marshall, N. (2008). Cognitive and practice-based theories of organizational knowledge and learning: Incompatible or complementary? *Management Learning, 39*(4), 413–435.

McAdam, M. & McAdam, R. (2006). The Networked Incubator: The Role and Operation of Entrepreneurial Networking with the University Science Park Incubator (USI). *The International Journal of Entrepreneurship and Innovation, 7*(2), 87–97.

McAdam, M., Miller, K. & McAdam, R. (2016). Situated regional university incubation: A multi-level stakeholder perspective. *Technovation, 50–51*, 69–78.

McDonald, J. & Cater-Steel, A. (Eds.). (2017). *Communities of Practice: facilitating social learning in higher education*: Singapore: Springer.

Mercieca, B. (2016). What Is a Community of Practice? In (pp. 3). Singapore: Springer Singapore.

Neck, H. M. & Corbett, A. C. (2018). The scholarship of teaching and learning entrepreneurship. *Entrepreneurship Education and Pedagogy, 1*(1), 8–41.

Nicholls-Nixon, C. L. & Valliere, D. (2020). A Framework for Exploring Heterogeneity in University Business Incubators. *Entrepreneurship Research Journal*, *10*(3). doi: 10.1515/erj-2018-0190

Nicholls-Nixon, C. L. & Valliere, D. (2021). Entrepreneurial logic and fit: a cross-level model of incubator performance. *International Journal of Entrepreneurial Behavior & Research* (ahead-of-print). doi:10.1108/IJEBR-11-2020-0801

Nicholls-Nixon, C. L., Valliere, D., Gedeon, S. A. & Wise, S. (2021). Entrepreneurial ecosystems and the lifecycle of university business incubators: An integrative case study. *International Entrepreneurship and Management Journal*, *17*(2), 809–837.

Nicolaou, N., Shane, S., Cherkas, L., Hunkin, J. & Spector, T. D. (2008). Is the Tendency to Engage in Entrepreneurship Genetic? *Management Science* (1), 167–179.

Nonaka, I. & Takeuchi, H. (1995). *The knowledge-creating company: how Japanese companies create the dynamics of innovation*. Oxford: Oxford University Press.

Pfeifer, S. & Borozan, D. (2011). Fitting Kolb's Learning Style Theory to Entrepreneurship Learning Aims and Contents. *International Journal of Business Research*, *11*(2), 216–223.

Piaget, J. (1926). *The language and thought of the child*. Oxford: Harcourt, Brace.

Pittaway, L. & Cope, J. (2007). Simulating Entrepreneurial Learning. *Management Learning*, *38*(2), 211–233.

Pittaway, L., Gazzard, J., Shore, A. & Williamson, T. (2015). Student clubs: experiences in entrepreneurial learning. *Entrepreneurship & Regional Development*, *27*(3/4), 127–153.

Pittaway, L., Rodriguez-Falcon, E., Aiyegbayo, O. & King, A. (2011). The role of entrepreneurship clubs and societies in entrepreneurial learning. *International Small Business Journal*, *29*(1), 37–57.

Pittaway, L. & Thorpe, R. (2012). A framework for entrepreneurial learning: A tribute to Jason Cope. *Entrepreneurship & Regional Development*, *24*(9/10), 837–859.

Pocek, J., Politis, D. & Gabrielsson, J. (2021). Entrepreneurial learning in extra-curricular start-up programs for students. *International Journal of Entrepreneurial Behavior & Research, ahead-of-print* (ahead-of-print). doi:10.1108/IJEBR-04-2020-0206

Politis, D. (2005). The Process of Entrepreneurial Learning: A Conceptual Framework. *Entrepreneurship: Theory & Practice*, *29*(4), 399–424.

Politis, D., Gabrielsson, J., Galan, N. & Abebe, S. A. (2019). Entrepreneurial Learning in Venture Acceleration Programs. *Learning Organization*, *26*(6), 588–603.

Preedy, S. & Jones, P. (2015). An Investigation into University Extracurricular Enterprise Support Provision. *Education & Training*, *57*(8–9), 992–1008.

Preedy, S. & Jones, P. (2017). Student-Led Enterprise Groups and Entrepreneurial Learning: A UK perspective. *Industry and Higher Education*, *31*(2), 101–112.

Preedy, S., Jones, P., Maas, G. & Duckett, H. (2020). Examining the perceived value of extracurricular enterprise activities in relation to entrepreneurial learning processes. *Journal of Small Business & Enterprise Development, 27*(7), 1085–1105.

Rae, D. (2004). Practical theories from entrepreneurs' stories: discursive approaches to entrepreneurial learning. *Journal of Small Business & Enterprise Development, 11*(2), 195–202.

Rae, D. (2012). Action learning in new creative ventures. *International Journal of Entrepreneurial Behavior & Research, 18*(5), 603–623.

Rae, D. & Carswell, M. (2001). Towards a conceptual understanding of entrepreneurial learning. *Journal of Small Business and Enterprise Development, 8*(2), 150–158.

Raelin, J. A. (2007). Toward an Epistemology of Practice. *Academy of Management Learning & Education, 6*(4), 495–519.

Ramoglou, S., Gartner, W. B. & Tsang, E. W. K. (2020). 'Who is an entrepreneur?' is (still) the wrong question. *Journal of Business Venturing Insights, 13*. doi:10.1016/j.jbvi.2020.e00168

Redondo, M. & Camarero, C. (2019). *Chapter 15: University business incubators: mechanisms to transform ideas into businesses*. In A Fayolle, DKariv and H Matlay (Eds.) *The Role and Impact of Entrepreneurship Education* (pp. 275–299). Cheltenham, UK: Edward Elgar Publishing

Redondo, M. & Camarero, C. (2019). Social Capital in University Business Incubators: dimensions, antecedents and outcomes. *International Entrepreneurship and Management Journal, 15*(2), 599–624.

Revans, R. (1978). Action learning and the nature of learning. *Education + Training, 20*(1), 8–11.

Sansone, G., Ughetto, E. & Landoni, P. (2021). Entrepreneurial intention: An analysis of the role of Student-Led Entrepreneurial Organizations. *Journal of International Entrepreneurship, 19*, 399–433.

Seet, P.-S., Jones, J., Oppelaar, L. & Corral de Zubielqui, G. (2018). Beyond 'know-what'and 'know-how'to 'know-who': enhancing human capital with social capital in an Australian start-up accelerator. *Asia Pacific Business Review, 24*(2), 233–260.

Shane, S., Nicolaou, N., Cherkas, L. & Spector, T. D. (2010). Genetics, the Big Five, and the Tendency to Be Self-Employed. *Journal of Applied Psychology, 95*(6), 1154–1162.

Shane, S. & Venkataraman, S. (2000). The Promise of Entrepreneurship as a Field of Research. *Academy of Management Review, 25*(1), 217–226.

Sørheim, R., Aadland, T. & Haneberg, D. H. (2021). Chapter 19: Venture creation programs: what kinds of ventures do students create? In H. Neck, J. Timmons & Y. Liu (Eds.), *Innovation in Global Entrepreneurship Education* (pp. 274–285). Cheltenham, UK: Edward Elgar Publishing.

Taylor, D. W. & Pandza, K. (Eds.). (2003). *Networking Capability: The Competitive Advantage of Small Firms*. Chichester: Wiley.

Taylor, D. W. & Thorpe, R. (2004). Entrepreneurial learning: a process of co-participation. *Journal of Small Business & Enterprise Development, 11*(2), 203–211.

Theodorakopoulos, N., K. Kakabadse, N. and McGowan, C. (2014). What matters in business incubation? A literature review and a suggestion for situated theorising. *Journal of Small Business and Enterprise Development, 21*(4), 602–622.

Tocher, N., Oswald, S. L. & Hall, D. J. (2015). Proposing Social Resources as the Fundamental Catalyst Toward Opportunity Creation. *Strategic Enterepreneurship Journal, 9*(2), 119–135.

van Weele, M. A., Steinz, H. J. & van Rijnsoever, F. J. (2018). Start-up Communities as Communities of Practice: Shining a Light on Geographical Scale and Membership. *Tijdschrift voor Economische en Sociale Geografie, 109*(2), 173–188.

van Weele, M. A., van Rijnsoever, F. J., Eveleens, C. P., Steinz, H. J., van Stijn, N. & Groen, M. (2018). Start-EU-up! Lessons from international incubation practices to address the challenges faced by Western European start-ups. *The Journal of Technology Transfer, 43*(5), 1161–1189.

Vygotsky, L. S. (1978). *Mind in Society: The Development of Higher Psychological Processes*. Cambridge: Cambridge University Press.

Wenger, E. C. & Snyder, W. M. (2000). Communities of Practice: The Organizational Frontier. *Harvard Business Review, 78*(1), 139–145.

Zellweger, T. M., Nason, R. S. & Nordqvist, M. (2012). From Longevity of Firms to Transgenerational Entrepreneurship of Families: Introducing Family Entrepreneurial Orientation. *Family Business Review, 25*(2), 136–155.

Social Capital as an Entrepreneurial Resource

6.1 Introduction

In this chapter we explore the links between entrepreneurial networks, the generation of social capital and access to resources. One of the most important changes in our understanding of entrepreneurship has been the shift away from seeing those engaged in business start-up as 'heroic' individuals (Conway & Jones, 2012; Jones, 2022). Birley (1985) was one of the first researchers to observe that the entrepreneurial ability to engage in networking was an essential skill for identifying opportunities[1] and accessing the resources necessary to develop new ventures. In the last 15 years the study of entrepreneurial networks has become one of the most important topics for improving our understanding of the way in which new businesses operate (Jones, 2022). It is well established that effective entrepreneurs need a mixture of both strong ties, based on family and close friends, and weaker ties based on professional and business contacts (Granovetter, 1973; Larson & Starr, 1993). Perhaps more importantly, entrepreneurial networks should be dynamic as the mix of strong and weak ties must change if the business is to access additional resources. As we discussed in Chapter 2 (skills and capabilities) developing the social and communication skills required to identify and access new network contacts is crucial for entrepreneurs who want to establish businesses which have longer-term potential for survival and growth (Honig & Hopp, 2019; Longva, 2021).

A related issue to the interest in networks has been the emergence of social capital as an important element in understanding entrepreneurship. Social capital refers to the outputs, both tangible and intangible, which emerge from relationships between social actors (Anderson & Jack, 2002;

DOI: 10.4324/9781003312918-7

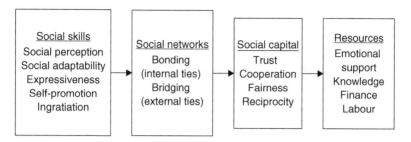

Figure 6.1 From Social Skills to Start-up Resources

Lans, Blok & Gulikers, 2015). Reciprocity is a key social capital term as it emphasizes the importance of cooperation and trust between actors. At a very pragmatic level, social capital concerns the economic benefits which entrepreneurs obtain from their social networks. At a broader level, building effective entrepreneurial communities means encouraging greater knowledge-sharing among a wider-range of individuals and groups. In Chapter 5 we explained how university incubators can facilitate the creation of social capital between those engaged in business start-up. In this chapter we demonstrate the ways in which nascent entrepreneurs can utilize their social networks as a means of 'creating' social capital that can add real value to their businesses. Figure 6.1 illustrates the links between social networks, social capital and the resources required by a new venture. The effectiveness with which would-be entrepreneurs exploit or mobilize their social networks depends, to a large extent, on how well they develop their social and communication skills (see Chapter 2).

6.2 Learning Objectives

- To understand the links between social networks and social capital.
- To be able to differentiate between the value of strong and weak network ties.
- To understand the role played by 'network brokers' in opening up links to professional and business networks.
- To understand the importance of social capital in accessing resources for new ventures.
- To understand the important of structural holes in the creation of social capital.

- To be aware of the dynamic nature of social networks and social capital during the start-up process.
- To recognize the role and nature of key social skills needed for the creation of social capital.
- To understand the importance of social media such as Facebook and LinkedIn for building large and diverse social networks that can provide invaluable social capital.

6.3 What are Social Networks?

The growing importance of social networks to entrepreneurship over the last 20 years signifies recognition that such relationships are essential for providing access to a wide range of resources (Aldrich, Rosen & Woodward, 1987; Cope, Jack & Rose, 2007; Elfring, Klyver & van Burg, 2021). The basic building block of any social network is the relationship between two social actors (A and B) known as a dyad. A social network is simply a series of dyadic relationships between the entrepreneur and other individuals in their social networks (Figure 6.2). The most familiar elements of a social network are those family members and close friends with whom individuals interact with on a regular basis. In it generally acknowledged that family and friends are most likely to provide finance, as well as other resources, for new businesses (Bhide, 2000; Brush, 2002; Brush, Greene & Hart, 2001; Jones & Giordano, 2021; Mason & Harrison, 1999). In social network terms such linkages are described as 'strong ties' which are favoured because they are readily accessibility to nascent entrepreneurs who find it difficult obtaining formal funding in the form of debt or equity.

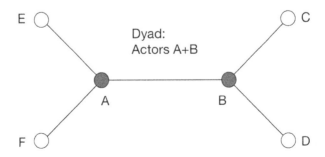

Figure 6.2 Dyadic Relationships

The entrepreneur's strong ties may have limited resources and it is important that they seek additional resources from their weaker network ties. Granovetter (1973) identified the 'strength of weak ties' as crucial in providing access to more contacts and a wider array of resources (Box 6.1). Relationship strength is important in determining the type and extent of resources which can be obtained through a network. For example, strong ties can provide funding, business-related knowledge, skills and information related to market opportunities as well as emotional support. Weak ties could be 'friends of friends' who are willing to provide the nascent entrepreneur with resources which are either free or charged at less than market price (Ruiz-Palomino & Martinez-Canas, 2021). Such resources include professional advice (legal, financial and managerial) as well as sharing office space, equipment or even employees (see Chapter 9 – Informal Finance). As entrepreneurs become more experienced their networks of business relationships will grow with a particular focus on customers and suppliers (Jones & Giordano, 2021). These weaker ties, based on non-affective relationships, provide the potential for access to a range of diverse information and resources (Figure 6.3).

Box 6.1

The weakness of strong ties: close contract with a small group of strong ties is likely, in most cases, to mean the individuals have limited access to knowledge, information and resources. While strong ties are important in the early stages of start-up they must be supplemented by weaker ties in the longer term.

The strength of weak ties: allow individuals access to a wider range of knowledge, information and resources. The disadvantage is that weaker ties will have less reason to share that knowledge with someone that they do not know very well. Therefore, effective social and communication skills help nascent entrepreneurs mobilize weaker ties.

Most would-be entrepreneurs have strong ties with other actors, particularly family and close friends, who can provide useful knowledge, information and external contacts. Open social networks which have

Closed networks   Open networks

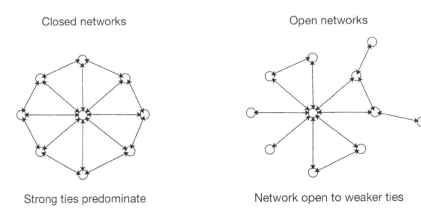

Strong ties predominate   Network open to weaker ties

Figure 6.3 Open and Closed Networks

significant numbers of weaker ties, provide access to a wider range of unique resources. There is an extensive literature that describes the process by which entrepreneurs gradually access additional resources by extending their strong ties into weaker networks (Elfring & Hulsink, 2008; Elfring et al., 2021; Smith & Lohrke, 2008). The relative importance of tie strength changes during different phases of the entrepreneurial process: emergence, newly established and maturity (Evald, Klyver & Svendsen, 2006). Strong ties (family and close friends) play a more important role than weaker ties during the emergence phase. At the 'newly established phase' it is important that entrepreneurs develop a mixture of strong and weak ties. A similar categorization also identified three distinct patterns of network development: evolution, renewal and revolution (Elfring & Hulsink, 2008). The different patterns are associated with various types of start-up businesses (independent, spin-off and incubatee) and two forms of innovation (incremental or radical). The authors go on to point out that strong and weak ties are important to the emergence and growth of firms, 'although they are beneficial in different ways and at different stages of a company's development' (Elfring & Hulsink, 2008, p. 1852).

The nature of closed (bonding) networks and open (bridging) networks is central to understanding how entrepreneurs make use of their strong and weak ties (Figure 6.3). Differences between bonding and bridging ties are similar to the distinction between strong and weak ties (Table 6.1). In the early stages of business creation, family and close friends will provide the most resources (Edelman, Manolova, Shirokova & Tsukanova, 2016), in the longer-term additional resources must be accessed by creating new

Table 6.1 Types of Network Ties

Bonding Ties	Bridging Ties
Homogeneous ties	Heterogeneous ties
Horizontal linkages (similar class, age, ethnicity & interests)	Vertical linkages (different, class, age, ethnicity & interests)
Similar moral values	Varied moral values
Trust and fair-play	Equivocal interests
Reciprocity	Negotiated reciprocity

network relationships. Sparse social networks in which there are less direct links between actors mean the inherent openness creates brokerage opportunities (Burt, 1992; Lee, 2017; Lee & Jones, 2008). Brokerage in this context means that entrepreneurs can obtain unique or privileged information about access to additional resources or new opportunities. Bonding ties based on family and close friends tend to have high levels of homogeneity with strong similarities in terms of class, ethnicity and interests. Because such groups are influenced by the same social norms and regular face-to-face interaction, they tend to have similar moral values based on trust, fair-play and reciprocity. In contrast, bridging ties are more heterogeneous and often cross 'boundaries' of class, age, ethnicity and interests. As these larger groups are subject to different social norm and tend to have irregular interaction which may be 'virtual' rather than face-to-face they are typified by different moral values and 'negotiated' reciprocity (that is, reciprocity will be more instrumental than is typical in bonding groups).

One important early study suggested that the entrepreneur's 'identity based' (internal/bonding) ties based on pre-existing social relationships provide the main support during the early stages of business start-up (Larson & Starr, 1993). As entrepreneurs become more experienced existing dyadic relationships are 'converted' into socio-economic exchanges[2] (see Section 6.4). For example, a friend may become an investor in the company or perhaps an employee. In essence, entrepreneurs must shift to 'calculative networks' (external/bridging) in which ties based on purpose and function are more important than identity ties (Jack, Drakopoulou-Dodd & Anderson, 2008). What this means in practice is that nascent entrepreneurs must try to identify those people (ties) who can provide them with the resources to establish and build their businesses. Brokering links between 'structural holes' (Burt, 1992) in external networks aids the identification of potential opportunities as well as providing access to knowledge, information and finance which are essential for successful growth (Hite, 2005; Lechner & Dowling, 2003).

There are studies which indicate that inexperienced nascent entrepreneurs can use more experienced intermediaries as brokers to access wider networks and resources (Batjargal, 2006; Burt, 1992; Ratzinger, Amess, Greenman & Mosey, 2018). The findings are confirmed by studies of incubators in which nascent entrepreneurs engaged in business start-up utilize 'boundary-spanners' to develop new network links (Hughes, Ireland & Morgan, 2007; Jones, Meckel & Taylor, 2021b). Taylor and Pandza (2003) discuss the importance of 'the professional periphery' which comprises business advisors, accountants, bank managers and solicitors. These professionals can link entrepreneurs to contacts who may be willing to provide support including finance. In a study based on over 660 Spanish undergraduate students, Ruiz-Palomino and Martinez-Canas (2021, p. 1177) found students who had entrepreneurs in their social networks were more likely to start a business than those relying on networks of family and friends. The main point of our argument, following many earlier studies, is that social networks provide access to a wide range of resources for new firms (Birley, 1985; Ostgaard & Birley, 1996).

There is a considerable amount of evidence that the networks of female entrepreneurs are very different from those of male entrepreneurs (Hamilton, 2006; Jayawarna, Jones & Marlow, 2015; Jones & Jayawarna, 2010; Manolova, Manev, Carter & Gyoshev, 2006). It appears that female entrepreneurs tend to have networks which are dominated by strong ties (Raven & Le, 2015). In contrast, male entrepreneurs appear more willing to establish network links with people they do not know (weak ties). On the other hand, women seem to be better than men at establishing and maintaining informal, rather than formal, networks (Burt, 2019; Jayawarna et al., 2015). Therefore, evidence suggests that in establishing new ventures there are significant male-female variations in nature of networks and access to resources (see Chapter 9 Informal Finance).

Recently Longva (2021, p. 1268) suggested that combining social network theory with the emerging literature on entrepreneurial ecosystems helps reveal the context where relationships are developed. Longva (2021) goes on to propose that an entrepreneurial ecosystem is defined as the set of actors and elements that promote or inhibit entrepreneurship within a particular region (Stam & van de Ven, 2021). According to Isenberg (2014), ecosystems are dynamic, self-regulating networks containing a variety of different actors including policymakers, venture capitalists, business angels, educators and those from various cultural sectors (Isenberg, 2010). While Stam and van de Ven (2021) propose that the quality of an entrepreneurial ecosystem is related to the number and survivability of start-up businesses. University students who are involved in business start-up activities during their studies are a part of a student entrepreneurial ecosystem (Morris, Shirokova & Tsukanova, 2017).

According to Wright, Siegel and Mustar (2017), there are a number of factors that influence the effectiveness of university-based ecosystems. For example, the extent to which entrepreneurship is embedded in all disciplines and courses, university support systems, presence of business incubators or accelerators as well as links to the regional ecosystem (Horner, Jayawarna, Giordano & Jones, 2019; Jones, Meckel & Taylor, 2021a; Wright et al., 2017). Data for Longva's (2021) study were collected from universities in three regions of Norway and included interview with student entrepreneurs, educators and ecosystem actors. The results indicated there was a clear division between internal (academic) and external (industry) ecosystems elements (Figure 6.4). The three most important internal factors were as follows:

- *Curricular activities* – entrepreneurial education was important to the students as it helped them develop business ideas as well as gaining

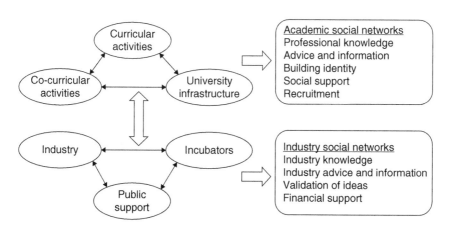

Figure 6.4 University and Industry Ecosystems

confidence in their ability to become entrepreneurs. Involvement in curricular activities also helped students build social networks with members of faculty and their peers. In the latter case, such networks became the basis of a community of like-minded students who were committed to entrepreneurship.

- *Co-curricular activities* – as we discuss in Section 5.5, involvement in entrepreneurship clubs and societies is important for developing an entrepreneurial mindset (see Section 1.5). Co-curricular activities also provide opportunities for informal mentoring, social support from fellow students and the opportunity to recruit students on temporary or part-time contracts to assist with the launch of a business.
- *University infrastructure* – includes the provision of incubation or accelerator facilities and links to experienced alumni. Alumni can provide a wide range of support to those wanting to become entrepreneurs including mentoring, coaching placements, finance and facilities as well as access to broader networks.

The three internal factors were complemented by three external factors associated with an entrepreneurial ecosystem:

- *Industry contacts* – exposure to experienced industry contacts is important for students who are trying to develop and test-out new ideas. Engaging with those who have 'real-world' experience helps students develop a more mature outlook. Those students who lacked such industry contacts during their education felt that it contributed to the failure to exploit their business ideas.
- *Industry incubators* – the ability to access an industry incubator provided students with knowledge and advice from experienced entrepreneurs. Industry incubators also inculcate more a professional attitude among incubatees than university-based incubators. Students and graduates tend to become more professional in their activities when they are exposed to those with more business experience.
- *Public support systems* – several students discussed accessing public support including funding and other forms of social support (coaching and mentoring) in the early stages of their business. Some regions may be keen to retain entrepreneurial talent by offering free or subsidized incubation facilities.

The study confirms that an effective ecosystem combining both internal and external features can have an extremely positive effect on students attempting to make the transition to entrepreneurship. Nevertheless, it is important to point out that a university ecosystem needs to be fully integrated internally as well as linked to the external ecosystem to ensure students obtain full value from their social networks. In practice, it is often the case that universities are limited in their ability to provide a coherent service to would-be entrepreneurs or to link to the regional business environment (Horner et al., 2019). Longva (2021, p. 1280) stresses the need for internal and external integration if the system is to provide useful support to students making the transition to entrepreneurs (Figure 6.4):

> This gives rise to important implications for policymakers, who must adapt policies and support systems carefully to fit existing entrepreneurial ecosystems. It further has important implications for universities and educators, who must consider the connection between internal ecosystem elements and the regional entrepreneurial ecosystem.

In summary, what Figure 6.4 indicates is the importance of students who wish to pursue entrepreneurial careers ensuring that they develop their industry/business networks as well as their academic networks. Making effective use of contacts with your fellow students, researchers and academic members of staff should be relatively straight-forward. Bridging out to industry and business contacts may be more difficult but ultimately is likely to be more rewarding. It will, of course, be easier to establish your own contacts with business if the university ecosystem overlaps with the local industry ecosystem. Even if those links are not formalized, there will certainly be individual members of staff who should be willing to broker links with appropriate business networks.

6.4 What is Social Capital?

Identification of the links between social networks and social capital has contributed to significant changes in the way that we think about entrepreneurship. Most early research concentrated on individual personality traits such as they need for achievement/autonomy, risk-taking and an internal locus of control (McClelland, 1967; Ndofirepi, 2020). As we have seen above, increasingly there was recognition that entrepreneurs' contacts via their networks were important to even the most individualistic entrepreneurs (Birley, 1985; Hite, 2005; Lans et al., 2015; Larson & Starr, 1993). It is generally acknowledged that use of the term social capital began with the work of Jane Jacobs (1965) in urban studies. James Coleman (1988) attempted to reconcile two conflicting explanations based on the distinction between individual social capital or social capital that advantages wider society. In other words, is social capital something which can be owned and exploited by individuals or is it something that is generated by a group or community? Developing relationships that encompass genuine shared values relies on processes of co-operation that create 'civic trust' (Coleman, 1988). Putnam (1995) who became an advisor to US President Bill Clinton, claimed that the decaying of social capital contributed to the decline of community spirit in the United States (hence the title of his book 'bowling alone'). Reciprocal relations based on mutual trust, obligations and expectations are central to the creation of social capital. Individuals help colleagues and friends because they believe that they will reciprocate and, consequently, both sides have expectations related to future behaviours (Lee, 2017). As we discuss in Chapter 5, this openness to knowledge-sharing is a particularly important feature of both entrepreneurial learning and the increase in provision of graduate incubation facilities (Jones et al., 2021a).

There are many different definitions of social capital, for example Davidsson and Honig (2003, p. 307) have a very instrumental perspective: 'the ability of actors to extract benefits from their social structures, networks and memberships'. An alternative view expressed by Nahapiet and Ghoshal (1998, p. 243) defines social capital as 'the sum of the actual and potential resources embedded within, available through, and derived from the network of relationships possessed by an individual or social unit'. The benefits associated with social capital can be extremely wide ranging and include tangible resources such as finance and facilities including equipment and buildings. Perhaps more significant are the intangible resources accessible via social capital such as knowledge and information about new opportunities, market changes, consumer needs and emotional support which is likely to be most important during the early stages of start-up (Edelman et al., 2016; Fisher, Neubert & Burnell, 2021).

Social capital, as well as social networks, can be distinguished between bonding and bridging linkages. Bonding social capital (internal/strong ties) concentrates attention on the collective rather than individuals and is concerned with linkages within groups or communities. The focus is on factors such as trust, obligations and reciprocity that contribute to the building of group cohesiveness and a sense of shared goals among nascent entrepreneurs (Box 6.2) based, for example, in an incubator (Jones et al., 2021a, 2021b). Bridging social capital (external/weak ties) focuses attention on the ways in which individuals utilize their egocentric links with other social actors. In essence, bridging social capital describes the way in which entrepreneurs access resources from those who are not part of their immediate group of family and friends (Lee, 2017; Lee & Jones, 2008). These ideas are associated with two views on the nature of networks and social capital (see Table 6.1). The first view suggests that social capital is mobilized via resources that accrue to individuals and groups because of long-standing network relationships. Closed networks based on strong cohesive social ties create an environment that facilitates trust and reciprocal relationships (Bourdieu, 1986; Coleman, 1988; Karatas-Ozkan & Chell, 2010). The other view is that the consistent norms fostered by cohesive networks limit the opportunities available to individual entrepreneurs (Burt, 1992, 2005, 2019). Hence, open networks with structural holes between actors present far more entrepreneurial opportunities than closed networks typified by bonding social capital (Figure 6.5). According to 'structural hole theory' consistent norms fostered by strong ties limit the opportunities for entrepreneurs to access unique resources such as knowledge and information (Burt, 1992, 2005, 2019). The openness associated with sparse social networks typified by 'spaces' between various actors, provide brokerage opportunities for those seeking to exploit 'structural holes'.

Box 6.2

Because it's hot-desking you basically meet a lot more people. The idea for MTL wouldn't have happened without Innospace full stop. Innospace gave me the opportunity to meet Neil, and without Neil, we wouldn't have that product [online workshop podcasting]. I wouldn't have had a website either. So it's the partnership with me, Neil, Dave and Val, as chains of business fundamentals. And that's really through Innospace.

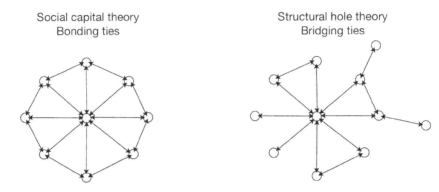

Figure 6.5 Bridging and Bonding Social Capital

Rather than making choices about either bonding or bridging social capital, effective entrepreneurs mobilize both internal (bonding) and external (bridging) social capital to ensure they successfully acquire and mobilize the appropriate knowledge-based resources. Therefore, it is increasingly acknowledged that, rather than being mutually exclusive, bonding and bridging ties are important to the success of entrepreneurial ventures. Internal (bonding) and external (bridging) social capital are essential for the successful acquisition and mobilization of knowledge-based resources (Crittenden, Crittenden & Ajjan, 2019; Smith, Smith & Shaw, 2017). As businesses begin to grow it is even more important to balance external relationships (with actors outside the firm) and internal relationships (within the firm). This distinction is fundamental to understanding the importance of social capital in growing businesses. Nascent entrepreneurs rely heavily for support on their 'identity-based' ties centred on family and friends (Larson & Starr, 1993). During growth, there is a shift to 'calculative networks' in which ties based on purpose and function become more important than identity ties (Hite & Hesterly, 2001; Jack et al., 2008). What this means in practice is that entrepreneurs begin to cultivate those contacts most useful to the survival of the business rather than relying on people they know and like. Hence, social capital can act as a form of 'glue' which bonds individuals together as well as a 'lubricant' which helps facilitate economic transactions (Anderson & Jack, 2002).

The core idea on which social capital is based concerns the need for successful entrepreneurs to develop and maintain relationships with a wide range of social actors. It is therefore important that entrepreneurs reflect on the efficacy of their internal and external network relationships.

Entrepreneurs also need the social skills to build and sustain bridging and bonding networks if they are to benefit from the acquisition of social capital (Lockett, Quesada-Pallarès, Williams-Middleton, Padilla-Meléndez & Jack, 2017; Rayna & Striukova, 2021). It seems clear that the structural and relational elements (see next section) of social capital are likely to directly influence the intellectual capital available to new entrepreneurs as they struggle to cope with uncertainty and ambiguity as well as making sense of existing practices and opportunities. The ability to retain and distribute this intellectual capital, and to make it more widely available within the ambit of the firm, is also important if both human and social capitals are to have more sustained and distributed benefits (Jones, Macpherson & Thorpe, 2010; Macpherson, Herbane & Jones, 2015).

One of the most significant advances in understanding the nature of entrepreneurial social capital was the idea that there are three underlying dimensions: structural, relational and cognitive (Lee, 2017; Lee & Jones, 2008; Nahapiet & Ghoshal, 1998; Shao & Sun, 2021). Structural social capital is essentially concerned with the nature of the entrepreneur's network based on size, density and diversity. As indicated earlier, smaller, closed homogeneous social networks in which all the actors know each other well are best for sharing knowledge and information. That is because norms associated with trust, reciprocity, mutual obligations and future expectations are more likely to be created within closed networks. The disadvantage is that access to social capital is likely to be limited because the network itself will have finite resources. Larger, more diverse and heterogeneous social networks will provide nascent entrepreneurs with access to a much wider array of social capital resources (Table 6.2). However, it may be more difficult to access those resources because actors do not have the same level of obligations to each other, nor can individuals be sure about the future

Table 6.2 Bonding and Bridging Social Capital

Network Tie	Group A High Human Capital	Group B Low Human Capital
Bonding (Close)	25	24
Bridging (Weak)	37	17
Bonding Resources	35	36
Bridging Resources	55	28

expectations of other actors in their network (Lee, Tuselmann, Jayawarna & Rouse, 2019).

Relational social capital refers to the norms of trust, reciprocity, mutual obligations and expectations which influence the behaviours of those belonging to network. Social capital is an intangible asset which relies on goodwill between the members of a network to ensure that there are effective flows of knowledge or meaningful discussions about new ideas. Without trust between those belonging to a network there will never be a basis for sharing valuable information such as new business opportunities or ways to improve some functional activity such as marketing or sales.

The third dimension, cognitive social capital has received less attention from researchers than either structural or relational social capital. Cognitive social capital refers to the way in which actors communicate via stories and narratives. Being able to communicate means we must have a 'shared language' and understand the codes which govern conversations. Clearly becoming an entrepreneur means acquiring the appropriate language in which to converse with other entrepreneurs and resource providers. At one level, that might simply mean understanding the differences between debt and equity funding. As we explain in the next section, enhancing your cognitive social capital skills means that the entrepreneur learns to communicate with other entrepreneurs as well as a wide-range of stakeholders including customers, competitors, suppliers and resource-providers (De Carolis & Saparito, 2006).

A study examined the role of cognitive social capital among two groups of nascent entrepreneurs who were attempting to access wider external resources (Lee & Jones, 2008). The research was based on two groups of students involved in business start-up programmes. Group A comprised well-qualified students undertaking a Master's in Entrepreneurship (high human capital). Group B comprised students from socially deprived areas who were undertaking a part-time business start-up course (low human capital) that was part of a programme known as the New Entrepreneur Scholarship [NES]. The study demonstrated that both groups were effective in utilizing their bonding (close) ties to access resources. However, those with lower levels of human capital were less willing or able to 'bridge out' of their bonding ties which limited access to bridging resources (28 compared to 55 for Group A). This is illustrated by the fact that those with low human capital on average had only 17 bridging ties compared to the 37 bridging ties of Group A. Hence, the study confirmed the importance of cognitive social capital for those nascent entrepreneurs who successfully access wider external resources (Table 6.2).

One other important outcome of the study were differences between the two groups in their use of online technologies (primarily email) to extend their networks and enhance their social capital (see Section 6.7). Group A (high human capital) students agreed that the use of devices such as cultural coded behaviour (online philosophies), online format-ting codes (short/brief messaging, text formatting, emphasis of words and symbols) and assertive language (formal, concise and questioning language) were important communication strategies and were effective for accessing diverse social ties. In contrast, students from Group B (low human capital) were reluctant users of electronic technologies, which restricted their ability to 'bridge' out of their close ties into broader networks of weaker ties with wider access to more extensive social capital (Lee & Jones, 2008, p. 579).

Shao and Sun (2021) examined the impact of the three forms of social capital on the ability of entrepreneurs in China to access venture capital funding. They were able to establish that structural and cognitive social capital had a positive impact on their ability to attract external finance. They explain this by stating that entrepreneurs with a larger social network (structural social capital) have access to a wider range of potential funders. Whereas cognitive social capital indicates that entrepreneurs and venture capitalists could engage in meaningful knowledge exchange based on their shared language. What this means in practice is that any would be entrepre-neur seeking external resources must develop the appropriate social skills to engage resource holders (Lans et al., 2015). Perhaps surprisingly, rela-tional social capital did not contribute to the ability of entrepreneurs to access external finance (Onginjo, Zhou, Berhanu & Belihu, 2021; Shao & Sun, 2021).

The key point to stress here is that there are very close links between the three forms of social capital. We can illustrate those links by referring to the network evolution model discussed above (Elfring & Hulsink, 2008; Elfring et al., 2021; Hite, 2005; Jayawarna, Jones & Macpherson, 2020). In the early stages of business start-up, the entrepreneur's strong ties (bonding) will be the most important in providing access to the resources needed for start-up (Figure 6.6). This means mobilizing the trust, mutual obligations and expectations with those whom the entrepreneur has the closest ties (family and friends). Hence, at this stage, relational social capital is the most important asset during the first phase of the start-up process. If the business is

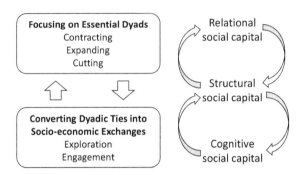

Figure 6.6 Social Capital and Network Evolution

to succeed, then the entrepreneur needs to open-up the network by bridging into new network ties. At this stage, structural social capital become more important as the network becomes larger and more diverse (weak ties). The entrepreneur must then identify those network ties that have access to the most useful resources. Cognitive social capital is key to building long-standing relationships with new members of the entrepreneur's network. So, the ability to construct joint narratives and stories helps turn weaker ties into strong ties which in the long-term will have most benefits for the entrepreneur (Lee & Jones, 2008; Shao & Sun, 2021).

6.5 Creating Social Capital during Business Start-up

As we have discussed in the previous sections, a key aspect of entrepreneurship is the ability to extend existing social networks in a way that provides the necessary resources to establish and grow a business. Nascent entrepreneurs have two major barriers to overcome in terms of establishing a viable new business: the liabilities of newness (Stinchcombe, 1965) and of smallness (Aldrich & Auster, 1986). Newness means that entrepreneurs lack a 'track record' and their business is unlikely to have visibility in the marketplace: potential customers will not know of the firm's existence. Smallness adds to the problems of visibility, but it also concerns the lack of knowledge, skills, information, finance and equipment which restricts entrepreneurial businesses during start-up. Based on three in-depth case studies, Fraccastoro, Gabrielsson and Chetty (2021) argue that use of social media

Equivocal reality: Unequivocal reality:
Does the business exist?   The business definitely exists

Figure 6.7 From Equivocal to Unequivocal Reality

(Facebook, Flickr, Instagram, LinkedIn, Twitter, YouTube etc.) can help new businesses overcome the liabilities of newness and smallness. The authors go on to point out that social media can help new businesses reach national and international markets comprising people of diverse ages and genders and can be 'localized' to specific parts of the world (Fraccastoro et al., 2021, p. 3). We suggest that social media can be an important aid in helping nascent entrepreneurs to move from an 'equivocal reality' to an 'unequivocal reality' (Figure 6.7). What this means is that entrepreneurs must give their businesses a tangible reality if they want to succeed. This can be done in several ways both physically and virtually. Physically means have premises, a trading name, telephone number, a web address. Virtually means that you should have a functional website as well as making regular use of various social media platforms (Box 6.3). It is important to acknowledge that many new businesses may not have a physical presence and, therefore, a strong focus on developing a presence on the appropriate social media is essential in overcoming the liabilities of newness and smallness.

Box 6.3

When you're trying to start a business it's important to have the kind of facilities that you've got in Innospace. Having access to meeting rooms and the networking areas, it's the kind of resources you might not have otherwise and I think it's also useful. It helps when you are dealing with customers or external bodies that you want to meet because its much more professional to have a place like this. Having a meeting room and have access to the projector and things like that. Its important that when you meet other people you present a professional

> image. It is also useful to have access to the Internet, computers, the printers, filing cabinet and those types of things which allow you to develop your business whereas if you didn't it would be less professional and more difficult.

Rae (2005) develops a conceptual framework that has three elements: personal and social emergence, contextual learning and negotiated enterprise. The first element focuses on the development of 'entrepreneurial identity' based on an individual's social, educational and career experiences. Second, contextual learning is related to social networks which help develop the skills associated with developing entrepreneurial opportunities. Third, negotiated enterprise is based on the recognition that any new business venture can only be established through 'negotiated relationships' with other people (Rae, 2005). Those who become successful entrepreneurs transform their experiences into new and useful knowledge. Entrepreneurs are action-oriented, and learning is largely experiential (see Chapter 5). Learning-by-doing is linked to what Cope (2003) describes as discontinuous events such as crises (failing to get an order or losing an existing customer) which promote higher level (double loop) learning. Such transformational learning relies on the individual entrepreneur's mental models which include their knowledge, experience and beliefs (Cope, 2003). Our view of entrepreneurship focuses on developing the most appropriate behaviours rather considering the individual's personality traits. The learning perspective which is adopted in this book complements the behavioural approach because, for example, it draws attention to the way in which nascent entrepreneurs mobilize their social capital.

The ability to extend personal relationships by bridging new networks is a crucial entrepreneurial skill (Larson & Starr, 1993). Research demonstrates how entrepreneurs transform different forms of media into 'knowable actions' to create meaningful communication patterns during business start-up. As demonstrated above, there are close links between human capital (education and experience), a willingness to learn and the creation of social capital. Human capital theory is based on the idea that increases in cognitive ability leads to higher levels of productivity and efficiency (Chapter 7). Furthermore, human capital incorporates experience and experiential learning as well as formal education. Cooperation from actors sharing similar interpretive frameworks during communication confirms the importance of cognitive social capital (De Carolis & Saparito, 2006). Entrepreneurial preparedness means that those engaged in business start-up can make use of previous experience to help acquire the skills to establish new businesses (Cope, 2003; Cope, 2005). The underlying links between structural capital (bonding and bridging) and cognitive social capital (language, codes and narrative) provides entrepreneurs with the means to access additional resources.

6.6 Social Capital and Access to Resources

Edith Penrose (1959) is a key figure in understanding the nature of resources which can be mobilized by entrepreneurs and owner-managers. Penrose suggested that the entrepreneurs' ability to exploit opportunities depends on the configuration of their resources (Kor, Mahoney & Michael, 2007; Pitelis, 2002). Researchers concerned with the development of entrepreneurial firms have been influenced by the resource-based view of the firm (Macpherson & Holt, 2007). The increasing focus on social capital has led to the recognition of how important network relationships are in providing resources for start-up businesses (Elfring et al., 2021; English, de Villiers Scheepers, Fleischman, Burgess & Crimmins, 2021).

To clarify how social capital contributes to entrepreneurial resources it is important to consider once again the distinction between bonding and bridging network ties. Bonding ties which are based on relationships with family members and close friends tend to be homogeneous. Whereas bridging ties are often based on professional or business relationship as well as 'friends of friends' therefore tend to be more heterogeneous. Heterogeneity is important because it exposes the entrepreneur to new ideas, new ways of thinking and new business opportunities as well as a wider array of more tangible resources (including finance). One of the most pressing problems for young entrepreneurs is that they lack business experience and, consequently, they also lack linkages to wider networks of professionals who can access to additional resources. Bonding and bridging social capital enable nascent entrepreneurs to obtain both tangible and intangible resources. As we discuss tangible resources in both Chapter 8 (Formal finance for a start-up business) and Chapter 9 (Informal finance for the start-up business) we focus on intangible resources in this section. Although, of course, it is important to acknowledge that family and friends are likely to provide some of the financial resources required to start a new business. Intangible resources include such factors as emotional support, business advice, potential referrals, business opportunities and new relationships.

It is generally agreed that there is a positive relationship between network size and access to resources: this is known as the 'network success hypothesis' (Birley, 1985; Elfring et al., 2021; Jones & Jayawarna, 2010). The network effect seems to be particularly powerful for bonding ties. The larger the network of family and close friends then the more likely entrepreneurs will be able to acquire useful resources. At the early stages of business start-up – having a large network of bridging ties does not appear to be so advantageous (Lee, 2017; Lee et al., 2019; Lee, Tüselmann, Jayawarna & Rouse, 2011). This may be because attempting to acquire resources from weaker ties during the crucial stages of business creation distracts the entrepreneur from their more important tasks of ensuring the business is functioning in an appropriate manner.

Importantly, bonding social capital also seems to be significantly more important in smaller communities than it is in large towns and cities. Entrepreneurs who live in rural communities mobilize social capital through their memberships of clubs and associations (sports clubs, youth clubs, civic societies and so on). For those attempting to start a rural business, social capital compensates for the lack of formal institutions which support businesses in urban environments (Bauernschuster, Falck & Heblich, 2010; Sørensen, 2012). Nevertheless, there are advantages to geographical concentrations in which entrepreneurs can share knowledge and information (Pitelis, 2012) this is particularly important in the case of technology-based firms (Maine, Shapiro & Vining, 2010)

Jones and Jayawarna (2010) examined the way in which social networks contributed to the performance of start-up firms which had existed for less than three years. The study confirmed that entrepreneurs used their strong ties to access a range of resources from their family and close friends. The study also demonstrated that weak ties were important in providing access to resources from suppliers and customers in terms of negotiating favourable trading relationship and securing working financial capital. Interestingly, the study also revealed that inexperienced entrepreneurs used experienced intermediaries to act as 'brokers' in negotiating access wider networks and resources (the results of this study are discussed in more detail in Chapter 9). The role of network brokers is very important in understanding how nascent entrepreneurs can access a wider range of social capital. As illustrated in

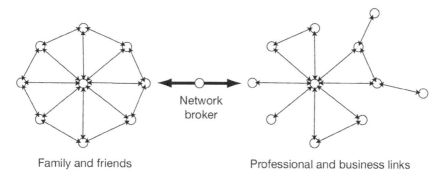

Family and friends   Professional and business links

Figure 6.8 The Role of Network Brokers

Figure 6.6, network evolution is linked to the way in which entrepreneurs make use of their structural, relational and cognitive social capitals. Using more experienced brokers is an effective way for those entrepreneurs who lack the necessary skills to bridge-out of their existing networks. Such brokers are important for two reasons: first, they can link new entrepreneurs into their own more extensive social networks. Secondly, brokers can help create social capital by using their own professional reputations to confirm the reliability of inexperienced entrepreneurs to a third-party business acquaintance. In other words, trust, reciprocity, mutual obligations and expectations between the broker and their networks ties can be 'transferred' to the new entrepreneur. University incubators are an effective way of mobilizing the professional links of an incubation manager for the benefit of incubatees (Box 6.4). Other studies have discussed the importance of students linking into professional networks that include business advisers, accountants, bank managers and solicitors (English et al., 2021; McDonald & Cater-Steel, 2017; Taylor & K. Pandza, 2003). These professionals can link entrepreneurs to contacts who may be willing to provide support including finance (Figure 6.8).

Box 6.4

A good example is that recently the Innospace manager suggested I spoke to an accountant who he knew. I was able to speak to her for about an hour and she advised me of the different ways that you go about issuing shares and how to factor in potential scenarios such as one director wanting to leave the company. As well as the legal implications of what the directors can decide on, what the shareholders can decide on and what percentages I needed to ensure a majority big enough to retain control. That directly influenced the way that we will be writing the legal documentation, the shareholders' agreement, the directors' service agreement, changing the memorandum and the articles of association. So these essential documents that determine how the company is run and by getting this advice we will be altering it in a way that better suits our needs.

As the topic of social skills has dealt with in Chapter 2, this section provides a very brief overview of the links between networks, social capital and resourcing a new business. Surprisingly, there has been a limited amount of research examining links between the entrepreneur's social skills and the success of their new venture (Baron & Markman, 2003; Zott & Quy Nguyen, 2007). There is, however, research which indicates that those employees with higher level social skills provide benefits to the individual and to the organization (Ferris, Davidson & Perrewé, 2005; Harris, Kacmar, Zivnuska & Shaw, 2007). Therefore, social skills are also likely to be of considerable benefit to those engaged in business start-up. Baron and Tang (2009) suggest that there are several social skills that are important for nascent entrepreneurs:

Social perception - refers to the ability to understand the motivations and attitudes of those people who are important during start-up. For example, potential working partners, employees and financial stakeholders.

Social adaptability – concerns the ability to adjust behaviours to a range of different social situations as well as being comfortable with people from different backgrounds, ages and social classes.

Expressiveness – it the individual's ability to express their feelings in an open and honest manner; that is, letting other people know how you feel about particular issues.

Self-promotion – means presenting your achievements and skills in a positive way to other people who have an influence on you and your business.

Ingratiation – the desire and the ability to encourage other people to have a positive attitude towards you by offering compliments and praise or doing personal favours.

Based on a study of 500 new ventures in Southern China it was established that social perception, expressiveness and self-promotion were all positively and directly linked to firm growth. Social perception and social adaptability were strong related to the acquisition of information including professional, managerial and marketing knowledge. Social adaptability and ingratiation were linked to effectiveness in acquiring resources including 'supply chain', human and financial resources (Figure 6.9). Hence, some social skills act on venture growth through access to information and resources. Baron and Tang (2009) conclude by stating that their study confirms that entrepreneurs' social skills play an important role in the performance and success of new ventures.

According to Lans et al. (2015), the ability of entrepreneurs to make best use of their social capital is related to what they describe as 'social competence'. Earlier work by Baron and colleagues (Baron & Markman, 2000, 2003; Baron & Tang, 2009) identified the most relevant entrepreneurial social skills: social perception, social adaptability, expressiveness, self-promotion and ingratiation (see above). Lans et al. (2015) examined the links between social competence and social capital by means of a study based on 130 MSc students in the Netherlands. The study confirmed that social competence had a significant impact on the social capital of early-stage entrepreneurs. In

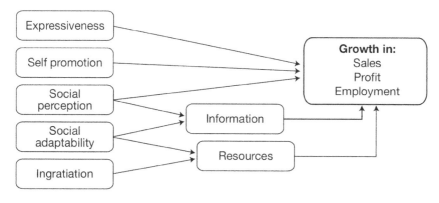

Figure 6.9 Social Skills and New Venture Growth

particular, structural social capital provided access to wider networks incorporating both strong and weak ties. That is, high levels of social competence enabled entrepreneurs to build larger and more diverse networks. Lans et al. (2015) go on to point out that 'self-promotion' appears to have a particularly strong impact on bridging social capital. While it is possible to view self-promotion from a negative perspective, the authors explain that it involves more than simply 'selling oneself' to others. Self-promotion also incorporates selling your business idea/model to other people and, therefore, having the appropriate social skills to communicate with various resource providers is clearly a major asset for young entrepreneurs.

6.7 Developing Social Capital via Social Media

We have established the importance of student and graduate entrepreneurs building up their social networks to ensure that they can create the social capital necessary to access additional resources. In recent years it has become apparent that social media technologies have a key role to play in the creation of social capital. As pointed out by Smith et al. (2017, p. 18), building, maintaining and using social networks online is very different from face-to-face communications. Smith et al. (2017, p. 22) draw on the work of (Kane, Alavi, Labianca & Borgatti, 2014) to suggest there are four factors that are central to online communication via social network sites (Facebook, LinkedIn, Instagram, Twitter, Pinterest and so on):

- *Digital user profiles* – refers to the content that entrepreneurs want to share with other users. Such profiles can include information about their entrepreneurial identities and values as well as an outline of their business model.
- *Digital search* – indicates the value of search engines which enable entrepreneurs to scan, see, review and extract network content.
- *Digital relations* - is a key feature of social network sites that help entrepreneurs interact with a wide range of weak and strong ties to grow their networks.
- *Network transparency* – all network connections are visible to the user.

The authors go on to argue that these four features are central to the creation of bridging and bonding social capital online. Twelve propositions are then developed to hypothesize the links between social media and social capital. To summarize, entrepreneurs can leverage vast amounts of network information using social media platforms. They can develop weak ties into stronger ties by sharing information on common interests and problems. They can also identify and broker structural holes in ways that would not be possible in conventional face-to-face social networks (Smith et al., 2017). Given the global reach of all the social media platforms it is also possible to establish a more diverse network of contacts.

In an attempt to clarify the role of social media in the creation of social capital, Zhao, Barratt-Pugh, Standen, Redmond and Suseno (2021) compared the online and offline networks of 35 entrepreneurs based in Western Australia who were involved with digital start-ups. In operational-izing social capital the authors draw on the three dimensions of social capital discussed above: structural, relational and cognitive (Nahapiet & Ghoshal, 1998). Zhao et al. (2021, p. 15) established that online social capital was different from off-line social capital and the impact on entrepreneurs was also different. Online social capital was primarily structural in nature as social media enabled entrepreneurs to rapidly extend and diversify their online social networks. Most of the entrepreneurs had a wide range of contacts on other continents and obtained regular information that had a positive impact on their business activities. In contrast, their face-to-face networks developed relational and cognitive social capital as contacts were local and often concentrated among those in co-working spaces. Consequently, off-line social networks were more important for developing the entrepreneurs' skills and knowledge as well as enhancing their self-confidence with posi-tive feedback (Zhao et al., 2021).

Wang, Liang, Mahto, Deng and Zhang (2020), in a study examining entrepreneurial entry, suggest that higher levels of social media usage help develop higher levels of social capital. Social media certainly allows indi-viduals to build networks that are not geographically constrained, and it should be relatively easy for most young entrepreneurs to establish many diverse contacts. Although regular interaction can help develop strong ties within a network it is likely that weak ties will dominate. Social media is increasingly important in helping younger people take the step into entre-preneurial entry (Wang et al., 2020). The authors go on to suggest that an individual's 'trust propensity' will mediate the impact of social media on their likelihood of starting a business. Data for the study were drawn from the China Panel Survey, which is carried out every two years and collects information on individuals and families. Focusing on those in the process of starting a business, Wang et al. (2020) were able to confirm a statistically significant link between the use of social media and the likelihood of starting a business. The authors suggest that their findings are consistent with the idea that larger social networks create higher levels of social capital. Interestingly, the study also confirmed that a larger online network had a positive influence on offline networks. In addition, the study established that an individuals' trust propensity does play a role in the use of social media as it can enhance or hinder entrepreneurial entry. Given the unreliability of social media, potential entrepreneurs should apply caution to information provided by online contacts if they are to benefit from the links between social media use and entrepreneurial entry (Wang et al., 2020).

The importance of building links to professional networks is also stressed in a recent study of alumni from an Australian university (English et al., 2021). Alumni had graduated on average three years previously giving them sufficient time to reflect on the important of developing professional networks during their time in academia. Many of the business graduates had entrepreneurial ambitions and they had made connections with guest speakers, business networking events and through external roles such as student ambassadors. The alumni also confirmed the importance of social networking sites for developing their professional networks. In particular, LinkedIn was regarded as the most useful asset in terms of building external connections and enhancing bridging social capital. As English et al. (2021, p. 656) go on to confirm: 'For those with entrepreneurial ambitions social media platforms provide the opportunity to find diverse connections who offer access to resources, support for their ventures as well as mentors who can provide guidance on start-up related challenges'.

To summarize, many students appear to believe creating a professional network is something that can be delayed until they have graduated (English et al., 2021). In this section we have stressed the importance of students using social media to bridge into professional networks during their studies. Most students will be familiar with using the most major social networking platforms for keeping in touch with friends and relatives (bonding social capital). Embarking on an entrepreneurial career means it is essential that you begin to build links to professional networks to create bridging social capital. As emphasized throughout this chapter, bonding social capital (strong ties) is important in the early stages of business start-up but longer-term survival and growth will be based on bridging social capital (weak ties). Initially, the focus of social media-based relationships is structural in term the size and diversity of network contacts. It is possible to forge stronger relationships (relational and cognitive social) by sharing knowledge and information with key online contacts (Smith et al., 2017).

6.8 Summary and Key Learning Points

Social networks, social/communications skills and social capital combine to provide access to a wide range of resources for nascent entrepreneurs. Resources include tangible assets such as finance and premises (a friend's garage or a converted bedroom in your parents' home) and intangible assets including emotional support, advice and links to other businesspeople. In the early stages of business start-up strong (bonding) ties which include your family and close friends are of most importance. Building a business which has the potential for long-term success means linking to weaker (bridging) ties who can provide access to a much wider range of resources. Social capital embodies trust, reciprocity, obligations and mutual expectations about future behaviours which facilitate the benefits of belonging to a larger, more diverse social network.

Links between the three dimensions of social capital (structural, relational and cognitive) are central to understanding how nascent entrepreneurs convert/extend their strong ties into more instrumental (economic) exchanges. In effect, this means that entrepreneurs must move from relationships based on strong emotional bonds with high levels of trust and mutual obligations to relationships that are more instrumental in nature. In relationships with weaker ties, both parties have expectations of future benefits in terms economic and financial benefits. In other words, your family and friends (bonding ties) will offer support without expecting a financial return because of strong emotional ties. Weaker ties will, in most cases, only provide valuable resources in exchange for specific assets such as a share in the business (see negotiations in Dragon's Den). Ultimately, an entrepreneur's ability to use their social network as a mechanism to mobilize social capital is only of use if it provided those resources necessary to develop their business.

In the final section of this chapter, we have identified the important role of social media in providing access to social capital. Making use of well-known platforms such as Facebook and LinkedIn is an important way of extending your social network as well as overcoming the dual liabilities of newness and smallness, which are associated with all new ventures. We have also stressed the key role of social competence (social skills) in building, maintaining and using your social network. It is certainly clear that those individuals with higher levels of social competence are best placed to build an extensive social network that provides access to a wide range of resources.

Key Learning Points:

- Understand the difference between social networks and social capital.
- Understand the three and differentiate between the dimensions of social capital: structural, relational and cognitive.
- Understand the differences between bonding and bridging relationships.
- Understand how the balance between strong (bonding) and weak (bridging) ties change as the entrepreneur gains in experience and the business begins to grow.
- Understand that the balance between strong-weak ties also vary according to males and females and whether the business is in an urban or rural area.
- Understand the importance of structural holes and the role of brokers in exploiting those structural holes.
- Understand which social skills are particularly important in extending your network and creating social capital.
- Understand the role of social media in providing access to social networks and social capital

6.9 Discussion Questions and Call to Action

1. What do you understand by the terms strong and weak ties?
2. Explain what is meant by the term 'the strength of weak ties' and why they are important to nascent entrepreneur.
3. Can you identify any individuals within your college/university who can act as network brokers?
4. How well do you think your university's ecosystem operates in support of student entrepreneurship (curricular, co-curricular and infrastructure)?
5. Explain the difference between the three forms of social capital: structural, relational and cognitive.

6. What is meant by the phrases liabilities of newness/liabilities of smallness and how can they be overcome by new entrepreneurs?

7. There are five different social skills discussed in Section 6.1, briefly explain what they are and the extent to which you are proficient in those skills.

8. How do you think that you could make better use of social media platforms to extend your social networks?

If you are thinking seriously about a career as an entrepreneur, then making good use of your social networks to access valuable social capital is of crucial importance. As stated at the beginning of this chapter, there has been a fundamental shift away from the idea of the entrepreneur as 'heroic' individuals. Most entrepreneurs are supported by a range of individuals belonging to their social networks. Even if you do not intend to start a business when you graduate, building a professional social network is likely to be useful in helping you obtain a good job. A key theme of this book is that your social skills are essential to your future career as an entrepreneur. As discussed in Chapter 5, engaging in experiential learning is certainly an effective way to develop your social skill/competence. You are unlikely to be able to build and make effective use of your social network without developing the appropriate social skills. In particular, the ability to promote yourself and your business is essential to accessing wider resources, which may be tangible but could equally be intangible. Therefore, you should be making good use of your time in college/university thinking about ways in which you can extend your social networks beyond the people you know at home and on campus. Starting to create a strong professional network will be invaluable whatever career you choose to pursue in the future.

Notes

1 As discussed in Chapter 3, our view is that opportunities are created by entrepreneurs rather than being discovered. Even if they are adopting an effectual approach, entrepreneurs still have to decide on an area of the market that they are intending to target (see the Jazooli case).

2 Larson and Starr (1993) include an additional stage – 'layering the exchanges' - which is concerned with the functional linkages as the firm grows. As we are dealing with the early stages of operation this phase does not apply here.

References

Aldrich, H. E. & Auster, E. R. (1986). Even Dwarfs Started Small: Liabilities of Age and Size and their Strategic Implications. *Research in Organizational Behavior*, *8*, 165–198

Aldrich, H. E., Rosen, B. & Woodward, W. (1987). *The impact of social networks on business foundings and profit: A longitudinal study*. Paper presented at the In Frontiers of entrepreneurship research, Wellesley, MA: Babson College.

Anderson, A. R. & Jack, S. L. (2002). The articulation of social capital in entrepreneurial networks: a glue or a lubricant? *Entrepreneurship & Regional Development*, *14*(3), 193–210.

Baron, R. A. & Markman, G. D. (2000). Beyond social capital: How social skills can enhance entrepreneurs' success. *Academy of Management Executive*, *14*(1), 106–116.

Baron, R. A. & Markman, G. D. (2003). Beyond social capital: the role of entrepreneurs' social competence in their financial success. *Journal of Business Venturing*, *18*(1), 41–60.

Baron, R. A. & Tang, J. (2009). Entrepreneurs' social skills and new venture performance: mediating mechanisms and cultural generality. *Journal of Management*, *35*(2), 282–306.

Batjargal, B. (2006). The dynamics of entrepreneurs' networks in a transitioning economy: the case of Russia. *Entrepreneurship & Regional Development*, *18*(4), 305–320.

Bauernschuster, S., Falck, O. & Heblich, S. (2010). Social capital access and entrepreneurship. *Journal of Economic Behavior and Organization*, *76*, 821–833.

Bhide, A. V. (2000). *The Origin and Evolution of New Businesses*. New York: Oxford University Press.

Birley, S. (1985). The Role of Networks in the Entrepreneurial Process. *Journal of Business Venturing*, *1*(1), 107–117.

Bourdieu, P. (Ed.) (1986). *The Forms of Capital*. New York: Greenwood.

Brush, C. G. (2002). The Role of Social Capital and Gender in Linking Financial Suppliers and Entrepreneurial Firms: A Framework for Future Research. *Venture Capital*, *4*(4), 305–323.

Brush, C. G., Greene, P. G. & Hart, M. M. (2001). From initial idea to unique advantage: The entrepreneurial challenge of constructing a resource base. *Academy of Management Executive*, *15*(1), 64–78.

Burt, R. S. (1992). *Structural holes: the social structure of competition*. Cambridge, MA: Harvard University Press.

Burt, R. S. (2005). *Brokerage and closure: an introduction to social capital*. Oxford: Oxford University Press.

Burt, R. S. (2019). The networks and success of female entrepreneurs in China. *Social Networks*, *58*, 37–49.

Coleman, J. S. (1988). Social capital in the creation of human capital. *The American Journal of Sociology: Supplement, Organizations and Institutions: Sociological and Economic Approaches to the Analysis of Social Structure*, *94*, S95–S120.

Conway, S. & Jones, O. (2012). Networks and the Small Business. In S. Carter & D. Jones-Evans (Eds.), *Enterprise and Small Business: Principles, Practice and Policy* (2nd ed. ed.) (pp. 338–361). Harlow: Pearson.

Cope, J. (2003). Entrepreneurial Learning and Critical Reflection: Discontinuous Events as Triggers for 'Higher-level' Learning. *Management Learning*, *34*(4), 429–450.

Cope, J. (2005). Toward a Dynamic Learning Perspective of Entrepreneurship. *Entrepreneurship: Theory & Practice*, *29*(4), 373–397.

Cope, J., Jack, S. & Rose, M. B. (2007). Social Capital and Entrepreneurship: An Introduction. *International Small Business Journal*, *25*(3), 213–219.

Crittenden, V. L., Crittenden, W. F. & Ajjan, H. (2019). Empowering women micro-entrepreneurs in emerging economies: The role of information communications technology. *Journal of Business Research*, *98*, 191–203.

Davidsson, P. & Honig, B. (2003). The role of social and human capital among nascent entrepreneurs. *Journal of Business Venturing*, *18*(3), 301–331.

De Carolis, D. M. & Saparito, P. (2006). Social Capital, Cognition, and Entrepreneurial Opportunities: A Theoretical Framework. *Entrepreneurship: Theory & Practice*, *30*(1), 41–56.

Edelman, L. F., Manolova, T. S., Shirokova, G. & Tsukanova, T. (2016). The impact of family support on young entrepreneurs' start-up activities. *Journal of Business Venturing*, *31*(4), 428–448.

Elfring, T. & Hulsink, W. (2008). Networking by entrepreneurs: Patterns of tie-formation in emerging organizations. *Organisation Studies*, *28*(12), 1848–1872.

Elfring, T., Klyver, K. I. M. & van Burg, E. (2021). *Entrepreneurship as Networking: Mechanisms, Dynamics, Practices, and Strategies*. New York: Oxford University Press.

English, P., de Villiers Scheepers, M. J., Fleischman, D., Burgess, J. & Crimmins, G. (2021). Developing professional networks: the missing link to graduate employability. *Education + Training*, *63*(4), 647–661.

Evald, M. R., Klyver, K. I. M. & Svendsen, S. G. (2006). The Changing Importane of the Strength of Ties Throughout the Entrepreneurial Process. *Journal of Enterprising Culture*, *14*(1), 1–26.

Ferris, G. R., Davidson S. L. & Perrewé, P. L. (2005). Political skill at work: Impact on effectiveness. Mountain View, CA: Davies-Black Publishing

Fisher, G., Neubert, E. & Burnell, D. (2021). Resourcefulness narratives: Transforming actions into stories to mobilize support. *Journal of Business Venturing*, *36*(4). doi:10.1016/j.jbusvent.2021.106122

Fraccastoro, S., Gabrielsson, M. & Chetty, S. (2021). Social Media Firm Specific Advantages as Enablers of Network Embeddedness of International Entrepreneurial Ventures. *Journal of World Business, 56*(3). doi:10.1016/j.jwb.2020.101164

Granovetter, M. S. (1973). The Strength of Weak Ties. *American Journal of Sociology, 78*(6), 1360–1380.

Hamilton, E. (2006). Whose Story Is It Anyway? Narrative Accounts of the Role of Women in Founding and Establishing Family Businesses. *International Small Business Journal, 24*(3), 253–271.

Harris, K. J., Kacmar, K. M., Zivnuska, S. & Shaw, J. D. (2007). The impact of political skill on impression management effectiveness. *Journal of Applied Psychology, 92*(1), 278–285.

Hite, J. M. (2005). Evolutionary Processes and Paths of Relationally Embedded Network Ties in Emerging Entrepreneurial Firms. *Entrepreneurship: Theory & Practice, 29*(1), 113–144.

Hite, J. M. & Hesterly, W. S. (2001). The Evolution of Firm Networks: From Emergence to Early Growth of the Firm. *Strategic Management Journal, 22*(3), 275–286.

Honig, B. & Hopp, C. (2019). Learning orientations and learning dynamics: Understanding heterogeneous approaches and comparative success in nascent entrepreneurship. *Journal of Business Research, 94*, 28–41

Horner, S., Jayawarna, D., Giordano, B. & Jones, O. (2019). Strategic choice in universities: Managerial agency and effective technology transfer. *Research Policy, 48*(5), 1297–1309.

Hughes, M., Ireland, R. D. & Morgan, R., E. (2007). Stimulating Dynamic Value: Social Capital and Business Incubation as a Pathway to Competitive Success. *Long Range Planning, 40*, 154–177.

Isenberg, D. J. (2010). How to Start an Entrepreneurial Revolution. *Harvard Business Review, 88*(6), 40–50.

Isenberg, D. J. (2014). What an Entrepreneurship Ecosystem Actually Is. *Harvard Business Review Digital Articles, 5*(1), 2–5.

Jack, S. L., Drakopoulou-Dodd, S. & Anderson, A. R. (2008). Change and the development of entrepreneurial networks over time: a processual perspective. *Entrepreneurship & Regional Development, 20*(2), 125–159.

Jacobs, J. M. (1965). *The death and life of great American cities Jane Jacobs*: Harmondsworth: Penguin.

Jayawarna, D., Jones, O. & Macpherson, A. (2020). Resourcing Social Enterprises: The Role of Socially Oriented Bootstrapping. *British Journal of Management, 31*(1), 56–79.

Jayawarna, D., Jones, O. & Marlow, S. (2015). The influence of gender upon social networks and bootstrapping behaviours. *Scandinavian Journal of Management, 31*(3), 316–329.

Jones, O. (2022). Academic engagement with small business and entrepreneurship: Towards a landscape of practice. *Industry and Higher Education, 36*(3), 279–293.

Jones, O. & Giordano, B. (2021). Family entrepreneurial teams: The role of learning in business model evolution. *Management Learning, 52*(3), 267–293.

Jones, O. & Jayawarna, D. (2010). Resourcing new businesses: social networks, bootstrapping and firm performance. *Venture Capital, 12*(2), 127–152.

Jones, O., Macpherson, A. & Thorpe, R. (2010). Learning in owner-managed small firms: Mediating artefacts and strategic space. *Entrepreneurship & Regional Development, 22*(7/8), 649–673.

Jones, O., Meckel, P. & Taylor, D. W. (2021a). *Creating Communities of Practice: Entrepreneurial Learning in a University-Based Incubator*. Cham (Switzerland): Springer.

Jones, O., Meckel, P. & Taylor, D. W. (2021b). Situated learning in a business incubator: Encouraging students to become real entrepreneurs. *Industry & Higher Education, 35*(4), 367–383.

Kane, G. C., Alavi, M., Labianca, G. & Borgatti, S. P. (2014). What's Different About Social Media Networks? A Framework and Research Agenda. *MIS Quarterly, 38*(1), 275–304.

Karatas-Ozkan, M. & Chell, E. (2010). *Nascent Entrepreneurship and Learning*: Cheltenham and Northampton, MA: Edward Elgar.

Kor, Y. Y., Mahoney, J. T. & Michael, S. C. (2007). Resources, Capabilities and Entrepreneurial Perceptions. *Journal of Management Studies, 44*(7), 1187–1212.

Lans, T., Blok, V. & Gulikers, J. (2015). Show Me Your Network and I'll Tell You Who You Are: Social Competence and Social Capital of Early-Stage Entrepreneurs. *Entrepreneurship and Regional Development, 27*(7–8), 458–473.

Larson, A. & Starr, J. A. (1993). A Network Model of Organization Formation. *Entrepreneurship: Theory & Practice, 17*(2), 5–15.

Lechner, C. & Dowling, M. (2003). Firm networks: external relationships as sources for the growth and competitiveness of entrepreneurial firms. *Entrepreneurship & Regional Development, 15*(1), 1–27.

Lee, R. (2017). *The Social Capital of Entrepreneurial Newcomers: Bridging, Status-power and Cognition*. London: Palgrave Macmillan.

Lee, R. & Jones, O. (2008). Networks, Communication and Learning during Business Start-up. *International Small Business Journal, 26*(5), 559–594.

Lee, R., Tuselmann, H., Jayawarna, D. & Rouse, J. (2019). Effects of structural, relational and cognitive social capital on resource acquisition: a study of entrepreneurs residing in multiply deprived areas. *Entrepreneurship & Regional Development, 31*(5/6), 534–554.

Lee, R., Tüselmann, H., Jayawarna, D. & Rouse, J. (2011). Investigating the social capital and resource acquisition of entrepreneurs residing in deprived areas of England. *Environment & Planning C: Government & Policy, 29*(6), 1054–1072.

Lockett, N., Quesada-Pallarès, C., Williams-Middleton, K., Padilla-Meléndez, A. & Jack, S. (2017). 'Lost in Space': The Role of Social Networking in University-Based Entrepreneurial Learning. *Industry and Higher Education, 31*(2), 67–80.

Longva, K. K. (2021). Student venture creation: developing social networks within entrepreneurial ecosystems in the transition from student to entrepreneur. *International Journal of Entrepreneurial Behavior & Research, 27*(5), 1264–1284.

Macpherson, A., Herbane, B. & Jones, O. (2015). Developing Dynamic Capabilities through Resource Accretion: Expanding the Entrepreneurial Solution Space. *Entrepreneurship and Regional Development, 27*(5–6), 259–291.

Macpherson, A. & Holt, R. (2007). Knowledge, Learning and Small Firm Growth: A Systematic Review of the Evidence. *Research Policy, 36*(2), 172–192.

Maine, E. M., Shapiro, D. M. & Vining, A. R. (2010). The role of clustering in the growth of new technology-based firms. *Small Business Economics, 34*(2), 127–146.

Manolova, T. S., Manev, I. M., Carter, N. M. & Gyoshev, B. S. (2006). Breaking the family and friends' circle: Predictors of external financing usage among men and women entrepreneurs in a transitional economy. *Venture Capital, 8*(2), 109–132.

Mason, C. M. & Harrison, R. T. (1999). 'Venture Capital': Rationale, Aims and Scope: Editorial. *Venture Capital, 1*(1), 1–46.

McClelland, D. C. (1967). *The Achieving Society*. New York: Free Press.

McDonald, J. & Cater-Steel, A. (2017). *Communities of Practice: facilitating social learning in higher education*: Cham Switzerland: Springer.

Morris, M. H., Shirokova, G. & Tsukanova, T. (2017). Student entrepreneurship and the university ecosystem: a multi-country empirical exploration. *European Journal of International Management, 11*(1), 65–85.

Nahapiet, J. & Ghoshal, S. (1998). Social Capital, Intellectual Capital, and the Organizational Advantage. *Academy of Management Review, 23*(2), 242–266.

Ndofirepi, T. M. (2020). Relationship between entrepreneurship education and entrepreneurial goal intentions: psychological traits as mediators. *Journal of Innovation & Entrepreneurship, 9*(1), 1–20.

Onginjo, J. O., Zhou, D. M., Berhanu, T. F. & Belihu, S. W. G. (2021). Analyzing the impact of social capital on US based Kickstarter projects outcome. *Heliyon, 7*(7). doi: 10.1016/j.heliyon.2021.e07425

Ostgaard, T. A. & Birley, S. (1996). New venture growth and personal networks. *Journal of Business Research, 36*(1), 37–50.

Penrose, E. (1959). *The theory of the growth of the firm*. Oxford: Oxford University Press.

Pitelis, C. (2012). Clusters, entrepreneurial ecosystem co-creation, and appropriability: a conceptual framework. *Industrial & Corporate Change, 21*(6), 1359–1388.

Pitelis, C. (Ed.) (2002). *The Growth of the Firm: the legacy of Edith Penrose.* Oxford: Oxford University Press.

Putnam, R. D. (1995). Bowling alone: America's declining social capital. *Current* (373), 3–10.

Rae, D. (2005). Entrepreneurial learning: a narrative-based conceptual model. *Journal of Small Business and Enterprise Development, 12*(3), 323–335.

Ratzinger, D., Amess, K., Greenman, A. & Mosey, S. (2018). The Impact of Digital Start-Up Founders' Higher Education on Reaching Equity Investment Milestones. *Journal of Technology Transfer, 43*(3), 760–778.

Raven, P. & Le, Q. V. (2015). Teaching business skills to women. *International Journal of Entrepreneurial Behavior & Research, 21*(4), 622–641. doi:10.1108/ IJEBR-06-2014-0099

Rayna, T. & Striukova, L. (2021). Fostering skills for the 21st century: The role of Fab labs and makerspaces. *Technological Forecasting & Social Change, 164.* doi: 10.1016/j.techfore.2020.120391

Ruiz-Palomino, P. & Martinez-Canas, R. (2021). From Opportunity Recognition to the Start-Up Phase: The Moderating Role of Family and Friends-Based Entrepreneurial Social Networks. *International Entrepreneurship and Management Journal, 17*(3), 1159–1182.

Shao, Y. & Sun, L. (2021). Entrepreneurs' social capital and venture capital financing. *Journal of Business Research, 136,* 499–512.

Smith, C., Smith, J. B. & Shaw, E. (2017). Embracing digital networks: Entrepreneurs' social capital online. *Journal of Business Venturing, 32*(1), 18–34.

Smith, D. A. & Lohrke, F. T. (2008). Entrepreneurial network development: Trusting in the process. *Journal of Business Research, 61*(4), 315–322.

Sørensen, J. F. L. (2012). Testing the Hypothesis of Higher Social Capital in Rural Areas: The Case of Denmark. *Regional Studies, 46*(7), 873–891.

Stam, E. & van de Ven, A. (2021). Entrepreneurial Ecosystem Elements. *Small Business Economics, 56*(2), 809–832.

Stinchcombe, A., L. (1965). Organizations as Social Structures. In J. March (Ed.), *Handbook of Organizations* (pp. 142–193). Chicago: Rand-McNally.

Taylor, D. & Pandza, K. (2003). *Networking Capability: The Competitive Advantage of Small Firms.* In O. Jones & F. Tilley, *Competitive Advantage in SMEs: Organising for Innovation and Change* (pp. 156–174), Chichester: Wiley.

Wang, W., Liang, Q., Mahto, R. V., Deng, W. & Zhang, S. X. (2020). Entrepreneurial entry: The role of social media. *Technological Forecasting & Social Change, 161.* doi:10.1016/j.techfore.2020.120337

Wright, M., Siegel, D. S. & Mustar, P. (2017). An Emerging Ecosystem for Student Start-Ups. *Journal of Technology Transfer*, *42*(4), 909–922.

Zhao, F., Barratt-Pugh, L., Standen, P., Redmond, J. & Suseno, Y. (2021). An exploratory study of entrepreneurial social networks in the digital age. *Journal of Small Business and Enterprise Development, ahead-of-print* (ahead-of-print). doi:10.1108/JSBED-10-2020-0359

Zott, C. & Quy Nguyen, H. (2007). How Entrepreneurs Use Symbolic Management to Acquire Resources. *Administrative Science Quarterly*, *52*(1), 70–105.

Human Capital and Business Start-up

7.1 Introduction

As we have discussed earlier, the resource-based view (RBV) promotes resources as central to the firm's capabilities for value-creation and long-term competitive advantage. The resources your firm has, or has access to, is a long-term process of resources accumulation, sometimes called resource assembly, that occurs throughout the entrepreneurial process. At the initial stages of venture creation, however, resources access is particularly crucial, since research evidence suggests that new ventures with a larger pool of resources are more likely to survive and display higher growth potential when compared to firms operating in resource poor environments. In the new venture context, resources encompass both tangible and intangible assets as well as capabilities that are available for entrepreneurs to exploit their new business ideas. As Sarasvathy (2001, p. 250) points out, all nascent entrepreneurs begin with three categories of 'means'; their own traits, tastes and abilities; their knowledge corridors; and their social networks.

Traditionally the literature advocates complete ownership control of all resources if firms are to gain competitive advantage. Depending on the scale and nature of the business and the abilities and starting endowments of the entrepreneur, however, gaining complete ownership of resources is a challenging task in most new ventures. Recent literature emphasizes the importance of developing behaviours that enhance the entrepreneurs' abilities to use and extract value from resources that are outside their control. 'Bootstrapping' describes the process that enables resource-constrained entrepreneurs to access resources relatively cheaply

DOI: 10.4324/9781003312918-8

and quickly to create, or respond to, market opportunities (see Chapter 9 for a discussion of bootstrapping). Once built into the fabric of the firm through its embedded routines, bootstrapping may also provide a way to remain responsive and agile by encouraging a lean approach to the firm's operating strategy (Timmons, 1999). Research also shows that not all entrepreneurs plan to grow their ventures and therefore resource assembly is also influenced by the purposeful decisions and expectations of the entrepreneur (Penrose, 1959).

In this chapter we introduce the resource-based view of the firm and examine the key resources required for entrepreneurs who are starting and running new venture. Burt (1992) proposed three essential resources for entrepreneurs during the venture founding stage: personal financial resources, personal skills and social resources. The importance of social and financial resources to the entrepreneur is discussed in more detail in Chapters 6, 8 and 9 respectively. In this chapter, we pay specific attention to the role of human capital in the entrepreneurial process. Most importantly, human capital is the first available resource for entrepreneurs, and it leads to the development and acquisition of other types of resources important for further venture development. The chapter also include a section that highlights the importance of recasting human capital in lifecycle terms and emphasizes the idea that children's education has far-reaching effects that become manifest in career paths related to entrepreneurship. Finally, we provide some research evidence that suggest entrepreneur human capital and new venture success/performance.

7.2 Learning Objectives

- To appreciate the relevance of the resource-based view to nascent entrepreneurs in their effort to accumulate appropriate resources at start-up.
- To recognize there are different types of resources that entrepreneurs require at the early stage of business development.
- To evaluate the role of human capital as a resource for entrepreneurs.
- To examine childhood opportunities for the accrual of human capital required to pursue a career in entrepreneurship.
- To learn from the evidence related to how human capital impacts on entrepreneurial potential and success.

7.3 Resource-based View of the Firm

The resource-based view (RBV) is built on the premise that all firms comprise bundles of resources (Penrose, 1959) and that resource accessibility will shape the firm's direction and ultimately determine performance (Barney, 1991). Barney (1991, p. 101) classifies resources as 'all assets, capabilities, organizational processes, firm attributes, information, knowledge, etc. controlled by the firm that enable the firm to conceive of and implement strategies that improve its efficiency and effectiveness'. Firms with stronger resource bases are better able to survive and grow irrespective of environmental change and business decisions. Critical to the theory is that resources that are valuable, rare, imperfectly inimitable and difficult to substitute provide firms with sustained competitive advantage (Barney, 1991). In a sustainable setting, substitution, duplication and imitation of resources is not possible due to the complexity associated with the processes that involve resource acquisition, management, reconfiguration and leverage (Sirmon & Hitt, 2003). Therefore, it is not only the resources themselves that determine a firm's competitive position but also how firms allocate and deploy resources for strategic activities. Because resource needs are idiosyncratic, there are variations in value creating actions and the competitive position derived from the entrepreneur's resource base (Arend & Lévesque, 2010).

Some writers have emphasized that while resources are necessary to deliver capability, the resource-based view (RBV) is too static for explaining how firms create new capabilities or exploit opportunities within dynamic and changing markets (see for example Coen & Maritan, 2011). In accordance with the dynamic capabilities theory, 'both the skills/resources and the way organizations use them must constantly change, leading to the creation of continuously changing temporary advantages' (Fiol, 2001, p. 692). As firms need to reconfigure opportunities through creative deployment of resources, it is the way in which owner-managers envisage and enact available resources that defines a firm's trajectory (See Chapter 10, Dynamic Capabilities).

Chrisman (1999) referred to the accumulation of resource stocks for new venture creation as a special case of resource-based theory. Because entrepreneurs begin with few, if any, stocks of resources other than their own knowledge and social networks. This knowledge is critical to make resource related decisions and to gain access to costly-to-duplicate resources that give the entrepreneur a competitive advantage (Foss, Klein, Kor & Mahoney, 2008). For new ventures, initial resources are particularly important as they not only act as a buffer against the liabilities of smallness, but they also provide strategic alternatives for the entrepreneur to develop their business.

7.4 Types of Resources

RBV is based on the potential for multiple types of resources including 'assets, capabilities, organizational processes, firm attributes, information and knowledge' (Barney, 1991, p. 101) that can be categorized as either tangible or intangible (Figure 7.1). Lichtenstein and Brush (2001) identify what they describe as 'salient resources' for entrepreneurial ventures which include: capital, social, organizational systems/structures, management know-how, technology, physical resources, leadership, culture and 'informal systems'. The authors go on to argue that, in new ventures, organizational resources evolve over a period of weeks, months and years (Figure 7.2 explains how the emphasis on human, social and financial resources change when nascent entrepreneurs set-up, run and develop their ventures). If new firms are to become established or self-sustaining then 'a series of resource acquisitions and combinations might be necessary' (Lichtenstein & Brush, 2001, p. 41). Interestingly, in their longitudinal analysis of three

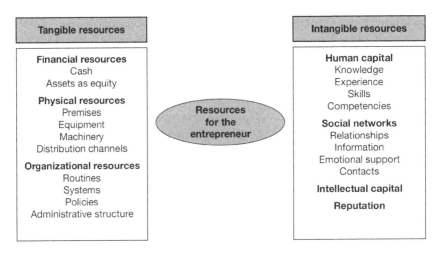

Figure 7.1 Tangible and Intangible Entrepreneurial Resources

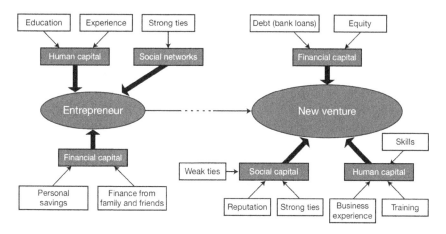

Figure 7.2 Resource Needs: From Entrepreneur to New Venture

firms, intangible resources (knowledge, expertise, relationships, sales/service delivery and decision-making) were found to be more salient than tangible resources. Newer studies in the field are examining resources as routines, such as marketing activities or exporting activities and measuring the effects of human capital as a resource. For example, a recent paper suggests the new firm survival is correlated with both exporting activity and human capital (Del Sarto, Di Minin, Ferrigno & Piccaluga, 2021). They argue that export activity provides the knowledge necessary to exploit the potential of qualified human capital. It is clear from the above discussion that what qualifies as a resource is complex and may involves the application of those resources using experience, judgement, knowledge and skills (human capital).

7.4.1 Tangible Resources

A firm's tangible resources include financial, physical and organizational resources (Barney, 1991). In terms of financial resources, during the stages of conception and gestation, entrepreneurs rely on their own funds plus those obtained from family and friends (Cassar, 2004). As firms grow there is a shift in focus from 'insider' to 'outsider' finance as investment becomes more attractive to business angels and venture capitalists (Bozkaya & De La Potterie, 2008). These financial resources are generally crucial to enable the acquisition of physical resources such as premises, machinery, equipment and distribution channels (see Chapter 8 and 9 for a fuller discussion on financial resources). In addition, policy support and Government funding can provide critical tangible resources for new firms (Pergelova & Angulo-Ruiz, 2014). Organizational capital includes routines, systems, policies and related firm's administrative structure within which other resources are applied to create value adding activities (Penrose, 1959). More specifically, these resources include a 'firm's formal reporting structure, its formal and informal planning, controlling and coordinating systems, as well as informal relations among groups within a firm and between a firm and those in its environment' (Barney, 1991, p. 101).

7.4.2 Intangible Resources

Intangible resources include social networks, intellectual property, reputation and human capital resources. Social capital includes the resource stocks embedded in the social networks that entrepreneurs can access. Networks are important because friendship and kinship ties provide access to resources at less than market price or even provide resources that are simply not available via market transactions (Baker, Miner & Eesley, 2003; Witt, Schroeter & Merz, 2008). Sparse social networks typified by weak ties also provide 'brokerage opportunities' to access unique resource providers (Burt, 1992, 2005) and therefore access to valuable resources. Entrepreneur's pre-existing networks and the capability to bridge into new networks are both important (Lee & Jones, 2008) because these shape the trajectory of a firm as they are the resources 'at hand' that entrepreneurs use when solving problems (Baker et al., 2003). Gaining access to value-rich networks depends on perceived legitimacy, the resources an entrepreneur has to exchange, their ability to bear the transaction costs involved in networking (Hanlon & Saunders, 2007) and skills necessary for creating quality engagement (Holt & Macpherson, 2010) [see Chapter 6 for a discussion of social networks]. Human capital resources include the knowledge, experience, judgement, intelligence, relationships and insight of people working in the firm and in particular the owner-manager/entrepreneur. Human capital delivers both functional capabilities (such as marketing), as well as the capability to innovate and solve organizational problems (Penrose, 1959). A recent study examined the specific relationship between human capital, entrepreneurial orientation and performance in 151 Swedish firms (Andersén, 2021). The conclusion was that firms with firm-specific human capital benefit from being highly entrepreneurial and relying on resource orchestration through collaborative human resource management. Clearly, knowledge in the form of specific human capital is significant but it is how those resources are integrated and orientated that is important for the delivery of functional competences necessary to run and grow a business.

Although tangible resources are important for survival and growth, intangible resources are viewed as being the principal drivers of competitive advantage. A study on Government support for new business found that while the tangible resources provided were important, these were moderated by the capabilities (human capital) available in the firm (Pergelova & Angulo-Ruiz, 2014). Intangible resources are embedded in organizational systems and processes and are not easily acquired in factor markets. They are largely related to the knowledge held by entrepreneurs, or the reputation and legitimacy acquired through social networks and are therefore difficult to replicate (Diaz Garcia & Jimenez Moreno, 2010). Transmission of such resources requires context specific tacit knowledge because it arises from situations that are idiosyncratic and complex (Shetty, Sundaram & Achuthan, 2020). Capabilities that intangible resources provide to the entrepreneur are particularly important for accessing tangible resources and managing innovatively through partnerships and knowledge exchange. Indeed, access to credit (tangible resources) was shown to be a function of human capital (business ownership experience) (Robson, Akuetteh, Stone, Westhead & Wright, 2013). According to Hitt et al. (2001, p. 14), 'intangible resources are more likely than tangible resources to produce competitive advantage'.

7.5 Human Capital and Entrepreneurship

Of the wide-ranging literature that discusses the relevance of intangible assets for start-up, a special emphasis has been placed on the human capital of the entrepreneur or the entrepreneurial team. Human capital is a powerful predictor of a person's propensity to establish a new venture. It encompasses the value creating skills, knowledge, competencies and talents acquired through formal and informal learning that resides within individuals (Becker, 1964) and relates to inter-generational transmission of knowledge and learning behaviours (Roberts, 2001). In addition to the human capital that entrepreneurs bring to their business, accumulation of human capital over time through training and work experience is also relevant. According to the labour economics literature, while human capital is a favourable resource for all employment the effects are more pertinent to some careers. Williams (2004) explains that individuals with higher stocks of human capital and varied skills are better able to make use of their resources in entrepreneurship than in salaried jobs. For example, a study found that there are synergistic effects that originate from a new venture creator's specific human capital factors (Ahmed & Brennan, 2019). They found that resources, learning and social network ties derived from specific human capital factors and this in turn influenced the ability to internationalize the business. The findings are consistent with other studies that show the importance of knowledge and relationships prior to the establishment a firm. Teece (2011) agrees that there are strong links between entrepreneurship and human capital. He draws on Schumpeter's concept of 'creative destruction' to identify the key role of well-educated individuals in entrepreneurs and in restructuring the economy:

> Whether one is focusing on creating value or capturing it, in recent decades the numerati and literati (expert talent) and entrepreneurs have become more important the creation and management of technology in the global economy.
>
> (Teece, 2011, p. 531)

At the same time, Teece acknowledges that the ability to create or sense new opportunities is not something that is 'universally distributed'. While *generic* human capital, such as education, knowledge and skills (acquired through formal education) can provide entrepreneurs with a relatively stable advantage over time, *specific* human capital accrued through on-the-job training and experience provides the capability for creating sustained competitive advantage. In terms of specific human capital, a recent large-scale study in the United States found that shared entrepreneurial competencies among the start-up management team were more important for firm performance than managerial competencies (Reese, Rieger & Engelen, 2021). Since specific human capital is inherently linked to the context of an opportunity, the associated knowledge is tacit and organizationally embedded making the firm's resource base inimitable and non-substitutable. Tacit knowledge is very relevant here, as entrepreneurship is usually developed through interaction with others (Rae & Carswell, 2001) as well as from the experiences of success and failure (Cope, 2011). Prior knowledge of markets and a clear understanding of how to address customer needs appear to aid this process of discovery (Shane, 2000). Therefore, while entrepreneurial competencies are essential in new venture management, it is also important that specialized expertise in managerial competencies, such as project management and managing customer relationships, are available to sustain new venture success (Reese et al., 2021). With time, entrepreneurs should draw upon additional human capital to gain greater diversity of skills and competences, as well as taking opportunities to build on their own human capital as their venture grows.

Existing stocks of human capital are the basis of sense-making resources through which appropriate actions are conceived and executed (Weick, 1995). Prior knowledge does have the potential to enable and constrain the ability of individuals to conceptualize alternative priorities. While human capital comprises an entrepreneur's knowledge and experience their learning trajectories also depend on motivation and resourcefulness (Hmieleski & Corbett, 2006). Learning from experience, through both reflection and reflexivity (Cunliffe, 2002) enhances an entrepreneur's human capital and provide opportunities to translate experience into innovation. Managerial and technical competences are important but the ability and willingness to engage in critical reflection provides the creativity necessary to promote organizational learning (Cope, 2003).

It is often argued that, in order for entrepreneurs to successfully manage the complexities of establishing a venture, previous education and work experience need to be supplemented by the advice and knowledge gained through networking (Shetty et al., 2020; West & Noel, 2009). Entrepreneurs must enlist the support of others to join their firms, to help make and sell their products or services, and to help them realize imagined futures (Gold, Holman & Thorpe, 2002). For that they must possess the social skills which enable them to interest other potential stakeholders in the potential of a new venture (Baron and Tang, 2009). Such social skills (human capital) are important for converting 'weak ties' into strong ties that provide access to valuable resources (Granovetter, 1973). Previous business experience helps create intangible assets (reputation) that give owner-managers credibility with other actors and therefore the potential to access valuable resources to the venture.

Entrepreneurs must be able to convince others that their chosen direction has merit and embed that vision in shared practices (Gold, Holt &

Thorpe, 2008). Analysis of entrepreneurial stories demonstrates the inter-dependence of the entrepreneur and employees within an institutional context (O'Connor, 2002). Thus, to enact change, entrepreneurs must use their human capital to engage with others and foster what Sadler-Smith et al. (2001) describe as a 'learning orientation'. Utilizing human capital requires entrepreneurs to collaborate with others to embed learning in shared activities (Macpherson & Jones, 2008; Reese et al., 2021). It is these collaborative routines that potentially support firm-level innovation and performance.

7.5.1 Experience as a Human Capital

The entrepreneur's ability to effectively engage in opportunity recognition and exploitation of ideas is largely influenced by previously acquired experience and abilities as well as the learning which takes place at each stage of the venture creation pathway (see Box 7.1) (Canavati, Libaers, Wang, Hooshangi & Sarooghi, 2021). However, accumulation of important human capital assets may start even earlier. Results from a study (Jayawarna, Jones & Macpherson, 2014) suggest that start-up is more likely for those who demonstrate higher levels of analytical and creative abilities in childhood, and who then invest in their human capital through gaining a range of diverse and longer work experience. Previous experience is not only a means to acquire the knowledge and skills required to manage a new business, but those experiences also act as a powerful factor for accessing additional resources. While inexperienced entrepreneurs rely more on personal sources such as family, friends and other business owners in their search for information, experienced entrepreneurs seek advice and support from more powerful and resource-rich sources (Cooper, Folta & Woo, 1995). Entrepreneurs whose business operations complement their previous employment can make use of the experience, knowledge and connections that are very relevant to the business in hand (Canavati et al., 2021).

Box 7.1

I remember being very young and going to Dad's office and him teaching me to do the very big A1 plans and also just being aware of the pressures he was under sometimes.

> I also did a bit of work for my father – he had an architect business at the time and so I did his website and did a few things like co-ordinating marketing activity. I probably did that for a few months – working off my kitchen table, pretty much, for most of that time and at that time I was generating enough business
>
> It is always around you and you are kind of aware of it – I had seen people fail, I had seen my dad fail, not fail, but the job come to a natural conclusion due to the market conditions, I had seen the businesses I had worked for when I was in University, get funding and go bump. So without that I don't think I wouldn't have learnt what I have. [Anna Heyes, Active Profile]

West and Noel (2009) provide a word of caution when they explain that the relatedness of experience to the new venture influences future performance. Politis et al. (2012) found that entrepreneurs with previous business experience or experience from same industry are capable of securing and using less costly resources during the new venture creation process. Experienced entrepreneurs were also found to be practicing bootstrapping in favour of traditional resource acquisition behaviours. Previous experience of the same industry in which the business is to function is considered particularly important for accessing the industry-specific knowledge necessary to become competitive (Canavati et al., 2021; Giones, Gozun & Miralles, 2019; Sharifi & Zhang, 2009). Such knowledge is especially beneficial to 'spot trends or generate a range of possible alternatives from which to make the best possible business decisions' (Boeker & Karichalil, 2002, p. 821). Additionally, experiences in different functional areas can provide the entrepreneurs with a wide breadth of management skills and know-how that is essential to manage and run their own businesses (Timmons & Spinelli, 2004).

7.5.2 *Knowledge as a Human Capital*

The resource-based view asserts that a firm's growth and competitive advantage arises from managerial knowledge (Esteve-Perez & Manez-Castillejo, 2008). In addition to knowledge relevant to the business, the knowledge to identify and evaluate those resources in which to invest and how to utilize them is a key task for the entrepreneur. Knowledge acquired by entrepreneurs through their idiosyncratic information gathering behaviours are particularly useful for acquiring and deploying resources in combinations that are difficult to copy (Giones et al., 2019). Tacit knowledge is more important than explicit knowledge for entrepreneurs who want to build long-term competitive advantage. Initially, internal knowledge largely resides with the individual entrepreneur and is central to managing the dynamics of setting up and developing the business opportunities they have. As the business develops, externally sourced knowledge in the form of partnerships with key stakeholders is important for enhancing the firm's resource capabilities (Jenssen & Koenig, 2002). In other words, to be successful, entrepreneurs must know how to integrate product specific knowledge, facts and management techniques with contextual experience (Alvarez & Busenitz, 2001) and combinations of human and social capital are related to survival (Linder, Lechner & Pelzel, 2020).

The knowledge resources necessary for entrepreneurs to set up and develop a new business are daunting. They include an understanding of the processes involved in business creation, people management, business growth, new technologies and new product development (Brush, Greene & Hart, 2001). The successful pursuit of these activities will depend on the entrepreneurs' understanding of the types and configurations of resources that are necessary to manage and develop their business and to deal with contingencies specific to their context. Wiklund and Shepherd (2003b) identified three types of procedural knowledge important to new venture founders: knowledge about the industry, knowledge about the type of business and knowledge about starting up new ventures. Thus, a wealth of experience-based knowledge, developed over time, exerts a central and often pivotal influence on your ability to engage effectively in setting up and developing your ideas into a successful venture.

As should be clear by now your opportunities as an entrepreneurs will significantly depend on the knowledge you acquire through occupations, job routines, social relationships and daily life (Linder et al., 2020; Venkataraman, 1997). High-tech entrepreneurs need specialized knowledge to understand and recognize unique business opportunities. As Grant (1996) proposes, knowledge is the foundation for the rent-earning potential of all resources and, therefore, during managing the early stages of venture development and growth entrepreneurs will need to draw in new members with new knowledge to deal with the changing circumstances they face (Jones & Macpherson, 2006; Tzabbar & Margolis, 2017). However, for new entrepreneurs, accumulation of human capital in the form of recruiting skilled and competent staff is a challenging task due to their limited financial capabilities. Therefore, 'an entrepreneur's expanding knowledge base and absorptive capacity becomes an entrepreneurial firm's competitive advantage' (Alvarez & Busenitz, 2001, p. 766). Therefore, pre-existing networks and the capability to bridge into new networks are both important. The first is a structural issue dependent on the number and depth of existing network ties (Elfring & Hulsink, 2003; Elfring & Hulsink, 2008) that have been developed prior to setting up the venture. The second is a capability issue that means an entrepreneur requires the skills to understand resource prospects available in more diverse network ties (Lee & Jones, 2008). For example, the ability of entrepreneurs to actively engage suppliers and customers as well as other business and social contacts can help support their emerging firm (Baker et al., 2003).

At an early stage, most entrepreneurs lack the necessary resources to build an internal knowledge base. Essentially, knowledge resources and capabilities need to be identified, borrowed, appropriated and integrated from outside the firm's boundaries. This is particularly important for technological entrepreneurs as the full range of knowledge resources necessary to create a successful business are unlikely to be readily available or possessed by the entrepreneurs themselves. For their ventures, high performance is more likely to be achieved if a range of skills are available via a start-up team or embedded in the firm's employees (Tzabbar & Margolis, 2017). If appropriate skills are absent, it is suggested that talented expertise may be recruited (Kaulio, 2003), developed within a wider managerial team (Littunen & Tohmo, 2003), obtained via external consultants or thorough alliance partners and other firms in close proximity (Fernhaber, McDougall-Covin & Shepherd, 2009). When entrepreneurship is team-based, it is important that knowledge and skills are complementary rather than dependent on a single individual with an absolute set of skills/knowledge (Jones, Macpherson & Thorpe, 2010). Brush et al. (2001) conclude that one of the biggest challenges facing new ventures is transforming the founding entrepreneur's personal knowledge of the industry, market and product into organizational resources, especially when the entrepreneur is working with a team.

7.6 Accumulation of Human Capital over the Life Course

Many researchers argue that the qualities entrepreneurs bring to new ventures largely depend on resources built up through their education and experience. While those with better education and experience have greater entrepreneurial intention (Kim, Aldrich & Keister, 2006) and more chance of succeeding, their opportunity costs for foregoing employment can be higher. Consequently, potential entrepreneurs with high human capital may not start a business or only start one with high earning prospects (Cassar, 2006). Despite being widely accepted that human capital is an essential entrepreneurial resource base, most start-ups are founded by those with limited educational qualifications (Henley, 2007). This distinction could be explained by differences between necessity-based entrepreneurship and opportunity-based entrepreneurship (Valliere & Peterson, 2009). Contradictions in the evidence base may also result from weak conceptualizations of how the process of accruing human capital and the experience of applying it in the labour market influences business start-up. Educational and sociological researchers focus on how social influences, including family, influence children's educational attainments (Hartas, 2011). Heinz (2002) argues that an individual's future outcomes arise from personal, family and work histories rather than from achievements fixed in time. Consequently, there has been growing interest in examining learning in a wider context, including on-the-job training as well as the role of family and community groups (Eraut & Hirsh, 2007). Most of an individual's personal qualities are established at early stages in life and therefore 'entrepreneurs are a product of their upbringing' and being born in a family with the 'right kind of parents' is important to the pursuit of a successful entrepreneurial career (Douglas & Shepherd, 2000, p. 233).

In this regard, life-course studies have promoted awareness in the potential links between human capital acquired in childhood with entrepreneurial potential (Jayawarna, Rouse & Macpherson, 2014). These life course studies explain the importance of conceptualizing age-appropriate human capital effects on entrepreneurship and suggest using life histories over an extended period. A recent study using longitudinal UK data [National Child Development Study (NCDS)] argues that the accumulation of entrepreneur human capital is a long-term outcome arising from the development of childhood cognitive abilities (education, subject know-ledge, intelligence) and advantages based on family resources (parents' education, occupation) combined with the cumulative 'events' and 'oppor-tunities' experienced during adulthood (Jayawarna et al., 2014). Empirical results suggest that there are powerful and previously unexplored, human capital effects that foster the development of skills and competence neces-sary to follow a career in entrepreneurship (see Figure 7.3 for the con-ceptual framework used in this study). More specifically the research emphasizes the importance of studying human capital as a resource that begins in childhood. Childhood literacy skills negatively affect business entry which suggests some support for the dyslexia thesis of entrepreneur-ship; numeracy skills although important are an inconsistent determinant of entrepreneurial status. The authors go on to argue that cognitive ability at early childhood and gifted outstanding ability identified in later childhood are strong positive predictors of entrepreneurship. The results further note that the importance of education in facilitating entrepreneurship operates not so much through the attainment of an outstanding education but rather through attainment of moderate achievements with a solid basic education (Jayawarna et al., 2014). More surprisingly were the strong links between human capital acquired through apprenticeship and the entrepreneurial

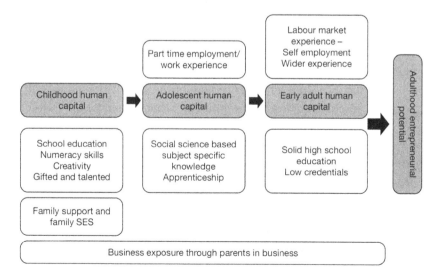

Figure 7.3 Accumulation of Human Capital over the Entrepreneurial Life-course

prospects of young people. The role apprenticeship programmes play in delivering human capital necessary to promote entrepreneurship was attributed to two factors: (1) apprenticeship endows people with specific skills and knowledge that give them advantages in setting up a business and (2) drop-outs from salaried employment may start an apprenticeship as an alternative route to increase the chances of employability and therefore have higher likelihood of starting a business.

Importantly, previous ownership experience (during early adulthood) has been found to account for a substantial portion of the human capital effects on entrepreneurship (Jayawarna et al., 2014). This emphasizes the importance of specific human capital developed through experience. In addition, role modelling through family-related entrepreneurship activities, such as parents with entrepreneurial experience, also facilitate the accumulation of business specific knowledge. It is certainly well established that those children whose parents are involved in small businesses are more likely to become entrepreneurs themselves (Zellweger, Sieger & Halter, 2011). This is generally attributed to the benefits of positive role-models and early exposure to the experience of business-related activities. Work experience gained during secondary education is also a strong predictor of entrepreneurial careers in adulthood. As Burchinal et al. (1997) point out, early work experience provides students with a variety of resources and skills that are distinct from those acquired in other pursuits such as conventional education. This experience not only provides students with knowledge in areas such as money, banking and consumer matters but also with additional responsibilities and practical life-skills. Resources associated with early employment have close links to adult wealth accumulation and are also important for the creation of new businesses. It is legitimate that high school employment is a stronger human capital predictor for entrepreneurship than for waged employment. Similarly, high school employment helps to develop social networks of those with similar interests (Painter, 2010) and social networks are valuable resources for future entrepreneurial endeavours. Painter (2010) also noted that an advantageous family socio-economic status (SES) can channel children with less cognitive ability into a more positive developmental pathway leading into a career in entrepreneurship. Children who grow-up in high SES families have more opportunities to convert negative human capital into positive entrepreneurial outcome and have more potential to nurture positive childhood human capital into positive entrepreneurial outcomes. Put simply, the broader and longer the experience and knowledge accumulation a person has about entrepreneurship, the more likely they are to develop knowledge relevant to starting their own business.

7.7 Effects of Human Capital on Entrepreneurial Success

Some studies have focused on measuring the effects of human capital endowments by examining the influence of educational attainment and organizational experience on financial performance, growth and innovation. Kim et al. (2006), using US data from a panel study including nascent entrepreneurs and a comparison group, conclude that actual entrepreneurial entry was influenced by human capital; both educational attainment and prior managerial experience. Indeed, a great deal of research in understanding success distinguishes between education and experience. According to Kim et al. (2006), attainment is normally a measure of the educational level (secondary or higher) rather than subject-specific such as entrepreneurship. Few studies provide an examination of entrepreneurship education and business start-up. Those that do often consider the effects of a specific education programme on the business outcomes (Jayawarna et al., 2014). This study found that human capital (degree-level education) provided access to a wide network of resources for the early-stage business which, in turn, facilitated development. It seems, therefore, that education is important, but the impact could be indirect since educational experience provides access to wider networks (see Chapter 6). A study by Colombo and Grilli (2010) focused on technology-based start-up firms also found that levels of founders' skills supported an argument of competence-based success in these businesses. Here though they also found that in venture-capitalized firms investors provided a coaching function that overrode the founder's skills deficits. In other words, human capital is still important; it just does not have to belong to the venture owner, but they can 'borrow' it from others.

Other studies that have examined the transition to self-employment consider human capital resources such as the non-financial motivation to be an entrepreneur and work experience. In one study, Burke et al. (2002) found that non-financial motivation was influential on success for male entrepreneurs, but not female; education and work-based human capital (experience) had similar gender differences. Wiklund and Shepherd (2003a) examined the relationship between growth aspirations and the success of small firms in 552 firms from four sectors in Sweden. They found that the cognitive resources available to a person, measured in terms of education and experience, magnified the effect of an entrepreneur's growth aspirations. In other words, motivation is not enough and personal aspirations are realized through the human capital available to the entrepreneur, since this provides the ability to manage a growing business and, as mentioned above, gain access to additional resources. However, another study by Jayawarna et al. (2014) propose that entrepreneurial human capital develops much earlier than is generally acknowledged. In a longitudinal study using data from a national child development study, they found that early childhood indicators of creative and analytical abilities, if encouraged in a supportive family and educational environment can have significant effects on the development of entrepreneurial potential. These childhood human capital endowments interact with general work experiences during adolescence to shape the development of entrepreneurial careers. Thus, opportunities to engage in entrepreneurial activities while still at school provide early experience with little real risk. In terms of developing childhood this human capital for future entrepreneurial careers, parental and family influences are very strong. Human capital development in childhood is widely centred in the family; the role of parents, their employment and economic status are decisive factors in tipping children into entrepreneurship as they mature. An entrepreneur's capabilities and motivation are in development very early in their lifecycle.

It might also be the case that such prior experience is both enabling and limiting. Eisenhardt and Schoonhoven (1990) address the impact of a firm's 'founding conditions' including the human capital embodied in the management team. In their study of 92 high-tech firms in Silicon Valley, they found that the management team's composition, including past, shared and broader experiences, were associated with links to higher growth. They argue that, regardless of market conditions, previous managerial experience enabled a defter and more nuanced navigation of the market. Experienced teams were particularly effective in exploiting growth markets, suggesting that they could make more able strategic choices; small differences multiplied significantly over time. That is, the effect of the human capital becomes more, not less, significant as ventures grow. Other studies have also found clear links between the founding management team's experiential and educational background and the subsequent dynamic development of the firm (Ensley & Hmieleski, 2005; Hmieleski & Ensley, 2007).

This suggests that the human capital available at start-up has a long-term influence on the trajectory of the firm. This is exactly what Baron et al. (1999) found in their study regarding the 'logics of organizing' implemented by a firm's founders. Their evidence suggests entrepreneurs influence not only organizational structures, but also the cultural fabric of the organization from the outset (Baron et al., 1999). They examined 76 growing technology start-ups in Silicon Valley California and found significant path-dependence in the way the firm developed from first principles, and this had a lasting effect on the intensity of bureaucracy. In essence, their findings suggest that the founder's organizational blueprints, theories, or 'recipes' (Spender, 1989) influence the rate of bureaucratization as the organization grows. Those firms that made early investment in 'cultural control' or softer management skills were able to economize on formal administrative systems. In other words, the early systems implemented create a culture that influences future organizational development. Such path dependencies are important since prior experience may not necessarily be relevant to developing a vibrant new firm. In that way, prior knowledge and skills gained through experience may impede longer-term development. Taken together, these findings suggest that that the early days of a new venture are particularly important, since entrepreneurs establish systems and activities quickly, which has a long-term influence on success.

So human capital in the form of prior education and experience is not only relevant because of the way in which new entrepreneurs apply it within the firm; human capital is also important because it mediates access to wider capital resources available from external networks (Chapter 6). However, contradictions in the evidence may be related to the difficult of conceptualizing (and testing) how human capital is both accrued and applied in the labour market and how that experience influences start-up (Unger, Rauch, Frese & Rosenbusch, 2011). Nevertheless, it seems that prior education and experience potentially provides the knowledge and skills required by new entrepreneurs to establish systems, structures and relationships; these initial structures then have a long-term effect on the trajectory of the firm, since they create path dependencies. This can be both positive and negative dependent on the range of skill brought to the venture (see Chapter 2 for a discussion of entrepreneur skills and competences).

7.8 Summary and Key Learning Points

RBV has focused attention on the role of firm resources as critical inputs and as a key source of competitive advantage. Prior research suggests that those with higher capital resources are more likely to establish successful new ventures since such capital endowments allow exploitation of the potential inherent in processes of production. Accumulation of resource stocks for new venture creation is a special case of resource-based theory as start-up resources are very limited and largely depend on the entrepreneur's original endowments (funds, education, experience, time and contacts). These entrepreneurial resources need to be combined with external resources acquired as the firm becomes established.

Primarily based on the resource-based view of the firm (Barney, 1991), research on entrepreneurship has attempted to link stocks of human capital to venture founding and success. Human capital is a valuable resource for the nascent entrepreneur as it is the first and sometimes the only resource available to them at start-up. Human capital not only includes the individuals' stock of knowledge and skills acquired through prior education and experience, but also their rhetorical and social skills which are necessary to persuade others about the potential of their proposed venture (Holt & Macpherson, 2010). Research has also explored the importance of conceptualizing age-appropriate human capital effects on entrepreneurship and suggests using life histories starting from childhood to fully appreciate its role. Taken together, the key learning points from this chapter are:

- Each business start-up is different as they possess unique bundles of tangible and intangible resources and capabilities that are acquired, developed and expand over time.
- Intangible resources are more important than tangible resources for entrepreneurs to achieve competitive advantage as these resources are developed internally and competitors cannot obtain them in the factor market or appropriate the same value in a new context.
- Human capital endowments are enhanced through experience, education and critical reflexivity and cannot be created or deployed in a vacuum. This accumulated human capital is central to enhancing absorptive capacity, social capital and, ultimately, firm performance.

- An individual's human capital accrued through cognitive developments and achievements in early childhood influence entrepreneurial potential in adulthood.
- Despite the wider recognition of the importance of the entrepreneur human capital and the development of firm knowledge base, research link between human capital and success is not as clear as we would expect.

7.9 Discussion Questions and Call to Action

1. What are the main types of resources that entrepreneurs require at the early stage of business development? What are the implications of resource-based theory of the firm for defining these resources within an entrepreneurial firm?

2. What are the key sources of human capital for the entrepreneur, and how does these sources help to understand the resource capability of the entrepreneur and the entrepreneurial venture?

3. What are the implications of seeing human capital of the entrepreneur as emerging from childhood? How might the human capital acquired during childhood and parental influence in childhood education influence entrepreneurial potential in adulthood?

4. Why is it challenging to link the knowledge and experience as human capital of the entrepreneur to new venture performance?

Human capital is the essential resource for new entrepreneurs as they engage on their business start-up journey. Human capital is a resource based on the cognitive abilities, experiences and skills developed during your life-course. The challenge for you as a new entrepreneur is to reflect on your stocks of human capital as a means of understanding your personal strengths and weaknesses. Identifying your personal knowledge gaps means that you can then consider how to engage your social networks (friends and family), employees and other business contacts to access the missing resources. As we emphasize throughout this book, experiential learning is a crucial ingredient for your future success as an entrepreneur. Early work experience, however mundane, is an effective way for gaining experience of dealing with customers and managing relationships with other people (your employer for example). Vicarious learning from experienced entrepreneurs via TV programmes such as Dragon's Den or Shark Tank, can also provide invaluable insights into dealing with potential resource providers. Engaging in extracurricular activities while in college or university is also an important mechanism for learning about entrepreneurship. In summary, if you are serious about becoming an entrepreneur then you should take every possible opportunity to improve your stocks of human capital.

References

Ahmed, F. U. & Brennan, L. (2019). The impact of founder's human capital on firms' extent of early internationalisation: Evidence from a least-developed country. *Asia Pacific Journal of Management, 36*(3), 615–659.

Alvarez, S. A. & Busenitz, L. W. (2001). The entrepreneurship of resource-based theory. *Journal of Management, 27*(6), 755–775.

Andersén, J. (2021). Resource orchestration of firm-specific human capital and firm performance – the role of collaborative human resource management and entrepreneurial orientation. *The International Journal of Human Resource Management, 32*(10), 2091–2123.

Arend, R. J. & Lévesque, M. (2010). Is the Resource-Based View a Practical Organizational Theory? *Organization Science* (4), 913–930.

Baker, T., Miner, A. S. & Eesley, D. T. (2003). Improvising Firms: Bricolage, Account Giving and Improvisational Competencies in the Founding Process. *Research Policy, 32*(2), 255–276.

Barney, J. (1991). Firm Resources and Sustained Competitive Advantage. *Journal of Management, 17*(1), 99–121.

Baron, J. N., Hannan, M. T. & Burton, M. D. (1999). Building the iron cage: Determinants of managerial intensity in the early years of organizations. *American Sociological Review, 64*(4), 527–547.

Baron, R. A. & Tang, J. (2009). Entrepreneurs' social skills and new venture performance: mediating mechanisms and cultural generality. *Journal of Management, 35*(2), 282–306.

Becker, G. S. (1964). *Human Capital: A Theoretical and Empirical Analysis, with Special Reference to Education*. New York: Columbia University Press.

Boeker, W. & Karichalil, R. (2002). Entrepreneurial Transitions: Factors Influencing Founder Departure. *The Academy of Management Journal, 4,* 818–826.

Bozkaya, A. & De La Potterie, B. (2008). Who Funds Technology-Based Small Firms? Evidence from Belgium. *Economics of Innovation and New Technology, 17*(1–2), 97–122.

Brush, C. G., Greene, P. G. & Hart, M. M. (2001). From initial idea to unique advantage: The entrepreneurial challenge of constructing a resource base. *Academy of Management Executive, 15*(1), 64–78.

Burchinal, M. R., Campbell, F. A., Bryant, D. M., Wasik, B. H. & Ramey, C. T. (1997). Early Intervention and Mediating Processes in Cognitive Performance of Children of Low-Income African American Families. *Child Development, 5,* 935–954.

Burke, A. E., FitzRoy, F. R. & Nolan, M. A. (2002). Self-employment Wealth and Job Creation: The Roles of Gender, Non-pecuniary Motivation and Entrepreneurial Ability. *Small Business Economics, 19,* 255–270.

Burt, R. S. (1992). *Structural holes: the social structure of competition.* Cambridge, MA [u.a.].

Burt, R. S. (2005). *Brokerage and closure: an introduction to social capital* / Ronald S. Burt. Oxford: Oxford University Press, 2005.

Canavati, S., Libaers, D., Wang, T., Hooshangi, S. & Sarooghi, H. (2021). Relationship between human capital, new venture ideas, and opportunity beliefs: A meta-analysis. *Strategic Entrepreneurship Journal, 15*(3), 454–477.

Cassar, G. (2004). The financing of business start-ups. *Journal of Business Venturing, 19,* 261–283.

Cassar, G. (2006). Entrepreneur opportunity costs and intended venture growth. *Journal of Business Venturing, 21,* 610–632.

Chrisman, J. J. (1999). The Influence of Outsider-Generated Knowledge Resources on Venture Creation. *Journal of Small Business Management, 37*(4), 42–58.

Coen, C. A. & Maritan, C. A. (2011). Investing in Capabilities: The Dynamics of Resource Allocation. *Organization Science, 1,* 99–117.

Colombo, M. G. & Grilli, L. (2010). On growth drivers of high-tech start-ups: Exploring the role of founders' human capital and venture capital. *Journal of Business Venturing, 25*(6), 610–626.

Cooper, A. C., Folta, T. B. & Woo, C. (1995). Entrepreneurial information search. *Journal of Business Venturing, 10,* 107–120.

Cope, J. (2003). Entrepreneurial Learning and Critical Reflection: Discontinuous Events as Triggers for 'Higher-level' Learning. *Management Learning, 34*(4), 429–450.

Cope, J. (2011). Entrepreneurial learning from failure: An interpretative phenomenological analysis. *Journal of Business Venturing, 26*(6), 604–623.

265

Cunliffe, A. L. (2002). Reflexive Dialogical Practice in Management Learning. *Management Learning, 33*(1), 35–61.

Del Sarto, N., Di Minin, A., Ferrigno, G. & Piccaluga, A. (2021). Born global and well educated: start-up survival through fuzzy set analysis. *Small Business Economics, 56*(4), 1405–1423.

Diaz Garcia, C. & Jimenez Moreno, J. (2010). The Impact of Legitimacy Building Signals on Access to Resources. In D. Smallbone, J. Leitao, M. Raposo & F. Welter (Eds.), *The Theory and Practice of Entrepreneurship: Frontiers in European Entrepreneurship Research* (pp. 215–235): Cheltenham, U.K. and Northampton, MA: Elgar.

Douglas, E. J. & Shepherd, D. A. (2000). Entrepreneurship as a utility maximizing response. *Journal of Business Venturing, 15*, 231–251. doi:10.1016/S0883-9026(98)00008-1

Eisenhardt, K. M. & Schoonhoven, C. B. (1990). Organizational Growth: Linking Founding Team, Strategy, Environment, and Growth among U.S. Semiconductor Ventures, 1978–1988. *Administrative Science Quarterly, 35*(3), 504–529.

Elfring, T. & Hulsink, W. (2003). Networks in Entrepreneurship: The Case of High-Technology Firms. *Small Business Economics, 21*(4), 409–422.

Elfring, T. & Hulsink, W. (2008). Networking by entrepreneurs: Patterns of tie-formation in emerging organizations. *Organisation Studies, 28*(12), 1849–1872.

Ensley, M. D. & Hmieleski, K. M. (2005). A comparative study of new venture top management team composition, dynamics and performance between university-based and independent start-ups. *Research Policy, 34*(7), 1091–1105.

Eraut, M. & Hirsh, W. (2007). The Significance of Workplace Learning for Individuals, Groups and Organizations. Retrieved from Oxford and Cardiff:

Esteve-Perez, S. & Manez-Castillejo, J. A. (2008). The Resource-Based Theory of the Firm and Firm Survival. *Small Business Economics, 30*(3), 231–249.

Fernhaber, S. A., McDougall-Covin, P. P. & Shepherd, D. A. (2009). International Entrepreneurship: Leveraging Internal and External Knowledge Sources. *Strategic Entrepreneurship Journal, 3*(4), 297–320.

Fiol, C. M. (2001). Revisiting an identity-based view of sustainable competitive advantage. *Journal of Management, 27*(6), 691–699.

Foss, N. J., Klein, P. G., Kor, Y. Y. & Mahoney, J. T. (2008). Entrepreneurship, subjectivism, and the resource-based view: toward a new synthesis. *Strategic Entrepreneurship Journal, 2*(1), 73–94.

Giones, F., Gozun, B. & Miralles, F. (2019). Unbundling the Influence of Human Capital on the New Venture's Performance. *DLSU Business & Economics Review, 28*(3), 47–51.

Gold, J., Holman, D. & Thorpe, R. (2002). The Role of Argument Analysis and Story Telling in Facilitating Critical Thinking. *Management Learning, 33*(3), 371–389.

Gold, J., Holt, R. & Thorpe, R. (2008). A Good Place for a CHAT: Activity Theory and MBA Education. In M. Reynolds & R. Vincent (Eds.), *The Handbook of Experiential Learning and Management Education*. Oxford: Oxford University Press

Granovetter, M. S. (1973). The Strength of Weak Ties. *American Journal of Sociology, 78*(6), 1360–1380.

Grant, R. M. (1996). Toward a Knowledge-Based Theory of the Firm. *Strategic Management Journal, 17*(SPI 2), 109–122.

Hanlon, D. & Saunders, C. (2007). Marshaling Resources to Form Small New Ventures: Toward a More Holistic Understanding of Entrepreneurial Support. *Entrepreneurship: Theory & Practice, 31*(4), 619–641.

Hartas, D. (2011). Families' Social Backgrounds Matter: Socio-Economic Factors, Home Learning and Young Children's Language, Literacy and Social Outcomes. *British Educational Research Journal, 37*(6), 893–914.

Heinz, W. R. (2002). Transition discontinuities and the biographical shaping of early work careers. *Journal of Vocational Behaviour, 60*(2), 220–240.

Henley, A. (2007). Entrepreneurial aspiration and transition into self-employment: evidence from British longitudinal data. *Entrepreneurship & Regional Development, 19*(3), 253–280.

Hitt, M. A., Biermant, L., Shimizu, K. & Kochhar, R. (2001). Direct and Moderating Effects of Human Capital on Strategy and Performance in Professional Service Firms: A Resource Based Perspective. *Academy of Management Journal, 44*(1), 13–28.

Hmieleski, K. M. & Corbett, A. C. (2006). Proclivity for Improvisation as a Predictor of Entrepreneurial Intentions. *Journal of Small Business Management, 44*(1), 45–63.

Hmieleski, K. M. & Ensley, M. D. (2007). A contextual examination of new venture performance: entrepreneur leadership behavior, top management team heterogeneity, and environmental dynamism. *Journal of Organizational Behavior, 28*(7), 865–889.

Holt, R. & Macpherson, A. (2010). Sensemaking, Rhetoric and the Socially Competent Entrepreneur. *International Small Business Journal, 28*(1), 20–42.

Jayawarna, D., Jones, O. & Macpherson, A. (2014). Entrepreneurial potential: The role of human and cultural capitals. *International Small Business Journal: Researching Entrepreneurship, 32*(8), 918–943.

Jayawarna, D., Rouse, J. & Macpherson, A. (2014). Life course pathways to business start-up. *Entrepreneurship & Regional Development, 26*(3–4), 282–312.

Jenssen, J. I. & Koenig, H. F. (2002). The Effect of Social Networks on Resource Access and Business Start-ups. *European Planning Studies, 10*(8), 1039–1046.

Jones, O. & Macpherson, A. (2006). Inter-organizational Learning and Strategic Renewal in SMEs: Extending the 4I Network. *Long Range Planning, 39*(2), 155–175.

Jones, O., Macpherson, A. & Thorpe, R. (2010). Learning in owner-managed small firms: Mediating artefacts and strategic space. *Entrepreneurship and Regional Development, 22*(7/8), 649–673.

Kaulio, M. A. (2003). Initial conditions or process of development? Critical incidents in the early stages of new ventures. *R&D Management, 33*(2), 165–176.

Kim, P. H., Aldrich, H. E. & Keister, L. A. (2006). Access (Not) Denied: The Impact of Financial, Human, and Cultural Capital on Entrepreneurial Entry in the United States. *Small Business Economics, 27*(1), 5–22.

Lee, R. & Jones, O. (2008). Networks, Communication and Learning during Business Start-up. *International Small Business Journal, 26*(5), 559–594.

Lichtenstein, B. M. & Brush, C. G. (2001). How do 'resource bundles' develop and change in New Ventures? A dynamic model and longitudinal exploration. *Entrepreneurship: Theory and Practice, 25*(3), 37–59.

Linder, C., Lechner, C. & Pelzel, F. (2020). Many Roads Lead to Rome: How Human, Social, and Financial Capital Are Related to New Venture Survival. *Entrepreneurship: Theory & Practice, 44*(5), 909–932.

Littunen, H. & Tohmo, T. (2003). The High Growth in New Metal-Based Manufacturing and Business Service Firms in Finland. *Small Business Economics* (2), 187–200.

Macpherson, A. & Jones, O. (2008). Object-mediated Learning and Strategic Renewal in a Mature Organization. *Management Learning, 39*(2), 177–201.

O'Connor, E. (2002). Storied Business: Typology, Intertextuality, and Traffic in Entrepreneurial Narrative. *Journal of Business Communication, 39*(1), 36–54.

Painter, M. A. (2010). Get a job and keep it! High school employment and adult wealth accumulation. *Research in Social Stratification and Mobility, 28*, 233–249.

Penrose, E. (1959). *The theory of the growth of the firm [electronic book]* / Edith Penrose: Oxford: Oxford University Press.

Pergelova, A. & Angulo-Ruiz, F. (2014). The impact of government financial support on the performance of new firms: the role of competitive advantage as an intermediate outcome. *Entrepreneurship & Regional Development, 26*(9/10), 663–705.

Politis, D., Winborg, J. & Dahlstrand, Å. L. (2012). Exploring the resource logic of student entrepreneurs. *International Small Business Journal, 30*(6), 659–683.

Rae, D. & Carswell, M. (2001). Towards a conceptual understanding of entrepreneurial learning. *Journal of Small Business and Enterprise Development, 8*, 150–158.

Reese, D., Rieger, V. & Engelen, A. (2021). Should competencies be broadly shared in new ventures' founding teams? *Strategic Entrepreneurship Journal, 15*(4), 568–589.

Roberts, J. (2001). *Class in Modern Britain*. Oxford: Open University Press.

Robson, P., Akuetteh, C., Stone, I., Westhead, P. & Wright, M. (2013). Credit-rationing and entrepreneurial experience: Evidence from a resource deficit context. *Entrepreneurship & Regional Development*, 25(5/6), 349–370.

Sadler-Smith, E., Spicer, D. P. & Chaston, I. (2001). Learning Orientations and Growth in Smaller Firms. *Long Range Planning*, 34, 139–158.

Sarasvathy, S. D. (2001). Causation and Effectuation: Toward a Theoretical Shift from Economic Inevitability to Entrepreneurial Contingency. *The Academy of Management Review*, 26(2), 243–263.

Shane, S. (2000). Prior Knowledge and the Discovery of Entrepreneurial Opportunities. *Organization Science*, 11(4), 448–469.

Sharifi, S. & Zhang, M. (2009). Sense-making and Recipes: Examples from Selected Small Firms. *International Journal of Entrepreneurial Behavior and Research*, 15(6), 555–571.

Shetty, S., Sundaram, R. & Achuthan, K. (2020). Assessing and Comparing Top Accelerators in Brazil, India, and the USA: Through the Lens of New Ventures' Performance. *Entrepreneurial Business & Economics Review*, 8(2), 153–177.

Sirmon, D. G. & Hitt, M. A. (2003). Managing Resources: Linking Unique Resources, Management, and Wealth Creation in Family Firms. *Entrepreneurship: Theory & Practice*, 27(4), 339–358.

Spender, J. C. (1989). *Industry Recipes: The Nature and Source of Management Judgement*. Oxford: Basil Blackwell.

Teece, D. J. (Ed.) (2011). *Human Capital, Capabilities, and the Firm: Literati, Numerati, and Entrepreneurs in the Twenty-First Century Enterprise*. Oxford.: Oxford University Press.

Timmons, J. A. (1999). *New Venture Creation: Entrepreneurship for the 21st Century* (Fifth ed.). New York: McGraw Hill.

Timmons, J. A. & Spinelli, S. (2004). *New Venture Creation* (6th ed.). Boston: Irwin McGraw-Hill. .

Tzabbar, D. & Margolis, J. (2017). Beyond the Startup Stage: The Founding Team's Human Capital, New Venture's Stage of Life, Founder – CEO Duality, and Breakthrough Innovation. *Organization Science*, 28(5), 857–872.

Tzabbar, D. & Margolis, J. (2017). Beyond the Startup Stage: The Founding Team's Human Capital, New Venture's Stage of Life, Founder-CEO Duality, and Breakthrough Innovation. *Organization Science*, 28(5), 857–872.

Unger, J. M., Rauch, A., Frese, M. & Rosenbusch, N. (2011). Human capital and entrepreneurial success: A meta-analytical review. *Journal of Business Venturing*, 26, 341–358.

Valliere, D. & Peterson, R. (2009). Entrepreneurship and Economic Growth: Evidence from Emerging and Developed Countries. *Entrepreneurship and Regional Development*, 21(5–6), 459–480.

Venkataraman, S. (Ed.) (1997). *The Distinctive Domain of Entrepreneurship Research: An Editor's Perspective* (Vol. 3). Greenwich, CT: JAI Press.

Weick, K. (1995). *Sensemaking in Organizations*. Thousand Oaks, CA: Sage.

West, G. P. & Noel, T. W. (2009). The Impact of Knowledge Resources on New Venture Performance. *Journal of Small Business Management, 47*(1), 1–22.

Wiklund, J. & Shepherd, D. (2003a). Aspiring for, and Achieving Growth: The Moderating Role of Resources and Opportunities. *Journal of Management Studies, 40*(8), 1919–1941.

Wiklund, J. & Shepherd, D. (2003b). Knowledge-Based Resources, Entrepreneurial Orientation, and the Performance of Small and Medium-Sized Businesses. *Strategic Management Journal* (13), 1307–1314.

Williams, D. R. (2004). Effects of Childcare Activities on the Duration of Self-Employment in Europe. *Entrepreneurship: Theory & Practice, 28*(5), 467–485. doi:10.1111/j.1540-6520.2004.00058.x

Witt, P., Schroeter, A. & Merz, C. (2008). Entrepreneurial resource acquisition via personal networks: an empirical study of German start-ups. *Service Industries Journal, 28*(7/8), 953–971.

Zellweger, T., Sieger, P. & Halter, F. (2011). Should I stay or should I go? Career choice intentions of students with family business background. *Journal of Business Venturing, 26*, 521–536.

Formal Finance for Business Start-up

8.1 Introduction

In this book, we suggest that most young entrepreneurs are best advised not trying to obtain formal finance in the shape of loans or equity. Harrison and Mason (2019, p. 3) point out that the traditional entrepreneurial finance relay race, 'in which funding from family and friends gives way to business angels who in turn hand over to venture capital before the IPO provides an exit opportunity for investors and a capital-raising opportunity for entrepreneurs', no longer exists. Research by Murzacheva and Levie (2020) questions the extent to which the traditional 'finance escalator' actually operates in practice. Business angels and venture capitalists focus on larger organizations requiring substantial amounts of funding rather than early-stage entrepreneurial ventures. For example, Jackson and Madison (2022) claim that a tiny proportion of US business start-ups (0.5%) obtain venture capital funding and the remainder use their own financial resources. Others argue that sources of entrepreneurial finance still include venture capital, private equity, private debt, trade credit, IPOs, business angel finance and crowdfunding as well as grants, funding from incubators/accelerators and family and friends (Cumming, Deloof, Manigart & Wright, 2019). Although it is certainly the case that the more sophisticated forms of funding will only become available well beyond the start-up stage. Nevertheless, it is important that you are familiar with the key concepts associated with formal finance and this chapter provides an introduction.

New entrepreneurs have to create a resource base to invest in assets, fund business operations and support growth agendas: decisions regarding tangible resources including finance are critical. Many young entrepreneurs start with low levels of capitalization, and this has a major influence on the survival and growth prospects of their ventures. Existing empirical evidence provides support for the assertion that new ventures face difficulties in acquiring external finance or lack of financial support discourages many people from starting businesses. The entrepreneur's personal financial capabilities are often limited and in the absence of internal cash generation young entrepreneurs are unlikely to have the capacity to self-fund their ventures.

There are a variety of forms of capital and several possible sources of finance including internal equity financing (i.e., money from the entrepreneurs, their family and friends), bank loans, trade credit, government grants, business angel investment and venture capital funds. Entrepreneurs in their early stage of business start-up however are regularly denied finance and working capital by external investors. This is the result of informational asymmetries associated with smallness and newness, which are the two main early-stage entrepreneurial firm specific financial constraints (Linder & Sperber, 2020). According to a report by the Department of Business, Innovation & Skills (BIS) less than 50% of small ventures in the UK utilize any form of external finance (including credit cards and overdrafts); only 11% of those ventures used bank loans (including commercial mortgage) and 1–2% attempted to obtain equity finance (Business, Innovation & Skills, 2012). Banks follow conservative, risk-mitigated lending approaches and therefore tend to pick entrepreneurs that are already successful or have assets (houses) to provide collateral. Traditional venture capitals and business angels represent only a minor proportion of the necessary capital for entrepreneurial ventures. Due to limited external finance options available to new ventures, entrepreneurs are forced to consider alternative sources including personal investments. Bootstrap financing enables entrepreneurs to access resources at 'little or no cost' (Harrison, Mason & Girling, 2004) and is a popular strategy for start-up and during the early stages of operation (see Chapter 9 for a fuller description of bootstrapping finance).

In this chapter, we provide an overview of different funding options that are potentially available for new entrepreneurs and discuss the various opportunities and challenges. Drawing insight from various empirical contributions to the subject of venture funding we then consider the difficulties entrepreneurs face when accessing external finance. We discuss information asymmetries and moral hazards which are barriers to accessing financial resources from external providers (Block, Colombo, Cumming & Vismara, 2018; Lee, Sameen & Cowling, 2015). While initial financial decisions are key for the pursuit of new opportunities, entrepreneurs need additional capital as their firm develops and therefore financing choices and lending relationships evolve over time. We also give an overview of the resourcing requirements of three specific types of venture: social enterprises, high-technology ventures and family businesses. We also introduce the topic of crowdfunding (Box 8.1) focusing on loan-based and equity-based (Landström, Parhankangas & Mason, 2019). Finally, we evaluate the current evidence, both academic and policy, on whether or not entrepreneurs face a funding gap in the current financial market.

Box 8.1

Crowdfunding is an alternative financing method that was originally used mainly by charities and social enterprises. Increasingly, it is relevant in resource–poor new ventures to raise the capital required to fund projects/enterprise. Here a large numbers of individuals network and pool small amounts of cash to support a worthy/interested cause by collective cooperation. This method of financing helps entrepreneurs to replace one large loan that demands higher returns by small amounts of donated money (or in some cases through selling small amounts of equity to investors). Although this is not an ideal financing options for all entrepreneurs, it gives some entrepreneurs, especially those who have a solid set of goals and principles but fail to access necessary finances, the opportunity to test their venturing ideas (see Sections 8.9 and 9.10.

8.2 Learning Objectives

- To learn about the challenges facing entrepreneurs in raising finance for their new ventures.
- To study different financing options for the entrepreneur.
- To review theoretical and empirical explanations of funding gap for new entrepreneurs at start-up stage.

- To understand the life-cycle aspect of a firm's financing and capital structure decisions.
- To learn how the context influences the finance choice of entrepreneurs.
- To understand the choices related to opportunities of obtaining crowdfunding finance.

8.3 Problems Financing Start-up Businesses

The resource-based view (RBV) refers to both tangible and intangible resources as important sources of capabilities that contribute to the value-creation process. Although intangible resources (see Chapter 10) are more likely to generate competitive advantage than tangible resources (Hitt, Ireland, Camp & Sexton, 2001), the latter are undeniably an essential entrepreneurial resource that contributes to survival and the performance of entrepreneurial activities. Tangible resources encompass financial, physical and organizational assets (Barney, 1991). Financial resources generally include the cash assets that are necessary to generate products and services and to acquire other essential resources. Financial resources can come from institutional investors (primarily banks, government agencies and venture capital funds,) and individual investors (the entrepreneur, family, friends and angel investors). While institutional investors make lending decisions based on hard information and arm-length principles, individual investor's use soft (private) information and relationship-based principles to guide their funding decisions (Nguyen & Canh, 2021). Physical resources for the firm include raw materials, equipment, technology, premises and geographic location. Organizational assets include the firm's formal and informal planning, controlling, coordinating and reporting systems. Both physical and organizational resources can potentially be used as collateral to secure financial capital.

The value and quality of an entrepreneur's ideas are difficult to judge and quantify. Without being able to accurately evaluate the viability of ideas, resource providers are faced with difficulties in judging whether entrepreneurs are capable of transforming resources into value-added activities (Jing, Pek-Hooi & Poh-kam, 2011). Investments in early-stage ventures are high-risk due to liabilities of newness, lack of prior financial history, limited business experience and untested markets. Unless the risk-returns of an investment can be accurately evaluated by appropriate due diligence resource providers are at risk of losing their investments (Shane & Stuart, 2002). In addition to uncertainty, resource acquisition is also complicated by information asymmetry. Information asymmetries arise when outside financiers do not have the same information about the quality of an investment as the entrepreneur (Granz, Henn & Lutz, 2020). Specifically, entrepreneurs possess more information about their own abilities and the prospects of their business ideas than external resource providers (Shane, 2000). Unless this information is credibly transferred, resource providers cannot appraise the viability of new ventures.

Entrepreneurs are often reluctant to fully disclose information to resource providers because of business confidentiality. Failure to communicate effectively with potential investors means that entrepreneurs face the risks of funders misinterpreting the information. This is particularly the case with evaluating technological innovations because of long product development times and the mismatch of the entrepreneur's scientific knowledge and the funder's commercial skills (Van Auken, 2002). In such events, as Dowd (2009) notes, it is essential that financial investors apply precautionary contractual restrictions in order to reduce risk exposure and it is a technique deployed by all reputable financial institutions. Empirical evidence suggests that businesses that have a high risk of failure and limited cash flow tend to seek more external funding. Therefore, applying such contractual restrictions is important mechanism for discouraging entrepreneurs with low survival prospects seeking debt finance (Vanacker & Manigart, 2010).

The other difficulty entrepreneurs face when obtaining external finance is related to the moral hazard problem (Block et al., 2018; Lee et al., 2015). Moral hazards occur in situations where 'one person makes the decision about how much risk to take, while someone else bears the cost if things go badly' (Krugman, 2009, p. 63). Essentially, it is asserted that because the capital risk is shared between lender and borrower, the latter takes higher risks than they would have done without external funding (Dowd, 2009). It also recognized that entrepreneurs may misuse or misallocate external funding for personal benefit. In order to ensure that this is not the case, financiers introduce complicated contracts with restrictive terms and conditions which are closely managed by costly and labour-intensive monitoring systems. However, it is acknowledged that while financial institutions can monitor the borrowers' activities throughout the duration of the facility, the cost of performing this role can be disproportionately high. Research also indicates that the cost of monitoring may lead to credit rationing even in circumstances where there is limited evidence of moral hazard and adverse selection (Dowd, 2009).

There are a number of strategies to mitigate the problems of information asymmetry and moral hazard to improve the probability of resource acquisition by entrepreneur (Block et al., 2018; Shane & Stuart, 2002). These include encouraging information transfer through social ties, introduction of intensive monitoring systems and credit subject to collateral provided by the entrepreneur. Interpersonal relationships with resource providers are also instrumental in helping entrepreneurs overcome their financing problems (Shane & Cable, 2002). Additionally, network ties are useful in mitigating the problem of information asymmetry faced by entrepreneurs when acquiring resources at the early stage of venture creation. Appropriate signals from the entrepreneur's social network are useful for potential investors to the venture (Jing et al., 2011).

8.4 Potential Sources of Finance for New Entrepreneurs

New entrepreneurs seek financial investment from both internal and external sources. Traditionally financial decisions have concentrated on choices between personal investments (savings, friends/relatives), debt finance (bank loans and government guaranteed loans), equity finance (business angel and venture capital funds) or a mix of all three (Klein, Neitzert, Hartmann-Wendels & Kraus, 2019). While each of these options have their pros and cons, a careful consideration of the capitalization configuration is essential to future success. The costs attached to some of these resources can be substantial and making repayments through retained earnings is often more a myth than a reality for most entrepreneurs.

Atherton (2012) provides two explanations for the capitalization structures of new ventures. First, a majority of firms suffer from under-capitalization at start-up and this not only limits venture growth prospects, but also makes ventures vulnerable to closure. Secondly, there is noticeable variation in the scale and nature of capitalization structures and new entrepreneurs tend to acquire 'bundles' of resources from a wide variety of sources. In practice, financing choices depend on multiple factors: the characteristics, preferences and aspirations of the entrepreneur, capital requirements (depending on the type of the venture), venture growth poten-tial and the availability of collateral (Granz et al., 2020; Klein et al., 2019). Atherton (2012) highlights the 'subjectivized influences' that determine new venture financing patterns. For example, entrepreneurs have different levels of risk-taking which has implications for their willingness to take on debt (Murzacheva & Levie, 2020). The stage of the business is also a decisive factor. Debt financing at the inception stage is riskier as repayment of loan instalments may not be possible due to limited cash flow. Equities can ease cash deficiencies, even though attracting equity funding is a difficult challenge for entrepreneurs without a strong capital base. Here the founder/team's ability to negotiate with funders and their own 'financial literacy' in relation to resourcing the start-up is particularly valuable.

8.4.1 Debt Finance

Debt finance includes loans provided by creditors including commercial banks, brokerage firms, credit unions and leasing companies as well as non-traditional lenders including family, friends, governments and other businesses (Cole & Sokolyk, 2018; Cumming et al., 2019). Three forms of debt financing are available for entrepreneurs in their early stage of ven-ture development: credit card or overdrafts from banks, asset-based finance (e.g. equipment-based loans) and supplier credit (credit offered by suppliers for inventory and equipment) (Baron, 2012). Credit cards are particularly useful because they require no explanation to lenders and are easier to obtain than other external funds. Overdrafts are also useful as they allow a flexible approach to borrow an agreed limit when needed by the entrepre-neur. In addition to its attractiveness as working capital, the flexibility allows entrepreneurs to use overdrafts to 'even out' any cash-flow changes (Storey & Greene, 2010). According to Scott (2009), nearly 60% of entrepreneurs use multiple credit card debt and overdraft facilities to fund approximately one third of their debt in their first year (Jackson & Madison, 2022).

The main source of capital debt (in terms of the amount borrowed) for entrepreneurs is bank loans. Banks are extremely conservative in their lending for early-stage businesses and therefore acquiring start-up finance from banks is not an easy process for new entrepreneurs. Usually, entrepreneurs have to offer collateral or personal guarantees to secure loans as banks regards new businesses as very risky given their high failure rates. Banks typically finance a smaller proportion of debt in the first year when entrepreneurs face potentially large adverse-selection and risk-shifting incentives (Huyghebaert, Van de Gucht & Van Hulle, 2007). At this stage, by lending on a short-term basis, banks retain more control over the firm and its investment decisions. Taking on short-term debt is riskier for entrepreneurs as it demands positive cash-flows in the short term to make the loan repayments. Banks increase the availability of credit to entrepreneurs, often offered as long-term debt, as the banking relationship develops (see Box 8.2). Long-term debt allows entrepreneurs to invest in projects that are of interest to them and have long-term prospects. Indeed, banks reward successful entrepreneurs with more credit at favourable repayment rates. The decision to grant a new loan or offer an extension to existing loans is decided by the level of current earnings, changes in earnings over time and the entrepreneur's debts with other lenders (Huyghebaert & Van de Gucht, 2007). Entrepreneurs in high-debt ventures and those who are keen to access future debt finance embark on projects that boost immediate profits to the detriment of projects with smaller initial earnings but larger future prospects. More positively, debt finance does not require entrepreneurs to give up any ownership in their business. However, it involves a financial obligation to return the capital together with an interest rate set by the bank which makes it an expensive funding option for most entrepreneurs (see Table 8.1 for a summary of debt and equity finance).

Box 8.2

It was about a year later – about a year on. I was always calling it, 'The business' it wasn't like it was just me calling it, 'the business' but it was probably about a year later when I had too much work and I needed to take somebody onto assist with that work and so I went to the bank and got £10,000 and I matched that. They could see I had work as I had proved I was kind of trading, and I matched that with about £6,000 from Merseyside Special Investment Fund at that time which opened up another door. *[Anna Heyes, Active Profile]*

As it is difficult to obtain reliable data on start-up firms, Cole and Sokolyk (2018) draw on the Kaufmann Firm Survey, which includes 5000

Table 8.1 Debt and Equity Finance: Advantages and Disadvantages

Funding type	Advantages	Disadvantages
Debt Finance	• Does not decrease/dilute the entrepreneur's equity position • Entrepreneur is singularly accountable for successes/failure • Entrepreneur is the sole recipient for all the ensuing profits. • Can enjoy the complete liberty to control the venture without any undue interference • Autonomy • As the interest repayed is tax-deductible, it shields part of the business income from taxes.	• Potential cost of financial distress • Agency costs arising between owners and financial creditors • High-risk strategy as far as company growth is concerned • Dept repayments can vary based on changes to interest rate • Additional management time to manage the debt • Failing to make repayments leading into firm liquidation • Demanding pay back schedule • Risk of losing collateral
Equity Finance	• Relatively large investments • Less restrictions on re-payments • Often are 'hands on' investors who are willingly contribute experience, knowledge and contacts • Equity providers are motivated by non-financial considerations • Receive close monitoring • Willing to take more risks	• Dilution of founder's share • Potential loss of control

US new businesses. The authors were able to identify the nature of debt obtained by start-up firms in their first year of operation. The average age of entrepreneurs (or primary owners) was 45 years of age, with 13 years' experience in the same industry and involvement with one previous start-up (approximately 25% were female). The median firm, firm generated $7500[1] (£5500) in revenues, reported a net loss of $300 (£222) and had $20,000 (£14,800) in total assets (Cole & Sokolyk, 2018). Despite the low level of revenue, these were not hobby businesses because they were registered on Dun & Bradstreet's Market Identifier (DMI)]. In terms of loans, 76% of firms had debt finance with a median sum of $20,000 (£14,800); 44% had business bank credit with a median figure of $10,000 (£7,400); and 24% had business trade credit with a median of $20,000 (£14,800). In addition, 55% of the entrepreneurs had taken out personal loans (in addition to business loans) with a median sum of $10,000 (£7,400). Comparing levels of debt with firm performance, 'better quality' start-up firms were more likely to obtain debt finance in the first year of operations. Debt finance was associated with higher success of the better-quality entrepreneurial firms in terms of survival and revenue growth. The less successful (lower-quality) start-ups were more likely to rely on personal debt in the initial year of operations. 'Importantly, it is business bank credit, but not business trade credit or personal debt, that drives the positive relation between debt financing and performance outcomes of young entrepreneurial firms' (Cole & Sokolyk, 2018, p. 611).

The data obtained by Cole and Sokolyk (2018) confirm the difficulties of obtaining debt finance for experienced entrepreneurs. Most entrepreneurs in the sample were mature with substantial amounts of previous business and start-up experience. In addition, they were also able to take on personal debt as well as business debt and this would be very difficult for any young entrepreneur without tangible assets.

8.4.2 Equity Finance

Equity finance can be obtained through internal and external sources; the choice depends on resource requirements, market conditions and the stage in venture development. Internal equity, primarily in the form of entrepreneur contributions (owned or accessed through relatives and partners) and retained profits are widely used by entrepreneurs. External equity can originate from informal angel investment or via venture capital markets. Access to these funding sources is, however, quite limited for new ventures or provides only a partial solution to capital requirements in the early stages of venture development.

8.4.2.1 Internal Equity (Personal Investment)

The most common source of new venture capital is the entrepreneur's personal finance. In additional to investing personal savings, entrepreneurs provide funding through credit cards, overdrafts and earnings from employment. Many entrepreneurs also turn to friends and family to raise the capital that they need to finance their businesses. These approaches to financing your business are forms of bootstrapping and they discussed in Chapter 9. According to Fraser (2009) personal savings are the most common source of internal finance (91% of all internal sources) followed by loans and gifts from family and friends, credit cards and home mortgage. Investment by family and friends are less expensive, have flexible return policies and make fewer demands in terms of equity. Although there is rarely sufficient funding from these sources it does provide the capital to set up and run the venture in the short term (Jackson & Madison, 2022). In the longer term these forms of capital can act as a signalling mechanism to investors and lenders about the entrepreneur's commitment to the new venture and its future prospects (Boudreau, Jeppesen, Reichstein & Rullani, 2021; Han, Fraser & Storey, 2009b). As discussed above, investment by the owner forms a major component of a start-up firm's collateral (Cole & Sokolyk, 2018).

8.4.2.2 External Equity

External equity finance is usually regarded as a preferred form of finance for entrepreneurs who have a viable business idea that involves high R&D (research and development) investment. Ou and Haynes (2006) give examples of two other situations when start-up ventures seek equity finance: first, when they experience financial distress and finance from alternative sources is lacking. Uncertainty about a firm's future discourages regular lenders from granting a loan and therefore equity would be the only viable alternative for working capital for some entrepreneurs. Secondly, when there is an imbalance between cash outflow from internal operations and cash inflow from regular financing sources. Here high growth demands new products and services for new and existing markets; equity capital is a useful resource to fill cash shortages for such expansion plans. Research also reveals that access to equity finance helps improve debt equity ratios that open the possibility of debt financing for expansion (Franck, Huyghebaert & D'Espallier, 2010).

Despite its benefits of faster business growth and increased value of the business, equity finance can put pressure on entrepreneurs to make immediate post-entry profits and also involves sharing of management control with equity providers. It is therefore important that entrepreneurs maintain a balance between the costs of losing control of the venture with the prospects for faster business growth. In the following sections we outline the different criteria used by business angels and venture capitalists when evaluating start-up companies (Granz et al., 2020).

8.4.2.3 Business Angels

Business angels are high net-worth private individuals who provide their own finance, time and expertise directly to new ventures with a view to financial gain (Giurca Vasilescu, 2009). Although typical business angels are former or current entrepreneurs themselves, they are extremely difficult to identify because of the private and unreported nature of their investment activities (Harrison & Mason, 2019; Mason & Harrison, 1995). Mason (2009) provided four reasons why informal business angel finance is important for entrepreneurs. First, business angels are often motivated by non-financial considerations and are, therefore, willing to make more risky investments. Their investment decisions are largely based on personal preferences which make them one of the few financing options available for entrepreneurs operating in the seed and start-up stages of venture creation. Secondly, business angels, for convenience, largely make investments locally and this not only helps to address regional gaps in the availability of finance it also helps entrepreneurs gain regional knowledge related to local markets. Thirdly, business angels are typically 'hands on' investors who are willingly contribute their experience, knowledge and contacts to the entrepreneur. Because business angels often come from an entrepreneurial background, they have high levels of commitment to contribute to venture success. Finally, due to the policy commitment to expand angel investment activity, there are more opportunities for entrepreneurs to access angel investments. This attempt however is hindered due to the lack of information relating to business angel existence and the impact of this form of investment.

There is some recent work examining the links between business angel behaviour performance of their portfolio companies (Block, Fisch, Obschonka & Sandner, 2019; Bonini & Capizzi, 2019; Bonini, Capizzi & Zocchi, 2019). Companies backed by syndicates of business angels (rather than individual business angels) are more likely to survive and have higher levels of performance (Block et al., 2019). Business angels who rate highly on extraversion prefer belonging to a syndicate. On the other hand, those with high levels of conscientiousness can restrict the flexibility of firms attempting to change quickly (Bonini et al., 2019). The so-called big-five personality traits of business angels do have an impact on some aspects of venture success but, overall, the results of link between business angel personality business success are inconclusive (Bonini et al., 2019).

Based on a review of the literature, Granz et al. (2020) compare the investment decisions made by business angels (BAs) and venture capitalists (VCs) according to three criteria: the management team (or the entrepreneur), the business and 'financial traction'. Business angels generally prefer to invest in entrepreneurs with whom they are familiar and levels of mutual compatibility are very important. Consequently, BAs use subjective criteria including the entrepreneur's trustworthiness, their commitment to the venture, their passion and persuasiveness. With regards to the business, BAs are concerned about the nature of the business opportunity and size of the potential market. Therefore, they examine levels of customer engagement, routes to market and competitive positioning. They also prefer to invest in sectors with which they are familiar and have reasonable levels of growth potential. In terms of 'financial traction', BAs do, 'to some extent' evaluate financial data but are not necessarily motivated by capital gains (as is the case with VCs). Rather, BAs are motivated by the satisfaction of their hands-on involvement with successful ventures. In other words, BAs will use their knowledge and experience to support the entrepreneur in their business decisions. VCs do not directly intervene in the management of ventures in which they invest. While business angels are more likely to invest in the early stages of a business compared to VC investors, they do not necessarily require greater financial compensation for their additional risk (Granz et al., 2020).

8.4.2.4 Venture Capitalists (VCs)

Venture capital funding constitutes investment from institutional investors (including pure VC firms, corporate VC units of large industrial companies, investment banks and private equity firms) who are interested in gaining equity stakes in entrepreneurial ventures with strong growth potential (Colombo, Grilli & Verga, 2007). The stage of venture development, levels of risk, the entrepreneur's background, geographic location and exit opportunities affect venture capitalists' assessment of potential returns and motivation to invest (Van Auken, 2002). As venture capitalists are keep to support high-growth enterprises that need large amounts of investment only a very small proportion of entrepreneurs meet their funding criteria (Timmons & Spinelli, 2004). VC funding therefore represents only a small percentage of total capital invested in entrepreneurial businesses. Moreover, due to high agency costs associated with due diligence, venture capital finance is an expensive solution for new entrepreneurs; only a limited number of VCs are involved in seed-stage funding (see Box 8.3). In general, venture capitalists expect a large share of ownership although the share depends on the perceived growth potential of the venture. Additionally, in riskier investments, venture capitalists impose restrictions on the actions of entrepreneurs to protect their financial investment. High-risk/high-return opportunities offered by venture capital investment can be suitable for young innovative entrepreneurs as traditional financing sources are unavailable, inadequate or inappropriate to fund risky business ideas. In this respect VC funding is generally considered as the most appropriate source of external finance for high-tech ventures with secure IPR (Colombo et al., 2007). Due to their sectoral knowledge VC investors are in a stronger position to distinguish between 'good' and 'bad' investment opportunities than any other external investors.

The evaluation criteria for venture capitalists are largely related to the characteristics of the entrepreneur, their background and experience rather than market or product characteristics (Pintado, de Lema & Van Auken, 2007). As there are information asymmetries between entrepreneurs and venture capital investors, they need to be embedded in local social networks to evaluate an investment opportunity efficiently (Ferrary, 2010). Venture capitalists who are involved in first-round funding at the seed stage learn-by-collaboration through their involvement in the venture management. This reduces information asymmetries between investor and entrepreneur.

Box 8.3

First Launched in Japan, Dragons Den, a reality show that is now airing in countries across the globe, showcases the venture capitalist investment and decision-making process for new entrepreneurial ventures.

Here Entrepreneurs pitch for investment in the Den from venture capitalists (called Dragons) willing to invest their money in exchange for equity from the venture, the amount of which is stipulated at the beginning of the discussion. Upon an agreed investment by a VC, entrepreneurs get the opportunity to accept the offer, negotiate further or simply walk away.

Recent research evidence from the recordings of the interactions from Dragons' Den suggests that the VCs do not use a fully compensatory decision-making model in the first selection stage and that they trade off speed for decision accuracy. One 'fatal flow' from the objective criteria in this initial stage can result in rejecting a good candidate and thereby filtering them out from the decisions in the subsequent stages, which are largely subjective (see more details in Maxwell et al., 2011).

In addition to finance, venture capitalists provide entrepreneurs with additional resources through their experience, knowledge, social networks and enhanced image and market creditability (Hanlon & Saunders, 2007). They add value to entrepreneurs' ideas by bringing investors and entrepreneurs together in an efficient manner and by making better investment decisions than entrepreneurs themselves. They do not, however, adopt a hand-on role in providing the entrepreneur/team with managerial guidance (Granz et al., 2020). Also venture capital investment essentially helps new ventures build reputation and achieving legitimacy. Large and Muegge (2008) point to the added value of successful mentoring which strengthens the entrepreneur's networks. The multifaceted forms of support that originate from venture capitals also include moral support to build the investor base and review and help to formulate strategy.

It is also important to remember that the institutional context determines the prospects of entrepreneurs receiving venture capital investment. Venture capital firms simultaneously manage a range of relationships with many stakeholders, including investors, investees, prospective buyers and co-investors and, therefore, investment decisions are not only shaped by individual and firm-specific factors (Sethuram, Taussig & Gaur, 2021). For example, Bonini and Alkan (2012) document how a positive socio political and entrepreneurial environment supports development of the venture capital industry. A number of macroeconomic factors such as GDP growth, tax rate, inflation, stock market value and interest rate are robust determinants of venture capital investment in Asia (Oino, 2014). In their study of venture capital investments in the US, Ning, Wang and Yu (2015) found a supportive macroeconomic and public market conditions to be the driving forces for entrepreneurs to access above average venture capital funding.

In terms of the criteria identified by Granz et al. (2020), VCs operate in a very different way than BAs. Venture capitalists place much greater emphasis on the prospects for short-term growth and the ability to 'cash-out' their investments. Much of the VC literature is focused on the 'entrepreneurial team', which indicates that they are very unlikely to invest in businesses established by single entrepreneurs. The team's human capital in the form their industry experience and their *complementary competences* are key factors for VCs. What this means in practice in that VCs prefer teams who have expertise in technology, sales, marketing, finance, operations and so on. Clearly it is very unlikely that a young, inexperienced entrepreneur will meet such exacting standards. In terms of business criteria, VCs usually invest where there is clear evidence of an ability to protect future competitive advantage by means of patents and other forms of intellectual property rights (design rights, trademarks etc). This means that, in general, VCs prefer to invest in technology or science-based businesses. In terms of financial traction, there is again a substantial variation in the criteria used by VCs compared to BAs. VCs only invest in those companies with the potential to grow rapidly in the short term (four to five years). Whereas BAs will apply their own skills to enhance business performance, VCs are much more likely to use *financial milestones* to exert control over the business. If a business does not meet its target in terms of growth/profitability, then the next stage of investment may be withheld.

Granz et al. (2020, p. 130) summarize their review: 'For entrepreneurs seeking venture funding, our results show that VCs and BAs have different preferences in terms of their investment policies. Entrepreneurs have only one opportunity to present their business idea to a VC or BA investor. Even though VCs and BAs place different weights on investment criteria, our review shows that they all holistically examine the management team, the business and the financial traction'.

8.5 Finance and Business Life Cycle

Literature on capital structure theory acknowledges that entrepreneurial financing choices evolve with the changing characteristics of their venture. The structure of finance at later stages is dependent on the initial conditions and financing decisions made at start-up (Lefebvre, 2021). Uncertainty and information asymmetries mean that entrepreneurs face difficulties in accessing finance during the start-up phase. At this stage entrepreneurs largely rely on interpersonal networks and resource their businesses through various financial bootstrapping methods (see Chapter 9). Personal finance and finance acquired through family and friends is a significant proportion of the initial investment for most entrepreneurs (Jackson & Madison, 2022). Own finance can act as collateral to secure bank borrowings for the entrepreneur once the business begins to operate. Although banks typically finance a smaller proportion of debt in the start-up year when firms face potentially large adverse-selection and risk-shifting incentives (Huyghebaert et al., 2007). Along with bank debt entrepreneurs can also approach leasing companies and form research and development partnerships for product development. Hence, start-ups can generally only access bank debt when they have established a track record by generating steady cash flow and have tangible assets on their balance sheets which can be used as collateral (Cumming et al., 2019). Other studies have found that bank debt can play a role in the start-up phase of some high-growth entrepreneurial firms (Deloof & Vanacker, 2018).

As ventures mature, entrepreneurs generate more stable earnings which helps them to develop a track record useful for future access to finance (Cumming et al., 2019; Franck et al., 2010). Those fortunate enough to gain bank finance at an early stage can develop an intense lending relationship with their banks thus helping to reduce information asymmetries. Consequently, banks will decrease credit terms and provide entrepreneurs with longer-term finance. This reduces the pressure on entrepreneurs enabling them to focus on more stable long-term income rather than riskier short-term earnings. Also, the availability of alternative financing sources – in particular internally generated cash – helps entrepreneurs focus on more innovative ideas which could be further funded by external equity. Additional capital required to fund high-risk projects and business expansion generally comes from business angels, venture capital funds, institutional investors and venture leasing companies (Nofsinger & Wang, 2011). High-growth technology

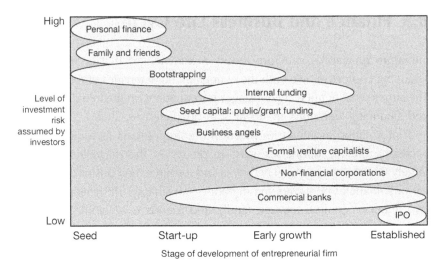

Figure 8.1 Changes in Financing Strategies during the Venture Lifecycle

firms have a substantially higher probability of acquiring external equity at a relatively early stage of venture development. Changes in financing strategies along the venture life cycle are depicted in Figure 8.1.

A recent literature review examining the financing of start-up businesses confirms that family and friends are the main sources of external funds at the start-up stage (Klein et al., 2019). Others suggest that there is less focus on family and friends at the early stage of business start-up because entrepreneurs recognize the limitations such funding can impose on their activities (Murzacheva & Levie, 2020). Entrepreneurs in this study preferred to use their own money in conjunction with public funds in the early stages and then seek bank loans as their need for finance increased. Murzacheva and Levie (2020, p. 209) do point out that the lack of interest in using informal funds (family & friends) by their sample of Scottish entrepreneurs 'may be rooted in the cultural setting, where mixing of personal and business lives is avoided, and the need for independence is dominant when launching a business'. During the business development phase when firms begin to generate revenue, leasing, factoring, supplier credit as well as bank loans and overdrafts are the main sources of external finance. During the growth phase it becomes possible to attract private equity and venture capitalist finance. As firms move towards maturity, then Bond Markets or an Initial Public Offering (IPO) may be a possibility for a small minority of businesses. If they have a strong personal connection, some entrepreneurs may be able to attract funding from a business angel in the early stages of start-up (Granz et al., 2020; Klein et al., 2019). If they do so, then it will certainly make attracting other external funding far easier in the future.

8.6 Variations in Financing Strategies

The life-cycle approach to business finance clearly indicates that smaller businesses do not have access to the same sources of finance as larger businesses. Firms utilize very different sources of finance depending on the stage of business development (Figure 8.1). Additionally, finance strategies for firms differ according to the type of entrepreneurial venture. The discussion that follows explains the financing strategies employed by entrepreneurs running social enterprises, high-technology ventures and family businesses (Figure 8.2).

8.6.1 Social Entrepreneurs

Existing strategy typologies (see, for example, Di Domenico, Haugh & Tracey, 2010; Moizer & Tracey, 2010) highlight the different combinations of financial and non-financial resources that social entrepreneurs draw on. Financial resources come in the form of (a) earned income; (b) government and other contracts; and (c) philanthropic capital. Earned income includes generating financial revenue from services, programmes or products provided by social ventures themselves or by their for-profit subsidiaries (at full, discounted or sliding-fee rates). These enterprises also create wealth through delivering

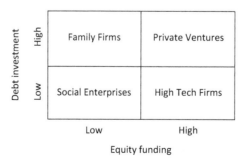

Figure 8.2 Debt and Equity Finance: Type of Venture

mission-related services funded through government and other contracts. The non-distribution restriction limits the ability of social entrepreneurs to access the same capital markets as commercial entrepreneurs and their ability to pay commercial rates for human and other resources (Austin, Stevenson & Wei-Skillern, 2006; Jayawarna, Jones & Macpherson, 2020).

Restricted access to capital markets means that social entrepreneurs are often reliant on philanthropic funding in the form of grants, goods and in-kind donations from private individuals, third party funding sources and membership fees. Philanthropic capital accounts for a considerable portion of the funding at start-up. The use of philanthropic capital raises a number of issues. First, the capacity to attract non-market sources of capital is tied to the social motives of the enterprise. Reliance on philanthropic funding can lead to what Teasdale (2010, p. 274) describes as 'coercive isomorphism' as social entrepreneurs tailor their processes, practices, objectives and goals to those prescribed by funding bodies. A corollary is that, because social entrepreneurs rarely recover the full cost of goods or services from con-sumers, funding bodies can become the most important clients. Hence, pro-curing resources can become the primary activity of social entrepreneurs (Austin et al., 2006). Secondly, limited access to capital markets means that it is essential for social entrepreneurs to engage with a wide range of stakeholders and develop substantial networks and partnerships if they are to leverage external resources (Austin et al., 2006; Khaire, 2010; Moizer & Tracey, 2010). Here the tensions between the social and economic imperatives of an enterprise become clear.

8.6.2 Family Business Finance

Entrepreneurs running family businesses follow a different strategies and financing structures to traditional entrepreneurs. The family business lit-erature provides both supply side (ability to borrow) and demand side (willingness to borrow) explanations for financing family businesses (Basu & Parker, 2008). The supply-side explanation uses the idea of gen-erational evolution in the family firm to argue that given a smooth tran-sition from one generation to the next, family firms have a better chance to access to debt financing. They have higher propensity to build long-term relationships with banks who consider them as less risky, profitable and more reliable. Arguably, these entrepreneurs have higher incentives to meet current and future obligations because failing to do so can damage the family name (Jones, Ghobadian, O'Regan & Antcliffe, 2013). Demand-side explanations on the other hand build on the premise that irrespective of access opportunities family-based entrepreneurs are reluctant to use external sources of capital as it dilutes family control. Interestingly, Romano et al. (2001) highlight the importance of studying the behavioural dimensions such as risk-taking, values and goals of family business owners. Although intergenerational differences can have an impact on the capital structure of family firms, they in general favour internal rather than external sources of finance. Formal and informal external equity investment is therefore very limited as these entrepreneurs see financing their firms through these sources as a riskier option. Bank funding on the other hand can form a part of the funding equation for those family businesses that pursue expansion plans.

In their study of a family-based start-up business, Jones and Giordano (2021) point out that a major advantage is that they have access to a wider range of resources including finance, skills and knowledge, compared with individual entrepreneurs. As *Jazooli* began to grow, the family members were determined to retain control of the business and retained profits were used to fund the growth. In addition, they also adopted a range of sophisticated financial techniques including foreign exchange hedging to mitigate risks associated with currency fluctuations (Jones & Giordano, 2021).

8.6.3 High-tech Firms

High research and development (R&D) costs, untested technology markets and long lead time in commercializing new products make technology-based firms very high-risk investments (Blank & Carmeli, 2021; Mason & Harrison, 1995). Entrepreneurs rarely have enough personal investment to fund expensive innovations. Access to external funds is problematic due to severe information asymmetries associated with new technologies. To overcome the problem of adverse selection, finance providers need a lengthy due-diligence process to access relevant information about the entrepreneur, the firm's scientific knowledge and intellectual property rights. Because large investments are required at an early-stage debt is not a suitable financing strategy for high-tech entrepreneurs. Short-term loans put unrealistic pressure on entrepreneurs to pay-off debts from internally generated cash.

Empirical evidence shows that high-tech ventures have a significantly lower probability of being successful with long-term loan applications; the probability of being successful with loan applications decreases as the R&D intensity increases (Freel, 2007). External equity investment is also a high risk for both entrepreneur and equity provider. The high risk-return characteristics of institutional investments however make venture capital funding sometimes the only suitable financing strategy for high-tech entrepreneurs (Irwin, Gilstrap, Drnevich & Tudor, 2019; Van Auken, 2002). VCs manage the risk of technology investments through close monitoring, personal involvement and through entering into legal and contractual agreements. Their sectoral specialization is particularly useful to overcome the information asymmetries between the entrepreneur and the VC investors and to highlight and support 'hidden values' of new technological innovations (Colombo et al., 2007). Research evidence however suggests that venture capitalists are reluctant to finance technology-based companies at a very early stage (Bottazzi & Da Rin, 2002).

The global dominance of Alphabet, Amazon, Apple, Facebook and Microsoft has limited the options for newer, fast-growing technology-based businesses (Irwin et al., 2019). This has led to a 'crowding-out' by the so-called 'Fearsome Five' who have the resources to acquire any new company that has growth potential. The downside of this dominance is that it has decreased merger and acquisitions (M&A) in the area of technology-based businesses because of the market concentration associated with the Fearsome Five. This is not a particularly healthy situation either for entrepreneurs or policymakers. Entrepreneurs have limited options for being bought-out by medium-sized technology firms. For policymakers it means that a lack of investor interest in small technology-based firms could restrict the number of new start-up businesses (Irwin et al., 2019).

Blank and Carmeli (2021) argue that the likelihood of a technology-based business obtaining external investment depends on the human capital of the founding team. There are three forms of previous experiences that are important: entrepreneurial, managerial and industry specific. *Entrepreneurial experience* refers to the previous creation of a new organization and the associated skills of opportunity identification/evaluation, resource acquisition and creation of the social networks that provide access to a range of finance providers. *Managerial experience* refers to the managerial positions held by team-members prior to establishing the current company. *Industry-specific (technological domain) experience* refers to previous work experience in a knowledge-intensive industry related to the technological domain in which the new firm operates (Blank & Carmeli, 2021, p. 1872). Based on their study of high-tech companies based in Israel, the authors confirm that the founding team's prior managerial and industry-specific experiences influenced the external investment in new ventures. Surprisingly, prior entrepreneurial experience did not influence the nature of external investment (Blank & Carmeli, 2021). Thus, the authors suggest that founders may have ambiguous feelings towards external funders because of their previous start-up experiences.

8.7 Is there a Funding Gap for New Entrepreneurs?

It is widely accepted that entrepreneurs find it increasingly difficult to acquire external funding and ways of improving the 'funding gap' has been a topic of national and international debate for some time. It is assumed that funding gaps arise where businesses are unable to access finance that they could use productively (Cressy, 2002; Năstase and Kajanus, 2009). Recently, it has been suggested that there are two funding gaps: 1) at the very early stages of business start-up (proof of concept) and 2) older, more mature firms that need funding to realize their growth potential (Cumming et al., 2019). There is a clearly recognized need to improve access to financing for new ventures on reasonable terms by banks and to set-up policies to ensure ventures with 'good growth prospects have access to appropriately structured risk capital at all stages of their development' (OECD, 2006). Although 'funding gaps' may be a global phenomenon, the theoretical justification is more controversial. Stiglitz and Weiss (1981) argued that small venture funding markets could be in a state of equilibrium yet still prevent access to finance for some ventures when banks *rationally* engage in processes of 'credit rationing'. According to Stiglitz and Weiss (1981), credit rationing occurs either when some receive credit while others do not; or there are identifiable groups in the population that are unable to obtain credit at any price. This asserts that asymmetric information and agency problems make it difficult for financial institutions to distinguish between 'good credit risks' and 'bad credit risks' (Han, Fraser & Storey, 2009a). Therefore, finance providers are often unwilling to provide funding or put prohibitive restrictions on the type and amount of funding for small firms (Blumberg & Letterie, 2008). These market failures create funding gaps for new ventures particularly in technology-based sectors.

Indeed, despite an agreement there is a shortage in the supply side of SMEs financing, there is an unquestionable need to understand the inter-play between supply and demand in the process of business creation and business growth (Han et al., 2009a). A review of public policies related to small firms confirms a common misconception that 'improving' the supply of finance will close the funding gap and thus solve the problem of small venture finance (Black & Strahan, 2002; Rahman & Jianchao, 2011). Recent research argues that this focus on funding supply is misguided for several reasons (Atherton, 2012). There is a challenge to the common assumption that the 'funding gap' is a supply-side problem and demand for finance is out of the owner's control. Lam (2010) for example, alludes to the 'funding gap' being just as much a supply side issue as a demand side issue. Nascent, or start-up, new ventures enact their environment by actively managing demand as well as supply of finance to narrow the 'funding gap'. For example, this narrowing is done by creating the required start-up capital themselves or relying on friends or family members to sub-sidize the venture. In other words, the 'funding gap' is not static or concrete but is dynamic and manageable in most cases (Lam, 2010). This is echoed by Harding (2002) who points out that it is the knowledge gap, rather than the funding gap, which needs to be addressed. Indeed, studies suggest that there are different banking and financial facilities (letters of credit, factoring, forfeiting – see Box 8.4) that business owners use to manage their financial needs without seeking external finance (bank loans, equity finance etc.). Yet many business owners are not aware of their existence or relevance to their businesses. In other words, addressing this knowledge gap (the gap between availability of financial facilities for small firms and the level of owner-managers awareness) appears to be a realistic way of addressing financing needs without substantial government investment. In addition, Cumming et al. (2019) point out that the funding gap may be helped by the emergence of new forms of finance such as crowdfunding (see Section 8.8).

Box 8.4

In issuing *letters of credit*, Banks acts as an uninterested party between customer and seller to assure payment to a seller of goods and/or services and therefor protects the sellers from illegitimate customers. This is particularly useful for inexperienced entrepreneurs as payments authorized in the letter of credit are paid by the Bank upon the delivery of the merchandise irrespective of any damages to the merchandise (which will be dealt with by the insurances).

Factoring releases the money tied up in customer invoices and help firms to prevent problems caused by late paying customers. This type of lending is important for firms to regulate their cash flows.

In international trading, *forfeiting* allows the exporter to receive immediate cash against its accounts receivable. Because the forfeiter takes on all the risks associated with the receivables (for a small return), like in factoring, forfeiting can make a direct contribution to the firm's immediate cash flow.

8.8 Formal Crowdfunding for Entrepreneurial Businesses

Crowdfunding is another avenue for financing start-up businesses as traditional funders including banks, business angels and venture capitalists increasingly focus on projects that are more mature, require large amounts of capital and entail lower levels of risk. Consequently, such organizations are generally unwilling to give a chance to inexperienced entrepreneurs (Popescul, Radu, Păvăloaia & Georgescu, 2020). In contrast to the professional investors associated with banks, business angels and venture capitalists, those investing via crowdfunding are likely to be relatively unsophisticated in financial terms. Crowdfunding has five distinct elements: (1) it is based on an Internet platform; (2) it aggregates funds from multiple individuals; (3) each individual generally contributes a relatively small amount of the total sum; (4) funders have a range of goals and objectives (making financial gains, seeking material gain or rewards, donating, towards a social cause and so on); and (5) funders make an assessment of the focal project (Dushnitsky & Zunino, 2019, p. 47). Crowdfunding can benefit entrepreneurs in ways that go beyond obtaining financial resources. Potentially, there are substantiated non-financial benefits, such as attracting employees, engaging the collective intelligence of the crowd, advanced promotion of products and services, obtaining feedback, attracting media attention and creating a pool of future customers (Popescul et al., 2020, p. 2).

According to Parhankangas, Mason and Landstrom (2019), crowdfunding has a long history of appeals to the public for support including providing finance for the Statue of Liberty in New York. Emergence of the Internet and particularly Web 2.0 has made bringing together those requiring finance and potential funders much simpler and more efficient. There are four basic models of crowding (Parhankangas et al., 2019, p. 3):

- Donation-based platforms such as *Justgiving.com* and *Gofundme.com*, in which individuals donate to what they perceive to be a worthy cause.
- Reward-based platforms which include US platforms such as *Kickstarter. com* and *Indiegogo.com*. Rewards usually take the form of early access to a product or service provided by the entrepreneur. Users may then be willing to provide feedback on the strengths and weaknesses of the offering.
- Loans (microfinance or peer-to-peer) are offered via platforms such as *Kiva* and *Prosper.com* and loans are offered to individuals and projects by funders whose financial compensation takes the form of interest payments (in the same way as banks).
- Equity-based finance offered by platforms such as *wefunder.com* and *localstake.com* in the US and *Crowdcube* and *Seedr* in the UK. Not surprisingly, equity-based crowdfunding transactions tend to be the most complex, both from a legal standpoint and in terms of the level of uncertainty.

Donation-based and reward-based platforms are regarded as 'bootstrapped' finance and are discussed in Chapter 9 (Section 9.8). Also, given the legal complexities associated with equity crowdfunding, this is extremely unlikely to be a realistic option for inexperienced entrepreneurs. Some suggest that equity crowdfunding should not be considered a substitute for business angel or venture capital investment even though both are in decline (Harrison & Mason, 2019). Investment by professionals (business angels and venture capitalists) is regarded as 'smart money' because they are more likely to invest in successful ventures. In comparison, equity crowdfunding is regarded as 'dumb money' that often is invested in projects that are not economically viable and, consequently, should be allowed to fail (Harrison & Mason, 2019).

Those entrepreneurs who have already raised some capital, even from family and friends, are more likely to succeed in crowdfunding (Klein et al., 2019). In addition, women are more successful in attracting funding via donation and reward platforms (Section 9.7) but are less likely to attract equity funding (Popescul et al., 2020). Once a crowdfunding campaign is launched it is essential to attract early investors who send signals to potential follow-on stakeholders. What this means is that social capital plays an important role in the success of crowdfunding campaigns (Cai, Polzin & Stam, 2021; Polzin, Toxopeus & Stam, 2018). Establishing a presence on social media platforms such as Facebook and Twitter is a critical success factor in generating interest in entrepreneurial projects. Social capital acts as the 'glue' which binds and bonds entrepreneurs and their funders (Onginjo, Zhou, Berhanu & Belihu, 2021). Human capital is also important in attracting crowdfunding. Having a track record (previous business experience), the ability to demonstrate a good understanding of the product/service as well as having convincing communication and presentation skills are all essential to successful crowdfunding campaigns (Parhankangas et al., 2019).

As mentioned above, it is extremely unlikely that inexperienced entrepreneurs will be able to access equity-based crowdfunding and, therefore, we outline details of loan-based crowdfunding. Zopa (UK) and Prosper (US) were lending crowdfunding platforms that emerged in 2005 and 2006 respectively (Ziegler & Shneor, 2020). Following the 2008 financial crises, digital financial platforms grew rapidly and crowdfunding became an important mechanism in filling the 'finance gap' for smaller firms. A key feature of lending platforms is that they by-passed traditional financial institutions and offered good returns to investors as well as low-cost loans to entrepreneurs (Ziegler & Shneor, 2020). The most common form of loan-based crowdfunding is *person-to-person (P2P)* in which the platform mediates interactions between investor and borrower. If the loan is not repaid, then the investor takes the loss rather than the digital intermediary. P2P lending platforms rely on traditional credit scoring facilities and financial information provided by the borrower to set interest rates and provide risk ratings for investors. Although, as pointed out by Ziegler and Shneor (2020), it is difficult to establish exactly how the various platforms carry out their loan risk assessments because of limited disclosures.

Balance sheet lending is the second most common form of loan-based crowdfunding. The digital lending platform retains all business loans and allocates funds directly from its own balance sheet. In contrast to the P2P model, balance sheet lenders are active in offering loans rather than acting as intermediaries. Consequently, the lending company, rather than the investor, bears the risk of financial loss if a loan is not repaid (Ziegler & Shneor, 2020). Therefore, balance sheet lenders act in a similar way to a conventional bank in offering loans directly to entrepreneurs and owner-managers. In addition to *P2P* and *balance sheet loan companies*, recently three other forms of loan-based crowdfunding have emerged: Invoice Trading, Debt-based Securities and Mini Bonds (Ziegler & Shneor, 2020). *Invoice trading* is similar to *Factoring* in which businesses sell off their invoices at a discount to an institutional investor. *Debt-based securities* and *mini bonds* are more sophisticated financial instruments where institutional funders purchase bonds or debentures at a fixed rate of interest (Ziegler & Shneor, 2020).

To restate our position, in the early stages of starting a new business trying to obtain external finance is likely to be more of a distraction than a benefit. It may be more practicable to make use of a crowdfunding platform once your business has begun to generate sales and income. Should you decide to pursue a crowdfunding campaign there are a number of factors which have a positive influence on the likelihood of success (Popescul et al., 2020):

- A professional presentation with a focus on detailed information about the project
- Frequent progress updates (related to funding and the project itself)
- The number of shares on social media
- Use of clear and unambiguous language
- Previous successful funding campaigns.

It should be clear from this list that attempting to obtain finance (loan or equity) via a crowdfunding platform will require a considerable amount of the entrepreneur's time and effort. If you are convinced that you do need external finance, then it may be better to consider either a donation-based or a reward-based platform and these are discussed in Section 9.7.

8.9 Summary and Learning Points

In this chapter we examine the types of finance inexperienced entrepreneurs can access to resource new ventures. Access to resources is one of the key ingredients that separate successful entrepreneurs from the unsuccessful. In most cases business failure can be traced to a lack of finance and many businesses are never started because of financial hardship. Using personal savings, assistance from family and friends and bootstrapping have become the best and sometimes the only way in which a new entrepreneur can raise capital. With regards to external finance, most entrepreneurs do not have much flexibility in their choices. If it is risky business with limited assets, it will be almost impossible to get bank debt without putting up some collateral other than business assets (usually personal property). Many start-ups do not have high-growth potential and will never be candidates for equity finance from venture capitalists. Innovation in digitization technologies have provided entrepreneurial start-ups potential investment opportunities via equity crowdfunding platforms (Parhankangas et al., 2019). Taken together the key learning points from this chapter are:

- For both nascent and early-stage entrepreneurs finding seed funding is a difficult task.
- Entrepreneurs acquire very different forms of finance in different configurations; the choice of which is influenced by multiple factors including type of company, founder's aspirations, growth potential, market sector and the availability of collateral. Finance choice also depends on the stage of business development.
- Most start-ups are initially funded by the entrepreneur and family and friends. Bootstrap resources (including overdrafts and credit cards) also form a major part of the initial capital base of new ventures.
- As a venture matures and requires investments for growth, use of external finance increases with debt financing (mainly bank loans) and equity finance (business angels and venture capitalists) taking a role in providing finance for the firm.
- Entrepreneurs must make a trade-off between paying interest and giving up some of their ownership when making a choice between debt or equity finance.
- Due to information asymmetries and the moral hazard problems, external funders (venture capitalists and business angels) are often unwilling to

provide finance or put prohibitive restrictions on the type and amount of finance for early entrepreneurial activities.

- Financing structure decisions for entrepreneurs vary based on the type of the venture they create. While early-stage social enterprises are largely funded through informal bootstrap finance and philanthropic capital (with very little bank loans or equity finance), high-growth businesses operating in high-tech industries often rely on equity finance (business angels and venture capitalists) for early-stage finance. Entrepreneurs from family businesses often rely on debt finance to promote growth; external equity is an uncommon form of funding for family firms as access to this finance can result in family members losing control of their business.
- Crowdfunding platforms connect entrepreneurs and investors who want to acquire equity shares in promising new ventures. Crowd due diligence reduces information asymmetries between entrepreneurs and funders thus enabling entrepreneurs to seek equity crowdfunding to invest in innovative projects.

8.10 Discussion Questions and Call to Action

- Why might financing strategies differ in early stages of a new venture from a more established venture?
- What are the key principles that differentiate debt finance from equity finance?
- An analysis of both the supply side and demand side issues related to financing behaviour of new ventures suggest that there is no evidence for venture funding gap. Discuss this issue.
- Is the business life cycle important for understanding the financing behaviour of entrepreneurial ventures?
- What are the key contextual characteristics that differentiate the financing patterns of different types of firms?
- What is the role of crowdfunding in the growth of start-up businesses?

As pointed out in the introduction to this chapter, it is unlikely that the majority of young people starting a business will be able to access formal finance in the form of bank loans or formal equity investment (business angels and venture capitalists). Nevertheless, it is important that you have a good understanding of the key issues associated with external finance.

Although it may be possible to fund future growth from retained profits, this is unlikely to be possible for all start-up firms. We want reading this book to inspire you to grow a business which will have a positive societal impact by creating new jobs and providing worthwhile products and services. Therefore, it is probable that at some stage in the future you will want or need to attract external funding. It may be that a business angel (or a syndicate of business angels) is the most likely route to external finance. Business angels generally prefer to invest in entrepreneurs with whom they already have a personal relationship. Consequently, as we stress throughout this book, developing your social networks will make attracting the right kind of external investment more likely. Crowdfunding is another possible avenue for obtaining external finance. However, as we discuss in the following chapter, crowdfunding is not an easy option and it may distract you from the real task of developing your business.

Note

1   The figure for mean revenue was $230,000 (£170,000) but this was skewed by 'significant outliers' and the median figure is more representative of typical revenue in first year.

References

Atherton, A. (2012). Cases of start-up financing: An analysis of new venture capitalisation structures and patterns. *International Journal of Entrepreneurial Behavior & Research, 18*(1), 28–47.

Austin, J., Stevenson, H. & Wei-Skillern, J. (2006). Social and Commercial Entrepreneurship: Same, Different, or Both? *Entrepreneurship: Theory & Practice, 30*(1), 1–22.

Barney, J. (1991). Firm Resources and Sustained Competitive Advantage. *Journal of Management, 17*(1), 99–121.

Baron, R. A. (2012). *Entrepreneurship: An evidence-based guide.* Northampton, MA: Edward Elgar Publishing.

Basu, A. & Parker, S. C. (2008). Family Finance and New Business Start-Ups. In P. Auerswald & A. Bozkaya (Eds.), *Financing Entrepreneurship* (pp. 335–360): Elgar Reference Collection. International Library of Entrepreneurship, vol. 12. Cheltenham, U.K. and Northampton, MA: Elgar.

Business, Innovation & Skills. (2012). SME Access to External Finance, BIS Economics Paper No. 16, Department for Business, Innovation and Skills, UK. Retrieved from http://search.ebscohost.com/login.aspx?direct=true&db=bth&AN=9607032 860&site=ehost-live

Black, S. E. & Strahan, P. E. (2002). Entrepreneurship and Bank Credit Availability. *The Journal of Finance, 57*(6), 2807–2833.

Blank, T. H. & Carmeli, A. (2021). Does founding team composition influence external investment? The role of founding team prior experience and founder CEO. *Journal of Technology Transfer, 46*(6), 1869–1888.

Block, J. H., Colombo, M. G., Cumming, D. J. & Vismara, S. (2018). New Players in Entrepreneurial Finance and Why They Are There. *Small Business Economics, 50*(2), 239–250.

Block, J. H., Fisch, C. O., Obschonka, M. & Sandner, P. G. (2019). A personality perspective on business angel syndication☆. *Journal of Banking and Finance, 100*, 306–327.

Blumberg, B. F. & Letterie, W. A. (2008). Business Starters and Credit Rationing. *Small Business Economics*(2), 187–200.

Bonini, S. & Alkan, S. (2012). The Political and Legal Determinants of Venture Capital Investments around the World. *Small Business Economics, 39*(4), 997–1016.

Bonini, S. & Capizzi, V. (2019). The Role of Venture Capital in the Emerging Entrepreneurial Finance Ecosystem: Future Threats and Opportunities. *Venture Capital, 21*(2–3), 137–175.

Bonini, S., Capizzi, V. & Zocchi, P. (2019). The performance of angel-backed companies. *Journal of Banking and Finance, 100*, 328–345.

Bottazzi, L. & Da Rin, M. (2002). Venture Capital in Europe and the Financing of Innovative Companies. *Economic Policy: A European Forum* (34), 229–263.

Boudreau, K. J., Jeppesen, L. B., Reichstein, T. & Rullani, F. (2021). Crowdfunding as Donations to Entrepreneurial Firms. *Research Policy, 50*(7), 104264.

Cai, W., Polzin, F. & Stam, E. (2021). Crowdfunding and social capital: A systematic review using a dynamic perspective. *Technological Forecasting & Social Change, 162*, 120412.

Cole, R. A. & Sokolyk, T. (2018). Debt financing, survival, and growth of start-up firms. *Journal of Corporate Finance, 50*, 609–625.

Colombo, M. G., Grilli, L. & Verga, C. (2007). High-tech Start-up Access to Public Funds and Venture Capital: Evidence from Italy. *International Review of Applied Economics, 21*(3), 381–402.

Cressy, R. (2002). Funding gaps: A symposium. *The Economic Journal, 112*, F1–F16.

Cumming, D., Deloof, M., Manigart, S. & Wright, M. (2019). New directions in entrepreneurial finance. *Journal of Banking and Finance, 100*, 252–260.

Deloof, M. & Vanacker, T. (2018). The recent financial crisis, start-up financing and survival. *Journal of Business Finance and Accounting, 45*(7–8), 928.

Di Domenico, M., Haugh, H. & Tracey, P. (2010). Social Bricolage: Theorizing Social Value Creation in Social Enterprises. *Entrepreneurship: Theory & Practice, 34*(4), 681–703

Dowd, K. (2009). Moral Hazard and the Financial Crisis. *Cato Journal, 29*(1), 141–166.

Dushnitsky, G. & Zunino, D. (2019). The Role of Crowdfunding in Entrepreneurial Finance. In H. Landstrom, A. Parhankangas & C. M. Mason (Eds.), *Handbook of Research on Crowdfunding* (pp. 46–92): Cheltenham, UK: Edward Elgar.

Ferrary, M. (2010). Syndication of Venture Capital Investment: The Art of Resource Pooling. *Entrepreneurship: Theory & Practice, 34*(5), 885–907.

Franck, T., Huyghebaert, N. & D'Espallier, B. (2010). How Debt Creates Pressure to Perform When Information Asymmetries Are Large: Empirical Evidence from Business Start-Ups. *Journal of Economics and Management Strategy, 19*(4), 1043–1069.

Fraser, S. (2009). *How Have SME Finance Been Affected by the Credit Crisis?* BERR/ESRC Seminar, March.

Freel, M. S. (2007). Are Small Innovators Credit Rationed? *Small Business Economics, 28*(1), 22.

Giurca Vasilescu, L. (2009). Business Angels: Potential Financial Engines for Start-Ups. *Economic Research, 22*(3), 86–97.

Granz, C., Henn, M. & Lutz, E. (2020). *Research on Venture Capitalists' and Business Angels' Investment Criteria: A Systematic Literature Review.* Cham: Springer International Publishing.

Han, L., Fraser, S. & Storey, D. J. (2009a). Are good or bad borrowers discouraged from applying for loans? Evidence from US small business credit markets. *Journal of Banking & Finance, 33*(2), 415–424.

Han, L., Fraser, S. & Storey, D. J. (2009b). The Role of Collateral in Entrepreneurial Finance. *Journal of Business Finance & Accounting, 36*(3/4), 424–455.

Hanlon, D. & Saunders, C. (2007). Marshaling Resources to Form Small New Ventures: Toward a More Holistic Understanding of Entrepreneurial Support. *Entrepreneurship: Theory & Practice, 31*(4), 619–641.

Harding, R. (2002). Plugging the knowledge gap: an international comparison of the role for policy in the venture capital market. *Venture Capital, 4*(1), 59–76.

Harrison, R. T. & Mason, C. M. (2019). Venture Capital 20 Years On: Reflections on the Evolution of a Field. *Venture Capital, 21*(1), 1–34. doi:www.tandfonline.com/loi/tvec20

Harrison, R. T., Mason, C. M. & Girling, P. (2004). Financial bootstrapping and venture development in the software industry. *Entrepreneurship & Regional Development, 16*(4), 307–333.

Hitt, M. A., Ireland, R. D., Camp, S. M. & Sexton, D. L. (2001). Guest Editors' Introduction to the Special Issue Strategic Entrepreneurship: Entrepreneurial Strategies for Wealth Creation. *Strategic Management Journal*, *22*(6), 479–491.

Huyghebaert, N., Van de Gucht, L. & Van Hulle, C. (2007). The Choice between Bank Debt and Trace Credit in Business Start-Ups. *Small Business Economics*, *29*(4), 435–452.

Huyghebaert, N. & Van de Gucht, L. M. (2007). The Determinants of Financial Structure: New Insights from Business Start-ups. *European Financial Management*, *13*(1), 101–133.

Irwin, K. C., Gilstrap, C. M., Drnevich, P. L. & Tudor, C. M. (2019). From start-up to acquisition: Implications of financial investment trends for small- to medium-sized high-tech enterprises. *Journal of Small Business Strategy*, *29*(2), 22–43.

Jackson, P. & Madison, F. (2022). Entrepreneurial finance and monetary policy. *European Economic Review*, *141*, 103961.

Jayawarna, D., Jones, O. & Macpherson, A. (2020). Resourcing Social Enterprises: The Role of Socially Oriented Bootstrapping. *British Journal of Management*, *31*(1), 56.

Jing, Z., Pek-Hooi, S. & Poh-kam, W. (2011). Direct ties, prior knowledge, and entrepreneurial resource acquisitions in China and Singapore. *International Small Business Journal*, *29*(2), 170–189.

Jones, O., Ghobadian, A., O'Regan, N. & Antcliffe, V. (2013). Dynamic Capabilities in a Sixth Generation Family Firm: Entrepreneurship and the Bibby Line. *Business History*, *55*(2), 910–941.

Jones, O. & Giordano, B. (2021). Family entrepreneurial teams: The role of learning in business model evolution. *Management Learning*, *52*(3), 267–293.

Khaire, M. (2010). Young and No Money? Never Mind: The Material Impact of Social Resources on New Venture Growth. *Organization Science*, *21*(1), 168–185.

Klein, M., Neitzert, F., Hartmann-Wendels, T. & Kraus, S. (2019). Start-up Financing in the Digital Age – A Systematic Review and Comparison of New Forms of Financing. *Journal of Entrepreneurial Finance*, *21*(2), 45–98.

Krugman, P. (2009). *The Return of Depression Economics and the Crisis of 2008*. New York: Norton Company Limited.

Lam, W. (2010). Funding gap, what funding gap?: financial bootstrapping; supply, demand and creation of entrepreneurial finance. *International Journal of Entrepreneurial Behavior & Research*, *16*(4), 268–295.

Landström, H., Parhankangas, A. & Mason, C. M. (2019). *Handbook of research on crowdfunding*. Cheltenham: Edward Elgar Pub.

Large, D. & Muegge, S. (2008). Venture capitalists' non-financial value-added: an evaluation of the evidence and implications for research. *Venture Capital*, *10*(1), 21–53.

Lee, N., Sameen, H. & Cowling, M. (2015). Access to Finance for Innovative SMEs since the Financial Crisis. *Research Policy, 44*(2), 370–380.

Lefebvre, V. (2021). Zero-debt capital structure and the firm life cycle: empirical evidence from privately held SMEs. *Venture Capital.* doi:10.1080/13691066.2021.2001700

Linder, C. & Sperber, S. (2020). 'Mirror, Mirror, on the Wall – Who Is the Greatest Investor of all?' Effects of Better-than-Average Beliefs on Venture Funding. *European Management Review, 17*(2), 407–426.

Mason, C. M. (2009). Public Policy Support for the Informal Venture Capital Market in Europe A Critical Review. *International Small Business Journal, 27*(5), 536–556.

Mason, C. M. & Harrison, R. T. (1995). Closing the Regional Equity Capital Gap: The Role of Informal Venture Capital. *Small Business Economics, 7*(2), 153–172.

Maxwell, A. L., Jeffrey, S. A. & Levesque, M. (2011). Business angel early stage decision making. *Journal of Business Venturing, 26*(2), 212–225.

Moizer, J. & Tracey, P. (2010). Strategy making in social enterprise: The role of resource allocation and its effects on organizational sustainability. *Systems Research & Behavioral Science, 27*(3), 252–266.

Murzacheva, E. & Levie, J. (2020). Entrepreneurial Finance Journeys: Embeddedness and the Finance Escalator. *Venture Capital, 22*(2), 185–214.

Năstase, C. & Kajanus, M. (2009). The impact of the global crisis on SME and entrepreneurship behavior–Romania and Finland cases. *Amfiteatru Economic, 3,* 752–753.

Nguyen, B. & Canh, N. P. (2021). Formal and Informal Financing Decisions of Small Businesses. *Small Business Economics, 57*(3), 1545–1567.

Ning, Y., Wang, W. & Yu, B. (2015). The Driving Forces of Venture Capital Investments. *Small Business Economics, 44*(2), 315–344.

Nofsinger, J. R. & Wang, W. (2011). Determinants of Start-Up Firm External Financing Worldwide. *Journal of Banking and Finance, 35*(9), 2282–2294.

OECD. (2006). *The SME Financing Gap – Theory and Evidence.* Retrieved from https://doi.org/10.1787/9789264029415-en

Oino, I. (2014). The macroeconomic and environmental determinants of private equity in emerging Asia market: The application of extreme bounds analysis. *Journal of Investment and Management, 3*(3), 51–60.

Onginjo, J. O., Zhou, D. M., Berhanu, T. F. & Belihu, S. W. G. (2021). Analyzing the impact of social capital on US based Kickstarter projects outcome. *Heliyon, 7*(7). Retrieved from https://doi.org/10.1016/j.heliyon.2021.e07425.

Ou, C. & Haynes, G. W. (2006). Acquisition of Additional Equity Capital by Small Firms – Findings from the National Survey of Small Business Finances. *Small Business Economics, 27*(2–3), 157–168.

Parhankangas, A., Mason, C. M. & Landstrom, H. (2019). Crowdfunding: An Introduction. In H. Landstrom, A. Parhankangas & C. M. Mason (Eds.), *Handbook of Research on Crowdfunding* (pp. 1–21): Cheltenham: Edward Elgar.

Pintado, T. R., de Lema, D. G. P. & Van Auken, H. E. (2007). Venture Capital in Spain by Stage of Development. *Journal of Small Business Management, 45*(1), 68–88.

Polzin, F., Toxopeus, H. & Stam, E. (2018). The wisdom of the crowd in funding: information heterogeneity and social networks of crowdfunders. *Small Business Economics, 50*(2), 251–273.

Popescul, D., Radu, L. D., Păvăloaia, V. D. & Georgescu, M. R. (2020). Psychological Determinants of Investor Motivation in Social Media-Based Crowdfunding Projects: A Systematic Review. *Frontiers in Psychology, 11* Retrieved from https://doi.org/10.3389/fpsyg.2020.588121.

Rahman, M. W. & Jianchao, L. (2011). The Development Perspective of Finance and Microfinance Sector in China: How Far Is Microfinance Regulations? *International Journal of Economics & Finance, 3*(1), 160–170.

Romano, C. A., Tanewski, G. A. & Smyrnios, K. X. (2001). Capital structure decision making: A model for family business. *Journal of Business Venturing, 16*(3), 285–310.

Scott, R. H. (2009). *The Use of Credit Card Debt by New Firms: Sixth in a Series of Reports Using Data from the Kauffman Firm Survey*. Ewing Marion Kauffman Foundation Research Paper Series, Retrieved from SSRN: http://dx.doi.org/10.2139/ssrn.1446780

Sethuram, S., Taussig, M. & Gaur, A. (2021). A multiple agency view of venture capital investment duration: The roles of institutions, foreignness, and alliances. *Global Strategy Journal, 11*(4), 578–619.

Shane, S. (2000). Prior Knowledge and the Discovery of Entrepreneurial Opportunities. *Organization Science, 11*(4), 448–469.

Shane, S. & Cable, D. (2002). Network Ties, Reputation, and the Financing of New Ventures. *Management Science, 48*(3), 364–381.

Shane, S. & Stuart, T. (2002). Organizational Endowments and the Performance of University Start-ups. *Management Science, 48*(1), 154–170.

Stiglitz, J. E. & Weiss, A. (1981). Credit Rationing in Markets with Imperfect Information. *American Economic Review, 71*(3), 393–410.

Storey, D. J. & Greene, F. J. (2010). *Small Business and Entrepreneurship*. Harlow: Pearson Education.

Teasdale, S. (2010). How can social enterprise address disadvantage? Evidence from an inner city community. *Journal of Nonprofit & Public Sector Marketing, 22*(2), 89–107.

Timmons, J. & Spinelli, S. (2004). *New Venture Creation* (6th ed.). Boston, MA: McGraw-Hill.

Van Auken, H. E. (2002). A Model of Community-Based Venture Capital Formation To Fund Early-Stage Technology-Based Firms. *Journal of Small Business Management, 40*(4), 287–301.

Vanacker, T. R. & Manigart, S. (2010). Pecking order and debt capacity considerations for high-growth companies seeking financing. *Small Business Economics, 1*, 53–69.

Ziegler, T. & Shneor, R. (2020). Lending Crowdfunding: Principles and Market Development. In R. Shneor, L. Zhao, & B-T. Flåten, *Advances in Crowdfunding: Research and Practice* (pp.63–92). Cham, Switzerland: Springer Nature.

Informal Finance and Business Start-up

9.1 Introduction

As pointed out by Miao, Rutherford and Pollack (2017), more than 75% of new firms make no use of external finance. Securing external finance to exploit a new business opportunity is simply not practical for most young entrepreneurs. In addition to facing disadvantage due to the liabilities of newness, such entrepreneurs often have limited potential for internal cash generation through realization of economies of scale. This puts pressure on young entrepreneurs to consider approaching institutional sources such as banks. When they are inexperienced and lack a reputation in debt markets, external finance is difficult to access, expensive and often makes a negligible contribution to the early-stage entrepreneur's resource base. More specifically, financial investors are sceptical of new entrepreneurial ventures' potential for success due to substantial information asymmetries. High monitoring cost, moral hazards and associated mistrust are overheads for financers who make unfavourable investment decisions. As a mechanism to shield them from financial risks and to recover overheads lenders often put additional constraints on lending terms, making external finance prohibitively expensive for the entrepreneur (Cassar, 2004). This puts more pressure on the entrepreneur as expensive repayments further limits the cash-flows which are essential to run a successful venture.

Given imbalances between the supply and demand for capital (Bruton, Ahlstrom & Si, 2015), problems in securing market solutions to early stage resource needs (Pollack, Maula, Allison, Renko & Gunther, 2021), and

DOI: 10.4324/9781003312918-10

improvements in technology it seems more realistic for inexperienced entrepreneurs to obtain resources by applying different kinds of financial bootstrapping methods. Bootstrapping promotes personal, intangible and opportunistic mechanisms to enhance entrepreneurs' ability to use and extract value from resources without necessarily gaining the ownership of the resource at hand (Rutherford, Pollack, Mazzei & Sanchez-Ruiz, 2017). These methods collectively reduce the need for outside finance, improve cash flow and enable entrepreneurs to operate their businesses in a resourceful and creative manner. Bootstrapping has become a vital part of entrepreneurial finance, with as many as 80–95% of entrepreneurs utilizing some form of bootstrapping at the early stages of business start-up (Bhide, 1992; Harrison, Mason & Girling, 2004; Winborg, 2015). The general assertion is that bootstrapping can be used effectively to improve the chances for entrepreneurial success and provide opportunities for future growth when managed strategically (Rutherford, 2015).

In this chapter we intend to demonstrate the use of bootstrapping as an alternative solution to conventional financing strategies such as banks, business angels and venture capitalists. We first provide our working definition for bootstrapping and the theoretical position we take in explaining bootstrap behaviour by new entrepreneurs. This is followed by a discussion of different types of bootstrapping techniques entrepreneurs can consider when resourcing their ventures. Understanding how choices are influenced by the entrepreneurs' financing preferences and the type of opportunities they are pursuing is important for those who wish to pursue a career in entrepreneurship. Also included in the discussion is a brief note about the gendered nature of bootstrapping and an explanation for how the preferences and the nature of bootstrapping vary over the course of the business life cycle. We discuss how a venture might be better positioned for growth by adopting a range of bootstrapping behaviours. We also introduce crowdfunding as a platform-mediated bootstrapping strategy that uses social networks as intermediaries to link communities of both entrepreneurs and investors. These online platforms facilitate participation, collection and transferring of small amounts of funds from large pool of investors to offer bootstrap resources to new ventures. Finally, we add a discussion in relation to how dependency and exchange relationships uniquely position social entrepreneurs to benefit from socially oriented bootstrapping.

9.2 Learning Objectives

- To investigate the importance of bootstrapping as an alternative resource strategy for those who face capital market imperfections.
- To learn different types of bootstrapping available for the entrepreneur to resource their ventures.
- To study how the entrepreneur's motives and gender roles influence the bootstrap decision.
- To study bootstrapping as relevant to the business life cycle
- To evaluate the potential of bootstrapping as a business growth strategy for the entrepreneur.
- To study how bootstrapped crowdfunding provides targeted support for early-stage ventures.
- To learn how and why social enterprises are uniquely positioned to benefit from social oriented bootstrapping.

9.3 Defining Bootstrapping: A Lean Approach

Financial bootstrapping has developed around the idea that resources not owned or controlled by the entrepreneur often play a key role in pursuing new opportunities for those who are resource-constrained (Lam, 2010). It essentially acknowledges resource acquisition which is either internally or externally generated are often available at zero cost, or at least, below market price. Harrison et al. (2004, p. 308) define bootstrapping as a venture strategy that involves creative and economical means for 'marshalling and gaining control of resources'. They highlight two forms of bootstrapping strategy which operate in practice. The first form involves being resource 'rich' without recourse to bank finance or external equity finance. There are instances where entrepreneurs have no alternatives other than to resource the venture activities through borrowings from personal credit cards or cash generated by cross-subsidizing from other activities. The second form includes strategies that minimize the need for finance by securing resources at little or no cost. Such strategies largely refer to network advantages as social contacts often provide the entrepreneur the access to free resources or resources accessed through subsidized rates (see Chapter 6 for a fuller discussion of entrepreneur networks).

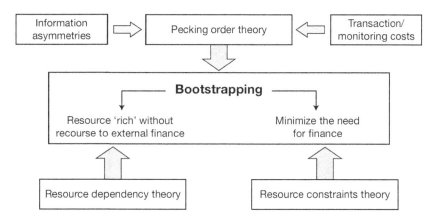

Figure 9.1 A Theoretical Explanation of Bootstrapping

The traditional view of bootstrapping coincides with a number of theoretical perspectives (see Figure 9.1). First, pecking order theory (Myers, 1984) indicates that due to the existence of asymmetric information and monitoring costs, the higher risks associated with start-ups mean higher returns are demanded by external financers. As a consequence, entrepreneurs are likely to resort to internal finance and will only raise external funds when retained earnings are depleted. Resource constraint theory provides another interesting perspective to the idea of bootstrapping. It argues that entrepreneurial ventures may grow despite owning a limited resource base through more efficient use of limited resources at hand. For example, entrepreneurs can exploit available resource inputs more effectively by recombining them to make unique resources useful to build competitive advantage (Baker & Nelson, 2005). Development of cash management skills and the use of network ties to gain access to resources are other typical examples within this context.

The third and the most widely used theoretical explanation for overcoming the inherent deficiencies of gaining access to formal finance and still running a successful venture is based on resource dependency theory (Pfeffer & Salancik, 1978). Resource dependency is based on the 'open systems' model and defines organizations as strategic agents that are strongly influenced by their external environment (Bretherton & Chaston, 2005). As entrepreneurs do not possess all the resources they need, the environment in which their firm operates is a very important resource base.

Indeed, the extent to which an entrepreneur is dependent upon a given environment/social group can be determined by the organization's need for the resource controlled by that environment/social group. Therefore, the types of responses that organizations exhibit depend on the level and nature of dependencies they develop (Villanueva, Van de Ven & Sapienza, 2012). As new ventures develop, dependencies will change and therefore some alteration to the availability and desirability of the bootstrapping techniques is inevitable. This suggests that organizational theory also plays an important role in explaining the bootstrapping behaviour in new ventures (Ebben & Johnson, 2006).

In their recent study, Michaelis, Scheaf, Carr and Pollack (2022) adopt social cognitive theory (Bandura, 1977) to obtain a better understanding of why some entrepreneurs enact resourcefulness behaviours. They suggest that those individuals with higher levels of frugality will have a strong orientation towards self-reliance and, therefore, be more resourceful when starting a business. According to Baker and Nelson (2005) resourcefulness is associated with innovative and creative behaviours in overcoming the liabilities of newness. Data from an online survey with 178 respondents enabled Michaelis et al. (2022) to examine the links between individual resourcefulness and the adoption of bootstrapping techniques. The results confirmed that individuals with high-levels of frugality saw the environment as hostile (lack of resources), which encouraged greater self-reliance in the form of customer-related and self-financing bootstrapping. The practical implications include encouraging entrepreneurs to make a self-assessment of their environmental perceptions and concerns for frugality. This will help determine their predisposition towards bootstrapping as a resourcing strategy. As the authors go on to state, 'it is especially relevant for nascent, aspiring, entrepreneurs who may need to develop an initial financial approach to new venture start-up' (Michaelis et al., 2022, p. 16).

9.4 Types of Entrepreneurial Bootstrapping

A number of models have emerged to explain the process of bootstrapping and the associated practices. Common to all these models is the view that entrepreneurs at inception are less likely to be funded through traditional sources and that capital minimization is a common practice. While the former rests on the notion that seeking alternative means to raise cash

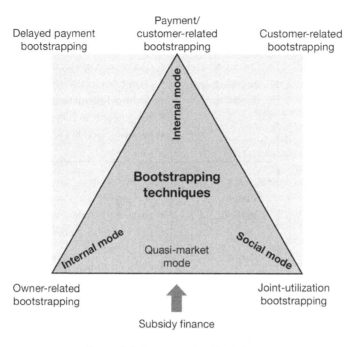

Delayed payment
bootstrapping

Payment/
customer-related
bootstrapping

Customer-related
bootstrapping

Internal mode

**Bootstrapping
techniques**

Internal mode

Quasi-market
mode

Social mode

Owner-related
bootstrapping

Joint-utilization
bootstrapping

Subsidy finance

Figure 9.2 Bootstrapping Techniques

are important start-up and survival strategies, the later recommend practices that minimize cash flow and business expenses and thereby opening up opportunities for exploring and expanding new ideas. Based on a study of over 800 small businesses, Winborg and Landstrom (2001) made a major contribution to understanding the various bootstrapping techniques (see Figure 9.2 for a summary). Winborg and Landström (2001) argued that the behaviours of financial bootstrappers differed according to the internal, social and quasi-market modes of resource acquisition patterns, which fall into five groups (Table 9.1).

The first group, 'owner-financed' bootstrapping includes methods the owner and his/her family and friends use to acquire necessary resources for the venture. These methods include personal loans, own savings, cross-subsidizing through multiple assignments, private credit card for business expenses, withholding salary and relatives working for the entrepreneur at free/below-market salary (Box 9.1). The second group, payment-related bootstrapping is a combination of the practices associated with 'minimization of accounts receivable' and 'delay payments'. These methods together provide cash-flow advantages to the entrepreneur through speeding up

Table 9.1 Bootstrapping: Internal, Social and Quasi-market Modes of Resource Acquisition

• Internal mode of resource acquisition	• Owner-related financing and resources.	• Use of manager's credit card . • Loan from relatives/friends. • Withholding manager's salary • Assignments in other businesses • Relatives working for non-market salary
	• Customer-related methods.	• Cease business relations with late payers • Lease equipment instead of buying • Best conditions possible with suppliers • Offer customers discounts if paying cash • Choose customer who pay quickly
	• Payment related	• Use routines for speeding up invoicing • Use interest on overdue payment • Delay payment to suppliers • Delay payment of value-added tax • Use routines in order to minimize stock
• Social mode of resource acquisition	• Joint-utilization of resources with other firms	• Borrow equipment from others • Own equipment in common with others • Co-ordinate purchases with others • Share premises with others • Share employees with others • Practice barter instead of buying/selling • Raise capital from a factoring company
• Quasi-market mode of resource acquisition.	• Subsidy finance	• Subsidy from County Administrative Board • Subsidy from Swedish National Board for

invoicing, using interest on overdue payments, negotiating longer terms with suppliers and practice leasing than making full payments during equipment purchase. Customer-related bootstrapping (Group 3) include practices such as obtaining advance payments, ceasing relations with late-paying customers, charging interest on overdue invoices. While all these methods tend to improve cash flow from customers, some of these can have a negative long-term effect in terms of maintaining customer relationships (Rutherford et al., 2017).

Box 9.1

With my computer recycling company, I was quite convinced that were was a viable enterprise in it and started working on it. My daughter had just been born and my wife wasn't happy as she wanted me to go and get a job with somebody else and I was convinced and I took on a supermarket free of charge an old derelict supermarket in Toxteth – 5000sqr feet and I filled it with computer equipment within weeks – just going out myself driving a van and picking stuff up and bringing it back, but those first 6 months were hard and I just deferred any salary and ended up building up £20,000 worth of debt on credit cards – in the next year we got £40,000 worth of grants from the Liverpool City Council and I was able to pay that back and I said, 'never again' but I have done it again since, particularly the salary deferment because when things are tight or when you are trying to get over a hump, par-ticularly with cash flow, but yes, all of the above salary deferment, credit cards, yes I've done them all.

(Paul – Wigan Recycling)

These three methods are more internally oriented as they involve actively seeking means to improve internal cash flow either through intro-ducing more discipline to entrepreneurial practices or through perseverance of the owner and his/her relatives. The fourth group, 'joint-utilization boot-strapping' consists of a range of activities aiming at absorbing and borrowing resources at no/low financial cost from the entrepreneurs' social networks. The presence of interpersonal relationships with resource owners is instru-mental in gaining access to this socially oriented resource acquisition. Some of the most common methods of joint resource utilization include bartering, sharing or borrowing employees, premises, equipment and other assets. Methods to take advantage of economies of scale, such as coordinating purchases with others, working in partnerships and outsourcing are also useful means of resource sharing for this relationship-based entrepreneurs. The degree of trust between parties appears to explain the level of usage and impact of this method of bootstrapping.

In addition to these four key bootstrapping methods, there are examples where subsidy finance or philanthropic capital from government and public organizations forms a major part of the resource formula for some entrepreneurs (Jayawarna, Jones & Macpherson, 2020). While this quasi-market mode of resource acquisition is particularly relevant for social entrepreneurs it is also relevant for conventional entrepreneurs.

9.5 Variations in Approaches to Bootstrapping

While all these methods are useful for gaining access to resources, it seems fair to assume a significant variability in the extent to which entrepreneurs rely on financial bootstrapping. Recent research shows how the use of boot-strap strategies varies per entrepreneur preferences, motives and business life-cycle stage. The following discussion addresses these contingency perspectives to bootstrapping.

9.5.1 Entrepreneurs' Financial Motives and the Use of Bootstrapping

Winborg (2009) provides empirical evidence to suggest three groups of new business founders differ in terms of the relative importance of their motives for bootstrapping. 'Cost-reducing bootstrappers'' choice of techniques are governed by their desire to minimize costs during financial or non-financial transactions. By minimizing outgoing, these entrepreneurs operate their businesses with low levels of resource demands. The second group, 'risk-reducing bootstrappers', prefer bootstrapping as it helps to reduce the risks of entering into contracts with formal financial providers. These entrepreneurs perceive their ventures to be risky and are more likely to pursue bootstrap-ping rather than more formal means of resourcing their ventures (Carter & Van Auken, 2005). Empirical evidence suggests that both these groups of entrepreneurs consider bootstrapping an effective resource acquisition strategy and therefore seek every opportunity to access additional resources rather than using it as a 'last resort'. The third group, 'capital constrained bootstrappers', choose to utilize bootstrapping as a means of overcoming financial constraints and, therefore, bootstrapping is very much a survival strategy for these entrepreneurs.

Based on a questionnaire survey of 91 small firms and interviews with ten entrepreneurs, Malmstrom (2014) developed a taxonomy of three distinct approaches to bootstrapping. *Quick fix* bootstrappers who adopted a reactive, internal approach by withholding or delaying payment of their own salaries. The second category, *proactive bootstrappers*, adopted a socially oriented approach, which involved building relationships with members of their networks. The main focus of their resourcing activities were the joint-utilization of resources and customer-related bootstrapping. The third type were the *efficient bootstrappers* who behaved opportunistically in minimizing costs by negotiating with customer and suppliers to improve their cash-flow. In most cases this meant delaying-payment to suppliers, which can be regarded as a risky approach because it creates a lack of trust with those suppliers. Interestingly, proactive bootstrappers had the highest growth levels of the three strategies. As stated by Malmstrom (2014, p. 45), 'this aligns with previous studies where, similar to the proactive bootstrappers, growth-achieving ventures have been found to more likely use collaborative bootstrapping activities (Harrison et al., 2004; Winborg & Landström, 2001)'.

9.5.2 Gendered Nature of Bootstrapping

It has been argued that obtaining external finance is much more difficult for female entrepreneurs than for male entrepreneurs. Traditionally, women have limited human capital and the general trend that they operate small, service-sector firms with less focus on growth are the main supply and demand side challenges for female-owned businesses. Since external finance is difficult and costly to obtain bootstrapping is vital for female entrepreneurs. There is also some variation in the type of bootstrapping techniques used by male and female entrepreneurs. Brush et al. (2006) revealed that while bootstrapping is a common phenomenon among female owners, how they use the various techniques is based on the type and the stage of their business development. At the emergent stage of their businesses, entrepreneurs min-imize capital by reducing labour costs, as they progress their emphasis changes to focus on minimizing capital by reducing operational costs. Jayawarna, Jones and Marlow (2015) also observed clear gender differences in the use of bootstrapping techniques. While men engaged in far more payment-related bootstrapping (customer and delay payment) activities than women, women made more use of joint-utilization and owner-related methods. Research evidence suggests that women have significantly higher tendency to withhold salary, forgo income and subsidize the business with their personal credit cards than men (Box 9.2).

Box 9.2

At the start, I charged ridiculous rates like £75 per day – stupid tiny amounts of money and got a few case studies of things that were working under my belt really. I think my first client was a photog-rapher, something like that. I was working for one-man bands really and charging ridiculous fees. I also did some work for the previous company I had worked for and that subsidised the work that I was doing in the business.

(Anna Heyes, Active Profile)

According to Gupta et al. (2009) entrepreneurship is a 'gendered pro-fession' (p.409) and gender stereotypical differences place limitations on women's ability to accrue necessary resources for their businesses. Following this line of arguments Jayawarna et al. (2015) studied how men and women bootstrap their resources following stereotypical views that female entrepreneurs are more cautious, have less business competence, are less strategic, less interested in growth and adopt a more participative management style compared to male entrepreneurs. The study confirms the importance of bootstrapping to both male and female businesses, but the techniques have distinct gender-related patterns. Women in gen-eral have a higher tendency to use owner-related and joint-utilization methods, whereas men's bootstrapping practices are largely limited to payment-related techniques. This supports the broader view that individ-uals draw upon their own personal values, preferences and ambitions when choosing among alternative strategies (Carter, Williams & Reynolds, 1997). The results also provide strong support for the gendered nature of resource acquisition through payment-related methods; men make greater use of payment-related methods than women. It is possible to argue that a risk-taking propensity, proactive thinking and perceived higher financial skills help men develop relationships with external parties and these relationships are beneficial to negotiate payment related resources with customers and suppliers. Similarly, behaviours associated with women, including low risk-taking, limited commitment to growth, participative management and limited business skills are linked with higher use of owner-related and joint-utilization methods by women.

The association between resource acquisition patterns, networking behaviour and generalized gender characteristics also confirms that there are clear structural barriers which mean that women are disadvantaged when starting new businesses (Greene, Brush, Hart & Saparito, 2001; Jayawarna et al., 2015; Manolova, Manev, Carter & Gyoshev, 2006). For example, negotiating competitively to acquire external finance through brokers and bootstrapping supplier and customer-related resources via weak ties appears to require stereotypical masculine behaviour. Clearly this presents problems if women are to acquire similar levels and types of resources as men. Concentration on strong ties means that female entrepreneurs will find it more difficult than men to obtain the resources necessary to grow their businesses (see Chapter 6 for a discussion of networking and resource acquisition).

Villaseca, Navío-Marco and Gimeno (2021) carried out a systematic review of the literature to obtain a better understanding of women's approaches to acquiring various resources, including finance, essential for closing the entrepreneurship gender gap. It appears that for most women, the simplest and preferred approach is to use self-finance (Myers, 1984). Clearly, relying on self-finance means there is a limitation to the amount of funds that female entrepreneur can access. The literature confirms that female entrepreneurs rely more heavily on internal bootstrapping than male entrepreneurs who find it easier to access external finance. According to Villaseca et al. (2021), whether women rely on internal finance because they are not focused on growth or because they are discriminated against by conventional financial institutions is not clear in the literature. Nevertheless, the data are unambiguous, a lower proportion of women obtain financial support from banks, venture capitalists, business angels or crowdfunding than their male counterparts (Villaseca et al., 2021).

9.5.3 Life Cycle Approach to Bootstrapping

Life cycle research suggests that the financial structure followed by the entrepreneur should differ across the stages of organizational life cycle as different approaches are needed to finance the growth of the business (see Chapter 8). Within this hierarchical financial structure, it is argued that entrepreneurs will first seek funding through flexible internal sources, followed by bank financing (debt) and, finally, expensive equity capital financing (Cassar, 2001). The administrative tasks of setting up a business are diverse and entrepreneurs need to produce products/services cost-effectively to minimize financial burdens. In addition, they have less formal organizational structures and therefore are resistant to formal contracts and relationships. Consequently, the use of informal, internal financing such as bootstrapping is more common among entrepreneurs in the emergent and early stages of business development. The purpose of bootstrapping at this stage is largely geared towards minimizing expenses and meeting short-term cash-flow needs. As firms move from these early stages to stages of stability and growth (Chapter 11), resource constraints are likely to ease. Therefore, resource acquisition behaviour changes from an internal reactive approach to an external proactive approach which minimizes the need for bootstrapping. During growth stages entrepreneurs rely more on formal rules and procedures to ensure organizational and administrative efficiency, which makes formal financing a possibility for the entrepreneurs.

While entrepreneurs may use diverse sets of activities, life-cycle theories imply that the stage of the firm should affect the type of bootstrapping used in the same way as it affects the actual use of bootstrapping as a resourcing strategy across various stages of business development (see Figure 9.3). In other words, the type of bootstrapping used in different life cycle phases should reflect differences in entrepreneurs' need for capital as suggested by organizational development theories. In terms of the type of bootstrapping utilized, the stage model suggests that the methods change as the business develops. Certain methods are more widely used at the beginning of the life cycle with different approaches becoming important as the entrepreneur gains experience in capital markets and building relationships with stakeholders.

Ebben and Johnson (2006) use resource dependence theory to explain why entrepreneurs use different types of bootstrapping at different stages of business; they also explain why certain bootstrapping methods are

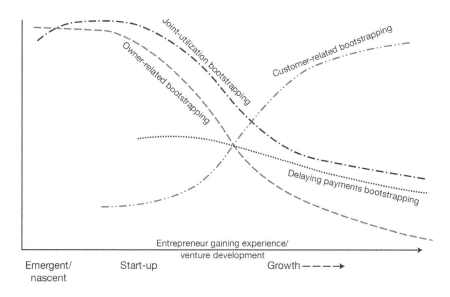

Figure 9.3 Bootstrapping and the Business Lifecycle

more prevalent than others. Their findings indicate that entrepreneurs who are forced to use bootstrapping methods at the early stages of start-up tend to adopt more attractive methods as they gain legitimacy and leverage. Resource dependency theory is very relevant in explaining why entrepreneurs rely heavily on owner-related bootstrapping at the start and why this trend declines over time. As entrepreneurs pass the hurdle of information asymmetry and establish close ties with investors, they are no longer keen to risk their personal wealth by making further financial investments. Resource dependence theory also predicts that joint-utilization bootstrapping techniques should decrease over time. The entrepreneur's personal credibility and the firm's legitimacy are valuable resources for those operating in resource poor environments. In the early stages, joint utilization of resources act as an effective way to obtain organizational legitimacy (through building relationships), which when developed could act as an effective way to access valuable resources from external parties as the business develops. Once the entrepreneur gains business credibility they reduce their dependency on others for resource access purposes.

Significant increases in the use of customer-related bootstrapping techniques over time explain the importance of maintaining strong relationships with customers. Initially, limited customer relationships mean imposing trading rules is not possible and instead entrepreneurs should consider offering credit terms to improve sales and thereby increasing working capital. With long-term customer relationships entrepreneurs can replace credit terms with credit rules as these relationships helps the firm to gain leverage to impose customer payment terms directed at enhancing cash-flow. In their study of Irish software start-ups, Mac an Bhaird and Lynn (2015) found that product development often occurred through a process of iterative improvement via their engagement with early customers who provided essential information. Moreover, formal organization systems developed over time should lead to structured approaches to managing the customer base, which includes implementing systems that speed up billing and provide incentives for upfront or earlier customer payments (Box 9.3). Unlike customer-related methods, explanation for the declining patter of payment-related methods is not straightforward; negative effects of compromising on-time and quality of supplier service for cost and cash-flow is a possible explanation for the limited acceptance for favourable payment arrangements with suppliers and customers as firm matures.

Box 9.3

We have moved on from our early suppliers. The thing with suppliers is there are a lot of agents who are middle men and they take a couple of per cent and unless you can get the factories, you can't build a relationship and make them understand about good quality and what you expect from them and so a lot of them we have moved away from and changed because other people will give us better prices- we now try to deal with the core factory that manufactures the product rather than those agents and buy bulk.

We've always been cash rich and have worked hard at chasing payments and things like that – we just run the business with commonsense. I think our systems contribute a lot in making that efficient because the systems we use invoice customers on the day which will then say you have 30 days to pay – it will then send reminders and issue a statement on the day saying we are now ready to collect money from you.

> We went from a very labour-intensive company to a systems base about six months before we moved here (to the warehouse). When we implemented the system it enabled us, from one stock source, to sell across all of our channels and to know at any point in time what we had in stock. When an item was sold it would be deducted, the system creates an invoice, prints a dispatch note and addresses. It is able to tell us our daily sales, plot a graph and basically took out 90% of the labour which was just incredible.
>
> (Ben Wilson, Jazooli)

9.6 Bootstrapping as a Growth Strategy

Resource availability continues to be the single largest predictor of entrepreneurial success and resource access through bootstrapping continues to contribute a major part in the formula for new entrepreneurs (Harrison et al., 2004). The main questions are:

1. does bootstrapping create value, or simply reduce costs?
2. is it practical to use bootstrapping as a substitute for more traditional sources of funding?

Thus far, research evidence attempting to check the relevance of bootstrapping as a firm performance indicator has been mixed at best (Rutherford et al., 2017). Accessing resources through bootstrapping is contrary to the traditional resource-based view which predicts that firm performance is based on the availability of *strategic resources*. Those who follow this view argue that while bootstrapping is a useful strategy for entrepreneurs to improve their chances of success, strategic approaches to bootstrapping are not practiced by most entrepreneurs (Rutherford, 2015). The practice is largely reactionary in nature; entrepreneurs who already have acquired external finance are less likely to consider bootstrapping (Myers, 1984). Many entrepreneurs use bootstrapping as a short-term reactive financing strategy largely focusing on cost reduction. Therefore, it is reasonable to assume that relying on bootstrapping may constrain firms from growing as fast as might otherwise be the case. Ebben (2009) also found detrimental returns from some forms of bootstrapping. The negative effects from higher levels of customer-related and delaying-payments bootstrapping on profitability is due to the breaking up of customer-supplier relationships due to the rules imposed for short-term cash flow advantages (Rutherford, 2015). Vanacker et al. (2011) provided at least five reasons that undermine the use of financial bootstrapping as a growth strategy for entrepreneurs:

1. as bootstrapped firms tend to be undercapitalized, the recourses acquired through financial bootstrapping will be largely insufficient to finance growth;

2. resources obtained through bootstrapping underestimates the ventures potential for future growth in the eyes of the stakeholders;

3. managing bootstrapping activities takes time and limits the entrepreneur's ability to concentrate on more critical tasks such as identifying and exploiting new opportunities;

4. obtaining access to cheap resources through social contacts may bring imperfect resources; and

5. the opportunity costs of identifying resource-rich social contacts is high; some techniques, such as delay-payments to suppliers can damage relationships with network providers.

Cornwall (2009, p. 6), using evidence from several case studies, however, provides three explanations to clarify some misinterpretations about the relevance of bootstrapping as a resourcing strategy. First, bootstrapping should not be seen as the cheapest way to resource a venture but as a creative way to access the full benefits from the limited resources available to new entrepreneurs. Secondly, evidence confirms that bootstrapping is not simply a survival strategy for new ventures but is a resourcing method for high-growth, high-potential ventures. Thirdly, bootstrapping is used as a resourcing strategy by businesses that make extensive use of debt and equity finance; it is not a choice between bootstrapping and gaining access to external funding through debt/equity.

Taken together the evidence suggests that bootstrapping should be used as a proactive strategy for preserving ownership and control of useful resources (Rutherford, 2015). At the emergent and start-up stages, entrepreneurs work in an environment characterized by resource constraints.

It is possible to argue that if the demand for resources exceeds availability, they need to be more efficient in the deployment of available resources. This causes entrepreneurs to develop cash management skills that help to exploit resource inputs from the external environment and effectively recombine those with the available internal resources (Smith & Smith, 2000). This practice stimulates entrepreneurs to find more innovative ways to achieve growth in areas that resource-rich entrepreneurs would not necessarily consider. The general contention is that the use of bootstrap strategies is desirable as it helps entrepreneurs to focus on the efficient and more creative use of resources (Bhide, 1992; Timmons, 1999). This is particularly the case with women entrepreneurs as it signals to potential investors that they have the ability to generate internal funds and control costs in creative ways when access to finance is limited. Effective execution of the start-up activities indirectly informs investors that the entrepreneur has the potential to satisfy their growth expectations that comes with their investments (Brush et al., 2006).

Interest in bootstrapping lies in the general agreement that there are benefits that go beyond its use as a creative means to access resources at the early stages of business start-up to greater opportunities for real growth. Jones et al. (2010) adopt the concept of bricolage (see Chapter 12) to suggest that bootstrapping is a dynamic capability in new ventures. Bricolage helps flexible and innovative adaptation of acquired bootstrap resources through learning processes embedded in a firm's routines (see Chapter 10 for a full discussion of dynamic capabilities in new ventures). There is evidence that bootstrapping contributes directly to entrepreneurs' resourcing formula for value creation. There are examples which indicate that many successful companies including Microsoft, Apple and Dell (Tomory, 2011) relied on bootstrap finance when they started as small ventures, and it was the foundation for achieving very high-growth [see Box 9.4]. The environment created through bootstrap practices encourages entrepreneurs to make the most efficient use of their limited resources. Bootstrapping not only introduces 'a discipline of leanness', which forces firms to spend wisely (Timmons, 1999, p. 39), it also promotes rapid growth using 'capital raising ingenuity' (Brush et al., 2006). This practice of leveraging and stretching available resources provides an explanation for why some apparently undercapitalized ventures outperform ventures that are resource rich (Baker, Pricer & Nenide, 2000).

Box 9.4

When the Altair deal inspired Bill Gates and Paul Allen to form their own software company, **Microsoft**, they were determined to build it without outside financing and followed a 'bootstrapping' model. To avoid unnecessary overheads, they moved into an inexpensive apartment and negotiated with MITS, the manufacturer of the Altair, for computer time and office space in their first years. Everything was funded through their savings from employments and 'late night poker games' (Gates et al., 1996, p.19). Human resource has been a major challenge: they were understaffed and hired students on a part-time basis. Everybody worked over long hours including the owners and were paid below industry averages.

Steve Wozniak and Steve Job raised $1,300 needed to get Apple started by selling Wosniak's scientific Hewlett-Packard calculator and Jobs's Volkswagen van. They were not only operating out of Jobs's parents' garage but received subsidized help from Jobs's family in the assembly line and in day-to-day business operations. Additionally, they relied on their network of friends who offered free service and financial assistance, which included $5,000 loan received from a friend of Wozniak's father. Invoices were largely paid by Wosniak's salary from his job at Hewlett-Packard. This bootstrapping model of financing at the inception stage helped Wozniak and Jobs to give a sound foundation for Apple, which eventually formed as **Apple Computer Inc** in 1977 after venture capitalist Mike Markkula underwrote a bank loan of $250,000.

At the age of 18 Michael Dell converted his informal business of upgrading IBM PC-compatible computers into an entrepreneurial venture, **Dell Computer Corporation**, using his savings of $1,000. Hit by cash deficiencies, Dell employed every measure to ensure minimum spending and cut unnecessary operating costs. Dell, together with an engineer hired to design his first computer, worked long hours in his own bedroom until he hired a few employees and moved to a 1,000-sqaure-foot office to start formal manufacturing operations. Rather than employing additional staff, the foundation team increased their work hours to save financial resources towards staff salaries.

Tomory (2011)

Bootstrapping strategies free new ventures from excessive debt and thereby take pressure off entrepreneurs when seeking growth opportunities. Most importantly bootstrapping is a less risky option than external debt for nascent entrepreneurs as they have limited experience of investing finance wisely when it is available. Bootstrapping helps nascent entrepreneurs learn financial discipline and provides valuable lessons in how to run a business with limited funding (Bhide, 1992). In the long run, bootstrapping can be the basis for acquiring other resources including outside equity investment or venture capital which can finance the next stage of growth (Brush et al., 2006; Carter, Brush, Greene, Gatewood & Hart, 2003). Also resourcing through bootstrapping provides flexibility to the entrepreneur in terms of the approach to the business. As informal options are often readily available and access to these options is dependent on short-term needs, bootstrapping helps embed dynamic capabilities within the nascent firm (see Chapter 10). Increased flexibility of resources (rather than the restriction of external resource providers) is particularly useful for nascent entrepreneurs who want to change the strategic direction of their ventures whenever they feel is necessary. Moreover, entrepreneurs who actively engage in bootstrapping are able to respond more effectively to their customers (Brush et al., 2006; Carter et al., 2003). Flexibility in acquiring resources is particularly helpful for dealing with unpredictable sales and acts as a survival strategy for firms in competitive markets (Baker et al., 2000; Bhide, 1992).

Based on their meta-analysis of the literature, Miao et al. (2017) found that bootstrapping was negatively related to profitability (especially return on assets). In contrast, three bootstrapping techniques (customer-related, delay payment and joint-utilization) had a positive relationship with performance (growth) while owner-related bootstrapping had a negative impact on performance. Both human capital and social capital were positively related to bootstrapping. It may very well be that bootstrapping's impact on firm performance and its inimitability is an idiosyncratic contingency. Following Ebben's (2009) research it is possible that bootstrapping only has a systematic impact on the bottom-line when it is imbedded in the firm's strategic objectives and provides solutions for strategic problems. A properly aligned process for bootstrap resources represents a core capability and can become a form of organizational capital. Jones and Jayawarna (2010) suggest that networking activity has strong mediating role on bootstrapping on the performance of start-up firms (see Chapter 6 for more details). The study was based on the argument that the decisions to use joint-utilization and payment-related methods (Winborg & Landström, 2001) are strategic while owner-related techniques are largely used in reaction to cash flow problems and have little impact on longer-term business outcomes. As discussed above, Miao et al. (2017) found that owner-related bootstrapping had a negative impact on the performance of new ventures. Joint-utilization techniques are particularly important for start-ups as they incur very limited costs. Techniques such as sharing staff can provide valuable human capital and equipment sharing can release capital to invest in resources essential for business development (Carter & Van Auken, 2005; Rutherford, 2015).

Rutherford (2015) agrees that most entrepreneurs adopt bootstrapping as a reactive response to their lack of finance (Neely & Van Auken, 2012) and suggests an approach he describes as 'strategic bootstrapping'. Adopting a strategic approach means beginning with a business plan even though it will not necessarily be used to access external finance. The business plan should be based on a number of key factors (Rutherford, 2015, p. 64):

- an outline of the firm's business model with clear identification of how you will make money (see Chapter 4)
- identification of your first customers and clear plan to expand to a wider marketplace
- an explicit statement of your source of competitive advantage
- a statement of your strategic approach – cost-based or differentiation?
- an industry analysis to identify your main competitors, barriers to entry and the potential for growth and profitability
- a plan to make effective use of various social media platforms to help build legitimacy
- a definitive evaluation of your existing capital resources: financial, human and social.

Rutherford (2015) goes on to explain that in the early stages of new business ventures, social capital will be the most valuable resource for the majority of entrepreneurs (Miao et al., 2017). Therefore, as we discussed in Chapter 6, you should adopt a strategic approach to developing your social networks (using social media where appropriate). Those entrepreneurs with the most diverse and extensive social networks have access to more resources and are more likely to succeed in the longer term (Lee, Tuselmann, Jayawarna & Rouse, 2019; Macpherson, Herbane & Jones, 2015; Smith, Smith & Shaw, 2017).

Jonsson and Lindbergh (2013) also draw heavily on the concept of social capital to examine the way in which entrepreneurs make the transition from bootstrapping to more formal debt finance. The authors suggest that while bootstrapping is useful in the early stages of start-up, developing a growing business requires external finance and the related expertise possessed by bankers. All six of the fashion-based start-ups in their study had bootstrapped their initial finance (own money or family and friends). In making the transition to external finance, entrepreneurs must develop their structural social capital (Lee & Jones, 2008; Nahapiet & Ghoshal, 1998) by extending the networks of professional contacts. Creating cognitive social capital by using the appropriate language codes (see Chapter 6) helps create shared values and meanings between entrepreneur and banker. Entrepreneurs must then develop the relational dimension to build trust with the banks to help smooth the flow of resources (finance and knowledge). As Jonsson and Lindbergh (2013, p. 681) go on to point out, 'developing relationships with banks signals other market participants that the firm is creditworthy and has the potential to prosper'. Establishing legitimacy with a bank also helps entrepreneurs acquire other sources of external financing (equity).

Based on a survey of almost 300 entrepreneurs participating in four major business planning competitions in Germany and one in Austria, Grichnik, Brinckmann, Singh and Manigart (2014) make a number of practical suggestions for those engaged in enterprise education. For example, they propose that there should be much more emphasis on the importance of bootstrapping. Instead, educators place far too much emphasis on how nascent entrepreneurs should engage in formal planning and fundraising activities. 'Our study highlights that providing specific business training and developing the professional network of nascent entrepreneurs enable them to engage in bootstrapping, which frequently might be a more economical and more promising solution in addressing resource constraints' (Grichnik et al., 2014, p. 323).

9.7 Entrepreneurial Bootstrapping via Crowdfunding

Crowdfunding as a formal financing strategy for start-up businesses is discussed in Chapter 8 (Landström, Parhankangas & Mason, 2019). Here we concentrate crowdfunding as an informal approach to obtaining the finance necessary for start-up businesses. What this means is that bootstrapped crowdfunding will be either donation-based or reward-based rather than loan-based or equity-based, which are formal forms of crowdfunding (Parhankangas, Mason & Landstrom, 2019). Donation-based platforms, such as Justgiving and Gofundme, are used for a variety of purposes as well as the funding of new businesses. Entrepreneurs using reward-based platforms, Kickstarter.com and Indiegogo.com, can offer early access to their products (new games, for example) as a reward to crowd funders. Until recently, entrepreneurs raised funds from small groups of sophisticated professional investors (business angels or venture capitalists). Emergence of the Internet meant that it became possible to obtain small sums of money from large numbers of non-professional investors known as 'the crowd' (Lynn, Rosati, Nair & Mac an Bhaird, 2020). It is likely that for most entrepreneurs, crowdfunding investors will be concentrated among family, friends and other close ties rather than professional investors. Lynn et al. (2020) suggest that Twitter is particularly useful for entrepreneurs seeking to extend their social networks because it is an open access platform. Online networks associated with Twitter represent a new form of habitus for the creation of entrepreneurial social capital (Smith et al., 2017). At the same time, inexperienced entrepreneurs need to develop the capabilities required to create and mobilize their new entrepreneurial networks (Lynn et al., 2020).

In many ways, crowdfunding is seen by inexperienced entrepreneurs as a panacea to the perennial problems of obtaining start-up funding. While it certainly has the potential to provide much needed financial resources to new businesses it is not a substitute for developing your business ideas and building feasible business models (see Chapters 3 and 4). Although informal crowdfunding is often associated with not-for-profit or social ventures (Renko, Moss & Lloyd, 2019), we believe that it is certainly something that every new entrepreneur should consider. Crowdfunding can help raise relatively small amounts of capital at an early stage of a business when formal investment from banks, business angels or venture capitalists is unlikely to be an option (Parhankangas et al., 2019). According to Foster (2019, p. 1) there are five main reasons why entrepreneurs should consider crowdfunding their start-up business. First, they can finance new projects while retaining their equity capital and avoiding debt. Secondly, they can generate interest in their products or services by creating a preliminary market among potential consumers. Thirdly, stimulating a conversation about their product/service helps get clients engaged by offering valuable feedback on design and functions. Fourthly, it can reduce negative implicit biases against entrepreneurs from underrepresented groups. Finally, it promotes efficient use of entrepreneurs' social networks in an inexpensive manner (Popescul, Radu, Păvăloaia & Georgescu, 2020). Social enterprises find it particularly difficult to obtain bank loans or access public funding because both local and national governments concentrate spending on essential services in response to Covid-19 (Renko et al., 2019). The authors claim that approximately 30% of the finance raised on crowdfunding platforms goes to social enterprises. Some crowdfunding platforms such as *Kiva* (www.kiva.org/) are themselves social enterprises and *Kickstarter.com* and *Indiegogo.com* also offer support to social enterprises. However, the funding for social ventures is far smaller, $6,000 from 55 backers, compared to commercial ventures, $66,000 from 2460 backers (Renko et al., 2019, p. 251). Engaging in crowdfunding activities can help social enterprises, as well as conventional start-up businesses, test their 'minimum viable products' (see Chapter 4). Crowdfunding provides potential users with the opportunity to give feedback to entrepreneur on the value of their product or service. Although, it is important to note that online 'advice' can be contradictory and, therefore, create confusion rather than providing clear guidance on improvements to the product/service. More positively, crowdfunding can help entrepreneurs build a loyal community who are willing to offer support in the future.

Dushnitsky and Zunino (2019) report on several studies that have examined the activities of Kiva.org, a loan-based platform. Entrepreneurs who emphasize their profit motive take far longer to reach their target funding than those who focus on the social value of their ventures (Allison, Davis, Short & Webb, 2015; Moss, Neubaum & Meyskens, 2015). As Dushnitsky and Zunino (2019, p. 58) go on to point out, crowd funders are motivated by pro-social considerations linked to intrinsically motivated entrepreneurs who have projects with a unique social value. To establish the motivations of those contributing to crowdfunding campaigns, Boudreau, Jeppesen, Reichstein and Rullani (2021) examine the launch of a game known at *Natural Selection* on Kickstarter.com. There are several non-pecuniary reasons why crowd funders contribute to specific appeals for funding. These include the *psychic rewards* of contributing to the public good, *signalling* to others that you are supporting a worthwhile project and the *reciprocity* associated with wanting to give something back to the 'community'. Therefore, financial rewards from early investment in a new business appear have a limited appeal to potential funders. It seems that there are strong similarities between the motivations of those contributing to small private ventures and donors to charities and philanthropic organizations.

Research has also explained how entrepreneurial narratives influence successful access to crowdfunding. Moss et al. (2015), for example, show that an entrepreneurial orientation that offer promise for innovative solutions in the crowdfunding narrative is more influential in determining funding success than is a virtuous orientation. Allison et al. (2015) provide evidence to suggest narratives using extrinsic cues such as profit driven motives for resource access are less likely to spark resource providers' interest for resource investment compared to intrinsic cues that support human engagement and cohesion. Taeuscher, Bouncken and Pesch (2021) portrayed crowd funders as novelty expecting resource providers and explained how distinctiveness of entrepreneurial stories can provide a source of normative legitimacy which is essential to achieve superior crowdfunding performance. Their analysis of 28,425 crowdfunding campaigns across 39 market categories revealed entrepreneurial stories with high distinctiveness attract 32% more backers and 47% higher funding pledges than those with low distinctiveness. Nielsen and Binder (2021) studied how egoistic, altruistic and biospheric values in crowdfunding campaign descriptions influence crowdfunders' willingness to support different projects. Their findings confirmed altruistic cues outperform egoistic and biospheric value frames. Hence, collectivistic cultures offer entrepreneurs more opportunity to win over resource providers compared to individualistic cultures. Taken together this empirical evidence explains non-pecuniary rewards in the form of reciprocity were a strong motivation for supporters of the entrepreneur responsible for developing *Natural Selection*. Boudreau et al. (2021) argue that their findings have implications for policy makers and entrepreneurs considering launching crowdfunding campaigns. In particular, entrepreneurs should (a) find ways to improve relationships that strengthen common cause with funders, for example, through strategic and 'inclusive' communications; (b) appeal to funder reciprocity motivations by, for instance, emphasizing the value (to be) delivered to funders; and (c) ensure that funders have the means to signal involvement, for example through a badge attached to user profiles (Boudreau et al., 2021, p. 12). In contrast, entrepreneurs should not pay too much attention to indicating positive future returns or their approaches to monitoring and control. Prędkiewicz and Kalinowska-Beszczyńska (2020) examined projects on a number of crowdfunding platforms to identify the key success factors (Box 9.5).

Box 9.5

As a result of their analysis of over 100 European crowdfunding platforms, the authors identified 37 equity-based, 20 donation-based, 35 reward-based and four revenue sharing crowdfunded investments. Although the focus of the research was eco-based projects, the findings are certainly relevant for all start-up businesses. Based on 41 active projects the most significant finding was that the higher the funding goal the lower the chances of success. Other studies have confirmed that less than 30% of projects on Kickstarter.com obtain more than $10,000 (£7,400). A detailed description of the individual (or team) associated with the start-up and their previous successful projects increased the likelihood of meeting funding targets. Progress updates and regular comments related to the project were also positively linked with success. In other words, simply posting details of the project on a funding platform is unlikely to lead to success. Constant updating of content related to your project will enhance the chances of a successful crowdfunding campaign.

Crowdfunding is not an easy solution to the problems associated with obtaining financial support for new business ventures. If you are seriously considering launching a crowdfunding campaign, then there are several steps that you need to take before deciding that it warrants committing your time and effort (which could be spent on the business itself rather than searching for funding). To begin, you should research the various crowdfunding platforms so that you find one that suits your purposes and your business model. If adopting a reward-based model, then you certainly need to consider what that will cost the business. You need to prepare very carefully by developing a convincing presentation, which is likely to appeal to your target audience. As pointed out above, this may mean concentrating the social value of your business (creating new jobs, providing a useful service to the community) rather than conventional financial outcomes such as profit and growth. Ensuring that you make your preparations in a professional manner will certainly give you a greater chance of meeting your financial targets. Developing both your human and social capital will also enhance the chances of meeting your crowdfunding targets (Onginjo, Zhou,

Berhanu & Belihu, 2021; Polzin, Toxopeus & Stam, 2018). In terms of your human capital, you should concentrate on getting as much experience as you can. As we discuss in Chapter 5, that means engaging in extracurricular activities organized by your university's enterprise club and societies such as Enactus. You should make regular use of social media (Facebook, Twitter etc.) to extend your social networks as a means of creating valuable social capital. The combination of social media and crowdsourcing solves two problems for new entrepreneurs by attracting external finance as well as early-stage customers (Lynn et al., 2020). One excellent way of reaching experienced businesspeople is to explore the potential of your Institution's alumni network using social media. Many alumni members will be willing to offer advice and support to current students and this is definitely a resource you should exploit (see Chapter 5, Section 5.5).

In summary, crowdfunding is certainly worth considering as your new business develops. There are a number of benefits associated with crowdfunding that go beyond finance including attracting potential customers (Foster, 2019). However, in the very early stages of setting up a new business we suggest your time will better spent working on the business itself rather than initiating a crowdfunding campaign.

9.8 Bootstrapping Social Ventures

Existing research notes that social ventures are more constrained in terms of their ability to attract both capital and talent (Austin, Stevenson & Wei-Skillern, 2006) and non-monetary, alternative sources of funding have become a major resourcing strategy for social enterprises. Resourcing actions in social ventures have therefore been conceptualized as a relational process centred on the practice of resource mobilization and resource access through social transactions, or what Starr and MacMillan (1990) term 'resource co-optation via social contracting'. Jayawarna et al. (2020) explained that, in refusing to enact resource limitations dictated by the environment social entrepreneurs display the character of 'socially oriented bootstrapping'. Khaire (2010) also argues that social entrepreneurs rarely take ownership of resources and success largely depends on their ability to effectively acquire and utilize external resources. There are a number of commonalities between resource-dependency and social exchange theories and bootstrapping practices in social enterprises.

First, according to resource dependency theory, resources are commodities with multiple ownerships (Pfeffer & Salancik, 1978), which coincides with the underlying principles of socially oriented bootstrapping. It also builds on the notion that resources are embedded in relationships between mutually dependent social actors and therefore these resources have multiple uses and common ownership (Fang, Chi, Chen & Baron, 2015; Grichnik et al., 2014). Secondly, it is widely acknowledged that social capital is a crucial factor in accessing bootstrap resources (Jones and Jayawarna, 2010; Jonsson and Linderg, 2013) and that relational and structural embeddedness have key roles in this process. Social exchange theory helps explain how regular interactions through strong relational embeddedness creates the obligations, expectations and trust that support mutual resource exchanges. While structural embeddedness helps to lower the cost of resources that are distributed in dependency relationships (Tornikoski & Newbert, 2013). Thirdly, the social exchange perspective, typified by group cohesion and bonding social capital (Lee & Jones, 2008), is also important in the case of social enterprise bootstrapping practices when there are likely to be positive outcomes for the community through mutual resource exchanges (Aryee, Walumbwa, Mondejar & Chu, 2015; Tornikoski & Newbert, 2013).

A study by Jayawarna et al. (2020) examined the bootstrapping activities of eight early-stage (one to five years) social enterprises. The study found multiple social contexts providing access, sharing and mobilization of bootstrap resources in the early stages of social enterprises (Jayawarna et al., 2020). Social enterprises use various managerial practices including legitimacy building, persuasion and strengthening community cohesion to attract resource providers and establish close relationships with those who have control over key bootstrap resources. Relationship formation is key to the accumulation and exploitation of social capital for social entrepreneurs as well as for them to broker structural holes with key stakeholders. This study provides strong support for the resource-dependency model as social enterprises cannot generate sufficient resources internally and therefore largely depend on their task environment for additional inputs. Jayawarna et al. (2020) identified three interrelated strategies that created both the enabling conditions and resource access opportunities for SEs: access to skilled voluntary labour (volunteer-based bootstrapping), competent, committed and ethical leadership (leadership-associated bootstrapping) and accumulation of social capital (relationship-oriented bootstrapping) (see Figure 9.4).

Figure 9.4 Non-monetary Resourcing in Social Enterprises

The study also found a wide variety of symbolic actions that generated visible signals conveying information to convince audiences that the social entrepreneur's activities fitted with normative expectation regarding 'the right thing to do' (Jayawarna et al., 2020). Symbolic actions help create a working space that promotes entrepreneurial activities by allowing staff and members of the support community to discover their resource access capacities. Voluntary labour formed a key alternative human resource for these entrepreneurs. In fact, the entire management team sometimes worked in a voluntary capacity and received no financial recompense beyond expenses. It was also found that leaders' social and ethical values helped develop collaborative relationships based on friendship and solidarity to generate change. The experience, skills and competence of leaders also helped the SEs to realize resource needs in the form of credibility, reputation and firm references. In addition, third-party affiliations that provided legitimacy based on symbolic gestures were particularly important in helping the early-stage SEs attract resource providers' attention. These third-party affiliations brought moral signals to the fore and thereby endorsed the fulfilment of social obligations. This actor-centred approach, where SEs control or manage the legitimization process, either by offering an accurate reflection of their conformance to a social mission or by adapting the image is particularly effective in the acquisition of bootstrap resources.

Jayawarna et al. (2020) conclude that the manner in which SEs and their communities attract bootstrap resources contrasts with the strategic approach adopted by commercial start-ups. Generally, in commercial ventures, resource providers are motivated by goal-oriented aims based on economic self-interest. Social entrepreneurs often place considerable emphasis on value creation at the system level – partly because they recognize that a viable ecosystem resulting from resource communities will have longer-term benefits for their own organizations and partly because they make use of underutilized resources from other organizations, which is unlikely to occur when 'for-profit' organizations are competing for resources. Volunteerism as a bootstrap resource is not normally found in conventional enterprises. As staff base in social enterprises do not make economically attractive returns and often work on a voluntary basis, volunteerism can be a key bootstrap resource for social ventures. However, in social enterprises it raises important organizational questions about addressing skill shortages and extra resource demands for voluntary management to gain full benefits of this resource (Guo & Acar, 2005).

9.9 Summary and Key Learning Points

It is commonly reported that new businesses have difficulty in accessing finance. Such businesses can engage in 'bootstrapping' activities as a way of compensating for the lack of finance and other resources. Defined as a creative means to exploit opportunities for the resource constraint entrepreneurs to launch and grow a successful venture, bootstrapping covers a variety of strategies and techniques for entrepreneurs who are either at the early stages of setting up a small business or running high-growth, high potential ventures. Techniques such as using parent's home as a base (see the Jazooli example), subsidising from other activities (as in Active Profile), salary deferment and use of credit cards (as in Wigan Recycling), bartering and sharing equipment are some of the bootstrap activities that entrepreneurs pursue when starting a new business. Although entrepreneurial finance has been widely studied, the use of bootstrapping as an alternative resourcing strategy has attracted much less interest from academic researchers. While the limited available literature largely agrees with the ideas put forward by

Winborg and Langstom (2001), new research evidence points to the import-ance of considering the business life-cycle, entrepreneurial motives and gender in explaining the usage of different bootstrapping methods, Taken together the key learning points from this chapter are:

- Bootstrapping is a key organizational capability, which influences the ability of new firms to respond to their resource needs in more efficient and cost-effective ways. It is focused on enhancing cash flow and min-imizing outgoing and maximizing income.
- The literature largely agrees that there are four different types of boot-strapping techniques for entrepreneurs to resource their ventures: owner-related, payment-related, customer-related and joint-utilization methods.
- Research categorizes bootstrapping into either internally or externally oriented activities. While internal activities aim at maximizing outcomes from the limited available resources, external methods of bootstrapping often target the securing of external sources of resources through sharing or jointly utilizing with other businesses or individuals.
- While the use of owner-related and joint-utilization techniques decline as venture matures, which fits with theories of entrepreneurial risk-taking, use of payment-related techniques tends to increase over time which coincides with theories of resource dependency (Pfeffer & Salancik, 1978) and organizational learning (Argyris, 1992).
- In addition to the direct benefit of gaining access to additional resources bootstrapping can indirectly benefit entrepreneurs through (1) encour-aging efficient use of resources; (2) overcoming the problem of infor-mation asymmetries; (3) introducing discipline to resource use; and (4) enabling flexible work delivery.
- Examples of the use of bootstrapping techniques can be found in ventures of all types and sizes, operating at different stages of venture development.
- Crowdfunding has emerged as an important bootstrapping strategy for entrepreneurs to access seed funds. The social value orientation of reward-based crowdfunding is particularly important to offer many non-pecuniary rewards for the entrepreneur.
- Social ventures offer a unique context to study socially oriented boot-strapping. In the practice of socially oriented bootstrapping, resource exchanges are facilitated through social embeddednessand reciprocal action to create social wealth.

9.10 Discussion Questions and Call to Action

1. What are the key reasons that influence new entrepreneurs to seek bootstrap resources to set up and run a new venture?
2. How does resource-based view of the firm, resource dependency theory and resource constraints theory help explain the need for boot-strapping in new ventures?
3. What are the bootstrapping techniques that nascent entrepreneurs can use to access additional resources for their businesses?
4. What are the short-term and long-term benefits of using bootstrap resources in the new venture?
5. How does the business life cycle help to understand dynamic and practical nature of bootstrap behavior by different entrepreneurs?
6. Why is it challenging to define a generic set of bootstrap techniques that an entrepreneur might use to start a new business? (use gender, business sector, business age and entrepreneur character, preferences and motivations in your discussion).
7. How does entrepreneurial bootstrapping via crowdfunding affect the mobilization of resources and what values entrepreneurs could gain through successful crowdfunding efforts?

As we stress throughout Chapters 8 and 9, the chances of young inexperienced entrepreneurs obtaining external funding for their start-up businesses are remote. The growth of Internet-based crowdfunding platforms over the last ten years certainly offers another potential avenue for funding in addition to the traditional sources of finance; banks, business angels and venture capitalists. While this may appear an attractive option, it takes time to put together a professional crowdfunding campaign and it is also important to provide regular updates that encourages potential funders to engage. In addition, you may only be able to raise relatively small amounts of funding via a crowdfunding campaign. We are committed to the concept of bootstrapping as a more realistic approach to starting a business for most young entrepreneurs. In fact, it is widely reported that most entrepreneurs do engage in bootstrapping behaviours (although they may not realize that they are 'bootstrapping'). Bootstrapping encourages a lean approach to start-up based on the development of higher levels of creativity and resourcefulness. Ideally, bootstrapping should be a proactive rather than a reactive process, which usually focuses on cost-reduction. Proactive boot-strapping means that you should take a strategic approach to developing your social networks by bridging out of your strong ties. Accessing a more diverse social network will enhance your prospects of obtaining additional valuable resources (Chapter 6). Bootstrapping means that your focus should be on collaboration rather than competition with other entrepreneurs within your ecosystem. There are lots of creative ways of obtaining add-itional resources for your business by sharing assets (including premises and employees) with other entrepreneurs. The important issue is to think about the positive ways in which bootstrapping can help develop your business without engaging in more negative aspects such as not taking a salary. For social entrepreneurs, bootstrapping practices are largely manifested in social exchange relationships, characterized by reciprocity, social pur-pose, empathy and altruistic behaviours. Donation-based or reward-based crowdfunding provide the best prospect for inexperienced entrepreneurs to bootstrap additional financial resources.

References

Allison, T. H., Davis, B. C., Short, J. C. & Webb, J. W. (2015). Crowdfunding in a Prosocial Microlending Environment: Examining the Role of Intrinsic Versus Extrinsic Cues. *Entrepreneurship Theory and Practice, 39*(1), 53–73.

Argyris, C. (1992). *On Organizational Learning*: Oxford: Blackwell.

Aryee, S., Walumbwa, F. O., Mondejar, R. & Chu, C. W. L. (2015). Accounting for the Influence of Overall Justice on Job Performance: Integrating Self-Determination and Social Exchange Theories. *Journal of Management Studies, 52*(2), 231–252.

Austin, J., Stevenson, H. & Wei-Skillern, J. (2006). Social and Commercial Entrepreneurship: Same, Different, or Both? *Entrepreneurship: Theory & Practice, 30*(1), 1–22.

Baker, T. & Nelson, R. E. (2005). Creating Something from Nothing: Resource Construction through Entrepreneurial Bricolage. *Administrative Science Quarterly, 50*, 329–366.

Baker, T., Pricer, R. & Nenide, B. (2000). *When less is more: undercapitalisation as a predictor of firm success*. Paper presented at the In Frontiers of Entrepreneurship Research.

Bandura, A. (1977). *Social learning theory*. Engetwood Cliffs, NJ: Prentice-Hall.

Bhide, A. (1992). Bootstrap Finance: The Art of Start-ups. *Harvard Business Review, 70*(6), 109–117.

Boudreau, K. J., Jeppesen, L. B., Reichstein, T. & Rullani, F. (2021). Crowdfunding as Donations to Entrepreneurial Firms. *Research Policy, 50*(7). doi:10.1016/j.respol.2021.104264

Bretherton, P. & Chaston, I. (2005). Resource dependency and SME strategy: an empirical study. *Journal of Small Business and Enterprise Development, 12*(2), 274–289.

Brush, C. G., Carter, N., Gatewood, E. J., Greene, P. G. & Hart, M. M. (2006). The use of bootstrapping by women entrepreneurs in positioning for growth. *Venture Capital, 8*(1), 15–31.

Bruton, G., Ahlstrom, D. & Si, S. (2015). Entrepreneurship, poverty, and Asia: Moving beyond subsistence entrepreneurship. *Asia Pacific Journal of Management, 32*(1), 1–22.

Carter, N., Brush, C., Greene, P., Gatewood, E. & Hart, M. (2003). Women entrepreneurs who break through to equity financing: the influence of human, social and financial capital. *Venture Capital, 5*(1), 1–28.

Carter, N., Williams, M. & Reynolds Paul, D. (1997). Discontinuance among new firms in retail: The influence of initial resources, strategy, and gender. *Journal of Business Venturing, 12*, 125–145.

Carter, R. B. & Van Auken, H. E. (2005). Bootstrap financing and owners' perceptions of their business constraints and opportunities. *Entrepreneurship & Regional Development, 17*(2), 129–144.

Cassar, G. (2001). The financing and capital structure of business start-ups: the importance of asset structure. *Frontiers of Entrepreneurship Research*, p. 252–263.

Cassar, G. (2004). The financing of business start-ups. *Journal of Business Venturing, 19*, 261–283.

Cornwall, J. R. (2009). *Bootstrapping*: Upper Saddle River, New Jersey: Prentice Hall

Dushnitsky, G. & Zunino, D. (2019). The Role of Crowdfunding in Entrepreneurial Finance. In H. Landstrom, A. Parhankangas & C. M. Mason (Eds.), *Handbook of Research on Crowdfunding* (pp. 46–92). Cheltenham, UK: Elgar.

Ebben, J. (2009). Bootstrapping and the financial condition of small firms. *International Journal of Entrepreneurial Behavior & Research, 15*(3/4), 346–363.,

Ebben, J. & Johnson, A. (2006). Bootstrapping in small firms: An empirical analysis of change over time. *Journal of Business Venturing, 21*, 851–865.

Fang, R., Chi, L., Chen, M. & Baron, R. A. (2015). Bringing Political Skill into Social Networks: Findings from a Field Study of Entrepreneurs. *Journal of Management Studies, 52*(2), 175–212.

Foster, J. (2019). Thank you for being a friend: The roles of strong and weak social network ties in attracting backers to crowdfunded campaigns. *Information Economics and Policy, 49*. doi:10.1016/j.infoecopol.2019.100832

Gates, B., Myhrvold, N. & Rinearson, P. (1996). *The Road Ahead*. New York: Penguin.

Greene, P. G., Brush, C. G., Hart, M. M. & Saparito, P. (2001). Patterns of venture capital funding: is gender a factor? *Venture Capital*, *3*(1), 63–83.

Grichnik, D., Brinckmann, J., Singh, L. & Manigart, S. (2014). Beyond environmental scarcity: Human and social capital as driving forces of bootstrapping activities. *Journal of Business Venturing*, *29*(2), 310–326.

Guo, C. & Acar, M. (2005). Understanding Collaboration among Nonprofit Organizations: Combining Resource Dependency, Institutional, and Network Perspectives. *Nonprofit and Voluntary Sector Quarterly*, *34*(3), 340–361.

Gupta, V. K., Turban, D. B., Wasti, S. A. & Sikdar, A. (2009). The Role of Gender Stereotypes in Perceptions of Entrepreneurs and Intentions to Become an Entrepreneur. *Entrepreneurship: Theory & Practice*, *33*(2), 397–417

Harrison, R. T., Mason, C. M. & Girling, P. (2004). Financial bootstrapping and venture development in the software industry. *Entrepreneurship & Regional Development*, *16*(4), 307–333.

Jayawarna, D., Jones, O. & Macpherson, A. (2020). Resourcing Social Enterprises: The Role of Socially Oriented Bootstrapping. *British Journal of Management*, *31*(1), 56–79.

Jayawarna, D., Jones, O. & Marlow, S. (2015). The influence of gender upon social networks and bootstrapping behaviours. *Scandinavian Journal of Management*, *31*(3), 316–329.

Jones, O. & Jayawarna, D. (2010). Resourcing new businesses: social networks, bootstrapping and firm performance. *Venture Capital*, *12*(2), 127–152.

Jones, O., Macpherson, A. & Jayawarna, D. (2010). *Bootstrapping as a Dynamic Capability: Innovation in TBSFs (technology-based start-up firms)*. Paper presented at the International Small Business and Entrepreneurship Conference (ISBE), London.

Jonsson, S. & Lindbergh, J. (2013). The Development of Social Capital and Financing of Entrepreneurial Firms: From Financial Bootstrapping to Bank Funding. *Entrepreneurship: Theory & Practice*, *37*(4), 661–686.

Khaire, M. (2010). Young and No Money? Never Mind: The Material Impact of Social Resources on New Venture Growth. *Organization Science*, *21*(1), 168–185.

Lam, W. (2010). Funding gap, what funding gap?: financial bootstrapping; supply, demand and creation of entrepreneurial finance. *International Journal of Entrepreneurial Behavior & Research*, *16*(4), 268–295.

Landström, H., Parhankangas, A. & Mason, C. M. (2019). *Handbook of research on crowdfunding*. Cheltenham: Edward Elgar Pub.

Lee, R. & Jones, O. (2008). Networks, Communication and Learning during Business Start-up. *International Small Business Journal*, *26*(5), 559–594.

Lee, R., Tuselmann, H., Jayawarna, D. & Rouse, J. (2019). Effects of structural, relational and cognitive social capital on resource acquisition: a study of entrepreneurs residing in multiply deprived areas. *Entrepreneurship & Regional Development,* *31*(5/6), 534–554.

Lynn, T., Rosati, P., Nair, B. & Mac an Bhaird, C. (2020). An Exploratory Data Analysis of the #Crowdfunding Network on Twitter. *Journal of Open Innovation, 6,* 80. doi:10.3390/joitmc6030080

Mac an Bhaird, C. & Lynn, T. (2015). Seeding the Cloud: Financial Bootstrapping in the Computer Software Sector. *Venture Capital, 17*(1–2), 151–170.

Macpherson, A., Herbane, B. & Jones, O. (2015). Developing Dynamic Capabilities through Resource Accretion: Expanding the Entrepreneurial Solution Space. *Entrepreneurship and Regional Development, 27*(5–6), 259–291.

Malmstrom, M. (2014). Typologies of Bootstrap Financing Behavior in Small Ventures. *Venture Capital, 16*(1), 27–50.

Manolova, T. S., Manev, I. M., Carter, N. M. & Gyoshev, B. S. (2006). Breaking the family and friends' circle: Predictors of external financing usage among men and women entrepreneurs in a transitional economy. *Venture Capital, 8*(2), 109–132.

Miao, C., Rutherford, M. W. & Pollack, J. M. (2017). An exploratory meta-analysis of the nomological network of bootstrapping in SMEs. *Journal of Business Venturing Insights, 8,* 1–8. doi:10.1016/j.jbvi.2017.04.002

Michaelis, T. L., Scheaf, D. J., Carr, J. C. & Pollack, J. M. (2022). An agentic perspective of resourcefulness: Self-reliant and joint resourcefulness behaviors within the entrepreneurship process. *Journal of Business Venturing, 37*(1). doi:10.1016/j.jbusvent.2020.106083

Moss, T. W., Neubaum, D. O. & Meyskens, M. (2015). The Effect of Virtuous and Entrepreneurial Orientations on Microfinance Lending and Repayment: A Signaling Theory Perspective. *Entrepreneurship Theory and Practice, 39*(1), 27–52.

Myers, S. C. (1984). The Capital Structure Puzzle. *Journal of Finance, 39*(3), 575–592.

Nahapiet, J. & Ghoshal, S. (1998). Social Capital, Intellectual Capital, and the Organizational Advantage. *Academy of Management Review, 23*(2), 242–266.

Neely, L. & Van Auken, H. (2012). An Examination of Small Firm Bootstrap Financing and use of Debt. *Journal of Developmental Entrepreneurship, 17*(01). doi:10.1142/S1084946712500021

Nielsen, K. R. & Binder, J. K. (2021). I Am What I Pledge: The Importance of Value Alignment for Mobilizing Backers in Reward-Based Crowdfunding. *Entrepreneurship Theory and Practice, 45*(3), 531–561.

Onginjo, J. O., Zhou, D. M., Berhanu, T. F. & Belihu, S. W. G. (2021). Analyzing the impact of social capital on US based Kickstarter projects outcome. *Heliyon, 7*(7). doi:10.1016/j.heliyon.2021.e07425

Parhankangas, A., Mason, C. M. & Landstrom, H. (2019). Crowdfunding: An Introduction. In H. Landstrom, A. Parhankangas & C. M. Mason (Eds.), *Handbook of Research on Crowdfunding* (pp. 1–21): Cheltenham, UK: Elgar.

Pfeffer, J. & Salancik, G. R. (1978). The external control of organizations: a resource dependence perspective. New York: Harper & Row.

Pollack, J. M., Maula, M., Allison, T. H., Renko, M. & Gunther, C. C. (2021). Making a Contribution to Entrepreneurship Research by Studying Crowd-Funded Entrepreneurial Opportunities. *Entrepreneurship: Theory and Practice, 45*(2), 247.

Polzin, F., Toxopeus, H. & Stam, E. (2018). The wisdom of the crowd in funding: information heterogeneity and social networks of crowdfunders. *Small Business Economics, 50*(2), 251–273.

Popescul, D., Radu, L. D., Păvăloaia, V. D. & Georgescu, M. R. (2020). Psychological Determinants of Investor Motivation in Social Media-Based Crowdfunding Projects: A Systematic Review. *Frontiers in Psychology, 11.* doi:10.3389/fpsyg.2020.588121.

Prędkiewicz, K. & Kalinowska-Beszczyńska, O. (2020). Financing eco-projects: analysis of factors influencing the success of crowdfunding campaigns. *International Journal of Entrepreneurial Behavior & Research, 27*(2), 547–566.

Renko, M., Moss, T. W. & Lloyd, A. (2019). Crowdfunding by Non-profit and Social Ventures. In H. Landstrom, A. Parhankangas & C. M. Mason (Eds.), *Handbook of Research on Crowdfunding* (pp. 249–268). Cheltenham: Elgar.

Rutherford, M. W. (2015). *Strategic bootstrapping* (First edition. ed.). New York: Business Expert Press.

Rutherford, M. W., Pollack, J. M., Mazzei, M. J. & Sanchez-Ruiz, P. (2017). Bootstrapping: Reviewing the Literature, Clarifying the Construct, and Charting a New Path Forward. *Group & Organization Management, 42*(5), 657–706.

Smith, C., Smith, J. B. & Shaw, E. (2017). Embracing digital networks: Entrepreneurs' social capital online. *Journal of Business Venturing, 32*(1), 18–34.

Smith, R. L. & Smith, J. K. (2000). *Entrepreneurial Finance.* New York: John Wiley & Sons.

Starr, J. A. & MacMillan, I. C. (1990). Resource Cooptation Via Social Contracting: Resource Acquisition Strategies for New Ventures. *Strategic Management Journal, 11*, 79–92.

Taeuscher, K., Bouncken, R. & Pesch, R. (2021). Gaining Legitimacy by Being Different: Optimal Distinctiveness in Crowdfunding Platforms. *Academy of Management Journal, 64*(1), 149–179.

Timmons, J. A. (1999). *New Venture Creation: Entrepreneurship for the 21st Century* (Fifth ed.). New York: McGraw Hill.

Tomory, E. M. (2011). Bootstrap Financing:Four Case Studies of Technology Companies. *International Journal of Management Cases, 13*(3), 531–538.

Tornikoski, S. L. & Newbert, E. T. (2013). Resource acquisition in the emergence phase: considering the effects of embeddedness and resource dependence. *Entrepreneurship: Theory and Practice, 37*(2), 249.

Vanacker, T., Manigart, S., Meuleman, M. & Sels, L. (2011). A longitudinal study on the relationship between financial bootstrapping and new venture growth. *Entrepreneurship & Regional Development, 23*(9/10), 681–705.

Villanueva, J., Van de Ven, A. H. & Sapienza, H. J. (2012). Resource mobilization in entrepreneurial firms. *Journal of Business Venturing, 27*(1), 19–30.

Villaseca, D., Navío-Marco, J. & Gimeno, R. (2021). Money for female entrepreneurs does not grow on trees: start-ups' financing implications in times of COVID-19. *Journal of Entrepreneurship in Emerging Economies, 13*(4), 698–720.

Winborg, J. (2009). Use of financial bootstrapping in new businesses: a question of last resort? *Venture Capital, 11*(1), 71–83.

Winborg, J. (2015). The role of financial bootstrapping in handling the liability of newness in incubator businesses. *International Journal of Entrepreneurship and Innovation, 16*(3), 197–206.

Winborg, J. & Landström, H. (2001). Financial bootstrapping in small businesses. Examining small business managers' resource acquisition behaviors. *Journal of Business Venturing, 16*, 235–254.

10 | Dynamic Capabilities in Entrepreneurial Ventures

10.1 Introduction

It is important to recognize, as we have argued elsewhere (see for example Chapter 2 and Chapter 12), that entrepreneurship is not necessarily an individual endeavour. We consider that you should think of entrepreneurship as a collective creative process. All the people with whom you have contacts, your network, can be used to help the venture grow. In the early stages of your venture resources are likely to be sparse and accessing resources available in your network is likely to be a more successful strategy than trying to achieve success alone (Foss, Klein, Kor & Mahoney, 2008). In other words, a firm has resources – including its management, employees, finances, equipment, premises, networks, etc. – which the entrepreneur will apply to solve problems or to try to leverage opportunities. In the initial stages of your venture, however, you may need to work to develop network contacts to gain access to the resources you need. The more resources, and the more a firm can renew and change those resources over time, the more opportunities there are for the firm to succeed. Zahra Sapienza and Davidsson (2006, p. 918) define the ability to renew and change those resources over time as dynamic capabilities: 'the abilities to reconfigure a firm's resources and routines in the manner envisioned and deemed appropriate by its principal decision makers'.

In the past two decades, the concept of dynamic capabilities has made a significant impact on our understanding of how firms maintain the capacity to innovate and grow. This concept has its roots in Edith Penrose's (1959) book *The Theory of the Growth of the Firm*, and the resource-based view of the firm (Barney, 1991). Barney suggested that firms' competitive

DOI: 10.4324/9781003312918-11

advantage depends on a unique set of resources that they have. The more unique those resources and the more difficult they are to copy, then the more likely you can successfully carve out a niche in the market. Penrose's (1959) contribution is to highlight that, whatever resources a firm holds, the application and renewal of those resources still depends on the skill and judgement of you, the entrepreneur, to act. From her perspective, higher profits and growth depend on the way those resources are used. In addition, while the application of resources to a particular problem or opportunity might initially provide some competitive advantage, to maintain that advantage you need to build in processes and routines into the design of the firm that allows those resources to be renewed, updated and reconfigured. The problem for new ventures is that, compared to large firms, they have fewer resources at hand, and thus the dynamic capabilities will likely be different (Zahra et al. 2006). One key dynamic capability, therefore, will be the ability to accumulate and integrate resources from outside of the firm to respond to problems or opportunities quickly and effectively (Macpherson, Herbane & Jones, 2015).

One other factor to consider is that, at the start of a venture, the principal decision maker is likely to have the most ability to influence how the capabilities of the firm are structured and embedded in the firm. For example, Baron, Hannan & Burton (1999) identified in their study of 76 firms in Silicon Valley that the 'logics of organizing' adopted in the early stage of venture creation had a long-term effect on the intensity and structures of bureaucracy within the firms. This means that organizational attitudes, processes and systems become embedded early in the creation of the venture and, unless entrepreneurs embed dynamic capabilities in the firm's blueprint at the outset, choices made early in the start-up process will endure and make it difficult create dynamic capabilities later without significant effort. You will need to consider very carefully how you might build in the types of capabilities into your venture that support the opportunities to renew and reconfigure as the venture grows.

In the remainder of this chapter, we explore an overview of dynamic capabilities drawing insights from theoretical and empirical studies to consider the types of processes or routines that might provide new ventures with the capacity to develop and renew their competencies. We highlight that resource deficiencies provide a particular challenge for new enterprises. Here, we discuss how the concept of bricolage, the art of making do with resources at hand or discarded by others (Baker, Miner & Eesley, 2003) can provide insight into the process of renewal and change. We also discuss the key role of learning processes that links the availability and adoption of resources to new configurations of routines and capabilities within the firm. We provide direct links to other chapters that reflect on the types of resources necessary to build a new venture but explore more how firms respond to changes in the environment and the key role of the entrepreneur in defining the trajectory of the firm.

10.2 Learning Objectives

- To explain the concept of dynamic capabilities.
- To explore the nature of dynamic capabilities in new ventures.
- To consider how bricolage can provide a creative way of managing and innovating, despite resource deficiencies.
- To consider the role of entrepreneurial action in focusing the trajectory of dynamic capabilities in new ventures.

10.3 From Resources to Dynamic Capabilities

Entrepreneurs managing new and small ventures will have to face the challenge of dealing with crises, obstacles and opportunities while working with limited resources (Brush, 2008). In other chapters (see Chapters 2, 5, 6, 7 and 9) we explored the types of resources that are necessary to start a new venture. We also explored how a nascent entrepreneur, with limited financial backing, might augment those initial resources by bootstrapping though networks (both close ties, such as family and looser ties, through business and education networks, or incubators). For example, research by Jayawarna, Jones & Macpherson (2020) demonstrates how early stage social enterprises overcome resource constraints by implementing organizational practices – building credibility, persuasion and creating resource communities – as bootstrapping strategies to access and mobilize resources available in the community.

This view, that the firm's success is dependent on the unique nature of the resources it can access, is called the resource-based view (RBV) of the firm (Barney, 1991). These resources include the financial capital that it holds, its access to raw materials that it needs for those products or services, the technology that it uses to create its products or services and the knowledge and experience employed to translate the materials into products and services. It is inevitable that as the venture grows, the resource needs change over time during the development process as the firm's offering is refined and changed to respond to market dynamics. What is interesting is that, in a longitudinal study of 3 firms by Lichtenstein and Brush (2001), they found that the most important assets were the intangible resources such as knowledge, expertise, relationships, sales and service delivery and decision making. This makes intuitive sense since, all things being equal and a firm has access to the same tangible resources (e.g., equipment and financial capital), it is the intangible soft skills and capabilities (such as relationship building) that is likely to make a significant difference.

Despite RBV's appeal (a firm with better resources is more competitive), it has been criticized as being too static and tautological. If a firm has better resources, then it will be more profitable; however, more profitable firms can invest in better resources. Others argue that while resources provide a set of assets essential for the firm to function, what is important is not those resources, but the way the entrepreneur and their strategic team deploy those assets creatively to configure and reconfigure opportunities. While resource dependence theory (Pfeffer & Salancik, 1978) suggests that a firm needs to structure the way it organizes in order to gain more control and power in accessing and controlling resources it needs to be competitive, an alternative view is that resources value is dependent on how they are used. For example, Lockett, Thompson & Morgenstern (2009: 13) note that:

> 'the role of the manager in the RBV is akin to that of a card player. The player is provided with a dealt hand of cards, the value of each card is determined *ex ante* by the rules of the game. Success depends on the relative skill with which that hand .... is played in competition against rivals'.

In other words, it is not the resources alone that are the source of value. What is important is how you deploy your resources. This same point was made in recent research of small enterprises in Australia which noted it is the performance and actions taken to deal with contingencies that is most important in the deployment of resources to create capabilities (Weaven et al., 2021). Moreover, this is a point that was made quite clearly by Penrose in 1959 (see the introduction). Resources, particularly tangible resources, are just things and the greater capacity, skill and creativity, or perhaps just some 'blind luck' (Storey, 2011), are required to get more from fewer resources. Success in deploying the resources requires capabilities such as making good decisions, leadership, skill and creativity to develop systems and processes necessary to get an attractive offering to market. For example, one study on the micro foundations of dynamic capabilities found that in some cases, perceived self-efficacy of the entrepreneur, their self-belief, was a crucial component or antecedent of dynamic capabilities (Kevill, Trehan & Easterby-Smith, 2017). This means that we cannot judge or measure intangible and tangible resources such as knowledge and capabilities as a proxy for potential success. The capacity to perform will depend on how you approach and apply your skills and knowledge to reconfigure your available resources in response to contingencies, such as changing markets, or other crises.

While resources alone are not a solution, the more resources you have will increases capacity and opportunities to be more creative and develop more options for crisis management. In a study of small and new ventures managing crises, Macpherson et al. (2015) noted that the firms were able to expand their opportunities to cope by gradually accumulating and integrating resources by extending their networks. This created the capacity within the case firms to develop new capabilities. These resource integration routines were an essential precursor to develop the types of capabilities that allowed them to survive the crises and flourish. Prior experience, relationships and knowledge of markets, or technical expertise and 'inside knowledge' provide an advantage; there are several studies that show how such experience is invaluable in successfully navigating the complex terrain of specific markets (Lockett et al. 2009). The bottom line is that resources matter, but managers must attend to the relevance, availability and deployment of such resources and they will need strategies and processes to do so.

For entrepreneurs to overcome the limitations of existing resources they need to extend the networks to ensure access to more resources, but perhaps more importantly it is suggested that their internal systems need to be flexible enough to deploy those resources effectively. In one study of technology-based start-ups, findings suggested that team building capabilities were an important precursor to rapid adaption to changing technologies and thus dynamic capabilities (Hernandez, Fernandez-Mesa &

Edwards-Schachter, 2018). Internal systems and processes that can renew and reconfigure exiting resources to environmental challenges are the 'dynamic capabilities' (Teece, 2007; Teece, Pisano & Shuen, 1997). The dynamic capabilities view of competitive advantages focuses more clearly on resource development and organization processes, which are argued to be fundamental to success. In their original conceptualization of 'dynamic capabilities', Teece and his colleagues argued that such a view of competitive advantage meant any strategy analysis must be sensitive to the actual situation of each firm and consider 5 key aspects:

1. Selecting and committing to a particular product portfolio means committing to developing path dependent competences.
2. Such entry decisions also depend on existing competences and capabilities of the entrants.
3. There are possibilities for organizations to expand when significant overlap exists between the core capabilities possessed within the firm and those needed in the market.
4. Therefore, such diversification must build on existing competences.
5. This means that specialization should be on competences not products, supported using internal processes for their deployment and evolution.

In other words, attention to knowledge, knowledge renewal, skills and capabilities that match the changing market needs is essential to stay relevant as a firm. For example, the evolution of the Internet and social media has meant that sourcing, marketing and advertising activity has fundamentally changed allowing small local firms the opportunities to source raw materials and products more widely and to reach new markets quickly. However, to do this requires new types of supply chain management competences and new types of marketing and advertising skills to be developed. It is this unique combination of competences and routines in a firm that Teece et al. (1997) suggest make success difficult to replicate. It has been argued that the core of entrepreneurship activity is actually dynamic capabilities because success and survival of your venture will depend on the redeployment of resources to create and adapt to opportunities (Arend, 2014). Therefore, it is not possible to just copy a template of success and deploy it to any market, you will need to be constantly aware of the changing market needs and maintain the capacity to adapt.

This view of a firm means that you need to understand what core competences you have in your venture. Also, when developing organizational processes and attitudes in your venture, you need to be continually open to learning new skills and capabilities. If you can embed a learning approach, routines and attitudes in your firm it is possible that you can create those 'dynamic capabilities' essential for success. Organizations confronted with changing markets or changing technologies must develop new capabilities to avoid the problem of 'core rigidities', where significant investment in past successes creates routines and path dependencies that become inflexible when dealing with changing contexts (Leonard-Barton, 1995). A classic example of such core rigidities is evident in the struggles many high street retail firms have had with the growth of online shopping. By maintaining a commitment to bricks and mortar, they were slow to transform to the digital age and, consequently, many struggled. For example, travel agencies and many travel companies have all but disappeared to be replaced by flight and travel consolidator businesses that only operate online, such as Expedia, Kayak or Booking.com. In short, 'dynamic capabilities' refers to the ability to create innovative responses to changing business environments and other crises. In other words, resources are necessary, but resource needs change over time. More importantly though are the types of organizational processes, attitudes and competences that you develop in your firm to encourage continued renewal, redeployment and reconfiguration of your venture's products and services (Colombo, Piva, Quas & Rossi-Lamastra, 2021), and which will enhance the possibilities of your venturing surviving jolts in the market (See Figure 10.1).

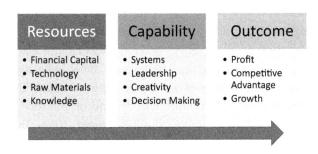

Figure 10.1 From Resources to Rents

10.4 Routines that Support Change

If it is important for you, as a new venture owner, to learn how to respond to changing contexts (Breslin & Jones, 2012), as proposed in the dynamic capabilities view, this raises the question: what are the types of processes in new firms that we can consider as 'dynamic'? Eisenhardt and Martin (2000, p. 1107) suggest that, while much of the strategy literature is 'vague' on the nature of dynamic capabilities, there are a number of specific examples of routines that support change from other areas, and which provide some insight. These include:

1. product development routines,
2. strategic decision-making routines,
3. resource-allocation routines,
4. and routines related to the acquisition and release of resources.

Zahra et al. (2006), on the other hand, make a distinction between substantive capabilities and dynamic capabilities. The former, they argue, are routines that contribute to the operational effectiveness and efficiency of the venture, while the latter provide the ability to renew such substantive capabilities. They comment:

> The challenge for new and established firms is to create – to a degree sufficient to meet the challenges of their environment – a systematic openness to upgrading and revising their substantive capabilities, through a variety of learning modes.
>
> (Zahra et al., 2006, p. 945)

In other words, they are higher order capabilities, that allow you to learn. However, it can be difficult to distinguish between those capabilities that provide incremental learning and those that create dramatic shifts in a firm's trajectory (Easterby-Smith, Lyles & Peteraf, 2009). In this regard, according to Bowman & Ambrosini (2003) dynamic capabilities have four main processes: reconfiguration, leveraging, learning and creative integration (see Table 10.1). Leveraging, which refers to the replication of processes or systems in another business unit, is unlikely to be relevant in the context of a new venture since the firm will not be large enough to have several

353

Table 10.1 Dynamic Capabilities in New Firms

Dynamic Capability	Types of Process
Reconfiguration	Reallocation of Resources Restructuring Recruitment Bootstrapping
Learning	Experimentation Improvisation Quality Management and Improvement Customer Relations Management New Product Development R&D Market Analysis
Integration	Embedding of New Routines, or Systems of Production

business units, but should be born in mind for the future. Reconfiguration involves the transformation of assets and resources; learning allows tasks to be performed more effectively because of previous experimentation; and creative integration refers to the firm's ability to combine assets and resources that leads to new resource configurations (Ambrosini & Bowman, 2009). Teece et al. (1997, p. 1319) in their contribution to the debate list three fundamental types of dynamic capabilities:

the capacity (1) to sense and shape opportunities and threats, (2) to seize opportunities and (3) to maintain competitiveness through enhancing, protecting and, when necessary, reconfiguring the business enterprise's intangible and tangible assets.

Like Bowman and Ambrosini (2003), Zollo and Winter (2002) specifically note the significance of learning mechanisms that are deliberately enacted to continually build experience and to change existing routines and practices. Indeed, Easterby-Smith and Prieto (2008, p. 245), in their conceptual paper, also propose that learning processes are 'a common theme underlying both dynamic capabilities and knowledge management'. Furthermore, they note that learning processes have an integrative and moderating influence that leads to the creative use of resources in dynamic firms.

The problem with a lot of these definitions is that they provide some rather vague conceptualizations of exactly what are dynamic capabilities. Nevertheless, underpinning each of them is a clear challenge to the entrepreneur that you must develop and maintain a deep knowledge of your product and markets, keep up with the latest innovations and technology, and maintain an operational flexibility to be able to pivot when new opportunities arise. However, all of these are dependent on the resources (such as time and expertise) to constantly review whether your venture is making the most out of its available resources or needs new resources. Taken together, then, there seems to be an agreement that dynamic capabilities 'as the capacity to effect change' are routines and processes that depend on managerial cognition and intangible knowledge to continually innovate to stay relevant (Easterby-Smith et al., 2009, p. S4).

This means that dynamic capabilities are exceedingly difficult to define but involve several functions within the firm such as product development, marketing and customer relations management. Initially, all these roles might be undertaken by a single person, the entrepreneur. However, as should be evident, dynamic capabilities are ultimately 'higher level capabilities which provide opportunities for knowledge gathering and sharing, continual updating of operational processes, interaction with the environment and decision-making evaluations' (Easterby-Smith et al., 2009, p. S7). It perhaps not surprising that many scholars have made the link between dynamic capabilities and learning processes, although the distinction between radical and incremental change is unclear. We discuss the issue and relevance of learning routines further in Section 10.4., and a fuller discussion of entrepreneurial learning is included in Chapter 5. However, it is also worth injecting a note of caution at this point. Successful outcomes of resource (re)configuration are not assured. The dynamic capabilities that lead to resource reconfigurations can just as easily destroy the routines and processes that provided competitive advantage in the first place (Ambrosini and Bowman, 2009). Inevitably making changes, and particularly radical ones, come with some risk for your venture.

10.5 Dynamic Capabilities in New Ventures

Given that most of the empirical research on dynamic capabilities is conducted on large firms, it is important to think about how dynamic capabilities might be important in small firms and what commonalities have been found. As a starting point, there are studies that have examined the entrepreneurial start-up process in detail, and they do provide some consensus on 'dynamic' factors that might be important (Carter, Gartner & Reynolds, 1996; Gatewood, Shaver & Gartner, 1995; Reynolds & White, 1997), and other studies draw on these findings to investigate these capabilities further. For example, drawing on the work of Reynolds and White (1997), Newbert's (2005) study of 817 US nascent entrepreneurs, using the panel study of entrepreneurial dynamics (PSED), combines gestation activities (including prepared business plan, developed model, hired employees etc.) with six measures of market dynamism. Several control variables are also incorporated, and these include race, gender, education, marital status and sector. Factors that were significant for all nascent entrepreneurs were: developing a model, purchasing materials, investing own money, committing full-time, hiring employees and engaging in promotional efforts. There were, however, interesting variations for high-tech entrepreneurs: develop models and purchasing materials were statistically significant with the likelihood of starting a business. Based on these results, Newbert (2005, p. 74) claims that a 'dynamic capabilities perspective provides a theoretical perspective by which to understand the process of new firm formation'. Other studies have also measured resource availability and integration to assess the relevance of dynamic capabilities. Wu's (2007) study of Taiwanese high-tech firms also confirmed that resource availability and their integration and reconfiguration were central to enhanced performance. A study of 'trans-generational value creation' in family firms also indicates that dynamic capabilities are the link between knowledge resources and entrepreneurial performance (Chirico & Nordqvist, 2010; Jones, Ghobadian, O'Regan & Antcliff, 2013). One study noted that team building was an important capability that facilitated collaboration in the venture and enhanced responsiveness early in venture formation (Hernandez et al., 2018)

In a case study approach, Macpherson, Jones & Zhang (2004) identify dynamic capabilities as a key antecedent to innovation and growth in a new, small and rapidly growing, technology-based entrepreneurial firm. The case demonstrates how building effective business networks helped to expand a firm's resource capacity (see Chapter 6), allowing it to respond flexibly to customers' needs and to exploit opportunities quickly by mobilizing external assets (Box 10.1). In RWL (the case company) new suppliers were identified through searches for companies with the capacity to provide innovative products and materials. Thus, initial weak ties (Granovetter, 1973) provided a 'loosely-coupled network' and the directors obtained access to critical resources that existed outside the firm's boundaries (Dyer & Singh, 1998). Routines of collaboration and problem solving within this network enabled the development of new products and solutions to technical problems for their main customer. In this instance, the dynamic capability was the effective coordination and integration of companies in its supply chain with existing processes at PPE Ltd. This allowed the firm to respond quickly to their main customer and supply technologically robust solutions (Macpherson et al. 2004). PPE Ltd essentially borrowed and shared resources to respond to a major new market opportunity. This bootstrapping of resources is discussed in detail Chapter 9, but there is also a discussion below in section 10.6, where we explore further the role of bootstrapping as a dynamic capability.

Box 10.1

At PPE Ltd, early in the development of the firm, they won a single source supply contract for their main customer. However, within the contract was a requirement to provide continuous improvement and innovation of products to meet the customer's changing requirements. This focus on value engineering and innovation meant that the firm's technical and creative resources were overloaded. In order to overcome this limitation they engaged in collaboration with the suppliers they managed as part of the contract. The directors established a number of close relationships and mutual trust grew through the exchange of ideas and knowledge with benefits for both parties. The network they created allowed the businesses able to share development time, costs, resources and expertise. In overcoming one particular problematic equipment failure, the directors noted that expertise from three firms was incorporated into the design, with each company benefitting from the improved finished product. This firm overcame its resource scarcity by seeking external expertise and support from a number of sources, including suppliers.

In another study that also involved accessing resources outside of the venture, Macpherson et al. (2015) found routines that enabled the creation and capturing of resources were essential in providing the capacity in a new and small venture for the entrepreneurs to cope with crisis. Entrepreneurs in this study went through a process of gradually accumulating and integrating resources depending on both the relevance and proximity of available resources within their network. Where resources were not immediately available, some entrepreneurs were able to extend their networks to capture more resources. The resources were an essential antecedent to being able to cope with the crisis and to reconfigure their businesses. The resources capturing gave the entrepreneurs the capacity to develop and apply dynamic solutions to their problems. Resource capturing thus seems to be an essential activity to provide the capacity to enact dynamic capabilities. Access to added resources helped entrepreneurs adapt to their crises by overcoming the firm's internal constraints (lack of foresight, technical knowledge, or risk management). The added resources allowed both structural and relational changes to their business models. The resource accretion actions provided them with capacity to change their firm's learning trajectory leading to the creation of new opportunities (Salge & Vera, 2013; Zhang, Macpherson & Jones, 2006).

These studies suggest that in your new resource-scarce firms (and almost all new firms are in this category) a key competitive capability will be for you to be able to gain access to the knowledge and information necessary to support the development of your venture. Thus, while a dynamic capabilities approach places more emphasis on internal activities and processes rather than the possession of resources (Ambrosini and Bowman, 2009), in small firms, resource scarcity is a significant problem. To have the capacity and capability to enact dynamic capabilities, resource capturing is important, and you will need to be alert to the potential resources not only in your firm, but in your networks. By creating and embedding resource search and integration strategies within the early development of your venture, you have the potential to create long-term resilience by embedding coping routines that, although they are not specifically dynamic capabilities, they provide access to the resources necessary to support reconfiguration, learning and creative integration (Ambrosini and Bowman, 2009).

10.6 Dynamic Capabilities and Learning Processes

We discussed in Chapter 5 that learning is a central activity for entrepreneurs, particularly in relationship to opportunity creation. As we note above, Zahra et al. (2006) also suggest that learning processes are central to the development and application of dynamic capabilities, while Bowman and Ambrosini (2003) propose that learning *is* a dynamic capability. However, because most new firms lack their own resources, new venture creators can leverage knowledge and learning from others, including feedback from customers and suppliers (Gibb, 1997; Pittaway et al., 2004) and advice and support from business and personal networks (see Chapter 6) to learn. Network interactions will provide you with many opportunities to engage and reflect on activities and discussions with others and they will provide you with opportunities to consider the relevance of your own firm's processes and routines. While these opportunities will be a valuable resource for you, the key challenge will be to assess whether what you learn is useful and if you can then integrate that learning into your own firm's routines. Moreover, it is not just your attitude to learning that is important. One study of 516 firms found that an organization's learning orientation (the structural and attitudinal approach to support learning) was a key factor in linking dynamic capabilities to firm performance (Mukhtar, Baloch & Khattak, 2019).

Jones and Macpherson (2006), for example, in their case study of three manufacturing firms stress that, if venture owners are to effectively embed and share their learning within the firm, they must create effective communication structures and repeatable routines. There are similar findings by Lans et al. (2008). In their study of 25 small horticulture businesses in the Netherlands, they distinguish between internal and external factors that promote learning. Formal internal communications included team meetings and clear communication lines. Informal communications include opportunities to obtain and provide feedback, trust and attention to cultural differences. External interactions had four elements: traders/buyers, consumers, suppliers and 'experts' (Lans et al. 2008, p. 6–7). In summary, the authors suggest that there are four features crucial to the entrepreneurial learning environment: support and guidance, task characteristics (division of labour), internal communication and external interaction. Also, in a study of the rise of Huawei, the researchers found that the organizations leaders' commitment to learning and innovation were key to underpinning the company's dynamic capabilities (Liang, Xiu, Fang & Wu, 2020). In other words, several studies identify practical activities, attitudes and commitment to learning are necessary for you to adapt consider if you are to develop a response to changes in your firm's environment (Breslin and Jones, 2012).

In a paper that specifically focuses on the importance of learning for dynamic capabilities, Zahra et al. (2006) suggest four distinct learning modes that can be sources of dynamic capabilities within entrepreneurial firms. These are: improvisation, trial and error, experimentation and imitation. They go on to suggest that, particularly in the early years of formation firms are more likely to engage in the first two: improvisation and trial and error (experiential) learning. The argument behind this is that, in the early days an entrepreneur is often dealing with major and minor crises, with limited resources. This means that they are often having to respond quickly with resources immediately available and adopt solutions immediately. These solutions may not be the best option, but only what can be done with limited time and resources. As Baker et al. (2003) note, this can lead to a 'just-in-time' mindset and a commitment to improvisational learning routines; the entrepreneur is constantly reconfiguring 'resources at hand' in the actual act of problem solving. This 'lean start-up' concept is discussed in some depth in Chapter 4. While the improvisation can deliver unplanned (potentially beneficial) organizational outcomes (Miner et al. 2001) in the short term, by using resources that they can redirect or borrow, improvisation and trial and error learning occurs unsystematically. There is no planning for the optimal solution and it seems likely that new firms will use these types of learning routines early in their formation to overcome resource scarcity. In the long-term, however, this improvisational learning might not be a good strategy. As they grow and have access to more resources it will be more important to develop learning opportunities that are structured, such as R&D, new product development, quality management systems and to engage in more formal experimentation (Baker et al. 2003). Zahra and colleagues (2006) suggest that imitation is not affected by age, since it can occur at any point

Table 10.2 Learning Modes and Activities

Learning Mode	Types of Activity
Improvisation and Trail and Error Learning	Problem Solving Responding to Crisis Making Do Experiences
Experimentation	R&D Processes Market Testing
Imitation	Quality Management and Assurance Continuous Improvement Techniques Regulation Compliance

in venture development. For example, venture owners will imitate norms within a sector, in response to accreditation bodies' requirements, based on prior experience within an industry sector, or to comply with exiting regulation. Each of these learning modes requires a change to substantive capabilities, but improvization and trial and error learning seem to be particularly important in the preliminary stages of venture formation (Table 10.2).

Although learning routines, as dynamic capabilities, tend to support renewal, there is a central tension: the balance between exploration of new learning and the exploitation of past learning (March 1991). As firms age, they begin to adopt specific processes, equipment and norms such that they become restricted by their path dependencies (David, 1985). Learning processes can facilitate a renewal of existing routines at the collective level, only if an entrepreneur, or others within the venture, share their individual learning and it becomes institutionalized into new norms, systems and routines (Crossan et al., 1999; Jones and Macpherson, 2006). This means that, while improvisation may lead to a new configuration of resources, this learning must be embedded if long run benefits are to be realized. Unfortunately, improvisation is often a fleeting solution that is adopted for a specific context or issue, and any learning from that event is lost once the issue has been resolved (Miner, et al., 2001). In terms of a dynamic capabilities perspective, systems and routines provide organizational learning and allow integration of learning into new routines (Popper and Lipshitz, 2000), and thus the renewal of existing capabilities. A longer term and more robust solution must be to develop the types of routines that allow for deliberate and structured experimentation, and the sharing of knowledge generated throughout the firm (Box 10.2). However, in all of this, it is worth remembering that if learning is embedded in existing systems and routines, the more rigid and embedded those routines become, they can then also actually block progress. At times, a radical shift from existing practices may be needed to create strategic renewal of your venture and to respond to changing market conditions. Making sense of the changing market environment will be essential to continual survival.

Box 10.2

When stating out, the technical director of PPE Ltd knew what he wanted to achieve in designing a new protection suit, but he did not have the technical materials expertise to do so. To begin with, he contacted a variety of suppliers and experimented with a range of material swatches they sent him, working out through trial and error what might work. Over time he became aware of the properties of different technical materials. He was then able to stipulate the hydrophilic properties of certain types of fibres and to become more specific in his requirements. At the same time, he was experimenting with different ways of 'welding' the materials together to create flexible, but strong, material joins. He developed a unique process for joining the material from which he was then able to create other products such as bespoke containment tenting and different types of suits. In other words, he embedded his trial and error learning within a manufacturing process that provided a new and unique scalable revenue stream.

In summary, because new firms are generally short of resources from which to generate new products and process, routines that support improvisation and experiential learning are likely to be the most common modes of learning that are used to support dynamic capabilities and renew existing capabilities in new ventures (Mukhtar et al., 2019). However, when entrepreneurs embed successful innovation in the firm, tensions between exploration and exploitation are likely to make improvisation less likely as the firm matures. This is because the institutionalization of learning creates path dependencies and rigidities (Leonard-Barton, 1995; David, 1985). As the firm grows, it will be important to develop the types of more formal and structured experimental learning routines. It is also worth remembering that any learning that is embedded in the DNA of the firm might disrupt the resource configurations that created favourable outcomes in the first place (Ambrosini, and Bowman, 2009). The creative aspect of learning can have negative effects on capabilities, but it is also essential to embed and exploit learning effectively for long-term survival of your venture (Jones and Macpherson, 2006). This takes us back to the point made by Penrose (1959), ultimately the success of the venture will likely be down to the knowledge, skills and choices you bring to your venture.

10.7 Bootstrapping and Bricolage: Entrepreneurs Acting Resourcefully

All of the forgoing discussion suggests that the way you as an entrepreneur act, your agency, is most important in understanding dynamic capabilities; any reconfiguration that takes place is fundamentally dependent on how you respond to what you perceive as the most important external changes or opportunities in your business context (Newey & Zahra, 2009). When your venture is newly being formed and small, your influence and decisions are particularly important because you are the principal decision maker. However, as in larger ventures, attitudes become more formalized or entrenched as an operating routine. Miner, Basoff & Moorman (2001) noted that quick responses to changing circumstances depended on improvisational competencies embedded in those organizational routines rather than residing with specific individuals. As Sullivan-Taylor and Branicki (2011, p. 5577) have found, it is important to consider that 'organizational resilience', the ability to bounce back and cope with change or shocks in the environment, is likely to depend on 'key strengths and capabilities already possessed by SMEs'. In other words, resilience and adaptability are developed early in your venture's formation and embedded in specific processes and practices. Baker and Nelson (2005, p. 232) also suggest that the resources available to new firms are idiosyncratic, as is the ability of the firm's principal decision makers to be able to make use of such resources. Therefore, they argue, there are three important implications for entrepreneurs engaged in business start-up:

1. All new firms are unique in their 'idiosyncratic' relationship with the resource environment.

2. There are substantial variations in the ability of such firms to survive even if they have access to 'ostensibly similar resource environments'.

3. Entrepreneurial firms can use resources that are worthless to one organization and make them extremely valuable if they are combined with existing internal knowledge and skills.

What this means is that resources have value only when they are used effectively, in a specific context. Indeed, one recent study suggests that the resources available within a specific spatial context are integrally intertwined with the resourcing strategies employed by the venture owners (Korsgaard, Müller & Welter, 2021). There are clear links here with Sarasvathy's (2001, 2008) articulation of effectuation (discussed in Chapter 12) in which entrepreneur's use the means at their disposal, combined with their ability and characteristics, to shape and exploit contingencies. However, one of the challenges faced by entrepreneurs when responding to changing environmental conditions is significant resource constraints (Brush, 2008) and the resource dispositions available in their immediate context (Korsgaard et al., 2021). The more resources to which you have access (both tangible and intangible), the more opportunities there are shape appropriate responses to changing circumstances.

Obtaining and developing adequate resources remains a key issue for any entrepreneur, but this is especially difficult for new entrepreneurs, and even harder in technology-based new firms that require higher capital investment, and generally longer lead times to get the product to market (Deeds, Decarolis & Coombs, 2000). Indeed, Davidsson, Achtenhagen & Naldi (2007) have demonstrated that low survival rates of new businesses can be attributed to their lack of resources. As noted in Chapter 9, bootstrapping refers to methods by which entrepreneurs access financial capital, but they can also 'bootstrap' other important resources (such as knowledge and information, materials and expertise), that are lacking for most new business ventures (Carter & Van Auken, 2005; Winborg, 2009). All organizations depend on external resources including human, materials, information and knowledge as well as finance. This is accentuated in the case of start-up businesses which are highly resource-deficient compared to their longer established rivals (Baker & Nelson, 2005; Katila & Shane, 2005; Lee, Tüselmann, Jayawarna & Rouse, 2011). Social enterprises and those facing recovery from disasters face particularly resource difficulties in their local context and have been found to create resource communities to help each other and to bootstrap among a network of enterprises (Jayawarna et al., 2020; Sarkar, 2018).

Given that we mentioned earlier it is the intangible resources (knowledge, expertise and experience) that can set ventures apart, as a new venture owner, it is essential to try to establish connections and access to both functional and technical expertise you might be missing. A systematic review of knowledge resources in small firms identifies a range of ways in which both human and social capital can help promote growth (Macpherson & Holt, 2007). By drawing on the experience available from your existing business relationships, prior employment, customer and supplier networks and non-executive directors, you can gain access to those scarce 'intangible' resources *and* tangible resources. This can include technological and managerial skills, information and knowledge and social networks which can then also provide access or the sharing of tangible assets such as labour, office space and equipment (Jenssen & Koenig, 2002). Networks are thus an essential 'means at hand' through which you can access a variety of resources that are either surplus to requirements or discarded by other firms (Baker et al., 2003). In other words, those firms that can bootstrap knowledge, equipment and financial resources may be able to respond more effectively to problems so that they can create opportunities. In short, increasing resource availability or bootstrapping, is an essential precursor to problem solving, particularly when your existing assets are in short supply.

The next step is to apply those untapped resources creatively. In explaining this process, Baker and Nelson (2005) note how entrepreneurs often use physical, social and institutional resources that more established firms disregard. Drawing on work by Lévi-Strauss (1967), Baker and Nelson (2005) adopt the concept of bricolage to suggest that entrepreneurs redefine these resources by enacting alternative practices and routines. Bricolage is, 'making do by applying combinations of resources at hand to new problems and opportunities' and this helps to conceptualize the flexible and innovative adaptation of entrepreneurs using all available resources (Baker and Nelson, 2005, p. 333) and the concept of bricolage fits very well with entrepreneurial activity. In their study, they note that bricolage relies on scavenging resources (bootstrapping) to extract use from goods that others do not value, or do not intend to use. Importantly, entrepreneurs who target this activity at a particular problem (selective bricolage) are more likely to be successful. In other words, while bricolage may provide a way of recombining and reconfiguring resources, entrepreneurs still must integrate the solution into the firm's existing routines if it is to provide long-term benefits. Baker and Nelson (2005) contrast this with 'parallel bricoleurs' who flit between projects depending on customer expectations and obligations. While entrepreneurs might take pride in being able to fashion something from nothing, in parallel bricolage they rarely generate substantial gains from their projects. Notwithstanding the differences between these types of bricolage, they both rely on improvisation, or trial and error learning, in order to create and test solutions; in so doing, resource combinations are broken down and/or reconfigured. In that sense, bricolage helps firms to explore new opportunities that might otherwise be too expensive to investigate by means that are used in more traditional and resource-rich enterprises, such as formal research and development (Miner et al. 2001, Baker and Nelson, 2005). This articulation of bricolage resonates with the dynamic capabilities literature above. Bootstrapping and bricolage can then be two routines that new ventures can develop as nascent dynamic capabilities. Studies have shown that applying bricolage behavior can allow a venture to break out of its path dependencies and to create and effective improvisational strategy to overcome external shocks (Ladstaetter, Plank & Hemetsberger, 2018).

By overcoming resource scarcity, Baker et al. (2003) and Baker and Nelson (2005) argue that entrepreneurs are essentially refusing to accept the resource limitations imposed by their constrained environment. They go on to suggest that resources available do not restrict such entrepreneur's understanding of opportunities. Not only is bricolage an important survival skill, but a study of 2489 Finnish entrepreneurs has shown that those who are passionate about inventing and developing their business are more likely to engage in bricolage (Stenholm & Renko, 2016). They found more 'make-do' behaviors among those firms that had longer survival rates. Resources and opportunities are therefore not an objective limitation but are (re)constructed through entrepreneurial ingenuity. If crises impact on entrepreneurial learning trajectories (Cope, 2005, 2010) and entrepreneurs creatively use resources to solve these crises (Baker and Nelson, 2005), it seems logical that that we need to understand better the routines and activity through which this learning is then realized at the firm level (Jones & Macpherson, 2006; Jones, Macpherson & Thorpe, 2010). Here the distinction noted above between parallel and selective bricolage is crucial. The later connotes an activity where the entrepreneur engages in tackling and learning from a particular problem. If it is to be effective, bricolage requires the entrepreneur to integrate learning outcomes into existing routines and to embed that learning in long-term activities. Entrepreneurial learning (Chapter 5) thus provides the dynamic capabilities to allow the firm to evolve in response to changing contexts (Breslin & Jones, 2012).

We have represented this argument in Figure 10.2. Entrepreneurs can bolster their limited resource base through bootstrapping. This need not be just financial resources, but could be material, knowledge (in the form of expertise), which can be applied to solve problems, or to improvise solutions. In this way, learning routines, such as improvisation and trial and error learning, potentially provide dynamic capabilities that support a reconfiguration of existing resource configurations and capabilities. Once embedded in the firm this creates a new resource base from which the next round of learning can occur. As such, learning routines that support the sharing and institutionalization of new routines from selective bricolage are likely to develop a revised resource base through which entrepreneurial firms deliver new products and services. However, resource reconfigurations over time and with growing success, become path dependencies that make future

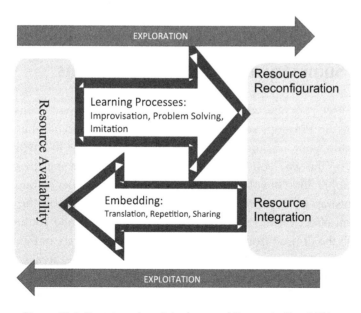

Figure 10.2 Bootstrapping, Bricolage and Dynamic Capabilities

innovations more challenging. It seems, as Zahra (2006) argue, that at this point more structured learning routines, such as experimentation, will be necessary to challenge embedded knowledge and routines.

In summary, in new ventures, the concept of bootstrapping suggests the entrepreneurs engage creatively with others to borrow, share, or appropriate resources. The concept of bricolage suggests that nascent entrepreneurs deploy and integrate resources in novel ways. Thus, bootstrapping and bricolage are potentially key dynamic capabilities that provide opportunities for new firms to enhance the value of external resources by extending and integrating such resources with the firm's limited internal resource base. However, the distinction between parallel and selective bricolage seems crucial. The former is a habituated process of making do and a modus operandi for some entrepreneurs. The latter is a way of targeting problems or opportunities such that entrepreneurs can generate long-run benefits from the solutions they create by embedding the outcomes in new processes and routines. In effect they are learning from their activity and updating knowledge, routines and processes in response to that learning. As indicated above, this view is consistent with conceptualizations of dynamic capabilities, which concentrates on the integration and reconfiguration of internal and external resources in response to environmental change (Teece, 2007; Wu, 2007). New resource configurations potentially provide increased profit, but, over time, they may also become liabilities.

10.8 Summary and Key Learning Points

At the outset, your new venture is likely to have to operate with constrained resources. To develop, your venture you will need to both enhance and reconfigure your resource base. The success is likely to involve and depend on the way you can engage in key activities of improvising the skillful application of your limited resources and any other resources you can bootstrap by networking. Your initial 'blueprint' for your firm has a long-term effect on the way administrative structures and routines will evolve in the firm, so from the outset you need to be aware of the importance of dynamic capabilities. Although research in the area is scarce, we can consider the types of activities that we might define as dynamic capabilities, the types of routines that allow a firm to sense and respond to the market changes and crises to reconfigure their assets for long-term survival and growth. If firms are to make best use of available resources, they need to be alert to changes in the market context and aware of what resource might be available within the firm and its network. This is a very human ability since it relies on your agency and your ability to pay attention to the market, to make decisions and to network. Given your limited resources you must be able to deftly adopt and adapt routines that allow your firm to generate and institutionalize learning gained as you engage in improvissation to cope with problems and opportunities that you encounter. Thus, the concepts of bootstrapping and bricolage highlight the areas in which you can target your activities to gain access to scarce resources and create new resource combinations. This exemplifies a Penrosian view of how firms create idiosyncratic solutions within similar resource and market constraints to create potential. Ultimately, with the same access to resources, it is the skill and capability (intangible resources) that provide competitive advantage.

In summary, the following key points are worth consideration:

- Every new firm's owner(s) have a unique resource base. To survive in the long-term, they will need to make the best use of this resource base, but they will also need to renew and reconfigure it in response to crises and changing market conditions.
- Renewal and reconfiguration require dynamic capabilities, higher-level routines that provide access to, reconfiguration and integration of novel resources. You need to embed these dynamic capabilities at the inception of the firm.
- Changing existing substantive capabilities inevitably involves learning, which in new ventures is most likely to involve, improvization and trial and error processes, although imitation is also a learning routine that can support change.
- Given that resources are likely to be scarce at the outset, the concept of bootstrapping highlights how new venture owners can be creative in sourcing necessary finance, material, information and knowledge, by getting access to and adopting or borrowing resources unused by others to create their solutions.
- Improvization and experiential learning routines can be transitory, but the concept of selective bricolage highlights the importance of embedding and integrating new processes to generate long-term profits and growth.

10.9 Discussion Questions and Call to Action

- What are the key principles of a dynamic capabilities view?
- Why might dynamic capabilities differ in a new firm from a larger, more established firm?
- What types of resources do you have immediately available in your venture and what types of resources might be available in your network?
- Why is networking important activity for both bootstrapping and bricolage?
- Why is learning important for understanding the role of dynamic capabilities in firms?
- How do the concepts of bricolage and improvisation help us to consider the types of dynamic capabilities a new firm might need to develop?

The ability to learn and adapt to changing circumstances, to evolve, is necessary for a firm to survive. In this chapter, we are asking you to consider how you can develop these capabilities very early in the development for your venture. More importantly, perhaps, as the firm grows you also need to pay attention to embedding knowledge capture and sharing, entrepreneurial mindsets and learning processes in the DNA of your firm. It is the commitment to learning that will help to create the types of high-level dynamic capabilities discussed here. This means establishing and maintaining network relationships and encouraging your employees and other stakeholders to do the same. It means inspiring your employees to share their ideas and improvise when necessary. Longer-term survival also means overcoming the various crises you will face in managing a growing business. Learning from the inevitable threats to your business (cashflow crises, lack of skills etc.) and embedding that learning in your firm's routines is essential for creating a resilient organization. Building the appropriate resources is necessary for new firms to survive and grow and those resources are based on the knowledge, skills and abilities of the people associated with your venture. We therefore encourage you to think about what you can do to create an open and innovative approach to managing and developing your venture as it moves from the survival phase to a focus on growth.

References

Ambrosini, V. & Bowman, C. (2009). What are dynamic capabilities and are they a useful construct in strategic management? *International Journal of Management Reviews, 11*(1), 29–49.

Arend, R. (2014). Entrepreneurship and dynamic capabilities: how firm age and size affect the 'capability enhancement-SME performance' relationship. *Small Business Economics, 42*(1), 33–57.

Baker, T., Miner, A. S. & Eesley, D. T. (2003). Improvising Firms: Bricolage, Account Giving and Improvisational Competencies in the Founding Process. *Research Policy, 32*(2), 255–276.

Baker, T. & Nelson, R. E. (2005). Creating Something from Nothing: Resource Construction through Entrepreneurial Bricolage. *Administrative Science Quarterly, 50*, 329–366.

Barney, J. (1991). Firm resources and sustained competitive advantage. *Journal of Management, 17*(1), 99–120.

Baron, J. N., Hannan, M. T. & Burton, M. D. (1999). Building the Iron Cage: Determinants of Managerial Intensity in the Early Years of Organizations. *American Sociological Review, 64*(4), 527–547.

Bowman, C. & Ambrosini, V. (2003). How the Resource-based and the Dynamic Capability Views of the Firm Inform Corporate-level Strategy. *British Journal of Management, 14*, 289–303.

Breslin, D. & Jones, C. (2012). The Evolution of Entrepreneurial Learning. *International Journal of Organizational Analysis, 20*(3), 294–308.

Brush, C. (2008). Pioneering strategies for entrepreneurial success. *Business Horizons, 51*, 21–27.

Carter, N., Gartner, W. & Reynolds, P. (1996). Exploring Start-up event sequences. *Journal of Business Venturing, 11*(3), 151–166.

Carter, R. B. & Van Auken, H. (2005). Bootstrap financing and owners' perceptions of their business constraints and opportunities. *Entrepreneurship & Regional Development, 17*(2), 129–144.

Chirico, F. & Nordqvist, M. (2010). Dynamic capabilities and trans-generational value creation in family firms: The role of organizational culture. *International Small Business Journal, 28*(5), 487–504.

Colombo, M. G., Piva, E., Quas, A. & Rossi-Lamastra, C. (2021). Dynamic capabilities and high-tech entrepreneurial ventures' performance in the aftermath of an environmental jolt. *Long Range Planning, 54*(3). doi:10.1016/j.lrp.2020.102026

Cope, J. (2005). Towards a dynamic learning perspective of entrepreneurship. *Entrepreneurship Theory and Practice, 29*(4), 373–397.

Cope, J. (2010). Entrepreneurial learning from failure: An interpretive phenomeno-logical analysis. *Entrepreneurship Theory and Practice*, 26, 604–623.

Crossan, M. M., Lane, H. W. & White, R. E. (1999). An Organizational Learning Framework: From Intuition to Institution. *Academy of Management Review*, 24(3), 522–537.

David, P. (1985). Clio and the Economics of Qwerty. *American Economic Review*, 75(2), 332–337.

Davidsson, P., Achtenhagen, L. & Naldi, L. (2007). What Do We Know About Small Firm Growth? In S. Parker (Ed.), *The Life Cycle of Entrepreneurial Ventures* (pp. 361–398). Boston: Springer.

Deeds, D. L., Decarolis, D. & Coombs, J. (2000). Dynamic capabilities and new product development in high technology ventures: An empirical analysis of new biotechnology firms. *Journal of Business Venturing*, 15(3), 211–229.

Dyer, J. & Singh, H. (1998). The relational view: cooperative strategy and sources of interorganizational competitive advantage. *Academy of Management Review*, 23(4), 660–679.

Easterby-Smith, M., Lyles, M. & Peteraf, M. (2009). Dynamic Capabilities: Current Debates and Future Directions. *British Journal of Management*, 20(SI), S1–8.

Easterby-Smith, M. & Prieto, I. (2008). Dynamic Capabilities and Knowledge Management: an Integrative Role for Learning. *British Journal of Management*, 19(3), 235–249.

Eisenhardt, K. & Martin, J. (2000). Dynamic capabilities: what are they? *Strategic Management Journal*, 21(10&11), 1105–1121.

Foss, N. J., Klein, P. G., Kor, Y. Y. & Mahoney, J. T. (2008). Entrepreneurship, sub-jectivism, and the resource-based view: toward a new synthesis. *Strategic Entrepreneurship Journal*, 2(1), 73–94.

Gatewood, E., Shaver, K. & Gartner, W. (1995). A longitudinal study of cognitive factors influencing start-up behaviors and success at venture creation. *Journal of Business Venturing*, 10, 371–391.

Gibb, A. (1997). Small Firms' Training and Competitiveness: Building upon the Small Firm as a Learning Organization. *International Small Business Journal*, 15(3), 13–29.

Granovetter, M. S. (1973). The Strength of Weak Ties. *American Journal of Sociology*, 78(6), 1360–1380.

Hernandez, A. K. L., Fernandez-Mesa, A. & Edwards-Schachter, M. (2018). Team collaboration capabilities as a factor in startup success. *Journal of Technology Management & Innovation*, 13(4), 13–22.

Jayawarna, D., Jones, O. & Macpherson, A. (2020). Resourcing Social Enterprises: The Role of Socially Oriented Bootstrapping. *British Journal of Management*, 31(1), 56–79.

Jenssen, J. I. & Koenig, H. F. (2002). The Effect of Social Networks on Resource Access and Business Start-ups. *European Planning Studies*, 10(8), 1039–1046.

Jones, O., Ghobadian, A., O'Regan, N. & Antcliff, V. (2013). Dynamic capabilities in a sixth-generation family firm: Entrepreneurship and the Bibby Line. *Business History*, *55*(6), 910–941.

Jones, O. & Macpherson, A. (2006). Inter-organizational Learning and Strategic Renewal in SMEs: Extending the 4I Network. *Long Range Planning*, *39*(2), 155–175.

Jones, O., Macpherson, A. & Thorpe, R. (2010). Learning in owner-managed small firms: Mediating artefacts and strategic space. *Entrepreneurship and Regional Development*, *22*(7/8), 649–673.

Katila, R. & Shane, S. (2005). When does lack of resources make new firms innovative? *Academy of Management Journal*, *48*(5), 814–829.

Kevill, A., Trehan, K. & Easterby-Smith, M. (2017). Perceiving 'capability' within dynamic capabilities: The role of owner-manager self-efficacy. *International Small Business Journal: Researching Entrepreneurship*, *35*(8), 883–902.

Korsgaard, S., Müller, S. & Welter, F. (2021). It's right nearby: how entrepreneurs use spatial bricolage to overcome resource constraints. *Entrepreneurship & Regional Development*, *33*(1/2), 147–173.

Ladstaetter, F., Plank, A. & Hemetsberger, A. (2018). The merits and limits of making do: bricolage and breakdowns in a social enterprise. *Entrepreneurship & Regional Development*, *30*(3/4), 283–309.

Lans, T., Biemans, H., Verstegen, J. & Mulder, M. (2008). The influence of the work environment on entrepreneurial learning of small business owners, *Management Learning*, *39*(5), 597–614.

Lee, R., Tüselmann, H., Jayawarna, D. & Rouse, J. (2011). Investigating the social capital and resource acquisition of entrepreneurs residing in deprived areas of England. *Environment & Planning C: Government & Policy*, *29*(6), 1054–1072.

Leonard-Barton, D. (1995) *Wellsprings of Knowledge: Building and Sustaining the Sources of Innovation*. Boston MA: Harvard Business School Press.

Lévi-Strauss, C. (1967). *The Savage Mind*. Chicago: University of Chicago Press.

Liang, X., Xiu, L., Fang, W. & Wu, S. (2020). How did a local guerrilla turn into a global gorilla? Learning how transformational change happened under dynamic capabilities from the rise of Huawei. *Journal of Organizational Change Management*, *33*(2), 401–414.

Lichtenstein, B. M. B. & Brush, C. G. (2001). How do 'resource bundles' develop and change in New Ventures? A dynamic model and longitudinal exploration. *Entrepreneurship: Theory and Practice*, *25*(3), 37–59.

Lockett, A., Thompson, S. & Morgenstern, U. (2009). The Development of the Resource-Based View of the Firm: a Critical Appraisal. *International Journal of Management Reviews*, *11*(1), 9–28.

Macpherson, A., Herbane, B. & Jones, O. (2015). Developing dynamic capabilities through resource accretion: expanding the entrepreneurial solution space. *Entrepreneurship & Regional Development*, *27*(5/6), 259–291.

Macpherson, A. & Holt, R. (2007). Knowledge, learning and small firm growth: A systematic review of the evidence. *Research Policy*, *36*, 172–192.

Macpherson, A., Jones, O. & Zhang, M. (2004). Evolution or revolution? Dynamic capabilities in a knowledge-dependent firm. *R & D Management*, *34*(2), 161–177.

Miner, A. S., Bassoff, P. & Moorman, C. (2001). Organizational Improvisation and Learning: A Field Study. *Administrative Science Quarterly*, *46*(2), 304–337.

Mukhtar, M. A., Baloch, N. A. & Khattak, S. R. (2019). Dynamic Capability & Firm Performance: Mediating Role Of Learning Orientation, Organizational Culture & Corporate Entrepreneurship: A Case Study Of Sme's Of Pakistan. *Journal of Managerial Sciences*, *13*(3), 119–128.

Newbert, S. (2005). New Firm Formation: A Dynamic Capability Perspective. *Journal of Small Business Management*, *43*(1), 55–77.

Newey, L. R. & Zahra, S. A. (2009). The Evolving Firm: How Dynamic and Operating Capabilities Interact to Enable Entrepreneurship. *British Journal of Management*, *20*, S81–S100.

Penrose, E. T. (1959). *The Theory of the Growth of the Firm*. Oxford: Basil Blackwell.

Pfeffer, J. & Salancik, G. (1978). *The External Control of Organizations*. New York: Harper and Row.

Pittaway, L., Robertson, M., Munir, K., Denyer, D. & Neely, A. (2004). Networking and innovation: A systematic review of the literature. *International Journal of Management Reviews*, *5/6*(3/4): 211–233.

Popper, M. & Lipshitz, R. (2000). Organizational learning: Mechanisms, culture and feasibility. *Management Learning*, *31*(2), 181-196.

Reynolds, P. D. & White, S. B. (1997). *The Entrepreneurial Process. Economic Growth, Men, Women, and Minorities*. Westport, CT: Quorum Books.

Salge, T. O. & Vera, A. (2013). Small Steps that Matter: Incremental Learning, Slack Resources and Organizational Performance. *British Journal of Management*, *24*(2), 156–173.

Sarasvathy, S. (2001). Causation and effectuation: towards a theoretical shift from economic inevitability to entrepreneurial contingency. *Academy of Management Review*, *26*(2), 243–263.

Sarasvathy, S. (2008). *Effectuation: elements of entrepreneurial expertise*. Cheltenham: Edward Elgar.

Sarkar, S. (2018). Grassroots entrepreneurs and social change at the bottom of the pyramid: the role of bricolage. *Entrepreneurship & Regional Development*, *30*(3/4), 421–449.

Stenholm, P. & Renko, M. (2016). Passionate bricoleurs and new venture survival. *Journal of Business Venturing*, *31*(5), 595–611.

Storey, D. J. (2011). Optimism and chance: The elephants in the entrepreneurship room *International Small Business Journal*, *29*(4), 303–321.

Sullivan-Taylor, B. & Branicki, L. (2011). Creating resilient SMEs: why one size might not fit all. *International Journal of Production Research*, *49*(18), 5565–5579.

Teece, D. (2007). Explicating dynamic capabilities: the nature and microfoundations of (sustainable) enterprise performance. *Strategic Management Journal*, *28*(13), 1319–1350.

Teece, D., Pisano, G. & Shuen, A. (1997). Dynamic Capabilities and Strategic Management. *Strategic Management Journal*, *18*(7), 509–533.

Weaven, S., Quach, S., Thaichon, P., Frazer, L., Billot, K. & Grace, D. (2021). Surviving an economic downturn: Dynamic capabilities of SMEs. *Journal of Business Research*, *128*, 109–123.

Winborg, J. (2009). Use of financial bootstrapping in new businesses: a question of last resort? *Venture Capital*, *11*(1), 71–83.

Wu, L. (2007). Entrepreneurial resources, dynamic capabilities and start-up performance of Taiwan's high-tech firms. *Journal of Business Research*, *60*, 549–555.

Zahra, S. A., Sapienza, H. & Davidsson, P. (2006). Enterpreneurship and Dynamic Capabilities: A Review, Model and Research Agenda. *Journal of Management Studies*, *43*(4), 917–955.

Zhang, M., Macpherson, A. & Jones, O. (2006). Conceptualizing the Learning Process in SMEs: Improving Innovation through External Orientation. *International Small Business Journal*, *24*(3), 299–323.

Zollo, M. & Winter, S. G. (2002). Deliberate Learning and the Evolution of Dynamic Capabilities. *Organization Science*, *13*, 339–351.

11 Growing New Businesses

11.1 Introduction

Once you have established your business, at some point it is likely that you may choose to grow the firm. Some new firms grow quickly but others, the majority, remain small. Understanding why this is the case has been a key issue in entrepreneurship research (Brush, Ceru & Blackburn, 2009). Also, it is a policy concern since national and supranational organizations consider small firm growth as a priority for sustaining the economy. Indeed, as we were writing this chapter the Chancellor of the Exchequer in the UK, Rishi Sunak, announced a £520 million Help to Grow Scheme for small businesses. The way policy makers understand and respond to the challenge, particularly for new firms, is discussed in detail in Chapter 13. In this Chapter, however, we concentrate on what the research tells us about how firms grow from inception.

Historically, there have been several theories of firm growth that focus on key transition points, or stages, where timely changes to resources and structures are required to develop the firm to continue their growth trajectory. Indeed, some stage models of growth now focus specifically on the stages of development for managing a social media business profile (Duane & O'Reilly, 2017), or engaging with customers relations management via Twitter (Yahav, Schwartz & Welcman, 2020). While stage model theories have face validity, some researchers have expressed concern that the evidence to support the theories is limited. There are criticisms that the underlying constructs lack any consensus, and that empirical confirmation of such models is inconclusive, at best (Levie & Lichtenstein, 2010). Rather than providing a useful tool to analyse transition states of firms, some argue

DOI: 10.4324/9781003312918-12

such models provide little explanatory power (Phelps, Adams & Bessant, 2007). Nevertheless, the idea of 'transition points' suggest that, as the firm grows, you will be faced with new challenges, or crises, in how you manage your firm's day-to-day operations. In other words, how successfully you respond to these challenges (getting resources through networks or innovating processes) will be crucial for survival. Growing a firm means you frequently must learn to do new things (Macpherson, 2005). The data on firm birth and death rates analysed by Anyadike Danes & Hart (2018) highlight a significant amount of 'churn' among new firms as many are established and die quite quickly (discussed further in Chapter 13). This means that, for new firms being responsive and innovative will be essential for you to deal with new challenges or crises to continue to grow. Paradoxically, the faster you grow, the faster you will need to adapt to new circumstances and to deal with crises this creates (Nicholls-Nixon, 2005).

As well as challenges, these crises, or tipping points, provide opportunities, if firms can embed and share learning across the firm (Jones, Macpherson & Thorpe, 2010). A crisis-based view of growth proposes that they are a day-to-day challenge for you and your senior team (Herbane, 2010; Macpherson, 2005). Such a dynamic view of growth recognizes that activities, resources and strategies are constantly evolving (Levie & Lichtenstein, 2010; Phelps et al., 2007), and that your current configuration of resources and processes will be your best efforts to match your current organizational capabilities to the market and customer demands. This means you will be facing a constant challenge to consider your potential to grow alongside a multi-level struggle for survival, one that requires a continual evolution of knowledge components, such as skill, competences, frameworks and routines (Breslin & Jones, 2012). To do so you will need to be sensitive to changing contexts and, probably more importantly, be willing to reflect on current practices and change if necessary. Fundamentally, if your firm is to survive and grow, it will be important to 'learn to learn' (Gartner, 1985) and embed dynamic learning into organizational routines to ensure that you can exploit tangible and intangible assets over the long term (see Chapter 10). So, it is not just resource appropriation that defines innovative capacity to grow, but resource integration and application (Cohen & Levinthal, 1990). In this chapter, we briefly review the legacy of business growth models, before exploring a more dynamic view of growth and suggesting growth involves continuous adaptation; crises are likely to recur and intensify during periods of growth.

11.2 Learning Objectives

- To review the contribution of traditional stage models of growth.
- To provide a more nuanced understanding of the processes that support growth.
- To explore an understanding of growth as a dynamic learning process.
- To explore the importance of institutionalizing learning to realize growth potential in a new venture.

11.3 Stages of Growth and Linear Growth Trajectories

As we have discussed in several other chapters, the link between management competences and growth is a legacy of Penrose's (1959) seminal text *The Theory of the Growth of the Firm*. For Penrose, growth is closely related to the processes through which entrepreneurs obtain and use knowledge. A shortfall in available suitable resources and/or managerial competences effectively undermine your firm's ability to grow (Goffee & Scase, 1995). Phase models of growth, normally representing several sequential periods through which a firm will develop, also highlight the role of knowledge resources in managing organizational growth (for example, Churchill & Lewis, 1983; Greiner, 1972; Scott & Bruce, 1987). Each of these models has a different conceptualization of growth, but they all generally discuss the accumulation of organizational resources and capabilities *in relation to the age and size of the firm*. In essence, such models highlight the difficulties a growing firm is likely to encounter at specific point in its growth curve and suggests a solution for you to apply to move on to the next phase of your business development. Primarily what these models suggest is that growth involves a predictable sequence of events. These models identify resource dependencies – physical, financial and human – that you will need to deal with at transition points if your firm is to grow successfully. Continued evolution or growth of your firm will depend on your ability to create the appropriate systems and processes to exploit opportunities and to move on to the next stage in your growth curve (Chandler, 1977).

While findings do suggest that age and size are related to growth and survival (Anyadike-Danes & Hart, 2018), a review of growth theories by Levie and Lichtenstein (2010) identified 104 different stage models in academic literature published between 1962 and 2006. They note these models continue to proliferate, and that the phases or stages of growth vary between three and six. Such models propose that each firm goes through identifiable points where transition is necessary to reach 'the next level' (Phelps et al., 2007). Consequently, at each stage of development firms will have to face and resolve similar problems. For example, Churchill and Lewis (1983, p42) note that 'issues of people, planning and systems gradually increase in importance as the company progresses from slow initial growth'. Burns (1996) defines four stages as existence, survival, success and take-off. During each of these phases, different strategies, management approaches, structures, marketing, accounting and finance models are necessary to sustain each phase of development. Stage or linear models thus imply that firms grow in a predictable way and that you should be able to diagnose a particular resource or systems deficiency at a specific stage in their development cycle and apply the appropriate solution.

Levie and Lichtenstein (2010) note that, while none of the models have gained theoretical primacy, perhaps the most influential model is the five-phase model of firm evolution and revolution provided by Greiner (1972). In this model, Greiner (1972) argues that the organizational systems that support the growth of the firm will eventually limit expansion. To continuing growing, entrepreneurs will have to implement new organizational systems. Greiner's linear model proposes organizational structures will go through phases of change as the firm ages and grows and that new co-ordination mechanisms will be essential to do so:

> each evolutionary period is characterized by the dominant *management style* used to achieve growth, while each revolutionary period is characterized by the dominant *management problem* that must be solved before growth can continue.
>
> (ibid, p40, original italics)

The crisis stages and their solution are included in Table 11.1. His main point is that while the firm is growing successfully this legitimates the dominant management approach at that time and the institutionalization of procedures, processes and rules. When this approach begins to fail, as it inevitably will, then a new organizational paradigm will be essential. Entrepreneurs will need to 'revolutionize' existing systems to enter the next

Table 11.1 Greiner's Growth Phases and Their Solutions

Growth Phase	Crisis
Creativity (implementing the new idea)	**Leadership** (the firm grows beyond the leadership capacity to manage informally)
Direction (the professionalization of management systems)	**Autonomy** (the systems become too complex for the capacity of the owner to manage)
Delegation (the responsibility for systems is devolved to middle managers)	Control (as the firm grows overview systems are required to monitor activity
Co-ordination (systems are designed to incentivize and manage performance in different business units)	**Bureaucracy** (the proliferation of systems stifles adaptability and responsiveness)
Collaboration (restructuring and development of a culture and systems to support cross functional and project work)	**Internal Growth** (limited internal capacity of the firm to achieve higher growth)
Alliances (engagement with consultants, alliances, mergers, networks and outsourcing)	

phase of growth. The length of time between evolutionary and revolutionary stages will depend on growth rate within the industry. To grow, Greiner argues that these new systems will inevitably fail and cause problems in the future and so on. Greiner updated his original model in 1998. He now proposes that the revolutionary phases may not be clean breaks; legacy systems may overlap between periods of evolution. He also alludes to the role of consultants in the later phases of evolution to provide new ideas, new knowledge resources, to facilitate the organizational revolution, since solutions to the crises involved in the latter stages of growth may lie outside of the organization (Greiner, 1998).

Stage models conceptualize management transitions as requiring access to specific knowledge resources that will solve predictable crises;

resource saliency will change depending on which crisis is being managed. In addition, stage models recognize that your previous experience will limit the available managerial and entrepreneurial resources, which can create barriers for change: '[h]olding onto old strategies and old ways ill serves a company that is entering the growth stages and can even be fatal' (Churchill & Lewis, 1983, pp 44–48). This suggests a paradoxical reliance on knowledge resources for growth. If management knowledge resources are fundamental to restructuring for growth, entrepreneurs in the early stages of firm inception are particularly vulnerable and may not be able to achieve transitions due to limited resources (Goffee & Scase, 1995). This seems to hold true as it has been found that business accelerators, which provide ready access to networks and resources, are a particularly useful tool in the development pipeline of firms in the early stages of venture development (Shu, Kher & Lyons, 2018) However, in later stages are still vulnerable as investment in past practices sets knowledge in organizational routines that create rigidities that are a challenge to change to new demands (David, 1985; Leonard-Barton, 1995). What is common in these phase models is that they identify the importance of watershed moments where management *must* alter their approach during transition periods. They also note to be successful during this transition period you will need additional resources in order to do so (Bessant, Phelps & Adams, 2005). Table 11.2 compares the two models and their transition points.

What stage theories do is exemplify Penrose's (1959) argument that increases in knowledge resources and managerial capacity are essential for managing growth. Greiner's (1972) model, for example, has three essential similarities to Penrose's theory. They both suggest that:

1. Systems of organizing are essential for the application of resources to achieve growth.
2. Entrepreneurial or managerial capabilities are fundamental resources that define the systems implemented.
3. Innovation to structures and systems are needed to both renew the organizational resources and to make best use of them.

While Greiner and other 'stage models' acknowledge that managerial competence and knowledge are important for enacting suitable organizational systems, they do not explore how these knowledge resources are acquired or

Table 11.2 Growth Stage Models and Processes

Churchill and Lewis (1983)		Scott and Bruce (1987)	
Stage	Key Challenges and Activities	Growth	Key Challenges and Activities
Existence	Owner manages everything and relies on close contacts for help.	Inception	Obtaining customers and demand placed on time and finances.
Survival	Simple organization with key challenge of managing cash flow – costs and revenues.	Survival	Balancing budgets and managing increasing complexity.
Success	Firm is managing cash flow and becomes more professional with established delegated management functions and appropriate systems.	Growth	Securing necessary resources, dealing with threats from competition, developing product portfolio.
Take off	Push for growth requires further access to finance and the ability to delegate and manage an increasingly complex organization	Expansion	Securing finance for growth and maintaining internal control. Maintaining market awareness.
Maturity	Owner has accumulated the financial, human, system and business resources necessary to trade effectively. Requires strategic abilities to look for future opportunities and threats.	Maturity	Managing expenses and productivity. Sustaining relevance of product portfolio.

altered during the transition period. What is not clear also is how managers are convinced of the need to innovate and change, or how they might identify and incorporate new knowledge. In Box 11.1 is a vignette that outlines the challenges an owner faced with incorporating the necessary new knowledge to move to 'just-in-time' production to sustain his growing business. What is interesting is the finding that business accelerators are particularly helpful in the early stages of a venture, since they provide access to knowledge and resources that would otherwise be difficult to achieve (Shu et al., 2018).

Box 11.1 Complex Crises of Co-ordination, Control and Leadership

Tony was a packaging manufacturer who provided packaging solutions for large corporate clients and small businesses. He set up the firm and was quickly successful in establishing a reputation for cost effective products and he grew the business quickly. He outgrew his premises, but was lucky when he heard a local competitor with larger premises was going out of business. He managed to buy out the failing firm and transferred his operations. However, as the business expanded he ran into further trouble. He quickly exceeded the storage capacity of his new premises and, although he knew about just in time production scheduling, he commented: 'I know the theory, but I have never done it and that would be really scary. It could be a real mess'. He struggled on and chose to cut his overheads to offset extra costs of material and product storage, by making some staff redundant. He also had some legacy human resource issues since he had hired new staff on different contracts to his old staff which was causing friction. Rather than replace his retiring salesman, he also took this job on as well as managing the company. Despite growth in employment and turnover, his gross value added per employee reduced. At one point he commented:

> Short-term, it's like we're in a hell of a lot of trouble. We've over-sold and we can't get the stuff out and we've got staff problems, production planning, we've got maintenance planning, distribution planning, storage and all of those are almighty great problems really

Tony was unable to recover from the multiple, human resource, production and operational crises he faced and went out of business six months later.

11.4 Critical Reflections on Stage Models

One of the key underpinning theoretical assumptions is that stage models are generally applicable to all growing firms. As noted above, however, Levie and Lichtenstein (2010), in their extensive review of 104 stage models, could not find a common template. Perhaps more concerning is the fact that when these theories have been tested (Birch, 1987; Birch, Haggerty & Parsons, 1995; Tushman, Newman & Romanelli, 1986) supporting evidence was very weak and did not validate stage model theories of growth. Perhaps particularly telling for understanding new ventures and their growth trajectories, McCann (1991) noted in his study of 100 high-tech firms that there was no predictable pattern of growth. A more recent study found that, while age and size do bear some relationship to survival and growth, this was not at a level that provides the ability to predict which firms would do so (Anyadike-Danes & Hart, 2018). More importantly perhaps, McCann (1991) also suggested that new ventures were able to make several choices at numerous different points in their development that influenced their growth trajectories and thus growth trajectories are also unpredictable. Thus, while stages of growth or transition points might be evident through large-scale analyses of such theories, they do not provide support a general model (Levie & Lichtenstein, 2010).

The Scott and Bruce (1987) model, which was initially developed though empirical research in the US in the 1970s, can only reflect the environmental influences that were present when the study was conducted. Even if the model were valid at that time, it would only be relevant in similar contexts. So, for example, structures of social capital are more formal in the German economic context than they are in the UK or US, and this will influence engagement with external knowledge resources to manage transitions (Spence & Schmidpeter, 2003). In China, the concept of Guanxi is important for appropriating resources and establishing firm legitimacy but is not appropriate for understanding growth in other contexts. In the US, Renski (2009) notes significant differences in growth trajectories depending on locations of firms in rural, suburban and urban environments, due to differences in market and resource opportunities. However, different types of new firm enjoy more growth potential (high-tech firms in particular) due to knowledge spillovers from clustering (Maine, Shapiro & Vining, 2010), or from an urban environment depending on if they are service rather than manufacturing firms (Raspe & Oort, 2011). While geography will have a significant impact, then also sector and entrepreneurial ecosystems will influence the potential for growth trajectories also (Shu et al., 2018). In other words, context is a significant factor that influences growth trajectories and growth strategies.

One of the things that has made stage models of growth so enduring is that they have significant face validity (Levie & Lichtenstein, 2010); most entrepreneurs can easily identify with the problems or crises they highlight, and indeed the solutions. Stage models are still included in almost every entrepreneurship textbook since they provide a helpful way of describing the challenges of developing a growing firm (Burns, 2007). However, despite their intuitive appeal, their underpinning assumptions that firm growth is sequential, predictable and universal has been increasingly scrutinized (Bessant et al., 2005). Emerging theoretical directions in entrepreneurial development attend to issues of ecology and focus primarily on how individual entrepreneurs make sense of the environment in which they are located (Breslin, 2008; Dutta & Crossan, 2005; Gregorio & Shane, 2003; Kitila & Shane, 2005; Sarasvathy, 2001, 2008). Contemporary research recognizes that analysis of entrepreneurial activity must appreciate the uneven distribution in society of knowledge and information (Shane, 2000), of reputation and ties to potential investors (Di Gregorio & Shane, 2003), and of market conditions (Kitila & Shane, 2005). Indeed, a study in the Caribbean found that one thing that marked out growing firms from others was approach and leadership of the owner, and their ability to develop significant networks, which allowed them access to more resources when managing growth (Williams & Ramdani, 2018). Thus, a condition of the entrepreneurial experience is the uneven access to resources and the fluidity of markets and potential opportunities creating different environments over time. Perhaps what is most striking about the entrepreneurial experience is a search for and recognition of how assets can be reconfigured to make the most of particular circumstances (Schumpeter, 1934). Taken together, this means that the process of firm evolution is dependent very much on responses to changing contexts, and that simple generalizations of stages of growth are likely to miss the dynamic and unpredictable nature of managing a growing firm (Breslin, 2008). Put simply, your challenges may not be unique in terms of requirements for knowledge, resources, personnel and markets, but your response to challenges or crises as you grow will very much be dependent on your own context, circumstances and opportunities.

11.5 Making Sense of Crisis in Context

Given the unpredictable nature of the economic environment and the uneven availability of resources, generalizing about phases of growth and specifics regarding resources needed should be done with great care. A study in China of 238 new high-tech firms, for example, found that the uneven availability of resources influenced the growth strategies adopted and achieved by these firms (Chen, Zou & Wang, 2009). This theme is taken up by Lichtenstein et al. (2006) who argue that although emergence or growth may be punctuated by significant events (such as crises noted by Greiner), the way entrepreneurs make sense of those events is crucial in determining the actions they take to resolve them. Rather than rational opportunity analysis, how your firm copes with the crisis or challenge is dependent on how you make sense out of what is happening, the process you put in place to cope, and the resources you available to act. All things are not equal, and your context and abilities will be a defining factor when coping. As Aldrich (1999, p40) notes, organizations are influenced by many forces, including:

> the competencies carried by experienced members, accumulated understandings within a work group, competitive and cooperative pressures from a population, and normative and regulatory obligations from a community and society.

He argues responses to uncertain situations are thus beyond the simple actions of the entrepreneur, and social norms and influential agents in effect construct the opportunities and the trajectory of a firm's evolution (Figure 11.1). Or to put it more simply, this means that firm growth is a more contextually sensitive process, rather than a predictable sequence of emergence events (Breslin, 2008).

Dodge, Fullerton & Robbins (1994) argue that, while crises act as focal points for action during transition, they do not occur in a predictable sequence. They suggest that crises occur and reoccur over time, are dependent on the state of the market, and can be both internal and external. Herbane (2010) takes a crisis management perspective to small businesses and argues that, when managing crises, both soft and hard systems interact with the internal and external environment in unpredictable ways to cause 'interruptions'. In dealing with these interruptions, the entrepreneur has

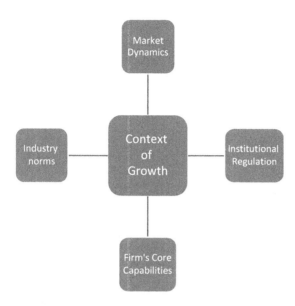

Figure 11.1 Growth in Contexts

limited resources and their responses are personalized, continuous and focused on a limited set of threats. Managing growth from a crisis perspective must recognize the dynamic, personal and active nature of coping (Cope, 2010). Moreover, to grow it is likely that a new firm will have to resolve recurring and concurrent crises across the full range of organizational activities rather than dealing with discrete problems and particular points in stages during a growth trajectory (Macpherson, 2005). Again, simply put, crises are unpredictable, and you will likely be dealing with similar crises repeatedly as the firm grows.

In addition, growth is not linear, but can be punctuated by growth spurts, plateaus or even regression depending on a number of factors such as fluctuations in the market, the skill of the management in dealing with crises and the availability of financial and other resources (Brush et al., 2009). If we take a more contextually sensitive approach to firm evolution, exactly what resources or capabilities are required for growth may be dependent on the specific challenges the firm's management is having to negotiate: 'growth and survival are inextricably linked to channelling organizational perceptions of the task environment' (Dodge et al., 1994, p131). Or, to put it another way, while crises occur during a firm's growth, their nature and solution is dependent on the context, the available experience embedded in organizational systems that sustain current activity and on relationships that provide access to alternative experience through business or social networks (see Chapters 2 and 6). Moreover, given that the environment will be constantly in flux and unpredictable, this means understanding the processes that support a dynamic view of growth (see also Chapter 10) might be a more fruitful undertaking rather than trying to identify a particular stage of transition.

11.6 Managing Growth Dynamically

What is clear from the review of stage models, and the empirical evidence, is that firms do operate in periods of relative stability. They also go through periods of flux when the operating systems and structures are incrementally or significantly revised (Levie & Lichtenstein, 2010). What is also clear is that these transitions are not predictable. Nevertheless, what may be common in all the growth models is that they identify crisis and crisis management as a function of managing growth transitions (Macpherson, 2005; Phelps et al., 2007). Dodge et al. (1994) suggest seven core crises that exist regardless of stage: customer networks, competition, leadership, financial management, organizational structures, organizational systems and human resources. They argue that managers perceive problems and then embed problem solutions in the institution, which guides future decisions. In a similar vein, Phelps et al. (2007) identify six key routines, or practices, that influence the trajectory of a growing firm:

1. People management (a focus on delegation, leadership, recruitment and training);

2. Strategy (the need to develop a more focused approach or alternative strategy);

3. Formalized systems (crucial to shift from informal approaches to data collection and knowledge acquisition to implementation of formal systems);

4. New market entry (the need to identify new customers and new areas through the modification of existing products and/or introduction of new products);

5. Obtaining finance (accessing external finance is central to effective growth in all SMEs);

6. Operational improvement (understanding process capabilities and best practices for such operations as sales, marketing, production etc.).

They argue that, at some point, and in no specific order, firms will approach a crisis, or 'tipping point' in one or all these key knowledge areas. They will have to address flaws in their current template of operations to continue to grow. Which part of their operations and how they adopt a solution will be dependent on context. In that regard, they will require access to resources and need to integrate new knowledge into their routines and develop new practices to overcome their difficulties (Khattak & Ullah, 2021). That knowledge and expertise is often not available inside the firm but may be available in their network. A study in Ireland, for example suggests that investors can bring professional expertise to help managing growing problems that cause personnel issues (Di Pietro, Monaghan & O'Hagan-Luff, 2022). These contributions draw on the work of Cohen and Levinthal (1990), since they effectively argue that solutions will depend on the 'absorptive capacity' of the firm: the ability to access, recognize, and integrate the appropriate knowledge to provide solutions. For example, an owner's previous experience in supply-chain management in a large manufacturing firm might be useful in searching for a solution when overcoming supply shortages or in developing lean manufacturing protocols to improve efficiency and reduce costs in their own firm. Had the owner of the Packaging Company discussed in Box 11.1 had that experience, or had access to someone who did, his firm might have had a better chance of survival. In managing such a crisis, if they do not have the expertise themselves, it might be available from their business network, or from relationships they had developed previously. In a different context, growing internationally, having access to those with prior experience of international business is shown to be a key criteria for managing this type of growth effectively (D'Angelo & Presutti, 2019).

Levie and Lichtenstein (2010) make similar arguments in their recent critique of the stage models of growth. In proposing a 'dynamic states' model, they recognize that firms do go through transition points, but argue that, the current 'state' of the firm represents management's attempts to provide the most efficient and effective organizational solutions to meet the challenges faced in the market and customer expectations – *at that time*. Since dynamic states (aim to) reflect an optimal relationship between the firm's business model and its environment, and since both sides of the equation can technically change *ad infinitem*, there can be any number of dynamic states in an organization's existence. Each solution can develop continually into any number of 'states' rather than go through a predictable sequence of stages, depending on how dynamic is the context in which the firm operates. In Box 11.2 is an example of an owner using his network resources to transition his firm into the next dynamic state.

Box 11.2 Overcoming a Crisis of Capacity

When he was setting up his fitness business Jerry spent some time establishing a clientele as a personal trainer, developing a network and reputation. However, he recognized that his business lacked the capacity to expand since he was the only fitness instructor and he did not have the time or resources to take the business to the next level. He was managing to survive, but he could not find a way to grow the business. He knew he lacked both the financial and business experience to convince the banks to lend him money and he did not have time to spend searching for premises or developing the business because all his time was spent running classes. He contacted an old school friend who he thought might be interested in investing in the business. Together they created a business plan and bought a gym in the local area that had been struggling for some time. With the new partner able to take care of the financial, infrastructure and marketing side of the business, Jerry was able to concentrate on the operational side, the delivery of classes and the hiring of instructors. His previous reputation and networks helped to establish a regular clientele quickly enough to ensure regular turnover. By solving his crisis, Jerry was able to grow the business, but his solution depended very much on the local network, extra resources and business acumen from his business partner and his own reputation.

Solutions, or developing appropriate 'states', will require access to salient resources such as finance, knowledge and experience. Firms that are more proactive and vigilant in identifying salient resources in their network are more successful in growing their business (Khattak & Ullah, 2021). For example, in addressing this issue of resource saliency, Lichtenstein and Brush (2001) conducted a study of three growing high-technology firms. They found that while traditional growth models concentrated on systems and financial capital to explain growth potential, in fact they found that social and organizational capital was more salient to the firms in their study. Intangible resources, Lichtenstein and Brush argue, suggest the importance of business relationships, alliances and tacit knowledge that help owner-managers strengthen their firm's position. Such intangibles provide access to scarce 'soft' resources, including skills, information and knowledge. In addition, they note how what entrepreneurs consider salient will depend on experience and access to alternative conceptions of a particular crisis. This again reinforces the view that a range of responses are available to any crisis; the actual response is dependent on how organizations, or the owner and senior management, perceive problems in their environment (Child, 1972; D'Angelo & Presutti, 2019). Perhaps then one of the most important resources is time to work *on* the business and not just *in* the business. Jones, Macpherson and Thorpe (2010) introduce the concept 'strategic space' to refer to the process by which entrepreneurs are able to access resources, motivation and capability to review existing practices. The starting point is the entrepreneur's existing human capital and their capacity to engage in critical reflection about their business. They highlight three related concepts central to the creation of strategic space:

- first, social capital (which refers to the network relationships that provide access to a wide range of resources and information);
- second, absorptive capacity (which describes the way in which organizational members identify, acquire and utilize knowledge from external sources);
- and third mediating artefacts (which represent existing knowledge but also facilitate the translation and transformation of understanding within and between communities of practice).

Their core argument is that growth and transitions in the business rely on the entrepreneur having the capacity and time to reflect on the current situation to respond to emerging crises or to pre-empt emerging trends so that the business has a chance to survive and grow. Breslin and Jones (2012), in their discussion of entrepreneurial learning, make the point that knowledge

Available Hard
and Soft
Resources

Focal crisis

New Systems
and
Procedures

Management
Perception
and Applied
Skills

Figure 11.2 Dealing with Crises during Growth

components must evolve to maintain pace with the changing environment in which firms operate; this requires that entrepreneurs continue to 'learn to learn' dynamically as they negotiate changing contexts and priorities (Figure 11.2). In another study involving three growing high-tech firms, Macpherson (2005) found that, while entrepreneurs faced crises of organization (such as collaboration, coordination, control and leadership), these were repeated issues that needed ongoing attention; they were never resolved, as suggested by Greiner. While, managing such crises required skill, an adept application of knowledge and the development and integration of new systems of organization (Breslin & Jones, 2012), the crises were concurrent, rather than sequential and (re)occurred in no specific order (Macpherson, 2005).

Crises, then, are not necessarily specific moments that occur within a particular linear trajectory of growth. They are haphazard, but they do provide an opportunity to martial resources, ideas and network to engage with changing the structures and systems of your business. Success or failure, and subsequent growth, may be influenced by the scope of resources, particularly intangible ones, that you can gain access to in a timely fashion. Success at navigating the crisis will also depend on your experience, skill and the adoption of appropriate systems that can support your ability to explore and adapt and break out of, your exiting practices that do not match your changing needs. Again, the vignette in Box 11.1 provides a good example of the challenge of being able to respond effectively to a crisis. Entrepreneurs who are in search of growth need to reflect on the support and constraints of their unique internal and external environment (Dutta & Crossan, 2005). Managing growth is a challenging and unpredictable journey that intensifies the challenges for entrepreneurs to establish appropriate systems to manage their business as it evolves.

11.7 Managing Growth through Resilience

To explain the unpredictability of the solutions and trajectories, some scholars have turned to re-thinking the assumptions that underpin stage growth models. One of these approaches, as alluded to above, is to contemplate the differences between a practice-based and a resource-based perspective of knowledge. In the resource-based view (see Chapter 10), knowledge is a resource that an entrepreneur can 'find' and 'apply' to resolve a crisis (Macpherson, Jones & Zhang, 2004). Resources, such as materials, finance and knowledge are available through networks. A practice-based view, which accepts the availability of tangible resources, considers knowledge, not as an entity waiting to be found and applied, but as an emergent capacity that is made relevant during application. In other words, you learn by doing and managing the crisis, through improvising, and thus your knowledge of how to manage the crisis evolves and emerges during the event (Macpherson, Herbane & Jones, 2015). This means that context is important and your specific issues, while they might be like others, will still require a unique solution.

This practice-based approach suggests that the most important quality for an entrepreneur to sustain growth is the capacity to be creative, and have the tenacity and resilience to manage get things done when current structures, systems and capabilities start to fail (Nicholls-Nixon, 2005). The qualities needed in an entrepreneur to achieve this means that not all new ventures will have the same capacities and motivations to engage in the crisis and to learn new ways of coping (Spicer & Sadler-Smith, 2006). A study on new high-tech firms in the US, for example, found that the financial competence of the firm's founders was a significant factor in managing successfully and coping with strategic growth (Brinckmann, Salomo & Gemuenden, 2011). The corollary of this is that managing growing firms may be less about creating a template for growth than it is about creating an infrastructure and culture that enables self-organized change to occur (Baron, Hannan & Burton, 1999; Lichtenstein, 2000). A practice perspective suggests that growth is more about practical coping and learning how to manage crises is a key attribute in an entrepreneur. It suggests that, rather than looking for growth stages and patterns, a more in depth understanding of the processes that support growth would be more beneficial. In other words, the solutions to crises are likely to be idiosyncratic rather than prescriptive responses to predict-able crises; 'stage of growth' will be less important than understanding your specific context so that you can be creative in shaping responses and developing solutions.

Taking a view of knowledge as a practical accomplishment, or knowing, means that entrepreneurial strategies for growth will require owners to make sense of, and deal with, particular problems as they arise (Dutta & Crossan, 2005) rather than to apply prescriptive solutions. Crises might provide the impetus to reconsider the effectiveness of existing activ-ities or the effectiveness of existing systems (Jason Cope, 2003, 2005), but the acknowledgement that entrepreneurs act in response to their perceptions of the challenges faced suggests a more dynamic and evo-lutionary understanding of managing growth (Breslin, 2008). What is important from this perspective is paying attention to both the processes that support innovation and improvisation, and a deep understanding of your context. This practice-based view suggests that transition through such crises will depend not on a prescriptive solution, but on your skill and ability to make sense of what are the key issues you face, and then to enact a response to crisis based on your strategic choices (Child, 1972; Weick, 1995). Understanding growth then is about more than searching for specific resources or solutions, it is seeing crisis as an opportunity and a period when you need to enact dynamic change to continue to grow (Nicholls-Nixon, 2005).

One of the concepts that helps us explore this dynamic and emergent relationship with crisis is *resilience*. Lengnick-Hall & Beck (2005) define 'resilience capacity', as a combination of cognitive, behavioural and con-textual factors (Figure 11.3). Their argument is that a venture develops its ability to cope with crises dependent on how the key members of your business can deploy these three properties. The ability to interpret ambiguous and uncertain situations creatively (cognitive resilience) helps you to con-ceive, develop and deploy both existing and unconventional activities or processes (behavioural resilience), to take advantage of, or develop new, relationships and resources (contextual resilience). Resilience 'involves more than simply knowing how to regroup during a crisis and keep going;

Figure 11.3 Resilience Capacity

it also means being able to come away from the event with an even greater capacity to prevent and contain future errors' (Weick, Sutcliffe & Obstfeld, 2002, p14). Managing crises and sustaining the firm's development requires the capability to innovate and adapt to rapid, turbulent changes in markets and technologies, but also to sustain the firm once the crisis has been resolved. This is a process that requires you to both mange the crisis, learn from the event and embed that learning within the new structures and processes of the firm. The challenge is to stay flexible enough to manage and cope with future crises. The problem for new venture owners is that it is unlikely that all the necessary competences and other resources will be immediately 'at hand'. This means that you must engage in improvization (using existing unused and discarded resources and capacity) and develop and use social capital available through your networks. Improvizational capacity and bricolage provide early building blocks to develop resilience and sustain the firm's growth.

How you solve crises and learn from them will be activities that provide seminal moments within your venture's operational and growth trajectory. Solving such crises is likely to require you to engage purposefully in the search for a solution. Furthermore, the crisis-induced learning processes in small firms are likely to resemble more closely real-time learning for adaptation and innovation. Such intra-crisis learning (Moynihan, 2008) takes place during the crisis episode (rather than between several episodes) and is suggested to be problematized by both the time constraints and the contextual ambiguities placed on those involved (Deverell, 2009). In other words, solutions may be short term and reactive, rather than result in learning and knowledge being embedded in the firm, as is suggested by such concepts as absorptive capacity (Cohen & Levinthal, 1990). However, the argument put forward by Baker and Nelson (2005), and discussed in Chapter 10, seems pertinent here. Such improvised solutions through bricolage might provide short-term relief from the current crisis but, if you are to gain long-term benefits through your solutions to crises, then they will have to embed them within the firm to capitalize on your efforts.

A practice-based view means that if existing resources within the firm are inadequate to manage a given problem, then reorganization and embedding of new practices will be necessary. Some entrepreneurs will be more capable than others of gaining access to new ideas and absorbing new knowledge in order to manage transformations (Bessant et al., 2005). Thus, access to knowledge resources is not enough. What will be a key factor in terms of both managing crisis and growing is your ability to put into practice ideas, knowledge and solutions that might be available through links you have in appropriate social and business networks (Aldrich, 1999; Cohen & Levinthal, 1990). So, for example, Bretherton and Chaston (2005) argue that resource-dependent firms (such as new firms) that could leverage their relational and structural ties achieved better access to scarce intangible and tangible resources and capabilities, and it was these firms that 'over-performed' in comparison to others. Moreover, as noted by Zhang, Macpherson & Jones (2006) in their study of 26 SMEs, some entrepreneurs can reflect on practical problems contemporaneously, to learn while working. Developing a capacity to learn while working enables entrepreneurs to modify their existing practices appropriately and to develop continually (Box 11.3). Those firms that are also open to learning and have systems and cultures that can support collective learning are more likely to be successful in managing transitions when faced with specific challenges (Lumpkin & Lichtenstein, 2005).

Box 11.3 Context, Learning and Embedding Change

David was aware that the reputation of his business was suffering through inconsistent quality of his products. As a fume cupboard manufacturer (Fume Co.), he also knew that in such a specialized and regulated industry, he had to maintain that reputation if he was to survive: 'It's all word of mouth you know and if people talk about you in a negative way it will kill the business'. He set about reorganizing the quality systems and in ensuring that his products met the needs of his customers: 'so we started having brainstorming sessions when we came up against a problem, because we have all worked in other places we can use that to help solve our problems'. The solutions were proposed by his staff and were then captured for future projects in systematic records: 'I make sure now that every one of our engineers uses the same sequence for their documentation. So one could pick up the contract off someone else and know exactly where everything is'. This standard process improved consistency. In generating ideas for continuing improvement he says that he reflects on his management education and that can stimulate him into action.

> Every so often if I think that something needs a shot in the arm, I read through my university notes and think, what about doing that? And it's surprising that you can always improve.

He was able to turnaround the firm and grow the order book based on a reputation for quality, consistency and customer service.

This perspective on managing growth, acknowledges that managers of small firms and entrepreneurs are likely to have their own quirky approach to running a business and that they will manage crises with their own perspectives on business concepts such as strategy, marketing, operations (Perks, 2006). These will not necessarily accord with existing management theory (Storey, 1994), and they are more likely to be improvised solutions they have developed to cope with a multitude of challenges across a whole range of issues. The robustness of these solutions will depend on the skills they have available, the resources they can deploy and the specific, and largely unique, contexts and challenges they face. Growth will depend on the resilience new firms have to cope practically with the current crisis and any solutions that you deploy will only ever be a temporary fix until the next crisis has to be (re)solved. Put bluntly, survival and growth depend on your capacity to enact creative solutions continually to ongoing and recurring, crises.

11.8 Summary and Key Points

Burns (2007), in reviewing selected growth models in his textbook notes that, despite significant criticisms of the models, they do highlight a process of growth that incorporates three linked elements: growth, crisis and consolidation. Perhaps, then, the usefulness of such models is not in providing a predictable sequence of events that can guide entrepreneurs, but in highlighting that entrepreneurship is a dynamic process and one that inevitably involves managing crises to survive. In managing this dynamic situation, entrepreneurs need to learn how to learn (Gartner, 1989), and the knowledge components of a firm, which exist at several levels, must be renewed to evolve to keep pace with changing circumstances (Breslin and Jones, 2012). This links specifically to the variety of economic, political and social contexts that entrepreneurs experience as they try to start their firms (see Chapter 13). While existing growth models might provide heuristics in which to make sense of experiences, the reality and variety of contexts make growth trajectories less predictable. With that in mind, it is important to consider emerging research and conceptualization of growth as managing 'dynamic states' and continual crisis. Here the view is that growth trajectories are not predictable but involve entrepreneurs reacting purposefully to contexts and crises by implementing their solutions. Evolution of the firm and its growth trajectory is a dynamic process. Moreover, studies show that venture owners who believe in their ability to network and expend effort in networking, can access resources that help them to manage the crisis transitions and continue to grow (Bratkovič Kregar, Antončič & Ruzzier, 2019; Macpherson et al., 2015). Crises provide the opportunity for a firm to look forward (Herbane, 2010), but the effectiveness of the solution will depend on access to appropriate resources and the ability to envision and enact solutions creatively. Essential to this transition is the application of your resources to (re)structure the firm appropriately to create opportunities in uncertain contexts.

In a dynamic states view, growth trajectories:

1. are idiosyncratic and influenced by context-dependent environmental and organizational challenges;
2. require the creative and improvizational skill of the ventures key actors in developing appropriate practical solutions;
3. depend on access to and innovative integration of the necessary resources, including knowledge; and
4. are temporary, since the current 'state' is only a provisional solution to the current problems faced by the firm.

Thus, continued growth of your venture will be dependent on the resilience capacity to manage crises dynamically and to develop practical solutions.

11.9 Discussion Questions and Call to Action

1. What are the main principles of stage or phase models of growth?
2. What are the main criticisms of the stage or phase models of growth?
3. How does a 'dynamic states' or crisis-based view of transition points differ from stage-based models?
4. What are the key elements of resilience, and how does that help to understand the dynamic and practical nature of growth?
5. What are the implications of knowledge as practical activity, rather than a fixed resource, in understanding how new firms cope with growth?

Growing your business will involve managing tipping points, or crises, where the current operations are not fit for purpose if you are to achieve scale, or at least they will need to be reviewed to see if they can continue to deliver your growth strategy. Your ability to build resilience and flexibility into your systems will be a key challenge, particularly if you are to be able to embed resources and learning into your venture. Building in capacity to scan your context, to sense changes in the market and respond will provide you with the opportunity to manage potential crises. Keeping your systems, processes, networks, supply chains and personnel needs under continual review will help to develop your firm's resilience. Flexibility and agility provide the capacity for your venture to evolve as it grows. Your challenges may not be unique in terms of requirements for knowledge, resources, personnel and markets, but your response to challenges or crises as you grow will very much be dependent on your own context, circumstances and opportunities. You need an intimate knowledge of your specific context and the ability to balance working *in* the business (to deliver for your current market), as well as working *on* the business (to ensure its viability in response to changing circumstances).

References

Aldrich, H. (1999). *Organizations Evolving*. London: Sage.

Anyadike-Danes, M. & Hart, M. (2018). All grown up? The fate after 15 years of a quarter of a million UK firms born in 1998. *Journal of Evolutionary Economics, 28*(1), 45–76.

Baker, T. & Nelson, R. E. (2005). Creating Something from Nothing: Resource Construction through Entrepreneurial Bricolage. *Administrative Science Quarterly, 50*, 329–366.

Baron, J. N., Hannan, M. T. & Burton, M. D. (1999). Building the Iron Cage: Determinants of Managerial Intensity in the Early Years of Organizations. *American Sociological Review, 64*(4), 527–547.

Bessant, J., Phelps, B. & Adams, R. (2005). *External Knowledge: A Review of the Literature Addressing the Role of External Knowlede and Expertise at Key Stages of Business Growth and Development*. Swindon: Advanced Institute of Management Research.

Birch, D. (1987). *Job Creation in America*. London: Free Press.

Birch, D., Haggerty, A. & Parsons, W. (1995). *Corporate evolution*. Cambridge, MA: Cognetics, Inc.

Bratkovič Kregar, T., Antončič, B. & Ruzzier, M. (2019). Linking a multidimensional construct of networking self-efficacy to firm growth. *Economic Research-Ekonomska Istrazivanja, 32*(1), 17–32.

Breslin, D. (2008). A review of the evolutionary approach to the study of entrepreneurship. *International Journal of Management Reviews, 10*(4), 399–423.

Breslin, D. & Jones, C. (2012). The Evolution of Entrepreneurial Learning. *International Journal of Organizational Analysis, 20*(3), 294–308.

Bretherton, P. & Chaston, I. (2005). Resource dependency and SME strategy: an empirical study. *Journal of Small Business and Enterprise Development, 12*(2), 274–289.

Brinckmann, J., Salomo, S. & Gemuenden, H. G. (2011). Financial Management Competence of Founding Teams and Growth of New Technology-Based Firms. *Entrepreneurship: Theory & Practice, 35*(2), 217–243.

Brush, C. G., Ceru, D. J. & Blackburn, R. (2009). Pathways to entrepreneurial growth: The influence of management, marketing, and money. *Business Horizons, 52*(5), 481–491.

Burns, P. (1996). Growth. In P. Burns & J. Dewhurst (Eds.), *Small Business and Enterpreneurship*. London: MacMillan.

Burns, P. (2007). *Entrepreneruship and Small Business* (2nd ed.). Basingstoke: Palgrave MacMillan.

Chandler, A. (1977). *The Visible Hand: The Managerial Revolution in American Business*. Cambridge, MA: Harvard University Press.

Chen, X., Zou, H. & Wang, D. T. (2009). How do new ventures grow? Firm capabilities, growth strategies and performance. *International Journal of Research in Marketing, 26*(4), 294–303.

Child, J. (1972). Organizational structure, environment and performance: the role of strategic choice. *Sociology, 6*, 1–22.

Churchill, N. C. & Lewis, V. L. (1983). The Five Stages of Small Business Growth. *Harvard Business Review, 61*(3), 30–50.

Cohen, W. & Levinthal, D. (1990). Absorptive Capacity: a new perspective on learning and innovation. *Administrative Science Quarterly, 35*(1), 128–152.

Cope, J. (2003). Entrepreneurial Learning and Critical Reflection. *Management Learning, 34*(4), 429–450.

Cope, J. (2005). Towards a Dynamic Learning Perspective of Entrepreneurship. *Entrepreneurship Theory and Practice, 29*(4), 373–397.

Cope, J. (2010). Entrepreneurial learning from failure: An interpretive phenomenological analysis. *Entrepreneurship Theory and Practice, 26*, 604–623.

D'Angelo, A. & Presutti, M. (2019). SMEs international growth: The moderating role of experience on entrepreneurial and learning orientations. *International Business Review, 28*(3), 613–624.

David, P. (1985). Clio and the Economics of QWERTY. *The American Economic Review, 75*(2), 332–337.

Deverell, E. (2009). Crises as Learning Triggers: Exploring a Conceptual Framework of Crisis-Induced Learning. *Journal of Contingencies and Crisis Management, 17*(3), 179–188.

Di Gregorio, D. & Shane, S. (2003). Why do some universities generate more start-ups than others? *Research Policy, 32*(2), 209–227.

Di Pietro, F., Monaghan, S. & O'Hagan-Luff, M. (2022). Entrepreneurial Finance and HRM Practices in Small Firms. *British Journal of Management*, *33*(1), 327–345.

Dodge, H. R., Fullerton, S. & Robbins, J. E. (1994). Stage of the Organizational Lifecycle and Competition as Mediators of Problem Perception for Small Business. *Strategic Management Journal*, *15*(2), 121–134.

Duane, A. & O'Reilly, P. (2017). A conceptual stages-of-growth model for managing a social media business profile. *Irish Journal of Management*, *36*(2), 78–98.

Dutta, D. K. & Crossan, M. M. (2005). The Nature of Entrepreneurial Opportunities: Understanding the Process Using the 4I Organizational Learning Framework. *Entrepreneurship Theory and Practice*, *29*(4), 425–449.

Gartner, W. B. (1985). A Conceptual Framework for Describing the Phenomenon of New Venture Creation. *The Academy of Management Review*, *4*, 696.

Gartner, W. B. (1989). 'Who Is an Entrepreneur?' Is the Wrong Question. *Entrepreneurship: Theory & Practice*, *13*(4), 47–68.

Goffee, R. & Scase, R. (1995). *Corporate Realities: The Dynamics of Large and Small Organizations*. London: Routledge.

Gregorio, D. D. & Shane, S. (2003). Why do some universities generate more start-ups than others? *Research Policy*, *32*(2), 209–227.

Greiner, L. E. (1972). Evolution and Revolution as Organizations Grow. *Harvard Business Review*, *50*(4), 37–46.

Greiner, L. E. (1998). Evolution and revolution as organizations grow. *Harvard Business Review*, *76*(3), 55–68.

Herbane, B. (2010). Small Business Research: Time for a Crisis-based View. *International Small Business Journal*, *28*(1), 43–64.

Jones, O., Macpherson, A. & Thorpe, R. (2010). Learning in owner-managed small firms: Mediating artefacts and strategic space. *Entrepreneurship and Regional Development*, *22*(7/8), 649–673.

Khattak, M. S. & Ullah, R. (2021). The role of entrepreneurial orientation in tangible and intangible resource acquisition and new venture growth. *Managerial & Decision Economics*, *42*(6), 1619–1637.

Kitila, R. & Shane, S. (2005). When Does Lack of Resources Make New Firms Innovate? *Academy of Management Journal*, *48*(5), 814–829.

Lengnick-Hall, C. A. & Beck, T. E. (2005). Adaptive Fit Versus Robust Transformation: How Organisations Respond to Environmental Change. *Journal of Management*, *31*, 738–757.

Leonard-Barton, D. (1995). *Wellsprings of Knowledge: Building and Sustaining the Sources of Innovation*. Boston: Harvard Business School Press.

Levie, J. & Lichtenstein, B. B. (2010). A Terminal Assessment of Stages Theory: Introducing a Dynamic States Approach to Entrepreneurship. *Entrepreneurship: Theory & Practice*, *34*(2), 317–350.

Lichtenstein, B. B. (2000). Self Organized Transitions: A Pattern Amid the Chaos of Transformative Change. *Academy of Management Executive, 14*(4), 128–141.

Lichtenstein, B. B., Dooley, K. J. & Lumpkin, G. T. (2006). Measuring Emergence in the Dynamics of New Venture Creation. *Journal of Business Venturing, 21,* 153–175.

Lichtenstein, B. M. & Brush, C. G. (2001). How do 'resource bundles' develop and change in New Ventures? A dynamic model and longitudinal exploration. *Entrepreneurship: Theory and Practice, 25*(3), 37–59.

Lumpkin, G. T. & Lichtenstein, B. B. (2005). The Role of Orgnaizational Learning in the Opportunity-Recognition Process. *Entrepreneurship Theory and Practice, 29*(4), 451–472.

Macpherson, A. (2005). Learning to Grow: Resolving the Crisis of Knowing. *Technovation, 25*(10), 1129–1140.

Macpherson, A., Herbane, B. & Jones, O. (2015). Developing dynamic capabilities through resource accretion: expanding the entrepreneurial solution space. *Entrepreneurship & Regional Development, 27*(5–6), 259–291.

Macpherson, A., Jones, O. & Zhang, M. (2004). Evolution or revolution? Dynamic capabilities in a knowledge-dependent firm. *R & D Management, 34*(2), 161–177.

Maine, E. M., Shapiro, D. M. & Vining, A. R. (2010). The role of clustering in the growth of new technology-based firms. *Small Business Economics, 34*(2), 127–146.

McCann, J. E. (1991). Patterns of Growth, Competitive Technology, and Financial Strategies in Young Ventures. *Journal of Business Venturing, 6*(3), 189–208.

Moynihan, D. (2008). Learning Under Uncertainty: Networks in Crisis Management. *Public Administration Review, 68*(2), 350–365.

Nicholls-Nixon, C. L. (2005). Rapid Growth and High Performance: The Entrepreneur's 'Impossible Dream?'. *Academy of Management Executive, 19*(1), 77–89.

Penrose, E. T. (1959). *The Theory of the Growth of the Firm*. Oxford: Basil Blackwell.

Perks, K. (2006). Influences on Strategic Management Styles Among Fast Growth Medium-Sized Firms in France and Germany. *Strategic Change, 15*(3), 153–164.

Phelps, R., Adams, R. & Bessant, J. (2007). Life cycles of growing organizations: A review with implications for knowledge and learning. *International Journal of Management Reviews, 9*(1), 1–30.

Raspe, O. & Oort, F. (2011). Growth of new firms and spatially bounded knowledge externalities. *Annals of Regional Science, 46*(3), 495–518.

Renski, H. (2009). New Firm Entry, Survival, and Growth in the United States: A Comparison of Urban, Suburban, and Rural Areas. *Journal of the American Planning Association, 75*(1), 60–77.

Sarasvathy, S. (2001). Causation and effectuation: towards a theoretical shift from economic inevitability to entrepreneurial contingency. *Academy of Management Review, 26*(2), 243–263.

Sarasvathy, S. (2008). *Effectuation: elements of entrepreneurial expertise* Cheltenham: Edward Elgar.

Schumpeter, J. (1934). *The Theory of Economic Development*. Cambridge, Mass: Harvard University Press.

Scott, M. & Bruce, R. (1987). Five Stages of Growth in Small Business. *Long Range Planning, 20*(3), 45–52.

Shane, S. (2000). Prior knowledge and the discovery of entrepreneurial opportunities. *Organization Science, 11*(4), 448–469.

Shu, Y., Kher, R. & Lyons, T. S. (2018). Where Do Accelerators Fit in the Venture Creation Pipeline? Different Values Brought by Different Types of Accelerators. *Entrepreneurship Research Journal, 8*(4), 1–13.

Spence, L. & Schmidpeter. (2003). SMEs, Social Capital and the Common Good. *Journal of Business Ethics, 45*(1), 93–108.

Spicer, D. P. & Sadler-Smith, E. (2006). Organizational Learning in Smaller Manufacturing Firms. *International Small Business Journal, 24*(2), 133–158.

Storey, D. J. (1994). *Understanding the Small Business Sector*. London: Routledge.

Tushman, M. L., Newman, W.H & Romanelli, E. (1986). Convergence and upheaval: managing the unsteady pace of change. *California Management Review, 19*(1), 29–44.

Weick, K. (1995). *Sensemaking in Organizations*. Thousand Oaks, CA: Sage.

Weick, K. E., Sutcliffe, K. M. & Obstfeld, D. (2002). High Reliability: The power of mindfulness. In F. Hesselbein & R. Johnson (Eds.), *On high performance organizations*. San Francisco: Jossey Bass.

Williams, D. A. & Ramdani, B. (2018). Exploring the characteristics of prosperous SMEs in the Caribbean. *Entrepreneurship and Regional Development, 30*(9/10), 1012–1026.

Yahav, I., Schwartz, D. G. & Welcman, Y. (2020). The journey to engaged customer community: Evidential social CRM maturity model in Twitter. *Applied Stochastic Models in Business & Industry, 36*(3), 397–416.

Zhang, M., Macpherson, A. & Jones, O. (2006). Conceptualizing the Learning Process in SMEs: Improving Innovation through External Orientation. *International Small Business Journal, 24*(3), 299–323.

Understanding Theories of Entrepreneurship

12

12.1 Introduction

This book is primarily intended for students who are studying entrepreneurship as a stand-alone module or as a degree programme. Therefore, our focus is on the things you, as a potential entrepreneur, need to know if you are seriously thinking about starting a business. Essentially, this means developing a strong commitment to learning about and for entrepreneurship. At the same time, we have drawn on a wide range of literatures to inform the material contained in the book. Consequently, we believe that *Resourcing the Start-up Business* will also be useful to those engaged in the academic study of entrepreneurship at postgraduate levels (MSc and PhD). To restate Kurt Lewin's well-known maxim, 'there is nothing as practical as a good theory' (Lewin, 1943, p. 118). We are steadfast in stating that theory and practice are inextricably linked – you cannot have one without the other! For example, there is no doubt that social network theory (Granovetter, 1973) and social capital theory (Coleman, 1988) have enhanced the academic and practical understanding of entrepreneurship over the last 20 years.

Entrepreneurial learning has also increased in importance among the academic research community (Hyams-Ssekasi & Caldwell, 2018). Lamont (1972) authored the first paper explicitly focusing on the topic of entrepreneurial learning and there was a rapid increase in the number of publications from 2000 onwards (Jones, 2022). Initially, approaches to entrepreneurial learning drew primarily on cognitive theory (Kohler, 1925; Piaget, 1926) and behaviourism (Pavlov, 1927; Skinner, 1938; Thorndike, 1913). In the UK, early attempts to improve 'learning' focused on management development programmes, which were underpinned by implicit learning theories including cognition, behaviourism, and experiential learning (Burgoyne & Stuart, 1977). Gradually, a number of innovative individuals promoted an explicit focus on learning for small firms (Gibb, 1997), individual entrepreneurs (Deakins & Freel, 1998) and enterprise education (Caird, 1990). As argued by Jones and Macpherson (2014, p. 304), there was a gradual shift from the relatively straight forward focus on individual entrepreneurs (cognition and behaviourism) to more sophisticated approaches in which individual entrepreneurs are seen as 'situated learners' who are part of a larger learning community (Jones, Meckel & Taylor, 2021a). Social learning theory is based on the idea that human development occurs as a result of observing what Bandura (1977) describes as 'credible and knowledgeable' individuals. Cultural-historical theory (Vygotsky, 1978) (Vygotsky, 1978), cultural-historical activity theory (Engestrom, 2014) and the communities of practice approach (Lave & Wenger, 1991) are all based on social learning theory and represent a reaction against the cognitive and behavioural approaches (Jones & Macpherson, 2014). Although experiential learning has been criticized for a reliance on cognition, Kolb (1984) was influenced by a number of other key theorists (Dewey, 1938; Lewin, 1951; Vygotsky, 1978). Raelin (2007) argued that growing interest so called 'practice turn' revitalized interest in the work of Dewey and Kolb. As recently argued by Jones (2022), academic engagement with entrepreneurs and owner-managers as well as entrepreneurship students has led to a more nuanced understanding of entrepreneurial learning, which complements social learning theories.

As briefly discussed in Chapter 1, there is increasing interest in the topic of entrepreneurship. Governments around the world have been keen to promote entrepreneurship as a way of responding to the decline of old industrial sectors as well as capturing the benefits from the emergence of new information and communication technologies (ICT). The academic study of entrepreneurship and new venture creation has also grown rapidly over the last 40 years. Landström et al. (2012) identify a number of key figures who defined the intellectual basis for future generations of academic researchers. It is widely acknowledged that Cantillon (1732/1931) first used the term entrepreneur in his *Essai Sur la Nature du Commerce en Général* where he outlined the importance of individual property rights, economic interdependency and the concept of arbitrage. Jean-Baptiste Say owned a cottonspinning mill as well as being Europe's first professor of economics and the entrepreneur was central to his explanation of how the economic system functioned. Say's (1880) ideas were also important because he recognized that human industry (knowledge) was the third factor of production in addition to land and capital (Pittaway, 2012).

Although the term entrepreneur was not used by Adam Smith's (1776) in *The Wealth of Nations*, his work was important in developing a deeper understanding of how a capitalist market economy operated. Joseph Schumpeter (1934) is by far the most important influence on contemporary understanding of the role played by entrepreneurs in capitalist economies. Even those with an extremely limited knowledge of Schumpeter's writing will be able to cite the crucial role of 'creative destruction' as the engine of economic change. *The Theory of Economic Development* (Schumpeter, 1934) remains the most cited publication in the entrepreneurship literature (Landström et al., 2012). Although it would be interesting to know how many of those citing Schumpeter have read any of his work. There were, of course, a number of other significant contributors to entrepreneurship during the course of the twentieth century and these include: Ludwig von Mises (1949), Fredrich von Hayek (1990), Frank Knight (1921) and Israel Kirzner (1973). The most widely known work other than Schumpeter's is almost certainly David McClelland (1961) whose ideas about entrepreneurial traits such as the need for achievement, risk-taking and a tolerance of ambiguity still have a seductive appeal for many students. However, research on traits has been inconclusive and, in contrast, many scholars have focused on the ambiguity and complexity associated with firm emergence (Baker & Nelson, 2005; Sarasvathy, 2008; Steyaert, 2007). It is the historical and institutional settings that actors occupy rather than specific psychological traits or resource bundles that determine entrepreneurial performance (Gartner & Shaver, 2012; Katz & Gartner, 1988)

Landstrom et al. (2012) argue that there have been three phases of entrepreneurship research since the 1970s. The *take-off phase* was stimulated by Birch's work in the US and the Bolton report in the UK. The *growth phase* of the 1990s involved both creation of a research infrastructure and greater fragmentation as the earlier economic assumptions were questioned by a new generation of researchers. From 2000 onwards, *the maturity phase* has incorporated much greater understanding of the phenomena of entrepreneurship with the emergence of various sub-groups who have continued to question the dominance of economic and psychological approaches to the study of entrepreneurship (Landström et al., 2012, p. 1156). A seminal article by Shane and Venkataraman (2000) based on the traditional, largely economic, view of entrepreneurship was followed by a series of publications that discussed alternative views about how entrepreneurs operate in practice (Alvarez & Busenitz, 2001; Baker, Miner & Eesley, 2003; Sarasvathy, 2001; Shah & Tripsas, 2007; Steyaert, 2007). In this chapter we provide an overview of the key ideas in entrepreneurship theory from Schumpeter (1934) to recent debates about the status of effectuation as a theory of entrepreneurship (Arend, Sarooghi & Burkemper, 2015; McKelvie, Chandler, DeTienne & Johansson, 2020; Read, Sarasvathy, Dew & Wiltbank, 2016a, 2016b).

We begin by examining individuals and opportunity identification, before opening the discussion out into new venture creation and exploring recent theoretical developments. We finish with a discussion about various practice-based theories that examine the context, ambiguity and variety of pathways to entrepreneurship in the early days of venture creation. The theoretical debates help to contextualize the earlier material contained in this book and provide grounding for some key debates associated with the study of entrepreneurs engaged in the process of establishing new businesses.

12.2 Learning Objectives

- To explain the differences between opportunity identification and opportunity creation.
- To describe and evaluate the key distinctions between the causal and effectuation theories of entrepreneurship.
- To understand the relevance of a range of alternative theories of entrepreneurship.
- To analyse the implications of entrepreneurship process theories for understanding new venture creation.

12.3 Individuals and Opportunities

In addition to advances in the theoretical understanding of entrepreneurship which are discussed below there have been some very important empirical studies (Landström et al., 2012). Research carried out by Birch in the US and the Bolton Commission in the UK laid the foundations for future empirical studies (see Chapter 13, Section 13.3). David Storey's *Understanding the*

Small Business Sector was the outcome of a major research project funded by the UK's ESRC (Economic and Social Research Council). Storey (1994) provided an in-depth account of research findings related to the birth, growth and death of small firms. This remains the only major study of entrepreneurship and the management of small firms carried out in the UK. In the US, Saxenian's (1996) book which examined the phenomenon of technology-based small firms in Silicon Valley and Route 128 was influential in identifying the role of culture in promoting entrepreneurship. There are also a large number of US studies which draw on the Panel Study of Entrepreneurial Dynamics (PSED I and PSED II) and these are summarized by Gartner et al. (2012) as well as work associated with the Global Entrepreneurship Monitor (GEM) studies (Kelley, Bosma & Amoros, 2011). According to Gartner and Shaver (2012) the PSED and GEM studies provide conclusive evidence that entrepreneurs are not born with specific attributes which distinguish them from the broader population.

The traditional view of entrepreneurship, described by Sarasvathy (2001) as the causal approach, adopts a linear perspective on the process of discovery, evaluation and exploitation of new ideas (Shane & Venkataraman, 2000). Within this field, early studies (Brockhaus, 1980; Chell, Haworth & Brearley, 1991; McClelland, 1961) focused in on the psychological traits of successful entrepreneurs in the belief that these distinguished them from the wider population. Alternatively, the resource-based view in management studies (Barney, 1991) suggests it is the arrangement of resource bundles internal to businesses that drive competitive advantage. This logic has developed into strategic entrepreneurship studies that analyse how competitive entrepreneurial opportunities are discovered and resources allocated to new business ventures (Hitt, Biermant, Shimizu & Kochhar, 2001; Zahra & Dess, 2001). Reflecting on these developments, Shane and Venkataraman (2000) introduced a distinct unifying construct into the domain of entrepreneurial study by focusing on the nature of opportunities. In contrast to Gartner (2006) who suggests that entrepreneurship is characterized by its messiness, Shane and Venkataraman (2000, p. 218) believe that the entrepreneurial process can be encapsulated in a relatively straightforward definition:

> the field involves the study of *sources* of opportunities; the *processes* of discovery, evaluation and exploitation of opportunities; and the set of *individuals* who discover, evaluate and exploit them.

There are a variety of ways in which business opportunities can be surfaced: new uses for existing resources; new products from existing resources; new resources for existing products; openings created through regulatory or demographic changes (Shane & Venkataraman, 2000, p. 220); creation of new information; and exploitation of market asymmetries (differences in information about potential opportunities) across space and time. Variations in the ability of individuals to exploit new opportunities are attributed to 'entrepreneurial alertness' (Kirzner, 2009; Shane & Venkataraman, 2000). Individual alertness depends on intuition and heuristics, as well as access to appropriate information and these factors determine who will become an entrepreneur (Shane, 2000). According to such writers, the nature of an opportunity is a 'concrete and real' space in a market that is ripe for exploitation. Focus on the nature of opportunity reduces the earlier emphasis of entrepreneurial traits such as the need for achievement and risk-taking (McClelland, 1961). While they shift the focus onto other individual characteristics, such as alertness and foresight, the entrepreneurial ability to discover, evaluate and exploit new opportunities, is retained (Shane, 2000; Shane & Venkataraman, 2000).

Shane (2012) also claimed credit for establishing the process perspective as the dominant approach in entrepreneurship (Shane & Venkataraman, 2000). He does, however, disagree with critics who believe that his model is based on a planned sequence of events which follow-on from opportunity identification. For example, he suggests that activities associated with the exploitation of an opportunity are simply 'sub-processes' which could occur in any order. Shane (2012) also takes issue with those who suggest that his view of entrepreneurial opportunities being objective phenomena is misguided. Instead, he argues that there is a clear conceptual distinction between opportunities and business ideas. It is acknowledged that business ideas are entrepreneurs' subjective interpretation of the resources required to pursue a particular opportunity (Shane, 2012, p. 15). Nevertheless, Shane's model (2003) is a deliberate attempt to reconcile the focus on either the individual or the environment (Figure 12.1). Hence, the model combines individual psychological attributes and demographic factors (age, education, experience) with environmental factors (sector and the macro environment). The underpinning ethos of the model is that entrepreneurs are driven by the profit-motive to identify and exploit opportunities. This illustrates the so-called causal approach in which opportunities are identified and then the entrepreneur acquires the resources needed to exploit that opportunity. Alvarez and Barney (2007) distinguish between the discovery

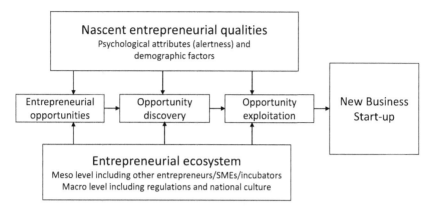

Figure 12.1 The Causal Model of Business Start-up

(causal) approach to new opportunities and the idea that opportunities are created by entrepreneurs themselves (see Section 12.6.5).

The work of Penrose and Gartner provides the foundation for the so-called 'narrative turn' in entrepreneurial studies. Three related themes in entrepreneurial narrative research have emerged in recent years. First, several scholars suggest entrepreneurial practice is a narrative pursuit through which actors create their life-stories (Rae, 2004, 2005; Rindova, Barry & Ketchen, 2009). Secondly, others focus on the metaphors (Cornelissen & Clarke, 2010; Cornelissen, Clarke & Cienki, 2012; Haslam, Cornelissen & Werner, 2017), plots (Hamilton, 2006) and clichés (Down & Warren, 2008) that are commonly employed when actors talk about their entrepreneurial actions. Thirdly, entrepreneurial storytelling and narratives articulate images of new business ventures, which emphasize their formality (Gartner, Bird & Starr, 1992) and their legitimacy (Lounsbury, Gehman & Glynn, 2019; Lounsbury & Glynn, 2001; Zott & Huy, 2007) rather than the informality and uncertainly usually associated with start-ups. There is a common focus on how opportunities emerge via exchanges made between creative actors and the historical and institutional settings in which they operate. Effectuation theory is also a narrative approach to understanding how entrepreneurial opportunities develop in actors' imaginations (Sarasvathy, 2001, 2008). Sarasvathy (2008, p. 13) suggests that opportunities emerge from a combination of history and identity: 'who actors are, what they know and who they know'. The effectual principles of design and creation in turn are propelled by the transformation of existing realities as actors attempt to create something from a limited set of resources. Effectuation enables prospective entrepreneurs to act in the face of *goal ambiguity* because opportunities emerge through practical engagement and experience. Sarasvathy's effectuation theory is described in more detailed in Section 12.6.4.

12.4 Creating New Ventures

Most writers take Low and Macmillan's seminal definition of entrepreneurship as the 'creation of a new venture' as their starting point (Low & MacMillan, 1988, p. 141). This definition suggests that entrepreneurship is a process, which takes months, or even years, rather than being an instantaneous event. The work of Katz and Gartner (1988, p. 433) is important here because they focused attention on to the processes by which 'an organization evolves from nothing to something'. What this means is that it is necessary to develop a better understanding of the 'territory between preorganization', before nascent entrepreneurs have initiated their venture, and the actual creation of a new organization (Katz & Gartner, 1988). Gartner (1985) developed a conceptual framework that describes new venture creation as an interaction between the environment, the organization, entrepreneurial behaviour and the process of business creation (Figure 12.2). Gartner's (1985) work was a direct response to the continuing focus on identifying entrepreneurial traits. This prompted a shift to much greater interest in the process-related aspects of entrepreneurial behaviour (Gartner et al., 1992). According to Gartner (1985) there are six processes associated with business creation and organizational emergence:

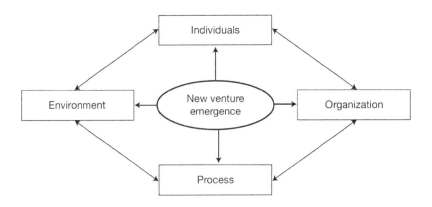

Figure 12.2 Gartner's Model of New Venture Emergence

1. Locate/identify a business opportunity.

2. Accumulate resources.

3. Market products or services.

4. Produce products or services.

5. Build the organization.

6. Respond to government (regulation/taxes) and society (the market).

From this perspective, the challenge is to understand exactly how new organizations are created, enacted (Weick, 1979) or socially constructed (Berger & Luckmann, 1966). The shift from the identification of an opportunity to a functioning business represents a quantum rather than an evolutionary change. Entrepreneurs attempting to set-up new businesses must 'talk and act "as if" equivocal events are non-equivocal' (Gartner et al., 1992, p. 17). In existing organizations, non-equivocal events are based on the routines and repertoires which individuals undertake that have meaning for other organizational actors (see Chapter 1). Organizational emergence is concerned with entrepreneurs generating a set of appropriate interactions that are convincing for actors such as potential customers, suppliers and employees as well as resource providers such as bankers, venture capitalists and business angels.

Starr and Fondas (1992) utilize theories of organizational socialization to illuminate the role of entrepreneurs in emerging organizations. Socialization is a useful concept because it specifies attitudinal and behavioural changes as well as revealing role relations between the entrepreneur and key outsiders who act as socializing agents (Starr & Fondas, 1992). A similar theme is pursued in a later paper in which Larson and Starr (1993) critically examine the role of network relations in organization formation. The network model has three stages that are important for the acquisition of the critical resources needed to start a new business. As pointed out by Kanter (1983) these resources include information, technical knowledge, capital, physical resources, as well as symbolic support such as endorsement, political backing, approval and legitimacy.

Stage one – focuses on essential dyads; relationships including family, friends and business contacts provide the basis for any entrepreneur seeking essential resources for a new firm. Effective entrepreneurs concentrate on the critical dyads by 'culling' those unlikely to provide sufficient resources to the venture.

Stage two – converting dyads to socioeconomic exchanges, is concerned with changing 'one dimensional' (social or economic) exchange processes into two dimensional exchange processes (social and economic).

Stage three – activities become more formalized through as functions such as finance, marketing and production are established. Development of organizational routines means that there is increasing interdependence with several key customers and suppliers who stabilize the network. Increasingly, relationships are not reliant on the entrepreneur's personal links but become part of repeated exchange cycles which typify established organizations.

Other studies confirm the importance of entrepreneurs recognizing that different resources can be accessed via strong and weak ties. Strong ties (essential dyads) are crucial in the early stages of business start-up. In the longer-term, entrepreneurs must develop their weaker ties if they want to access the resources necessary to build a sustainable business (Lee, 2017; Lee & Jones, 2008; Lee, Tuselmann, Jayawarna & Rouse, 2019). Other studies demonstrate there are clear links between the ability of entrepreneurs to extend their networks and the financial performance of early-stage businesses (Jayawarna, Jones & Macpherson, 2020; Jones & Jayawarna, 2010).

While a wide range of authors have suggested frameworks for the process of new venture creation (Gartner, 1985; Greenberger & Sexton, 1988; Katz & Gartner, 1988; Mazzarol, Volery, Doss & Thein, 1999; Vesper, 1990) there is little evidence to suggest a common pattern of events. Carter et al. (1996) draw on a theory of organizing (Weick, 1979) as the conceptual basis for their exploration of business start-ups. The process of new business creation is analogous to the concept of 'enactment' which refers to the generation of specific patterns of interlocking behaviours among individuals. The study was based on the analysis of two existing datasets; (Curtin, 1982; Reynolds & Miller, 1992; Reynolds & White, 1997) which provided a total of 71 nascent entrepreneurs. Interviews identified a list of 14 'precursor behaviours' associated with new venture creation which were categorized according to the time between initiation and completion (3-month periods up to 5 years). Precursor behaviours included: prepared plan, invested money, bought/rented facilities, devoted fulltime. The authors were able to discriminate between three distinct groups (started, still trying and given up). Those still trying were differentiated from the other two groups by being less likely to have obtained financial support or bought equipment. Secondly, those who had given-up were less likely to have obtained financial support or developed models or prototypes (Carter et al., 1996, p. 158).

In explaining these results, the authors summarize each of the three groups. Successful entrepreneurs were more aggressive in making their business tangible to others by obtaining equipment, finance, organizing their team and in establishing a legal entity. Those who gave-up were quite similar in their activities to the first group, but their early enthusiasm soon dissipated. Emphasis on the development of a 'model' suggested that 'testing' may have indicated that the concept/idea did not work in a way that matched the entrepreneurs' expectations. The 'still-trying' group seemed to lack motivation because they had undertaken fewer activities and those activities were 'internal' such as saving money and preparing a business plan. Significantly, they put much less effort into the more 'external' activities likely to make the business real to others.

> In terms of advice to individuals considering starting a business, it would seem that the results provide evidence that nascent entrepreneurs should aggressively pursue opportunities in the short term, because they will quickly learn that these opportunities will either reveal themselves as worthy of start-up or as poor choices that should be abandoned.
>
> (Carter et al., 1996, p. 163).

Reynolds (2011) re-examined precursor behaviours by interviewing a representative sample of those in the process of starting a business. The results are summarized in Table 12.1 and provide some insight into the way in which US entrepreneurs establish new businesses. The main precursor of setting up a business was 'serious thoughts about business' for 99% of entrepreneurs. A total of 11 precursor behaviours were new in the 2011 survey (not mentioned in the 1996 study) and these included 'began talking to customers', 'use of physical space' and 'collect competitor information'.

Muller et al. (2012) describes a rather different approach to identifying what entrepreneurs actually do when engaged in business start-up. This study is based on a detailed observation of six entrepreneurs engaged in the process of business start-up, which has similarities to a classic study of

Table 12.1 Start-up Activities

	Survey 2011	Survey 1999
Serious thoughts about business	99%	99%
Invested own money	79%	68%
Began taking to customers	76%	NA
Developed model/prototype	65%	35%
Initiated business plan	64%	56%
Use of physical space	62%	NA
Collect competitor information	62%	NA
Created inventory	59%	NA
Generated income	56%	NA
Phone book/Internet	55%	NA
Defined market	54%	NA
Bought facilities/equipment	53%	50%
Examined regulatory requirements	53%	NA
Promotion of good/services	49%	NA
Business bank account	39%	NA
Registered business	36%	NA

managerial work (Mintzberg, 1973). The six businesses had been established between three months and 12 months at the time of the study. Work undertaken by the entrepreneurs was characterized by 'brevity and high levels of fragmentation' (Fritsch & Mueller, 2004, p. 1004). Actions undertaken by the entrepreneurs were organized under three headings:

* **activities** – primarily concerned with exchanging information, undertaking analytical and conceptual work and networking/maintaining relationships (75%[1]).

- **functions** – marketing, sales, PR; product/service development; administration; finance; environmental monitoring (62%).
- **exploitation/exploration** – the former refers to activities which are aimed at improving efficiencies within the business (65%); the latter involves activities focused on experimentation and innovation (33%).

12.5 The Entrepreneurial Process

One of the common elements, which underpin the various academic attempts to understand new venture creation, is that it is described as a process rather than a single event. In fact, questions about the activities in which entrepreneurs engage during business start-up is central to the interest of academics and policymakers. Low and MacMillan (1988) set out a detailed account of the business creation process which still influences entrepreneurial scholars. In recent years, several new theoretical approaches have been developed to provide a better understanding of the behaviour associated with the entrepreneurial process. As Fisher (2012) points out, these new theoretical perspectives have taken very different approaches to the traditional causal explanation of how new ventures are created. In the causal approach, entrepreneurs follow a linear process of opportunity identification and evaluation, the setting of goals to exploit that opportunity and the identification of means by which to achieve the goals (Shane, 2003). In contrast, the process perspective pays attention to entrepreneurial actions which are based on an interrelated set of creative activities.

Evolutionary perspectives have strongly influenced the process view of entrepreneurship. Nelson and Winter (1982) developed the concept of organizational routines which have been influential in understanding how existing firms change as well as how new firms are created (see Chapter 1). The work of Aldrich (1999) extended the evolutionary approach by introducing ideas related to variation, selection and retention (Jones & Li, 2017). Moroz and Hindle (2012) identified 32 'scholarly works' which focus on the entrepreneurial process and examined four of those 'theories' in greater depth: Gartner (1985), Bruyat and Julien (2001), Sarasvathy (2001) and Shane (2003). In their conclusions Moroz and Hindle (2012, p. 811) suggest that there are important points of agreement based on their analysis of the four process models:

1. The relationship between individual and opportunity is crucial (not all entrepreneurs can exploit all opportunities).

2. Time matters as opportunities do not last forever and market receptiveness changes.

3. Action is crucial to the exploitation of any opportunity.

4. Understanding the context in which the entrepreneurial action takes place is essential.

According to Fisher (2012, p. 1020) a range of new theoretical perspectives emerged early in the twenty-first century outlining behaviours associated with the entrepreneurial process: effectuation theory (Sarasvathy, 2001), entrepreneurial bricolage (Baker & Nelson, 2005), the creation perspective (Alvarez & Barney, 2007) and user entrepreneurship (Shah & Tripsas, 2007). In addition, there is a largely European approach that draws on the practice perspective and is known as 'entrepreneuring' (Steyaert, 2007). Based on a detailed study of six entrepreneurial ventures, Fisher (2012) attempted to establish whether traditional theory (the casual model) or more *modern* behavioural theories (effectuation and bricolage) provide the better explanation of real-life entrepreneurial activities. A cohort of six web-based companies[2] founded in the early 2000s were analysed using multiple data sources and Fisher (2012) attempted to match the data to the behaviours associated with each theory. Only two of the start-ups, Flickr and Tripadvisor, adopted approaches to business start-up that fitted with causation theory: the entrepreneurs identified and evaluated the opportunity, gathered the required resources and then began to exploit the opportunity. There was no evidence that any of the other four start-up ventures adopted behaviours associated with causation. Although effectuation and bricolage are largely independent theories, there are many consistencies in terms of entrepreneurial behaviours during business start-up. Fisher (2012, p. 1024) concludes that there are four strong similarities associated with the two modern process theories:

1. Existing resources are important for the exploitation of opportunities.

2. Action helps overcome resource constraints.

3. Community is the catalyst for venture emergence.

4. Resource constraints are a source of creative innovation.

Fisher (2012) goes on to suggest that 'the behaviors associated with effectuation and bricolage appeared to be more representative of what entrepreneurs do in building their businesses'. The findings of this study have many practical implications for the way in which most entrepreneurs start new businesses. Certainly, contemporary theories such as effectuation and bricolage are useful alternative ways of thinking about how entrepreneurs engage with the start-up process.

Davidsson and Gruenhagen (2021) carried out a systematic review of literature focused on the new venture creation process, which is used interchangeably with 'the entrepreneurial process'. Their study updates earlier reviews examining the start-up process (Bygrave & Hofer, 1991; Fisher, 2012; McMullen & Dimov, 2013; Moroz & Hindle, 2012; Steyaert, 2007). The authors identify a range of key contributions to process theory beginning with Gartner's influential framework of the new venture creation process (Gartner, 1985) to a recent contribution introducing the importance of time and temporality (Wood, Bakker & Fisher, 2021).[3] The research, covering a 30-year period of published work in leading entrepreneurship and management journals, identified 116 contributions to the new venture creation process. Given the centrality of business start-up to any understanding of entrepreneurship, Davidsson and Gruenhagen (2021) expressed surprise at what they describe as the limited literature base. In addition, the focus and terminology are highly variable, and the field is divided into two distinct groups. First, research described as 'deeply process engaged' (qualitative) with a strong focus on in-depth case studies and, secondly, hypotheses-based articles (quantitative) many of which utilized PSED data (Davidsson & Gruenhagen, 2021, p. 1093). Although they agree that the literature review provides considerable insight into the entrepreneurial process, overall, the lack of communication between the two research paradigms (van Burg & Romme, 2014) restricts a more coherent understanding of the new venture creation process.

The problem is that after over 30 years of testimony to the centrality of a process view of new venture creation to our domain (Bygrave & Hofer, 1991; (Dimov, 2020): Gartner, 1985; Low & MacMillan, 1988; McMullen & Dimov, 2013; Shane & Venkataraman, 2000), the field of entrepreneurship does not have much of a unified body (or parallel, alternative bodies of significant magnitude) of knowledge about the NVC process which we discuss in a broadly shared terminology.

(Davidsson & Gruenhagen, 2021, p. 1094)

The authors conclude by pointing out the 'dwindling role' of the leading entrepreneurship journals (Entrepreneurship: Theory and Practice, Journal of Business Venturing) in this core research topic. They also acknowledge that there may well be important contributions to understanding the process of new venture creation in journals not covered by their review (Davidsson & Gruenhagen, 2021).

12.6 Alternative Theories of Entrepreneurship and Opportunities

Based on a study of 20 start-up companies in the Swedish mobile Internet industry, Sanz-Velasco (2006, p. 267) suggests that in most cases the opportunities were 'rudimentary' and in need of further development. Hence, even in a strongly technology-based sector opportunity creation was more likely to be the approach than opportunity discovery. A later study based on a random sample of 114 nascent entrepreneurs also found support for the view that opportunities are based on the entrepreneurs' subjective perceptions rather than having an objective reality (Edelman & Yli-Renko, 2010). The study also demonstrated that those entrepreneurs who actively engaged in 'venture-creation activities' are more likely to establish successful firms. As Edelman and Yli-Renko (2010, p. 850) go on to state: 'It is through these efforts that entrepreneurs reduce subjective uncertainty regarding opportunities and mobilize resources to start a venture'. What these studies indicate is that the conventional rational, planned execution *causal model* (Shane, 2003, 2012; Shane & Venkataraman, 2000) does not capture the messiness associated with the reality of trying to start new businesses (Moroz & Hindle, 2012). In this section, we examine five alternative approaches to understanding the ways in which entrepreneurs identify or create new opportunities: entrepreneuring (Steyaert, 2007), bricolage (Baker et al., 2003), effectuation (Sarasvathy, 2001), user entrepreneurship (Shah & Tripsas, 2007), creation entrepreneurship (Alvarez & Barney, 2007) and bootstrapping (Winborg & Landström, 2001).

12.6.1 Entrepreneuring as Practice

Process theorists argue that entrepreneurship is dominated by equilibrium-based theories, which focus on entrepreneurial performance (Steyaert, 2007; Steyaert & Katz, 2004). Consequently, entrepreneurship is perceived as an activity which can be defined in terms of profit and status. In contrast, Steyaert (2007) uses the verb entrepreneuring to focus attention on entrepreneurship as a deeply processual activity involving social creativity, dialogue and imagination. As an open-ended concept, entrepreneuring extends possibilities for understanding entrepreneurial experience through the creative perspective represented by effectuation theory (Sarasvathy, 2001, 2008). To make sense of the notion of relationality, Steyaert adopts the term prosaic to capture the ordinary everyday experience of entrepreneurial practices. Intertextualities extend entrepreneurial practice away from isolated actors to involve conversational processes of 'co-authorship' (Steyaert & Katz, 2004, p. 9). Entrepreneurial practices and opportunities cannot be reduced to objective entities because they are always unfinished and constantly emerging during the process of entrepreneuring (Poldner, Branzei & Steyaert, 2019; Steyaert, 2007; Weiskopf & Steyaert, 2009). To engage with entrepreneurial prosaics and experience as 'becoming', processual research is promoted as the narrative analysis and discursive interpretation of entrepreneurial storytelling (Johannisson, 2011; Steyaert, 2004). Weiskopf and Steyaert (2009) conclude that entrepreneurial practice becomes a subversive form of social creativity that is characterized by movement, life, and change so that 'selves' are always unfinished.

In a study of a family-based start-up business, Jones and Li (2017) link entrepreneuring (Steyaert, 2007), effectuation theory (Sarasvathy, 2001) and the concept of sensemaking (Weick, 1995). Two young brothers were still at school when they started their business and certainly did not set out with clear goals. Instead, the business opportunity gradually evolved as a result of the younger brother's online trading activities, which brought his money-making activities his parents' attention. Jones and Li (2017) contend that the brothers' ability to manage the transition from a lucrative supplement to their pocket-money into a rapidly growing business was shaped by the habits, heuristics and nascent routines inculcated by their parents as well as the sensemaking processes of enactment, selection and retention (Aldrich & Yang, 2012; Weick, Sutcliffe & Obstfeld, 2005). As effective entrepreneurs, they understood that the process of starting a new business was based on making the best of ambiguous information and limited resources (Macpherson, Herbane & Jones, 2015).

Entrepreneuring is strongly associated with what is known as the 'practice turn' in organization theory (Nicolini, 2017; Whittington, 1996). Adopting a practice perspective means rejecting explanations of entrepreneurship based on either individual agency or societal structures (Lee & Jones, 2015). Instead, it is important to focus on the basic activities underpinning the creation of new opportunities: 'the meetings, the talking, the selling, the form-filling and the number-crunching' (Thompson, Verduijn & Gartner, 2020, p. 247). There appears to be little agreement about what constitutes 'a practice' and there are even some scholars such as Nicolini (2017) who suggest that attempting a definition will inevitably mean 'reifying' the concept (Burrell & Morgan, 1979). Nevertheless, Thompson et al. (2020, p. 249) suggest that 'most practice theorists loosely conceive of a 'practice' as an array of sequentially ordered activity – 'doings' and 'sayings' – that are (a) relational; (b) embodied; (c) mediated and (d) organized around shared practical understanding. Practices are relational in that the actions that compose them are enacted by multiple practitioners but are organized and connected through their sequence. In their systematic review of the entrepreneurship as practice (EaP) literature, Champenois, Lefebvre and Ronteau (2020) found there were neither quantitative data nor mixed method approaches among the 48 empirical papers. There were, however, a range of qualitative research approaches ranging from use of biographies (Goss, Jones, Betta & Latham, 2011), open-ended interviews or in-depth semi-structured interviews (Holt & Macpherson, 2010), to 'quasi' ethnographic approaches (Chalmers & Shaw, 2017). They then identified the most common practices: narratives, discursive, sensegiving, sensemaking practices [12 articles], resource acquisition/use [8], gendered practices, becoming [6], social resourcing [6], networking [5], practice renewal [5], effectuation [4], learning everyday entrepreneurial practices [4] and organizing [4]. Practitioners were concentrated on the following: women entrepreneurs [8 articles], bundle of practitioners, different types of entrepreneurs or mix of entrepreneurs, other practitioners such as mentors, or co-workers [7], social entrepreneurs [6], cultural industries entrepreneurs [4], disadvantaged/minority entrepreneurs' [4], successful entrepreneurs [4], tech entrepreneurs [4] and service entrepreneurs [4] (Champenois et al., 2020, p. 289). The literature review revealed that the work of most

EaP researchers was informed by 'prominent practice theories' including Bourdieu (1977) Giddens (1987) and Schatzki (1996).

As a recent review of the EaP literature confirms (Champenois et al., 2020), this approach is in direct opposition to conventional positivistic research which dominates output in leading journals (Soto-Simeone, Siren & Antretter, 2020). Of the 76 papers included in their review only two appeared in *Entrepreneurship: Theory & Practice* and five in the *Journal of Business Venturing* and most of those seven papers were published at least ten years ago. Thompson et al. (2020, p. 252) point out that the practice tradition sits uneasily with academic publishing where articles are valued for their 'theoretical contributions'. Theories of practice do not explain causal relations and cannot be tested in the positivist sense. Teague, Tunstall, Champenois and Gartner (2021, p. 570) in their introduction to a special issue explain that 'social practice theory, is not a singular theory but a group of theories that share ontological assumptions'. The authors go on to explain that practices are repeated patterns of behaviour that are distinct from both the individual and the behaviour as units of inquiry (Teague et al., 2021, p. 570). Finally, Antonacopoulou and Fuller (2020) argue that the EaP perspective should be extended by focusing on the 'lived experience' of entrepreneurs. They suggest that the concept of emplacement draws attention to the enactment and embodiment of entrepreneurship 'from which judgements, intentions, choices, actions and their impact emanate' (Antonacopoulou & Fuller, 2020, p. 257).

12.6.2 Bricolage

The term bricolage means making the best use of the resources you have in your possession. According to Baker and Nelson (2005) *bricoleurs* use resources in ways for which they were not originally intended in a process they describe as 'creative reinvention'. In entrepreneurial terms bricolage means that individuals use the resources to which they have access in a creative way to uncover and exploit new business opportunities. In attempting to exploit opportunities by adopting a bricolage approach entrepreneurs can use a combination of five activities: 1) *physical inputs* – making use of unwanted materials; 2) *labour inputs* – encouraging customer or suppliers to work in the business; 3) *skills input* – encouraging the use of amateur or self-taught skills; 4) *customers/markets* – supplying products or services that would otherwise be unavailable; 5) *institutional/regulatory environment* – not seeing rules and regulations as constraining (Fisher, 2012). The ideas underpinning bricolage are linked to the work of Penrose (1959) who suggested that resource environments are idiosyncratic to the individual entrepreneur or firm. What this means is that resources, equipment, or even skills, which are worthless to one entrepreneur can be extremely valuable to someone else.

Baker and Nelson (2005) note that bricolage relies on scavenging resources in order to extract use from goods that others do not value or do not intend to use. Importantly, entrepreneurs who target this activity at a particular problem (selective bricolage) are more likely to be successful. While bricolage provides a way of recombining and reconfiguring resources the solution must be embedded into the firm's existing routines if it is to provide long-term economic benefit. In contrast, 'parallel bricoleurs' move between projects responding to customer expectations and obligations without a clear focus (Baker & Nelson, 2005). Notwithstanding the differences between these types of bricolage, they both rely on experimentation or improvisation to test new solutions; in so doing resource combinations are broken down and/or reconfigured. In that sense, bricolage helps entrepreneurs to explore and exploit new opportunities that might otherwise be too expensive to investigate by more traditional means (Baker & Nelson, 2005; Miner, Bassoff & Moorman, 2001). The process of entrepreneurial bricolage is illustrated in Figure 12.3.

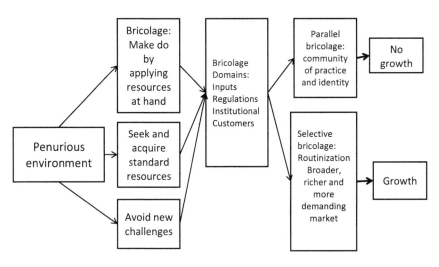

Figure 12.3 Entrepreneurial Bricolage

Stenholm and Renko (2016) link passion and bricolage in their study based on a large sample of (2489) Finnish entrepreneurs. They draw on the work of Cardon and colleagues (Cardon, Gregoire, Stevens & Patel, 2013; Cardon, Wincent, Singh & Drnovsek, 2009; Murnieks, Cardon & Haynie, 2020) to suggest that passion has three dimensions: inventing new products or services, founding new organizations and developing these organizations beyond initial survival. The research was designed to investigate how passionate entrepreneurs used bricolage as a means of helping their firms survive the early stages of business start-up (Stenholm & Renko, 2016). Bricolage is associated with entrepreneurial resourcefulness (Fisher, Neubert & Burnell, 2021) in making use of existing assets and creativity in accessing new resources. The results of the study confirmed that higher levels of bricolage were associated with improved chances of business survival. Stenholm and Renko (2016, p. 606) found that those entrepreneurs with a passion for developing a business or passion for inventing new solutions made use of bricolage to supplement their existing resources. The authors explain the results by suggesting that passionate individuals are less likely to give up and to use bricolage as part of their sustained efforts to succeed (Stenholm & Renko, 2016).

Bernardi and Pedrini (2020) extend bricolage theory by examining the way in which environmental entrepreneurs obtain access to additional resources. As we discuss throughout this book, all entrepreneurs have to deal with resource scarcity, but environmental entrepreneurs try to limit the natural resources used in their businesses. For example, Di Domenico, Haugh and Tracey (2010) created the concept of 'social bricolage', which is associated with communities lacking in facilities and services (Cheung et al., 2019; Jayawarna et al., 2020). Similarly environmental entrepreneurs aspire to preserve the natural environment and encourage biodiversity (Fisher, 2012). In their study, Bernardi and Pedrini (2020) interview 20 'biodynamic entrepreneurs' in the Italian wine producing industry. The cultivation of grapes is associated with environmental degradation and a lack of biodiversity, hence the interest in organic/biodynamic viticultures. The study established that the environmental entrepreneurs tailored their activities to make a positive impact on the environment while resisting environmental degradation, preserving the ecosystem and encouraging biodiversity (Bernardi & Pedrini, 2020). In terms of their theoretical contribution, the authors confirmed that 'typical' aspects of bricolage such as making do, refusal to accept limitations and a focus on improvisation were also relevant for environmental entrepreneurs. In addition, they identified three new constructs: environmental gain, sensibilization and network establishment (Bernardi & Pedrini, 2020, p. 8). 'Environmental gain' refers to generating a positive impact on the environment by recycling and selecting equipment that does not damage the environment. 'Sensibilization' means attempting to change people's mind-sets and encourage them to align their goals with protection of the environment. 'Network establishment' focuses on uses new contacts to acquire valuable resources including knowledge, information and natural resources (Bernardi & Pedrini, 2020). The authors also note that as the firms they studied were well established, their study confirms that bricolage is not only relevant to new ventures.

12.6.3 Effectuation Theory

Sarasvathy (2001) set out what she describes as an alternative approach to the traditional causal perspective. According to Sarasvathy (2001, p. 250) all nascent entrepreneurs begin with three categories of 'means'; their own traits, tastes and abilities; their particular set of knowledge; and their social networks (Galkina & Atkova, 2020). Hence, 'effectuation' is 'a tool for problem solving when the future is unpredictable, our goals unspecified or simply unknown and when the environment is not independent of our decisions' (Sarasvathy, 2004, p. 525). The key point in effectuation theory is that entrepreneurs begin with the means in their possession rather than establishing a set of end goals. The process is illustrated in Figure 12.4 in which the actual means at the entrepreneur's disposal influence their possible courses of action (that is, the type of business they can establish). Effectual entrepreneurs engage in activities associated with starting their business and allow longer-term goals to emerge as they exploit the means under their control. The basic premise is that opportunities are *actively created* rather than being identified before the business is started as per the Shane model. Goals evolve over time as the business develops rather than being established at the outset. The factors which underpin effectuation theory are as follows (Fisher, 2012, p. 1024):

1. Start with means rather than end goals (bird-in-hand principle).
2. Apply affordable loss rather than expected returns (risk little, fail cheap).

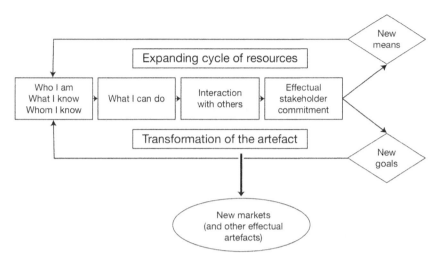

Figure 12.4 Effectual Entrepreneurship

3. Leverage relationships rather than carrying competitive analysis (crazy quilt principle).

4. Entrepreneurs exploit rather than avoid contingencies (lemonade principle).

The theory of effectuation is based on Simon's (1959) decision theory, which indicates that rather than trying to predict future trends in an uncertain environment it is more effective to acquire information through experiential and iterative learning. Sarasvathy (2001) argues that one of the main benefits of an effectuation approach is that entrepreneurs who fail will fail very early and with much lower levels of investment than if they had pursued an opportunity based on the causal approach (Read, Sarasvathy, Dew, Wiltbank & Ohisson, 2011). As noted in Section 2.4, there are strong similarities between the effectual and bricolage approaches to starting a business. In Chapter 10, we combined these ideas together with bootstrapping to provide our own process of business creation.

The five principles underpinning effectuation theory are described in Section 2.4. Also, as we discuss in Section 12.6.7, there has been an extensive debate between the proponents of effectuation theory and those who oppose Sarasvathy's ideas. Therefore, here we highlight some recent work that has attempted to extend the original model of effectuation theory. Sarasvathy and Ramesh (2019) link effectuation theory to the concept of institutional analysis and development (IAD) (Ostrom, 2011) to explain how collective action can help deal with 'market failure' in terms of global warming and climate change. It is suggested that effectuation and IAD are complementary because the design principles (Ostrom, 2011) help explain the local and micro level factors that encourage collective action. Sustainable entrepreneurship is given a central role in the process of creating solutions to various environmental problems without ascribing particular entrepreneurial characteristics or motivations. 'Instead, it recognizes sustainable entrepreneurship as a process that involves any and all stakeholders who are willing to self-select into the process' (Sarasvathy & Ramesh, 2019, p. 421). Based on a longitudinal study of six high-technology firms, Jiang and Rüling (2019) identify differences in the ways entrepreneurs engage with the five process characteristics: perception of uncertainty, nature of aspirations, information processing, orientation of new goals and attention to new goals. As Jiang and Rüling (2019, p. 193) go on to point out: 'entrepreneurs may perform an effectuation activity such as building strategic alliances in response to their different perceptions of uncertainty about the market and their ability to respond'.

The role of national culture (Hofstede, 2001, 2015) in shaping collective identity and effectual entrepreneurial behaviour is examined by Strauß, Greven and Brettel (2021). The authors use the concepts of Power Distance, Individualism, Masculinity and Long-term Orientation (Hofstede, 2001) to examine differences between entrepreneurs in Germany and Thailand. The research demonstrates that national culture influences effectual entrepreneurs. As stated by the authors: 'We showed that the usage of experimentation and flexibility during the entrepreneurial process is significantly influenced by cultural conditioning. Thereby, our findings support the existing theory that national culture has a significant influence on entrepreneurial processes' (Strauß et al., 2021, p. 1001). Finally, Hensel and Visser (2020) examine the links between personality and effectual behaviour based on a study of 128 students participating in a university-based 'pre-launch' programme. They found that three factors provided a comprehensive measure of effectual behaviour: bird-in-the-hand, pilot-in-the-plane and crazy quilt principles (see Section 2.4). The first two principles (bird-in-the-hand, pilot-in-the-plane) were positively influenced by sensitivity to feedback, sociability and ambition while the pilot-in-the-plane was influenced by extraversion (enjoying social interaction). The authors note Sarasvathy's argument that effectuation is a manifestation of entrepreneurial experience and expertise rather than being trait-based (Sarasvathy, 2001, 2008). 'The results of this study seem to cast serious doubt on this claim, based on the model revealing a strong and significant relationship between effectuation principles and personality' (Hensel & Visser, 2020, p. 477). Zhang, Foo and Vassolo (2021) surveyed a group of 143 entrepreneurs to examine the links between effectuation and cognition. The study revealed that exposure to the principles of effectuation increased illusions of control and reduced their overconfidence. While acknowledging the limitations of their study based on a relatively small sample, Zhang et al. (2021) point out the importance of integrating effectuation and cognitive science to better understand entrepreneurial decision-making.

12.6.4 User Entrepreneurship

In developing their concept of 'user entrepreneurship' Shah and Tripsas (2007) point out that many new ventures are founded by individuals who respond to needs identified in their daily lives. Such individuals then go on to create a solution to the problem which is eventually commercialized. The concept of a 'lead user' is well known in the innovation literature and is primarily associated with the work of Eric von Hippel (Morrison, Roberts & Von Hippel, 2000; von Hippel, 1986). The rise of user entrepreneurs is linked to universities in the UK and the US trying to be more effective in exploiting their knowledge base (Shah & Tripsas, 2007). The authors also suggest that prior experience and knowledge gained from previous experience also feature in user entrepreneurship. Shah and Tripsas (2007, p. 124) provide the following definition:

> We define user entrepreneurship as the commercialization of a new product and/or service by an individual or group of individuals who are also users of that product and/or service. We distinguish between two categories of user entrepreneurs: professional-users and end-users.

Professional users refer to those employed in organizations, including universities, who experience a product in their working lives and identify a need for improvement. End-users could be any consumer who experiences a product in their day-to-day lives. One well-known example is the British entrepreneur, James Dyson, who became frustrated with the inefficiency of the conventional vacuum cleaner he was using and developed his 'dual-cyclone' model (Conway & Jones, 2012). One of the ways in which user entrepreneurship differs from conventional entrepreneurship is that discoveries are often accidental and development of the idea occurs before any formal evaluation of the opportunity has taken place. Nevertheless, Shah and Tripsas (2020) point out that 46% of innovative start-ups (and 10.7% of all start-ups) that survive five years or more are founded by user entrepreneurs.

To investigate the phenomenon of user entrepreneurship Shah and Tripsas (2007) studied 263 firms operating in the 'juvenile products' sector because parents and grandparents are often responsible for new products. In total, 84% of the firms were founded by user entrepreneurs (all the firms had been established in the previous 18 years) and most of those were parents. Some products were radically new such as the 'baby stroller' while others were incremental changes – child car seats for underweight babies (Shah & Tripsas, 2007). The authors then go on to contrast their model with the 'classic Austrian' approach in which opportunities exist because of inefficiencies in the market and they are identified by alert entrepreneurs (Shane & Venkataraman, 2000). Shah and Tripsas (2007) go on to explain that there are two key differences associated with their concept of user entrepreneurs. First, it is an emergent process as entrepreneurs develop new products without first evaluating the market. Secondly, users are often embedded with a community who often play an active role in developing and diffusing the innovation. The idea of the user entrepreneur being part of a community who are willing to share information and knowledge is particularly important as pointed out by Morrison et al. (2000). Two other factors that are important elements of user entrepreneurship are information asymmetries and sticky knowledge. Because of their engagement with practical problems, user entrepreneurs have a unique position that helps them spot new opportunities. At the same time, that engagement with problems means that the knowledge is 'sticky' (Von Hippel, 1994) and difficult for outsiders to access.

A systematic review of the user entrepreneurship literature was carried out to establish the current state of knowledge (Escobar, Schiavone, Khvatova & Maalaoui, 2021). Adopting a bibliometric coupling approach, the authors were able to identify four distinct research clusters based on 69 papers (1991 to 2020) included in the review. The clusters were as follows: 1) entrepreneurial marketing, customer orientation and entrepreneurial personality (32 papers), 2) user knowledge and new ventures (25 papers), 3) entrepreneurial and innovation ecosystems (7 papers), 4) lead user innovation (5 papers). Escobar et al. (2021, p. 13) suggest that several issues emerge from their study including confirmation that most research has focused on entrepreneurial marketing and customer orientation in smaller firms. Secondly, the review confirms the important role played by communities of practice in supporting user entrepreneurs. Identifying obvious knowledge gaps, Escobar et al. (2021) point out that there has been limited research attention given to the role of the latest digital technologies on user entrepreneurship. In terms of influence, Shah and Tripsas (2007) published the single most cited paper while Lettl and colleagues (Hienerth & Lettl, 2017; Lettl, Hienerth & Gemuenden, 2008) have amassed the most citations (Escobar et al., 2021).

In a short 'reflective' article, Shah and Tripsas (2020) suggest that user entrepreneurs had important role to play in responding to recent disasters including climate change and the Covid-19 pandemic. The original model of user entrepreneurs is extended by identifying the importance of the open-source software movement, which encourages the free exchange of information and knowledge. They give the example of how openly available designs were important in the development of personal protective equipment (PPE) and ventilators in response to Covid-19. Doctors and nurses lacking essential PPE, developed their own products as protection against the virus and then freely shared their designs (Shah & Tripsas, 2020). This inventiveness when faced with unforeseen crises confirms the importance of acting collectively rather than individually. Shah and Tripsas (2020, p. 568) summarize as follows: 'The examples of user entrepreneurship that we observe showcase human ingenuity, need and compassion while also illuminating the importance of informed adaptation, open design and collaboration'.

Kalisz, Schiavone, Rivieccio, Viala and Chen (2021) examine the influence of national culture on user entrepreneurship. They suggest that various microlevel factors are proved to be inadequate for explaining user entrepreneurship. Their extensive data provide a two-factor solution: innovation-driven innovation and health-culture driven user entrepreneurship.

12.6.5 Creation Entrepreneurship

Another alternative approach to the opportunity identification (causal) view is that potential entrepreneurs use their knowledge and experience to *create* opportunities (Gartner et al., 1992; Macpherson & Holt, 2007). Alvarez and Barney (2007) suggest that various elements of creation theory have been described by a range of authors (Alvarez & Busenitz, 2001; Baker & Nelson, 2005; Gartner, 1985; Sarasvathy, 2001; Schumpeter, 1934). Rather than opportunities being exogeneous to the entrepreneur (causal theory), in the creation approach opportunities are endogenous to the actions and activities of the entrepreneur. The linking of experience to the creation of new opportunities can also be traced to the work of Edith Penrose (1959) who laid the foundations for the resource-based view of the firm (Barney, 1991). The legacy of Penrose can be found in a range of approaches to understanding the entrepreneur-opportunity interface: entrepreneurial embeddedness (Anderson & Jack, 2002; Anderson & Miller, 2003), entrepreneurial learning (Cope, 2005; Rae, 2004, 2005) and entrepreneurial practice (Fletcher, 2007; Katz & Gartner, 1988; Sarason, Dean & Dillard, 2006). Penrose (1959) is important because she rejected the idea that entrepreneurs are rational economic actors arguing that opportunities are created (rather than discovered) during the day-to-day practices of being an entrepreneur.

Discovery theory is based on the assumption that entrepreneurs are different from non-entrepreneurs because they are more alert to the potential of objective opportunities (Shane, 2000). In creation theory there are assumed to be limited differences between entrepreneurs and non-entrepreneurs at the start of the process particularly in terms of their cognitive abilities (Alvarez & Barney, 2007). However, Alvarez and Barney (2007) go on to suggest that as entrepreneurs engage in the creation process their cognitive abilities will be positively reinforced, gradually accentuating differences with non-entrepreneurs. The decision-making process will also be very different from the discovery approach because opportunities do not exist until they have been created. Consequently, when deciding to 'create' a new opportunity, there are limited data and information available to the entrepreneur. Hence, it is not possible to develop an elaborate business plan based on a detailed analysis of the opportunity as is the cased in the discovery approach. This means that entrepreneurs attempting to create an opportunity will find it difficult to access external finance from banks or venture capitalists. As Alvarez and Barney (2007, p. 20) point out, 'Bootstrapping' is likely to be a much more common way to finance activities taking place under creation conditions'. Bootstrapping refers to informal sources of finance and was discussed in Chapter 9 as well as in Section 12.6.6. At the time of writing, Alvarez and Barney (2007) argued that 'discovery theory' was the only opportunity formation and exploitation process that had been extensively discussed in the literature. Therefore, to encourage a broader debate in the field of entrepreneurship it was necessary to develop other theorical perspectives beginning with creation theory (Alvarez & Barney, 2007).

As pointed out by Alvarez and Barney (2013), the idea that both entrepreneurial opportunities and markets are socially constructed is fundamental to the creation perspective. Drawing on this idea, Goss and Sadler-Smith (2018) examine the different degrees of *agency* displayed by individuals during opportunity creation based on their previous social experiences rather than entrepreneurial cognition. Goss and Sadler-Smith (2018) adopt what they describe as a 'micro-sociology' perspective centred on 'affect', which incorporates both short-term moods and longer-term emotions (Baron & Tang, 2009). For example, there is increasing research interest in links between affect and motivation in the form of entrepreneurial passion (Cardon et al., 2013; Murnieks et al., 2020). The concept of 'interaction ritual chains' (Collins, 2004) illustrates how social interaction helps create a collective sense of identity leading to emotional energy and motivation. According to Goss and Sadler-Smith (2018, p. 223) interaction ritual chains provide 'an explicit and comprehensive formulation' of the intersubjective and affective bases of individual and collective agency. The authors then use the well-known case of Richard Branson to demonstrate the value of their model incorporating interaction rituals, emotional energy and opportunity-creating agency. Goss and Sadler-Smith (2018, p. 232) summarize the value of their approach: 'It broadens significantly the scope of opportunity creation research by making the roles of intersubjective and affective processes central, explicit, amenable to operationalization, and, hence, empirical testing'.

Alvarez and Barney (2020b) reflect on the uncertainty associated with the Covid-19 crisis for creation theory. They suggest that uncertainty (Knight, 1921) is fundament to Creation Theory in exploring the formation and exploitation of entrepreneurial opportunities (Alvarez & Barney, 2007, 2013, 2020a). Creation theory is based on the idea that forming opportunities often begins with limited information about the nature or extent of the opportunities. Alvarez and Barney (2020b) argue that 'rational analysis', based on existing theories is not helpful in dealing with high levels of uncertainty. Instead, it is necessary to examine the actions that started the uncertainty: 'By understanding what happened and the specific actions that started the uncertainty, individuals can shape the uncertainty and create opportunities for the betterment of humankind' (Alvarez & Barney, 2020b, p. 554). The links between Knightian uncertainty (Ramoglou, 2021) and the creation of opportunities are also addressed by Arikan, Arikan and Koparan (2020). Rather than the creation process being initiated by entrepreneurial alertness, Arikan et al. (2020) propose that entrepreneurial curiosity is the spark for the creation of opportunities. In addition, the 'entrepreneur's cognitive generative processes' are the basis for explaining how individuals 'create' the various ways by which to exploit opportunities (Arikan et al., 2020, p. 819).

12.6.6 A Social Theory of Bootstrapping

The idea of bootstrapping[4] has its conceptual roots in resource dependency theory (Pfeffer & Salancik, 1978), which suggests that firms rely on their abilities to acquire external resources. Winborg and Landström (2001) examined the techniques adopted by 262 Swedish small businesses and identified four distinct bootstrapping approaches: customer related, delay payments, owner related and joint utilization. In their study, Jones and Jayawarna (2010, p. 145) confirmed the presence of joint utilization and owner related bootstrapping techniques but found that customer related and delay payment formed a single construct which they termed 'payment related' (Ebben, 2009; Ebben & Johnson, 2006). At a conceptual level, bootstrapping is seen as a useful strategy for acquiring resources as a basis for helping new ventures succeed (Brush, Carter, Gatewood, Greene & Hart, 2006; Harrison, Mason & Girling, 2004; Timmons & Spinelli, 2004). Brush et al. (2006) studied the bootstrapping activities of 88 women-led high growth technology firms and found those using 'capital raising ingenuity' achieved rapid growth. Timmons notes that bootstrapping introduces 'a discipline of leanness' which encourages entrepreneurs to spend wisely and use resources to promote shareholder responsiveness (Timmons, 1999, p. 37). In their longitudinal study of early-stage start-up business, Jones and Jayawarna (2010) identified a link between the ability to bootstrap additional resources and entrepreneurs' social networks. Importantly, obtaining resources from their networks was dependent on entrepreneurs' ability to deploy the appropriate social skills (Baron & Tang, 2009). The results confirmed the findings of Carter, Brush, Greene, Gatewood and Hart (2003) who established that managerial skills and social networks were foundational to effective bootstrapping techniques. Brush (2008) also recognized that entrepreneurs relied on their social skills to engage with those stakeholders able to provide appropriate resources.

Rutherford, Pollack, Mazzei and Sanchez-Ruiz (2017, p. 658) begin their review of the bootstrapping literature by stating: 'this is an important contribution because, in some ways, bootstrapping is a construct in search of a theory to better explain its important role for new ventures'. The study was based on 60 articles all published in peer-reviewed journals and the authors identify a number of problems with the existing bootstrapping literature. Primarily, they argue, because the concept of bootstrapping lacks clarity the results have proved to be ambiguous particularly in relationship to the performance of new ventures. Therefore, Rutherford et al. (2017, p. 674) review the most widely used definitions of bootstrapping: 'launching ventures with modest personal funds' (Bhide, 1992, p. 110); 'highly creative ways of acquiring the use of resources without borrowing money or raising equity financing from traditional sources' (Freear, Sohl & Wetzel, 1995, p. 102); 'capital acquired from sources other than traditional providers of capital' (Van Auken & Neeley, 1996, p. 236); 'financial bootstrapping refers to the use of methods for meeting the need for resources without relying on long-term external finance from debt holders and/or new owners' (Winborg & Landström, 2001, p. 238); 'bootstrapping involves imaginative and parsimonious strategies for marshalling and gaining control of resources' (Harrison et al., 2004, p. 308). These definitions are regarded as too broad to be useful and Rutherford et al. (2017, p. 675) propose a more precise definition: 'starting a business with only financial capital possessed by the owners of the business or family members of the owners'. They suggest that this definition provides greater clarity and establishes boundaries with related concepts including bricolage and effectuation.

Rutherford et al. (2017) then go on to identify the three most widely used theoretical frameworks in the bootstrapping literature: transaction costs economics (TCE) (Williamson, 1993), resource dependency theory (RDT) (Pfeffer & Salancik, 1978) the resource-based view (RBV) (Barney, 1991). The problem, according to the authors, is that all three theories can lead to the identification of positive or negative relationships between boot-strapping and performance. Consequently, this has contributed to a lack of consistency and generalizability based on existing empirical data. The root problem with all three theories is they share a 'common ontological and epistemological fallacy that new firms are simply scaled-down versions of large and old firms' (Rutherford et al., 2017, p. 686). The authors suggest that signalling theory (Spence, 1973, 2002) resolves many of the problems associated with TCE, RDT, RBV. New and inexperienced entrepreneurs must send signals to various stakeholders about the viability of their ventures. The process of signalling overcomes problems of information asymmetry, which are inevitably associated with business start-ups (Franck, Huyghebaert & D'Espallier, 2010).

While we acknowledge that signalling theory is a useful adjunct to bootstrapping, we believe that it ignores the creative processes associated with learning to bootstrap by applying the appropriate social skills to relationships with resource providers. Furthermore, we do not see boot-strapping as 'one-off' event that takes place when the business is founded as Rutherford et al. (2017) appear to suggest. Rather, bootstrapping is a process that can underpin a firm's business model as it moves to maturity based on the principles of 'leanness' (Timmons, 1999). We also suggest that not all bootstrapping necessarily involve economic transactions as they can be based on trust, shared values and feelings of obligation and reciprocation (Jayawarna et al., 2020). Social capital is a crucial factor in accessing external resources (Granovetter, 1973, 2005) and relational and structural embed-dedness have a key role in this process (Nahapiet & Ghoshal, 1998). While social exchange theory helps explain how regular interactions through strong relational embeddedness create the obligations, expectations and trust that support mutual resource exchanges (Blau, 1964), structural embedded-ness helps to lower the cost of resources that are distributed in dependency relationships (Tornikoski & Newbert, 2013). Ozdemir, Moran, Xing and Bliemel (2014) explain that 'meshed networks' combine the benefits of rela-tional and structural embeddedness and provide the best access to entrepre-neurial resources. Here we argue that combining the theoretical arguments from each perspective offers a better conceptualization of resource access and mobilization for entrepreneurial resources. There are similarities with the idea of a communities of practice (Section 5.6) in which various actors share knowledge, information and other resources freely (Jones, Meckel & Taylor, 2021b). Drawing on ideas discussed in Chapters 2, 5 and 6, we

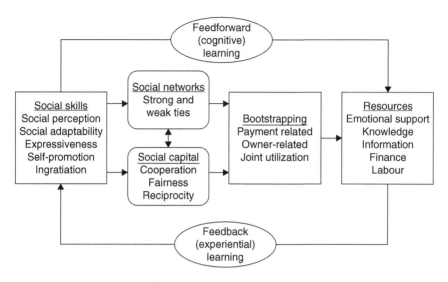

Figure 12.5 The Bootstrapping Process

suggest a model which links social skills, social networks, social capital and bootstrapping as a way of accessing various resources (Figure 12.5).

The acquisition of various social skills (perception, adaptability, expressiveness, self-promotion and ingratiation) will enable entrepreneurs to develop their social networks (strong and weak ties) to help create social capital (cooperation, fairness, reciprocity) as a means of bootstrapping additional resources for their business. Those resources could be as simple as friends and family providing emotional support (Jones & Li, 2017), information about new opportunities, new skills/knowledge and so on. As discussed in Section 5.3, the 'bootstrapping process' is reinforced by two complementary forms of learning. Feedforward or cognitive learning refers to the ways in which entrepreneurs deliberately plan to extend their social skills as a means of creating a larger and more diverse social network. While we acknowledge that some networks contacts can be made as a result of serendipitous meetings those entrepreneurs who have the appropriate social skills as more likely to benefit from those meetings (Conway & Jones, 2012). Secondly, experiential learning means that the entrepreneur acquires a better understanding of the bootstrapping process by reflecting on their earlier experience. To state this process more formally:

Developing the appropriate social skills will enable entrepreneurs to establish more extensive social networks/social capital as a basis for bootstrapping activities that provides access to additional resources. This process will be reinforced by cognitive and experiential learning.

12.6.7 Summary: Comparing Theories

Very few new businesses started by young people taking courses in higher education will be based on the kind of tangible market opportunities described by scholars such as Shane and Venkataraman (Shane, 2000, 2012; Shane & Venkataraman, 2000). Even if they were able to identify an objective opportunity, the chances of them obtaining the necessary financial resources would be remote. Adopting an approach in which young, nascent entrepreneurs make the best of the resources to which they have access means they will have more chance of success and they will be exposed to much less financial risk. Therefore, we suggest that most 'alternative' theories, discussed above, provide a better understanding of the way in which inexperienced entrepreneurs create opportunities as they attempt to set-up new businesses. While it is not impossible for younger people to start their businesses as 'user entrepreneurs' the evidence suggests that those with some work experiences are more likely to take this route (Escobar et al., 2021; Shah & Tripsas, 2007, 2020).

As several authors confirm, there are considerable overlaps in the newer theoretical perspectives on business start-up (Edelman, Manolova, Shirokova & Tsukanova, 2016; Fisher, 2012; Fisher et al., 2021; Sanz-Velasco, 2006). In Table 12.2, we compare the six alternative approaches to opportunity discovery based on seven dimensions: creation/discovery, low-cost resources, networking, process-driven, social practices, improvision and level of information. Five of the theories are based on the creation approach to opportunities with only Bootstrapping the outlier. This is primarily the case because the bootstrapping literature concentrates on the acquisition of resources rather than the nature of opportunities (Jones & Jayawarna, 2010). In addition, four of the six theories feature low-cost of resources as a key factor in the start-up process. While it is possible to speculate that both entrepreneuring-as-practice (EaP) and user-entrepreneurship will often involve businesses started with minimum external funding, this is not specified in either theoretical approach. With regards to the remaining four factors, there is consistency across all six alternative theories. For example, in discovery theory (Shane, 2000), the collection of data on the extent of the opportunity and the likely

Table 12.2 Comparing Alternative Theories of Entrepreneurship

Theory	Creation/discovery	Low-cost resources	Social networks	Process-driven	Social practices	Improvis-ation	Information
EAP	Create	N	Y	Y	Y	Y	Limited
Bricolage	Create	Y	Y	Y	Y	Y	Limited
Effectuation	Create	Y	Y	Y	Y	Y	Limited
User Ent	Create	N	Y	Y	Y	Y	Limited
Creation Ent	Create	Y	Y	Y	Y	Y	Limited
Bootstrap	C&D	Y	Y	Y	Y	Y	Limited

financial returns are crucial activities if entrepreneurs are to obtain external funding. In contrast, all the alternative theories suggest that entrepreneurs can and do proceed based on limited information about the extent of the opportunity.

Despite strong similarities, the six alternative theories seek to explain very different elements of the entrepreneurial process as illustrated in Table 12.3. As pointed out above, there are several publications reviewing literature focused on the entrepreneurial process (Fisher, 2012; Moroz & Hindle, 2012; Steyaert, 2007). Based on their recent review of literature examining the new venture creation process published in leading journals over the past 30 years, Davidsson and Gruenhagen (2021, p. 1104) reach the following conclusion:

Table 12.3 Main Focus of the Alternative Theories

Theory	Main Focus of the Theory	Research Approach
Enterpreneuring-as-practice	Entrepreneurship is a deeply processual activity involving social creativity, dialogue and imagination.	Qualitative
Bricolage	Entrepreneurs in penurious environment make do with the resources at hand + combine resources for new purposes	Mainly qualitative
Effectuation	Using own means, entrepreneurs identify and exploit opportunities in markets with high levels of uncertainty	Mainly qualitative
User Entrepreneurs	New ventures are founded by individuals who create and commercialize solutions to problems in their daily lives.	Qualitative
Creation Entrepreneurs	Potential entrepreneurs use knowledge and experience to *create* opportunities that are endogenous to their actions and activities	Qualitative
Bootstrapping	Entrepreneurs obtain additional resources either free (sharing) or well below the market price	Qualitative & quantitative

At the outset of this article, we asked whether entrepreneurship research has been making satisfactory progress in building insights, concepts, theories and shared understandings about new venture creation as a process. What we found in our review is a rich and varied literature offering many excellent and enticing studies, but which – despite notable growth in quality and quantity – is surprisingly limited in volume and sometimes frustratingly difficult to integrate.

Building on their earlier work (Landström et al., 2012), Landstrom and Harirchi (2018) point out that the study of entrepreneurship emerged because of its practical and political relevance. Consequently, the field is fragmented with scholars from a wide range of disciplinary backgrounds engaged in the study of entrepreneurship. In an attempt to map the 'social structure' of the field, Landstrom and Harirchi (2018) obtained 870 responses to a web-based survey from the global entrepreneurial community. Their data revealed three distinct clusters: entrepreneur conferences, entrepreneurial economics and entrepreneurial journals. The conference cluster had two main sub-clusters; a North American cluster associated with the International Confederation of Small Business (ICSB) at Babson College and a European cluster involving the RENT and ISBE conferences. The economic cluster has three sub-clusters; strategic entrepreneurship, economic entrepreneurship and a Schumpeterian policy cluster. The journal cluster also had three sub-clusters. Two of those were dominated by north American scholars associated with the *Journal of Business Venturing* and *Entrepreneurship: Theory and Practice*. The third cluster was primarily associated with northern European scholars publishing in *Entrepreneurship & Regional Development*. The authors conclude that it would be difficult to argue that entrepreneurship is a 'coherent scholarly community' as there is a diversity of approaches, theoretical frameworks and even definitions of entrepreneurial activities (Landstrom & Harirchi, 2018, p. 661).

12.7 Debates about Entrepreneurial Theory

Lee and Jones (2015) identify a number of dualisms in entrepreneurship research including the key distinction between qualitative and quantitative approaches to data collection. They also suggest these two approaches are linked to another well-known dualism; the different research traditions associated with Europe and the United States (Down, 2013). Although Davidsson (2013) argues that the two traditions are more heterogeneous than classifying US entrepreneurship research as largely quantitative while the European tradition is regarded as largely qualitative. It is certainly the case that most articles in the leading US entrepreneurship journals (ETP, JBV, SEJ) follow in the broadly positivist tradition and are firmly located within the functionalist paradigm. A recent review of literature related to new venture survival identified 205 studies of which 75% (153) were quantitative, only 10% qualitative and less than 2% (4) used mixed methods. As the authors go on to state: 'suggesting that this field has been dominated by positivistic research approaches' (Soto-Simeone et al., 2020, p. 7). In total, 97 of the studies were published in the entrepreneurship journals and the majority (96%) were in 3 or 4 rated journals (Soto-Simeone et al., 2020). According to Al-Amoudi and Willmott (2011) these deep-seated philosophical differences can be summarized as variations between constructionism and positivism with a mid-point occupied by critical realism. Studies based on the critical realist perspective are starting to emerge in the entrepreneurship arena (Kitching and Rouse, 2020; Ramoglou, 2013; Ramoglou and Tsang, 2016). Although, these publications are primarily critiques of existing research approaches without offering empirical studies based on critical realist methods. To some extent, the debate between the two opposing camps can be explained by the discussion about the status of 'effectuation' as a legitimate theory of entrepreneurship.

Arend et al. (2015) provide a comprehensive critique of effectuation theory, which was found to be 'ineffectual' based on a 'comprehensive theory-assessment framework'. While Arend et al. (2015, p. 544) are positive about some elements of effectuation theory, overall they suggest that there is substantial amount of work to be done before effectuation can become a 'solid theory'. The main weaknesses[5] in effectuation theory (Sarasvathy, 2001) are as follows. First, there is a failure to acknowledge previous process-driven research (Aldrich & Martinez, 2001; Gartner, 1989; Low & MacMillan, 1988) work on social networks (Uzzi, 1997) as well as bricolage (Baker & Nelson, 2005; Lévi-Strauss, 1967). Secondly, there is a lack of diversity and depth in the original sample of 27 experienced entrepreneurs (Sarasvathy, 2001) as well as in other attempts (Dew, Read, Sarasvathy & Wiltbank, 2009) to verify effectuation theory (Baron, 2009). Thirdly, effectuation theory is missing a number of important 'units' such as contextual competition and industry forces including rivalry and competition, which 'casts doubt on the validity of the model' (Arend et al., 2015, p. 639). Fourthly, effectuation theory focuses on a descriptive account of how, rather than why, various entrepreneurial actions take place. Fifthly, there are a number of 'questionable' assumptions underpinning effectuation theory including the lack of any explanation of how new value and longer-term business sustainability are created. Sixthly, rather than being a single construct, effectuation is an amalgam of several different cognitive processes and behaviours. Finally, because of the weaknesses discussed above, it is claimed that testing effectuation theory based on large-scale surveys would be difficult. The authors then examine a small number of published papers attempting to validate effectuation theory: 'In sum, we do not find strong evidence of a meaningful impact of effectuation on the thinking of the wider field in terms of its diffusion to top business journals' (Arend et al., 2015, p. 643).

In response, Read et al. (2016b) contend that Arend and colleagues (referred to as ASB) create a 'strawman' by assessing effectuation theory according to positivistic criteria such as falsifiability and theory testing. In particular, Arend et al. (2015) assume human action takes place within a world of 'stable states' whereas effectuation is based on 'a pragmatist stance of seeing the world as in-the-making and therefore makeable through human action' (Read et al., 2016b, p. 528). A further problem with ASB's critique is that they base many of their arguments on a sample of 26 empirical papers drawing on effectuation theory. Read et al. (2016b) conducted their own search of the literature and selected 85 articles not cited by ASB in their paper. They then suggest that many of the issues raised by ASB have, in fact, already been dealt with in the literature. Furthermore, this literature includes scholars who are seeking to take the field of entrepreneurship beyond the positivist perspective.

Gupta, Chiles and McMullen (2016) critique ASB because they ignore the fact that effectuation is a process theory of entrepreneurship. They explain that Sarasvathy (2001) based her ideas on the work of key figures associated with process theory (March & Simon, 1958; Mintzberg, 1973; Weick et al., 2005). Because ASB's theory-assessment framework uses 'variance criteria' to assess Sarasvathy's work, their thesis is subject to 'erroneous inferences' about the status of effectuation as a theory. According to Gupta et al. (2016) variance theory is concerned with explanations of change in outcomes (growth, profitability etc) based on a set of independent variables. In contrast, process theory attempts to explain how a phenomenon evolves as a result of 'temporal ordering and sequential interactions of myriad events and activities' (Gupta et al., 2016, p. 541). The authors also found that many studies applying effectuation theory used variance methods rather than process approaches. Gupta et al. (2016) suggest there are a number of reasons why variance methods are applied to the study of effectuation including a concentration on a positivist philosophy of science, which informs most published work in the leading entrepreneurship journals (Soto-Simeone et al., 2020; Soto-Simeone, Sirén & Antretter, 2021).

In their response to ASB's critique, Reuber, Fischer and Coviello (2016) broadly agree with Read et al. (2016b) that positivist criteria are used to evaluate effectuation theory. They point out that social science theories 'evolve through a process of selection and retention whereby revisions and modifications occur as theorists articulate, disseminate, apply, refine and repurpose them' (Reuber et al., 2016, p. 536). Consequently, the purpose of academic debate should be to reflect on the value of a specific theory rather than making judgements about whether that theory is 'true'. Reuber et al. (2016) do, however, suggest that effectuation theory's origin in pragmatism is focused primarily on individual creativity to the exclusion of habit. All human agency incorporates habitual behaviours which are shaped by previous experiences and helps inform decisions about future actions. In fact, creativity is seen to be based on the intelligent adaption to the prevailing conditions (Dewey, 1922). Therefore, rather than finding fault with effectuation theory, Reuber et al. (2016, p. 538) make the following suggestion: 'incorporating notions of habitual response into effectuation theory would involve examining the interplay between creativity and habit, rather than viewing them as substitutes'. For example, Jones and Li (2017) do incorporate habits, heuristics and routines (Aldrich & Yang, 2012) into their explanation of how 'effectual entrepreneurs' make the best of ambiguous information and limited resources in a process of enactment, selection and retention (ESR), which form the basis of nascent organizational routines.

Arend, Sarooghi and Burkemper (2016) provide a detailed reply to the various issues raised by supporters of effectuation theory in response to their original critique (Arend et al., 2015). In many ways, this illustrates the gap between the two sides of the argument in which groups belong to different research paradigms (Burrell & Morgan, 1979; Perry, Chandler & Markova, 2012; van Burg & Romme, 2014). Reed and Burrell (2019) reject the desire for an integrated theory of organizations (and entrepreneurship) in favour of contesting the dominant orthodoxy. As pointed out above, Lee and Jones (2015) identify a range of dualisms in the study of entrepreneurship and the causation-effectuation dichotomy symbolizes the fundamental ontological, epistemological and methodological chasm that exists between the largely qualitative and quantitative research traditions (Davidsson & Gruenhagen, 2021; Gupta et al., 2016).

12.8 Summary and Key Learning Points

The precursor to the setting up any new business is the would-be entrepreneur's ability to locate an appropriate business opportunity. The debate about whether entrepreneurs identify of create opportunities is one of the most important topics in the study of entrepreneurship. Neo-classical economic theory is based on the concept of market equilibrium, which is maintained by the 'invisible hand' of market forces (Renko, Shrader & Simon, 2012). While temporary disequilibrium resulting from changes in supply or demand may lead to some entrepreneurial opportunities in general there is no place for entrepreneurs in neo-classical theory. Schumpeter's work was located in neo-classical theory although he suggested that major technological change could lead to market disequilibrium and provide significant entrepreneurial opportunities via creative destruction (Schumpeter, 1934). In recent years, those belonging to the Austrian school has been influential in defining the nature of entrepreneurial opportunities (Chiles, Vulture, Gupta, Greening & Tuggle, 2010; Elias, Chiles & Qian, 2020; Renko et al., 2012; Shane & Venkataraman, 2000). As discussed above, the work of Shane/Venkataraman is the most important in bringing this view into the mainstream of entrepreneurship research. The Austrian view of markets is that they are in a constant state of disequilibrium and are characterized by dynamic competition. Entrepreneurial opportunities are created because of these constant disturbances to the market. The nature of those opportunities is that they have an objective reality, a reality that is distinct from the entrepreneurs who identify them as new business opportunities. Those subscribing to this view are described by Sarasvathy (2001) as the 'causal school'.

The alternative view rejects the idea that profitable opportunities are 'out there' waiting for entrepreneurs to discover them. Those who focus on the creation of opportunities do not accept that entrepreneur's base new businesses on a clear objective opportunity. Sanz-Velasco (2006) suggests that the differences between 'discovery' and 'creation' is reflected in differences between what Sarasvathy (2001) describes as 'causation' and 'effectuation'. The creation perspective proposes that, during the emergence of the firm, entrepreneurs' activities create the opportunities that they exploit (Alvarez & Barney, 2007, 2020a, 2020b). As discussed above, such a perspective draws heavily on the ideas of Penrose (1959) and Weick (1995). These theorists see the process of opportunity creation as a 'sensemaking process' in which entrepreneurs slowly develop an image of how they might start a new business. That 'image' influences entrepreneurial behaviours during an iterative process involving the matching of perceived means and perceived ends. Thus, the creation perspective is based on the principle that entrepreneurs make decisions based on their own subjective judgements rather than the evaluation of objective environmental factors (which underpin the causation perspective).

The creation perspective is linked to five other process theories of entrepreneurship (discussed above). Baker and Nelson (2005) use the terms improvization and bricolage to explain how opportunities are 'created and enacted idiosyncratically' by entrepreneurs making the best of limited resources (Bernardi & Pedrini, 2020). There are strong similarities between the bricolage and bootstrapping perspectives (Winborg & Landström, 2001). Bootstrapping focuses attention on the ways in which entrepreneurs with limited means make best the use of existing resources and access external resources (Rutherford et al., 2017). Effectuation theory (Sarasvathy, 2001) provides the intellectual bedrock for what we regard as a more realistic perspective on the entrepreneur-opportunity interface (Chen, Liu & Chen, 2021). For most entrepreneurs, the information available when they are considering starting a new venture is both incomplete and overwhelming. As described by Read et al. (2011, p. 5) data are confusing and conflicting, which means that entrepreneurs generate opportunities from a number of possibilities. Entrepreneuring (Steyaert, 2007) is closely associated with the so-called 'practice turn' (Nicolini, 2017) and focuses on the microprocesses associated with entrepreneurial activities (Champenois et al., 2020). The user perspective is concerned with the way in which opportunities are discovered when individuals are involved in their day-to-day activities (Shah & Tripsas, 2007). The term 'user entrepreneurship' suggest a close interaction with customer and lead users (von Hippel, 1986) as new opportunities are created (Escobar et al., 2021).

Therefore, the approach adopted in this book fits with the opportunity creation and effectuation/bricolage perspectives. We are certainly willing to acknowledge that on some occasions entrepreneurs do identify objective opportunities and then follow a conventional causal approach to the exploitation of that opportunity. However, such cases will, we suggest, be in a minority as most young entrepreneurs will adopt a more effectual approach to entrepreneurial development. Key Learning Points in this chapter are:

- You should be able to explain the key differences between the causal approach to understanding entrepreneurship and the bricolage/effectuation perspectives.
- You should be able to articulate the differences between opportunity identification and opportunity creation.
- You should be able to explain why understanding entrepreneurship as a process is important.
- You should be able to explain why the trait approach has been superseded by the narrative approach based on the work of Gartner.

12.9 Discussion Questions and Call to Action

- To what extent has the 'trait-based' approach contributed to a better understanding of entrepreneurship?
- What do you consider to be the main weaknesses in Shane's ideas about the entrepreneur-opportunity interface?
- What is the significance of Scott Shane's work to the theory of entrepreneurial opportunities?
- What are the core ideas that underpin effectuation theory?
- Can you explain the strengths and weaknesses of the 'alternative' theories of entrepreneurship discussed about (entrepreneuring, bricolage, effectuation, user entrepreneurship, creation entrepreneurship and bootstrapping)?

As indicated in the introduction to this chapter, we are committed to the idea that theory and practice are the opposite sides of the same coin. Theories of entrepreneurial learning (Wang & Chugh, 2014), social networks (Granovetter, 1973) and social capital (Coleman, 1988) have certainly enhanced the academic understanding of entrepreneurs and owner-managers. This deeper understanding is also reflected in enterprise education (Fayolle, Kariv & Matlay, 2019) in universities/colleges as well as practical courses for those already managing their own businesses (Kempster, Smith & Barnes, 2018). Therefore, even if you are not interested in articulating the differences between Shane's view of the entrepreneurial process (Shane, 2003) and Sarasvathy's contrasting perspective (Sarasvathy, 2008), we still believe that familiarity with key concepts discussed in this chapter will be of value to you in your entrepreneurial career. For example, as we stress throughout this book, the idea of bootstrapping (Jones & Jayawarna, 2010; Politis, Winborg & Dahlstrand, 2012) and the associated concept of bricolage (Baker & Nelson, 2005; Bernardi & Pedrini, 2020) are certainly of practical value to those students who are serious about starting their own businesses. On the other hand, for students undertaking postgraduate study, this chapter provides an overview of some of the most recent theories of entrepreneurship as well as the associated debates.

Notes

1 Percentages refer to the amount of time taken-up by these activities and functions during the working day.
2 The case study companies were 37signals, Bloglines, del.icio.us, Six Apart, Flickr and Tripadvisor.
3 Available online in 2019.
4 The practical issues associated with bootstrapping are discussed in Chapter 9, here we concentrate on a 'theory' of bootstrapping.
5 This is a very brief summary of the various weaknesses identify by ASB.

References

Aldrich, H. E. (1999). *Organizations Evolving*. London: Sage.
Aldrich, H. E. & Martinez, M. (2001). Many are Called, but Few are Chosen: An Evolutionary Perspective for the Study of Entrepreneurship. *Entrepreneurship: Theory & Practice*, 25(4), 41.
Aldrich, H. E. & Yang, T. (2012). Lost in translation: Cultural codes are not blueprints. *Strategic Entrepreneurship Journal*, 6(1), 1–17.

Alvarez, S. A. & Barney, J. B. (2007). Discovery and creation: alternative theories of entrepreneurial action. *Strategic Entrepreneurship Journal*, *1*(2), 11–26.

Alvarez, S. A. & Barney, J. B. (2013). Epistemology, Opportunities, and Entrepreneurship: Comments on Venkataraman et al. (2012) and Shane (2012). *Academy of Management Review*, *38*(1), 154–157.

Alvarez, S. A. & Barney, J. B. (2020a). Has the Concept of Opportunities Been Fruitful in the Field of Entrepreneurship? *Academy of Management Perspectives*, *34*(3), 300–310.

Alvarez, S. A. & Barney, J. B. (2020b). Insights from creation theory: The uncertain context rendered by the COVID-19 pandemic. *Strategic Entrepreneurship Journal*, *14*(4), 552–555.

Alvarez, S. A. & Busenitz, L. W. (2001). The entrepreneurship of resource-based theory. *Journal of Management*, *27*(6), 755–775.

Al-Amoudi, A. & Willmott, H. (2011) Where constructionism and critical realism converge: interrogating the domain of epistemological relativism, *Organization Studies*, *32*(1): 27–46.

Anderson, A. R. & Jack, S. L. (2002). The articulation of social capital in entrepreneurial networks: a glue or a lubricant? *Entrepreneurship & Regional Development*, *14*(3), 193–210.

Anderson, A. R. & Miller, C. J. (2003). 'Class matters': human and social capital in the entrepreneurial process. *Journal of Socio-Economics*, *32*, 17–36.

Antonacopoulou, E. P. & Fuller, T. (2020). Practising entrepreneuring as emplacement: the impact of sensation and anticipation in entrepreneurial action. *Entrepreneurship & Regional Development*, *32*(3/4), 257–280.

Arend, R. J., Sarooghi, H. & Burkemper, A. (2015). Effectuation as ineffectual? Applying the 3e theory-assessment framework to a proposed new theory of entrepreneurship. *Academy of Management Review*, *40*(4), 630–651.

Arend, R. J., Sarooghi, H. & Burkemper, A. C. (2016). Effectuation, Not Being Pragmatic or Process Theorizing, Remains Ineffectual: Responding to the Commentaries. *Academy of Management Review*, *41*(3), 549–556.

Arikan, A. M., Arikan, I. & Koparan, I. (2020). Creation Opportunities: Entrepreneurial Curiosity, Generative Cognition, and Knightian Uncertainty. *Academy of Management Review*, *45*(4), 808–824.

Baker, T., Miner, A. S. & Eesley, D. T. (2003). Improvising Firms: Bricolage, Account Giving and Improvisational Competencies in the Founding Process. *Research Policy*, *32*(2), 255–276.

Baker, T. & Nelson, R. E. (2005). Creating Something from Nothing: Resource Construction through Entrepreneurial Bricolage. *Administrative Science Quarterly*, *50*, 329–366.

Bandura, A. (1977). *Social learning theory*. Engelwood Cliffs, New Jersey: Prentice-Hall.

Barney, J. (1991). Firm Resources and Sustained Competitive Advantage. *Journal of Management, 17*(1), 99–121.

Baron, R. A. (2009). Effectual versus predictive logics in entrepreneurial decision making: Differences between experts and novices: Does experience in starting new ventures change the way entrepreneurs think? Perhaps, but for now, 'Caution' is essential. *Journal of Business Venturing, 24*(4), 310–315.

Baron, R. A. & Tang, J. (2009). Entrepreneurs' social skills and new venture performance: mediating mechanisms and cultural generality. *Journal of Management, 35*(2), 282–306.

Berger, P. L. & Luckmann, T. (1966). *The Social Construction of Reality: A Treatise in the Sociology of Knowledge.* New York: Doubleday.

Bernardi, C. D. & Pedrini, M. (2020). Transforming water into wine: Environmental bricolage for entrepreneurs. *Journal of Cleaner Production, 266.* doi:10.1016/j.jclepro.2020.121815

Bhide, A. (1992). Bootstrap Finance: The Art of Start-ups. *Harvard Business Review, 70*(6), 109–117.

Blau, P. M. (1964). *Exchange and power in social life.* New York: Wiley.

Bourdieu, P. (1977). *Outline of a theory of practice [by] Pierre Bourdieu; translated by Richard Nice*: Cambridge: Cambridge University Press.

Brockhaus, S. R. H. (1980). Risk Taking Propensity of Entrepreneurs. *Academy of Management Journal, 23*(3), 509–520.

Brush, C. G. (2008). Pioneering strategies for entrepreneurial success. *Business Horizons, 51*, 21–27.

Brush, C. G., Carter, N. M., Gatewood, E. J., Greene, P. G. & Hart, M. M. (2006). The use of bootstrapping by women entrepreneurs in positioning for growth. *Venture Capital, 8*(1), 15–31.

Bruyat, C. & Julien, P. A. (2001). Defining the field of research in entrepreneurship. *Journal of Business Venturing, 16*(2), 165–180.

Burgoyne, J. & Stuart, R. (1977). Implicit Learning Theories as Determinants of the Effect of Management Development Programmes. *Personnel Review, 6*(2), 5–14.

Burrell, G. & Morgan, G. (1979). *Sociological paradigms and organisational analysis: elements of the sociology of corporate life.* (Heinemann), Reprinted 2016, New York: Routledge.

Bygrave, W. D. & Hofer, C. W. (1991). Theorizing about Entrepreneurship. *Entrepreneurship: Theory & Practice, 16*(2), 13–22.

Caird, S. (1990). What Does it Mean to be Enterprising? *British Journal of Management, 1*(3), 137–145.

Cantillon, R. (1732/1931). *Essai Sur la Nature du Commerce General.* London: Macmillan.

Cardon, M. S., Gregoire, D. A., Stevens, C. E. & Patel, P. C. (2013). Measuring entrepreneurial passion: Conceptual foundations and scale validation. *Journal of Business Venturing*, *28*(3), 373–396.

Cardon, M. S., Wincent, J., Singh, J. & Drnovsek, M. (2009). The nature and experience of entrepreneurial passion. *Academy of Management Review*, *34*(3), 511–532.

Carter, N., Brush, C., Greene, P., Gatewood, E. & Hart, M. (2003). Women entrepreneurs who break through to equity financing: the influence of human, social and financial capital. *Venture Capital*, *5*(1), 1–28.

Carter, N., Gartner, W. B. & Reynolds, P. D. (1996). Exploring Start-up event sequences. *Journal of Business Venturing*, *11*(3), 151–166.

Chalmers, D. M. & Shaw, E. (2017). The endogenous construction of entrepreneurial contexts: a practice-based perspective. *International Small Business Journal*, *35*(1), 19–39.

Champenois, C., Lefebvre, V. & Ronteau, S. (2020). Entrepreneurship as Practice: Systematic Literature Review of a Nascent Field. *Entrepreneurship and Regional Development*, *32*(3–4), 281–312.

Chell, E., Haworth, J. & Brearley, S. (1991). *The entrepreneurial personality: Concepts, cases and categories*: Routledge Small Business Series. London and New York: Routledge.

Chen, J., Liu, L. & Chen, Q. (2021). The effectiveness of effectuation: a meta-analysis on contextual factors. *International Journal of Entrepreneurial Behavior & Research*, *27*(3), 777–798.

Cheung, C. W. M., Kwong, C., Manzoor, H., Rashid, M. U., Bhattarai, C. & Kim, Y. (2019). The co-creation of social ventures through bricolage, for the displaced, by the displaced. *International Journal of Entrepreneurial Behavior & Research*, *25*(5), 1093–1127.

Chiles, T. H., Vulture, D. M., Gupta, V. K., Greening, D. W. & Tuggle, C. S. (2010). The Philosophical Foundations of a Radical Austrian Approach to Entrepreneurship. *Journal of Management Inquiry*, *19*(2), 138–164.

Coleman, J. S. (1988). Social capital in the creation of human capital. *The American Journal of Sociology: Supplement, Organizations and Institutions: Sociological and Economic Approaches to the Analysis of Social Structure*, *94*, S95–S120.

Collins, R. (2004). *Interaction Ritual Chains*. Princeton, NJ: Princeton University Press.

Conway, S. & Jones, O. (2012). Networks and the Small Business. In S. Carter & D. Jones-Evans (Eds.), *Enterprise and Small Business: Principles, Practice and Policy* (3rd ed. pp 338–361). Harlow: Pearson.

Cope, J. (2005). Toward a Dynamic Learning Perspective of Entrepreneurship. *Entrepreneurship: Theory & Practice*, *29*(4), 373–397.

Cornelissen, J. P. & Clarke, J. S. (2010). Imagining and rationalizing opportunities: Inductive reasoning and the creation and justification of new ventures. *The Academy of Management Review*, *35*(4), 539–557.

Cornelissen, J. P., Clarke, J. S. & Cienki, A. (2012). Sensegiving in entrepreneurial contexts: The use of metaphors in speech and gesture to gain and sustain support for novel business ventures. *International Small Business Journal*, *30*(4), 213–241.

Curtin, R. (1982). Indicators of Consumer Behavior: The University of Michigan Survey of Public Consumers. *Public Opinion Quarterly*, *46*, 340–362.

Davidsson, P. & Gruenhagen, J. H. (2021). Fulfilling the Process Promise: A Review and Agenda for New Venture Creation Process Research. *Entrepreneurship: Theory & Practice*, *45*(5), 1083–1118.

Davidsson, P. (2013). Some reflection on research 'schools' and geographies, *Entrepreneurship & Regional Development*, *25*(1/2): 100–110.

Deakins, D. & Freel, M. (1998). Entrepreneurial learning and the growth process in SMEs. *Learning Organization*, *5*(3), 144–155.

Dew, N., Read, S., Sarasvathy, S. D. & Wiltbank, R. (2009). Effectual versus predictive logics in entrepreneurial decision-making: Differences between experts and novices. *Journal of Business Venturing*, *24*(4), 287–309.

Dewey, J. (1922). *Human nature and conduct: an introduction to social psychology*. New York: H. Holt and Co.

Dewey, J. (1938). *Experience and education*. New York: Macmillan Publishing.

Di Domenico, M., Haugh, H. & Tracey, P. (2010). Social Bricolage: Theorizing Social Value Creation in Social Enterprises. *Entrepreneurship: Theory & Practice*, *34*(4), 681–703.

Dimov, D. (2020). Opportunities, Language, and Time. *Academy of Management Perspectives*, *34*(3), 333–351.

Down, S. (2013). The distinctiveness of the European tradition in entrepreneurship research, *Entrepreneurship & Regional Development*, *25*(1/2), 1–4.

Down, S. & Warren, L. (2008). Constructing narratives of enterprise: cliches and entrepreneurial self-identity. *International Journal of Entrepreneurial Behavior and Research*, *14*(1), 4–23.

Ebben, J. J. (2009). Bootstrapping and the financial condition of small firms. *International Journal of Entrepreneurial Behavior & Research*, *15*(3/4), 346–363.

Ebben, J. J. & Johnson, A. (2006). Bootstrapping in small firms: An empirical analysis of change over time. *Journal of Business Venturing*, *21*, 851–865.

Edelman, L. F., Manolova, T. S., Shirokova, G. & Tsukanova, T. (2016). The impact of family support on young entrepreneurs' start-up activities. *Journal of Business Venturing*, *31*(4), 428–448.

Edelman, L. F. & Yli-Renko, H. (2010). The impact of environment and entrepreneurial perceptions on venture-creation efforts: Bridging the discovery and creation views of entrepreneurship. *Entrepreneurship: Theory and Practice*, *34*(5), 833–856.

Elias, S. R., Chiles, T. H. & Qian, L. I. (2020). Austrian economics and organizational entrepreneurship: a typology. *Quarterly Journal of Austrian Economics*, *23*(3/4), 313–354.

Engestrom, Y. (2014). *Learning by Expanding: An Activity-Theoretical Approach to Developmental Research* (2nd ed.). Cambridge: Cambridge University Press.

Escobar, O., Schiavone, F., Khvatova, T. & Maalaoui, A. (2021). Lead user innovation and entrepreneurship: Analyzing the current state of research. *Journal of Small Business Management*, *35*(1) 19–39.

Fayolle, A., Kariv, D. & Matlay, H. (2019). *The role and impact of entrepreneurship education: methods, teachers and innovative programmes.* Cheltenham: Edward Elgar.

Fisher, G. (2012). Effectuation, Causation, and Bricolage: A Behavioral Comparison of Emerging Theories in Entrepreneurship Research. *Entrepreneurship: Theory & Practice*, *36*(5), 1019–1051.

Fisher, G., Neubert, E. & Burnell, D. (2021). Resourcefulness narratives: Transforming actions into stories to mobilize support. *Journal of Business Venturing*, *36*(4). doi:10.1016/j.jbusvent.2021.106122

Fletcher, D. (2007). 'Toy Story': The narrative world of entrepreneurship and the creation of interpretive communities. *Journal of Business Venturing*, *22*, 649–672.

Franck, T., Huyghebaert, N. & D'Espallier, B. (2010). How Debt Creates Pressure to Perform When Information Asymmetries Are Large: Empirical Evidence from Business Start-Ups. *Journal of Economics and Management Strategy*, *19*(4), 1043–1069.

Freear, J., Sohl, J. E. & Wetzel, W. E. (1995). Angels: personal investors in the venture capital market. *Entrepreneurship & Regional Development*, *5*(1), 85–94.

Fritsch, M. & Mueller, P. (2004). Effects of New Business Formation on Regional Development over Time. *Regional Studies*, *38*(8), 961–975.

Galkina, T. & Atkova, I. (2020). Effectual Networks as Complex Adaptive Systems: Exploring Dynamic and Structural Factors of Emergence. *Entrepreneurship: Theory & Practice*, *44*(5), 964–995.

Gartner, W. B. (1985). A Conceptual Framework for Describing the Phenomenon of New Venture Creation. *The Academy of Management Review* (4), 696–706.

Gartner, W. B. (1989). 'Who Is an Entrepreneur?' Is the Wrong Question. *Entrepreneurship: Theory & Practice*, *13*(4), 47–68.

Gartner, W. B. (2006). Entrepreneurial narrative and a science of the imagination. *Journal of Business Venturing*, *22*(5), 613–627.

Gartner, W. B., Bird, B. J. & Starr, J. A. (1992). Acting As If: Differentiating Entrepreneurial From Organizational Behavior. *Entrepreneurship: Theory & Practice*, *16*(3), 13–31.

Gartner, W. B., Frid, C. J. & Alexander, J. C. (2012). Financing the Emerging Firm. *Small Business Economics*, *39*(3), 745–761.

Gartner, W. B. & Shaver, K. G. (2012). Nascent Entrepreneurship Panel Studies: Progress and Challenges. *Small Business Economics*, *39*(3), 659–665.

Gibb, A. (1997). Small Firms' Training and Competitiveness: Building upon the Small Firm as a Learning Organization. *International Small Business Journal*, *15*(3), 13–29.

Giddens, A. (1987). *Social theory and modern sociology*. Cambridge: Polity Press.

Goss, D., Jones, R., Betta, M. & Latham, J. (2011). Power as Practice: A Micro-Sociological Analysis of the Dynamics of Emancipatory Entrepreneurship. *Organization Studies*, *32*(2): 211–229.

Goss, D. & Sadler-Smith, E. (2018). Opportunity creation: Entrepreneurial agency, interaction, and affect. *Strategic Entrepreneurship Journal*, *12*(2), 219–236.

Granovetter, M. S. (1973). The Strength of Weak Ties. *American Journal of Sociology*, *78*(6), 1360–1380.

Granovetter, M. S. (2005). The impact of social structure on economic outcomes. *Journal of Economic Perspectives*, *19*(1), 33.

Greenberger, D. B. & Sexton, D. L. (1988). An interactive model of new venture initiation. *Journal of Small Business Management*, *26*(3), 1–7.

Gupta, V. K., Chiles, T. H. & McMullen, J. S. (2016). A Process Perspective on Evaluating and Conducting Effectual Entrepreneurship Research. *Academy of Management Review*, *41*(3), 540–544.

Hamilton, E. (2006). Whose Story Is It Anyway? Narrative Accounts of the Role of Women in Founding and Establishing Family Businesses. *International Small Business Journal*, *24*(3), 253–271.

Harrison, R. T., Mason, C. M. & Girling, P. (2004). Financial bootstrapping and venture development in the software industry. *Entrepreneurship & Regional Development*, *16*(4), 307–333.

Haslam, S. A., Cornelissen, J. P. & Werner, M. D. (2017). Metatheories and Metaphors of Organizational Identity: Integrating Social Constructionist, Social Identity, and Social Actor Perspectives within a Social Interactionist Model. *International Journal of Management Reviews*, *19*(3), 318–336.

Hayek, F. v. (1990). Economics and Knowledge. In M. Casson (Ed.), *Entrepreneurship* (pp. 33–80). Aldershot: Edward Elgar.

Hensel, R. & Visser, R. (2020). Does personality influence effectual behaviour? *International Journal of Entrepreneurial Behavior & Research*, *26*(3), 467–484.

Hienerth, C. & Lettl, C. (2017). Perspective: Understanding the Nature and Measurement of the Lead User Construct. *Journal of Product Innovation Management*, *1*, 3–12.

Hitt, M. A., Biermant, L., Shimizu, K. & Kochhar, R. (2001). Direct and Moderating Effects of Human Capital on Strategy and Performance in Professional Service

Firms: A Resource Based Perspective. *Academy of Management Journal*, *44*(1), 13–28.

Hofstede, G. (2001). *Culture's consequences: comparing values, behaviors, institutions, and organizations across nations* (2nd ed.). Thousand Oaks, CA: Sage.

Hofstede, G. (2015). Culture's causes: the next challenge. *Cross Cultural Management*, *22*(4), 545–569.

Holt, R. & Macpherson, A. (2010). Sensemaking, Rhetoric and the Socially Competent Entrepreneur. *International Small Business Journal*, *28*(1), 20–42.

Hyams-Ssekasi, D. & Caldwell, E. F. (2018). *Experiential Learning for Entrepreneurship: Theoretical and Practical Perspectives on Enterprise Education*: Cham (Switzerland): Springer International Publishing.

Jayawarna, D., Jones, O. & Macpherson, A. (2020). Resourcing Social Enterprises: The Role of Socially Oriented Bootstrapping. *British Journal of Management, 31*(1), 56–79.

Jiang, Y. & Rüling, C. C. (2019). Opening the Black Box of Effectuation Processes: Characteristics and Dominant Types. *Entrepreneurship: Theory & Practice, 43*(1), 171–202.

Johannisson, B. (2011). Towards a practice theory of entrepreneuring. *Small Business Economics*, *36*(2), 135–150.

Jones, O. (2022). Academic engagement with small business and entrepreneurship: Towards a landscape of practice. *Industry and Higher Education*, *36*(3), 279–293.

Jones, O. & Jayawarna, D. (2010). Resourcing new businesses: social networks, bootstrapping and firm performance. *Venture Capital, 12*(2), 127–152.

Jones, O. & Li, H. (2017). Effectual Entrepreneuring: Sensemaking in a Family-Based Start-Up. *Entrepreneurship and Regional Development*, *29*(5–6), 467–499.

Jones, O. & Macpherson, A. (2014). Research perspectives on learning in small firms. In D. Rae & C. L. Wang (Eds.), *Entrepreneurial Learning: New Perspectives in Research, Education and Practice* (pp. 289–312). Cheltenham: Edward Elgar Publishing.

Jones, O., Meckel, P. & Taylor, D. (2021a). *Creating Communities of Practice: Entrepreneurial Learning in a University-Based Incubator.* Cham (Switzerland): Springer.

Jones O, Meckel P, Taylor D. (2021) Situated learning in a business incubator: Encouraging students to become real entrepreneurs. *Industry and Higher Education*, *35*(4), 367–383.

Kalisz, D., Schiavone, F., Rivieccio, G., Viala, C. & Chen, J. (2021). Analyzing the Macro-level Determinants of User Entrepreneurship: The Moderating Role of the National Culture. *Entrepreneurship and Regional Development*, *33*(3–4), 185–207.

Kanter, R. M. (1983). *The change masters: Innovation for productivity in the Americancorporation*. New York: Simon & Schuster.

Katz, J. & Gartner, W. B. (1988). Properties of Emerging Organizations. *The Academy of Management Review*, 13(3), 429–441.

Kelley, D., Bosma, N. & Amoros, J. E. (2011). *Global Entrepreneurship Monitor: 2010 Global Report*. Global Entrepreneurship Research Association (www.gemconsort ium.org).

Kempster, S., Smith, S. & Barnes, S. (2018). *Chapter 14: A review of entrepreneurial leadership learning: an exploration that draws on human, social and institutional capitals*. Cheltenham: Edward Elgar Publishing.

Kirzner, I. M. (1973). *Competition and Entrepreneurship*. Chicago: University of Chicago.

Kirzner, I. M. (2009). The Alert and Creative Entrepreneur: A Clarification. *Small Business Economics* (2), 145–152.

Kitching, J. & Rouse, J. (2020). Contesting effectuation theory: Why it does not *explain* new venture creation. *International Small Business Journal*, 38(6), 515–535.

Knight, F. (1921). *Risk, Uncertainty and Profit*. New York: Houghton Mifflin.

Kohler, W. (1925). *The Mentality of Apes*. Norwood, NJ: Ablex

Kolb, D. A. (1984). Experiential learning: experience as the source of learning and development. Englewood Cliffs, N.J.: Prentice-Hall.

Lamont, L. M. (1972). What Entrepreneurs Learn from Experience. *Journal of Small Business Management*, 10(3), 36–41.

Landstrom, H. & Harirchi, G. (2018). The Social Structure of Entrepreneurship as a Scientific Field. *Research Policy*, 47(3), 650–662.

Landström, H., Harirchi, G. & Åström, F. (2012). Entrepreneurship: Exploring the knowledge base. *Research Policy*, 41, 1154–1181.

Larson, A. & Starr, J. A. (1993). A Network Model of Organization Formation. *Entrepreneurship: Theory & Practice*, 17(2), 5–15.

Lave, J. & Wenger, E. (1991). *Situated learning: Legitimate peripheral participation*. New York: Cambridge University Press.

Lee, R. (2017). *The Social Capital of Entrepreneurial Newcomers: Bridging, Status-power and Cognition*. London: Palgrave Macmillan.

Lee, R. & Jones, O. (2008). Networks, Communication and Learning during Business Start-up. *International Small Business Journal*, 26(5), 559–594.

Lee, R. & Jones, O. (2015). Entrepreneurial social capital research: resolving the structure and agency dualism. *International Journal of Entrepreneurial Behavior & Research*, 21(3), 338–363.

Lee, R., Tuselmann, H., Jayawarna, D. & Rouse, J. (2019). Effects of structural, rela-tional and cognitive social capital on resource acquisition: a study of entrepreneurs residing in multiply deprived areas. *Entrepreneurship & Regional Development*, 31(5/6), 534–554.

Lettl, C., Hienerth, C. & Gemuenden, H. G. (2008). Exploring How Lead Users Develop Radical Innovation: Opportunity Recognition and Exploitation in the Field of Medical Equipment Technology. *IEEE Transactions on Engineering Management, Engineering Management, IEEE Transactions on, IEEE Trans. Eng. Manage.*, *55*(2), 219–233.

Lévi-Strauss, C. (1967). *The Savage Mind*. Chicago: University of Chicago Press.

Lewin, K. (1943). Psychology and the Process of Group Living. *Journal of Social Psychology*, *17*(1), 113–131.

Lewin, K. (1951). *Field Theory in Social Science*. London: Harper Row.

Lounsbury, M., Gehman, J. & Glynn, M. A. (2019). Beyond Homo Entrepreneurus: Judgement and the Theory of Cultural Entrepreneurship. *Journal of Management Studies*, *56*(6), 1214.

Lounsbury, M. & Glynn, M. A. (2001). Cultural Entrepreneurship: Stories, Legitimacy and the Acquisition of Resources. *Strategic Management Journal*, *22*, 545–564.

Low, M. B. & MacMillan, I. C. (1988). Entrepreneurship: Past Research and Future Challenges. *Journal of Management*, *14*(2), 139–161.

Macpherson, A., Herbane, B. & Jones, O. (2015). Developing Dynamic Capabilities through Resource Accretion: Expanding the Entrepreneurial Solution Space. *Entrepreneurship and Regional Development*, *27*(5–6), 259–291.

Macpherson, A. & Holt, R. (2007). Knowledge, learning and small firm growth: A systematic review of the evidence. *Research Policy*, *36*, 172–192.

March, J. G. & Simon, H. A. (1958). *Organizations*. Oxford England: Wiley.

Mazzarol, T., Volery, T., Doss, N. & Thein, V. (1999). Factors influencing small business start-ups: A comparison with previous research. *International Journal of Entrepreneurial Behavior & Research*, *5*(2), 48.

McClelland, D. C. (1961). *The Achieving Society*. New York: Free Press.

McKelvie, A., Chandler, G. N., DeTienne, D. R. & Johansson, A. (2020). The measurement of effectuation: highlighting research tensions and opportunities for the future. *Small Business Economics: An Entrepreneurship Journal*, *54*(3), 689.

McMullen, J. S. & Dimov, D. (2013). Time and the Entrepreneurial Journey: The Problems and Promise of Studying Entrepreneurship as a Process. *Journal of Management Studies*, *50*(8), 1481–1512.

Miner, A. S., Bassoff, P. & Moorman, C. (2001). Organizational Improvisation and Learning: A Field Study. *Administrative Science Quarterly*, *46*(2), 304–337.

Mintzberg, H. (1973). *The Nature of Managerial Work*. New York: Harper & Row.

Mises, L. v. (1949). *Human Actions: A Treatise on Economics*. New Haven, CT: Yale University Press.

Moroz, P. W. & Hindle, K. (2012). Entrepreneurship as a Process: Toward Harmonizing Multiple Perspectives. *Entrepreneurship: Theory and Practice*, *36*(4), 781–818.

Morrison, P. D., Roberts, J. H. & Von Hippel, E. (2000). Determinants of User Innovation and Innovation Sharing in a Local Market. *Management Science*, *46*(12), 1513.

Mueller, S., Volery, T. & von Siemens, B. (2012). What do entrepreneurs actually do? An observational study of entrepreneurs' everyday behavior in the start-up and growth stages. *Entrepreneurship: Theory and Practice, 36*(5), 995–1017

Murnieks, C. Y., Cardon, M. S. & Haynie, J. M. (2020). Fueling the fire: Examining identity centrality, affective interpersonal commitment and gender as drivers of entrepreneurial passion. *Journal of Business Venturing, 35*(1). doi:10.1016/j.jbusvent.2018.10.007

Nahapiet, J. & Ghoshal, S. (1998). Social Capital, Intellectual Capital, and the Organizational Advantage. *Academy of Management Review, 23*(2), 242–266.

Nelson, R. R. & Winter, S. G. (1982). *An evolutionary theory of economic change.* Cambridge, MA: Belknap Press of Harvard University Press.

Nicolini, D. (2017). Practice theory as a package of theory, method and vocabulary: affordances and limitations. In M. Jonas, B. Littig & A. Wroblewski (eds.) *Methodological reflections on practice oriented theories* (pp. 19–34). Cham (Switzerland): Springer.

Ostrom, E. (2011). Background on the Institutional Analysis and Development Framework. *Policy Studies Journal, 39*(1), 7–27.

Ozdemir, S. Z., Moran, P., Xing, Z. & Bliemel, M. (2014). An Analytical Investigation of The Entrepreneur's Ability to Acquire Valued Resources From Others. *Academy of Management Annual Meeting Proceedings.* doi:10.5465/AMBPP.2014.15188abstract

Pavlov, I. P. (1927). *Conditioned Reflexes: An Investigation of the Physiological Activity of the Cerebral Cortex:* Translated and Edited by G. V. Anrep. London: Oxford University Press.

Penrose, E. (1959). *The theory of the growth of the firm.* Oxford: Oxford University Press.

Perry, J. T., Chandler, G. N. & Markova, G. (2012). Entrepreneurial Effectuation: A Review and Suggestions for Future Research. *Entrepreneurship: Theory & Practice, 36*(4), 837–861.

Pfeffer, J. & Salancik, G. R. (1978). *The external control of organizations: a resource dependence perspective.* New York: Harper & Row.

Piaget, J. (1926). *The language and thought of the child.* Oxford: Harcourt, Brace.

Pittaway, L. (2012). The Evolution of Entrepreneurship Theory. In S. Carter & D. Jones-Evans (Eds.), *Entrepreneurship and Small Business: Principles, Practice and Policy* (pp. 9–26). Harlow: Pearson.

Poldner, K., Branzei, O. & Steyaert, C. (2019). Fashioning ethical subjectivity: The embodied ethics of entrepreneurial self-formation. *Organization, 26*(2), 151–174.

Politis, D., Winborg, J. & Dahlstrand, Å. L. (2012). Exploring the resource logic of student entrepreneurs. *International Small Business Journal, 30*(6), 659–683.

Rae, D. (2004). Practical theories from entrepreneurs' stories: discursive approaches to entrepreneurial learning. *Journal of Small Business & Enterprise Development, 11*(2), 195–202.

Rae, D. (2005). Entrepreneurial learning: a narrative-based conceptual model. *Journal of Small Business and Enterprise Development, 12*(3), 323–335.

Raelin, J. A. (2007). Toward an Epistemology of Practice. *Academy of Management Learning & Education, 6*(4), 495–519.

Ramoglou, S. (2013). On the misuse of realism in the study of entrepreneurship. *Academy of Management Review, 38*(3): 463–465.

Ramoglou, S. (2021). Knowable opportunities in an unknowable future? On the epistemological paradoxes of entrepreneurship theory. *Journal of Business Venturing, 36*(2). doi:10.1016/j.jbusvent.2020.106090

Ramoglou, S. & Tsang, E. W. (2016) A realist perspective of entrepreneurship: Opportunities as propensities. *Academy of Management Review, 41*(3): 410–434.

Read, S., Sarasvathy, S. D., Dew, N. & Wiltbank, R. (2016a). Response to Arend, Sarooghi, and Burkemper (2015): Cocreating Effectual Entrepreneurship Research. *Academy of Management Review, 41*(3), 528–536.

Read, S., Sarasvathy, S. D., Dew, N. & Wiltbank, R. (2016b). Straw man at sea: positivist critique of a pragmatist theory. *Academy of Management Review, 41*(3), 528–536.

Read, S., Sarasvathy, S. D., Dew, N., Wiltbank, R. & Ohisson, A. V. (2011). *Effectual Entrepreneurship*. London and New York: Routledge Taylor and Francis.

Reed, M. & Burrell, G. (2019). Theory and Organization Studies: The Need for Contestation. *Organization Studies, 40*(1), 39–54.

Renko, M., Shrader, R. C. & Simon, M. (2012). Perception of entrepreneurial opportunity: A general framework. *Management Decision, 50*(7), 1233–1251.

Reuber, A. R., Fischer, E. & Coviello, N. (2016). Deepening the Dialogue: New Directions for the Evolution of Effectuation Theory. *Academy of Management Review, 41*(3), 536–540.

Reynolds, P. D. (2011). Informal and Early Formal Financial Support in the Business Creation Process: Exploration with PSED II Data Set. *Journal of Small Business Management, 49*(1), 27–54.

Reynolds, P. D. & Miller, B. (1992). New firm gestation: Conception, birth, and implications for research. *Journal of Business Venturing, 7*, 405–417.

Reynolds, P. D. & White, S. B. (1997). *The Entrepreneurial Process. Economic Growth, Men, Women, and Minorities*. Westport, CT: Quorum Books.

Rindova, V., Barry, D. & Ketchen, J. D. J. (2009). Entrepreneuring as emancipation. *Academy of Management Review, 34*(3), 477–491.

Rutherford, M. W., Pollack, J. M., Mazzei, M. J. & Sanchez-Ruiz, P. (2017). Bootstrapping: Reviewing the Literature, Clarifying the Construct, and Charting a New Path Forward. *Group & Organization Management, 42*(5), 657–706.

Sanz-Velasco, S. (2006). Opportunity development as a learning process for entrepreneurs. *International Journal of Entrepreneurial Behavior & Research, 12*(5), 251–271.

Sarason, Y., Dean, T. & Dillard, J. F. (2006). Entrepreneurship as the nexus of individual and opportunity: A structuration view. *Journal of Business Venturing, 21*(3), 286–305.

Sarasvathy, S. D. (2001). Causation and Effectuation: Toward a Theoretical Shift from Economic Inevitability to Entrepreneurial Contingency. *The Academy of Management Review, 26*(2), 243–263.

Sarasvathy, S. D. (2004). Making it happen: Beyond theories of the firm to theories of firm design. *Entrepreneurship: Theory and Practice, 28*(6), 519–531.

Sarasvathy, S. D. (2008). *Effectuation: elements of entrepreneurial expertise.* Cheltenham: Edward Elgar.

Sarasvathy, S. D. & Ramesh, A. (2019). An Effectual Model of Collective Action for Addressing Sustainability Challenges. *Academy of Management Perspectives, 33*(4), 405–424.

Saxenian, A. (1996). *Regional Advantages: Culture and Competition in Silicon Valley and Route 128.* Cambridge, MA: Harvard University Press.

Say, J.-B. (1880). *A Treatise on Political Economy.* Philadephia, PA: Claxton, Remsen and Haffelfinger.

Schatzki, T. R. (1996). *Social Practices: A Wittgensteinian Approach to Human Activity and the Social.* Cambridge: Cambridge University Press.

Schumpeter, J. (1934). *The Theory of Economic Development.* Cambridge, MA: Harvard University Press.

Shah, S. K. & Tripsas, M. (2007). The accidental entrepreneur: the emergent and collective process of user entrepreneurship. *Strategic Entrepreneurship Journal, 1*(2), 123–140.

Shah, S. K. & Tripsas, M. (2020). User entrepreneurs in times of crisis: Innovators you can count on. *Strategic Entrepreneurship Journal, 14*(4), 566–569.

Shane, S. (2000). Prior Knowledge and the Discovery of Entrepreneurial Opportunities. *Organization Science, 11*(4), 448–469.

Shane, S. (2003). *A General Theory of Entrepreneurship: The Individual-Opportunity Nexus.* Cheltenham: Edward Elgar.

Shane, S. (2012). Reflections On The 2010 AMR Decade Award: Delivering on the Promise of Entrepreneurship as Field of Research. *Academy of Management Review, 37*(1), 10–20.

Shane, S. & Venkataraman, S. (2000). The Promise of Entrepreneurship as a Field of Research. *Academy of Management Review, 25*(1), 217–226.

Simon, H. A. (1959). Theories of Decision Making in Economics and Behavioral Science. *American Economic Review, 49*, 253–283.

Skinner, B. F. (1938). *The Behavior of Organisms*. New York: Crofts-Crofts.

Smith, A. (1776). *The Wealth of Nations*. London: Strahan & Cadell.

Soto-Simeone, A., Siren, C. & Antretter, T. (2020). New Venture Survival: A Review and Extension. *International Journal of Management Reviews*, *22*(4), 378–407.

Soto-Simeone, A., Sirén, C. & Antretter, T. (2021). The role of skill versus luck in new venture survival. *International Journal of Management Reviews*. doi:10.1111/ijmr.12262

Spence, M. (1973). Job Market Signaling. *Quarterly Journal of Economics*, *87*(3), 355–374.

Spence, M. (2002). Signaling in Retrospect and the Informational Structure of Markets. *American Economic Review*, *92*(3), 434–459.

Starr, J. A. & Fondas, N. (1992). A Model of Entrepreneurial Socialization and Organization Formation. *Entrepreneurship: Theory & Practice*, *17*(1), 67–76.

Stenholm, P. & Renko, M. (2016). Passionate bricoleurs and new venture survival. *Journal of Business Venturing*, *31*(5), 595–611.

Steyaert, C. (2004). The Prosaics of Entrepreneurship. In D. Hjorth & C. Steyaert (Eds.), *Narrative and Discursive Approaches in Entrepreneurship* (pp. 8–21). Cheltenham: Edward Elgar.

Steyaert, C. (2007). 'Entrepreneuring' as a conceptual attractor? A review of process theories in 20 years of entrepreneurship studies. *Entrepreneurship & Regional Development*, *19*(6), 453–477.

Steyaert, C. & Katz, J. A. (2004). Reclaiming the space of entrepreneurship in society: geographical, discursive and social dimensions. *Entrepreneurship & Regional Development*, *16*(3), 179–196.

Storey, D. J. (1994). *Understanding the small business sector*. London: International Thompson Business Press.

Strauß, P., Greven, A. & Brettel, M. (2021). Determining the influence of national culture: insights into entrepreneurs' collective identity and effectuation. *International Entrepreneurship & Management Journal*, *17*(2), 981–1006.

Teague, B., Tunstall, R., Champenois, C. & Gartner, W. B. (2021). Editorial: An introduction to entrepreneurship as practice (EAP). *International Journal of Entrepreneurial Behavior & Research*, *27*(3), 569–578.

Thompson, N. A., Verduijn, K. & Gartner, W. B. (2020). Entrepreneurship-as-practice: grounding contemporary theories of practice into entrepreneurship studies. *Entrepreneurship & Regional Development*, *32*(3/4), 247–256.

Thorndike, E. L. (1913). *Educational Psychology*. New York: Teachers College.

Timmons, J. A. (1999). *New Venture Creation: Entrepreneurship for the 21st Century* (Fifth ed.). New York.: McGraw Hill.

Timmons, J. A. & Spinelli, S. (2004). *New Venture Creation* (6th ed.). Boston: Irwin McGraw-Hill.

Tornikoski, S. L. & Newbert, E. T. (2013). Resource acquisition in the emergence phase: considering the effects of embeddedness and resource dependence. *Entrepreneurship: Theory and Practice*, *37*(2), 249–280.

Uzzi, B. (1997). Social Structure and Competition in Interfirm Networks: The Paradox of Embeddedness. *Administrative Science Quarterly*, *42*(1), 35–67.

Van Auken, H. E. & Neeley, L. (1996). Evidence of bootstrap financing among small start-up firms. *Journal of Entrepreneurial & Small Business Finance*, *5*(3), 233.

Van Burg, E. & Romme, A. G. L. (2014). Creating the future together: toward a framework for research synthesis in entrepreneurship. *Entrepreneurship: Theory and Practice*, *38*(2), 369–397.

Vesper, K. (1990). *New Venture Strategies*. Englewood Cliffs, NJ: Prentice-Hall.

von Hippel, E. (1986). Lead Users: A Source of Novel Product Concepts. *Management Science*, *32*(7), 791–805.

Von Hippel, E. (1994). 'Sticky Information' and the Locus of Problem Solving: Implications for Innovation. *Management Science*, *40*(4), 429–439.

Vygotsky, L. S. (1978). *Mind in Society: The Development of Higher Psychological Processes*. Cambridge: Cambridge University Press.

Wang, C. L. & Chugh, H. (2014). Entrepreneurial Learning: Past Research and Future Challenges. *International Journal of Management Reviews*, *16*(1), 24–61.

Weick, K. (1979). *The Social Psychology of Organizing* (2nd ed.). Reading, MA: Addison-Wesley.

Weick, K. (1995). *Sensemaking in Organizations*. Thousand Oaks, CA: Sage.

Weick, K., Sutcliffe, K. & Obstfeld, D. (2005). Organizing and the Process of Sensemaking. *Organization Science*, *16*(4), 409–421.

Weiskopf, R. & Steyaert, C. (2009). Metamorphoses in Entrepreneurship Studies: Towards an Affirmative Politics of Entrepreneuring. In D. Hjorth & C. Steyaert (Eds.), *The Politics and Aesthetics of Entrepreneurship: A Fourth Movement in Entrepreneurship* (pp. 183–201). Cheltenham: Edward Elgar.

Whittington, R. (1996). Strategy as Practice. *Long Range Planning*, *29*(5), 731–735.

Williamson, O. E. (1993). Transaction Cost Economics and Organization Theory. *Industrial & Corporate Change*, *2*(2), 107–156.

Winborg, J. & Landström, H. (2001). Financial bootstrapping in small businesses. Examining small business managers' resource acquisition behaviors. *Journal of Business Venturing*, *16*, 235–254.

Wood, M. S., Bakker, R. M. & Fisher, G. (2021). Back to the Future: A Time-Calibrated Theory of Entrepreneurial Action. *Academy of Management Review*, *46*(1), 147–171.

Zahra, S. & Dess, G. G. (2001). Entrepreneurship as a Field of Research: Encouraging Dialogue and Debate. *The Academy of Management Review*, *26*(1), 8–10.

Zhang, S. X., Foo, M.-D. & Vassolo, R. S. (2021). The ramifications of effectuation on biases in entrepreneurship – Evidence from a mixed-method approach. *Journal of Business Venturing Insights*, *15*. doi:10.1016/j.jbvi.2021.e00238

Zott, C. & Huy, Q. N. (2007). How Entrepreneurs Use Symbolic Management to Acquire Resources. *Administrative Science Quarterly*, *52*(1), 70–105.

13 Business Start-up and Economic Development

13.1 Introduction

For the governments of developed countries such as the UK, the US, France and Germany, as well as developing countries such as Brazil, China and India, entrepreneurship is seen as a 'silver bullet' for economic growth. Consequently, most governments have been concerned to encourage entrepreneurship both directly and indirectly. The UK has initiated several schemes to support those engaged in business start-up (Mallett & Wapshott, 2020). For example, the 'New Entrepreneur Scholarship' helped those from disadvantaged areas establish new businesses (Jayawarna, Jones & Macpherson, 2011; Lee, Tuselmann, Jayawarna & Rouse, 2019). Whereas the United States has a strong political aversion to the provision of direct support and entrepreneurship is promoted indirectly through government funding of major projects in the defence industries and space exploration. Such funding has certainly helped provide support for many of the high-technology businesses associated with Silicon Valley (Castells, 2000; Irwin, Gilstrap, Drnevich & Tudor, 2019).

Our purpose in writing this book is to concentrate on the crucial early stages of entrepreneurship: identifying or creating an opportunity, starting the business and ensuring that is it still operating after 12 months. Clearly, we believe that the principles on which this book is based, entrepreneurial learning and bootstrapping, mean that businesses will have the potential for long-term growth. However, as we are primarily concerned with the shorter-term survival of new firms, we intend to focus on government policies which encourage, promote and support early-stage entrepreneurship. We acknowledge that there is not a clear distinction between policies aimed

DOI: 10.4324/9781003312918-14

at nascent entrepreneurs and policies designed to support more established SMEs (small and medium-sized enterprises). A dynamic small firm sector depends on an inflow of viable new businesses. Equally, there will be a greater incentive for potential entrepreneurs to start new businesses when they can see that there is a thriving small firm ecosystem (Stam & van de Ven, 2021). Therefore, in this chapter we are mainly concerned with the links between the creation of new businesses and the impact on economic development.

There is a considerable debate about the extent to which new firms contribute to economic growth. As we discuss below, much of this debate was prompted by David Birch's work which suggested that new firms were responsible for most of the growth in jobs (Birch, 1979, 1987). Birch's basic proposition that entrepreneurial firms lead to the creation of new jobs has proved to be extremely seductive to politicians and policymakers. This debate is important because it is fundamental to questions about whether governments should provide financial support for entrepreneurs and SMEs. To offer greater clarity on the debate about the extent to which new firms are responsible for job creation and, therefore, the extent to which government should support entrepreneurial activity we draw on three bodies of evidence. First, the OECD (organization for economic collaboration and development) suggests there are six determinants of entrepreneurship which are the basis of public policy initiatives (OECD, 2017). The GEM (global entrepreneurship monitor) studies also focus on policy initiative at three different levels of economic activity: factor-driven (less developed countries), efficiency-driven (rapidly developing countries) and innovation-driven (the most highly developed countries). Finally, the World Bank concentrates on links between entrepreneurship and economic development by examining the 'barriers to doing business' in 190 countries.

In this chapter we examine the findings from these three organizations to establish the links between entrepreneurship and economic development. We also investigate the extent to which governments can implement the appropriate policies to stimulate productive entrepreneurship.

13.2 Learning Objectives

- To understand the evolution of UK entrepreneurship policies over the last 40 years.

- To understand the different stages in the creation of a new business.
- To be able to explain the differences between necessity-based and opportunity-based entrepreneurship.
- To understand the different prescriptions for promoting entrepreneurship offered by the OECD, GEM and the World Bank.
- To differentiate between various international context of entrepreneurship – with particular emphasis on policies designed to promote new business creation.
- To be able to differentiate between factors which promote entrepreneurship and inhibiting factors.

13.3 UK Policy Initiatives from 1970 to 2021

Post-war 'industrial policy' in the UK concentrated on those larger organizations believed to typify 'modern' economies (Jones & Tang, 1998). Gradually, during the 1960s and 1970s there was recognition that the successful post-war economies of Germany and Japan had thriving small business sectors. In the late 1960s, the Labour Prime Minister, Harold Wilson, commissioned a report on the state of the small firm sector in the UK. Publication of the Bolton Report (1971) stimulated greater interest in small firms and entrepreneurship from both academics and policy makers (Jones, 2022; Wapshott & Mallett, 2021). Around the same time as the Bolton Report (1971) Birch (1979) published his influential work on the role of small firms in generating new jobs in the US. Birch claimed that 3% of small firms were responsible for creating 70% of the net new jobs in the US economy across all sectors. Such firms, described as 'gazelles', were growing at 20% or more a year and had at least $100,000 in annual sales (Birch, 1979). In subsequent years Birch's (1979) study was widely criticized for its methodological and analytical failings (Storey, 1994, p. 163). In addition, Wapshott and Mallett (2021, p. 109) point out the limitations of Bolton: 'it became apparent that acknowledging the importance of small firms and the difficulties they faced would not extend to recommending positive discrimination and would not entail working outside the established institutional framework for government–industry relations'. Nevertheless, the work of Bolton and Birch did have major implications for both policymakers and for the academic community (Bennett, 2008; Huggins & Williams, 2009).

The first Thatcher government in 1979 saw a determination to create an 'enterprise culture' in the UK with more focus on self-employment and entrepreneurship. Mallett and Wapshott (2020) explain that this led to several policy initiatives including the Enterprise Allowance Scheme, the Small Firms Loan Guarantee Scheme, Business Start-up Scheme, Local Enterprise Agencies and the Training and Enterprise Councils. Although the authors argue that it was not clear how much difference these schemes really made to economic activity (Mallett & Wapshott, 2020). In the late 1980s, the Economic and Social Research Council (ESRC) launched a small business research project which helped legitimize the study of entrepreneurship and small business in the UK. According to Storey (1994) this initiative was a direct political response to David Birch's work in the US. The initiative led to the creation of three small firm research centres: Kingston Polytechnic (now University), University of Cambridge and University of Sussex. More than 10,000 small firms participated in the research between 1989 and 1992 and the results were contained in three edited books (Atkinson & Storey, 1993; Curran & Storey, 1993; Hughes & Storey, 1994). In addition, David Storey (1994), the programme coordinator, provided his own influential interpretation of the research findings. Storey (1994) argued that government intervention should be restricted to creating the appropriate macroeconomic conditions in which small firms could thrive. In essence this meant low inflation, low interest rates, economic growth and high aggregate demand (Storey, 1994, p. 513). At one level such arguments are not contentious but at the same time David Storey's prescriptions were not accepted by all those operating within the academic small business community. For example, the work of Allan Gibb was a direct challenge to the 'free market' policies espoused by Storey (Gibb, 1987, 2002; Gibb & Ritchie, 1982). As we have stated earlier, this book is underpinned by a 'Gibbsian' view of the world in which there is an important role for both policymakers and academics in promoting the success of entrepreneurial businesses.

While the election of New Labour in 1997 continued the focus on an enterprise culture in the UK, there were several new initiatives. The Small Business Service (SBS), introduced in 1999, was intended to act as a bridge between government and the small business community as well as providing a more coherent service to those small businesses. Gradually, however, the SBS was replaced by the Regional Development Agencies (RDA) which 'were designed to lead on regional investment and identify skills training needs appropriate to the local economy' (Mallett & Wapshott,

2020, p. 177). The election of a coalition government (Conservatives and Liberal Democrats) in 2010 meant RDAs were replaced by Local Enterprise Partnerships (LEPs). From 2000 onwards, European Structural Funds (European Regional Development Fund and European Social Fund) became increasingly important in providing training for the small business community particularly in areas with high levels of social deprivation (Jones, 2022).

Rostow (1960) an economic historian, suggested that countries go through five stages of economic growth: traditional society, preconditions for takeoff, takeoff, drive to maturity and mass consumption. Porter (1998) updated Rostow's work by identifying three stages of economic development: factor-driven, investment-driven and innovation-driven. As discussed below, it is generally accepted that there is a U-shaped relationship between entrepreneurial activity and economic growth (Wennekers, van Stel, Thurik & Reynolds, 2005). Entrepreneurship tends to be at a high level in factor-driven economies and then declines during the transition to an efficiency-driven economy, entrepreneurship then increases during the innovation-driven phase. Although there are high levels of entrepreneurship (or self-employment) at the factor-driven stage it tends to be low-value and makes little real contribution to economic development. During the innovation-driven phase there is a switch from 'necessity' entrepreneurship to 'opportunity' entrepreneurship (Block & Sandner, 2009; Dencker, Bacq, Gruber & Haas, 2021). This is characterized by Wennekers et al. (2005) as the difference between unproductive (necessity) entrepreneurship and productive (opportunity) entrepreneurship. Therefore, one of the key issues which must be addressed by policymakers is how to discourage unproductive entrepreneurship while encouraging productive entrepreneurship.

Bridge (2010) examines the nature of policy initiatives and their impact on economic performance. Although the primary focus is UK policy, Bridge (2010, p. 34) asserts that policy recipes adopted by most countries are created from a set of common components:

- Finance programmes (loans and grants)
- Premises such as incubators and hatcheries
- Advice and mentoring programmes
- Business training usually associated with preparing a business plan
- Marketing programmes including support for exporting
- Management development programmes
- Support for innovation and R&D

- Start-up support programmes
- Awareness raising (advertising)
- Programmes for specific sectors (digital for example)
- The Government desire to be seen to be doing something

There are few useful evaluations of policies designed to create new businesses and generate employment (Bridge, 2010; Bridge & O'Neill, 2018). However, studies which have rigorously assessed the impact of government policies indicate that they have had 'little or no impact' on relative levels of entrepreneurship. As we will demonstrate below, data available from sources such as the OECD, the GEM studies and the World Bank are largely contradictory. This appears to confirm that links between government policy, entrepreneurship and economic growth are poorly understood. Or, as Bridge (2010) claims, based on inappropriate models of entrepreneurship. We return to this issue at the end of the chapter.

13.4 Promoting and Supporting Entrepreneurship

The Organization for Economic Co-operation and Development (OECD) established an Entrepreneurship Indicators Programme (EIP) in 2006 to build an internationally comparable database related to entrepreneurship. The following year, Eurostat joined with the OECD to create an OECD-Eurostat EIP based on standard definitions as a basis for the collection of empirical data (OECD, 2009). Definitions were based on a combination of 'available empirical indicators and 'conceptual contributions' from key figures in the field of entrepreneurship such as Richard Cantillon, Adam Smith, Jean-Baptiste Say, Alfred Marshall, Joseph Schumpeter, Israel Kirzner and Frank Knight:

- *Entrepreneurs* are those persons (business owners) who seek to generate value through the creation or expansion of economic activity by identifying and exploiting new products, processes or markets.
- *Entrepreneurial activity* is enterprising human action in pursuit of the generation of value through the creation of expansion of economic activity by identifying and exploiting new products, processes or markets.

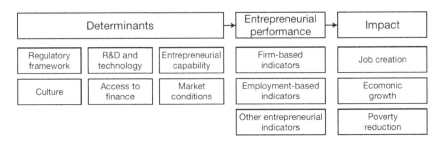

Figure 13.1 OECD Determinants of Entrepreneurship

The OECD (2006) developed a framework that identified six determinants of entrepreneurship. This model was updated in 2017 to provide more details on entrepreneurial performance as well as the impact on job creation and economic growth (Figure 13.1). Firm-based performance is measured in terms of birth-rates (number of new firms founded), death rates (number of firm closures), the related 'business churn' (birth rates compared to death rates), the net population growth or decline, and finally the survival rates for three and five years. Employment is measured by the number of high-growth firms, employment in three- and five-year-old firms and average firm size after three and five years. Finally, wealth is measured by turnover of high-growth firms, value-added, productivity, innovation and export performance of young/small firms.

The underlying principle of this book is that nascent entrepreneurs must make the best of the resources that they have without seeking external funding from banks, venture capitalists or business angels. In Chapters 9 and 12 we suggest that there are several ways to describe this approach: effectuation, bricolage and the term we use most widely, bootstrapping. Therefore, our view is that access to formal finance is not an important factor to most entrepreneurs starting new businesses. Similarly, while R&D investment may be crucial to a small number of high-technology start-ups, technology diffusion or technological cooperation between firms are unlikely to be directly relevant to the majority of new entrepreneurs. We also believe that issues concerning regulation will not concern most nascent entrepreneurs if there are not too many barriers related to setting up new businesses. The other three factors, entrepreneurial capabilities, entrepreneurial culture and market conditions, illustrated in Figure 13.1 are certainly directly relevant to those actively engaged in business start-up (all six factors are discussed below).

13.4.1 *Entrepreneurial Capabilities*

Entrepreneurial capabilities refer to the education and training that is available to those who are considering setting up their own businesses. The OECD places particular emphasis on the numbers participating in tertiary education and proportions of the population with training in business start-up. Focusing on the development of entrepreneurial capabilities among younger people has become increasingly important for most counties. For example, in the last 15 years, UK universities have placed much more emphasis on enterprise education designed to develop and enhance the skills of students (Hägg & Kurczewska, 2021; Hyams-Ssekasi & Caldwell, 2018; Preedy, Jones, Maas & Duckett, 2020). US institutions such as Babson College have long been at the forefront of promoting education for entrepreneurs. In Chapters 1, 2 and 5 we discuss the main mechanisms for helping students 'learn' to become more enterprising.

13.4.2 *Entrepreneurial Culture*

Culture focuses attention on perceptions of entrepreneurship or self-employment as a real alternative to conventional employment (or unemployment). In other words, the extent to which, within a particular population, there is a positive image of entrepreneurs and entrepreneurship. An entrepreneurial culture can be enhanced or restricted by institutional factors such as laws relating to the legality of private enterprise as well as by informal norms and attitudes which encourage or discourage entrepreneurship (Lounsbury, Cornelissen, Granqvist & Grodal, 2019). For example, in state-regulated economies such as the USSR and China private enterprise was illegal until reforms at the end of the twentieth century and the beginning of the twenty-first century (Jiangyong & Zhigang, 2008; Rogers, 2006). During the early 1980s Margaret Thatcher's government instigated several political initiatives which were explicitly designed to create an entrepreneurial culture within the UK (Wapshott & Mallett, 2021). These initiatives included paying an 'enterprise allowance' to those willing to set-up their own businesses and attempts to remove the stigma of failure by reducing the penalties for bankruptcy (Storey, Greene & Mole, 2007).

13.4.3 Market Conditions

The OECD concentrates on indicators such as competition law, policy indicators and import and export burdens on small firms. While we acknowledge that such macro-level factors are important in promoting entrepreneurship, we believe that more general market conditions will have a greater impact on promoting new business creation. The availability of business opportunities is likely to have much more positive impact on the propensity of individuals to start their own business than policies designed to 'stimulate' greater levels of competitiveness within an economy. For example, UK data indicates that the likelihood of starting a business is twice as great in the Southeast of England as it is in the Northwest of England (100 start-ups per 10,000 head of population compared to 50 start-ups per 10,000). It is widely acknowledged that there are far more business opportunities within the southeast which have very little to do with variations in access to finance, variations in the regulatory framework or knowledge creation and diffusion.

13.4.4 Knowledge Creation and Diffusion

This factor includes a number of technology-based indicators such as 'business R&D intensity', firms with 'new to market innovations', firms 'collaborating on innovation' and 'turnover from e-commerce'. As indicated above, our view is that these measures will have very little direct impact on most new businesses. However, we do acknowledge that 'knowledge creation and diffusion' are central to the creation of a healthy and growing small firm sector. In fact, knowledge creation and diffusion are central to the idea of effective entrepreneurial learning which is the principle on which this book is based (Chapter 5). As discussed in Chapter 5, establishing thriving entrepreneurial communities via the creation of incubators such as Innospace is an extremely effective mechanism for promoting entrepreneurial learning (Jones, Meckel & Taylor, 2021).

13.4.5 Regulatory Framework

We seriously doubt whether either 'top statutory personal income tax rate' or 'top statutory corporate income tax rate' are likely to be important factors in decisions about whether individuals decide to become entrepreneurs. Although in the longer term personal and corporate tax rates may influence where a successful entrepreneur decides to reside or to locate their main business activities. Other factors such as 'ease of doing business' and 'barriers to entrepreneurship' will be much more significant in terms of influencing potential entrepreneurs. For example, many European countries have extremely onerous and time-consuming regulations for those who want to establish a new business. As we discuss in section 13.5, the World Bank uses four measures of entry barriers: start-up costs, number of procedures required to establish a business, number of days required to start a business and the difficulty of hiring/redundancy.

13.4.6 Access to Finance

Ease of access to loans, business angel networks, venture capital investments and share of high-technology sectors in total venture capital are the main indicators of access to finance. However, it is widely acknowledged (see Chapters 8 and 9) that only a very small proportion of new entrepreneurs seek external finance. Therefore, we suggest that, in fact, access to finance is not a major barrier for most new businesses. In fact, it is our contention that 'learning' to manage without the need for loans or equity is likely to have a positive influence on the longer-term success of most start-up ventures (Jayawarna, Jones & Macpherson, 2020; Jones & Jayawarna, 2010).

Following the 2008 financial crisis, which had a negative impact on entrepreneurship, the OECD (2017) reports a recovery in the levels of new firm creation and a decline in bankruptcy rates in most OECD countries. The report also notes that new firms were concentrated in service sectors rather than manufacturing. The other clear trend across most countries was a growth in the numbers of self-employed, part-time workers based in the 'gig economy'. Although whether gig workers can really be classed as 'entrepreneurs' is certainly open to debate. However, the OECD (2017) points out that greater flexibility associated with gig-employment does offer opportunities for nascent entrepreneurs to implement their start-up ideas while covering their living expenses; so-called hybrid entrepreneurs (Pollack, Carr, Michaelis & Marshall, 2019). As a result of the Covid-19 pandemic, the most recent OECD report in conjunction with Facebook (Facebook, 2020), confirms that most smaller businesses faced falling demand for their products and services. Micro businesses (less than 10 employees) were disproportionately affected with 21% closing compared to 13% of small firms (more than 10 employees). Not surprisingly, an 34% of small businesses had reduced their levels of employment.

13.5 The GEM Studies

At the publication of its most recent report (2020/2021) the GEM (global entrepreneurship monitor) Research Association had existed for 22 years. The GEM team has been responsible for comparing entrepreneurial activity in 120 countries and numerous reports have been published in that time (www.gemconsortium.org/reports/latest-global-report). Although the survey-based data are based on limited samples, GEM does provide an extremely useful way of comparing entrepreneurial activity across a wide-range of countries. The survey examines entrepreneurial activity at two levels which combine to give an overall index (TEA):

- Nascent entrepreneurs – those individuals who are actively committing resources to start their own businesses. Payment of a wage for more than three months (including the owner) is regarded as the birth of the firm.
- New Business Ownership – those who have established businesses which have paid salaries for more than three months but less than 42 months.
- Total entrepreneurial activity (TEA) is the total of nascent entrepreneurs and new business owners in any country.

Figure 13.2 illustrates the entrepreneurial process in which potential entrepreneurs with the appropriate skills take the step into nascent entrepreneurship. When the business begins trading, entrepreneurs are classified as 'new business owners' for 3.5 years. Many businesses will fail during this stage and some entrepreneurs will, with the benefit of experience gained from failure, begin new businesses. Those firms that continue to trade after 3.5 years are known as established businesses. Early stage (nascent) entrepreneurs are classified according to their age, gender and motivation for starting a business (necessity or opportunity based).

Until recently, the GEM approach to country classification was based on Porter's (1998) ideas about three distinct phases of economic development: factor-driven, efficiency enhancers and entrepreneurship &

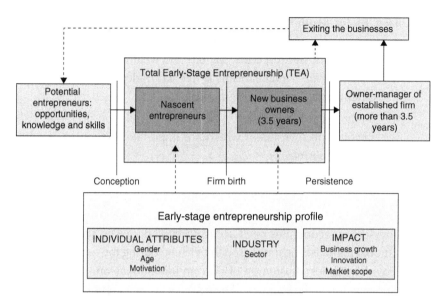

Figure 13.2 The GEM Entrepreneurial Process

innovation. Factor-driven countries (least developed) included India, Iran, Cameroon, Senegal, Kazakhstan and the Russian Federation; efficiency-driven economies included rapidly developing countries such as Argentina, Brazil, China, Poland, South Africa and Saudi Arabia; the innovation-driven economies included the most developed countries such as Australia, France, Germany, Italy, Ireland, Portugal, the US and the UK. According to the GEM studies, whatever the economic stage of development, entrepreneurs are influenced by prevailing attitudes, activities and aspirations which, in turn, influence national economic growth (Figure 13.3). Consequently, countries can be at the same stage of economic development but have very different levels of entrepreneurship.

Factor-driven economies require the creation of several basic institutional factors if entrepreneurship is to contribute to real economic development. Potential entrepreneurs are unlikely to risk starting a (legal) business unless they can access appropriate resources and know that the legal system will be able to offer them protection. Most entrepreneurial opportunities tend to be associated with subsistence agriculture – 'necessity' entrepreneurship. If entrepreneurs are to become more productive then it is essential there is a functioning market whereby, they can trade their produce for cash which can be reinvested in the business.

475

1. **Basic Factor Requirements**
    *   *Institutions* – including property rights, an effective legal system, regulations, start-up costs, savings and wealth creation, taxation.
    *   *Infrastructure* – mechanisms by which trade can take place – in other words – functioning markets.
    *   *Macroeconomic stability* – low levels of inflation promote trade, savings and investment which are important to support new and growing businesses.
    *   *Health and primary education* – the population must be healthy and have reasonable levels of education.

Efficiency-driven economies need access to large domestic and, if possible, international markets. The rapid growth of China during the twenty-first century provides the best illustration of how an initial focus on exports helped stimulate demand in the home market as Chinese consumers had increasing levels of disposal income and ready access to consumer goods. A highly mobile labour force was also important as the population moved to the larger, rapidly developing cities in the South of China. The transition from factor-driven to efficiency-driven economy presents opportunities for small manufacturing firms to enter the supply chain and the emergence of entrepreneurial opportunities to offer professional services.

2. **Efficiency Enhancers**
    *   *Higher education and training* – there is a need for courses and programmes to provide higher level scientific, technical and managerial skills.
    *   *Goods and market efficiency* – needs effective supply chains (national and international) and appropriate retail outlets
    *   *Labour market efficiency* – the labour market must have high levels of mobility (from rural to urban) as well as the appropriate skills and motivation.
    *   *Financial markets* – the availability of loans and credit for individuals and for businesses.
    *   *Technological readiness* – individuals and businesses must have the knowledge and skills to exploit existing technologies.
    *   *Market size* – high levels of efficiency depend on economies of scale in markets; hence the rapid development of Brazil, Russia, India, China and South Africa (BRICS) in the early 2000s.

Innovation-driven economies are associated with higher levels of commitment to the creation of new technologies via investment in R&D (research and development). There is also a more rigorous approach to the protection of intellectual property to encourage universities, businesses and individuals to invest in knowledge creation. Policy makers generally place a considerable amount of attention on technology-based new firms as these are seen to be the drivers of economic success. While innovation-driven economies have higher levels of 'opportunity' entrepreneurship there is still a substantial amount of necessity entrepreneurship as developed economies increasingly suffer from high levels of unemployment. Of the 22 countries originally classified as innovation-driven, according to the latest figures, the US has the highest rate of new business formation as measured by TEA with a figure of 17.4%. This compares with figures of 10.4% for the Netherlands, 9.3%, for the UK, 8.3% for Sweden, 7.6% for Germany, 5.7% for France, 5.4% for Japan and 2.8% for Italy.

3. Innovation and Entrepreneurship

- *Entrepreneurial finance* – obtainable from a variety of sources including banks, business angels and venture capitalists.
- *Government policy* – providing support for nascent entrepreneurs and growing businesses (information etc).
- *Entrepreneurship programmes and education* – encouraging entrepreneurial activity via primary, secondary and tertiary education.
- *R&D transfer* – appropriate mechanisms to transfer knowledge from universities to the private sector.
- *Legal infrastructure* – an effective system of intellectual property rights including patents, copyrights and trademarks.
- *Market openness* – the effective operation of markets ensures that efficient companies survive and inefficient companies fail.
- *Physical infrastructure* – a developed economy needs high-quality infrastructure including roads, rail, airports and communication technologies (broadband).
- *Cultural and social norms* – these must be supportive of innovation and entrepreneurship.

The GEM Conceptual Framework (Figure 13.3) illustrates the relationship between entrepreneurship and the local, regional and national environments. The broader economic, social and cultural context has a direct

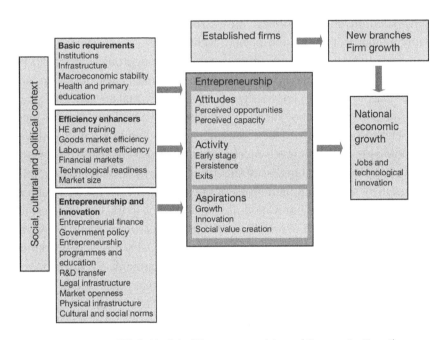

Figure 13.3 GEM's Model of Entrepreneurship and Economic Growth

and indirect influence on individual perception of the values placed on entrepreneurship. For the 2020/21 Report,[1] 46 countries were evaluated by their national teams in two ways. First, the adult population survey (APS) is based on random samples of at least 2000 people in each country. This survey asks questions about the ease of starting a business, the extent of business opportunities, their 'fear of failure' and whether they are currently engaged in starting a business. Secondly, the national expert survey (NES) is created by 36 national experts who rate each country based on the framework conditions (see Appendix 13.1). Based on these two surveys, entrepreneurial activity in each country is established by phase (nascent, new, established, exit), by impact (high-growth, innovation, market scope and by type (total entrepreneurial activity [TEA], established business ownership [EBO] and employee entrepreneurial activity [EEA]. These factors are influenced by the levels of economic activity discussed above: factor-driven (basic requirements), efficiency-driven (efficiency enhances) and innovation and entrepreneurship-driven (innovation and business sophistication).

Necessity-driven entrepreneurship refers to those individuals who resort to business start-up because they have no alternatives for paid employment

(Audretsch, Belitski, Chowdhury & Desai, 2021). In general, necessity-based entrepreneurship is unlikely to have a significant economic impact as it acts as a substitute for low-wage or subsistence employment. Opportunity-based entrepreneurship describes individuals who start new businesses because they identify genuine opportunities which will improve their incomes and independence. According to GEM (2019/20) the level of necessity entrepreneurship certainly decreases, and opportunity-based entrepreneurship increases among the high-income economies (Appendix 13.2). There is, however, less clarity in the differences between the middle-income and the low-income economies in terms of both necessity and opportunity entrepreneurship (Appendices 13.3 and 13.4). Also, Columbia has extremely low levels of necessity entrepreneurship (12.2%) and high levels of opportunity entrepreneurship (85.5%). It is impossible to claim that the GEM data[2] provide conclusive evidence that necessity-based entrepreneurship is concentrated in factor-driven (low-income) economies and declines in efficiency-driven (middle-income) and innovation-driven (high-income) economies. Clearly there are other factors which influence the TEA scores as well as the balance between necessity-based and opportunity-based entrepreneurship in addition to the stage of economic development. Some of these factors will be discussed in the next section.

The GEM studies do provide some interesting data on variations according to both age and gender. Based on five age groups (18–24; 25–34; 35–44; 45–54; 55–65) the proportions remain largely similar across all levels of economic activity. Those in the 25–34 age group generally have the highest levels of entrepreneurship and they are followed by the 18–24, 35–44, 45–54 and 55–64 groups. There are, of course, some notable exceptions to this pattern: in the US entrepreneurs in the 35–44 age group have higher levels of start-up than the 25–34 group. This may indicate the higher proportion of technology-based start-ups in the US which demand more extensive resources than new businesses started in other countries. Among other countries in the high-income category, Canada, Greece, Italy, the Slovak Republic and Sweden all have the highest levels of entrepreneurship in the youngest (18–24) age group as does the Russian Federation from the middle-income group. The pandemic generally had a negative influence on entrepreneurship as TEA declined across four of the five age groups between the 2019 and 2020 GEM surveys. There was one exception as most economies saw an increase in TEA among the 55–64 age group

Generally, across all three levels of economic activity men are more likely than women to start their own businesses. Italy, Poland and India have very low rates of female early-stage entrepreneurship and a further six European economies (Germany, Slovenia, Sweden, Norway, Luxembourg and Austria) have less than 5% of women starting or running new businesses. Countries from Middle East and Africa have the highest rates of female entrepreneurship. More than 50% of women in Angola, 35% in Togo and over 20% in Burkina Faso are starting or running new businesses. While more than 15% of women are starting their own businesses in Kuwait, Oman and Saudi Arabia. The Latin American countries (Brazil, Chile, Columbia, Guatemala, Panama and Uruguay) all have female participation rates of between 20% and 30%. Italy (3.5%), Poland (5.7%) and Spain (6.3%) have the lowest rates of European male entrepreneurship together with Pakistan (5.5%) and Japan (7.8%). In most other countries male TEA is at least 10% of the population with some Latin American countries having very high rates: Chile (41.1%), Ecuador (38.5%) and Panama (26.0%). The UK has a male participation rate of 11.7% and a female rate of 7.0% compared to the US with 18.3% male and 16.6% female.

Bosma and Kelley (2019) describe one of GEM's recent initiative, the National Entrepreneurship Context Index (NECI), which ranked 54 countries based on a range of factors including: finance, Government policies, entrepreneurship education, R&D transfer, physical infrastructure as well as culture & social norms (Appendix 13.1). Interestingly, the UK was ranked 34th of 54 countries on NECI, lagging other European countries such as the Netherlands (third), France (tenth) and Germany (19th) as well as the US, which was ranked in sixth place. In the 2021 GEM report, there were several significant changes with the UK rising to 15th place and the US falling to 12th place from the 44 countries surveyed (Table 13.1). It is difficult to make direct comparisons as the list of countries surveyed changes annually. It is also difficult to reconcile the figures for some of the countries with their TEA scores. For example, India has a high NECI score but very low levels of female entrepreneurship.

In summary, according to the GEM studies, there is a progression in the levels of economic activity from factor-driven (low-income) to efficiency-driven (middle-income) and eventually innovation-driven (high-income). This progression is summarized in Figure 13.4. It is also anticipated that higher levels of economic development will be associated with a move to much greater focus on opportunity-based entrepreneurship with declining

Table 13.1 NECI Rankings

NECI RANK	COUNTRY
1	Indonesia
2	Netherlands
3	Taiwan
4	UAE
5	India
6	Norway
7	Saudi Arabia
8	Qatar
9	Republic of Korea
10	Switzerland
11	Israel
12	United States
13	Oman
14	Luxembourg
15	United Kingdom

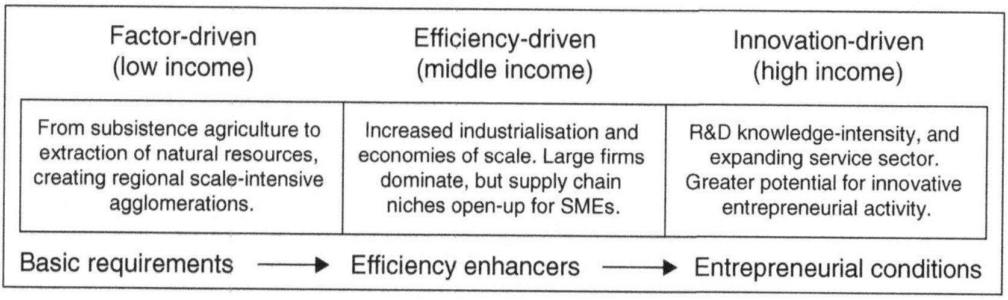

Factor-driven (low income)	Efficiency-driven (middle income)	Innovation-driven (high income)
From subsistence agriculture to extraction of natural resources, creating regional scale-intensive agglomerations.	Increased industrialisation and economies of scale. Large firms dominate, but supply chain niches open-up for SMEs.	R&D knowledge-intensity, and expanding service sector. Greater potential for innovative entrepreneurial activity.

Basic requirements ──→ Efficiency enhancers ──→ Entrepreneurial conditions

Figure 13.4 Economic Groups and Entrepreneurship

levels of necessity-based entrepreneurship. While innovation-driven economies do tend to have higher levels of opportunity-based entrepreneurship, as discussed above, there is little difference between the two forms of entrepreneurship in the efficiency-driven and factor-driven economies.

13.6 Factors Influencing New Firm Formation

In addition to the two organizations already discussed (OECD and GEM) the World Bank examines the extent to which entrepreneurship contributes to economic development. The World Bank's *Doing Business Project* was launched in 2002 to examine how business regulation impacts on small and medium-sized companies. The 2020 edition of the *Doing Business Project* includes measures of regulation and their enforcement across 190 economies. The *Doing Business* index is constructed from ten measures of business activity: starting a business, construction permits, registering property, getting credit, protecting investors, paying taxes, trading across borders, enforcing contracts, resolving insolvency and getting electricity. Based on these ten measures the top ten and the bottom ten countries for ease of doing business are shown in Table 13.2.

All countries in the top ten for ease of doing business are in the highest income bracket except for Georgia, which is in the upper middle-income bracket. In fact, 22 of the top 25 countries are in the highest income bracket with the other exceptions being Malaysia and Mauritius. Equally, of the bottom ten countries, eight are in the lowest income bracket with the exceptions of Timor-Leste (lower middle income) and Libya (upper middle income). Clearly these data are consistent with the most developed, richest countries having the most sophisticated institutions for regulating their economies. This is confirmed in the 2020 World Bank report: 'a considerable disparity persists between low- and high-income economies on the ease of starting a business. An entrepreneur in a low-income economy typically spends about 50% of income per capita to launch a company, compared to just 4.2% for an entrepreneur in a high-income economy'. In addition, on average, it takes nearly six times longer to start a business in economies ranked in the bottom 50 than it does in the top 20.

According to the 2020 report, there have been almost 4,000 changes in regulations since the World Bank's first report in 2003. Those reforms were implemented in four key areas that act as barriers to entrepreneurship: starting

Table 13.2 Ease of Doing Business

Top ten countries		Bottom ten countries	
Country	Ease of doing business	Country	Ease of doing business
New Zealand	1	Timor-Lestre	181
Singapore	2	Chad	182
Hong Kong	3	Congo Democratic Rep	183
Denmark	4	Cen. African Republic	184
Republic of Korea	5	South Sudan	185
United States	6	Libya	186
Georgia	7	Yemen Republic	187
UK	8	Venezuela, RB	188
Norway	9	Eritrea	189
Sweden	10	Somalia	190

a business, getting credit, paying taxes and resolving insolvency. With regards to starting a business, at the time of the first report, many countries required 'paid-in minimum capital' as security for creditors before anyone could start a business. Since 2003, 58 countries, including most in Europe and North America, have eliminated the requirement for paid-in minimum capital. Many middle-income and lower-income countries have also eliminated the need for paid-in minimum capital (Jordan and Saudi Arabia) or significantly reduced the amount of capital required. For example, all 17 members of the Organization for the Harmonization of Business Law in Africa (OHADA) agreed to allow member states to set paid-in minimum requirements nationally, with a minimum of $9 per share.

The second barrier to entrepreneurship is the lack of a reliable credit-scoring system. Such systems indicate an individual's or firm's credit worthiness and, hence, the level of risk to potential lenders (banks, business angels, venture capitalists etc). In 2004, 67% of economies had a private credit bureau or a public credit registry and that figure had risen to 88% by 2019.

For example, 15 of the 39 new credit registries launched since the World Bank's 2004 report were established in Sub-Saharan Africa, although this region still has the least developed credit information system. In general, the presence of either a public or private credit-rating agency is associated with lower default levels and lower interest rates. Consequently, in those economies with a credit-scoring system, entrepreneurs are less likely to report access to finance as a constraint on their business activities.

Thirdly, establishing an efficient system for the payment of taxes helps ease the administrative burden on entrepreneurs and smaller business owner-managers. Electronic systems for filing and paying taxes have reduced compliance times from almost 500 hours to 225 hours in the last 15 years. Most high-income economies (97%) use electronic filing or payments. In contrast, Sub-Saharan Africa has the lowest share of economies (17%) using electronic tax returns. The World Bank (2020, p. 51) goes on to state that countries with high tax compliance costs are generally associated with larger informal sectors, higher levels of corruption and less investment. Modernization of the IT infrastructure increases efficiency of tax collection, reduces physical interactions between officials and taxpayers, eliminates the physical exchange of cash and reduces the likelihood of corruption. At the same time, it is important that tax revenues are converted into public goods and services to ensure that entrepreneurs and small businesses remain committed to the payment of their taxes.

Finally, the World Bank (2020) points out that reorganizing insolvency procedures helps reduce the failure rates of small and medium-size enterprises and prevents the liquidation of insolvent but viable businesses. Establishing 'modern' insolvency regimes means that there are restructuring tools to support economically viable businesses facing temporary financial problems while quickly liquidating nonviable businesses. Generally, those countries with effective insolvency regimes have much higher rates of domestic investment. In contrast, countries without reorganization procedures have seen domestic investment as a percentage of GDP decline between 2004 and 2019.

There have been several publications which have analyse the results of the 'doing business survey' and they can be found on the World Bank website.[3] For example, Klapper et al. (2009) found that the barriers to starting a business were significantly and negatively related to both entry rate (business start-up) and density (number of small businesses). Quite simply, more procedures required to start a new business lead to lower new business entry rates. There is also an inverse relationship between political risk/instability and business start-up. Those countries which suffer from poor governance and/or political instability have the lowest rates of business start-up. This is largely confirmed by data in Table 13.2 which compares the ease of doing business in the top and bottom ten countries. Certainly, most of the bottom ten countries are typified by conflict and poor, unstable government. In contrast, all the top ten countries, except for Georgia, are stable with little internal conflict or external threats. More recently, Rocha, Ulyssea and Rachter (2018) examine the impact of taxes on entrepreneurship, Harju, Matikka and Rauhanen (2019) focus on the cost of compliance, Belitski, Chowdhury and Desai (2016) examine the links between taxes and business entry (Audretsch et al., 2021)

13.7 The Economic Contribution of New Businesses

In a special issue of the journal *Small Business Economics* Acs and Szerb (2007) examined links between entrepreneurship, economic growth and public policy (Figure 13.5). There is empirical evidence to demonstrate that entrepreneurial activity varies according to the stage of economic development. In particular, the data suggest that there is a U-shaped curve linking the level of economic development and the rate of entrepreneurship (Acs & Szerb, 2007, p. 109). Entrepreneurship appears to have a positive effect on developed economies and a negative effect on the economies of developing countries. Wennekers et al. (2005) used GEM data to examine

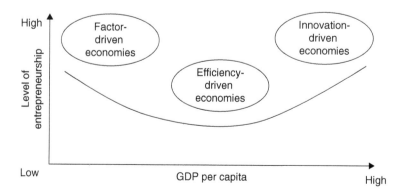

Figure 13.5 The U-Shaped Entrepreneurship Curve

links between nascent entrepreneurship and the level of economic development. They were particularly concerned to establish whether there was empirical evidence for U-shaped relationship between entrepreneurship and economic development (Figure 13.5). Essentially, their hypothesis was that as a country's economy begins to grow (moving from factor-driven to efficiency-driven) the rate of business start-up will decline.

One of the key reasons for declining levels of self-employment (entrepreneurship) during the shift to higher levels of economic activity is that employment moves from agriculture to large-scale manufacturing (efficiency-driven). Those engaged in poorly paid agricultural self-employment find more opportunities for waged employment; marginal entrepreneurs become employees thereby increasing their income. Essentially factor-driven (low-income) countries are dominated by necessity (unproductive) entrepreneurship while innovation-driven (high-income) countries have far greater levels of opportunity (productive) entrepreneurship (Audretsch et al., 2021; Dencker et al., 2021). The shift from efficiency-driven to innovation-driven leads to increased entrepreneurial activity (see Figure 13.4). At this stage, technological innovation is an important driver of economic activity in a number of key clusters such as biotechnology and information and communication technologies (Porter, Takeuchi & Sakaibara, 2000). It is also important that there are generally high levels of cooperation between government, business and universities in a process described by Etzkowitz and Leydersdorf (2000) as the 'triple helix'. Innovation-driven economies are typified by a declining employment in manufacturing and a corresponding increase in service-sector activity together with a rise in the 'creative class' (Florida, 2002). As economic activity increases higher levels of per capita income create niche markets for entrepreneurial businesses (see Acs, Audretsch & Feldman, 1994).

Based on 36 countries which participated in the 2002 GEM study Wennekers et al. (2005) confirmed that there was a U-shaped relationship between entrepreneurship and economic development (Figure 13.5). As well as identifying variations in the levels of entrepreneurial activity Wennekers et al. (2005) also identified significant changes in the relationship between necessity and opportunity-based entrepreneurship. In less developed nations (factor-driven economies) at least 50% of entrepreneurial activity is necessity-based. This drops to less than 20% in the most advanced economies based on GEM data. One of the main conclusions drawn from this study is that entrepreneurship is not an effective mechanism for promoting economic development in low-income countries. Instead, governments should encourage foreign direct investment (FDI), develop the physical infrastructure, promote education, create access to capital markets and ensure the macro-economic conditions are stable. In high-income countries government should encourage opportunity-based entrepreneurship by fostering expenditure on research and development (R&D), improve incentives for self-employment, stimulate entrepreneurship education, enhance intellectual property rights and stimulate a healthy venture capital market (Wennekers et al., 2005, p. 306).

Stel et al. (2007) use data related to rates of entrepreneurship from 39 countries participating in the GEM studies and data from the World Bank's 'doing business' survey to examine the impact of regulation on business start-up. According to Stel et al. (2007) governments have three main policy options related to the support of new and established small firms:

- Lowering the entry barriers to new firm foundation (time taken to register business for example)
- Reduce the burdens of those operating small firms (hiring and firing employees, access to credit)
- Use public funds to provide information, training and advice to those engaged in business start-up

Examining the entry barriers and regulatory burdens revealed several important facts about the relationship between regulation and business start-up (Stel et al., 2007). First the impact of regulation on entrepreneurship rates was found to be 'limited' with 'minimum-capital requirement' the only obstacle to start-up (see Section 13.6). Second, labour market rigidity did have a negative relationship with entrepreneurship rates; higher levels of labour market regulation mean lower rates of business start-up. If, for example, job security is low (less regulation) then there may be more incentive to start a business. Third, not surprisingly, countries with high rates of nascent entrepreneurship had more 'young' businesses (up to 42 months). However, 'necessity-based' nascent entrepreneurs were more likely to establish businesses than those with an opportunity-based motive. As the authors point out, this likely to be because necessity-based entrepreneurs have less alternative employment opportunities and, therefore, are 'forced' into starting a business. Fourth, there were links between GDP growth and the rates of opportunity and necessity entrepreneurship. Growth in GDP had a positive influence on rates of opportunity-based entrepreneurship but no impact on necessity entrepreneurship as this group of entrepreneurs are not influenced by market demand. In addition, increased participation in tertiary education had a positive impact on opportunity entrepreneurship but no influence on necessity entrepreneurship. Those with experience of higher education are more likely to start new businesses. Finally, the data suggest that neither taxation levels nor bankruptcy regulations influence business start-up rates. In summary, Stel et al. (2007, p. 183) conclude: 'the study finds no significant impact on nascent or young business formation of administrative considerations such as the time, cost, or the number of procedures needed to start a business'. Based on data from 25 EU counties, Bosma, Content, Sanders and Stam (2018) found that the quality of institutions stimulates (productive) entrepreneurship, which contributes to economic growth. The most important predictors of entrepreneurship included financial stability, the size of government and perceived skills to start a business.

Recently, Stoica, Roman and Rusu (2020, p. 1186) examined links between entrepreneurship and economic growth based on 22 European countries; five in transition from efficiency-driven to innovation-driven (Croatia, Hungary, Latvia, Poland and Romania) and 17 innovation-driven countries (Belgium, Denmark, Finland, France, Germany, Greece, Ireland, Italy, Netherlands, Norway, Portugal, Slovakia, Slovenia, Spain, Sweden, Switzerland and the UK) for the period 2002–2018. The results confirmed that higher levels of total early-stage (TEA) entrepreneurship were positively related to increases in GDP per capita regardless of the level of development of the 22 European countries. Higher levels of opportunity-motivated entrepreneurship had a significant and positive influence on economic growth but only for the five transition countries. Valliere and Peterson (2009) suggest that it is possible that opportunity-based entrepreneurs in innovation-driven countries do not have high-growth expectations because of obstacles in the economic environment or because they are focused on gradually growing their businesses. Higher levels of necessity-motivated entrepreneurship did have a statistically significant negative influence on the economic growth of innovation-driven countries. Surprisingly, necessity entrepreneurship did not have a negative impact on the economic growth of the five transition economies. Stoica et al. (2020, p. 1202) conclude that 'sustained economic growth has positive long-term effects on businesses. Thus, a high quality of the entrepreneurial activities, at present, generates positive effects on the economic growth and subsequently determines an improvement on the business environment'.

Based on data from 79 diverse countries, Reynolds (2020) identified a correlation of 0.51 between business creation and GDP growth. Although Reynolds (2020) points out that it is difficult to determine whether a growing economy (GDP) encourages more new businesses or whether those new businesses promote economic growth. He goes on to state that there is also a very strong relationship between firm births and firm deaths: higher levels of start-ups are associated with more firms going out of business. This so-called 'churn' means that there is a high correlation between firm births and firm deaths, which reaches a top figure of 0.85 after a four-year lag (based on US regional data). Hence, the relationship between firm births and future firm deaths takes several years for the maximum rate to become apparent. The correlation between firm churn and economic growth is the same as for firm births. There is a strong association in the first three years, a low association four to eight years in the future and a positive association after ten years (Reynolds, 2020, pp. 39–40). What this means is that large numbers of new businesses add to GDP, but that impact starts to decline as increasing number of firms fail. In the longer run, however, the surviving firms begin to have a positive impact on economic growth. We discuss the policy implications of this churning in the next section.

13.8 Do New Businesses Create New Jobs?

Finally, we return to the crucial question concerning the extent to which new firms are responsible for the creation of new jobs. Anyadike-Danes, Bonner and Hart (2011) suggest that Birch's work on the links between entrepreneurship and job creation led to a long-standing and acrimonious debate (Birch, 1979, 1987). Despite many attempts to replicate Birch's (1987) findings there is still limited consensus about the links between entrepreneurial activity and job creation. Although, as demonstrated in the previous section, there certainly appear to be strong links between new firms and economic growth (Stoica et al., 2020). According to Reynolds (2020), in the US firms less than one year old provided 3.5 million jobs, one-third of the total net gain (in 2005). In the US, as in most other countries, sole-proprietorships and self-employment are not responsible for large-scale job creation. A small number of new firms create most new jobs although firms with five or fewer employees create 40% of US new jobs (Reynolds, 2020, p. 63).

Anyadike-Danes et al. (2011) draw on a database of firms founded in 1998, which was created by the UK Office for National Statistics (ONS). The Business Structure Database (BSD) relies on VAT (value added tax) and PAYE (pay as you earn) to provide the basis for firm-level longitudinal data. The BSD contains five million firm-level records detailing number of employees, turnover, sector and location. UK private-sector employment increased from 17.3 million to 18.6 million (7.6%) and the number of firms increased by 250,000 (20%) between 1998 and 2010. During that 12-year period, growth was concentrated in the 0–1 size-band (the self-employed and firms with just one employee). Excluding the small size-band there was a negative relationship between firm size and the number of firms. For example, large firms employing 250+ were responsible for the largest proportionate decline with a fall from 6600 to 4600 firms. In total, the stock of firms increased in the 12-year period (1998–2010) meaning that 'birth-rate' exceeded 'death-rate' by an average of 19,200 firms per year. Importantly, we stress again, all that growth occurred in the very smallest size-band. An important issue for policymakers is the fact that there was a substantial decline in the number of small (10 to 49) and medium-sized (50–249) enterprises. What this indicates is that most start-up businesses are unlikely to grow into successful and viable SMEs. Anyadike-Danes et al. (2011) then go on to deal with the issue raised by Birch; the extent to which entrepreneurship leads to job creation. The number of private sector employees in the UK grew by 1.3 million between 1998 and 2010 (Table 13.3). As suggested above, employment growth was concentrated in the smallest (0–1) firms with an increase of 1.287 million jobs and a further 1.176 million created by micro firms. Employment in medium-sized firms (10–49) also increased by 195 thousand. Significantly, medium-sized firms (50 to 249) and large firms (250+) both suffered decreases in the numbers employed, 238 thousand and 1.10 million respectively. However, as we discuss below, the situation in the last 10 years has been very different in terms of which firms were responsible for job creation.

Anyadike-Danes and Hart (2018) constructed job creation and destruction metrics based on surviving firms from the original cohort (Anyadike-Danes et al., 2011). Fifteen years later, only 26,162 (10.9%) of the original 239,600 firms established in 1998 still existed. At birth, those 239,600 firms were responsible for 1.12 million jobs, 15 years later the remaining 26,162

Table 13.3 UK Job Creation 1998–2010

SIZE-BAND	INCREASE IN EMPLOYEE NUMBERS (1998–2010)
0–1	1,287,000
2–9	1,176,000
10–49	195,000
50–249	-238,000
250+	-1,103,000
Total New Jobs	1,317,000

firms were contributing almost 400,000 jobs: 'So in just 15 years 213,000 firms died and almost three quarters of a million jobs were lost' (Anyadike-Danes & Hart, 2018, p. 55). More positively, the number of jobs in the surviving firms increased from 163,000 at birth to 395,000 thousand in 2013, as Anyadike-Danes and Hart (2018, p. 57) point out, a 'net job creation of almost a quarter of a million jobs'. Table 13.4 illustrates whether the 26,162 firms increased or decreased in size over the 15-year period. Of the 22,229 firms in the 0–4 size-band in 1998,[4] 15011 (67.5%) remained in that size-band, while 3,974 moved to size-band 5–9, 1997 moved to size-band 10–19 and 1,248 moved to the 20+ size-band. In the other size-bands, the majority of firms remained the same size or moved into a larger size-band. For example, of the 2,259 firms in size-band 5–9, 642 remained in the same size-band, 896 increased in size and 721 dropped into size-band 1–4. Similarly, in size-band 10–19, 560 (226 + 334) remained the same or grew compared to 376 that declined in size. In the 20+ size-band, 508 remained and 230 (84, 55 and 91) declined in size (Table 13.4). As mentioned above, these 26,132 firms created 231,500 jobs over the 15-year period of which over 60% (139,300) were generated by firms in size-band 0–4.

Finally, we draw on recent UK government statistics[5] to look at changes in the population of firms by size and by number of employees[6] from 2010 to 2021. As Table 13.5 illustrates, the UK population of private-sectors firms grew by 1.1 million between 2010 and 2021. Of course, the vast majority of those firms were in the smallest (0–1) size-band, which accounted for 838,000 (75.8%). The other most notable fact is that population of large firms (250+) also increased by a ratio of 1.29 (from 5,940 to 7,655). It is

Table 13.4 Surviving Firms 15 Years Later

Firm Size at Start-up in 1998	Firm Size 15 Years Later				
	1–4	5–9	10–19	20+	TOTAL
1–4	15011 (67.5%)	3974 (17.9%)	1997 (9.0%)	1248 (5.6%)	22229 (100%)
5–9	721 (31.9%)	642 (28.4%)	489 (21.7%)	407 (18.0%)	2259 (100%)
10–19	196 (20.9%)	180 (19.2%)	226 (24.2%)	334 (35.7%)	936 (100%)
20+	84 (11.4%)	55 (7.4%)	91 (12.3%)	508 (68.9%)	738 (100%)
Total	16012 (61.3%)	4850 (18.5%)	2803 (10.7%)	2497 (9.5%)	26,162 (100%)

Table 13.5 Increase in Number of Firms 2010–2021

	2010 Number of Firms	2021 Firms	Change in Number of Firms	2021/ 2010 Ratio Employees
0–1	3,471,000	4,309,000	838,000	1.39
2–4	589,830	765,000	175,000	1.19
5–9	220,000	262,000	42,000	1.16
10–19	111,000	137,000	26,000	1.21
20–49	59,300	73,670	14,370	1.23
50 – 249	27,715	35,620	7,905	1.28
>250–499	5,940	7655	1,715	1.29
Total	4,484,500	5,590,900	1,105,500	1.20

Table 13.6 Change in Number of Employees (2010–2021)

Size-band	2010 Employee Numbers	2021 Employee Numbers	Total Change	2010/2021 Ratio
0–1	3,941,000	4,837,000	896,000	1.23
2–4	1,786,000	2,135,000	349,000	1.19
5–9	1,523,000	1,776,000	253,000	1.16
10–19	1,545,000	1,875,000	330,000	1.21
20–49	1,818,000	2,236,000	418,000	1.23
50–249	2,704,000	3,474,000	770,000	1.28
>250	9,199,000	10,638,00	1,439,000	1.15
Total	22,500,000	26,972,000	4,472,000	1.20

worth noting that after the 2008 financial crash, large firms decreased in number and the more recent figures represent a recovery to pre-crash levels.

Table 13.6 indicates employee numbers per size-band for the years 2010/2021 and there were consistent growth ratios across all seven size-bands. Micro-firms (0–nine employees) created 1,498,000 (896,000+ 349,000+253,.000) new jobs in that time-period (Table 13.6). However, in complete contrast to the 1998 to 2010 time-period, not only was there a substantial increase in the number of large firms, the number of employees also increased by 1,439,000. While this increase in jobs created by large firms is clearly important for the UK economy, our focus is on those jobs created by the smallest firms. Therefore, even with all the problems associated with Covid-19, small firms continued to be an extremely important source for the creation of new jobs.

Several implications flow from the various data presented above. First, many jobs within the UK economy are created by very small firms. It should also be noted that these small firms are also responsible for large numbers of job losses which lead to considerable amounts of 'churn' in private sector employment. The second major implication is that most new firms simply do not grow; there is very little evidence of UK start-up businesses becoming 'gazelles' (Aldrich & Ruef, 2018). We believe that this is an important issue which needs to be addressed at the early stages of entrepreneurial careers. Building a viable business rather than simply becoming self-employed (or undertaking 'necessity entrepreneurship') means that nascent entrepreneurs should acquire the appropriate skills, competence and personal resilience to deal with the setbacks they will inevitably face. It our contention that understanding the nature of bootstrapping, bricolage and dynamic learning helps create that right conditions for longer-term business growth.

13.9 Summary and Key Learning Points

The priority for factor-driven economies (low-income) is the need to establish the basic institutional arrangements associated with property rights, rule of law and the minimization of start-up costs (Naudé, 2011). At the efficiency-driven stage (middle-income) the state should adopt a more interventionist approach to encourage development of domestic technological capabilities. In addition, provision of financial support can strengthen the entrepreneurial base as achieved by countries such as Korea and Singapore. Innovation-driven economies (high-income) should focus on innovation and the development of new technologies as well as improving competitiveness through the entry of new entrepreneurial firms. However, Naudé (2011, p. 329) does acknowledge that the design of entrepreneurial policies relative to the stage of economic development 'is still a relatively unchartered area'.

One of the key outcomes of this overview of the policy literature is that there are substantial variations in the links between nascent entrepreneurship and the stage of economic development. Consequently, there are no simple and straightforward conclusions that can be drawn about the relationship between government support, nascent entrepreneurship and economic development. In fact, data provided by the three institutions discussed above (OECD, GEM and the World Bank) are often contradictory. For example, Wennekers et al. (2005) claim that their empirical data confirm that there is a U-shaped relationship between entrepreneurship and economic growth. In contrast, the GEM data suggest that 'total entrepreneurial activity' (TEA) is, in fact, highest for efficiency-driven economies and then undergoes a substantial decline for innovation-driven economies. However, as we have discussed in Section 13.4 there is probably too much variation in TEA for the GEM data to provide any useful insight into links between entrepreneurship and economic development. Significantly, in September 2021, the World Bank withdrew its 'ease of doing business' publication because of 'ethical concerns' about the collection and presentation of their data.

There are tenuous links between the nature of the regulatory environment and the levels of business start-up (Wennekers et al., 2005). The UK, Norway and Sweden are in the top ten of countries for 'ease of doing business' (Table 13.2), their TEA (total entrepreneurial activity) scores of 9.3, 8.4 and 8.3 respectively are low compared to South Korea (14.9) and the US (17.4). In contrast, is Brazil ranked 124/190 for ease of doing business and had a TEA of 23.3 (the fourth highest ranked country in 2020). India also has a high TEA score (15.0) and is ranked 63/190 in terms of the ease of doing business. Despite this conflicting evidence, it does appear, at least as far as the UK is concerned, that there is support for Birch's hypothesis that new firms are responsible for many new jobs. Unfortunately for the UK, few new firms develop into rapidly-growing 'gazelles' which have the potential for a stronger impact on longer-term economic growth.

We now return to what Bridge (2010) describes as his alternative approach to enterprise policy which rejects ideas associated with 'standard economic theory'. What this means is that individuals are assumed to make rational economic choices about engaging in business start-up based on risk assessments of the expected returns from entrepreneurship. In contrast, Bridge claims that social factors are a much more important than economic factors in terms of influencing whether individuals engage in entrepreneurship. He also suggests that the population can be divided into three distinct groups: 1) an active group of entrepreneurs 2) a group who will never consider entrepreneurship 3) those who could be encouraged to become entrepreneurial (Figure 13.6). An individual's decision to become an entrepreneur is primarily influenced by what we describe in Chapter 5 as their close ties

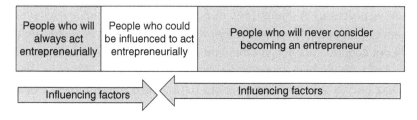

Figure 13.6 Levels of Entrepreneurship in a Population

(family, friends and other influential people such as teachers). Conventional factors designed to promote entrepreneurship including various enterprise support agencies, training, finance and reductions in 'red-tape' are unlikely to change attitudes to entrepreneurship. This model certainly goes some way in explaining the discrepancies we have discussed in relationship to the OECD, GEM and World Bank data (Bridge, 2010). It also helps explain why there are substantial regional variations in the levels of entrepreneurship. As we discuss above, start-up rates are twice as high in the Southeast of the UK compared to the Northwest. According to Bridge, areas which have high levels of entrepreneurship will continue to have high start-up rates while the reverse will be true for areas which have low levels of entrepreneurship.

We largely agree with Bridge's assertion that social influences are important in terms of encouraging individuals to consider entrepreneurship. Our view is that in addition to family and friends, higher education has an increasingly important role to play in promoting entrepreneurship to younger people (Chapter 5). As a result of participating in enterprise-related courses at university or by belonging to societies, such as Liverpool Enterprise Network, students are exposed to lecturers and guest speakers who are enthusiastic about entrepreneurship (Fearon, Furlotti, van Vuuren & McLaughlin, 2021; Pittaway, Rodriguez-Falcon, Aiyegbayo & King, 2011; Preedy et al., 2020). Lourenco et al. (2013) evaluated the extent to which exposure to enterprise-related courses influenced students' attitudes and behaviours. The study was informed by the theory of planned behaviour (Ajzen, 1991) which suggests that behaviours are influenced by intentions which, in turn, are influenced by three sets of beliefs: behavioural, normative and control (Figure 13.7). The study indicates that students' perceptions of benefits are a major driver of intentions to exploit their classroom learning. It also suggests that introducing fewer complex techniques are important in terms of raising students' perceptions of the benefits of learning about entrepreneurship. This finding extends the theory of planned behaviour by clarifying the role of perceived ease-of-use as a significant driver of the learning processes. Although, perceived 'ease-of-use' did not in itself predict intentions to exploit learning. In other words, potential student entrepreneurs will not acquire knowledge unless they perceive that it has real benefits in terms of helping them start their own businesses (Anjum, Farrukh, Heidler & Díaz Tautiva, 2021; Lourenço et al., 2013). The positive influence of education on entrepreneurship is confirmed by an extensive study of more than 10,000 individuals in Europe and the US (Block., Hoogerheide & Thurik,

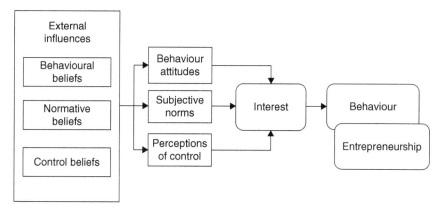

Figure 13.7 The Theory of Planned Behaviour

2011). Such studies support Ajzen's (1991) theory that attitudes (perception of benefits) are a strong influence on behavioural intentions. Hence, when students perceive there are real benefits in learning about entrepreneurship, they are more likely to have intentions to exploit their learning.

Key Learning Points are:

- You should be able to explain how the work of Birch in the US and Bolton in the UK influenced the development of policies related to business start-up
- You should be able to explain the ways in which UK policies designed to enhance entrepreneurship have evolved over the last 40 years
- You should be able to explain why entrepreneurship varies according to the stages of economic development – particularly the balance between necessity-based and opportunity-based entrepreneurship
- You should be able to explain why the OECD, GEM and the World Bank offer different prescriptions for promoting entrepreneurship – it is important to understand the extent to which the various policies promoted by these institutions make a difference to entrepreneurial activity.
- You should be able to explain why most governments are keen to promote the importance of entrepreneurship.
- You should be able to explain how the theory of planned behaviour complements the various policies promoted by the OECD, GEM and the World Bank.

13.10 Discussion Questions and Call to Action

- To what extent is access to finance a barrier to business start-up?
- According to the OECD, what are the most important determinants of entrepreneurship?
- What is your evaluation the entrepreneurial process described by GEM (Figure 13.2)?
- How and why do the levels of entrepreneurship vary according to the three stages of economic development – factor-driven (low-income), efficiency-driven (middle-income) and innovation-driven (high-income)?
- What do you regard as the most important factors in promoting entrepreneurship?
- What is meant by the terms firm and employment 'churn' and why are these factors so important in the context of small firms?
- What is the relationship between business regulation (World Bank) and entrepreneurship?
- How does the theory of planned behaviour complement the various policies designed to promote entrepreneurship?

As reiterated throughout the previous 12 chapters, this book is focused on the early stages of business start-up. This is largely encompassed by what the GEM studies describe as total entrepreneurial activity (TEA). In this chapter we have examined policy prescriptions from three organizations: the Organization for Economic Cooperation and Development (OECD), the Global Entrepreneurship Monitor (GEM) and the World Bank. All three organizations have very different views about the best ways in which to promote entrepreneurship and business start-up. The GEM studies are probably the most interesting because they evaluate entrepreneurship according to age, education and gender. The GEM organization is also keen to promote entrepreneurship to young people. For example, it is useful to understand why, in most developed countries, the highest rates of entrepreneurial activity are in the 25–34 age group (rather than the 18–24 or the 35–44 age groups). Our view is that having a better understanding of the barriers to business start-up are an important element in learning to become an entrepreneur. So, if you are participating in entrepreneurship education in college or university, you may feel that learning about 'policy' is not important for your future as an entrepreneur. We believe that developing an entrepreneurial mindset is an essential element in building your future career as an entrepreneur. Being able to explain the differences between the OECD, GEM and the World Bank is unlikely to make you a better entrepreneur. But understanding the various barriers to business start-up and developing strategies to overcome those barriers will certainly aid your entrepreneurial career.

Notes

1 www.gemconsortium.org/report/gem-20202021-global-report
2 The GEM data are extremely detailed, and you should examine their most recent reports to gain a full understanding of the complexity associated with starting and growing a new business.
3 https://data.worldbank.org/indicator/IC.BUS.EASE.XQ
4 Firms above the diagonal line moved up a size-band and those below moved down a size-band.
5 www.gov.uk/government/statistics/business-population-estimates-2021
6 www.gov.uk/government/statistics/bis-business-population-estimates

References

Acs, Z. J., Audretsch, D. B. & Feldman, M. P. (1994). R&D Spillovers and Innovative Activity. *Managerial and Decision Economics* (2), 131–138.

Acs, Z. J. & Szerb, L. (2007). Entrepreneurship, Economic Growth and Public Policy. *Small Business Economics* (2/3), 109–122.

Ajzen, I. (1991). The Theory of Planned Behavior. *Organizational Behavior & Human Decision Processes, 50*(2), 179–211.

Aldrich, H. E. & Ruef, M. (2018). Unicorns, Gazelles, and Other Distractions on the Way to Understanding Real Entrepreneurship in the United States. *Academy of Management Perspectives, 32*(4), 458–472.

Anjum, T., Farrukh, M., Heidler, P. & Díaz Tautiva, J. A. (2021). Entrepreneurial Intention: Creativity, Entrepreneurship, and University Support. *Journal of Open Innovation, 7*(1), 1–13.

Anyadike-Danes, M., Bonner, K. & Hart, M. (2011). *Job Creation and Destruction in the UK: 1998–2012*. Retrieved from Department for Business Innovation and Skills, UK

Anyadike-Danes, M. & Hart, M. (2018). All grown up? The fate after 15 years of a quarter of a million UK firms born in 1998. *Journal of Evolutionary Economics, 28*(1), 45–76.

Atkinson, J. & Storey, D. J. (1993). *Employment, the small firm and the labour market / Beschäftigung, Kleinbetriebe und Arbeitsmarkt*. London: Routledge and Kegan Paul.

Audretsch, D. B., Belitski, M., Chowdhury, F. & Desai, S. (2021). Necessity or opportunity? Government size, tax policy, corruption, and implications for entrepreneurship. *Small Business Economics*. doi:10.1007/s11187-021-00497-2

Belitski, M., Chowdhury, F. & Desai, S. (2016). Taxes, Corruption, and Entry. *Small Business Economics*, *47*(1), 201–216.

Bennett, R. (2008). SME Policy Support in Britain since the 1990s: What Have We Learnt? *Environment and Planning C: Government and Policy*, *26*(2), 375–397.

Birch, D. L. (1979). *The job generation process*. M.I.T. Program on Neighborhood and Regional Change. Cambridge, MA: M.I.T.

Birch, D. L. (1987). *Job Creation in America*. London: Free Press.

Block, J. & Sandner, P. (2009). Necessity and Opportunity Entrepreneurs and Their Duration in Self-employment: Evidence from German Micro Data. *Journal of Industry, Competition & Trade, 9*(2), 117–137.

Block., J., H., Hoogerheide, L. & Thurik, R. (2011). Education and Entrepreneurial Choice: An Instrumental Variables Analysis. *International Small Business Journal*, *31*(1), 23–33.

Bolton, J. E. (1971). *Report of the Committee of Enquiry on small firms*. Retrieved from London: HMSO.

Bosma, N., Content, J., Sanders, M. & Stam, E. (2018). Institutions, Entrepreneurship, and Economic Growth in Europe. *Small Business Economics, 51*(2), 483–499.

Bosma, N. & Kelley, D. (2019) *Global Entrepreneurship Monitor (GEM) Report 2019*. Global Entrepreneurship Research Association (www.gemconsortium.org).

Bridge, S. (2010). *Rethinking enterprise policy [electronic book]: Can failure trigger new understanding? / Simon Bridge*. Houndmills, Basingstoke: Palgrave Macmillan

Bridge, S. & O'Neill, K. (2018). *Understanding enterprise: entrepreneurs & small business*. London: Red Globe Press.

Castells, M. (2000). *The rise of the network society*. Oxford: Blackwell Publishers.

Curran, J. & Storey, D. J. (1993). *Small firms in urban and rural locations*. London and New York.: Routledge Small Business Series.

Dencker, J. C., Bacq, S., Gruber, M. & Haas, M. (2021). Reconceptualizing Necessity Entrepreneurship: A Contextualized Framework of Entrepreneurial Processes Under the Condition of Basic Needs. *Academy of Management Review, 46*(1), 60–79.

Etzkowitz, H. & Leydesdorff, L. (2000). The dynamics of innovation: from National Systems and 'Mode 2' to a Triple Helix of university-industry-government relations. *Research Policy, 29*(2), 109–123.

Facebook (2020). *Global State of Small Business Report*. Retrieved from https://data forgood.fb.com/global-state-of-smb

Fearon, C., Furlotti, M., van Vuuren, W. & McLaughlin, H. (2021). Developing new opportunities, entrepreneurial skills and product/service creativity: a 'Young Enterprise' (YE) perspective. *Studies in Higher Education, 46*(6), 1081–1098

Florida, R. (2002). *The Rise of the Creative Class and how it's Transforming Work, Life, Leisure, Community and Everyday Life*. New York: Perseus Books.

Gibb, A. (1987). Education for Enterprise: Training for Small Business Initiation – Some Contrasts. *Journal of Small Business and Entrepreneurship, 4*(3), 42–47.

Gibb, A. (2002). In pursuit of a new 'enterprise' and 'entrepreneurship' paradigm for learning: creative destruction, new values, new ways of doing things and new combinations of knowledge. *International Journal of Management Reviews, 4*(3), 213–232.

Gibb, A. & Ritchie, J. (1982). Understanding the Process of Starting Small Businesses. *International Small Business Journal, 1*(1), 26–45.

Hägg, G. & Kurczewska, A. (2021). *Entrepreneurship Education – Scholarly Progress and Future Challenges*. New York: Routledge.

Harju, J., Matikka, T. & Rauhanen, T. (2019). Compliance costs vs. tax incentives: Why do entrepreneurs respond to size-based regulations? *Journal of Public Economics, 173*, 139–164.

Huggins, R. & Williams, N. (2009). Enterprise and Public Policy: A Review of Labour Government Intervention in the United Kingdom. *Environment and Planning C: Government and Policy, 27*(1), 19–41.

Hughes, A. & Storey, D. J. (1994). *Finance and the small firm*: London [u.a.].

Hyams-Ssekasi, D. & Caldwell, E. F. (2018). *Experiential Learning for Entrepreneurship: Theoretical and Practical Perspectives on Enterprise Education*. Cham: Springer International Publishing.

Irwin, K. C., Gilstrap, C. M., Drnevich, P. L. & Tudor, C. M. (2019). From start-up to acquisition: Implications of financial investment trends for small- to medium-sized high-tech enterprises. *Journal of Small Business Strategy, 29*(2), 22–43.

Jayawarna, D., Jones, O. & Macpherson, A. (2011). New business creation and regional development: enhancing resource acquisition in areas of social deprivation. *Entrepreneurship and Regional Development, 23*(9–10), 735–761.

Jayawarna, D., Jones, O. & Macpherson, A. (2020). Resourcing Social Enterprises: The Role of Socially Oriented Bootstrapping. *British Journal of Management, 31*(1), 56–79.

Jiangyong, L. & Zhigang, T. (2008). Determinants of entrepreneurial activities in China. *Journal of Business Venturing, 25*, 261–273.

Jones, O. (2022). Academic engagement with small business and entrepreneurship: Towards a landscape of practice. *Industry and Higher Education, 36*(3), 279–293.

Jones, O. & Jayawarna, D. (2010). Resourcing new businesses: social networks, bootstrapping and firm performance. *Venture Capital, 12*(2), 127–152.

Jones, O., Meckel, P. & Taylor, D. (2021). *Creating Communities of Practice: Entrepreneurial Learning in a University-Based Incubator*. Cham (Switzerland): Springer.

Jones, O. & Tang, N. (1998). Mature Firms in the Mid-Corporate Sector: Strategies for Innovation and Employment. In R. Delbridge & J. Lowe (Eds.), *Manufacturing in Transition*. London: MacMillan.

Klapper, L., Laeven, L. & Rajan, R. (2009). Entry Regulation as a Barrier to Entrepreneurship. In T. Beck (Ed.), *Entrepreneurship in Developing Countries* (pp. 340–378): Elgar Reference Collection. International Library of Entrepreneurship, vol. 15. Cheltenham and Northampton, MA: Elgar. (Reprinted from: [2006]).

Lee, R., Tuselmann, H., Jayawarna, D. & Rouse, J. (2019). Effects of structural, relational and cognitive social capital on resource acquisition: a study of entrepreneurs residing in multiply deprived areas. *Entrepreneurship & Regional Development, 31*(5/6), 534–554.

Lounsbury, M., Cornelissen, J., Granqvist, N. & Grodal, S. (2019). Culture, innovation and entrepreneurship. *Innovation: Organization & Management, 21*(1), 1–12.

Lourenço, F., Jones, O. & Jayawarna, D. (2013). Promoting sustainable development: The role of entrepreneurship education. *International Small Business Journal, 31*(8), 841–865.

Mallett, O. & Wapshott, R. (2020). *A History of Enterprise Policy: Government, Small Business and Entrepreneurship*. London: Routledge.

Naudé, W. (2011). Entrepreneurship is Not a Binding Constraint on Growth and Development in the Poorest Countries. *World Development, 39*, 33–44.

OECD (2006). *The SME Financing Gap – Theory and Evidence*. Retrieved from https://doi.org/10.1787/9789264029415-en

OECD (2009). *The impact of the global crisis on SME and entrepreneurship financing and policy responses*. Retrieved from Paris: www.oecd.org/cfe/smes/43183090.pdf

OECD (2017). *Entrepreneurship at a Glance* (22266941). Retrieved from Paris: http://dx.doi.org/10.1787/entrepreneur_aag-2017-en

Pittaway, L., Rodriguez-Falcon, E., Aiyegbayo, O. & King, A. (2011). The role of entrepreneurship clubs and societies in entrepreneurial learning. *International Small Business Journal, 29*(1), 37–57.

Pollack, J. M., Carr, J. C., Michaelis, T. L. & Marshall, D. R. (2019). Hybrid entrepreneurs' self-efficacy and persistence change: A longitudinal exploration. *Journal of Business Venturing Insights, 12*. doi:10.1016/j.jbvi.2019.e00143

Porter, M. (1998). *The Competitive Advantage of Nations*. Basingstoke: Macmillan Press.

Porter, M., Takeuchi, H. & Sakaibara, M. (2000). *Can Japan Compete?* New York: Basic Books.

Preedy, S., Jones, P., Maas, G. & Duckett, H. (2020). Examining the perceived value of extracurricular enterprise activities in relation to entrepreneurial learning processes. *Journal of Small Business & Enterprise Development, 27*(7), 1085–1105.

Reynolds, P. D. (2020). *The truth about entrepreneurship: policy making and business creation*. Cheltenham: Edward Elgar.

Rocha, R., Ulyssea, G. & Rachter, L. (2018). Do lower taxes reduce informality? Evidence from Brazil. *Journal of Development Economics, 134*, 28–49.

Rogers, N. (2006). Social Networks and the Emergence of the New Entrepreneurial Ventures in Russia: 1987–2000. *American Journal of Economics & Sociology, 65*(2), 295–312.

Rostow, W. W. (1960). *The stages of economic growth: a non-communist manifesto by W.W. Rostow*. Cambridge: Cambridge University Press.

Stam, E. & van de Ven, A. (2021). Entrepreneurial Ecosystem Elements. *Small Business Economics, 56*(2), 809–832.

Stel, A., Storey, D. J. & Thurik, A. R. (2007). The Effect of Business Regulations on Nascent and Young Business Entrepreneurship. *Small Business Economics* (2/3), 171–186.

Stoica, O., Roman, A. & Rusu, V. D. (2020). The Nexus between Entrepreneurship and Economic Growth: A Comparative Analysis on Groups of Countries. *Sustainability, 12*(3), 1186. doi:10.3390/su12031186

Storey, D. J. (1994). *Understanding the small business sector*. London: International Thompson Business Press.

Storey, D. J., Greene, F. J. & Mole, K. (2007). *Three decades of enterprise culture? [electronic book]: entrepreneurship, economic regeneration and public policy*. Basingstoke: Palgrave Macmillan.

Valliere, D. & Peterson, R. (2009). Entrepreneurship and Economic Growth: Evidence from Emerging and Developed Countries. *Entrepreneurship and Regional Development, 21*(5–6), 459–480.

Wapshott, R. & Mallett, O. (2021). *Small Business, Big Government and the Origins of Enterprise Policy: The UK Bolton Committee*. London: Routledge.

Wennekers, S., van Stel, A., Thurik, R. & Reynolds, P. D. (2005). Nascent Entrepreneurship and the Level of Economic Development. *Small Business Economics* (3), 293–309.

World Bank (2020). *Doing Business 2020*. Washington, DC: World Bank. DOI:10.1596/978-1-4648-1440-2. License: Creative Commons Attribution CC by 3.0 IGO.

Appendices

Appendix 13.1 GEM Entrepreneurial Framework Conditions

1. **Access to entrepreneurial finance.** Sufficient funds are available to new start-ups, from informal investment and bank loans to government grants and venture capital.
2. **Government policy: support and relevance.** Government policies promote Entrepreneurship and support those starting a new business venture.
3. **Government policy: taxes and bureaucracy.** Business taxes and fees are affordable for the new enterprise. Rules and regulations are easy to manage, without undue burden on the new business.
4. **Government entrepreneurship programs.** Quality support programs are available to the new entrepreneur at local, regional and national levels.
5. **Entrepreneurial education at school.** Schools are introducing ideas of entrepreneurship and instilling students with entrepreneurial values such as enquiry, opportunity recognition and creativity.
6. **Entrepreneurial education post-school.** Colleges, universities and business schools offer effective courses in entrepreneurial subjects, alongside practical training in how to start a business.
7. **Research and development transfer.** Research findings, including from universities and research centres, can readily be translated into commercial ventures.
8. **Commercial and professional infrastructure.** There are sufficient affordable Professional services such as lawyers and accountants to support the new venture, within a Framework of property rights.
9. **Ease of entry: market dynamics.** There are free, open and growing markets where no large businesses control entry or prices.
10. **Ease of entry: market burdens and regulations.** Regulations facilitate, rather than restrict, entry.
11. **Physical infrastructure.** Physical infrastructure (such as roads), Internet access and speed, the cost and availability of physical spaces, is adequate and accessible to entrepreneurs.
12. **Social and cultural norms.** National culture encourages and celebrates entrepreneurship, including through the provision of role models and mentors, as well as social support for risk-taking.

The scale of measurement on which these averages are given is from 0 to 10 points, whereby 0 = completely insufficient and 10 = completely sufficient.

Appendix 13.2 Innovation-Driven (High-income) Economies

Country	TEA	EBO	Necessity % TEA	Opportunity % TEA
South Korea	14.9%	13.0%	21.0%	77.7%
US	12.4%	8.2%	8.1%	78.3%
Netherlands	10.4%	10/8%	9.1%	62.3%
UK	9.3%	8.2%	12.9%	84.2%
Sweden	8.3%	4.9%	9.3%	73.4%
Germany	7.6%	5.2%	16.7%	69.8%
Spain	6.2%	6.3%	22.6%	70.7%
France	5.7%	6.0%	22.3%	72.9%
Japan	5.4%	7.0%	20.2%	69.5%
Italy	2.8%	4.7%	11.4%	81.0%

Note: Ranked according to TEA

Appendix 13.3 Efficiency-Driven (Middle-income) Economies

Country	TEA	EBO	Necessity % TEA	Opportunity % TEA
Guatemala	25.1%	14.8%	37.7%	46.1%
Brazil	23.3%	16.2%	37.5%	61.8%
Columbia	22.3%	4.3%	12.2%	85.5%
Russia	9.3%	5.1%	39.8%	52.2%
China	8.7%	9.3%	27.8%	70.5%

Appendix 13.4 Factor-Driven (Low-income) Economies

Country	TEA	EBO	Necessity % TEA	Opportunity % TEA
Angola	49.6%	9.2%	38.8%	57.0%
Madagascar	19.5%	20.2%	31.3%	67.2%
Morocco	10.4%	10.8%	31.2%	64.5%
Indonesia	9.6%	11.4%	25.2%	73.0%
Egypt	6.7%	1.5%	47.6%	47.5%

Conclusions
Dynamic Entrepreneurial Learning

14.1 Introduction

In this book we concentrate on the first 12 months of operation as we regard this as the crucial period in the life of any entrepreneurial business. As discussed in Chapter 13, most new entrepreneurs do not get beyond the self-employment stage. We acknowledge that there is an important role for those individuals who operate as sole-traders whether offering craft-based services (hairdressing/plumbing) or providing technical services such as web design, software engineering, consultancy, environmental monitoring and so on. However, it is our view that establishing a business according to the principles outlined in this book provides a sound basis for future growth – as outlined in Chapters 10 and 11. Successful entrepreneurship is important to those individuals who start their own businesses as well as their families. Improving the performance of start-up businesses is also the focus of policymakers and politicians in mature, innovation-based economies including the UK and the US, efficiency-driven economies (Brazil, China, Columbia, Russia) and factor-driven economies such as Egypt, Indonesia and Morocco. Every country and region would like to recreate the success of Silicon Valley (Castells, 2000; Saxenian, 1996) and establish a base for the emergence of gazelles and unicorns (Aldrich & Ruef, 2018).

Of course, one of the problems for less-developed countries is making the shift from unproductive necessity entrepreneurship to the higher productivity associated with opportunity entrepreneurship (Dencker, Bacq, Gruber & Haas, 2021; Valliere & Peterson, 2009). Such a shift relies on developing countries making a real effort to improve educational levels among the population as demonstrated by highly successful economies

DOI: 10.4324/9781003312918-15

such as South Korea or China. As illustrated in Figure 10.2, entrepreneurial resources are the starting point for understanding effective new venture creation. Knowledge or, more formally, human capital is the most important of the resources, which any entrepreneur can mobilize (see Chapter 7).

In addition to knowledge, Aldrich and Yang (2012) point out the importance of three dispositions: routines, habits and heuristics (Jones & Li, 2017). Rather than being fixed psychological attributes these dispositions are outcomes of learned behaviours. Such learning can come from many sources including your family (see the Jazooli case), friends, role models, TV programmes such as Dragon's Den and from lecturers who offer courses dealing with entrepreneurship and business start-up. Potential entrepreneurs should also take the opportunity to learn from a wide-range of experiences, which are part of our development during the early stages of the human life-course (Jayawarna, Jones & Macpherson, 2014, 2015). Learning can come from part-time work during school or university when there are many opportunities to observe the real-life management of small businesses (newsagents, restaurants, bars, retail outlets, etc.). Learning can also come from your experiences as a consumer when the provision of inadequate offerings from existing companies could help you identify business opportunities. Analysing the activities of existing organizations provides you with the opportunity to identify the routines that underpin any successful business.

In the remainder of this chapter, we intend to briefly summarize the main factors that we believe contribute to dynamic entrepreneurial learning capabilities. It is our belief that these factors will lead the creation of new business ventures that have real potential for future growth and, hopefully, meaningful employment creation.

14.2 Learning Objectives

- To be able to articulate the basic principles on which this book is based.
- To distinguish between the causal and effectual approaches to business start-up and explain the implications of both approaches for opportunity identification and creation.
- To explain why social skills are so important for young, inexperienced entrepreneurs.

- To explain how effective entrepreneurs can combine bootstrapping and bricolage to compensate for their lack of resources.
- To explain the links between enterprise education and the development of an entrepreneurial mindset.
- To understand the importance of resourcefulness and resilience to new entrepreneurs.

14.3 Theory, Practice and Learning

In Chapter 12, we discussed changes to the nature of entrepreneurial theory over the last 15 years (Landström, Harirchi & Åström, 2012). The most significant issue for the would-be entrepreneur relates to ideas about the nature of business opportunities. The traditional, largely economic, view suggests that new opportunities have an objective reality, which means they are 'out there' awaiting entrepreneurial discovery (Shane, 2000). This is strongly linked to the idea that there are a small group of individuals who possess the necessary 'entrepreneurial alertness' to identify and exploit those opportunities (Kirzner, 1973). The view expressed by the 'causal school' has been increasingly challenged by a number of competing theories including bricolage (Baker & Nelson, 2005) effectuation (Sarasvathy, 2001; Sarasvathy, 2008) and the narrative approach (Fisher, Neubert & Burnell, 2021; Fletcher, 2007). A common theme in these theories is that entrepreneurs create opportunities through a process of sensemaking. What this means is that the entrepreneur's own resources and interests provide the basis of a business opportunity (Baker & Nelson, 2005). This approach is clearly illustrated by Ben and Sam Wilson's experience of establishing Jazooli, which began as a hobby and has grown into a company that has ten employees with a turnover of £3 million (Jones & Li, 2017).

There are many implications arising from an acceptance of the idea that entrepreneurs create rather than discover opportunities. Starting at a relatively small-scale enables entrepreneurs to develop the appropriate skills and knowledge as they establish the business. As outlined in Chapter 2, the nature of skills and capabilities depend on the entrepreneur's education and previous experience. The type of business and the type of the opportunity are also crucial factors to consider. Many start-ups established by young entrepreneurs replicate existing businesses and therefore do not require specialist knowledge, skills, or capabilities. We accept that such businesses can still be extremely demanding for inexperienced entrepreneurs, as you must develop the appropriate organizational routines by which to deliver their products/services. However, if you are introducing a product or service that redefines an existing market then, in addition to basic organizational skills, nascent entrepreneurs will need to be creative and innovatory. It is also likely that such ventures demand far higher levels of financial resources (see Chapter 8). Although there is little agreement on the exact nature of the appropriate skills and competences, we suggest that functional skills including marketing, finance, sales, planning and customer relationship management are likely to be highly relevant whatever the type of start-up.

It is also increasingly recognized that social skills are important for successful entrepreneurship (Cornelissen, Clarke & Cienki, 2012; Rayna & Striukova, 2021). We suggest that developing the appropriate social skills is central to the effective mobilization of entrepreneurial social capital (Anderson, Jack & Drakopoulou-Dodd, 2009; Shao & Sun, 2021). This is particularly important in terms of accessing wider resources (finance, knowledge, information and business opportunities) by moving beyond the 'strong ties' which are important in the very early stages of start-up to 'weaker ties' associated with professional networks (English, de Villiers Scheepers, Fleischman, Burgess & Crimmins, 2021). Figure 6.6 illustrates this process of converting 'essential dyads' into socio-economic exchanges. We also suggest that there are three forms of social capital, structural, relational and cognitive, which enable entrepreneurs to access wider, more resource-rich social networks. Cognitive social capital illustrates the forms of communication used by nascent entrepreneurs to build relationships with resource providers (Lee & Jones, 2008; Zhao, Barratt-Pugh, Standen, Redmond & Suseno, 2021).

Entrepreneurial learning underpins the process of accessing a wider range of social contacts. Building dynamic entrepreneurial learning capabilities is of central importance to young entrepreneurs wanting to establish successful businesses. As described in Chapters 2 and 5, we believe that 'learning-to-learn' is an important capacity for any potential entrepreneur studying in higher education (McDonald & Cater-Steel, 2017). Furthermore, we see the Kolb cycle, which is based on two dialectical processes (prehension and transformation), as an essential tool for understanding learning activities (Baker, Jensen & Kolb, 2005; Honig & Hopp, 2019; Kolb, 1984). What this means in practice is that courses/modules designed to develop entrepreneurial skills and capabilities must have an experiential element in which students can gain experience of what it means to be an entrepreneur (Hyams-Ssekasi & Caldwell, 2018; Jones, Meckel & Taylor, 2021). Courses can promote such learning in a variety of ways including writing business plans, engaging in simulation games such as SimVenture (Kriz & Auchter, 2016), starting a small-scale business, as well as joining enterprise clubs and societies (Landoni, Bolzani & Baroncelli, 2021). Our view is that the more 'real' such experiences are then the more likely students are to develop the appropriate skills and competences (Pittaway, Gazzard, Shore & Williamson, 2015; Pittaway, Rodriguez-Falcon, Aiyegbayo & King, 2011). In the previous Chapter (13), we describe how this approach fits with Ajzen's theory of planned behaviour (Figure 13.6), which suggests that behaviours are influenced by intentions which, in turn, are shaped by behavioural, normative and control beliefs (Ajzen, 1991; Lourenço, Jones & Jayawarna, 2013). Students who perceive there are real benefits in learning about entrepreneurship are more likely to have intentions to exploit their learning (Bandura, 1997; Lourenço et al., 2013). This view is based on the concept of self-efficacy; individuals are more likely to undertake particular tasks when they believe they have the appropriate knowledge and skills (Bandura, 1997).

14.4 Resources, Bootstrapping and Bricolage

Creating opportunities, and learning from experience, requires the application of human capital and other resources to establish and develop new ventures. While highly capitalized start-ups may have an abundance of resources, the reality is that most new entrepreneurs have a limited ability to attract funding from external sources and rely mainly on the creative energy of one or two people. This means that, in new firms, resource capacity is generally limited. Financial and other tangible resources are clearly necessary to be able to start and maintain the venture (Irwin, Gilstrap, Drnevich & Tudor, 2019). However, as Hitt et al. (2001) argue, it is the intangible resources that distinguish successful firms since these assets are more difficult to replicate (Flechas Chaparro, Kozesinski & Camargo Júnior, 2021). In addition, despite similar resource endowments, some firms prosper while others decline and go out of business. Penrose (1959) attributes this to the unique capabilities and capacity of entrepreneurial individuals. At the start of any venture, Sarasvathay (2001) argues that nascent entrepreneurs have three categories of means – their own personal traits, tastes and abilities, their own knowledge gained through education and experience and their social networks (Elfring, Klyver & van Burg, 2021). As suggested by Read, Sarasvathy, Dew, Wiltbank and Ohisson (2011) and discussed in Chapter 7, an entrepreneur's human capital is an important foundational capability. It is this resource that provides access to social networks and the purposeful capacity and capability to transform resources into rents (Penrose, 1959). Human capital resources include the knowledge, experience, judgement, intelligence, relationships and insight of people working in the firm and in particular the entrepreneur. These are not static attributes; effective entrepreneurs are continually developing their capabilities through experience and learning (see Section 12.1). New entrepreneurs can develop, acquire, appropriate, or borrow capabilities from others within their social network (Fayolle, Kariv & Matlay, 2019; Lans, Blok & Gulikers, 2015; Xiangyang, Frese & Giardini, 2010).

Although Teece (2011) recognizes that such human capital resources are not equally distributed, he argues that they can be enhanced through education (generic human capital) and, more importantly, through experience, to create specific and unique capabilities (Seet, Jones, Oppelaar & Corral de Zubielqui, 2018). If resource poor new firms are to become established and self-sustaining then 'a series of resource acquisitions and combinations might be necessary' (Lichtenstein & Brush, 2001, p. 41). Here the concepts of bootstrapping and bricolage help us explore resource development and enhancement through the dynamic capabilities that provide opportunities for new firms to learn to grow (Bernardi & Pedrini, 2020; Ghezzi, 2019; Jayawarna, Jones & Macpherson, 2020; Rutherford, Pollack, Mazzei & Sanchez-Ruiz, 2017). Entrepreneurs who successfully manage the complexities of establishing new ventures do so by supplementing their human capital through resources, advice and knowledge available in their networks (Macpherson, Herbane & Jones, 2015; West & Noel, 2009). Since new entrepreneurs are unlikely to have all the resources they need to establish and grow their business, the environment (and particularly networks) in which they operate is a vital resource base. While traditional financial resources may be available, they are difficult for young entrepreneurs to access (Chapter 8) and financial bootstrapping can provide many tangible resources at little or no cost (Block, Fisch & Hirschmann, 2021; Harrison, Mason & Girling, 2004). As noted above, social skills and the ability to manage relationships to establish and extend networks is a particularly useful capability, since this gives access, potentially at least, to a broader array of resources (Cornelissen et al., 2012; Fearon, Furlotti, van Vuuren & McLaughlin, 2021).

While many routes and options exist to 'bootstrap', most rely on the availability, strength and diversity of network ties entrepreneurs can leverage (Jayawarna et al., 2020; Rutherford, 2015). This means that the extent to which entrepreneurs are reliant on a given environment or social group can determine their capacity for resource acquisition. Therefore, the growth trajectory and opportunities that new entrepreneurs generate depend on the level and nature of relationships and dependencies they develop (Fisher et al., 2021; Villanueva, Van de Ven & Sapienza, 2012). These relationships will change as the firm grows, and therefore there will inevitably be some alteration to the availability and desirability of the various bootstrapping techniques (Malmstrom, 2014; Michaelis, Scheaf, Carr & Pollack, 2022). Human capital in the form of prior education and experience is not only relevant because of the way in which new entrepreneurs apply it to manage their business; it is also important because it can mediate access to wider capital resources available within internal and external networks (Seet et al., 2018). This also highlights how, in different social contexts and cultures, some social groups will have a significant advantage in terms of bootstrapping their business (see Chapter 9). In developing countries and regions with high levels of social deprivation, most new enterprises arise out of necessity entrepreneurship and have limited capacity to grow (Stoica, Roman & Rusu, 2020). Moreover, as pointed out by Gupta, Turban, Wasti and Sikdar (2009, p. 409) this social dimension, makes entrepreneurship a 'gendered profession' since societies place limitations on women's ability to accrue necessary resources for their businesses (Jayawarna, Woodhams & Jones, 2012).

Social networks can also provide access to knowledge, experience and capabilities not possessed by new, young entrepreneurs (English et al., 2021). This may be particularly useful when, in dynamic contexts, entrepreneurs must respond to market changes to create opportunities (Arikan, Arikan & Koparan, 2020). In larger firms the strategic ability to manage these volatile contexts has been termed dynamic capabilities (Teece, Pisano & Shuen, 1997), the ability to reconfigure and integrate both internal and external resources in response to environmental shifts (Jones, Ghobadian, O'Regan & Antcliffe, 2013). However, new firms lack the resource capacity and resource slack, to manage such situations (Arikan et al., 2020).

In this regard, the concept of bricolage is particularly useful. Bricolage is the art of making do with resources at hand or discarded by others (Baker & Nelson, 2005; Stenholm & Renko, 2016). Given the limited resources with which most new ventures operate, being able to scrounge or borrow resources discarded by others or being able to access knowledge and capabilities available in social networks is potentially a resource multiplier (Bernardi & Pedrini, 2020; Ghezzi, 2019). In new firms, the application of these resources is likely be through improvization and trial and error (or experiential) learning (Hyams-Ssekasi & Caldwell, 2018; Zahra, Sapienza & Davidsson, 2006). Thus, the effective, evolution of new firms depends on the ability of entrepreneurs to develop the ability to problem-solve when responding to changing contexts (Breslin & Jones, 2012; Macpherson et al., 2015). Bricolage is thus intimately linked to the learning ability of the entrepreneur (developing their human capital) and the capability to bootstrap both tangible and intangible resources. Thus, bootstrapping, bricolage and the social skills to navigate network relationships are the most important capabilities nascent entrepreneurs bring to their venture. If new businesses are to grow, new entrepreneurs will need to overcome their resource constraints. In doing so, Baker and Nelson (2005) argue that entrepreneurs are essentially refusing to accept the resource limitations imposed by their situation. Establishing a new firm, from this perspective, is a dynamic creative process, one that requires tenacity and the ability to learn (from others) while working on the business (Kempster, Smith & Barnes, 2018; Zhang, Macpherson & Jones, 2006).

14.5 Resourcefulness and an Entrepreneurial Mindset

As stated in Chapter 1, this book is based on the idea that the 'blue-print' or template established in the pre- and immediate post-start-up phases will have significant implications for the future of your business (Baron, Hannan & Burton, 1999). Hence, the importance of entrepreneurial learning and the need to create new businesses based on the principles associated with 'lean start-ups' (Bortolini, Nogueira Cortimiglia, Danilevicz & Ghezzi, 2021). In Chapter 4, we discuss the links between the ideas of lean start-ups and business modelling. Young entrepreneurs adopting a lean start-up approach should translate their business concept into a basic business model. We suggest the following three element are the essential elements of a basic business model: customer-value proposition (CVP), market segment and revenue (Section 4.2). The lean approach is intended to reduce the time and resources you invest in non-viable business ideas. Adopting a lean approach means minimizing the time spent on product/service development and obtaining early customer feedback (Ries, 2011). The key idea associated with lean start-ups is that you should obtain feedback from potential customers as early as you can. Ries (2011) describes the lean 'build-measure-learn' approach, as early engagement with customers enables you to adjust your business model before committing too many resources.

Having the appropriate mindset will help you adopt a lean approach to your new business. Figure 1.1 illustrates the five core attributes associated with an entrepreneurial mindset as well as two meta-cognitive factors: meta-cognitive and cognitive adaptability (Naumann, 2017). It would be useful revision if you return to Section 1.5 and review the five attributes described in Figure 1.1. Another approach to the entrepreneurial mindset suggests that there are three distinct factors: cognition, behaviours and emotions (Kuratko, Fisher & Audretsch, 2021). Although we are committed to the importance of social learning, it is important to acknowledge the central role of cognition, which focuses on your mental abilities to understand, store and recall new knowledge as well as your problem-solving and decision-making skills (Cope & Down, 2010; Gregoire, Cornelissen, Dimov & Burg, 2015; Santos, Costa, Neumeyer & Caetano, 2016). Entrepreneurial cognition is regarded as particularly important for identifying new opportunities and making decisions about how to develop business ideas (Kuratko et al., 2021). Hence, entrepreneurial cognition with a focus on opportunity spotting suggests a *mindset* that distinguishes entrepreneurs from non-entrepreneurs (Arikan et al., 2020).

Entrepreneurial behaviour directs attention to activities associated with identifying or creating opportunities as well as the actions required to obtain the resources necessary for business start-up (the entrepreneurial process). This is the crucial period when you learn whether you have the motivation, self-efficacy, resilience and resourcefulness to pursue a career in entrepreneurship. Starting a new business will lead stressful emotions you will be exposed to high levels of risk and uncertainty. A willingness to accept that your day-to-day life will be typified by stressful situations is a crucial element in becoming an entrepreneur. In addition to the risk of failure, you will have to adopt a range of different roles and rapidly acquire new skills. You will certainly need basic technical skills including financial management, business planning, competitor analysis and the digital skills (see Tables 2.1, 2.2 and 2.3) that are increasingly important for new entrepreneurs (Peschl, Deng & Larson, 2021; Rayna & Striukova, 2021). You will also need to develop the 'softer' entrepreneurial skills including creativity, collaboration, networking and effective communications (McCallum, Weicht, McMullan & Price, 2018). As your business begins to operate, you will need to acquire higher-level skills such as strategic decision-making, negotiation, financial planning (see Chapters 2, 10 and 11).

In many ways, debates about cognition are like the question about whether entrepreneurs are 'born or made'. Our view (otherwise we would not have written this book) is that you can certainly learn to become an entrepreneur and develop a more entrepreneurial mindset. While there are undoubtably social and familial influences on 'entrepreneurial behaviour', individual cognition also has a role to play. As set out in Section 1.5.1, there are several ways in which enterprise (or entrepreneurship) education can help develop your entrepreneurial mindset. Fostering a more entrepreneurial mindset means becoming aware of your own enterprise and entrepreneurial capabilities. The QAA (2018, p. 19) presents a list of factors associated with an entrepreneurial mindset, which include a self-awareness of your personality and social identity as well as being motivated to achieve your personal ambitions and goals. A range of recent studies confirm the importance of entrepreneurship education in developing an entrepreneurial mindset (Cui, Sun & Bell, 2021; Inada, 2020; Kwapisz, Schell, Aytes & Bryant, 2021; Lindberg, Bohman, Hulten & 2017). Experiential learning combined with extracurricular activities that encourage enterprising behaviour have a positive influence on the entrepreneurial mindset (Bignotti & le Roux, 2020; Pocek, Politis & Gabrielsson, 2021; Preedy, Jones, Maas & Duckett, 2020).

Becoming an entrepreneur by establishing your own business will inevitably mean that you will be confronted with many challenges and setbacks. Those who do not have high levels of resourcefulness and resilience are unlikely to succeed. Overcoming difficulties or even what may appear to be insoluble problems requires you to develop a cognitive adaptability based on your prior knowledge. Creating resourcefulness narratives is important for encouraging resource providers to support your business (Fisher et al., 2021). Other people, including family and friends, are more likely to offer support if you are seen to be a resourceful individual who is not easily discouraged. Building resilience, mental toughness or grit helps you overcome difficulties as you make the transition from student to entrepreneur (Chadwick & Raver, 2020; Mooradian, Matzler, Uzelac & Bauer, 2016).

We suggest that it would be useful revision to undertake the two exercises at the end of Chapter 1. Ideally, you will be able to identify clear changes in your entrepreneurial mindset.

14.6 Conclusions

As discussed in Chapter 5, the idea that entrepreneurs are born remains an issue of some contention (Ramoglou, Gartner & Tsang, 2020). The debate has largely moved on from the idea that entrepreneurs have specific psychological attributes such as a tolerance of ambiguity and a high need for achievement (McClelland, 1961) to a search for the 'entrepreneurial gene' (Nicolaou, Shane, Cherkas, Hunkin & Spector, 2008; Shane, Nicolaou, Cherkas & Spector, 2010). Our view is that anyone attending college or university has the potential to start their own business. We acknowledge that there are a range of skills and competences that students should acquire if they are intending to start their own business (Chapter 2). At least as important is that students should learn-to-learn so that they can make sense of an environment that is rapidly changing. Anyone starting a business will be confronted with a large number of crises in the first twelve months of operation (Deverell, 2009). Such crises will be particularly challenging for young people who are gaining their first exposure to the 'real world' of business and have little previous experience on which to draw. According to a study of young entrepreneurs (Hickie, 2011), those who were the most successful initiated entrepreneurial ventures while still at school. The *Jazooli case* also illustrates the benefits of gaining early trading experience as well as having supportive parents with appropriate business expertise (Jones & Li, 2017). Aldrich and Yang (2012) suggest that family members are crucial influences on the 'substrate of individual habits' which help new entrepreneurs embed their learning as they build a set of routines, habits and heuristics. Such dispositions help new entrepreneurs use their rules-of-thumb to make decisions when they do not possess the time or resources required for optimal solutions.

The majority of those studying enterprise/entrepreneurship courses/modules are unlikely to have had previous experience of operating a business or have family members willing to share their experience of self-employment or managing a small firm. Therefore, encouraging students to gain real benefits from their educational experiences is an important contribution to establishing new businesses with the potential to survive and grow. As outlined in Chapter 5, our view is that the delivery of conventional lectures has to be supplemented by more active approaches to learning (Pfeifer & Borozan, 2011) including various extracurricular activities (Bignotti & le Roux, 2020; Pocek et al., 2021; Preedy & Jones, 2015). We believe that entrepreneurship can be learned as long as modules, courses and programmes are designed in such a way that students are provided with the opportunities to engage in meaningful experiential learning (Corbett, 2005; Deema & Rita, 2016; Higgins & Elliott, 2011; Hyams-Ssekasi & Caldwell, 2018; Politis, Gabrielsson, Galan & Abebe, 2019) and are encouraged to engage in extracurricular activities (Pocek et al., 2021; Preedy et al., 2020). At the same time, students of entrepreneurship should be prepared to continue their learning outside the classroom by joining enterprise clubs and societies as well as contacting alumni members (Landoni et al., 2021; Pittaway et al., 2015). Other potential learning experiences include trading goods on *eBay*, observing organizational routines in places of employment such as bars, restaurants and retail outlets, as well as learning vicariously from TV programmes (*Dragon's Den*) and experienced entrepreneurs. In Hickie's (2011) study, fourteen of his 15 high-growth young entrepreneurs had acquired previous work experience before starting their businesses. In most cases, this experience was mundane involving the kind of retail activities familiar to most of those studying at school, college, or university. The point of this experience was that it provided insight into key factors such as understanding customers, working in teams and the basic routines of business. In more formal terms, these experience made a significant contribution to the development of their human capital (Hahn, Minola, Bosio & Cassia, 2020; Jayawarna et al., 2014, 2015; Unger, Rauch, Frese & Rosenbusch, 2011) which, in turn, contributed to the creation of businesses with real growth potential (Bosma, Content, Sanders & Stam, 2018; Chen, Zou & Wang, 2009; Piispanen, Paloniemi & Simonen, 2017; Zimmerman & Zeitz, 2002). Our ultimate objective is students reading this book should acquire the dynamic entrepreneurial learning capabilities that will enable them to establish businesses that have real potential for growth and the creation of employment opportunities for others.

14.7 Key Learning Points

- Developing your dynamic learning capabilities is central to the message of this book. In practice, that means taking every opportunity to learn the skills and competences you need to become an entrepreneur.
- You are unlikely to benefit from any course on entrepreneurship and business start-up if you are a passive learner. Experiential learning means that you must actively engage in the acquisition of knowledge.
- Acquiring an entrepreneurial mindset is crucial if you are seriously considering starting your own business or working for yourself. Even if you decide that entrepreneurship is not for you, we suggest that developing an entrepreneurial mindset will be invaluable in whatever future career you decide to pursue.
- Resourcefulness and resilience are important attributes for any would-be entrepreneur. Taking every opportunity to enhance your skills, knowledge and competences will help improve your resourcefulness and resilience. If you are able to face crises with confidence in your own abilities, then you are more likely to overcome those difficulties.
- Adopting a 'lean' approach to business start-up means you should be familiar with the principles of bootstrapping, bricolage and effectuation theory.

14.8 Discussion Questions and Call to Action

- Why is engaging in extracurricular learning as important as classroom-based learning for young, inexperienced entrepreneurs?
- To what extent do the entrepreneur's social skills contribute to the success of new business ventures?
- What are the key differences between bootstrapping and bricolage?
- What do you understand by the term 'dispositions' and why are they important in the context of starting a new business?
- Do you think that enterprise education can contribute to the development of an entrepreneurial mindset?
- Why do you think that the distinction between opportunity identification and opportunity creation is such an important theme in this book?

Over the last 20 years, entrepreneurship has increasingly become a legitimate career for those graduating from colleges and universities. In part this was a response to a decline in graduate job opportunities in larger organizations. On a more positive note, the importance of entrepreneurship for economic growth encouraged universities and colleges to offer courses on self-employment and business start-up (Jones, 2022). Increasingly, universities are also offering incubation facilities to help make the transition from student to entrepreneur (Jones et al., 2021). The Covid-19 pandemic has certainly created major problems for all organizations as well as seriously disrupting education since it was first identified in 2019 (Haneberg, 2021). As we discussed in Chapter 13, recent data from the Global Entrepreneurship Monitor (GEM) studies do indicate declining levels of early-stage entrepreneurial activity. Although some have suggested that the pandemic has led to the emergence of new business opportunities (Alvarez & Barney, 2020; Kuckertz et al., 2020). We believe that if you are committed to starting your own business then the core principles of this book; entrepreneurial learning, bootstrapping/bricolage as well as building extensive and diverse social networks will help you to overcome the difficulties all young entrepreneurs are likely to face in the early stages of their entrepreneurial careers.

References

Ajzen, I. (1991). The Theory of Planned Behavior. *Organizational Behavior & Human Decision Processes*, *50*(2), 179–211.

Aldrich, H. E. & Ruef, M. (2018). Unicorns, Gazelles, and Other Distractions on the Way to Understanding Real Entrepreneurship in the United States. *Academy of Management Perspectives*, *32*(4), 458–472.

Aldrich, H. E. & Yang, T. (2012). Lost in translation: Cultural codes are not blueprints. *Strategic Entrepreneurship Journal*, *6*(1), 1–17.

Alvarez, S. A. & Barney, J. B. (2020). Insights from creation theory: The uncertain context rendered by the COVID-19 pandemic. *Strategic Entrepreneurship Journal*, *14*(4), 552–555.

Anderson, A. R., Jack, S. L. & Drakopoulou-Dodd, S. (2009). Social capital in the capitalisation of new ventures: accessing, lubricating and fitting. In M. Bergmann and T. Faust (Eds.), *Handbook of Business and Finance* (pp. 293–300). New York: Nova Science Publishers Inc.

Arikan, A. M., Arikan, I. & Koparan, I. (2020). Creation Opportunities: Entrepreneurial Curiosity, Generative Cognition, and Knightian Uncertainty. *Academy of Management Review, 45*(4), 808–824.

Baker, A. C., Jensen, P. J. & Kolb, D. A. (2005). Conversation as Experiential Learning. *Management Learning, 36*(4), 411–427.

Baker, T. & Nelson, R. E. (2005). Creating Something from Nothing: Resource Construction through Entrepreneurial Bricolage. *Administrative Science Quarterly, 50*, 329–366.

Bandura, A. (1997). *Self-efficacy: the exercise of control.* New York: W.H. Freeman, 1997.

Baron, J. N., Hannan, M. T. & Burton, M. D. (1999). Building the Iron Cage: Determinants of Managerial Intensity in the Early Years of Organizations. *American Sociological Review, 64*(4), 527–547.

Bernardi, C. D. & Pedrini, M. (2020). Transforming water into wine: Environmental bricolage for entrepreneurs. *Journal of Cleaner Production, 266.* doi:10.1016/j.jclepro.2020.121815.

Bignotti, A. & le Roux, I. (2020). Which types of experience matter? The role of prior start-up experiences and work experience in fostering youth entrepreneurial intentions. *International Journal of Entrepreneurial Behavior & Research, 26*(6), 1181–1198.

Block, J. H., Fisch, C. & Hirschmann, M. (2021). The determinants of bootstrap financing in crises: evidence from entrepreneurial ventures in the COVID-19 pandemic. *Small Business Economics.* doi:10.1007/s11187-020-00445-6.

Bortolini, R. F., Nogueira Cortimiglia, M., Danilevicz, A. d. M. F. & Ghezzi, A. (2021). Lean Startup: a comprehensive historical review. *Management Decision, 59*(8), 1765–1783.

Bosma, N., Content, J., Sanders, M. & Stam, E. (2018). Institutions, Entrepreneurship, and Economic Growth in Europe. *Small Business Economics, 51*(2), 483–499.

Breslin, D. & Jones, C. (2012). The Evolution of Entrepreneurial Learning. *International Journal of Organizational Analysis, 20*(3), 294–308.

Castells, M. (2000). *The rise of the network society*: Oxford: Blackwell Publishers.

Chadwick, I. C. & Raver, J. L. (2020). Psychological Resilience and Its Downstream Effects for Business Survival in Nascent Entrepreneurship. *Entrepreneurship: Theory & Practice, 44*(2), 233–255.

Chen, X., Zou, H. & Wang, D. T. (2009). How do new ventures grow? Firm capabilities, growth strategies and performance. *International Journal of Research in Marketing, 26*(4), 294–303.

Cope, J. & Down, S. (2010). *I think therefore I learn? Entrepreneurial Cognition, Learning and Knowledge and Knowing in Practice.* Paper presented at the Babson College Entrepreneurship Research Conference, Lausanne, Switzerland.

Corbett, A. C. (2005). Experiential Learning Within the Process of Opportunity Identification and Exploitation. *Entrepreneurship: Theory & Practice, 29*(4), 473–491.

Cornelissen, J. P., Clarke, J. S. & Cienki, A. (2012). Sensegiving in entrepreneurial contexts: The use of metaphors in speech and gesture to gain and sustain support for novel business ventures. *International Small Business Journal, 30*(4), 213–241.

Cui, J., Sun, J. & Bell, R. (2021). The impact of entrepreneurship education on the entrepreneurial mindset of college students in China: The mediating role of inspiration and the role of educational attributes. *The International Journal of Management Education, 19*(1). doi:10.1016/j.ijme.2019.04.001

Deema, R. & Rita, K. (2016). Enterprise education in pharmacy schools: Experiential learning in institutionally constrained contexts. *International Journal of Entrepreneurial Behavior & Research, 22*(4), 485–509.

Dencker, J. C., Bacq, S., Gruber, M. & Haas, M. (2021). Reconceptualizing Necessity Entrepreneurship: A Contextualized Framework of Entrepreneurial Processes Under the Condition of Basic Needs. *Academy of Management Review, 46*(1), 60–79.

Deverell, E. (2009). Crises as Learning Triggers: Exploring a Conceptual Framework of Crisis-Induced Learning. *Journal of Contingencies and Crisis Management, 17*(3), 179–188.

Elfring, T., Klyver, K. & van Burg, E. (2021). *Entrepreneurship as Networking: Mechanisms, Dynamics, Practices, and Strategies*. New York: Oxford University Press.

English, P., de Villiers Scheepers, M. J., Fleischman, D., Burgess, J. & Crimmins, G. (2021). Developing professional networks: the missing link to graduate employability. *Education + Training, 63*(4), 647–661.

Fayolle, A., Kariv, D. & Matlay, H. (2019). *The role and impact of entrepreneurship education: methods, teachers and innovative programmes*. Cheltenham: Edward Elgar Pub.

Fearon, C., Furlotti, M., van Vuuren, W. & McLaughlin, H. (2021). Developing new opportunities, entrepreneurial skills and product/service creativity: a 'Young Enterprise' (YE) perspective. *Studies in Higher Education, 46*(6), 1081–1098.

Fisher, G., Neubert, E. & Burnell, D. (2021). Resourcefulness narratives: Transforming actions into stories to mobilize support. *Journal of Business Venturing, 36*(4). doi:10.1016/j.jbusvent.2021.106122

Flechas Chaparro, X. A., Kozesinski, R. & Camargo Júnior, A. S. (2021). Absorptive capacity in startups: A systematic literature review. *Journal of Entrepreneurship, Management & Innovation, 17*(1), 57–95.

Fletcher, D. (2007). 'Toy Story': The narrative world of entrepreneurship and the creation of interpretive communities. *Journal of Business Venturing, 22*, 649–672.

Ghezzi, A. (2019). Digital startups and the adoption and implementation of Lean Startup Approaches: Effectuation, Bricolage and Opportunity Creation in practice. *Technological Forecasting & Social Change*, *146*, 945–960.

Gregoire, D. A., Cornelissen, J., Dimov, D. & Burg, E. (2015). The Mind in the Middle: Taking Stock of Affect and Cognition Research in Entrepreneurship. *International Journal of Management Reviews*, *17*(2), 125–142.

Gupta, V. K., Turban, D. B., Wasti, S. A. & Sikdar, A. (2009). The Role of Gender Stereotypes in Perceptions of Entrepreneurs and Intentions to Become an Entrepreneur. *Entrepreneurship: Theory & Practice*, *33*(2), 397–417.

Hahn, D., Minola, T., Bosio, G. & Cassia, L. (2020). The Impact of Entrepreneurship Education on University Students' Entrepreneurial Skills: A Family Embeddedness Perspective. *Small Business Economics*, *55*(1), 257–282.

Haneberg, D. H. (2021). Interorganizational learning between knowledge-based entrepreneurial ventures responding to COVID-19. *Learning Organization*, *28*(2), 137–152.

Harrison, R. T., Mason, C. M. & Girling, P. (2004). Financial bootstrapping and venture development in the software industry. *Entrepreneurship & Regional Development*, *16*(4), 307–333.

Hickie, J. (2011). The Development of Human Capital in Young Entrepreneurs. *Industry and Higher Education*, *25*(6), 469–481.

Higgins, D. & Elliott, C. (2011). Learning to Make Sense: What Works in Entrepreneurial Education? *Journal of European Industrial Training*, *35*(4), 345–367.

Hitt, M. A., Biermant, L., Shimizu, K. & Kochhar, R. (2001). Direct And Moderating Effects Of Human Capital on Strategy and Performance in Professional Service Firms: A Resource-Based Perspective. *Academy of Management Journal*, *44*(1), 13–28.

Honig, B. & Hopp, C. (2019). Learning orientations and learning dynamics: Understanding heterogeneous approaches and comparative success in nascent entrepreneurship. *Journal of Business Research*, *94*, 28–41.

Hyams-Ssekasi, D. & Caldwell, E. F. (2018). *Experiential Learning for Entrepreneurship: Theoretical and Practical Perspectives on Enterprise Education*. Cham: Springer.

Inada, Y. (2020). The Impact of Higher Education Entrepreneurship Practical Courses: Developing an Entrepreneurial Mindset. *Journal of Applied Business & Economics*, *22*(8), 161–176.

Irwin, K. C., Gilstrap, C. M., Drnevich, P. L. & Tudor, C. M. (2019). From start-up to acquisition: Implications of financial investment trends for small- to medium-sized high-tech enterprises. *Journal of Small Business Strategy*, *29*(2), 22–43.

Jayawarna, D., Jones, O. & Macpherson, A. (2014). Entrepreneurial potential: The role of human and cultural capitals. *International Small Business Journal*, *32*(8), 918–943.

Jayawarna, D., Jones, O. & Macpherson, A. (2015). Becoming an Entrepeneur: The Unexplored Role of Childhood and Adolescent Human Capital. In C. L. Wang & D. Rae (Eds.), *Entrepreneurial Learning: New Perspectives in Research, Education and Practice*, (pp. 45–71). Abingdon: Taylor and Francis Inc.

Jayawarna, D., Jones, O. & Macpherson, A. (2020). Resourcing Social Enterprises: The Role of Socially Oriented Bootstrapping. *British Journal of Management, 31*(1), 56.

Jayawarna, D., Woodhams, C. & Jones, O. (2012). Gender and Alternative Start-Up Business Funding. *Competition & Change, 16*(4), 303–322.

Jones, O. (2022). Academic engagement with small business and entrepreneurship: Towards a landscape of practice. *Industry and Higher Education, 36*(3), 279–293.

Jones, O., Ghobadian, A., O'Regan, N. & Antcliffe, V. (2013). Dynamic Capabilities in a Sixth Generation Family Firm: Entrepreneurship and the Bibby Line. *Business History, 55*(2) 910–941.

Jones, O. & Li, H. (2017). Effectual Entrepreneuring: Sensemaking in a Family-Based Start-Up. *Entrepreneurship and Regional Development, 29*(5–6), 467–499.

Jones, O., Meckel, P. & Taylor, D. (2021). *Creating Communities of Practice: Entrepreneurial Learning in a University-Based Incubator*. Cham (Switzerland): Springer.

Kempster, S., Smith, S. & Barnes, S. (2018). *Chapter 14: A review of entrepreneurial leadership learning: an exploration that draws on human, social and institutional capitals*. Cheltenham: Edward Elgar.

Kirzner, I. M. (1973). *Competition and Entrepreneurship*. Chicago: University of Chicago.

Kolb, D. A. (1984). *Experiential learning: experience as the source of learning and development*. Englewood Cliffs, NJ: Prentice-Hall.

Kriz, W. C. & Auchter, E. (2016). 10 Years of Evaluation Research Into Gaming Simulation for German Entrepreneurship and a New Study on Its Long-Term Effects. *Simulation & Gaming, 47*(2), 179–205.

Kuckertz, A., Brändle, L., Gaudig, A., Hinderer, S., Morales Reyes, C. A., Prochotta, A., Berger, E. S. C. (2020). Startups in times of crisis – A rapid response to the COVID-19 pandemic. *Journal of Business Venturing Insights, 13*. doi:10.1016/j.jbvi.2020.e00169

Kuratko, D. F., Fisher, G. & Audretsch, D. B. (2021). Unraveling the entrepreneurial mindset. *Small Business Economics, 57*(4), 1681–1691.

Kwapisz A, Schell WJ, Aytes K, Bryant S. (2021) Entrepreneurial Action and Intention: The Role of Entrepreneurial Mindset, Emotional Intelligence, and Grit. Entrepreneurship. *Education and Pedagogy*. doi:10.1177/2515127421992521

Landoni, M., Bolzani, D. & Baroncelli, A. (2021). The Role of Alumni Clubs in the Universities' Entrepreneurial Networks: An Inquiry in Italian Universities. In P. Jones, N. Apostolopoulos, A. Kakouris, C. Moon, V. Ratten & A. Walmsley (Eds.),

Universities and Entrepreneurship: Meeting the Educational and Social Challenges (Vol. 11, pp. 49–63). Bingley: Emerald Publishing Limited.

Landström, H., Harirchi, G. & Åström, F. (2012). Entrepreneurship: Exploring the knowledge base. *Research Policy, 41*, 1154–1181.

Lans, T., Blok, V. & Gulikers, J. (2015). Show Me Your Network and I'll Tell You Who You Are: Social Competence and Social Capital of Early-Stage Entrepreneurs. *Entrepreneurship and Regional Development, 27*(7–8), 458–473.

Lee, R. & Jones, O. (2008). Networks, Communication and Learning during Business Start-up. *International Small Business Journal, 26*(5), 559–594.

Lichtenstein, B. M. & Brush, C. G. (2001). How do 'resource bundles' develop and change in New Ventures? A dynamic model and longitudinal exploration. *Entrepreneurship: Theory and Practice, 25*(3), 37–59.

Lindberg, E., Bohman, H., Hulten, P., &, W., Timothy. (2017). Enhancing students' entrepreneurial mindset: a Swedish experience. *Education + Training, 59*(7/8), 768–779.

Lourenço, F., Jones, O. & Jayawarna, D. (2013). Promoting sustainable development: The role of entrepreneurship education. *International Small Business Journal*, 31(8), 841–865.

Macpherson, A., Herbane, B. & Jones, O. (2015). Developing Dynamic Capabilities through Resource Accretion: Expanding the Entrepreneurial Solution Space. *Entrepreneurship and Regional Development, 27*(5–6), 259–291.

Malmstrom, M. (2014). Typologies of Bootstrap Financing Behavior in Small Ventures. *Venture Capital, 16*(1), 27–50.

McCallum, E., Weicht, R., McMullan, L. & Price, A. (2018*). EntreComp into Action – Get inspired, make it happen: A user guide to the European Entrepreneurship Competence Framework*. Luxembourg: Publications Office of the European Union.

McClelland, D. C. (1961). *The Achieving Society*. New York US: Free Press.

McDonald, J. & Cater-Steel, A. (2017). *Communities of Practice: facilitating social learning in higher education*: New York: Springer.

Michaelis, T. L., Scheaf, D. J., Carr, J. C. & Pollack, J. M. (2022). An agentic perspective of resourcefulness: Self-reliant and joint resourcefulness behaviors within the entrepreneurship process. *Journal of Business Venturing, 37*(1). doi:10.1016/j.jbusvent.2020.106083

Mooradian, T., Matzler, K., Uzelac, B. & Bauer, F. (2016). Perspiration and inspiration: Grit and innovativeness as antecedents of entrepreneurial success. *Journal of Economic Psychology, 56*, 232–243.

Naumann, C. (2017). Entrepreneurial Mindset: A Synthetic Literature Review. *Entrepreneurial Business and Economics Review, 5*(3), 149–172.

Nicolaou, N., Shane, S., Cherkas, L., Hunkin, J. & Spector, T. D. (2008). Is the Tendency to Engage in Entrepreneurship Genetic? *Management Science* (1), 167–179.

Penrose, E. T. (1959). *The Theory of the Growth of the Firm*. Oxford: Basil Blackwell.

Peschl, H., Deng, C. & Larson, N. (2021). Entrepreneurial thinking: A signature pedagogy for an uncertain 21st century. *The International Journal of Management Education, 19*(1). doi:10.1016/j.ijme.2020.100427

Pfeifer, S. & Borozan, D. (2011). Fitting Kolb's Learning Style Theory to Entrepreneurship Learning Aims and Contents. *International Journal of Business Research, 11*(2), 216–223.

Piispanen, V.-V., Paloniemi, K. & Simonen, J. (2017). Entrepreneurs' business skills and growth orientation in business development. *International Journal of Entrepreneurship and Small Business, 32*(4), 515–536.

Pittaway, L., Gazzard, J., Shore, A. & Williamson, T. (2015). Student clubs: experiences in entrepreneurial learning. *Entrepreneurship & Regional Development, 27*(3/4), 127–153.

Pittaway, L., Rodriguez-Falcon, E., Aiyegbayo, O. & King, A. (2011). The role of entrepreneurship clubs and societies in entrepreneurial learning. *International Small Business Journal, 29*(1), 37–57.

Pocek, J., Politis, D. & Gabrielsson, J. (2021). Entrepreneurial learning in extra-curricular start-up programs for students. *International Journal of Entrepreneurial Behavior & Research* (ahead-of-print).

Politis, D., Gabrielsson, J., Galan, N. & Abebe, S. A. (2019). Entrepreneurial Learning in Venture Acceleration Programs. *Learning Organization, 26*(6), 588–603.

Preedy, S. & Jones, P. (2015). An Investigation into University Extracurricular Enterprise Support Provision. *Education & Training, 57*(8–9), 992–1008.

Preedy, S., Jones, P., Maas, G. & Duckett, H. (2020). Examining the perceived value of extracurricular enterprise activities in relation to entrepreneurial learning processes. *Journal of Small Business & Enterprise Development, 27*(7), 1085–1105.

Ramoglou, S., Gartner, W. B. & Tsang, E. W. K. (2020). 'Who is an entrepreneur?' is (still) the wrong question. *Journal of Business Venturing Insights, 13*. doi:10.1016/j.jbvi.2020.e00168

Rayna, T. & Striukova, L. (2021). Fostering skills for the 21st century: The role of Fab labs and makerspaces. *Technological Forecasting & Social Change, 164*. doi:10.1016/j.techfore.2020.120391

Read, S., Sarasvathy, S. D., Dew, N., Wiltbank, R. & Ohisson, A. V. (2011). *Effectual Entrepreneurship*. Routledge Taylor and Francis London and New York.

Ries, E. (2011). *The lean startup: how today's entrepreneurs use continuous innovation to create radically successful businesses*. New York: Crown Business.

Rutherford, M. W. (2015). *Strategic bootstrapping* (First edition. ed.). New York: Business Expert Press.

Rutherford, M. W., Pollack, J. M., Mazzei, M. J. & Sanchez-Ruiz, P. (2017). Bootstrapping: Reviewing the Literature, Clarifying the Construct, and Charting a New Path Forward. *Group & Organization Management, 42*(5), 657–706

Santos, S. C., Costa, S. F., Neumeyer, X. & Caetano, A. (2016). *Bridging entrepreneurial cognition research and entrepreneurship education: What and how*: Cheltenham: Edward Elgar.

Sarasvathy, S. D. (2001). Causation and Effectuation: Toward a Theoretical Shift from Economic Inevitability to Entrepreneurial Contingency. *The Academy of Management Review* (2), 243–263.

Sarasvathy, S. D. (2008). *Effectuation: elements of entrepreneurial expertise*. Cheltenham: Edward Elgar.

Saxenian, A. (1996). *Regional Advantages: Culture and Competition in Silicon Valley and Route 128*. Cambridge, MA.: Harvard University Press.

Seet, P.-S., Jones, J., Oppelaar, L. & Corral de Zubielqui, G. (2018). Beyond 'know-what' and 'know-how' to 'know-who': enhancing human capital with social capital in an Australian start-up accelerator. *Asia Pacific Business Review, 24*(2), 233–260.

Shane, S. (2000). Prior knowledge and the discovery of entrepreneurial opportunities. *Organization Science, 11*(4), 448–469.

Shane, S., Nicolaou, N., Cherkas, L. & Spector, T. D. (2010). Genetics, the Big Five, and the Tendency to Be Self-Employed. *Journal of Applied Psychology, 95*(6), 1154–1162.

Shao, Y. & Sun, L. (2021). Entrepreneurs' social capital and venture capital financing. *Journal of Business Research, 136*, 499–512.

Stenholm, P. & Renko, M. (2016). Passionate bricoleurs and new venture survival. *Journal of Business Venturing, 31*(5), 595–611.

Stoica, O., Roman, A. & Rusu, V. D. (2020). The Nexus between Entrepreneurship and Economic Growth: A Comparative Analysis on Groups of Countries. *Sustainability, 12*(3), 1186. doi:10.3390/su12031186

Teece, D. (Ed.) (2011). *Human Capital, Capabilities, and the Firm: Literati, Numerati, and Entrepreneurs in the Twenty-First Century Enterprise*. Oxford: Oxford University Press.

Teece, D., Pisano, G. & Shuen, A. (1997). Dynamic Capabilities and Strategic Management. *Strategic Management Journal, 18*(7), 509–533.

Unger, J. M., Rauch, A., Frese, M. & Rosenbusch, N. (2011). Human capital and entrepreneurial success: A meta-analytical review. *Journal of Business Venturing, 26*, 341–358.

Valliere, D. & Peterson, R. (2009). Entrepreneurship and Economic Growth: Evidence from Emerging and Developed Countries. *Entrepreneurship and Regional Development, 21*(5–6), 459–480.

Villanueva, J., Van de Ven, A. H. & Sapienza, H. J. (2012). Resource mobilization in entrepreneurial firms. *Journal of Business Venturing, 27*(1), 19–30.

West, G. P. & Noel, T. W. (2009). The Impact of Knowledge Resources on New Venture Performance. *Journal of Small Business Management, 47*(1), 1–22.

Xiang-yang, Z., Frese, M. & Giardini, A. (2010). Business owners' network size and business growth in China: The role of comprehensive social competency. *Entrepreneurship & Regional Development, 22*(7/8), 675–705.

Zahra, S. A., Sapienza, H. & Davidsson, P. (2006). Enterpreneurship and Dynamic Capabilities: A Review, Model and Research Agenda. *Journal of Management Studies, 43*(4), 917–955.

Zhang, M., Macpherson, A. & Jones, O. (2006). Conceptualizing the Learning Process in SMEs: Improving Innovation through External Orientation. *International Small Business Journal, 24*(3), 299–323.

Zhao, F., Barratt-Pugh, L., Standen, P., Redmond, J. & Suseno, Y. (2021). An exploratory study of entrepreneurial social networks in the digital age. *Journal of Small Business and Enterprise Development, 29*(1), 147–173.

Zimmerman, M. A. & Zeitz, G. J. (2002). Beyond Survival: Achieving New Venture Growth by Building Legitimacy. *Academy of Management Review, 27*(3), 414–431.

Index

Note: Figures are shown in *italics* and tables in **bold type**. Endnotes consist of the page number followed by 'n' and the endnote number e.g., 151n2 refers to note 2 on page 151.

Printed in the United States
by Baker & Taylor Publisher Services